all-time top 1000 ALBUMS

Colin Larkin

First published in Great Britain in 2000 by
Virgin Publishing Ltd
Thames Wharf Studios
Rainville Road
London W6 9HA

A catalogue record for this book is available
from the British Library

ISBN 0 7535 0493 6

muze

Conceived, written, edited and produced
by Colin Larkin for MUZE UK Ltd
to whom all editorial enquiries should be sent
nic@muze.co.uk
www.muze.com

Editor In Chief: Colin Larkin
Assistant Editor: Nic Oliver
Production Editor: Susan Pipe
Editorial Assistant: Kelly Larkin
Design and Typesetting: Roger Kohn
Design Assistant: Aku Young
Special thanks to: Trev Huxley and Paul Zullo
of Muze Inc., Neal Goddard of Muze UK
and to Rob Shreeve, David Gould and
Roz Scott of Virgin Publishing.
Printed and bound in Great Britain by
Butler & Tanner Ltd, Frome and London

Contents

Dedicated to Johnnie Walker
Who still hasn't sent his bloody voting form back

Introduction

The third edition proper of the *All-Time Top 1000 Albums* arrives seven years after the original concept. As long as there continues to be a market there will be a new edition every two years. I find it fascinating to view people's changing tastes (or, some critics would say, the lack of change). Over the past two years there has been a gamut of All-Times polls and lists. I wish I could have copyrighted that hyphenated word, as I would be stinking rich by now. Most music magazines have produced their own polls, and, within reason, they are all similar. We claim, with some justification, that ours is the first, the biggest, and naturally the best. I decided to expand upon Paul Gambaccini's excellent *Top 100 Albums* book, but poll as large an audience as I could physically handle. The total votes now exceed 200,000, and I have factored in every poll that has appeared in the press since 1974.

If I kept the age groups of voters in different sections we would get a completely different picture. Once again the age range was considerable, from 9 to 65. The main body of voters falls into the 20 to 45 age group. Additionally, many votes have been received from music literate schoolchildren, and, believe me, 10 to 15-year olds really know and love their music. Although it must play a small part, these kids are not exclusively indoctrinated by the tastes of their parents. It goes without saying that a household bought up hearing the Beach Boys or Miles Davis will naturally form a familiarity and affection with that music, which will often lead to lead to them acquiring the particular family favourite. The writer and ex-punk Tony Parsons is proud of his love for Frank Sinatra, which certainly came from being initially exposed to the music by his dad. That music will be passed on in this way, to future generations, not in a forceful way, but by way of sharing something that is great. I hope my own tin lids will appreciate their exposure to the Beatles and Bob Dylan. If the music is great then it will surely endure. Today's young parents will do their own part in passing on the music of Radiohead or Nirvana.

Within reason, musical fashion comes and goes very quickly. When we were collecting the bulk of the votes for 1997's 2nd edition the much-hyped Britpop scene was still prevalent. That was reflected in the unnaturally high positions for artists such as Ocean Colour Scene (*Moseley Shoals*), Supergrass (*In It For The Money*), and Kula Shaker (*K*). Now the dust has settled most of these albums have dropped out of people's minds and opinions have polarized.

The other significant change is the increase in votes from outside the UK. I took votes from visitors to the MIDEM music festival in Cannes in 1999 and 2000. MIDEM is a showcase that brings together people from all over the world, and as a result we have a clutch of votes from places such as Poland, Russia and, indeed, most countries in the world including one from the only bookseller from a tiny island located off New Zealand.

On the web site which is maintained by my colleagues at MUZE Inc. in New York we received over 12,000 online votes from an American contingent. That batch of votes has reshaped our book, and the inclusion of more hip-hop and alternative rock has given the chart a much more universal flavour. Pearl Jam, Pavement and the Smashing Pumpkins compete with Blur and Oasis. Strangely, bands such as the Byrds, Steely Dan and the Beach Boys find little favour in their homeland. On the other hand, most of the votes for the Cure, Depeche Mode, Leftfield and Underworld came from the USA. I also suspect that the dangerously high showing of albums by Boston was not down to European taste.

One of my American colleagues also had a justifiable gripe about our standing on 'Best Of' and 'Greatest Hits' albums. We do not allow them to be counted because the idea is for the album to really be a showcase of songs put together by an artist at a particular time. Artists such as Madness, the Kinks, the Hollies, the Impressions, Neil Diamond, Hall and Oates, Bobby Darin, the Four Tops and the Four Seasons have a formidable catalogue of hit singles, and all have outstanding 'Best Of' albums currently available. It is impossible to nail one or even two 'great' albums by these artists, because if they ain't got the hits then it ain't good enough. My erstwhile colleague then immediately challenged me on the inclusion of the odd renegade like *Legend* by Bob Marley and The Wailers or *Big Ones* by Aerosmith. My lame answer is that there were so many votes for these 'carefully created compilations' that I would have distorted the final picture if I had not included them. Albums such as *Forrest Gump* and *Dirty Dancing* were allowed because they were film soundtracks.

The jazz showing is much stronger and more polarized. It is clear that most jazz votes are from rock fans who like a bit of jazz. Interestingly, the choices are steeped in the 50s and 60s. M young jazz lovers I have met are more interes in this era than anything recent, hence the go showing for Charles Mingus, Duke Ellingto Thelonious Monk, as well as Miles and Coltran

Rap, meanwhile, is fast becomin establishment music. A few albums have show longevity, especially Public Enemy's *It Takes Nation Of Millions To Hold Us Back* which ha now become the *Revolver* of rap music.

This time all the albums in the list ar available on CD, except for the odd one such a Neil Young's *On The Beach*, a bizarre situatio that finds the artist holding up the reissue Occasionally some early albums have beer packaged as two for one, and this represent amazing value. Two such items are Gram Parsons' *Grievous Angel/GP* and Jimmy Smith's *Got My Mojo Workin'/Hoochie Coochie Man*. The CD medium is able to give us twice the length of an album from the 50s and 60s. Some reissue companies like Ace Records are putting out entire catalogues as two-for-ones. The votes cast were for *Grievous Angel* and *Got My Mojo Workin'*, but the extra album is a fantastic bonus.

As for the chart commentary itself, I would dearly love to orally reel it off in the style of UK DJ Alan 'Fluff' Freeman or the US jock Russ 'Weird Beard' Knight. Sadly, I do not have their talent. In the final list, the most interesting stuff for me is always at the tail end. I hope very much that new readers will benefit from picking up a few classics that may have passed them by, or they may never have heard of.

Last time around I confessed that my favourite album of all-time was David Crosby's *If I Could Only Remember My Name*. It still is, but I received about a dozen positive letters from people who had bought the album on my recommendation and thanked me for opening a door for them. This time around I am thrilled at Dennis Wilson's 'solo' solo album *Pacific Ocean Blue* has snuck in. Get it, it's a joy.

This time there were about 300 new entries, though none of these charted as ridiculously high as albums in the previous edition by artists associated with the hysteria surrounding britpop. The highest new entry was Air's *Moon Safari* (68), which has captured the voters' hearts along with the Stereophonics' *Performance and Cocktails* (69), Travis' *The Man Who* (75), and the Corrs' *Talk On Corners* (78). The next highest entry is *Americana* from the Offspring.

The biggest surprises came about as a result of the new American vote which dramatically pushed up the Who's *Tommy* (257 to 52) and *Who's Next* (133 to 48), Led Zeppelin's debut (212 to 61), and My Bloody Valentine's *Loveless*, an incredible jump from 472 to 65. Another serious rise was for the often ignored *Saint Dominic's Preview* by Van Morrison (324 to 71). I'd like to think my past whingeing has helped cause this happy event, at the expense of a few *Astral Weeks* votes.

The big droppers are of major proportions. How about these for LPs that received fantastic over-the-top reviews when they were first released, but have now settled down in most people's minds as good, bad or indifferent. Oasis' *Be Here Now* (36 to 459, oops), the Verve's *A Northern Soul* (81 to 289, oops), the Manic Street Preachers' *The Holy Bible* (56 to 272, oops), the Spice Girls' *Spice* (101 to 493, oops), Paul Weller's *Stanley Road* (66 to 589, oops), Suede's *Coming Up* (195 to 695, oops), Ocean Colour Scene's *Moseley Shoals* (60 to 811, blimey), Black Grape's *It's Great When You're Straight, Yeah!* (127 to 878, oops), Kula Shaker's *K* (55 to 879, wow), the Charlatans' *Tellin' Stories* (180 to 889, oops), and finally the Stone Roses' *The Second Coming* (137 to 920, ouch).

They should not feel so terrible, because even Tina Turner (*Private Dancer*) grazes her bum as she slides from 242 to 969, and Sly Stone (*There's A Riot Goin' On*) comes down to reality from 216 to 978.

The cult acts have generally held their own, although Nick Drake has gained considerably, especially *Five Leaves Left* (197 to 55). *Pink Moon* (221 to 131) is at odds with *Bryter Layter* (118 to 306). Prince is about to join the dinosaur footsie, as *Sign 'O' The Times* climbs from 47 to 19.

Rap and dance genres have pushed down reggae and soul. Strong new contenders include 2Pac (*All Eyez On Me*), the Beastie Boys (*Licensed To Ill*), and Massive Attack (*Protection*).

All the major dinosaur artists, David Bowie, Elton John, Van Morrison, U2 and Neil Young, have improved their overall showing. For some reason their most popular work has suffered. Shock horror drops from *Pet Sounds* (6 to 18), *Hunky Dory* (16 to 23), *The Rise and Fall Of Ziggy Stardust and The Spiders From Mars* (11 to 27), *Rubber Soul* (20 to 34), *Blonde On Blonde* (17 to 33), and even *Never Mind The Bollocks Here's The Sex Pistols* (13 to 29).

Equally perplexing is the sudden rise of the dinosaur. *Blue* (53 to 24), *A Hard Day's Night* (142 to 22, thanks to the USA vote), *Born To Run* (63 to 20) although Springsteen's other work has tumbled dramatically. *The Unforgettable Fire* (169 to 15, quite astonishing!), *Forever Changes* (40 to 12, justice at last) and *The Queen Is Dead* (23 to 10). Miles Davis' classic *Kind Of Blue* also surprises with a leap from 48 to 14, although the remastered CD is pretty amazing and recently topped the *Billboard* chart for an age.

The three most notable changes near the top concern two artists. After years of slowly gaining popularity, Bob Dylan's *Blood On The Tracks* has finally become his highest album. In spectacular fashion it leap frogs *Highway 61 Revisited* and *Blonde On Blonde* to number 7.

The other feat is left to the remarkable Radiohead who have shot up with *OK Computer* (21 to 4) and *The Bends* (10 to 2). No other band (not even Pink Floyd) has ever come so close to giving the fab four a seeing to.

Without wishing to act as a record company plugger it is quite amazing that artists on the Parlophone Records label occupy the top five positions. Incredible to think that all their A&R man George Martin had in 1959 was the Goons and Adam Faith.

There is enough change in this edition to make it worthwhile, but there are some things that will never alter. I really can't imagine a Top Ten without the Beatles; they really justify my belief in the greatness of pop music. If they were to disappear from the list I really think it would be time for me to give up and go back to my Moby Grape albums. I try not to let my opinions and feelings get the better of me, but the older I get the more I quite fancy being a curmudgeon. There are a few reviews this time around from which the reader will deduce I will not be having the albums in question played at my funeral.

What does it all mean? Absolutely nothing really, except the immense pleasure people like me seem to get from stupid obsessions with lists, numbers and positions. At the end of it all, the best part is to grab a fistful of CDs, find yours a spare few hours on the sofa, and play t bloody things. Only then do you realise th listening to a recent 'great' album such as Be Orton's *Central Reservation* is the only importa thing. The fact that it is position 982 completely irrelevant. The music is the re driving force, and that is why people have the favourite album of all time. It is something yc can go back to time and time again and it wi never let you down. Relationships may come an go, best friends may betray you, but you favourite album will always be there to lift you spirits or make you feel melancholy. There is n more powerful force in my opinion. A fascinating as watching this chart unfold is, th real reward is for it to be some real help ir assembling a pretty amazing record collection Not for the sake of just building a collection tc impress the neighbours, but to find some new music that really moves you and in some way becomes part of your life. If this book helps sell an extra copy of XTC's *Oranges & Lemons* or John Martyn's *One World* then I will feel ecstatic. So once again, this really is the absolute, final *All-Time Top 1000 Albums*. Until next time.

Colin Larkin,
July 2000

Acknowledgements

The best thing about finishing a book is getting to the acknowledgements. At that point you know the book really is almost finished and you can start the massive clean-up process. On a book such as this that involves getting all the scanned CD covers back from the designer and then matching them up to the relevant CD, which will either: A) be lying out flat on the floor of the upstairs office, spine to view if it's a new entry, or B) in various piles, skyscraper style, downstairs, separated from the others. Locating the CD can take anything up to half an hour, especially if either pile has been disturbed by either: A) my own tin lids, or B) new stepson, or C) new stepson's girlfriend. This time I also had the bright idea to do a Top 100 Singles list, which involved another unmanageable pile of vinyl. A few items were loaned to me; many thanks to Dan Larkin, Tom Larkin, Carmen Larkin and Simon Dekker for lending CDs from their own collection. Also, thanks to the unbelievably warm-hearted Pete Frame for sticking Jimmy Jones in the post so promptly after I had interrupted his gardening.

A project like this can only work with the co-operation of record companies. Fortunately, most seem to realise the logic of the book helping to promote their product. Top of the pile is Warners catalogue manager Stuart Batsford and his colleagues Mike Bartlett and Florence Halfon. Batty or Stewball, as he prefers to be known, is not only incredibly knowledgeable about music but passionate about it. His company and associated labels have the largest slice of the 1000 albums.

Other thanks are due to Murray Chalmers, Chris Latham and Sarah Bleach at the Parlophone/Capitol press office (numbers 1-5, well done), Alan Robinson at Castle Music, Joanna Kalli at Beggars Banquet, Julia Honeywell at Ace Records, James at Arista Records, Jason Day at Virgin Records, and Matt Wheeler at Polydor Records.

Other help came in the shape of compliment slips containing indecipherable names from Mute Records, Mercury Records, Columbia Records, Epic Records, ZTT Records, Jeepster Recordings, Warp Records, 4AD Records, Fiction Records, Music For Nations, A&M Records, RCA Records, Rykodisc, Grapevine, Universal Music, Island Records, BGO and See for Miles. Slipped Discs II in Chelmsford was my first port of call for other CDs, and the manager Carl Newsum and his Tonto, Dennis Eastgate, were always very helpful. Slipped Discs is exactly what you want an independent record shop to be like.

Past help came from Alex Ogg, Jon Staines, Marc Miller, Mark Simpson, Peter Doggett, Trevor Dann, Neil Slaven, Tony Russell, Richard Cook, Harry Hawke, David Crosby, Alan Hull, Salsri Nyah, Roy Sheridan, Mike Nevins, Sarah Lavelle, David Gritten, Brian Hogg, John Martland, Spencer Leigh, Phil Wilding, Bruce Crowther, Linton Chiswick, Paul Toal of Audio T in Brentwood, Essex, Dorothy Howe, Sue and Dave Williams at Frontier Promotions, and Danny Sperling at New Meeja. Encouragement was provided by Johnny Rogan, Chris

Charlesworth and Johnny Black, while promotion came from the Quite Great Company in the shape of Pete Bassett and Dave Clarke. Computer programming as always from Michael Kaye, and general help and advice from John Burton, Bert Lynch, Kathleen Dougherty, Mad Fred & Dawn Nelson, Dave Larkin and Sabra Larkin.

The two main reference bibles for chart information are Joel Whitburn's *Billboard Top Pop Singles* and *Billboard Top Pop Albums*, and the new UK industry standard *The Complete Book Of The British Charts* by Tony Brown, Jon Kutner and Neil Warwick.

Additionally, thanks to everybody who took the time and inclination to vote this time. I believe the entire Vlemmicks family was the first off the grid. Graham the village postman is responsible for safely delivering over 40 music magazines and a pile of CDs every month. The book was designed by the exceptional Aku, an African Grey parrot who was occasionally assisted by her owner Roger Kohn. Supp came from the *grande fromage* Rob Shreeve, delectable Roz Scott, the always reassuring Dav Gould, and all the others at Virgin Publishi My own highly accomplished team of Susan P and Nic Oliver did their editorial stuff as usu Kelly Larkin inputted all the new charts, tra listings and located the CD sleeves. I colleagues at MUZE Inc. and MUZE UK we quite outstanding in leaving well alone a allowing me the freedom to get stuck in writing the book. At MUZE UK, thanks to Wi Commander Neal Goddard and flight stewa Stephanie Jones and Mark Rigby. Thanks to usual crowd in the USA, including Phil Fletch Matt Puccini, Scott Lehr, Gary Geller, Steph Hughes, Adam Silver, Raisa Howe, Paul Parrei Phil Antman, Jennifer Rose, Marc Miller, and founding dewds, Paul Zullo and the charisma Mark T. Huxley. Lastly, to the family closest my heart and nearest to the CD player, To Dan, Carmen and Kelly.

TOP 50 Artists Of All Time

The Top 50 All Time Artists are listed below. Positions are calculated by the cumulative votes for each artist's albums that appear in the Top 1000 albums. The number of albums by each artist is shown on the right, after the votes total. We set the minimum amount to qualify as three proper albums. It is possible therefore that if Alanis bloody Morissette makes another half-decent album she will qualify. One can only hope that common sense will prevail.

Once again the Beatles win by a mile; they are so far ahead that it is hard to imagine anybody ever being able to overtake them. Bob Dylan also looks pretty safe at the moment.

Of the newer artists it would seem that Radiohead and R.E.M. are the only two that stand any chance of overtaking the top three. Radiohead in particular have made massive inroads with just three albums, and with a new one on the way, we could see some amazing changes. After two less than perfect albums and a ton of internal strife Oasis can no longer be considered.

And still Captain Beefheart and Frank Zappa are in there, yipee! With the latter artist we could compile an all-time Zappa Top 50. We could probably do it with John Coltrane, Miles Davis and Frank Sinatra as well.

1 (1) **The Beatles** – 21,372 (14 albums)	26 (28) **Michael Jackson** – 3,204 (5 albums)
2 (2) **Bob Dylan** – 10,300 (13 albums)	27 (24) **Joni Mitchell** – 3,140 (6 albums)
3 (3) **Pink Floyd** – 9,235 (10 albums)	28 (18) **Manic Street Preachers** – 3,079 (4 albums)
4 (6) **R.E.M.** – 7,857 (12 albums)	29 (29) **Elvis Costello** – 2,959 (8 albums)
5 (7) **U2** – 7,600 (9 albums)	30 (22) **Frank Sinatra** – 2,920 (8 albums)
6 (5) **David Bowie** – 7,279 (9 albums)	31 (31) **The Who** – 2,881 (5 albums)
7 (9) **The Rolling Stones** – 6,940 (11 albums)	32 (37) **The Doors** – 2,808 (6 albums)
8 (4) **Oasis** – 6,895 (3 albums)	33 (26) **The Byrds** – 2,760 (6 albums)
9 (11) **Led Zeppelin** – 6,235 (8 albums)	34 (34) **Stevie Wonder** – 2,657 (5 albums)
10 (8) **Radiohead** – 6,231 (3 albums)	35 (–) **Metallica** – 2,651 (7 albums)
11 (16) **Miles Davis** – 5,104 (14 albums)	36 (30) **Paul Simon** – 2,616 (5 albums)
12 (13) **Van Morrison** – 5,052 (9 albums)	37 (45) **Grateful Dead** – 2,348 (9 albums)
13 (10) **Nirvana** – 5,031 (4 albums)	38 (–) **Pulp** – 2,309 (3 albums)
14 (12) **The Beach Boys** – 4,839 (7 albums)	39 (–) **Aerosmith** – 2,307 (8 albums)
15 (20) **Neil Young** – 4,682 (11 albums)	40 (39) **Steely Dan** – 2,298 (6 albums)
16 (14) **Jimi Hendrix** – 4,544 (4 albums)	41 (–) **Madonna** – 2,288 (6 albums)
17 (15) **The Smiths** – 3,994 (5 albums)	42 (32) **Captain Beefheart** – 2,281 (4 albums)
18 (21) **Fleetwood Mac** – 3,832 (5 albums)	43 (40) **Smashing Pumpkins** – 2,226 (3 albums)
19 (25) **Bruce Springsteen** – 3,812 (8 albums)	44 (–) **Pearl Jam** – 2,141 (5 albums)
20 (19) **Velvet Underground** – 3,588 (4 albums)	45 (–) **The Eagles** – 2,138 (5 albums)
21 (35) **Bob Marley** – 3,474 (9 albums)	46 (38) **Frank Zappa** – 2,076 (7 albums)
22 (17) **The Clash** – 3,392 (3 albums)	47 (33) **The Band** – 2,021 (3 albums)
23 (23) **Marvin Gaye** – 3,305 (6 albums)	48 (–) **Massive Attack** – 1,956 (3 albums)
24 (–) **Blur** – 3,248 (4 albums)	49 (–) **Tori Amos** – 1,903 (4 albums)
25 (27) **Prince** – 3,230 (4 albums)	50 (46) **John Coltrane** – 1,877 (5 albums)

● The 1998 positions are shown in brackets

All-Time Favourite Decades

The 90s leapt from fourth position to become the most popular. The 60s receded even further so that it now trails the 80s. Surely this is a horrible mistake? The 1998 percentages are in brackets.

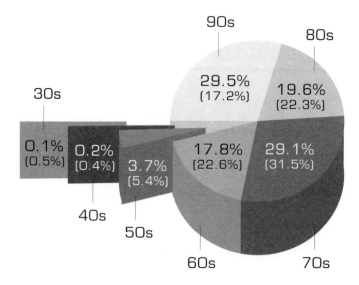

90s

80s

30s

0.1%
(0.5%)

0.2%
(0.4%)

3.7%
(5.4%)

29.5%
(17.2%)

19.6%
(22.3%)

17.8%
(22.6%)

29.1%
(31.5%)

40s

50s

60s

70s

All-Time Favourite Genres

We divided the albums into 13 categories. Interestingly, although both rap and dance have a bigger slice, it is heavy metal which makes a startling comeback. This is primarily due to the inclusion of American hardcore and alternative rock under this banner. The indie section has exactly the same percentage this time, although the albums have been shuffled quite a bit. Likewise, my own lack of comprehension for 'what is dance' probably sells the genre short. Folk, Stage and Film continue to decline, or maybe I am just not finding the people out there. The previous 1998 percentages are in brackets.

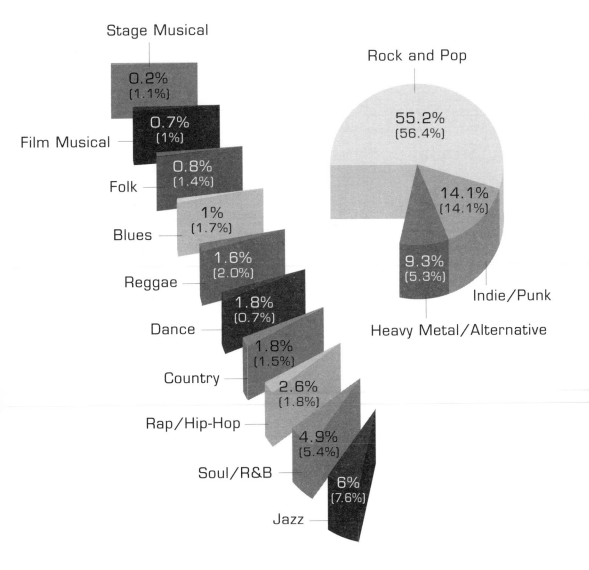

Stage Musical

0.2%
(1.1%)

Film Musical

0.7%
(1%)

Folk

0.8%
(1.4%)

Blues

1%
(1.7%)

Reggae

1.6%
(2.0%)

Dance

1.8%
(0.7%)

Country

1.8%
(1.5%)

Rap/Hip-Hop

2.6%
(1.8%)

Soul/R&B

4.9%
(5.4%)

Jazz

6%
(7.6%)

Rock and Pop

55.2%
(56.4%)

14.1%
(14.1%)

9.3%
(5.3%)

Indie/Punk

Heavy Metal/Alternative

The All-Time 50 Albums
Bubbling Under

Just a few more votes, or in the case of the top few, just one more would have done the trick. Many of these are the ones kicked out by new entries, others were the also-rans who just needed that extra support.

1001 **Rio** – Duran Duran
1002 **Blizzard Of Oz** – Ozzy Osbourne
1003 **The Sun Collection** – Elvis Presley
1004 **Trans-Europe Express** – Kraftwerk
1005 **A Swingin' Affair!** – Frank Sinatra
1006 **Indigo Girls** – Indigo Girls
1007 **Rapture** – Anita Baker
1008 **All Change** – Cast
1009 **Elegantly Wasted** – INXS
1010 **Diva** – Annie Lennox
1011 **Texas Flood** – Stevie Ray Vaughan
1012 **Gish** – The Smashing Pumpkins
1013 **The Who Sings My Generation** – The Who
1014 **Charlie Parker On Dial, Vols 1-6** – Charlie Parker
1015 **Cuckoo** – Curve
1016 **Fashion Nugget** – Cake
1017 **Thick As A Brick** – Jethro Tull
1018 **Sublime** – Sublime
1019 **Fragile** – Yes
1020 **Gordon** – The Barenaked Ladies
1021 **Electric Music For The Mind and Body** – Country Joe and The Fish
1022 **Listen Like Thieves** – INXS
1023 **Searching For The Young Soul Rebels** – Dexys Midnight Runners
1024 **Operation: Mindcrime** – Queensrÿche
1025 **Double Live** – Garth Brooks
1026 **The Fantastic Expedition Of Dillard and Clark** – Doug Dillard & Gene Clark

1027 **The Final Cut** – Pink Floyd
1028 **Let It Be** – The Replacements
1029 **Cosmo's Factory** – Creedence Clearwater Revival
1030 **Black Sabbath** – Black Sabbath
1031 **Heart** – Heart
1032 **Misplaced Childhood** – Marillion
1033 **Brain Salad Surgery** – Emerson, Lake and Palmer
1034 **Pronounced Leh-Nerd Skin-Nerd** – Lynyrd Skynyrd
1035 **Rites Of Passage** – The Indigo Girls
1036 **A Kind Of Magic** – Queen
1037 **Red Headed Stranger** – Willie Nelson
1038 **Shout At The Devil** – Mötley Crüe
1039 **Future Days** – Can
1040 **Star** – Belly
1041 **Breezin'** – George Benson
1042 **Live At Red Rocks 8.15.95** – The Dave Matthews Band
1043 **Come Dance With Me** – Frank Sinatra
1044 **Middle Of Nowhere** – Hanson
1045 **A Salty Dog** – Procol Harum
1046 **Time Out** – Dave Brubeck
1047 **New Miserable Experience** – The Gin Blossoms
1048 **L.A.M.F.** – The Heartbreakers
1049 **The Man-Machine** – Kraftwerk
1050 **Hellbilly Deluxe** – Rob Zombie

50 All-Time Hit Albums
Absolutely Nobody Voted For

These were mega-selling albums by highly successful artists. Some were successful for half an hour, others like Barbra Streisand, Mariah Carey, Donna Summer, and even dear old Perry Como were/are simply huge. Multi-platinums and Number 1's abound, but astonishingly, not one vote was recorded for any of them. What does this say about the taste of the experts and fans? Do the voters have short memories, or ultimately do the people know best? How many records in your own collection are you ashamed of? Even when prompted by a drunken dinner party guest, who has been poking through your record collection, to put on a Thompson Twins album there is still a stigma attached to a dead and buried album. Just remember, 'highly successful' and 'popular' does not necessarily mean 'good'.

All of us have these dark secrets. I can recall in the mid-70s putting on a Barclay James Harvest album to entertain a few friends. I'll get me coat . . .

1   **Music Box** – Mariah Carey
2   **Jane McDonald** – Jane McDonald
3   **Hangin' Tough** – New Kids On The Block
4   **Non-Stop Erotic Cabaret** – Soft Cell
5   **Forever and Ever** – Demis Roussos
6   **Guilty** – Barbra Steisand
7   **Daydream** – Mariah Carey
8   **So Good** – Mica Paris
9   **Blue Jays** – Justin Hayward & John Lodge
10 **My Name Is Barbra, Two** – Barbra Streisand
11 **Robson & Jerome** – Robson and Jerome
12 **Into The Gap** – The Thompson Twins
13 **Rock Of The Westies** – Elton John
14 **True** – Spandau Ballet
15 **Vital Idol** – Billy Idol
16 **Discovery** – ELO
17 **Flying Colours** – Chris De Burgh
18 **I Remember Yesterday** – Donna Summer
19 **When The World Knows Your Name** – Deacon Blue
20 **It's Better To Travel** – Swing Out Sister
21 **Popped In Souled Out** – Wet Wet Wet
22 **Hello** – Status Quo
23 **Fantastic** – Wham!
24 **Heaven On Earth** – Belinda Carlisle
25 **And I Love You So** – Perry Como

26 **Slade Alive** – Slade
27 **Turn Back The Clock** – Johnny Hates Jazz
28 **Real Love** – Lisa Stansfield
29 **A Little Bit More** – Dr. Hook
30 **Shaky** – Shakin' Stevens
31 **Back To Front** – Gilbert O'Sullivan
32 **The Jazz Singer** – Neil Diamond
33 **Love Over Gold** – Dire Straits
34 **Love Hurts** – Cher
35 **Beverley Craven** – Beverley Craven
36 **The Crossing** – Big Country
37 **Close** – Kim Wilde
38 **Rollin'** – Bay City Rollers
39 **Up** – Right Said Fred
40 **Soul Provider** – Michael Bolton
41 **Manilow Magic** – Barry Manilow
42 **No Parlez** – Paul Young
43 **Time, Love and Tenderness** – Michael Bolton
44 **Go West** – Go West
45 **Pearls** – Elkie Brooks
46 **Everything Changes** – Take That
47 **Endless Flight** – Leo Sayer
48 **American Pie** – Don McLean
49 **The Innocents** – Erasure
50 **Step By Step** – New Kids On The Block

BLUES
The All-Time Top 50

1 (2) **Bluesbreakers With Eric Clapton** – John Mayall and The Bluesbreakers

2 (4) **The Healer** – John Lee Hooker

3 (5) **Peter Green's Fleetwood Mac** – Fleetwood Mac

4 (10) **The Sky Is Crying** – Stevie Ray Vaughan

5 (16) **Bare Wires** – John Mayall

6 (6) **Live At The Regal** – B.B. King

7 (1) **King Of The Delta Blues Singers** – Robert Johnson

8 (9) **A Hard Road** – John Mayall and the Bluesbreakers

9 (7) **Damn Right, I've Got The Blues** – Buddy Guy

10 (46) **Mr Lucky** – John Lee Hooker

11 (11) **In Step** – Stevie Ray Vaughan

12 (12) **Born Under A Bad Sign** – Albert King

13 (13) **The Blues Of Lightnin' Hopkins** – Lightnin' Hopkins

14 (14) **Couldn't Stand The Weather** – Stevie Ray Vaughan

15 (15) **Muddy Waters At Newport** – Muddy Waters

16 (3) **Texas Flood** – Stevie Ray Vaughan

17 (–) **Lie To Me** – Jonny Lang

18 (18) **Moanin' In The Moonlight** – Howlin' Wolf

19 (–) **Just Like You** – Keb' Mo'

20 (8) **Getting Ready** – Freddie King

21 (50) **Live At St Quentin** – B.B. King

22 (–) **The Real Folk Blues** – Howlin' Wolf

23 (27) **The Complete Chess Folk Blues Sessions** – John Lee Hooker

24 (–) **The Legendary Modern Recordings 1948-1954** – John Lee Hooker

25 (29) **Muddy Waters Folk Singer** – Muddy Waters

26 (–) **Deuces Wild** – B.B. King

27 (22) **The Late Fantastically Great** – Elmore James

28 (34) **The Blues Of Otis Spann** – Otis Spann

29 (31) **The London Howlin' Wolf Session** – Howlin' Wolf

30 (20) **The Complete Recordings** – Bessie Smith

31 (–) **Phantom Blues** – Taj Mahal

32 (37) **Hooker 'N' Heat** – John Lee Hooker and Canned Heat

33 (45) **Iceman** – Albert Collins

34 (43) **Showdown!** – Albert Collins, Robert Cray, Johnny Copeland

35 (26) **My Kind Of Blues** – B.B. King

36 (42) **Strong Persuader** – Robert Cray

37 (–) **There Is Always One More Time** – B.B. King

38 (23) **Just Jimmy Reed** – Jimmy Reed

39 (21) **Complete Library Of Congress Recordings** – Lead Belly

40 (–) **Keb' Mo'** – Keb' Mo'

41 (25) **Sings Down and Out Blues** – Sonny Boy Williamson

42 (–) **Chill Out** – John Lee Hooker

43 (39) **Ice Pickin'** – Albert Collins

44 (–) **A Ass Pocket Of Whiskey** – R.L. Burnside

45 (44) **Taj Mahal** – Taj Mahal

46 (–) **The Natch'l Blues** – Taj Mahal

47 (–) **Willie's Blues** – Willie Dixon and Memphis Slim

48 (–) **The Blues Never Die!** – Otis Spann

49 (48) **The Truth** – T-Bone Walker

50 (–) **Wander This World** – Jonny Lang

● The 1998 positions are shown in brackets

COUNTRY
The All-Time Top 50

1 (3) **Sweetheart Of The Rodeo** – The Byrds
2 (1) **Grievous Angel** – Gram Parsons
3 (–) **Come On Over** – Shania Twain
4 (–) **Wrecking Ball** – Emmylou Harris
5 (4) **Copperhead Road** – Steve Earle
6 (9) **Patsy Cline Showcase** – Patsy Cline
7 (14) **Modern Sounds In Country and Western Music** – Ray Charles
8 (2) **The Gilded Palace Of Sin** – Flying Burrito Brothers
9 (15) **I Still Believe In You** – Vince Gill
10 (7) **Johnny Cash At Folsom Prison** – Johnny Cash
11 (–) **Wide Open Spaces** – The Dixie Chicks
12 (–) **The Woman In Me** – Shania Twain
13 (29) **No Fences** – Garth Brooks
14 (30) **Ropin' The Wind** – Garth Brooks
15 (–) **Everywhere** – Tim McGraw
16 (–) **Car Wheels On A Gravel Road** – Lucinda Williams
17 (16) **Come On Come On** – Mary-Chapin Carpenter
18 (–) **Mermaid Avenue** – Billy Bragg and Wilco
19 (–) **Did I Shave My Legs For This?** – Deana Carter
20 (10) **Old No. 1** – Guy Clark
21 (13) **Moanin' The Blues** – Hank Williams
22 (11) **Johnny Cash At St Quentin** – Johnny Cash
23 (12) **Blue** – LeAnn Rimes
24 (6) **Guitar Town** – Steve Earle
25 (5) **Red Headed Stranger** – Willie Nelson

26 (8) **Shotgun Willie** – Willie Nelson
27 (25) **Hank Williams Sings** – Hank Williams
28 (19) **Ramblin' Man** – Hank Williams
29 (23) **Gunfighter Ballads and Trail Songs** – Marty Robbins
30 (21) **Waylon & Willie** – Waylon Jennings and Willie Nelson
31 (–) **Double Live** – Garth Brooks
32 (27) **City Of New Orleans** – Willie Nelson
33 (–) **When Love Finds You** – Vince Gill
34 (17) **Country Music Hall Of Fame** – Jimmie Rodgers
35 (22) **Ol' Waylon** – Waylon Jennings
36 (28) **Songs Our Daddy Taught Us** – The Everly Brothers
37 (24) **Always On My Mind** – Willie Nelson
38 (32) **Quarter Moon In A Ten Cent Town** – Emmylou Harris
39 (20) **Memorial Album** – Hank Williams
40 (33) **Guitars Cadillacs Etc. Etc.** – Dwight Yoakam
41 (34) **When Tragedy Struck** – Hank Snow
42 (35) **Killin' Time** – Clint Black
43 (–) **High Mileage** – Alan Jackson
44 (36) **If There Was A Way** – Dwight Yoakam
45 (37) **Always and Forever** – Randy Travis
46 (–) **Faith** – Faith Hill
47 (40) **Trio** – Dolly Parsons, Linda Ronstadt, Emmylou Harris
48 (42) **Songs Of Tragedy** – Hank Snow
49 (–) **Music For All Occasions** – The Mavericks
50 (–) **Not A Moment Too Soon** – Tim McGraw

● The 1998 positions are shown in brackets

DANCE
The All-Time Top 50

1 (–) **Blue Lines** – Massive Attack
2 (–) **Leftism** – Leftfield
3 (–) **Moon Safari** – Air
4 (–) **Dig Your Own Hole** – The Chemical Brothers
5 (–) **Endtroducing ...** – DJ Shadow
6 (–) **Dubnobasswithmyheadman** – Underworld
7 (–) **Protection** – Massive Attack
8 (–) **The Orb's Adventures Beyond The Ultraworld** – The Orb
9 (–) **The Fat Of The Land** – Prodigy
10 (–) **Music For The Jilted Generation** – The Prodigy
11 (–) **Maxinquaye** – Tricky
12 (–) **Club Classics Vol. 1** – Soul II Soul
13 (–) **The Cross Of Changes** – Enigma
14 (–) **Mezzanine** – Massive Attack
15 (–) **You've Come A Long Way, Baby** – Fatboy Slim
16 (–) **Play** – Moby
17 (–) **Selected Ambient Works: 1985-1992** – Aphex Twin
18 (–) **Surrender** – The Chemical Brothers
19 (–) **Remedy** – Basement Jaxx
20 (–) **Swass** – Sir Mix-A-Lot
21 (–) **Modus Operandi** – Photek
22 (–) **In Sides** – Orbital
23 (–) **Let's Get Killed** – David Holmes
24 (–) **MCMXC AD** – Enigma
25 (–) **New Forms** – Roni Size
26 (–) **Northern Exposure 2** – Sasha and John Digweed
27 (–) **Rafi's Revenge** – Asian Dub Foundation
28 (–) **Global Underground 006: Sydney** – John Digweed
29 (–) **Orbus Terrarum** – The Orb
30 (–) **Prince Blimey** – Red Snapper
31 (–) **All In The Mind** – Bucketheads
32 (–) **Tripomatic Fairytales 2001** – Jam and Spoon
33 (–) **Global Underground 009: San Francisco** – Sasha
34 (–) **Snivilisation** – Orbital
35 (–) **Orblivion** – The Orb
36 (–) **Beaucoup Fish** – Underworld
37 (–) **Exit Planet Dust** – The Chemical Brothers
38 (–) **Goldie Presents Metalheadz: Timeless** – Goldie
39 (–) **Prodigy Present The Dirtchamber Sessions Volume One** – Prodigy
40 (–) **Second Toughest In The Infants** – Underworld
41 (–) **Animal Rights** – Moby
42 (–) **Essential Mix** – David Holmes
43 (–) **Accelerator** – Future Sound Of London
44 (–) **Le Roi Est Mort, Vive Le Roi!** – Enigma
45 (–) **Community Music** – Asian Dub Foundation
46 (–) **Sinking** – Aloof
47 (–) **Sunday 8pm** – Faithless
48 (–) **Electro Boogie** – Dave Clarke
49 (–) **Dreamland** – Robert Miles
50 (–) **Trip On This** – Technotronic

● The 1998 positions are shown in brackets

HEAVY METAL/ALTERNATIVE ROCK
The All-Time Top 50

1 (–)   **Nevermind** – Nirvana
2 (1)   **Led Zeppelin IV** – Led Zeppelin
3 (6)   **Led Zeppelin** – Led Zeppelin
4 (–)   **Ten** – Pearl Jam
5 (–)   **Mellon Collie and The Infinite Sadness** – The Smashing Pumpkins
6 (3)   **Led Zeppelin II** – Led Zeppelin
7 (5)   **Metallica** – Metallica
8 (9)   **Van Halen** – Van Halen
9 (7)   **Master Of Puppets** – Metallica
10 (8) **Back In Black** – AC/DC
11 (10) **Houses Of The Holy** – Led Zeppelin
12 (13) **Hysteria** – Def Leppard
13 (4) **Appetite For Destruction** – Guns N'Roses
14 (–) **Americana** – The Offspring
15 (–) **Siamese Dream** – The Smashing Pumpkins
16 (2) **Physical Graffiti** – Led Zeppelin
17 (21) **Machine Head** – Deep Purple
18 (22) **Toys In The Attic** – Aerosmith
19 (17) **Nothing's Shocking** – Jane's Addiction
20 (–) **Rage Against The Machine** – Rage Against The Machine
21 (–) **Mechanical Animals** – Marilyn Manson
22 (32) **Superunknown** – Soundgarden
23 (29) **Pyromania** – Def Leppard
24 (–) **Escape** – Journey
25 (14) **Highway To Hell** – AC/DC

26 (–) **In Utero** – Nirvana
27 (39) **Dirt** – Alice In Chains
28 (–) **Pretty Hate Machine** – Nine Inch Nails
29 (33) **Get A Grip** – Aerosmith
30 (50) **Use Your Illusion II** – Guns N'Roses
31 (–) **MTV Unplugged In New York** – Nirvana
32 (11) **Slippery When Wet** – Bon Jovi
33 (18) **Paranoid** – Black Sabbath
34 (16) **The Number Of The Beast** – Iron Maiden
35 (15) **Led Zeppelin III** – Led Zeppelin
36 (26) **1984** – Van Halen
37 (–) **Foo Fighters** – Foo Fighters
38 (–) **My Own Prison** – Creed
39 (–) **... And Justice For All** – Metallica
40 (–) **Vs.** – Pearl Jam
41 (31) **Dressed To Kill** – Kiss
42 (–) **The Downward Spiral** – Nine Inch Nails
43 (34) **These Days** – Bon Jovi
44 (–) **Yield** – Pearl Jam
45 (–) **Sixteen Stone** – Bush
46 (35) **Permanent Vacation** – Aerosmith
47 (–) **Keep The Faith** – Bon Jovi
48 (–) **Burn** – Deep Purple
49 (38) **Rocks** – Aerosmith
50 (30) **Unleashed In The East** – Judas Priest

● The 1998 positions are shown in brackets

INDIE/PUNK
The All-Time Top 50

1 (2) **The Bends** – Radiohead
2 (5) **OK Computer** – Radiohead
3 (6) **The Queen Is Dead** – The Smiths
4 (4) **The Stone Roses** – The Stone Roses
5 (1) **(What's The Story) Morning Glory?** – Oasis
6 (3) **Never Mind The Bollocks Here's The Sex Pistols** – The Sex Pistols
7 (8) **London Calling** – The Clash
8 (10) **Dummy** – Portishead
9 (7) **Definitely Maybe** – Oasis
10 (32) **Marquee Moon** – Television
11 (16) **Odelay** – Beck
12 (38) **The Smiths** – The Smiths
13 (–) **Loveless** – My Bloody Valentine
14 (26) **Debut** – Björk
15 (–) **Disintegration** – Cure
16 (9) **Parklife** – Blur
17 (47) **Garbage** – Garbage
18 (28) **Doolittle** – The Pixies
19 (–) **Meat Is Murder** – The Smiths
20 (12) **Screamadelica** – Primal Scream
21 (–) **Slanted and Enchanted** – Pavement
22 (37) **Blood Sugar Sex Magik** – The Red Hot Chili Peppers
23 (–) **Fresh Fruit For Rotting Vegetables** – The Dead Kennedys
24 (21) **Dog Man Star** – Suede
25 (48) **Surfer Rosa** – The Pixies

26 (24) **The Clash** – The Clash
27 (–) **Setting Sons** – The Jam
28 (–) **Pornography** – The Cure
29 (39) **Hatful Of Hollow** – The Smiths
30 (–) **Sandinista!** – The Clash
31 (–) **Dookie** – Green Day
32 (13) **Everything Must Go** – The Manic Street Preachers
33 (15) **Urban Hymns** – The Verve
34 (14) **Different Class** – Pulp
35 (–) **Heaven Or Las Vegas** – The Cocteau Twins
36 (29) **Suede** – Suede
37 (–) **Viva Hate** – Morrissey
38 (43) **The Ramones** – The Ramones
39 (–) **Crooked Rain, Crooked Rain** – Pavement
40 (–) **Exile In Guyville** – Liz Phair
41 (36) **Unknown Pleasures** – Joy Division
42 (44) **Placebo** – Placebo
43 (34) **All Mod Cons** – The Jam
44 (35) **His 'N' Hers** – Pulp
45 (–) **Kiss Me Kiss Me Kiss Me** – The Cure
46 (19) **Blur** – Blur
47 (18) **The Holy Bible** – The Manic Street Preachers
48 (–) **Version 2.0.** – Garbage
49 (22) **Closer** – Joy Division
50 (25) **A Northern Soul** – The Verve

● The 1998 positions are shown in brackets

JAZZ
The All-Time Top 50

1 (1)   **Kind Of Blue** – Miles Davis
2 (2)   **A Love Supreme** – John Coltrane
3 (3)   **In A Silent Way** – Miles Davis
4 (6)   **Sketches Of Spain** – Miles Davis
5 (39) **Mingus Ah Um** – Charles Mingus
6 (4)   **The Blanton-Webster Years** – Duke Ellington
7 (7)   **Bitches Brew** – Miles Davis
8 (9)   **Blues and The Abstract Truth** – Oliver Nelson
9 (10) **Blue Train** – John Coltrane
10 (5) **Birth Of The Cool** – Miles Davis
11 (29) **The Köln Concert** – Keith Jarrett
12 (–) **My Favorite Things** – John Coltrane
13 (17) **Miles Smiles** – Miles Davis
14 (11) **Genius Of Modern Music Vols 1 & 2** – Thelonious Monk
15 (18) **Saxophone Colossus** – Sonny Rollins
16 (12) **The Atomic Mr. Basie** – Count Basie
17 (14) **The Complete Savoy Sessions** – Charlie Parker
18 (19) **The Black Saint and The Sinner Lady** – Charles Mingus
19 (20) **Maiden Voyage** – Herbie Hancock
20 (24) **Gerry Mulligan Meets Ben Webster** – Gerry Mulligan and Ben Webster
21 (36) **At Newport** – Duke Ellington
22 (35) **Waltz For Debby** – Bill Evans
23 (43) **My Funny Valentine** – Miles Davis
24 (40) **The George and Ira Gershwin Songbook** Ella Fitzgerald
25 (21) **Milestones** – Miles Davis

26 (23) **Body and Soul** – Coleman Hawkins
27 (27) **Ella Fitzgerald Sings The Cole Porter Songbook** – Ella Fitzgerald
28 (26) **Mingus Mingus Mingus Mingus Mingus** – Charles Mingus
29 (–) **Round About Midnight** – Miles Davis
30 (13) **Lady In Autumn** – Billie Holiday
31 (31) **Money Jungle** – Duke Ellington
32 (33) **Ellington Indigos** – Duke Ellington
33 (49) **Organ Grinder Swing** – Jimmy Smith
34 (–) **Sonny Rollins Vol. 2** – Sonny Rollins
35 (–) **Travels** – Pat Metheny
36 (46) **Our Man In Paris** – Dexter Gordon
37 (28) **The Sidewinder** – Lee Morgan
38 (30) **Song For My Father** – Horace Silver Quintet
39 (–) **Ella and Louis** – Ella Fitzgerald and Louis Armstrong
40 (–) **Ella Fitzgerald Sings The Rodgers and Hart Songbook** – Ella Fitzgerald
41 (–) **The Complete Live At The Plugged Nickel 1965** – Miles Davis
42 (–) **Offramp** – Pat Metheny
43 (–) **Got My Mojo Workin'** – Jimmy Smith
44 (–) **Impressions** – John Coltrane
45 (–) **The Cat** – Jimmy Smith
46 (–) **Solo Monk** – Thelonious Monk
47 (15) **Giant Steps** – John Coltrane
48 (–) **Porgy and Bess** – Miles Davis
49 (44) **Heavy Weather** – Weather Report
50 (–) **Monk's Music** – Thelonious Monk

● The 1998 positions are shown in brackets

RAP/HIP-HOP
The All-Time Top 50

1 (1) **It Takes A Nation Of Millions To Hold Us Back** – Public Enemy

2 (18) **Licensed To III** – The Beastie Boys

3 (3) **Paul's Boutique** – The Beastie Boys

4 (6) **The Chronic** – Dr. Dre

5 (4) **3 Feet High and Rising** – De La Soul

6 (10) **Enter The Wu-Tang (36 Chambers)** – Wu-Tang Clan

7 (–) **Check Your Head** – The Beastie Boys

8 (–) **All Eyez On Me** – 2Pac

9 (11) **Straight Outta Compton** – N.W.A.

10 (15) **Life After Death** – The Notorious B.I.G.

11 (–) **Doggystyle** – Snoop Doggy Dogg

12 (16) **The Low End Theory** – A Tribe Called Quest

13 (7) **Paid In Full** – Eric B & Rakim

14 (–) **Big Willie Style** – Will Smith

15 (12) **Hypocrisy Is The Greatest Luxury** – The Disposable Heroes of Hiphoprisy

16 (17) **E.1999 Eternal** – Bone Thugs-N-Harmony

17 (2) **Fear Of A Black Planet** – Public Enemy

18 (–) **Slim Shady LP** – Eminem

19 (14) **One For All** – Brand Nubian

20 (–) **Hello Nasty** – The Beastie Boys

21 (–) **The Score** – Fugees

22 (9) **Ready To Die** – The Notorious B.I.G.

23 (–) **III Communication** – The Beastie Boys

24 (–) **No Way Out** – Puff Daddy and The Family

25 (–) **Me Against The World** – 2Pac

26 (5) **Follow The Leader** – Eric B & Rakim

27 (8) **By All Means Necessary** – Boogie Down Productions

28 (19) **The Message** – Grandmaster Flash and The Furious Five

29 (20) **Raising Hell** – Run DMC

30 (21) **Apocalypse '91 ... The Enemy Strikes Black** – Public Enemy

31 (22) **Of The Heart, Of The Soul and Of The Cross: The Utopian Experience** – P.M. Dawn

32 (23) **Straight Out The Jungle** – The Jungle Brothers

33 (24) **Strictly Business** – EPMD

34 (25) **3 Years, 5 Months, and 2 Days In The Life Of** – Arrested Development

35 (26) **Ghetto Music: The Blueprint Of Hip Hop** Boogie Down Productions

36 (27) **People's Instinctive Travels and The Paths Of Rhythm** – A Tribe Called Quest

37 (28) **All Hail The Queen** – Queen Latifah

38 (29) **Yo! Bum Rush The Show** – Public Enemy

39 (30) **Mama Said Knock You Out** – LL Cool J

40 (–) **2Pacalypse Now** – 2Pac

41 (32) **Cypress Hill** – Cypress Hill

42 (34) **Wanted: Dead Or Alive** – Kool G Rap and DJ Polo

43 (–) **The Don Killuminati: The 7 Day Theory** – Makaveli

44 (35) **AmeriKKKa's Most Wanted** – Ice Cube

45 (–) **Hell On Earth** – Mobb Deep

46 (41) **Criminal Minded** – Boogie Down Productions

47 (–) **No Limit Top Dogg** – Snoop Dogg

48 (–) **In My Lifetime, Vol 1 ...** – Jay-Z

49 (–) **I Am ...** – Nas

50 (–) **Doc's Da Name 2000** – Redman

● The 1998 positions are shown in brackets

REGGAE
The All-Time Top 50

1 (1)   **Legend** – Bob Marley and The Wailers
2 (4)   **Live!** – Bob Marley and The Wailers
3 (2)   **Catch A Fire** – Bob Marley and The Wailers
4 (3)   **Natty Dread** – Bob Marley and The Wailers
5 (5)   **Burnin'** – The Wailers
6 (10) **Rastaman Vibration** – Bob Marley and The Wailers
7 (12) **African Herbsman** – Bob Marley and The Wailers
8 (11) **Kaya** – Bob Marley and The Wailers
9 (19) **Reggae Greats** – Toots and The Maytals
10 (15) **Operation Radication** – Yellowman
11 (8) **Dreadlocks Dread** – Big Youth
12 (9) **Dread Inna Babylon** – U-Roy
13 (14) **Equal Rights** – Peter Tosh
14 (43) **Black Woman and Child** – Sizzla
15 (6) **Exodus** – Bob Marley and The Wailers
16 (7) **Marcus Garvey** – Burning Spear
17 (27) **Screaming Target** – Big Youth
18 (13) **Social Living** – Burning Spear
19 (22) **Gussie Presenting** – I. Roy
20 (16) **Mr. Mention** – Buju Banton
21 (29) **Funky Kingston** – Toots and The Maytals
22 (17) **Labour Of Love** – UB40
23 (44) **Survival** – Bob Marley and The Wailers
24 (33) **Blackheart Man** – Bunny Wailer
25 (26) **The Wailing Wailers** – The Wailers

26 (–) **Super Ape** – Lee Perry
27 (–) **Midnite Lover** – Shaggy
28 (28) **Soon Forward** – Gregory Isaacs
29 (23) **King Tubby Meets Rockers Uptown** – Augustus Pablo
30 (–) **The Upsetter** – Lee Perry
31 (–) **Many Moods Of Moses** – Beenie Man
32 (24) **Wolf & Leopards** – Dennis Brown
33 (46) **This Is Augustus Pablo** – Augustus Pablo
34 (–) **Inna Heights** – Buju Banton
35 (30) **Version Galore** – U-Roy
36 (21) **Right Time** – The Mighty Diamonds
37 (49) **Many Moods Of** – I. Roy
38 (32) **Flesh Of My Skin, Blood Of My Blood** – Keith Hudson
39 (–) **Think Like A Girl** – Diana King
40 (–) **Jamaica's Most Wanted** – Bounty Killer
41 (37) **Skylarking** – Horace Andy
42 (–) **Babylon By Bus** – Bob Marley and The Wailers
43 (40) **Uprising** – Bob Marley and The Wailers
44 (–) **Yardcore** – Born Jamaicans
45 (41) **Blackboard Jungle Dub** – The Upsetters
46 (–) **Three Against War** – Beenie Man
47 (–) **Chant Down Babylon** – Various
48 (–) **U-Roy** – U-Roy
49 (45) **Cool Ruler** – Gregory Isaacs
50 (47) **Choice Of Version** – Prince Jazzbo

● The 1998 positions are shown in brackets

SOUL/R&B
The All-Time Top 50

1 (1) **What's Going On** – Marvin Gaye
2 (2) **Thriller** – Michael Jackson
3 (3) **Songs In The Key Of Life** – Stevie Wonder
4 (4) **Otis Blue** – Otis Redding
5 (6) **Innervisions** – Stevie Wonder
6 (14) **Dusty In Memphis** – Dusty Springfield
7 (9) **Off The Wall** – Michael Jackson
8 (7) **Live At The Apollo Vol. 1** – James Brown
9 (12) **Lady Soul** – Aretha Franklin
10 (16) **HIStory: Past, Present and Future – Book 1** – Michael Jackson
11 (5) **Bad** – Michael Jackson
12 (10) **Talking Book** – Stevie Wonder
13 (42) **Dangerous** – Michael Jackson
14 (18) **I Never Loved A Man The Way I Loved You** – Aretha Franklin
15 (20) **Genius + Soul = Jazz** – Ray Charles
16 (15) **Let's Get It On** – Marvin Gaye
17 (–) **On How Life Is** – Macy Gray
18 (22) **The Genius Of Ray Charles** – Ray Charles
19 (37) **Fulfillingness' First Finale** – Stevie Wonder
20 (27) **I Want You** – Marvin Gaye
21 (34) **The Genius Hits The Road** – Ray Charles
22 (30) **The Man and His Music** – Sam Cooke
23 (38) **Trouble Man** – Marvin Gaye
24 (46) **Midnight Love** – Marvin Gaye
25 (33) **Complete & Unbelievable: The Otis Redding Dictionary Of Soul** – Otis Redding

26 (41) **Here, My Dear** – Marvin Gaye
27 (17) **Can't Slow Down** – Lionel Richie
28 (44) **What's The 411?** – Mary J. Blige
29 (45) **Janet** – Janet Jackson
30 (–) **Baduizm** – Erykah Badu
31 (50) **Aretha Now** – Aretha Franklin
32 (49) **The Soul Album** – Otis Redding
33 (47) **Hot Buttered Soul** – Isaac Hayes
34 (11) **Secrets** – Toni Braxton
35 (–) **The Great Otis Redding Sings Soul Ballads** – Otis Redding
36 (–) **Music Of My Mind** – Stevie Wonder
37 (40) **Tell Mama** – Etta James
38 (–) **The Miseducation Of Lauryn Hill** – Lauryn Hill
39 (25) **Crazy Sexy Cool** – TLC
40 (–) **Whitney Houston** – Whitney Houston
41 (32) **Backstabbers** – The O'Jays
42 (19) **Let's Stay Together** – Al Green
43 (35) **The Dock Of The Bay** – Otis Redding
44 (–) **Janet Jackson's Rhythm Nation 1814** – Janet Jackson
45 (8) **Stand!** – Sly and The Family Stone
46 (–) **Fanmail** – TLC
47 (13) **There's A Riot Goin' On** – Sly and The Family Stone
48 (21) **Superfly** – Curtis Mayfield
49 (24) **3+3** – The Isley Brothers
50 (48) **You Got My Mind Messed Up** – James Carr

● The 1998 positions are shown in brackets

The All-Time 50 Box Sets
To Enhance Every Collection

To qualify they have to be three CDs or more, and they have to include a descriptive book with the package. This is a totally subjective list and my own recommendation, but taken as a whole covers a pretty wide range of music that I am happy to stand by.

1 **Nuggets – Original Artyfacts From The First Psychedelic Era 1965-1968** – Various
2 **The Chess Story 1947-1975** – Various
3 **The Complete Columbia Studio Recordings** – Miles Davis & Gil Evans
4 **30 Years Of Maximum R&B** – The Who
5 **Queen Of Soul: The Atlantic Recordings** – Aretha Franklin
6 **The Birth Of Soul: The Complete Atlantic R&B '52-'59** – Ray Charles
7 **The Complete Stax/Volt Singles 1959-1968** – Various
8 **The Bootleg Series, Volumes 1-3, Rare and Unreleased 1961-1991** – Bob Dylan
9 **Atlantic Rhythm and Blues 1947-1974** – Various
10 **Hitsville USA: The Motown Singles Collection 1959-1971** – Various
11 **The Byrds** – The Byrds
12 **Otis! The Definitive Otis Redding** – Otis Redding
13 **The Complete Muddy Waters 1947-1967** – Muddy Waters
14 **Peel Slowly and See** – Velvet Underground
15 **The Specialty Story** – Various
16 **The Complete Hank Williams** – Hank Williams
17 **CSN** – Crosby, Stills and Nash
18 **The Rolling Stones Singles Collection: The London Years** – The Rolling Stones
19 **The Doo-Wop Box** – Various
20 **Tracks** – Bruce Springsteen
21 **The Specialty Sessions** – Little Richard
22 **Fruit Tree** – Nick Drake
23 **Harvest Festival 1969-1979** – Various
24 **Heartaches and Harmonies** – Everly Brothers
25 **King Of The Blues** – B.B. King
26 **Zombie Heaven** – The Zombies
27 **Good Vibrations: Thirty Years Of The Beach Boys** – The Beach Boys

28 **They Call Me The Fat Man: The Legendary Imperial Recordings** – Fats Domino
29 **The John Lennon Anthology** – John Lennon
30 **The Patsy Cline Collection** – Patsy Cline
31 **Guilty: 30 Years Of Randy Newman** – Randy Newman
32 **The Sue Records Story: The Sound Of Soul** – Various
33 **Remasters** – Led Zeppelin
34 **The King Of Rock 'n' Roll: The Complete '50s Masters** – Elvis Presley
35 **Star Time** – James Brown
36 **Playback** – Tom Petty and The Heartbreakers
37 **Bo Diddley: The Chess Years** – Bo Diddley
38 **Poet Of Rock 'N' Roll** – Chuck Berry
39 **The Complete Prestige/Bluesville Recordings** – Lightnin' Hopkins
40 **As Long As I'm Singing: The Bobby Darin Collection** – Bobby Darin
41 **The Heavyweight Champion: The Complete Atlantic Recordings** – John Coltrane
42 **Those Were The Days** – Cream
43 **Keith Jarrett At The Blue Note: The Complete Recordings** – Keith Jarrett
44 **Crossroads** – Eric Clapton
45 **Monterey International Pop Festival** – Various
46 **The Complete Blue Horizon Sessions 1967-1969** – Fleetwood Mac
47 **Direction, Reaction, Creation** – The Jam
48 **The Pet Sounds Sessions** – Beach Boys
49 **Long Train Runnin': 1970-2000** – The Doobie Brothers
50 **The Look Of Love: The Burt Bacharach Collection** – Various

50 All-Time Overlooked Jazz Albums

Overlooked in the opinion of the author, but very difficult to narrow down to just 50.

These are jazz albums I know well, and in a short time have grown to love. I came to jazz quite late, but that does not exclude me from having an opinion. This list is not for the jazz buff – I have experienced enough of them to know that their list would be deliberately different and elitist. This 50 is meant for the ordinary person who discovered Kind Of Blue and wants to find out more, but is so intimidated by jazz that he or she does not know where to go. Having experienced this painful transition, I know how it feels. Once you get stuck into this, and assuming you enjoy it, you can hold your head up with confidence.

1   **Gettin' Together** – Paul Gonsalves
2   **Music For Loving: Ben Webster With Strings** – Ben Webster
3   **Everybody Digs Bill Evans** – Bill Evans Trio
4   **Jeru** – Gerry Mulligan
5   **Know What I Mean?** – Julian 'Cannonball' Adderley
6   **Electric Bath** – Don Ellis Orchestra
7   **Newk's Time** – Sonny Rollins
8   **Full View** – Wynton Kelly Trio
9   **Big Music** – Mike Gibbs
10 **Alone With The Blues** – Ray Bryant
11 **The Sermon** – Jimmy Smith
12 **Work Song** – Nat Adderley
13 **The Amazing Adventures Of Simon Simon** – John Surman
14 **Meant To Be** – John Scofield Quartet
15 **Into The Hot** – Gil Evans Orchestra
16 **Quartets: Live At The Village Vanguard** – Joe Lovano
17 **It's OK To Listen To The Gray Voice** – Jan Garbarek
18 **King Of The Tenors** – Ben Webster
19 **Standards Volume 1** – Keith Jarrett Trio
20 **Mulligan Meets Monk** – Gerry Mulligan & Thelonious Monk
21 **Fluid Rustle** – Eberhard Weber
22 **Unity** – Larry Young
23 **Such Sweet Thunder** – Duke Ellington
24 **As Falls Wichita, So Falls Wichita Falls** – Pat Metheny & Lyle Mays
25 **Mulligan Plays Mulligan** – Gerry Mulligan
26 **Love Scenes** – Diana Krall
27 **Solo Concerts: Bremen and Lausanne** – Keith Jarrett
28 **Jimmy & Wes The Dynamic Duo** – Jimmy Smith & Wes Montgomery
29 **Bass Desires** – Marc Johnson
30 **We Free Kings** – Rahsaan Roland Kirk
31 **Little Susie** – Ray Bryant Trio
32 **Michel Plays Petrucciani** – Michel Petrucciani
33 **Matador** – Grant Green
34 **Oh, Yeah!** – Charles Mingus
35 **Portrait In Jazz** – Bill Evans Trio
36 **Soul Station** – Hank Mobley
37 **Soulville** – Ben Webster
38 **Groovin' With Jug** – Richard Holmes & Gene Ammons
39 **A Night At Birdland Volume 1** – Art Blakey Quintet
40 **Getz Meets Gerry Mulligan In Hi-Fi** – Stan Getz & Gerry Mulligan
41 **Misterioso** – Thelonious Monk
42 **African Waltz** – Cannonball Adderley & Orchestra
43 **Mercy Mercy Mercy!** – Cannonball Adderley
44 **The Jimmy Giuffre 3** – Jimmy Giuffre
45 **Jazz In Silhouette** – Sun Ra
46 **How My Heart Sings!** – Bill Evans Trio
47 **Go** – Dexter Gordon
48 **The Hawk Flies High** – Coleman Hawkins
49 **Ray Charles and Betty Carter** – Ray Charles & Betty Carter
50 **Street Dreams** – Lyle Mays

All-Time 50 Long Forgotten Gems

ome slipped the net, even when first released on vinyl. Many have since become cult classics but have never sold in any quantity. Others recently released and deemed unhip should be investigated immediately and reappraised. I would not lie to you. Some are yet to be reissued on CD, or have been included on a decent compilation. Take Moby Grape, for example. I suggest you direct your attention to Vintage Grape, a fantastic compilation. I will continue to annoy my chum at Warners for the CD issue of Earth Opera, Bernie Leadon/Michael Georgiades and Rhinoceros. The latter have just had the intro of 'Apricot Brandy' stolen by Ocean Colour Scene for the Lock Stock theme.

All come highly recommended. Don't turn your nose up at artists you would normally not cross the street for. Give it a listen first, then turn your nose up and fire off a 'come off it' letter to me.

1   **Quah** – Jorma Kaukonen
2   **Recall The Beginning … A Journey From Eden** – Steve Miller Band
3   **Halfbreed** – The Keef Hartley Band
4   **A Long Time Comin'** – The Electric Flag
5   **Sea Shanties** – High Tide
6   **Fame At Last** – Georgie Fame
7   **Ace** – Bob Weir
8   **Moby Grape '69** – Moby Grape
9   **Super Session** – Al Kooper, Mike Bloomfield, Stephen Stills
10 **A Good Feelin' To Know** – Poco
11 **Natural Progression** – Bernie Leadon & Michael Georgiades
12 **Ferguslie Park** – Stealers Wheel
13 **Hums Of The Lovin' Spoonful** – Lovin' Spoonful
14 **Ennismore** – Colin Blunstone
15 **Ahead Rings Out** – Blodwyn Pig
16 **Piece By Piece** – John Martyn
17 **Would You Believe?** – The Hollies
18 **Tim Rose** – Tim Rose
19 **Waterloo Lily** – Caravan
20 **The Great American Eagle Tragedy** – Earth Opera
21 **Child Is Father To The Man** – Blood, Sweat and Tears
22 **Five Bridges** – The Nice
23 **Those Who Are About To Die Salute You** – Jon Hiseman's Colosseum
24 **Fully Qualified Survivor** – Michael Chapman
25 **Wanted: One Soul Singer** – Johnnie Taylor
26 **Four Sail** – Love
27 **Stormcock** – Roy Harper
28 **America's Choice** – Hot Tuna
29 **Rhinoceros** – Rhinoceros
30 **Born Walden Robert Cassotto** – Bobby Darin
31 **Get It While You Can** – Howard Tate
32 **N.R.P.S.** – New Riders Of The Purple Sage
33 **Everyone Is Everybody Else** – Barclay James Harvest
34 **Sittin' In** – Loggins and Messina
35 **Wasa Wasa** – Edgar Broughton Band
36 **Warren Zevon** – Warren Zevon
37 **Whatevershebringswesing** – Kevin Ayers
38 **Egyptology** – World Party
39 **Thought Talk** – Starry Eyed and Laughing
40 **The Smoker You Drink, The Player You Get** – Joe Walsh
41 **Pelican West** – Haircut 100
42 **Spooky Two** – Spooky Tooth
43 **Introducing The Hardline According To** – Terence Trent D'Arby
44 **Loose Salute** – Michael Nesmith
45 **Zen Arcade** – Hüsker Dü
46 **The Fence** – Harold McNair
47 **Robbie Robertson** – Robbie Robertson
48 **Marjory Razorblade** – Kevin Coyne
49 **Expressway To Your Skull** – Buddy Miles Express
50 **Woyaya** – Osibisa

The 10 All-Time Worst Albums Ever Made

There is always at least one per collection. You know, the one to bring out and play to your friends. The one that is truly wretched, but you actually went out and paid money for it! I did that with the Jefferson Starship, out of loyalty for the Airplane. Enough was enough, even I could not continue to torture myself beyond *Freedom At Point Zero*.

I continued to shell out many times for absolute stinkers. What about Crosby, Stills & Nash's *Live It Up* (the cover with the hot dogs stuck on the moon), David Peel's worthy but hard going *Have A Marijuana*. How about the turgid *Iron Butterfly Live* or Love's bitterly disappointing *False Start?*, that even a guest appearance from Jimi Hendrix could not save. None of these were so terrible however; there was a tiny glimmer of hope in them.

Sadly, I cannot say the same for the ten below. For once your own nominations left me underwhelmed. Most of the votes were for popular albums people loved to hate. Top of the list were Oasis (*Be Here Now*), Blur (*Parklife*) and Suede (*Suede*). I had to put the votes in the bin, because they were not generally seen as 'really' bad albums. The number one is likely to remain, unless you can do better (I really want a worse album to knock it off). The late David Sutch was interviewed when I made his album the all-time worst. In typical Sutch fashion, he said it was one of the highlights of his career.

1 **Lord Sutch and His Heavy Friends** – Screaming Lord Sutch
2 **Metal Machine Music** – Lou Reed
3 **The Transformed Man** – William Shatner
4 **Initiation** – Todd Rundgren
5 **10cc Live** – 10cc
6 **Electric Light Orchestra Part Two** – ELO
7 **Quick Change World** – Ric Ocasek
8 **Two Sides Of The Moon** – Keith Moon
9 **Dance Into The Light** – Phil Collins
10 **Time** – Fleetwood Mac

The 10 All-Time Most Consistently Overrated Albums

Does it irritate you as much as it does me, that albums like the ones below, sell billions of copies, and yet other excellent albums by the same artists get overlooked, and often ignored? My own opinion varies with the general public. I do actually think *Brothers in Arms* is a load of overrated tosh, and I suggest the debut as being fresh, innocent, and much better. When it comes to the Beach Boys, I do agree that *Pet Sounds* is an all-time classic, but *Sunflower*, which I believe to be equally as good, remains one of their worst-selling and least appreciated albums. The Santana effect really does puzzle me, more than any other album of all-time. Surely not even multi-Grammy Carlos can comfortably go to bed at night thinking *Supernatural* comes remotely near his first four albums.

1 For Santana **Supernatural** read **Abraxis**
2 For Dire Straits **Brothers In Arms** read **Dire Straits**
3 For Fleetwood Mac **Rumours** read **Fleetwood Mac**, (the dustbin album)
4 For Beach Boys **Pet Sounds** read **Sunflower**
5 For Eagles **Hotel Bloody California** read **Desperado**
6 For Simon & Garfunkel **Bridge Over Troubled Water** read **Bookends**
7 For Lou Reed **Transformer** read **New York**
8 For Paul Simon **Graceland** read **Hearts and Bones**
9 For Stevie Wonder **Songs in The Key Of Life** read **Music Of My Mind**
10 For Joni Mitchel **Blue** read **Hissing Of Summer Lawns**

1 REVOLVER ←
The Beatles

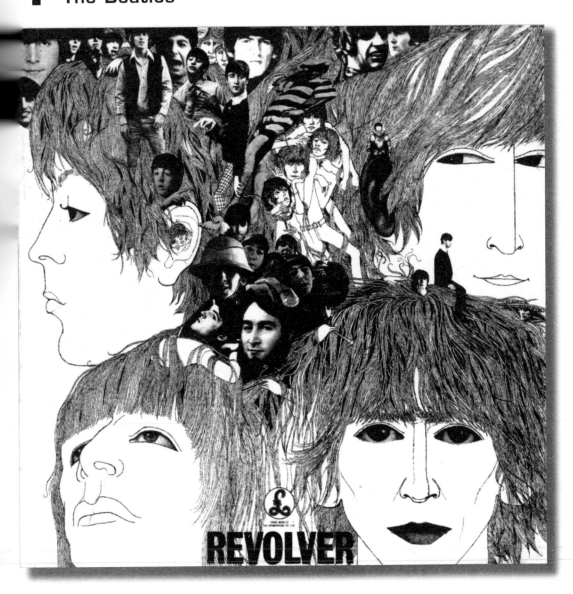

A shamelessly perfect record, its position fully justified. Music critics have always preferred *Revolver* to its famous successor, while fans were at first a little wary of the brilliantly bizarre 'Tomorrow Never Knows', the eastern promise of 'Love You To' or the goodtime brass of 'Got To Get You Into My Life'. Years of repeated listening unfolds quiet gems such as George Harrison's exceptional 'I Want To Tell You' and John Lennon's wondrously hazy 'I'm Only Sleeping', or as he sings 'I'm only seeping'. Paul McCartney was also on a creative roll with the unabashed and brave romanticism of 'Here There and Everywhere' and the classical sadness of 'Eleanor Rigby'. Subtly original and beautifully recorded.

» Tracks: *Taxman; Eleanor Rigby; I'm Only Sleeping; Love You To; Here, There and Everywhere; Yellow Submarine; She Said She Said; Good Day Sunshine; And Your Bird Can Sing; For No One; Dr. Robert; I Want To Tell You; Got To Get You Into My Life; Tomorrow Never Knows.*

★ First released 1966
★ UK peak chart position: 1
★ USA peak chart position: 1
★ Previous Top 1000 position: 1998 [1]: 1994 (5)

2 THE BENDS ↑
Radiohead

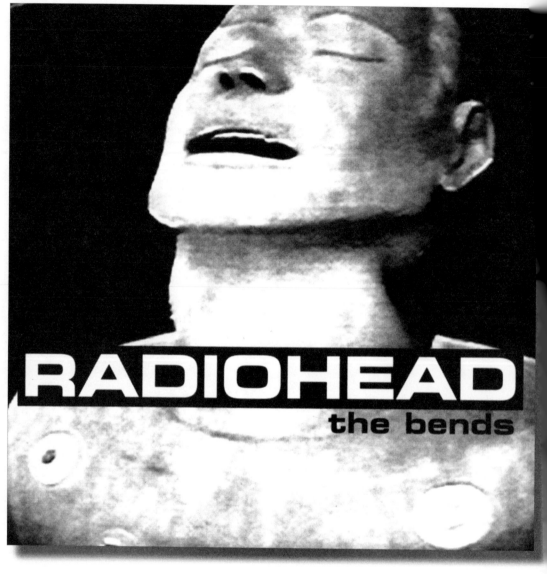

The progress that this scruffy but brainy bunch have made is phenomenal. On only their second LP Oxford's Radiohead fulfilled their huge potential, fashioning an album whose relentlessly downbeat tone was offset by an ability to formulate consistently winning melodies. The title track and 'Just' throw some customary rock poses, but for the most part the band displayed a far more expansive approach. Thom Yorke emerged from with a new-found vocal confidence, revealing a striking but frail falsetto on two of the album's strongest tracks, 'Fake Plastic Trees' and 'High & Dry'. In five years this album has become a modern classic, that is already doomed for a *Dark Side Of The Moon* dinosaur status.

》 Tracks: *Planet Telex; The Bends; Fake Plastic Trees; High & Dry; Bones; (Nice Dream); My Iron Lung; Just (You Do It To Yourself); Bullet Proof ... I Wish I Was; Black Star; Sulk; Street Spirit (Fade Out).*

★ First released 1995
★ UK peak chart position: 6
★ USA peak chart position: 88
★ Previous Top 1000 position: 1998 (10): 1994 (–)

3 SGT. PEPPERS LONELY HEARTS CLUB BAND ↓ The Beatles

The Beatles reached for the sky, and they got it. This one album revolutionized, altered and reinvented the boundaries of 20th century popular music, style and graphic art. More than 30 years on, this four-track recording is still a masterpiece. Equal credit is now justifiably placed with the elegant George Martin. He was the chemist who made their crazy ideas work. He shaped their glorious songs and fantasmagorical lyrics with melody and harmony, pushing recording technique into unknown waters. Most of late 60s pop was fashioned out of this one record; a wave of fifth rate pink-coated-marshmallow-airship-jasmine-mushroomhead-spineless-jackass-patchouli followed. Nothing came near it, its influence is inestimable.

» Tracks: *Sgt. Pepper's Lonely Hearts Club Band; With A Little Help From My Friends; Lucy In The Sky With Diamonds; Getting Better; Fixing A Hole; She's Leaving Home; Being For The Benefit Of Mr. Kite; Within You Without You; When I'm Sixty-Four; Lovely Rita; Good Morning Good Morning; Sgt. Pepper's Lonely Hearts Club Band (Reprise); A Day In The Life.*

★ First released 1967
★ UK peak chart position: 1
★ USA peak chart position: 1
★ Previous Top 1000 position: 1998 (2): 1994 (1)

4 OK COMPUTER ↑
Radiohead

Having seemingly peaked with *The Bends*, Radiohead emerged two years later with a spiky and 'difficult' collection of songs far removed from the epic rock of the previous album. Eschewing the easy option of grafting stadium choruses onto every track, *OK Computer* is an album of distorted guitars and eerie atmospherics, welded together by Thom Yorke's acutely modern lyrics. The album's first single, 'Paranoid Android', perfectly encapsulated the band's new agenda: a stunning tri-part song whose aura of restlessness is captured by its thrilling musical adventure. With this extraordinary album, they dragged intelligent rock music kicking and screaming into a new millennium.

» Tracks: *Airbag; Paranoid Android; Subterranean Homesick Alien; Exit Music (For A Film); Let Down; Karma Police; Fitter Happier; Electioneering; Climbing Up The Walls; No Surprises; Lucky; The Tourist.*

★ First released 1997
★ UK peak chart position: 1
★ USA peak chart position: 21
★ Previous Top 1000 position: 1998 (21): 1994 (–)

5 THE BEATLES (WHITE ALBUM)
The Beatles

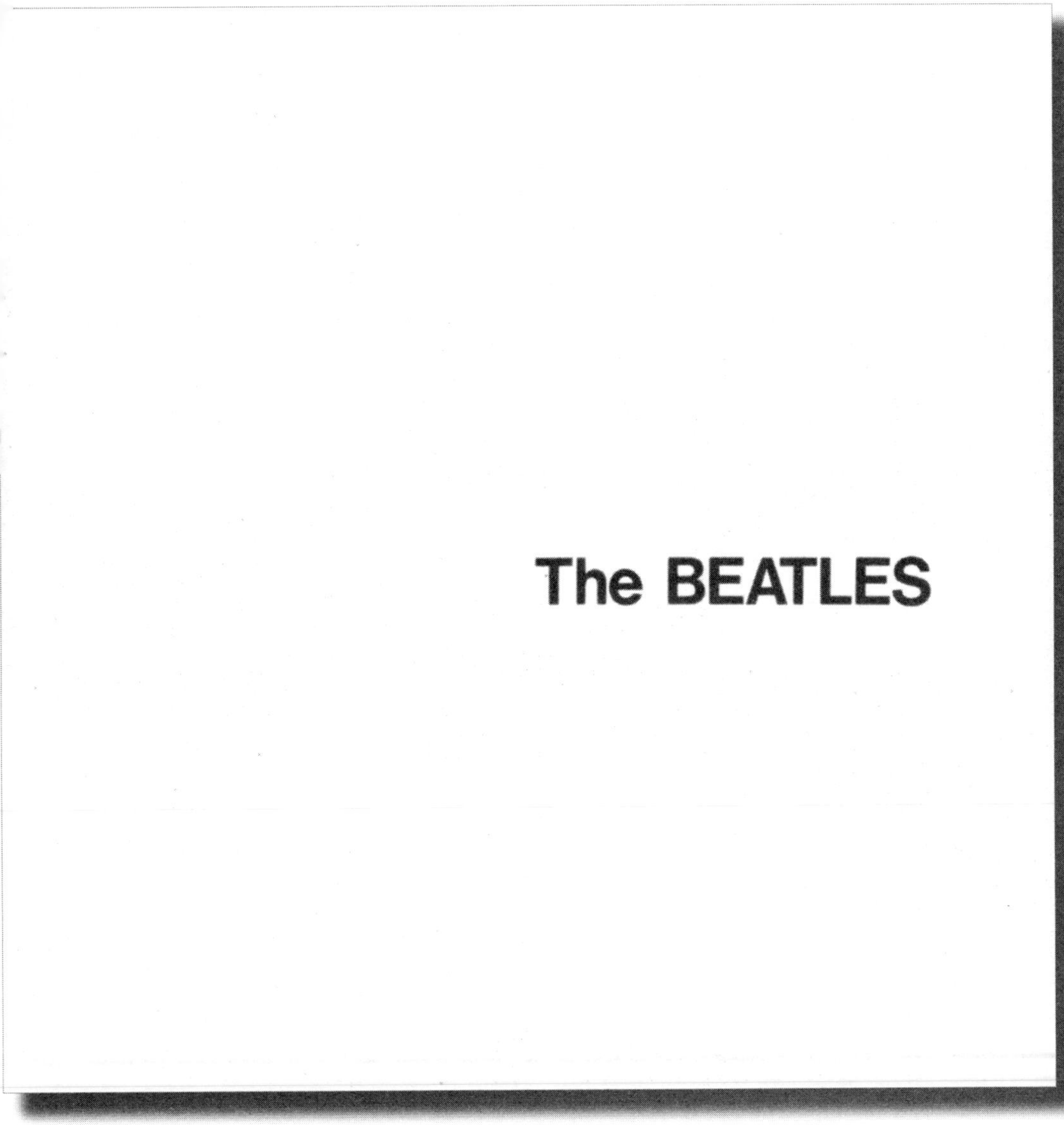

The BEATLES

While it was mooted that this could have been edited to make a great single album instead of a double, we did at least get the efforts of four different, yet troubled, individuals. The Beatles demonstrated that they could be way above our heads with items such as 'Revolution No. 9', and downright kitsch with 'Martha My Dear' and 'Good Night'. Lennon excelled with 'Happiness Is A Warm Gun' and McCartney tore his throat with 'Birthday'. Above all, and for the first time on record, they showed that they could really play, as displayed by 'Helter Skelter' and 'Back In The USSR', even though they enlisted Eric Clapton for support on 'While My Guitar Gently Weeps'.

》 Tracks: *Back In The USSR; Dear Prudence; Glass Onion; Ob La Di, Ob La Da; Wild Honey Pie; The Continuing Story Of Bungalow Bill; While My Guitar Gently Weeps; Happiness Is A Warm Gun; Martha My Dear; I'm So Tired; Blackbird; Piggies; Rocky Raccoon; Don't Pass Me By; Why Don't We Do It In The Road?; I Will; Julia; Birthday; Yer Blues; Mother Nature's Son; Everybody's Got Something To Hide Except Me and My Monkey; Sexy Sadie; Helter Skelter; Long, Long, Long; Revolution 1; Honey Pie; Savoy Truffle; Cry Baby Cry; Revolution 9; Good Night.*

★ First released 1968

★ UK peak chart position: 1 ★ USA peak chart position: 1

★ Previous Top 1000 position: 1998 (3): 1994 (15)

6 AUTOMATIC FOR THE PEOPLE
R.E.M.

Not yet a decade old, and already established as a classic of modern rock. Released soon after *Out Of Time* it shows the band on a creative roll with no shortage of original ideas. Bold songs such as 'Drive' and 'Everybody Hurts' demonstrated that the band were not reluctant to experiment, while the Karl Denver 'Wimoweh' opening on 'The Sidewinder Sleeps Tonite' and Michael Stipe's magnificent hare-lip Elvis on 'Man On The Moon' were as good as anything they have recorded. Even with the departure of Bill Berry, R.E.M. are still very much alive, but it would be asking a lot to expect any future album to top this.

>> Tracks: *Drive; Try Not To Breathe; The Sidewinder Sleeps Tonite; Everybody Hurts; New Orleans Instrumental No. 1; Sweetness Follows; Monty Got A Raw Deal; Ignoreland; Star Me Kitten; Man On The Moon; Nightswimming; Find The River.*

★ First released 1992
★ UK peak chart position: 1
★ USA peak chart position: 2
★ Previous Top 1000 position: 1998 (7): 1994 (27)

7 BLOOD ON THE TRACKS ↑
Bob Dylan

A slow but sure change has come, and this masterpiece has now eclipsed all of Dylan's albums, to become the people's unanimous choice. Where he had once obscured personal feelings in simile and metaphor, here he articulates disintegrating relationships with a painful, harrowing, honesty. There are fleeting moments of optimism, but overall the atmosphere is one of loss and the quest to come to terms with it. Lyrically, Dylan takes the specific to declare the universal, no more so than on 'If You See Her, Say Hello', one of the saddest love songs ever. And you can briefly smile at the ironic delivery of the lyric 'got all them buckets coming outta my ears' on 'Buckets Of Rain'. All spelt out with amazing clarity.

» Tracks: *Tangled Up In Blue; Simple Twist Of Fate; You're A Big Girl Now; Idiot Wind; You're Gonna Make Me Lonesome When You Go; Meet Me In The Morning; Lily, Rosemary and The Jack Of Hearts; If You See Her, Say Hello; Shelter From The Storm; Buckets Of Rain.*

★ First released 1975
★ UK peak chart position: 4
★ USA peak chart position: 1
★ Previous Top 1000 position: 1998 (24): 1994 (98)

8 ABBEY ROAD ↓
The Beatles

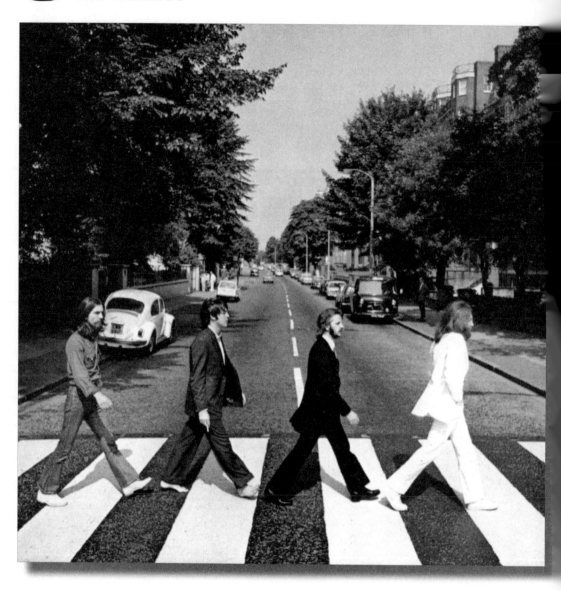

The product of their last recording session, *Abbey Road* transcends the internecine strife gripping its participants. Individuality triumphs on side one, as each group member pursues specific callings, be it classic rock 'n' roll, Lear-like nonsense verse, riff-laden *cris de coeur* or simple, sumptuous pop. Wait for the sudden silence after 'I Want You' halts, or simply count the 'she's so heavys'. Later on the partworks and fragments of Pam and Mr Mustard are fused together to perfection to construct a breathtaking suite. Characters are cast and melodies envelop until the final experience is of a seamless whole, a proclamation of the ultimate joy of pop itself. 'And in the end, the love you make . . .'

▶▶ Tracks: *Come Together; Something; Maxwell's Silver Hammer; Oh! Darling; Octopus's Garden; I Want You (She's So Heavy); Here Comes The Sun; Because; You Never Give Me Your Money; Sun King; Mean Mr. Mustard; Polythene Pam; She Came In Through The Bathroom Window; Golden Slumbers; Carry That Weight; The End; Her Majesty.*

★ First released 1969
★ UK peak chart position: 1
★ USA peak chart position: 1
★ Previous Top 1000 position: 1998 (5): 1994 (58)

9 THE DARK SIDE OF THE MOON ↓ Pink Floyd

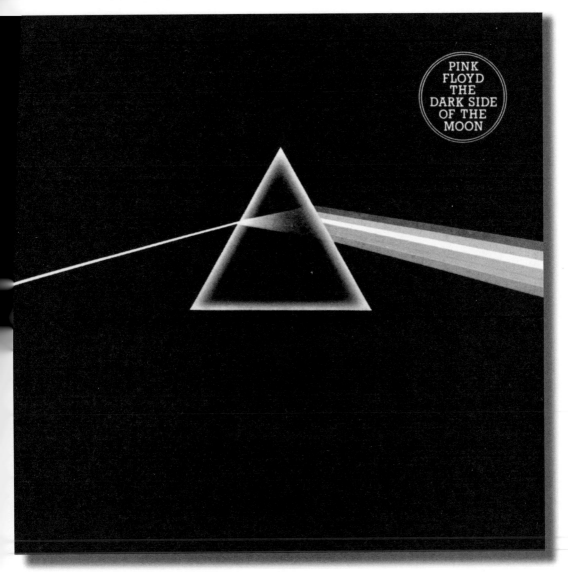

PINK
FLOYD
THE
DARK SIDE
OF THE
MOON

Try to tuck it away in the collection, but your dinner guests will still seek it out. Nearly thirty years on, it still sets standards of recording excellence for today's digitally minded customers. Dave Gilmour's piercing guitar solo on 'Money' will still make you shiver, Clare Torry's wailing vocal on 'The Great Gig In The Sky' is still remarkable and Roger Waters' lyrics remain relevant in the 90s. Once the album coveted by cosy Habitat catalogue 70s couples as an essential purchase for their new home. It is now recognized by succeeding generations as a magnificent, pristine rock record. It is OK to have it out on full display. Unlike *The Final Cut*, this gets played.

▶ Tracks: *Speak To Me; Breathe; On The Run; Time; The Great Gig In The Sky; Money; Us and Them; Any Colour You Like; Brain Damage; Eclipse.*

★ First released 1973
★ UK peak chart position: 2
★ USA peak chart position: 1
★ Previous Top 1000 position: 1998 (8): 1994 (6)

10 THE QUEEN IS DEAD ↑
The Smiths

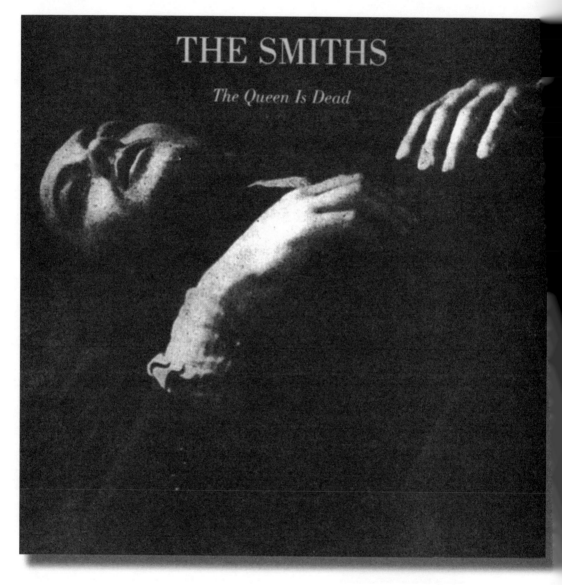

Growing in popularity over the years, this is definitely the Smiths' masterpiece album, this shows a group expanding horizons without sacrificing their unique sound. Vocalist Morrissey retains his self-centred romanticism, but articulates his anguish through a succession of engaging melodies, most notably 'The Boy With The Thorn In His Side'. The singer's flippant persona surfaces on 'Frankly, Mr. Shankly' and 'Vicar In A Tutu', while Johnny Marr's multi-layered jangling guitarwork is best heard on the abrasive title track. This LP shows a group aware of its strengths, but unafraid to build and expand upon them. On which Morrissey melody met Marr's music, magnificently. Marvelous.

▶▶ Tracks: *The Queen Is Dead; Frankly, Mr. Shankly; I Know It's Over; Never Had No One Ever; Cemetery Gates; Big Mouth Strikes Again; The Boy With The Thorn In His Side; Vicar In A Tutu; There Is A Light That Never Goes Out; Some Girls Are Bigger Than Others.*

★ First released 1986
★ UK peak chart position: 2
★ USA peak chart position: 70
★ Previous Top 1000 position: 1998 (23): 1994 (62)

11 THE STONE ROSES ↑
The Stone Roses

Quite simply, this debut album is a superlative record. Manchester's most likely to, who escaped independent status after a lengthy court battle, signed to Geffen Records and then promptly disappeared for five years. The Stone Roses came back, and then went pop. A Byrds-like listlessness caused listeners to swoon in wonder and slip quietly beneath the surface. 'Waterfall' and 'She Bangs The Drums' were sublime and quietly brilliant, 'I Wanna Be Adored' teased with its epic intro, and, of course, created incredible and impossible pressure for that all-important second album. A classic album, already seen as one of the finest records of the past 30 years.

))) Tracks: *I Wanna Be Adored; She Bangs The Drums; Waterfall; Don't Stop; Bye Bye Badman; Elizabeth My Dear; (Song For My) Sugar Spun Sister; Made Of Stone; Shoot You Down; This Is The One; I Am The Resurrection.*

★ First released 1989
★ UK peak chart position: 19
★ USA peak chart position: 86
★ Previous Top 1000 position: 1998 (14): 1994 (47)

12 FOREVER CHANGES ↑
Love

For anybody not familiar with this record, it is unconditionally recommended as one of the finest albums ever. The continuing deep affection for this gem is no fluke. Its universal appeal to rock critics earns its position even though total sales have yet to exceed a million. The enigmatic Arthur Lee created the perfect hippie album, with joyous acoustic melody, strings and occasional biting guitars. The paradox was for Lee to sing a line such as 'oh the snot has caked against my pants, it has turned into crystal' and for it to sound absolutely right and sincere. The equally arresting 'Alone Again Or' features the line 'I could be in love with almost everyone', yet it somehow avoids sounding like a hippie cliché.

))) Tracks: *Alone Again Or; A House Is Not A Motel; Andmoreagain; The Daily Planet; Old Man; The Red Telephone; Maybe The People Would Be The Times Or Between Clark and Hilldale; Live and Let Live; The Good Humor Man He Sees Everything Like This; Bummer In The Summer; You Set The Scene.*

★ First released 1967
★ UK peak chart position: 24
★ USA peak chart position: 154
★ Previous Top 1000 position: 1998 (40): 1994 (32)

13 THE VELVET UNDERGROUND & NICO ↑ The Velvet Underground

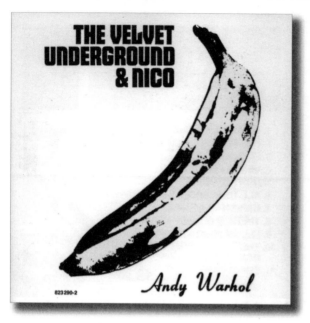

This dark, decadent and steamy album failed to sell whe it was first released, in deference to what was happenir on the hippie-laden west coast of America. Andy Warho pets unconsciously produced one of the most influenti rock albums of all time. Openly addressing drugs, se and everything that was sub-culture, this album sti smells bad. Lou Reed's brilliantly uncompromising lyric together with the band's sloppy sexuality, continue t influence. 'Venus In Furs', 'Heroin', 'Black Angel's Deat Song' and the magnificent 'I'm Waiting For The Man', is all here in 45 minutes of untouchable debaucher Beautifully bent, like the banana on the cover.

» Tracks: *Sunday Morning; I'm Waiting For The Man; Femme Fatale; Venus In Furs; Run, Run, Run; All Tomorrow's Parties; Heroin; There She Goes Again; I'll Be Your Mirror; Black Angel's Death Song; European Son (To Delmore Schwartz).*

★ First released 1967
★ UK peak chart position: did not chart
★ USA peak chart position: 171
★ Previous Top 1000 position: 1998 (22): 1994 (20)

14 KIND OF BLUE ↑
Miles Davis

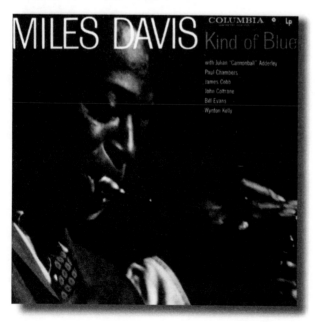

Advocates from the many corners of jazz will argue their points, some with bigoted passion and self righteousness. When you find jazzers, rock and popular music followers unanimously united over one record, then you know something must be right. This album contains only five tracks, with musicians the calibre of Cannonball Adderley (alto), Coltrane (tenor), Wynton Kelly & Bill Evans (piano), Paul Chambers (bass), James Cobb (drums) and Miles on trumpet. It is played with absolute cool perfection, not a drop of sweat or cigarette ash. There can be no debate, this is the greatest jazz album in the world ever. Start with this, get hooked, and then come back to it time and time again. It never disappoints.

» Tracks: *So What; Freddie Freeloader; Blue In Green; Al Blues; Flamenco Sketches.*

★ First released 1960
★ UK peak chart position: did not chart
★ USA peak chart position: did not chart
★ Previous Top 1000 position: 1998 (48): 1994 (28)

15 THE UNFORGETTABLE FIRE ↑
U2

Not an album packed with songs of romance, but each one a powerful statement. The title of this album was taken from an exhibition of paintings by survivors of Hiroshima and Nagasaki. It confirmed U2 as one of a handful of bands able to tackle such vast and emotive subjects with dignity and musical integrity. There are few artists capable of writing about religion, war, race, the Irish problem and life with such ferocity and global commercial success. 'Pride (In The Name Of Love)', a hymn to Martin Luther King, was a worldwide hit, and almost every track is an anthem sung by millions. The production by Brian Eno and Daniel Lanois was a taste of things to come.

)) Tracks: *A Sort Of Homecoming; Pride (In The Name Of Love); Wire; The Unforgettable Fire; Promenade; Fourth Of July; Bad; Indian Summer Sky; Elvis Presley and America; MLK.*

★ First released 1984
★ UK peak chart position: 1
★ USA peak chart position: 12
★ Previous Top 1000 position: 1998 (169): 1994 (18)

16 ASTRAL WEEKS ↓
Van Morrison

Quoted, recommended and worshipped by the critics for over 30 years, this underground masterpiece has now become part of the establishment. It cries out to be listened to without interruption, which may explain why it failed to reach either the UK or US charts. It wanders and weaves, repeating themes and lyrics as if one song, yet we never tire of 'gardens wet with rain', 'champagne eyes' or the wonder of how Van Morrison can make a place like Ladbroke Grove seem so hauntingly evocative. The record is also a great educator in opening our eyes beyond pop to soul and jazz, and although Morrison continues to return to its themes time and time again, this is his core.

)) Tracks: *Astral Weeks; Beside You; Sweet Thing; Cyprus Avenue; Young Lovers Do; Madame George; Ballerina; Slim Slow Slider.*

★ First released 1968
★ UK peak chart position: did not chart
★ USA peak chart position: did not chart
★ Previous Top 1000 position: 1998 (15): 1994 (7)

17 NEVERMIND ↓
Nirvana

Historically, America's north-west coast has produced edgy, rebellious music, of which grunge was one manifestation. An offspring of punk, speed metal and the 'slacker' lifestyle, it found an apotheosis in Nirvana, who combined such elements with a faultless grasp of hooklines. On *Nevermind*, group leader Kurt Cobain unleashed frustrated alienation, his ravaged rasp and bone-crunching guitar soaring through a tight, intensive sound, courtesy of former hardcore producer Butch Vig. Cobain's solipsism proved tragically prophetic and his suicide elevated him to cultural icon status. This should not obscure the singer's empathy for the mechanics of classic rock, reworked and infused with new life on this emphatic statement.

» Tracks: *Smells Like Teen Spirit; In Bloom; Come As You Are; Breed; Lithium; Polly; Territorial Pissings; Drain You; Lounge Act; Stay Away; On A Plain; Something In The Way; Endless Nameless.*

★ First released 1991
★ UK peak chart position: 33
★ USA peak chart position: 1
★ Previous Top 1000 position: 1998 (4): 1994 (57)

18 PET SOUNDS ↑
The Beach Boys

This group, and more specifically, their acknowledged leader Brian Wilson, worked too hard to try to make this the greatest pop record of all time. At the time of recording Brian was experiencing a creative growth from which he never recovered. The intense beauty of this record grows with age and Brian Wilson should not feel any failure or under achievement in the face of the four mop-tops from Liverpool. They had George Martin; Brian had only himself, some rival siblings and a cousin to deal with. The orchestral arrangements remain magnificently lush but never sickly, a sound that has influenced many. Still one of the worst album covers of all time.

» Tracks: *Wouldn't It Be Nice; You Still Believe In Me; That's Not Me; Don't Talk (Put Your Head On My Shoulder); I'm Waiting For The Day; Let's Go Away For Awhile; Sloop John B; God Only Knows; I Know There's An Answer; Here Today; I Just Wasn't Made For These Times; Pet Sounds; Caroline, No.*

★ First released 1966
★ UK peak chart position: 2
★ USA peak chart position: 10
★ Previous Top 1000 position: 1998 (6): 1994 (3)

19 SIGN 'O' THE TIMES ↑
Prince

A gleefully adventurous double album from Prince. Considered in some quarters as a little too ambitious at the time, it has come to be regarded as probably his greatest album. Drawing on nearly every influence with which he had previously toyed in his career, here he wove them together and created a palette rich with colour, style and life: the title track, a snapshot of modern life and its slow erosion; 'Starfish and Coffee', a precise and neat piece of storytelling; 'U Got The Look', all swagger and poise, Prince verbally jousting with Sheena Easton. Magnificent, and one recording the former artist surely would never disown.

➽ Tracks: *Sign 'O' The Times; Play In The Sunshine; Housequake; The Ballad Of Dorothy Parker; It; Starfish and Coffee; Slow Love; Hot Thing; Forever In My Life; U Got The Look; If I Was Your Girlfriend; Strange Relationship; I Could Never Take The Place Of Your Man; The Cross; It's Gonna Be A Beautiful Night; Adore.*

★ First released 1987
★ UK peak chart position: 4
★ USA peak chart position: 6
★ Previous Top 1000 position: 1998 (47): 1994 (84)

20 BORN TO RUN ↑
Bruce Springsteen

After 25 years, still the Springsteen album to come back to, and for the listener never to be let down. The punch, the verve and the youthful freshness still have incredible impact. This album lives up to the hype we experienced about the future of rock 'n' roll. The title track still makes hairs stand on end, with the images conveyed in the lyrics having an enduring power. Saxophones came back into fashion thanks to the blistering Clarence Clemons, as did forgotten 50s images of cars and drive-ins. Springsteen, meanwhile, exhumed his youth and reminded us of ours with honest tales of growing up in post-Eisenhower America. Just the title track would have been enough.

➽ Tracks: *Thunder Road; Tenth Avenue Freeze-out; Night; Backstreets; Born To Run; She's The One; Meeting Across The River; Jungleland.*

★ First released 1975
★ UK peak chart position: 17
★ USA peak chart position: 3
★ Previous Top 1000 position: 1998 (63): 1994 (16)

21 (WHAT'S THE STORY) MORNING GLORY? ↓ Oasis

The second album from the most written-about pop band since the Beatles was an assured collection. There were enough brilliant hooks and choruses to make it instantly sound like a great record. 'Roll With It' is a prime example, being an automatically familiar and accessible pop song. Liam Gallagher was happy to have the mighty 'Wonderwall', complete with *Sgt. Pepper*-style cellos and singalong chorus, but brother Noel gave him a run for his money with the epic 'Don't Look Back In Anger', borrowing on this occasion from Pachelbel's 'Canon & Gigue'. Despite accusations that Oasis were taking their 'influences' a step too far, this was undeniably a gigantic album.

▶▶ Tracks: *Hello; Roll With It; Wonderwall; Don't Look Back In Anger; Hey Now!; Some Might Say; Cast No Shadow; She's Electric; Morning Glory; Champagne Supernova.*

★ First released 1995
★ UK peak chart position: 1
★ USA peak chart position: 4
★ Previous Top 1000 position: 1998 (9): 1994 (−)

22 A HARD DAY'S NIGHT ↑
The Beatles

This timeless album is only now being appreciated for what it is and not for what it purported to be. The 'songs from the motion picture' was usually a hastily assembled group of songs for inclusion in a film. This film remains a classic of happy 60s naivety. The songs flow like the absolute finest red wine. The title track leads to the glorious harmonica of 'I Should Have Known Better' (remember the guards van scene) to the powerfully poignant 'If I Fell' (remember Ringo suddenly relenting and picking up his drumsticks). This period represents the Beatles at their happiest, and can now be spoken of in the same breath as *Revolver* and *Pepper*.

▶▶ Tracks: *A Hard Day's Night; I Should Have Known Better; If I Fell; I'm Happy Just To Dance With You; And I Love Her; Tell Me Why; Can't Buy Me Love; Any Time At All; I'll Cry Instead; Things We Said Today; When I Get Home; You Can't Do That; I'll Be Back.*

★ First released 1964
★ UK peak chart position: 1
★ USA peak chart position: 1
★ Previous Top 1000 position: 1998 (142): 1994 (−)

23 HUNKY DORY ↓
David Bowie

Bowie's most eclectic album acknowledged his 60s mentors and prepared this artist for subsequent musical directions. Andy Warhol, Bob Dylan and the Velvet Underground were canonized, and a veneer of menace bubbled beneath the surface of several sweet pop songs, especially 'Life On Mars'. Is it Lennon or Lenin that is on sale again? The subject matter embraced transexuality, Nietzsche and science fiction. Guitarist Mick Ronson proved a sympathetic foil amid a support cast that understood Bowie's chameleon-like qualities and reacted accordingly. The singer's eclectic interests have never been captured so confidently, even though he sings 'didn't know what I was looking for' in 'Changes'.

» Tracks: *Changes; Oh! You Pretty Thing; Eight Line Poem; Life On Mars?; Kooks; Quicksand; Fill Your Heart (Biff); Andy Warhol; Song For Bob Dylan; Queen Bitch; The Bewlay Brothers.*

★ First released 1971
★ UK peak chart position: 3
★ USA peak chart position: 93
★ Previous Top 1000 position: 1998 (16): 1994 (34)

24 BLUE ↑
Joni Mitchell

Mitchell's fourth album maintained the confessional style of its predecessors, but her biographical epistles were here infused with greater maturity. Although her lyrics remained personal, Mitchell drew upon their described scenarios to express a greater context. Stephen Stills and James Taylor added sympathetic accompaniment, but the album's musical textures were defined by the singer's use of guitar, piano and dulcimer. Mitchell's vocals showed a new depth and range absent from earlier work, but it is the use of a great lyric that makes the collection so memorable. Conversational, descriptive yet powerful; 'sitting in bar in Paris, France' ('California'), 'I could drink a case of you, and still be on my feet' ('A Case Of You'). etc. No pretensions, nothing oblique.

» Tracks: *All I Want; My Old Man; Little Green; Carey; Blue; California; This Flight Tonight; River; A Case Of You; The Last Time I Saw Richard.*

★ First released 1971
★ UK peak chart position: 3
★ USA peak chart position: 15
★ Previous Top 1000 position: 1998 (53): 1994 (89)

25 THE JOSHUA TREE ↓
U2

After their arresting appearance at Live Aid, U2 album sales went crazy across the globe, and the world waited impatiently for their next release. *The Joshua Tree* did not disappoint. There are few weaknesses, musical or lyrical, in this album. The pure power of the music and patent honesty of the lyrics steer the band clear of whimsy and self-indulgence. The anguish and questioning is shot through with faith as they chant and stomp and batter their way through instant classics such as 'I Still Haven't Found What I'm Looking For', 'Where The Streets Have No Name' and 'With Or Without You', leaving the listener bruised but elated.

» Tracks: *Where The Streets Have No Name; I Still Haven't Found What I'm Looking For; With Or Without You; Bullet The Blue Sky; Running To Stand Still; Red Hill Mining Town; In God's Country; Trip Through Your Wires; One Tree Hill; Exit; Mothers Of The Disappeared.*

★ First released 1987
★ UK peak chart position: 1
★ USA peak chart position: 1
★ Previous Top 1000 position: 1998 (18): 1994 (48)

26 HIGHWAY 61 REVISITED ←
Bob Dylan

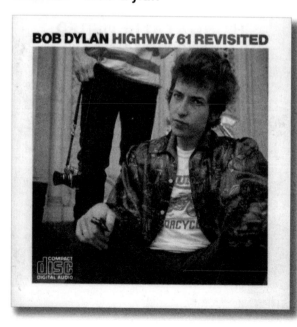

Dylan's first fully fledged electric album engendered considerable controversy. Folk purists had already waved goodbye to him, but rock had become the métier through which the singer could now best express his vision. Session organist Al Kooper and blues guitarist Michael Bloomfield were among those providing free-spirited accompaniment to a collection of songs that redefined pop music. Wrapped in a raw, driving sound, Dylan's poems – part beat, part symbolist, part concrete – ensured that contemporaries could no longer rely on traditional forms, an influence immediately apparent on recordings by the Beatles and the Rolling Stones. There are lyrics of a generation still to be found on this album, only now can we really understand them; 'do you Mr Jones?'

» Tracks: *Like A Rolling Stone; Tombstone Blues; It Takes A Lot To Laugh, It Takes A Train To Cry; From A Buick Six; Ballad Of A Thin Man; Queen Jane Approximately; Highway 61 Revisited; Just Like Tom Thumb's Blues; Desolation Row.*

★ First released 1965
★ UK peak chart position: 4
★ USA peak chart position: 3
★ Previous Top 1000 position: 1998 (26): 1994 (2)

27 THE RISE AND FALL OF ZIGGY STARDUST AND THE SPIDERS FROM MARS ↓ David Bowie

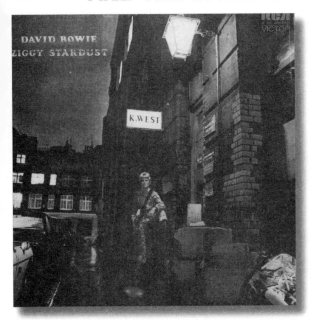

This artist's penchant for reinvention has allowed the singer to follow a fascinating chameleon career. The blend of rock star persona and alien creature defining *Ziggy Stardust* was probably his finest creation. Buoyed by the support of guitarist Mick Ronson, Bowie produced some of his finest songs, from the raucous 'Suffragette City' to the prophetic 'Rock 'n' Roll Suicide' – the singer would famously declare Ziggy dead during a live concert. Bowie failed miserably, of course Ziggy is immortal. Androgyny and science fiction combined with the artist's love of theatre to bring a visual nature to an album that remains central to Bowie's wide-ranging catalogue.

❱❱ Tracks: *Five Years; Soul Love; Moonage Daydream; Starman; It Ain't Easy; Lady Stardust; Star; Hang On To Yourself; Ziggy Stardust; Suffragette City; Rock 'n' Roll Suicide.*

★ First released 1972
★ UK peak chart position: 5
★ USA peak chart position: 75
★ Previous Top 1000 position: 1998 (11): 1994 (19)

28 BLUE LINES ↑
Massive Attack

Bristol's Massive Attack were pioneers of the 'trip-hop' genre, an ambient form of hip-hop. Born from the ashes of pioneering sound system unit the Wild Bunch, the core trio of Daddy-G, Mushroom and 3-D were joined on *Blue Lines* by soul diva Shara Nelson, reggae singer Horace Andy and a young Tricky. Together they fashioned a strikingly modern urban soundtrack that added an emotional intensity to the sparseness and studied cool of hip-hop, with Nelson's impassioned vocals on 'Unfinished Sympathy' helping to create one of the decade's definitive songs. As slow and sweet as toffee.

❱❱ Tracks: *Safe From Harm; One Love; Blue Lines; Be Thankful For What You've Got; Five Man Army; Unfinished Sympathy; Daydreaming; Lately; Hymn Of The Big Wheel.*

★ First released 1991
★ UK peak chart position: 13
★ USA peak chart position: did not chart
★ Previous Top 1000 position: 1998 (43): 1994 (–)

29 NEVER MIND THE BOLLOCKS HERE'S THE SEX PISTOLS ↓ Sex Pistols

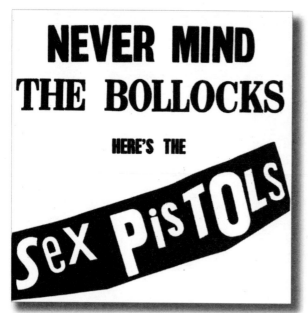

In the same way that *Sgt Pepper...* and *Revolver* are cast in stone at the top of the pop/rock genre, so this milestone stands above any other punk record of its kind. Seen by some snobs at the time as musical illiterates, the Sex Pistols legend continues as strong as ever. The music was in such stark contrast to what we had previously been enjoying that a backlash was inevitable. This will stay as a classic because it will not date. The power of tracks such as 'Pretty Vacant' or 'No Feelings' is as strong as in 1977. This pivotal record has not mellowed with age, thankfully.

» Tracks: *Holidays In The Sun; Bodies; Liar; No Feelings; God Save The Queen; Problems; Seventeen; Anarchy In The UK; Submission; Pretty Vacant; New York; EMI.*

★ First released 1977
★ UK peak chart position: 1
★ USA peak chart position: 106
★ Previous Top 1000 position: 1998 (13); 1994 (12)

30 THE WALL ↑
Pink Floyd

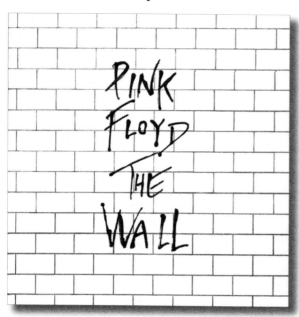

There are hidden depths to this remarkable album which fans and critics have at times dismissed. It is not the concept of tearing down the wall, of opposition to the educational system or even Roger Waters becoming intolerable for the others to work with. It is a double album that contains some outstanding songs. For example, 'Nobody Home' highlights the frustration of Waters' rock star lot, but for all the luxury we can sense his appalling frustration at finding nobody home and of sitting in his hotel room with 'thirteen channels of shit on the TV, to choose from. Similarly, the epic 'Comfortably Numb': 'the child is gone, the dream is gone, and I have become comfortably numb'.

» Tracks: *In The Flesh; Thin Ice; Happiest Days Of Our Lives; Another Brick In The Wall (Part 2); Mother; Goodbye Blue Sky; Empty Spaces; Young Lust; One Of My Turns; Don't Leave Me Now; Another Brick In The Wall (Part 3); Goodbye Cruel World; Hey You; Is There Anybody Out There?; Nobody Home; Comfortably Numb; Show Must Go On; Run Like Hell; Waiting For The Worms; Stop; The Trial; Outside The Wall.*

★ First released 1980
★ UK peak chart position: 3
★ USA peak chart position: 1
★ Previous Top 1000 position: 1998 (46); 1994 (176)

31 RUMOURS ↓
Fleetwood Mac

The reviewers tell us what to buy, but the public actually part with the cash. Surely twenty-six million people cannot be wrong, as Peter Green's Frankenstein became the prime example of AOR in the 70s. The inner strife and turmoil of the band is credited as having helped to make this many-headed beast into such a success. Christine sparred with John McVie and Stevie scrapped with Lindsay Buckingham. Mick Fleetwood held the emotional mess together with the same confident steadiness as he demonstrated in his drumming throughout the record. Stevie Nicks' fiery vocals on 'Go Your Own Way' complemented Christine McVie's beautifully understated 'You Make Loving Fun'. The people have chosen, but don't ignore other important albums in their catalogue.

» Tracks: *Second Hand News; Dreams; Never Going Back Again; Don't Stop; Go Your Own Way; Songbird; The Chain; You Make Loving Fun; I Don't Want To Know; Oh Daddy; Gold Dust Woman.*

★ First released 1977
★ UK peak chart position: 1
★ USA peak chart position: 1
★ Previous Top 1000 position: 1998 (19): 1994 (17)

32 ELECTRIC LADYLAND ↓
The Jimi Hendrix Experience

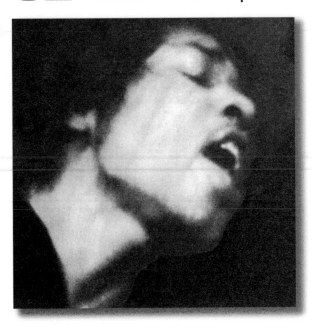

The last official Experience band contained contributions from both Traffic and Jefferson Airplane members, and presented an unrivalled collection of songs, including a brilliant rendition of Bob Dylan's 'All Along The Watchtower', an interpretation that Dylan was later to adopt live. 'Crosstown Traffic', 'Gypsy Eyes', and 'Burning Of The Midnight Lamp', as well as the posthumous number one, 'Voodoo Chile (Slight Return)'. This and the brilliant improvisation (with Steve Winwood, Jack Casady) showed an incredible clarity in Jimi Hendrix's musical thinking. His vision had already moved beyond the musical confines of the trio. A rich and still somehow contemporary record. Now with de-breasted cover.

» Tracks: *. . . And The Gods Made Love; Have You Ever Been (To Electric Ladyland); Crosstown Traffic; Voodoo Chile; Little Miss Strange; Long Hot Summer Night; Come On (Let The Good Times Roll); Gypsy Eyes; Burning Of The Midnight Lamp; Rainy Day, Dream Away; 1983 (A Merman I Should Turn To Be); Moon, Turn The Tides ... Gently Gently Away; Still Raining, Still Dreaming; House Burning Down; All Along The Watchtower; Voodoo Chile (Slight Return).*

★ First released 1968
★ UK peak chart position: 6
★ USA peak chart position: 1
★ Previous Top 1000 position: 1998 (12): 1994 (72)

33 BLONDE ON BLONDE ↓
Bob Dylan

Just a year after *Highway 61 Revisited*, the polka-dotte thin one repeated the act with further epitaphs of creativ malarkey and intrigue. Listeners were spoilt with double album, longer than anything they had previousl heard, yet still destined to endure. The punishing tourin and high profile drove Dylan to be creative beyond belie as he scribbled these gems in his hotel rooms Surrounding himself with the likes of Al Kooper, Robbi Robertson, Charlie McCoy and Kenny Buttrey, these seasoned musicians gave this album a relaxed confidence quite unlike the youthful energy of *Highway 61 Revisited* Possibly the chemicals coursing through his body had something to do with all this.

» Tracks: *Rainy Day Woman Nos 12 & 35; Pledging My Time; Visions Of Johanna; One Of Us Must Know (Sooner Or Later); I Want You; Stuck Inside Of Mobile With The Memphis Blues Again; Leopard-Skin Pill-Box Hat; Just Like A Woman; Most Likely You Go Your Way (And I'll Go Mine); Temporary Like Achilles; Absolutely Sweet Marie; Fourth Time Around; Obviously Five Believers; Sad-Eyed Lady Of The Lowlands.*

★ First released 1966
★ UK peak chart position: 3
★ USA peak chart position: 9
★ Previous Top 1000 position: 1998 (17): 1994 (4)

34 RUBBER SOUL ↓
The Beatles

The album that put the Beatles into the hearts and minds of middle-class, quality Sunday newspaper readers. The working-class lads won over a new audience with a mature collection of songs that belied their age. As the art and literary worlds moved away from polo-necked bohemian jazz, the Beatles wooed them with simple melodies and clever lyrics. This album also demonstrated that the Beatles were not without their own demons as unparalleled success took its toll – witness John Lennon's illicit affair in 'Norwegian Wood', Paul McCartney's profound 'I'm Looking Through You' and George Harrison's continuing growth with the thoughtful 'Think For Yourself'. Lennon owned the jewel, however, with the prophetic 'In My Life'.

» Tracks: *Drive My Car; Norwegian Wood (This Bird Has Flown); You Won't See Me; Nowhere Man; Think For Yourself; The Word; Michelle; What Goes On; Girl; I'm Looking Through You; In My Life; Wait; If I Needed Someone; Run For Your Life.*

★ First released 1965
★ UK peak chart position: 1
★ USA peak chart position: 1
★ Previous Top 1000 position: 1998 (20): 1994 (10)

35 EXILE ON MAIN STREET ↓
The Rolling Stones

The Rolling Stones entered the 70s as 'the world's greatest rock 'n' roll band', an epithet confirmed by this album. Where its predecessor, *Sticky Fingers*, boasted a clear production, this rampaging double set offered a thick, muddy mix that adds an air of mystery to the proceedings. Up-tempo material, laden with riffs ('All Down The Line', 'Happy', 'Soul Survivor'), contrasts with loose, unhinged performances drawn from the rich textures of delta blues. Hedonism and bacchanalia ooze from every pore, emphasizing an air of sexual degeneracy encapsulating the Rolling Stones' appeal. This expansive and important LP is now rightly regarded as one of the pinnacles of their incredible career.

» Tracks: *Rocks Off; Rip This Joint; Hip Shake; Casino Boogie; Tumbling Dice; Sweet Virginia; Torn and Frayed; Black Angel; Loving Cup; Happy; Turd On The Run; Ventilator Blues; Just Wanna See His Face; Let It Loose; All Down The Line; Stop Breaking Down; Shine A Light; Soul Survivor.*

★ First released 1972
★ UK peak chart position: 1
★ USA peak chart position: 1
★ Previous Top 1000 position: 1998 (27): 1994 (114)

36 ACHTUNG BABY ↓
U2

From their Trabant period, this album presents U2 at their most powerful and eloquent. The ace production team of Daniel Lanois, Steve Lillywhite and Brian Eno is raw and uncompromising. On the opening track, 'Zoo Station', the VU meters are driven mercilessly into the red by Larry Mullen's percussive attack. The words are equally potent, creating the lyrical equivalent of a Hieronymous Bosch painting – a tangled steel web of tortured love and urban nightmare. This spawned numerous hit singles, including 'Even Better Than The Real Thing', 'One', 'The Fly', 'Mysterious Ways' and 'Who's Gonna Ride Your Wild Horses'. In this mood, U2 were untouchable.

» Tracks: *Zoo Station; Even Better Than The Real Thing; One; Until The End Of The World; Who's Gonna Ride Your Wild Horses; So Cruel; The Fly; Mysterious Ways; Tryin' To Throw Your Arms Around The World; Ultra Violet (Light My Way); Acrobat; Love Is Blindness.*

★ First released 1991
★ UK peak chart position: 2
★ USA peak chart position: 1
★ Previous Top 1000 position: 1998 (28): 1994 (162)

37 LONDON CALLING ↓
The Clash

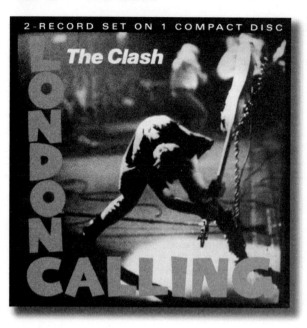

2-RECORD SET ON 1 COMPACT DISC

The Clash

LONDON CALLING

If punk rejected pop history, *London Calling* reclaimed albeit with a knowing perspective. The scope of th double set is breathtaking, encompassing reggae rockabilly and the group's own furious mettle. Wher such a combination might have proved over-ambitiou the Clash accomplish it with swaggering panache. Gu Stevens, who produced the group's first demos, returns t the helm to provide a confident, cohesive sound equal t the set's brilliant array of material. Boldly assertive an superbly focused, this contains many of the quartet finest songs and is, by extension, virtually faultless. The title track is a sharp reminder of the turmoil in the street of the main cities of the UK.

» Tracks: *London Calling; Brand New Cadillac; Jimmy Jazz; Hateful; Rudie Can't Fail; Spanish Bombs; The Right Profile; Lost In The Supermarket; Clampdown; The Guns Of Brixton; Wrong 'Em Boyo; Death Or Glory; Koka Kola; The Card Cheat; Lover's Rock; Four Horsemen; I'm Not Down; Revolution Rock; Train In Vain.*

★ First released 1979
★ UK peak chart position: 9
★ USA peak chart position: 27
★ Previous Top 1000 position: 1998 (29): 1994 (54)

38 WISH YOU WERE HERE ↓
Pink Floyd

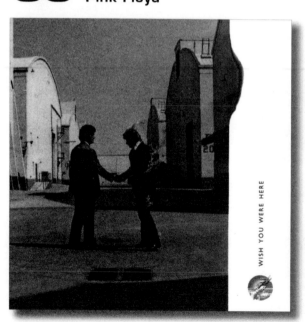

WISH YOU WERE HERE

The Floyd reaped massive commercial acclaim with *Dark Side Of The Moon*, but it was on *Wish You Were Here* that the quartet reached an artistic maturity. The album revolves around 'Shine On You Crazy Diamond', a lengthy suite devoted to founder-member Syd Barrett, whose fragile ego snapped at the earliest whiff of success. This in mind, the group addresses music business exploitation in 'Welcome To The Machine', particularly pithy given their new-found status. A quiet determination marks this set. Roger Waters contributes some of his most openly heartfelt lyrics, while guitarist Dave Gilmour proved both economical and incisive. Free of the self-indulgence marking later work, Pink Floyd emerge as thoughtful technocrats, amalgamating and contextualizing new possibilities, rather than being swamped by them.

» Tracks: *Shine On You Crazy Diamond (Parts 1-5); Welcome To The Machine; Have A Cigar; Wish You Were Here; Shine On You Crazy Diamond (Parts 6-9).*

★ First released 1975
★ UK peak chart position: 1
★ USA peak chart position: 1
★ Previous Top 1000 position: 1998 (31): 1994 (127)

39 WHAT'S GOING ON ↓
Marvin Gaye

The best soul album in the world, for always. Prior to this monumental release, albums recorded for Tamla/Motown Records were largely adjuncts to successful singles, rather than independent projects. Despite pressure to conform, Marvin Gaye was determined not only to break with tradition but also to comment on social topics. Through a seamless suite of songs the singer addressed issues including ecology, poverty and the Vietnam War, yet polemics did not deflect his artistic strengths, and 'Inner City Blues (Make Me Wanna Holler)' and 'Mercy Mercy Me (The Ecology)' boast hypnotic melodies and vocals. Gaye's sinewy voice retained its distinctive qualities and his vision was rewarded with both critical and commercial success. In turn the course of black music was irrevocably changed.

》 Tracks: *What's Going On; What's Happening Brother; Flyin' High (In The Friendly Sky); Save The Children; God Is Love; Mercy Mercy Me (The Ecology); Right On; Wholy Holy; Inner City Blues (Make Me Wanna Holler).*

★ First released 1971
★ UK peak chart position: did not chart
★ USA peak chart position: 6
★ Previous Top 1000 position: 1998 (32): 1994 (9)

40 LET IT BLEED ↑
The Rolling Stones

The last Rolling Stones album to feature the presence of the band's creator, Brian Jones, was a brilliant culmination of all their musical influences over the previous monumental decade. The power of the opening track, 'Gimme Shelter', will haunt many of us forever with the memory of the Altamont murder, Mick Jagger's top hat and scarf and the death of the 60s. The repeated line, 'It's just a shot away', complements the repetition of the naïvely profound lyric of the album's last track: 'you can't always get what you want'. The filling in between, like the layered cake on the cover, is equally delectable but never sticky.

》 Tracks: *Gimme Shelter; Love In Vain; Country Honk; Live With Me; Let It Bleed; Midnight Rambler; You Got The Silver; Monkey Man; You Can't Always Get What You Want.*

★ First released 1969
★ UK peak chart position: 1
★ USA peak chart position: 3
★ Previous Top 1000 position: 1998 (44): 1994 (8)

41 DUMMY ↓
Portishead

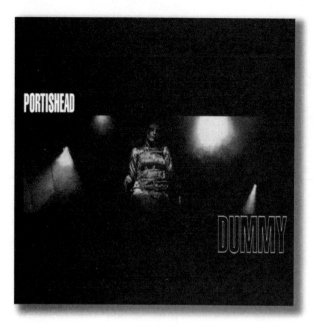

They emerged from Bristol's thriving trip-hop scene wit little fanfare, but produced an understated, remarkabl album that was lavished with critical praise and awards Beth Gibbons' moody vocals made her the obvious focus turning from haunting, otherworldly angel to snarlin witch within a moment, the Portishead sound wa completely original. Much of the credit was also due to the programming of Geoff Barrow, which combined hip hop scratching with science-fiction samples and dense orchestration. Not an immediately accessible record, it has, nevertheless, become a 90s classic 'dinner-party favourite' – arguably a waste for such an unsettling and cinematic album.

» Tracks: *Mysterons; Sour Times; Strangers; It Could Be Sweet; Wandering Star; Numb; Roads; Pedestal; Biscuit; Glory Box.*

★ First released 1994
★ UK peak chart position: 2
★ USA peak chart position: 79
★ Previous Top 1000 position: 1998 (34): 1994 (–)

42 LED ZEPPELIN IV ↓
Led Zeppelin

Its unscripted sleeve design suggested anonymity, but nothing was left to question over this album's content. Led Zeppelin were never so strident as on 'Rock 'n' Roll' and 'Black Dog', two selections of undiluted urgency. Blues standard 'When The Levee Breaks' is recast as a piece of unremitting power, particularly through John Bonham's expansive drumming, and the group's love of folk forms surfaces on the graceful 'Battle Of Evermore', complete with a cameo from Fairport Convention's Sandy Denny. 'Stairway To Heaven' has, of course, become the album's best-known track, but the anthem-like stature it has since assumed should not obscure its groundbreaking companion selections. *Led Zeppelin IV* left much of heavy metal, and indeed rock itself, trailing in its wake.

» Tracks: *Black Dog; Rock 'n' Roll; The Battle Of Evermore; Stairway To Heaven; Misty Mountain Hop; Four Sticks; Going To California; When The Levee Breaks.*

★ First released 1971
★ UK peak chart position: 1
★ USA peak chart position: 2
★ Previous Top 1000 position: 1998 (39): 1994 (38)

43 GRACELAND ↓
Paul Simon

Through the mist of subsequent pale imitations, it is difficult now to recall the enormous impact of this transcultural album. The mould-breaking blend of rock and African rhythms is exemplified by 'Homeless', an exquisitely melancholic evocation of African beauty and desolation. The stirring harmonies of Ladysmith Black Mambazo illuminate 'Homeless' and 'Diamonds On The Soles Of Her Shoes'. The element of humour in the latter is echoed in 'You Can Call Me Al', a hit single and now overplayed on the radio. The lyrics are finely crafted and the result is a structure of impeccable proportions. There are angels in the architecture.

» Tracks: *The Boy In The Bubble; Graceland; I Know What I Know; Gumboots; Diamonds On the Soles Of Her Shoes; You Can Call Me Al; Under African Skies; Homeless; Crazy Love Vol. 2; All Around The World Or The Myth Of Fingerprints.*

★ First released 1986
★ UK peak chart position: 1
★ USA peak chart position: 3
★ Previous Top 1000 position: 1998 (38): 1994 (93)

44 DEFINITELY MAYBE ↓
Oasis

Even though they did not go supernova until 1995's (What's The Story) Morning Glory ?, Oasis never bettered the sheer swagger and panache of their debut. The rousing statement of intent on the opening track, 'Rock 'n' Roll Star', presaged a collection of songs that brilliantly reclaimed rock music for the 90s, with both a sneer and a nod of respect to their spiritual predecessors the Beatles. An indication of the impact this album made on release was the way a whole generation seemed instantly to connect with the sentiments of 'Live Forever', and the group did not hesitate to seize the opportunity it gave them to reach for the stars.

» Tracks: *Rock 'n' Roll Star; Shakermaker; Live Forever; Up In The Sky; Columbia; Sad Song; Supersonic; Bring It On Down; Cigarettes & Alcohol; Digsy's Dinner; Slide Away; Married With Children.*

★ First Released 1994
★ UK peak chart position: 1
★ USA peak chart position: 58
★ Previous Top 1000 position: 1998 (25): 1994 (–)

45 THE BAND ↑
The Band

Initially renowned as Bob Dylan's backing group, the Band emerged from the singer's shadow to proclaim a distinctive talent. Drawing upon a musical canon embracing soul, country, folk and rock 'n' roll, the quintet created a unique sound that was quintessentially American. Its rustic qualities were enhanced by principle songwriter Robbie Robertson who created vistas suggestive of a pre-industrial age, and as such, captured the restlessness of the late 60s without the need for explicit manifestos. Expressive singing, sublime melodies and telepathic musicianship instils *The Band* with quality, but its adult themes and perspectives ensure an absolute timelessness. An all-time critics' favourite.

» Tracks: *Across The Great Divide; Rag Mama Rag; The Night They Drove Old Dixie Down; When You Awake; Up On Cripple Creek; Whispering Pines; Jemima Surrender; Rockin' Chair; Look Out Cleveland; Jawbone; The Unfaithful Servant; King Harvest (Has Surely Come).*

★ First released 1969
★ UK peak chart position: 25
★ USA peak chart position: 9
★ Previous Top 1000 position: 1998 (49): 1994 (35)

46 THE DOORS ↑
The Doors

The Doors were the antithesis of windblown Californian pop. Dark, brooding and alienated, every element of the quartet's métier was unveiled on their debut album. In Jim Morrison they possessed one of rock's authoritative voices, while the group's dense instrumental prowess reflected his lyrical mystery. Highly literate, they wedded Oedipean tragedy to counter-culture nihilism and, in 'Light My Fire', expressed erotic images previously unheard in pop. Howlin' Wolf, Brecht and Weill are acknowledged as musical reference points, a conflict between the physical and cerebral that gives *The Doors* its undiluted tension. Or you can just enjoy it as a brilliant album that sucks you in as it breathes out the 60s.

» Tracks: *Break On Through; Soul Kitchen; The Crystal Ship; Twentieth Century Fox; Alabama Song; Light My Fire; Back Door Man; I Looked At You; End Of The Night; Take It As It Comes; The End.*

★ First released 1967
★ UK peak chart position: 43
★ USA peak chart position: 2
★ Previous Top 1000 position: 1998 (67): 1994 (63)

47 LOW ↑
David Bowie

The first (*Heroes* and *Lodger* would follow) of David Bowie's three Berlin albums. Living there as a semi-recluse for three years, he worked with svengali/producer Brian Eno and the results of their collaborations helped change the face of the European mainstream. Artists such as Gary Numan, Ultravox and OMD were indebted to the sound Bowie had created with the synthesizer to build a somewhat terse wall of sound. It was critically acclaimed, but a relative commercial failure, apart from the surprise 'Sound and Vision' hit single. It remains as a pertinent reminder of Bowie's ability to surprise and enlighten, and gains popularity with age.

❯❯ Tracks: *Speed Of Life; Breaking Glass; What In The World; Sound and Vision; Always Crashing In The Same Car; Be My Wife; A New Career In A New Town; Warszawa; Art Decade; Weeping Wall; Subterraneans.*

★ First released 1977
★ UK peak chart position: 2
★ USA peak chart position: 11
★ Previous Top 1000 position: 1998 (120): 1994 (216)

48 WHO'S NEXT ↑
The Who

The follow-up to *Tommy* would always provide Pete Townshend with an artistic dilemma, and two years passed before the Who unleashed this. The wait proved worthwhile and taking the best from the aborted *Lifehouse* project, Townshend added a handful of urgent new songs to create one of his group's finest releases. Synthesizer obbligatos and acoustic guitars provide occasional counterpoints to the quartet's accustomed power, a contrast emphasizing their sense of dynamics. 'Behind Blue Eyes' and 'Baba O'Riley' were each destined to become integral parts of the Who's 70s lexicon, as vital as 'My Generation' had proved from the previous decade. It set a hard rock standard that even its creators struggled to emulate, and 'Won't Get Fooled Again' is probably the greatest of rock anthems.

❯❯ Tracks: *Baba O'Riley; Bargain; Love Ain't For Keeping; My Wife; Song Is Over; Getting In Tune; Going Mobile; Behind Blue Eyes; Won't Get Fooled Again.*

★ First released 1971
★ UK peak chart position: 1
★ USA peak chart position: 4
★ Previous Top 1000 position: 1998 (133): 1994 (140)

49 OUT OF TIME ↑
R.E.M.

R.E.M. are one the world's most successful band in recent years, and their stream of acclaimed albums illustrates their importance as America's greatest post-Springsteen export. Michael Stipe's thinking person's lyrics are almost buried by the band's Byrds-like arrangements of the notable 'Radio Song' and 'Shiny Happy People'. There are those that have criticized R.E.M. for stepping out of a parochial indie scene, but their impact in the 90s was as welcome as the Sex Pistols were in the 70s. Their catalogue is destined to endure as critics reluctantly accept their considerable importance in the history of rock.

» Tracks: *Radio Song; Losing My Religion; Low; Near Wild Heaven; Endgame; Shiny Happy People; Belong; Half A World Away; Texarkana; Country Feedback; Me In Honey.*

★ First released 1991
★ UK peak chart position: 1
★ USA peak chart position: 1
★ Previous Top 1000 position: 1998 (51): 1994 (13)

50 TROUT MASK REPLICA ↑
Captain Beefheart and The Magic Band

There is nothing like this is the world, this Frank Zappa-produced extravaganza remains a classic of lyrical malarkey. Accompanied by his finest ever Magic Band, the Captain entered the recording studio (actually a rented house) with a few ideas for songs. What came out is still to this day, quite astonishing. Ornette Coleman wildness and guitars thrashing in tune but deliberately off key. At times, it was alleged, Beefheart's mum sent them food parcels. The good Captain's retirement from the music world to take up painting is a great loss. This record is living proof of his bizarre genius. A challenging and unbelievable record. A squid eating dough in polyethylene bag is fast n' bulbous, got me?

» Tracks: *Frownland; The Dust Blows Forward 'N The Dust Blows Back; Dachau Blues; Ella Guru; Hair Pie: Bake 1; Moonlight On Vermont; Pachuco Cadaver; Bill's Corpse; Sweet Sweet Bulbs; Neon Meate Dream Of A Octafish; China Pig; My Human Gets Me Blues; Dali's Car; Hair Pie: Bake 2; Pena; Well; When Big Joan Sets Up; Fallin' Ditch; Sugar 'N Spikes; Ant Man Bee; Orange Claw Hammer; Wild Life; She's Too Much For My Mirror; Hobo Chang Ba; The Blimp; Steal Softly Thru Snow; Old Fart At Play; Veteran's Day Poppy.*

★ First released 1969
★ UK peak chart position: 21
★ USA peak chart position: did not chart
★ Previous Top 1000 position: 1998 (61): 1994 (153)

51 JAGGED LITTLE PILL ↓
Alanis Morissette

One wondered how on earth she could have followed this remarkable debut. She did, but it was a pale shadow. Alanis Morissette defined the independent rock chick genre started, but not completed, by Suzanne Vega and Sheryl Crow. They like men, but they don't need 'em. Most major record companies have now been signing up Morissette soundalikes for the past two years, but the popularity of this album is inflated because it caught the mood at the right time. There is no doubt that 'Ironic' and 'Hand in My Pocket' are great songs, but radio almost killed them off. Morissette is ballsy and this was a very fine rock album. but that's about it for now.

》》 Tracks: *All I Really Want; You Oughta Know; Perfect; Hand In My Pocket; Right Through You; Forgiven; You Learn; Head Over Feet; Mary Jane; Ironic; Not The Doctor; Wake Up.*

★ First released 1995
★ UK peak chart position: 1
★ USA peak chart position: 1
★ Previous Top 1000 position: 1998 (35): 1994 (–)

52 TOMMY ↑
The Who

The definitive rock opera, *Tommy* liberated the Who from a 'singles band' stigma, and made them an international attraction. Composer Pete Townshend had flirted with the genre on two previous releases; here his vision was spread over two ambitious albums that played to his group's main strengths. Memorable songs were matched by pulsating musicianship, which emphasized the Who's internal kineticism, while the cast of characters unleashed revealed an unconventional imagination. Townshend even incorporates 'Eyesight To The Blind', first recorded by Sonny Boy Williamson, as part of his fable about the 'deaf, dumb and blind kid', a rare but successful reference to the past in what is a forward-looking achievement.

》》 Tracks: *Overture; It's A Boy; 1921; Amazing Journeys; Sparks; Eyesight To The Blind; Miracle Cure; Sally Simpson; I'm Free; Welcome; Tommy's Holiday Camp; We're Not Gonna Take It; Christmas; Cousin Kevin; The Acid Queen; Underture; Do You Think It's Alright; Fiddle About; Pinball Wizard; There's A Doctor; Go To The Mirror; Tommy Can You Hear Me; Smash The Mirror; Sensation.*
★ First released 1969
★ UK peak chart position: 2 ★ USA peak chart position: 4
★ Previous Top 1000 position: 1998 (257): 1994 (423)

53 MARQUEE MOON ↑
Television

New York's 70s punk was markedly different to that of the UK. Rather than reject the past, American groups deconstructed its forms and rebuilt them with recourse to the music's strengths. Television's leader, Tom Verlaine, professed admiration for Moby Grape and the folk rock of early Fairport Convention. Elements of the latter appear on this album's title track, which offers a thrilling instrumental break, built upon a modal scale. Verlaine's shimmering guitar style provides the set's focus, but his angular compositions are always enthralling. A sense of brooding mystery envelops the proceedings, and *Marquee Moon* retains its standing as another of the era's pivotal releases that missed the *Billboard* chart.

》》 Tracks: *See No Evil; Venus; Friction; Marquee Moon; Elevation; Guiding Light; Prove It; Torn Curtain.*

★ First released 1977
★ UK peak chart position: 28
★ USA peak chart position: did not chart
★ Previous Top 1000 position: 1998 (103): 1994 (467)

54 ODELAY ←
Beck

His previous album *Mellow Gold* had been overshadowed by the huge success of the slacker anthem 'Loser', but on this 1996 major label follow-up, Beck Hansen corralled his wildly imaginative talent into a stunning collection of tracks that has made the skinny white *wunderkind* one of contemporary music's most important artists. *Odelay* is a potent mix of the new and the old, sampling from the deep wells of hip-hop, electronica, funk, blues and folk to create a multi-layered post-modern masterpiece. The album's surreal air, however, does not detract from the accessibility of songs such as 'Jack-Ass' and 'The New Pollution'. One of the albums of the 90s.

» Tracks: *Devils Haircut; Hotwax; Lord Only Knows; The New Pollution; Derelict; Novacane; Jack-Ass; Where It's At; Minus; Sissyneck; Readymade; High 5 (Rock The Catskills); Ramshackle.*

★ First released 1996
★ UK peak chart position: 18
★ USA peak chart position: 16
★ Previous Top 1000 position: 1998 (54): 1994 (–)

55 FIVE LEAVES LEFT ↑
Nick Drake

Drake's debut encapsulates a marriage between folk music and the singer-songwriter genre. Part Donovan, part Jimmy Webb, he articulated an aching romanticism at a time when progressive rock ran rampant. Beautiful melodies and fragrant accompaniment, in particular Robert Kirby's stunning string arrangements, enhance the artist's sense of longing in which warm, but understated, vocals accentuate the album's passive mystery. An aura of existential cool envelops the proceedings, accentuated by Danny Thompson's sonorous bass lines and Drake's poetic imagery. The result is a shimmering, autumnal collection, reflective but never morbid. It's a tragedy that Drake never lived to see how important his slim catalogue has become.

» Tracks: *Time Has Told Me; River Man; Three Hours; Way To Blue; Day Is Done; 'Cello Song; The Thoughts Of Mary Jane; Man In A Shed; Fruit Tree; Saturday Sun.*

★ First released 1969
★ UK peak chart position: did not chart
★ USA peak chart position: did not chart
★ Previous Top 1000 position: 1998 (197): 1994 (130)

56 THE SMITHS ↑
The Smiths

As great first albums go, *The Smiths* remains a perfect bedsitter moment, cultivated from a batch of Morrissey's diaries then uplifted and exonerated on Marr's guitar. Their juxtaposing of a lopsided grin of gloom and the light doodling of an almost always perfectly placed guitar was virtually unheard of. Marr just jangled in and out like a dog at a fair (Pete Frame acknowledged). Reference points were rare, apart from Morrissey's adopted Oscar Wilde demeanour, to which the press clung with a morbid fascination. It remains a delicate set of knowing quiffs and rounded, innocent eyes, beguiling the listener with some wonderfully crafted pop – when they weren't laughing behind their hands.

» Tracks: *Reel Around The Fountain; You've Got Everything Now; Miserable Lie; Pretty Girls Make Graves; The Hand That Rocks The Cradle; Still Ill; Hand In Glove; What Difference Does It Make?; I Don't Owe You Anything; Suffer Little Children.*

★ First released 1984
★ UK peak chart position: 2
★ USA peak chart position: 150
★ Previous Top 1000 position: 1998 (115): 1994 (75)

57 PARALLEL LINES ↑
Blondie

Madonna and Michael Jackson aside, this is supreme pop music and as good as the genre can ever get. Everybody loved Blondie; fans, children, critics, other musicians and senior citizens – and not just because the pouting gorgeous little Debbie Harry was its frontperson. This is an unintentional greatest hits record that never lets up until the last note of 'Just Go Away' has died. If one wanted to carp, you could have asked for 'Denis' and 'Call Me' to have been included, but that would be just plain greedy. One of the greatest 'up' pop records of all time that can be put on repeat play.

》 Tracks: *Fade Away; Hanging On The Telephone; One Way Or Another; Picture This; Pretty Baby; I Know But I Don't Know; 11.59; Will Anything Happen; Sunday Girl; Heart Of Glass; I'm Gonna Love You Too; Just Go Away.*

★ First released 1978
★ UK peak chart position: 1
★ USA peak chart position: 6
★ Previous Top 1000 position: 1998 (166): 1994 (108)

58 TRANSFORMER ↑
Lou Reed

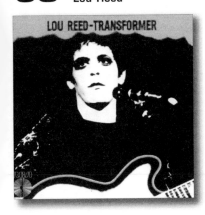

Having quit the Velvet Underground, a disillusioned Lou Reed came to the UK to rethink his musical career. A low-key solo debut was followed by this highly successful release, which combined the artist's narrative compositions with the lure of contemporaneous fashions, glam-rock and androgyny. Long-time fan David Bowie co-produced the set, which emphasized the commercial nature of Reed's work without sacrificing his individuality or authenticity. Members of Andy Warhol's entourage were described graphically in 'Walk On The Wild Side'. And in 'Vicious', to qualify the power of the word vicious, with 'you hit me with a flower' is priceless cheek.

》 Tracks: *Vicious; Andy's Chest; Perfect Day; Hangin' Around; Walk On The Wild Side; Make Up; Satellite Of Love; Wagon Wheel; New York Telephone Conversation; I'm So Free; Goodnight Ladies.*

★ First released 1972
★ UK peak chart position: 13
★ USA peak chart position: 29
★ Previous Top 1000 position: 1998 (69): 1994 (95)

59 LEFTISM ↑
Leftfield

With this recording Leftfield made the crossover of techno into the pop mainstream two years before the likes of the Chemical Brothers. Embarking on a series of high-profile collaborations, they introduced to the charts a musical manifesto that had been popular in the clubs for years – including ambient ('Song Of Life'), pure techno, ragga, African tribal chants ('Afro-Left') and the all-important remix. The pumping, snarling 'Open Up', featuring John Lydon, predated the Prodigy in its blend of punk and dance, and 'Original', with Curve's Toni Halliday, ironically inspired a multitude of imitators. Most of these tracks have become ubiquitous through mainstream television and film, and it is easy to forget that, before Leftfield, techno music had only rarely stepped outside clubland.

》 Tracks: *Release The Pressure; Afro-Left; Melt; Song Of Life; Original; Black Flute; Space Shanty; Inspection (Check One); Storm 3000; Open Up; 21st Century Poem.*

★ First released 1995
★ UK peak position: 3 ★ USA peak position: did not chart
★ Previous Top 1000 position: 1998 (78): 1994 (–)

60 LEGEND ↑
Bob Marley

Although reggae is still perceived as a minor specialist genre, when it presses th
button right, the music captures the hearts of the masses. Bob Marley is a giant, simil
to Elvis Presley: both continue to sell vast numbers of records long after their death
and both are clear leaders of their respective genres. This album is the most perfec
selection of hits. The running order is unbeatable, each track is made for the nex
There is a superb four-CD box set available for serious collectors, but for those wh
want to put on a Marley CD at any time of the day this will always hit the spot.

» Tracks: *Is This Love; Jamming; No Woman No Cry; Stir It Up; Get Up and
Stand Up; Satisfy My Soul; I Shot The Sheriff; One Love; People Get Ready; Buffalo
Soldier; Exodus; Redemption Song; Could You Be Loved; Want More.*

★ First released 1984
★ UK peak chart position: 1
★ USA peak chart position: 54
★ Previous Top 1000 position: 1998 (80): 1994 (29)

61 LED ZEPPELIN ↑
Led Zeppelin

The greatest heavy rock group ever emerged from the ashes of the Yardbirds, but their self-
assured debut album immediately established them in their own right. Right from the
opening note of a track such as 'Communication' you feel their confident power. Faultless
musicianship combined with strong material to create a real assertive statement of
purpose. Blues standards are extensively reworked and original songs either acknowledge
pop/rock structures or allow the quartet to extend itself musically. Robert Johnson would
surely have acknowledged their interpretations with approval. Guitarist Jimmy Page
explored the instrument's potential with dazzling runs of sonic inventiveness, while
Robert Plant took the notion of vocalist into new realms of expression.

» Tracks: *Good Times Bad Times; Babe I'm Gonna Leave You; You Shook Me;
Dazed and Confused; Your Time Is Gonna Come; Black Mountain Side;
Communication Breakdown; I Can't Quit You Baby; How Many More Times.*

★ First released 1969
★ UK peak chart position: 6 ★ USA peak chart position: 10
★ Previous Top 1000 position: 1998 (212): 1994 (209)

62 AFTER THE GOLDRUSH ↑
Neil Young

Young's first solo release since joining Crosby, Stills and Nash, *After The Goldrush*
confirmed the singer's talent in the full glare of the public eye. His most eclectic set to
date encompassed the delicate wistfulness of 'I Believe In You' and 'Only Love Can
Break Your Heart', as well as the electric anger of 'Southern Man', a raging *tour de force*
that captured the special tension generated between Young and backing group Crazy
Horse. Stills and Nils Lofgren also provided support on an album that consolidated a
talent while also extending its range. The transformation of Don Gibson's 'Oh
Lonesome Me' from canter to ballad confirmed an original musical vision, but the
album owes its continued strength to Young's own remarkable compositions.

» Tracks: *Tell Me Why; After The Goldrush; Only Love Can Break Your Heart;
Southern Man; Till The Morning Comes; Oh Lonesome Me; Don't Let It Bring You
Down; Birds; When You Dance I Can Really Love; I Believe In You; Cripple Creek Ferry.*

★ First released 1970
★ UK peak chart position: 7
★ USA peak chart position: 8
★ Previous Top 1000 position: 1998 (73): 1994 (106)

63 ARE YOU EXPERIENCED ↑
The Jimi Hendrix Experience

By 1967 Jimi Hendrix was fêted as a genius by audiences and contemporary musicians alike. His innovative, evolving guitar prowess was captured to perfection on this, his album debut. At times audacious, at others lyrical, Hendrix brought new perspectives to every style he chose to play, be it blues, pop or psychedelia. This contains a wide range of material, on which Noel Redding (bass) and Mitch Mitchell (drums) provide the ideal springboard for the master's flights. Each format offered avenues for experiment, none more so than the vibrant 'Red House', on which the standard 12-bar blues is teased and twisted to new heights. Hendrix was clearly enraptured by a new-found artistic freedom, a joy that pervades this entire album. The 1997 MCA Records reissue with extra tracks is a treat for sore ears.

)) Tracks: *Foxy Lady; Manic Depression; Red House; Can You See Me; Love Or Confusion; I Don't Live Today; May This Be Love; Fire; 3rd Stone From The Sun; Remember; Are You Experienced?*

★ First released 1967
★ UK peak chart position: 2 ★ USA peak chart position: 5
★ Previous Top 1000 position: 1998 (70): 1994 (39)

64 THRILLER ↓
Michael Jackson

The finest example of perfect disco pop, and a record that should be prescribed to musical snobs and manic depressives. The album is a true ambassador of what pop music can sometimes be. Jacko whoops and dances through a suite of unforgettable melodies that should be danced to with a smile on your face. While many listeners will lapse into UK comedian Lenny Henry's 'Aston Villa' lyric to replace 'thriller'. Most people are touched by this quite magnificent record. Each track offers at least one musical hook, whether it is the beauty of 'Human Nature' (who can resist the 'dada dada da da da da') or the 'whoo whoo' of 'Billie Jean'. It's all so very good.

)) Tracks: *Wanna Be Startin' Somethin'; Baby Be Mine; The Girl Is Mine; Thriller; Beat It; Billie Jean; Human Nature; PYT (Pretty Young Thing); The Lady In My Life.*

★ First released 1982
★ UK peak chart position: 1
★ USA peak chart position: 1
★ Previous Top 1000 position: 1998 (58): 1994 (14)

65 LOVELESS ↑
My Bloody Valentine

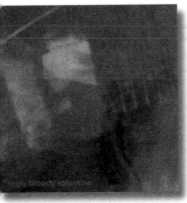

'The last word in noise-pop' was how this release was reviewed on release in 1991, but that is a somewhat simplistic response. Creation Records must have been relieved, having invested some £200,000 over three years indulging their notoriously workshy recluses. The results are well worth the price, at least in artistic terms. Eighteen sound engineers are credited on the LP sleeve and the group's huge, luminous soundscapes now involved everything from guitars to bagpipes. At one turn the Jesus and Mary Chain, at others Philip Glass or the Beach Boys, *Loveless* is a colossal achievement, and by necessity one constructed by the most ambitious studio band of their generation. It demands your attention.

)) Tracks: *Only Shallow; Loomer; Touched; To Here Knows When; When You Sleep; I Only Said; Come In Alone; Sometimes; Blown A Wish; What You Want; Soon.*

★ First released 1991
★ UK peak chart position: 24
★ USA peak chart position: did not chart
★ Previous Top 1000 position: 1998 (472): 1994 (–)

66 BRIDGE OVER TROUBLED WATER ↓
Simon and Garfunkel

The measured beauty of its opening title track set the tone for this album's quie authority. International acclaim immediately ensued and the duo's passage from fol act to popular singers was confirmed through a series of stellar, Paul Simon-penne compositions. Alternately reflective, then bubbling, the collection revealed a growir maturity and, in 'El Condor Pasa', the first flowering of his infatuation with worl music styles. Art Garfunkel's angelic tenor was never so perfect; when combined wit Simon's lower register it created a seamless resonance, redolent of the Everly Brother It is no surprise that this album features a rendition of the latter's 'Bye Bye Love'.

» Tracks: *Bridge Over Troubled Water; El Condor Pasa; Cecilia; Keep The Customer Satisfied; So Long, Frank Lloyd Wright; The Boxer; Baby Driver; The Only Living Boy In New York; Why Don't You Write Me; Bye Bye Love; Song For The Asking.*

★ First released 1970
★ UK peak chart position: 1 ★ USA peak chart position: 1
★ Previous Top 1000 position: 1998 (52): 1994 (97)

67 HOTEL CALIFORNIA ↑
The Eagles

A steady growth suddenly mushroomed into a monster as the Eagles, along wit Fleetwood Mac, epitomized cosy AOR in the early 70s. This record is supposedly concept album but most of the purchasers merely enjoyed the accessible songs whi driving down to the coast in their Volvo estates with 2.4 children. Joe Walsh wa added to give gutsy guitar in the wake of the departed country flavour of Bern Leaden, while Randy Meisner grew in stature as a writer with 'Try and Love Again' an 'New Kid In Town'. The title track still bites as Henley's stretched voice blends wit Walsh's epic trebly guitar solo.

» Tracks: *Hotel California; New Kid In Town; Life In The Fast Lane; Wasted Time Wasted Time (Reprise); Victim Of Love; Pretty Maids All In A Row; Try and Love Again; The Last Resort.*

★ First released 1976
★ UK peak chart position: 2
★ USA peak chart position: 1
★ Previous Top 1000 position: 1998 (162): 1994 (171)

68 MOON SAFARI ↑
Air

Just to confirm that melody will out, Air took ambient dance/space pop/electronica ou of the air and into the mainstream smog. Synth and moog critics were stopped in thei tracks as they were charmed by irresistible melody. From the Bacharach flavour of 'C Matin La' to the gentle FatBoy Slim soundalike, 'Kelly, Watch The Stars', it's all ver agreeable, easy on the ear and maddeningly addictive. Those who are unable to read French will only be able to surmise what the chanteuse Beth Hirsch is saying on 'Sex Boy'. Something about 'òu sont tes héros aux corps d'athlètes'.

» Tracks: *La Femme D'Argent; Sexy Boy; All I Need; Kelly Watch The Stars; Talisman; Remember; You Make It Easy; Ce Matin La; New Star In The Sky; Le Voyage De Penelope.*

★ First released 1998
★ UK peak chart position: 6
★ USA peak chart position: did not chart
★ Previous Top 1000 position: 1998 (–): 1994 (–)

69 PERFORMANCE AND COCKTAILS ↑
Stereophonics

With their second album the Stereophonics raised their patriotic Welsh flag with a degree of justified pride. Following on from the success enjoyed by the Manic Street Preachers and Super Furry Animals, Stereophonics ended the century out front. They combined gritty rock songs with sudden bursts of fantastic pop melody, notable in their middle eights. Alert your ears to 'roll out the shock parade, free falling from a stage' on 'Roll Up and Shine', and 'the bartender and the thief are lovers steal what they need like sisters and brothers' on the chorus of 'The Bartender and The Thief'. It is hoped they don't run out of hooks.

» Tracks: *Roll Up and Shine; The Bartender and The Thief; Hurry Up and Wait; Pick A Part That's New; Just Looking; Half The Lies You Tell Ain't True; I Wouldn't Believe Your Radio; T-Shirt Sun Tan; Is Yesterday, Tomorrow, Today?; A Minute Longer; She Takes Her Clothes Off; Plastic California; I Stopped To Fill My Car Up.*

★ First released 1999
★ UK peak chart position: 1
★ USA peak chart position: did not chart
★ Previous Top 1000 position: 1998 (–): 1994 (–)

70 TEN ↑
Pearl Jam

Formed from the ashes of Seattle's Band-Most-Likely-To, Mother Love Bone, who quietly fell to pieces after the untimely overdose of vocalist Andrew Wood, Stone Gossard and Jeff Ament unearthed vocalist Eddie Vedder and rescued him from a job as an all-night petrol pump attendant. The result was a most curious multi-platinum album that, like its predecessor's attempts, drew on 70s rock as a major influence. Vedder's lyrical insights were as beguiling as they were obtuse; however, they captured a disenchanted nation's imagination and success came running. Angst rock pretenders came out of the woodwork with their cassette demos, after this succeeded so well.

» Tracks: *Once; Even Flow; Alive; Why Go; Black; Jeremy; Oceans; Porch; Garden; Deep; Release; Master; Slave.*

★ First released 1992
★ UK peak chart position: 18
★ USA peak chart position: 2
★ Previous Top 1000 position: 1998 (83): 1994 (124)

71 SAINT DOMINIC'S PREVIEW ↑
Van Morrison

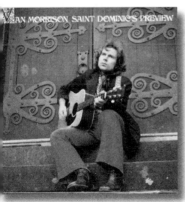

The cover depicts a troubled soul sitting on the church steps strumming his Martin guitar, probably unaware of the P. J. Proby split in his pants. The music inside is varied, as if Morrison is still feeling his way. He places the soul/jazz of 'Jackie Wilson Said' and 'I Will Be There' next to the delicious 12-string acoustic ramblings of 'Almost Independence Day' and 'Listen To The Lion'. It is the latter two that make this album so special. Van can knock off a soul song every time he opens his mouth, but 'Listen To the Lion' opens his soul. In addition to *Astral Weeks*, please don't miss out on this album.

» Tracks: *Jackie Wilson Said; Gypsy; I Will Be There; Listen To The Lion; St. Dominic's Preview; Redwood Tree; Almost Independence Day.*

★ First released 1972
★ UK peak chart position: did not chart
★ USA peak chart position: 15
★ Previous Top 1000 position: 1998 (324): 1994 (241)

72 PURPLE RAIN ↑
Prince and The Revolution

A soundtrack to a movie so disappointing that it is infinitely wiser to let the record stand on its own merits. While Prince cavorted in purple kitchen foil and rode his Harley in high heels, the real star of the film, the music, was doing all the talking. A knit of funk and rock, a heavily stylized Hendrix guitar lick here and there, and a wilfully danceable backbeat all made for a huge commercial smash, and the first real international introduction for many people to a star-in-waiting. 'Darling Nikki' accidentally set the Prince musical caravan rolling, but the heady lilt of the title track and the crushing 'When Doves Cry' can pardon him that.

➠ Tracks: *Let's Go Crazy; Take Me With U; The Beautiful Ones; Computer Blue; Darling Nikki; When Doves Cry; I Would Die 4 U; Baby I'm A Star; Purple Rain.*

★ First released 1984
★ UK peak chart position: 7
★ USA peak chart position: 1
★ Previous Top 1000 position: 1998 (79): 1994 (44)

73 LITTLE EARTHQUAKES ↑
Tori Amos

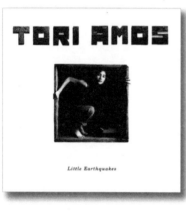

With this debut, Tori Amos rose above the inevitable Kate Bush/Joni Mitchell comparisons, producing a stunning set of brutally honest and emotionally wrought songs. A skilled and imaginative pianist, Amos also proved a versatile vocalist, moving from whisper to scream in an instant. She concentrates on intimate stories of her religious upbringing, childhood traumas, and predominantly, sex, self-discovery and unhappy relationships. 'Silent All These Years' was the first to hit a nerve with the public on single release, but all the tracks – memories of her father in 'Winter', the bittersweet 'Happy Phantom', the harrowing account of her own rape, 'Me and A Gun' – combine to make this inspiring, if rarely comfortable, listening.

➠ Tracks: *Crucify; Girl; Silent All These Years; Precious Things; Winter; Happy Phantom; China; Leather; Mother; Tear In Your Hand; Me and A Gun; Little Earthquakes.*

★ First released 1992
★ UK peak position: 14 ★ USA peak position: 54
★ Previous Top 1000 position: 1998 (98): 1994 (–)

74 TAPESTRY ↑
Carole King

During the 60s Carole King was renowned for composing a succession of classic pop songs. A low-key recording career blossomed with the release of this album which successfully married this skill with the contemporary singer-songwriter movement. *Tapestry* is comprised of self-penned material and collaborations with either ex-husband Gerry Goffin or lyricist Toni Stern. King's unfussy vocal style enhances the simply stated yet astute material and in 'It's Too Late' the singer expresses the breakdown of a relationship with percipient incisiveness. Such skill ensures the album's lasting popularity, and a sad reminder to some who have grown older and forgotten to be in love.

➠ Tracks: *I Feel The Earth Move; So Far Away; It's Too Late; Home Again; Beautiful; Way Over Yonder; You've Got A Friend; Where You Lead; Will You Love Me Tomorrow; Smackwater Jack; Tapestry; (You Make Me Feel Like) A Natural Woman.*

★ First released 1971
★ UK peak chart position: 4 ★ USA peak chart position: 1
★ Previous Top 1000 position: 1998 (102): 1994 (183)

75 THE MAN WHO ↑
Travis

One of the brightest hopes for quality guitar based rock in the new millennium. In 1999, Scotland's Travis stormed the airwaves with their second album and continued to stay on top during 2000. Their success is well deserved, as *The Man Who* is a reassuring reminder that songs with fresh uplifting melodies still exist. The only cause for concern is that radio overplay might kill these stars. Already the slightly grating 'Why Does It Always Rain On Me' deserves a nice rest, closely followed by the ever so slightly Radioheadish 'As You Are' and the anthemic 'Turn'. By the time this is read they may well have conquered America.

» Tracks: *Writing To Reach You; The Fear; As You Are; Driftwood; The Last Laugh Of The Laughter; Turn; Why Does It Always Rain On Me?; Luv; She's So Strange; Slide Show.*

★ First released 1999
★ UK peak chart position: 1
★ USA peak chart position: 135
★ Previous Top 1000 position: 1998 (–): 1994 (–)

76 MELLON COLLIE AND THE INFINITE SADNESS ↓
Smashing Pumpkins

A double album was always risky business in the days of vinyl; some of those pompous 70s efforts contained only four tracks. A double album in the CD age, with so much recordable time available (and expected) is potentially suicidal. Billy Corgan had no such concerns when he formulated the lyrics to over two dozen songs. Part 1, 'Dawn To Dusk', and Part 2, 'Twilight To Starlight', contain few potato peelings, and the project was deemed an unmitigated success. Despite the heavy nature of much of the music, the Smashing Pumpkins refused to resort to formulaic riffs, and the occasional use of exquisite strings was an inspired decision.

» Tracks: *Mellon Collie and The Infinite Sadness; Tonight, Tonight; Jellybelly; Zero; Here Is No Why; Bullet With Butterfly Wings; To Forgive; An Ode To No One; Love; Cupid de Locke; Galapogos; Muzzle; Porcelina Of The Vast Oceans; Take Me Down; Where The Boys Fear To Tread; Bodies; Thirty-Three; In The Arms Of Sleep; 1979; Tales Of A Scorched Earth; Thru The Eyes Of Ruby; Stumbleine; X.Y.U.; We Only Come Out At Night; Beautiful; Lily (My One and Only); By Starlight; Farewell and Goodnight.*

★ First released 1995 ★ UK peak chart position: 4 ★ USA peak chart position: 1
★ Previous Top 1000 position: 1998 (71): 1994 (–)

77 DEBUT ↑
Björk

One of the most pleasingly quizzical and quite unexpected first albums. Although Björk's animated meanderings with the Sugarcubes hinted at a deeply singular approach to songwriting, the depth and inventiveness employed on *Debut* went far beyond what had been imagined or expected. Bringing new meaning to the word unorthodox, the record offered gems such as 'There's More To Life Than This', recorded live in the toilet of a club, replete with slamming doors. Meanwhile, the fragility of the human condition was expounded on in reflections on love and sex, each point wonderfully adorned by the rise and fall of her yearning vocal. A true delight.

» Tracks: *Human Behaviour; Crying; Venus As A Boy; There's More To Life Than This; Like Someone In Love; Big Time Sensuality; One Day; Aeroplane; Come To Me; Violently Happy; The Anchor Song; Play Dead.*

★ First released 1993
★ UK peak chart position: 3
★ USA peak chart position: 61
★ Previous Top 1000 position: 1998 (85): 1994 (539

78 TALK ON CORNERS ↑
The Corrs

A perfect blend of 90s super pop, mixed with just enough credibility, pushes Ireland's Corrs that little bit ahead of the pack. They seem destined to be here for the long run, not just because they are precociously talented musicians, but because you get the strong feeling they will move on and develop in other directions, all hinted at on this important album. They tackle traditional folk really well on 'Paddy McCarthy', an unmitigated celebration of their homeland. Similarly, their interpretations of two rock classics, Fleetwood Mac's 'Dreams' and Jimi Hendrix's 'Little Wing', are immaculate and respectfully unthreatening. The special edition CD is the one to own.

» Tracks: *What Can I Do (Tin Tin Out Remix); So Young (K-Klass Remix); Only When I Sleep; When He's Not Around; Dreams (Tee's Radio); I Never Loved You Anyway; Don't Say You Love Me; Love Gives, Love Takes; Runaway (Tin Tin Out Remix); Hopelessly Addicted; Paddy McCarthy; Intimacy; Queen Of Hollywood; No Good For Me; Little Wing.*

★ First released 1998
★ UK peak chart position: 1 ★ USA peak chart position: 72
★ Previous Top 1000 position: 1998 (–): 1994 (–)

79 MOONDANCE ↑
Van Morrison

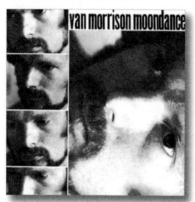

Where on previous recordings Van Morrison had implied soul and R&B roots, on *Moondance* he set them free. He had rarely sounded so relaxed, whether on the bubbling joy of 'And It Stoned Me', the finger-popping ease of the title track or the celebratory bliss of 'Caravan'. Morrison revelled in the music's tight arrangements, clearly enjoying the punchy horn section ('Glad Tidings') and empathizing with quieter, acoustic settings ('Crazy Love'). Where *Astral Weeks* was a cathartic stream-of-consciousness, *Moondance* shows an artist enraptured by a new-found musical freedom. From this moment on everything he sang had soul, without even thinking about it.

» Tracks: and *It Stoned Me; Moondance; Crazy Love; Caravan; Into The Mystic; Come Running; These Dreams Of You; Brand New Day; Everyone; Glad Tidings.*

★ First released 1970
★ UK peak chart position: 32
★ USA peak chart position: 29
★ Previous Top 1000 position: 1998 (113): 1994 (152)

80 WOODFACE ↓
Crowded House

The third and best album from the finest rock band New Zealand has yet produced. A good second would have been Split Enz, but they split up to become errr . . . Crowded House. The Finn brothers have been writing songs for many years and it is encouraging to see that their lyrics are as sharp, fresh and perceptive as ever. The opener 'Chocolate Cake' starts with 'not everyone in New York would pay to see Andrew Lloyd Webber, may his trousers fall down as he bows to the Queen and the crown'. Nothing lapses, no standards are dropped. No worries mate. This one should be around as long as the Beatles.

» Tracks: *Chocolate Cake; It's Only Natural; Fall At Your Feet; Tall Trees; Weather With You; Whispers and Moans; Four Seasons In One Day; There Goes God; Fame Is; All I Ask; As Sure As I Am; Italian Plastic; She Goes On; How Will You Go.*

★ First released 1991
★ UK peak chart position: 6
★ USA peak chart position: 83
★ Previous Top 1000 position: 1998 (72): 1994 (167)

31 LED ZEPPELIN II ↑
Led Zeppelin

Having declared an individual brand of blues rock on their debut album, Led Zeppelin significantly expanded musical horizons on its successor. The now famous opening riff to 'Whole Lotta Love' declared a strength of intent and excitement and the song quickly achieved anthem-like proportions. *Led Zeppelin II* personifies the entire heavy metal spectrum, from guitar hero to virile vocalist. Sexual metaphor ('The Lemon Song') collides with musical dexterity ('Moby Dick') and the faintest whiff of sword and sorcery to create one of the most emphatic and celebratory heavy rock albums. Many copied the formula, but nobody quite had a Page and a Plant.

》 Tracks: *Whole Lotta Love; What Is and What Should Never Be; The Lemon Song; Thank You; Heartbreaker; Livin' Lovin' Maid (She's Just A Woman); Ramble On; Moby Dick; Bring It On Home.*

★ First released 1969
★ UK peak chart position: 1
★ USA peak chart position: 1
★ Previous Top 1000 position: 1998 (105): 1994 (26)

32 SO ↑
Peter Gabriel

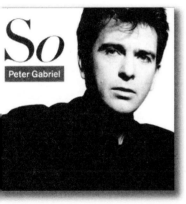

This consolidated Peter Gabriel's reputation as an original and exciting composer, capable of projecting sophisticated lyrics on accessible melodies. 'Sledgehammer' was a massive hit (number one in the USA), as was 'Don't Give Up', with Kate Bush's vocals adding extra pathos. 'This Is The Picture' clearly shows the slightly surreal influence of co-writer Laurie Anderson, and the whole is given flight by Daniel Lanois' impeccable production. The unsung towering achievement, however, is 'Mercy Street', a sparsely orchestrated and perfectly constructed tribute to the late poet Anne Sexton. To date, as admirable as his Real World projects have been, Gabriel has been unable to come anywhere near the power of this album.

》 Tracks: *Red Rain; Sledgehammer; Don't Give Up; That Voice Again; In Your Eyes; Mercy Street; Big Time; We Do What We're Told; This Is The Picture.*

★ First released 1986
★ UK peak chart position: 1
★ USA peak chart position: 2
★ Previous Top 1000 position: 1998 (123): 1994 (78)

33 CROSBY STILLS & NASH ↑
Crosby, Stills and Nash

This beautiful example of 'wooden music' is pining for a reappraisal after being abused by critics in recent years in favour of the more varied *Déjà Vu*. Although the badly recorded bass still booms throughout, and yes, frankly Graham Nash is a bit twee, the quality of the harmonies remains breathtaking. Three youthful men singing songs about their relationships and changing partners deserve a better press in 2000, they were after all, pretty nifty songwriters. Graham Nash's coy 'Lady Of The Island' (about Joni Mitchell), Stephen Stills' opus-like 'Suite: Judy Blue Eyes' (about Judy Collins) and a slim David Crosby singing of his sadly deceased sweetheart Christine on 'Guinnevere'. Be brave, there is more than just 'Marrakesh Express' on this timeless record.

》 Tracks: *Suite: Judy Blue Eyes; Marrakesh Express; Guinnevere; You Don't Have To Cry; Pre Road Downs; Wooden Ships; Lady Of The Island; Helplessly Hoping; Long Time Gone; 49 Bye Byes*

★ First released 1969
★ UK peak chart position: 25 ★ USA peak chart position: 6
★ Previous Top 1000 position: 1998 (126): 1994 (43)

84 STICKY FINGERS ↑
The Rolling Stones

The cheek and arrogance of the Rolling Stones came of age with this work, comple
with zip-fly cover and 'up yours' tongue and lips. Crushing any doubts that they ha
gone soft with *Satanic Majesties*, the guitars of Keith Richards and Mick Taylor rocke
together while Mick Jagger spat out some of his foxiest lyrics. Never had the
sounded so loose, yet so together, with examples such as 'Bitch', 'Sister Morphine', t
country-tinged 'Wild Horses' and the perennial 'Brown Sugar'. Downright dirty, fun
rock 'n' roll like this has still to be bettered, and there is, as yet, no real rival in sig

➤➤ Tracks: *Brown Sugar; Sway; Wild Horses; Can't You Hear Me Knocking; You
Gotta Move; Bitch; I Got The Blues; Sister Morphine; Dead Flowers; Moonlight
Mile.*

★ First released 1971
★ UK peak chart position: 1
★ USA peak chart position: 1
★ Previous Top 1000 position: 1998 [107]: 1994 [11]

85 A LOVE SUPREME ↑
John Coltrane

John Coltrane's great masterpiece and one of the most profoundly moving records
all of jazz, *A Love Supreme* was recorded in December 1964 by Coltrane's clas
quartet (with pianist McCoy Tyner, bassist Jimmy Garrison and drummer Elvin Jone
It is a brilliantly integrated jazz suite examining four distinct stages of spiritu
development, represented by four movements entitled 'Acknowledgemen
'Resolution', 'Pursuance' and 'Psalm'. The music is intense and gripping, and builds
a head on the fast and aggressive 'Pursuance' before the beautiful and soothing 'Psalr
A Love Supreme is without doubt one of the most profound instrumental statements
religious conviction to have emerged in this century.

➤➤ Tracks: *Part 1 Acknowledgement; Part 2 Resolution; Part 3 Pursuance; Part
4 Psalm.*

★ First released 1965
★ UK peak chart position: did not chart
★ USA peak chart position: did not chart
★ Previous Top 1000 position: 1998 [122]: 1994 [40]

86 GOODBYE YELLOW BRICK ROAD ↑
Elton John

An ambitious and bold attempt to produce a double album with no fillers, and Elt
John succeeded better than most. This is an excellent package of sadness and patho
notably 'Funeral For A Friend', 'Love Lies Bleeding', 'Candle In The Wind' an
'Goodbye Yellow Brick Road'. Both Taupin and John were able to change mood for t
perennial encore 'Benny and The Jets'. Quite why 'Benny' is so liked is a mystery; it
usually followed by 'Saturday Night's Alright For Fighting', which is a much mo
substantial song. Note that this album contains the original 'Candle In The Win
written for Marilyn Monroe, not that 1997 version.

➤➤ Tracks: *Funeral For A Friend; Love Lies Bleeding; Benny and The Jets; Candle
In The Wind; Goodbye Yellow Brick Road; This Song Has No Title; Grey Seal;
Jamaica Jerk Off; I've Seen That Movie Too; Sweet Painted Lady; Ballad Of Danny
Bailey; Dirty Little Girl; All The Girls Love Alice; Your Sister Can't Twist (But She
Can Rock 'N' Roll); Saturday Night's Alright For Fighting; Roy Rogers; Social
Disease; Harmony.*

★ First released 1973 ★ UK peak chart position: 1 ★ USA peak chart position:
★ Previous Top 1000 position: 1998 [179]: 1994 [30]

87 HOUNDS OF LOVE ↓
Kate Bush

Kate Bush

Hounds Of Love

Though not the most prolific of album artists, Kate Bush's works make up in impact what they lack in frequency. Her style and material has always been unique, eccentric even, but *Hounds Of Love* is probably the strongest mix of controlled musical experimentation and lyrical expression. It deals with big issues – childhood fantasy and trauma, conflict, sexuality – but rarely lapses into pretension. The intense arrangements are perfectly matched to the subjects: 'Running Up That Hill' climactically erotic, 'Cloudbusting' broodingly triumphant, and 'The Big Sky' just … big. It would be nice to think she has some more albums in her, maybe she could get one out soon.

》 Tracks: *Running Up That Hill (A Deal With God); Hounds Of Love; The Big Sky; Mother Stands For Comfort; Cloudbusting; And Dream Of Sheep; Under Ice; Waking The Witch; Watching You Without Me; Jig Of Life; Hello Earth; The Morning Fog.*

★ First released 1985
★ UK peak chart position: 1 ★ USA peak chart position: 30
★ Previous Top 1000 position: 1998 (59): 1994 (385)

88 METALLICA ↑
Metallica

For the band who helped change the traditional face of contemporary heavy metal, Metallica were never found wanting in innovation. Nevertheless, 1991's album of the same name appeared as a significant burst of ideas, surprising even their most ardent of fans. Songs were stripped down to comparatively palatable lengths and subtle orchestration was introduced, with vocalist James Hetfield dropping his infamous growl for a warm, accomplished vocal. 'Enter Sandman' and the lilting 'Nothing Else Matters' revealed both sides of their clever songwriting temperament, contributing to this unabashed masterstroke of sincerity and overwhelming musical confidence. They have now proved themselves the leaders of the genre.

》 Tracks: *Enter Sandman; Sad But True; Holier Than Thou; The Unforgiven; Wherever I May Roam; Don't Tread On Me; Through The Never; Nothing Else Matters; Of Wolf and Man; The God That Failed; My Friend Of Misery; The Struggle Within.*

★ First released 1991 ★ UK peak chart position: 1 ★ USA peak chart position: 1
★ Previous Top 1000 position: 1998 (165): 1994 (234)

89 SONGS IN THE KEY OF LIFE ↓
Stevie Wonder

An ambitious double vinyl set (plus a further freebie EP) that represented the culmination of Stevie Wonder's second golden period which started with *Music Of My Mind*. Now firmly established as a musical genius, Wonder gave us longer and stronger songs. Although the hits such as the unremarkable 'Sir Duke', 'Another Star' and 'I Wish' are more often remembered, it is the overall incredibly high standard of all the songs that makes this such an outstanding achievement. Featuring beautiful gems such as 'Joy Inside My Tears', the brassy and funky 'Black Man', and the cloying but unforgettable 'Isn't She Lovely'. Coolio took his ace reworking of 'Pastime Paradise' into the charts in 1996.

》 Tracks: *Love's In Need Of Love Today; Have A Talk With God; Village Ghetto Land; Confusion; Sir Duke; I Wish; Knocks Me Off My Feet; Pastime Paradise; Summer Soft; Ordinary Pain; Isn't She Lovely; Joy Inside My Tears; Black Man; Ngiculela – Es Una Historia – I Am Singing; If It's Magic; As; Another Star.*

★ First released 1976 ★ UK peak chart position: 2 ★ USA peak chart position: 1
★ Previous Top 1000 position: 1998 (65): 1994 (45)

90 OTIS BLUE ↑
Otis Redding

The man who bought classic soul music to the white masses at the Monterey Pop Festival died later that year, just as he was really gearing up for a creative burst that included 'Dock Of The Bay'. This is the finest of many classic Otis Redding albums in the soul genre and an automatic recommendation for anyone's playlist. Redding could make you dance and scream and the next minute have you crying yourself to sleep, such was his wide emotional range. Compare the power of 'Respect' and 'Shake' to the passion of 'I've Been Loving You Too Long' and 'My Girl'. Untouchable for its heartfelt emotion.

» Tracks: *Ole Man Trouble; Respect; Change Gonna Come; Down In The Valley; I've Been Loving You Too Long; Shake; My Girl; Wonderful World; Rock Me Baby; Satisfaction; You Don't Miss Your Water.*

★ First released 1966
★ UK peak chart position: 6
★ USA peak chart position: 75
★ Previous Top 1000 position: 1998 (116): 1994 (21)

91 SYNCHRONICITY ↑
The Police

Fancy knowing you were going to break up and yet be able to record and produce this masterpiece. The world domination of the Police was as calculated and planned as was their departure. Each of the intervening albums have something special but the power of tracks such as 'Synchronicity II', and the haunting quality of 'Every Breath You Take' (you really believe Sting when he says, 'I'll be watching you') give this record the edge. The only tracks less than brilliant are Andy Summers' and Stewart Copeland's offerings, a fact of which they must all have been aware. They bowed out while they were still winning. That is commendable and brave.

» Tracks: *Synchronicity I; Walking In Your Footsteps; O My God; Mother; Miss Gradenko; Synchronicity II; Every Breath You Take; King Of Pain; Wrapped Around Your Finger; Tea In The Sahara.*

★ First released 1983
★ UK peak chart position: 1
★ USA peak chart position: 1
★ Previous Top 1000 position: 1998 (336): 1994 (113)

92 IT TAKES A NATION OF MILLIONS TO HOLD US BACK ↑ Public Enemy

The title says it all. In 1988, when this album was released, Public Enemy's music cut with a wholly revolutionary edge. Rarely has fear, anger, paranoia and anxiety been so masterfully compressed onto a record's grooves. The Bomb Squad's artistry is the keynote to the hard, lean delivery, while Chuck D.'s supremely pointed lyrics leave no stone of the black experience unturned. It is not comfortable listening, but on tracks such as 'Don't Believe The Hype', 'Night Of The Living Baseheads' and 'Rebel Without A Pause' the listener is left in no doubt that they are facing a fantastically potent force. A starting point for your rap collection.

» Tracks: *Countdown To Armageddon; Bring The Noise; Don't Believe The Hype; Cold Lampin With Flavor; Terminator X To The Edge Of Panic; Mind Terrorist; Louder Than A Bomb; Caught, Can We Get A Witness?; Show Em Whatcha Got; She Watch Channel Zero?!; Night Of The Living Baseheads; Black Steel In The Hour Of Chaos; Security Of The First World; Rebel Without A Pause; Prophets Of Rage; Party For Your Right To Fight.*

★ First released 1988 ★ UK peak chart position: 8 ★ USA peak chart position: 42
★ Previous Top 1000 position: 1998 (131): 1994 (541)

93 HARVEST ↓
Neil Young

Only after the release of *Harvest Moon* in 1993 did Neil Young aficionados reluctantly admit that this was a delightful album in deference to the depressing *Tonight's The Night* and symbolic *On The Beach*.. Young knew he had a commercial winner when he recorded it, and revisited it 20 years later. Using the Stray Gators as his foils and even recording two tracks with the London Symphony Orchestra in Barking Town Hall, Essex, Young sounds wonderfully old before his time. Introspective and pleading, he has to remind listeners in 'Old Man' that he is 'twenty-four and there's so much more'; well over 24 more glorious albums, 29 to be precise.

➡ Tracks: *Out On The Weekend; Harvest; A Man Needs A Maid; Heart Of Gold; Are You Ready For The Country?; Old Man; There's A World; Alabama; The Needle and The Damage Done; Words (Between The Lines Of Age).*

★ First released 1972
★ UK peak chart position: 1 ★ USA peak chart position: 1
★ Previous Top 1000 position: 1998 (92): 1994 (115)

94 DISINTEGRATION ↑
The Cure

Dark, despairing, dreamlike and magical, *Disintegration* surely represents one of the Cure's finest hours. Although retaining the darkest elements of the earlier albums, it pointed the way towards the band's later, more commercial work on *Wish*. The intoxicating music draws the listener inexorably downwards, but somehow one remains buoyant – rarely since this album has Robert Smith surpassed the beauty and yearning of 'Pictures Of You', or the poignant pop of 'Love Song'. The nightmarish 'Lullaby', however, increases the pressure, and by the final tracks, all hope quite literally disintegrates. A unique and emotionally raw album, this evokes the sensation of inevitable, but desirable, death by drowning.

➡ Tracks: *Plainsong; Pictures Of You; Closedown; Love Song; Last Dance; Lullaby; Fascination Street; Prayers For Rain; The Same Deep Water As You; Disintegration; Homesick; Untitled.*

★ First released 1990
★ UK peak position: 3 ★ USA peak position: 12
★ Previous Top 1000 position: 1998 (746): 1994 (–)

95 PARKLIFE ↓
Blur

Just as the Kinks' Ray Davies distilled 'Englishness' on *Something Else* in 1967, so two of Davies' greatest admirers took it a step further in 1994. Damon Albarn and Graham Coxon wrote a 'chirpy cheeky chappie' concept album without any deliberate concept. True, the pseudo-Cockney narratives frequently seemed contrived, but overall the set gelled perfectly. From the cynical 'Girls & Boys', through the punk sensibilities of 'Bank Holiday', to the sadness of 'This Is A Low', *Parklife* was a stunning album of high-quality, undeniably English pop. The title track quickly became a ubiquitous (and many would argue, highly irritating) anthem, but with this album Blur firmly established themselves as a major talent.

➡ Tracks: *Girls & Boys; Tracy Jacks; End Of A Century; Parklife; Bank Holiday; Badhead; The Debt Collector; Far Out; To The End; London Loves; Trouble In The Message Centre; Clover Over Dover; Magic America; Jubilee; This Is A Low; Lot 105.*

★ First released 1994
★ UK peak chart position: 1 ★ USA peak chart position: did not chart
★ Previous Top 1000 position: 1998 (30): 1994 (–)

96 A NIGHT AT THE OPERA ↓
Queen

The album that gave the world the inimitable 'Bohemian Rhapsody', and it pioneering video, is still a record that exhibits every aspect of a true and timeless classic. Queen's sheer inventiveness, collective contribution and the original verve and displays of ingenuity that they brought to this album were immense, with the dramatic and quite theatrical strut of 'Death On Two Legs (Dedicated To...)', the graceful 'Love Of My Life', and the ritz and panache of 'I'm In Love With My Car'. Without measure, equal, or boundaries – every home should have one. The finest Queen album without a shadow of a doubt.

» Tracks: *Death On Two Legs (Dedicated To...); Lazing On A Sunday Afternoon; You're My Best Friend; I'm In Love With My Car; Sweet Lady; Seaside Rendezvous; Good Company; '39; The Prophet's Song; Love Of My Life; Bohemian Rhapsody; God Save The Queen.*

★ First released 1975
★ UK peak chart position: 1
★ USA peak chart position: 4
★ Previous Top 1000 position: 1998 (87); 1994 (164)

97 LICENSED TO ILL ↑
The Beastie Boys

Wholly original, the first and the best rap group to make the genre universally palatable. These Brooklyn boys succeeded with a combination of tremendously exciting backgrounds, from straight riff metal (on 'Rhymin' & Stealin'' and 'She's Crafty') to sample ('The New Style'). Having learnt their art by observing rather than participating while at NYU, they sounded street-cred, even though they were positively middle-class. The Volkswagen badge-stealing craze was unknowingly started by the band, who wore the pendant merely in order to mock the hippies who had worn the ban-the-bomb medallion. The rap album for people who think they don't like rap.

» Tracks: *Rhymin' & Stealin'; The New Style; She's Crafty; Posse In Effect; Slow Ride; Girls; Fight For Your Right; No Sleep Till Brooklyn; Paul Revere; Hold It Now, Hit It; Brass Monkey; Slow and Low; Time To Get Ill.*

★ First released 1986
★ UK peak chart position: 7
★ USA peak chart position: 1
★ Previous Top 1000 position: 1998 (948); 1994 (–)

98 MOBY GRAPE ↑
Moby Grape

Time and time again this album is cited as the finest debut of all time. But just who were Moby Grape? They were a stellar San Francisco rock band who became appalling victims of record company hype followed by their own excesses, as they were lulled into believing they were more than they were. Loopy Skip Spence, growling Bob Mosley and talented bluesman Jerry Miller were but three-fifths of a great band. Every track could have been issued as a single, which is exactly what CBS did when they released five on the same day, with disastrous results. An indispensable collection and superseded in 1993 by the even more indispensable *Vintage Grape*.

» Tracks: *Hey Grandma; Mr. Blues; Fall On You; 8.05; Come In The Morning; Omaha; Naked, If I Want To; Someday; Ain't No Use; Sitting By The Window; Changes; Lazy Me; Indifference.*

★ First released 1967
★ UK peak chart position: did not chart
★ USA peak chart position: 24
★ Previous Top 1000 position: 1998 (134); 1994 (159)

99 GRACE ↓
Jeff Buckley

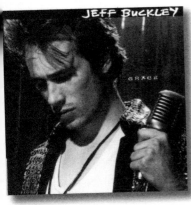

Jeff Buckley's tragic death means there will now never be an official follow-up to this astonishing album, which has already gained classic status four years on from its release. On *Grace* Buckley played up to his heartbroken troubadour image, but managed to avoid cliché by virtue of the seductive power of his multi-octave voice and a remarkably assured grasp of song structure. The album's three cover versions ('Lilac Wine', 'Hallelujah' and 'Corpus Christi Carol') showcase Buckley's ability to make a song his own, but they pale beside the inventiveness of his own material. On the title track and 'So Real', his music achieved a perfection that was staggering for a debut album.

➡ Tracks: *Mojo Pin; Grace; Last Goodbye; Lilac Wine; So Real; Hallelujah; Lover; You Should've Come Over; Corpus Christi Carol; Eternal Life; Dream Brother.*

★ First released 1994
★ UK peak chart position: did not chart
★ USA peak chart position: 149
★ Previous Top 1000 position: 1998 (82): 1994 (–)

100 SONGS FOR SWINGIN' LOVERS! ↓
Frank Sinatra

The most familiar Frank Sinatra album and one that captured a generation of music lovers in the 50s; it is unquestionably his most perfect work. No album could begin to encapsulate quality lounge pop more than this. Quite apart from his graceful vocals, the orchestral arrangements are immaculate and crisp 40 years later. The band, conducted by Nelson Riddle, gave Sinatra such space and freedom that he was able to make already established songs his own. The 15 songs contained on this record should serve to educate élitists that pop music has to swing before it rocks. Nobody should be too proud to have this indispensable record in their collection.

➡ Tracks: *You Make Me Feel So Young; It Happened In Monterey; You're Getting To Be A Habit With Me; You Brought A New Kind Of Love To Me; Too Marvellous For Words; Old Devil Moon; Pennies From Heaven; Love Is Here To Stay; I've Got You Under My Skin; I Thought About You; We'll Be Together Again; Makin' Whoopee; Swingin' Down The Lane; Anything Goes; How About You.*

★ First released 1958
★ UK peak chart position: 8
★ USA peak chart position: 2
★ Previous Top 1000 position: 1998 (97): 1994 (22)

101 PAUL'S BOUTIQUE ↑
Beastie Boys

Dismissed by some as zeitgeist-mugging white rap fakers after the huge commercial success of their debut album, the Beastie Boys' later work could hardly be said to reveal musical depth or sophistication either. However, thanks to an overdose of cultural reference points (via samples and brilliant lyrical cut-ups) and the Dust Brothers' pungent production, they were still big fun compared to hip-hop's new orthodoxy. At times ('Shake Your Rump', '3-Minute Rule') the sound is pure bedlam, but rap's most hilarious trio of b-boys just about keep the thread going through the montage of in-jokes and namechecks. Like all the best records, *Paul's Boutique* was a de facto commercial non-event.

» Tracks: *To All The Girls; Shake Your Rump; Johnny Ryall; Egg Man; High Plains Drifter; The Sounds Of Science; 3-Minute Rule; Hey Ladies; 5-Piece Chicken Dinner; Looking Down The Barrel Of A Gun; Car Thief; What Comes Round; Shadrach; Ask For Janice; B-Boy Bouillabaisse a) 59 Christie Street b) Get On The Mic c) Stop That Train d) A Year and A Day e) Hello Brooklyn f) Dropping Names g) Lay It On Me h) Mike On The Mic i) A.W.O.L.*

★ First released 1989
★ UK peak chart position: 44
★ USA peak chart position: 14
★ Previous Top 1000 position: 1998 (395): 1994 (–)

102 TUBULAR BELLS ↓
Mike Oldfield

Still a firm favourite of the class of 1973, which was given a huge lease of life in 1992 with the dreaded sequel. It was further followed by the dancier 1998 version, 'Tubular Bells III'. The aphorism of 'the original is always the best' can be applied here, as Virgin Records V2001 set Richard Branson down a very lucrative road. There is no denying that it is an excellent piece of instrumental music. The inspired choice of using Viv Stanshall as the orchestra master gives the album greater strength. Studying the credits we are reminded that Edgar Broughton's brother Steve plays drums. Mike Oldfield, meanwhile, plays just about every instrument he can lay his hands on.

» Tracks: *Tubular Bells Part I; Tubular Bells Part II.*

★ First released 1973
★ UK peak chart position: 1
★ USA peak chart position: 3
★ Previous Top 1000 position: 1998 (76): 1994 (220)

103 AMERICAN BEAUTY ↑
Grateful Dead

Following on from *Workingman's Dead*, their beautiful country-tinged exercise in sounding like Crosby, Stills and Nash, the Grateful Dead gave us an even mellower set with this exemplary record. The album's stand-out track was the introspective 'Ripple'; for once, Jerry Garcia actually sang one of Robert Hunter's lyrics as though he meant it. Other excellent supporting numbers included 'Box Of Rain' and the overwhelmingly sad 'Attics Of My Life'. Although the Grateful Dead were always a mellow band, they never recorded another album as light and emotional as this. There are no overlong solos on this absolutely charming record. Imagine 'Ripple' being adopted as the new American national anthem, it could happen you know.

» Tracks: *Box Of Rain; Friend Of The Devil; Operator; Sugar Magnolia; Ripple; Brokedown Palace; Till The Morning Comes; Attics Of My Life; Truckin'.*

★ First released 1970
★ UK peak chart position: did not chart
★ USA peak chart position: 30
★ Previous Top 1000 position: 1998 (208): 1994 (255)

104 VAN HALEN ↑
Van Halen

Quite simply put, no-one had seen or heard anything like it. David Lee Roth's flamboyant showmanship, with the microphone dangling provocatively between his legs on the cover, and Eddie Van Halen's monstrously inventive guitar playing became a textbook for air guitarists the world over. From the instrumental blow-out of 'Eruption', the gritty teen pop of 'Feel Your Love Tonight', to the strutting riff around which 'Ain't Talkin' Bout Love' was built and the grandiose reworking of the Kinks' 'You Really Got Me', Van Halen set their own absurd standards. One of the truly great rock and roll/metal debut albums of all time.

» Tracks: *You Really Got Me; Jamie's Cryin'; On Fire; Runnin' With The Devil; I'm The One; Ain't Talkin' Bout Love; Little Dreamer; Feel Your Love Tonight; Atomic Punk; Eruption; Ice Cream Man.*

★ First released 1978
★ UK peak chart position: 34
★ USA peak chart position: 19
★ Previous Top 1000 position: 1998 (293): 1994 (177)

105 MASTER OF PUPPETS ↑
Metallica

Metallica's irresistible rise to the top continued with this enigmatic 1986 album. A constant touring unit by this point, their combination of light and dark and their deft staccato delivery, especially on the title track, came brusquely through. Their lengthy arrangements, bolstered by the precise snap of Hetfield's vocals, testified to their undeniable power. The striding 'Battery', the darkly lit 'Welcome Home (Sanitarium)', as well as the complex instrumental, 'Orion', all gave powerful testament to their ever-developing skill and vision. Still on catalogue, this may not be the first Metallica purchase on a wants list, but once hooked it will creep up on you.

》 Tracks: *Battery; Master Of Puppets; The Thing That Should Not Be; Welcome Home (Sanitarium); Disposable Heroes; Leper Messiah; Orion; Damage Inc.*

★ First released 1986
★ UK peak chart position: 41
★ USA peak chart position: 29
★ Previous Top 1000 position: 1998 (217): 1994 (625)

106 DÉJÀ VU ↑
Crosby, Stills, Nash and Young

With the inspired decision to add Neil Young to the ranks, Crosby, Stills, Nash and Young became America's biggest attraction for a short time. While the results on this excellent record show four individuals, rather than the vocal unity of the Crosby, Stills and Nash debut, it still holds up to repeated listening. Young contributed 'Country Girl', with a wonderful John Sebastian harmonica solo added, and the aching 'Helpless'. His colleagues pitched in with notable songs from David Crosby ('Almost Cut My Hair'), Stephen Stills ('Carry On' and '4+20') and Graham Nash, who has subsequently grabbed the radio play with 'Our House,' and 'Teach Your Children', the latter featuring Jerry Garcia's piercing but beautiful pedal steel guitar.

》 Tracks: *Carry On; Teach Your Children; Almost Cut My Hair; Helpless; Woodstock; Déjà Vu; Our House; 4+20; Country Girl; Everybody I Love You.*

★ First released 1970
★ UK peak chart position: 5
★ USA peak chart position: 1
★ Previous Top 1000 position: 1998 (163): 1994 (157)

107 BACK IN BLACK ↑
AC/DC

After the untimely death of former enigmatic vocalist Bon Scott, AC/DC finally chanced upon a worthy replacement in the shape of former Geordie frontman, Brian Johnson. The result was more than the formal pastiche some expected, with Johnson stamping his own personality, not to mention distinctive rasp, on the record. The band's staple lyrical diet of sex and the general pursuit of happiness, however, remained very much intact. Highlights include the stomping 'Hell's Bells' and 'You Shook Me All Night Long', the quiet build of the title track, and the chuckling insolence of 'Rock and Roll Ain't Noise Pollution'. A winning return.

》 Tracks: *Back In Black; Hell's Bells; Shoot To Thrill; Give The Dog A Bone; What Do You Do For Money Honey?; Rock and Roll Ain't Noise Pollution; Let Me Put My Love Into You; You Shook Me All Night Long; Shake A Leg; Have A Drink On Me.*

★ First released 1980
★ UK peak chart position: 1
★ USA peak chart position: 4
★ Previous Top 1000 position: 1998 (247): 1994 (173)

108 HYSTERIA ↑
Def Leppard

Four years after *Pyromania*, Def Leppard were a comparative write-off. Dismissed by critics, seemingly dogged by bad luck, with drummer Rick Allen losing an arm in a car accident, *Hysteria* had to be an album to turn heads. In retrospect, it sounded like the first true hard rock record for the CD generation. Ambitious arrangements and remixes on songs such as 'Rocket' and 'Armageddon It', a crisp single in 'Animal', and a dense paean to love with 'Love Bites', all bets were off. Def Leppard had created an intriguing language of ideas that still speaks volumes more than a decade on.

》 Tracks: *Women; Rocket; Animal; Love Bites; Pour Some Sugar On Me; Armageddon It; Gods Of War; Don't Shoot Shot Gun; Run Riot; Hysteria; Excitable; Love and Affection; I Can't Let You Be A Memory.*

★ First released 1987
★ UK peak chart position: 1
★ USA peak chart position: 1
★ Previous Top 1000 position: 1998 (323): 1994 (607)

109 SIAMESE DREAM ↓
Smashing Pumpkins

The hardness of the grunge guitar and metal drums of the Smashing Pumpkins are always tempered by an incredibly mellow and soft centre. Billy Corgan has a fantastic ability to find great chords to put in sequence, as in the opening track 'Cherub Rock'. This album received a new lease of life following the huge success of the Mellon Collie album. All the signs were here of a monster in the making. 'Quiet' is a joy and 'Hummer' has some wonderful peaks and troughs. Has anybody else ever noticed the incredible similarity in style between guitarist James Iha and the late Randy California of Spirit?

➤ Tracks: Cherub Rock; Quiet; Today; Hummer; Rocket; Disarm; Soma; Geek USA; Mayonaise; Spaceboy; Silverfuck; Sweet Sweet; Luna.

★ First released 1993
★ UK peak chart position: 4
★ USA peak chart position: 89
★ Previous Top 1000 position: 1998 (99): 1994 (–)

110 AUGUST AND EVERYTHING AFTER ↑
Counting Crows

Angst rock usually features a male vocalist with a thin voice, whingeing about a series of women who done him wrong. The head whiner of this exciting outfit from California is Adam Duritz, whose dreadlocks and pained expressions belie his youth. He does sing and write some excellent yet intense songs. This album remained on the US chart for an age, and it can be only a matter of time before irresistible tracks such as 'Omaha' and 'Mr. Jones' find their way on to 'classic rock tracks' playlists. Duritz is clearly a major talent, and it is hoped that this sparkling debut can be bettered in the future.

➤ Tracks: Round Here; Omaha; Mr. Jones; Perfect Blue Building; Anna Begins; Time and Time Again; Rain King; Sullivan Street; Ghost Train; Raining In Baltimore; A Murder Of One.

★ First released 1994
★ UK peak chart position: 16
★ USA peak chart position: 4
★ Previous Top 1000 position: 1998 (148): 1994 (747)

111 PHYSICAL GRAFFITI ↓
Led Zeppelin

One of the strongest hard rock albums ever, over 20 years later it is still much imitated and sampled, and, quite rightly, stands as the major contemporary reference point in rock music. The heavily stylized 'Kashmir', allegedly the starting point for a war of words between Plant and David Coverdale, after a very similar refrain appeared in Whitesnake's 'In The Heat Of The Night'. The blissful 'Bron-Y-Aur', which followed their limo through New York during The Song Remains The Same, 'Custard Pie', with its legendary intro, and the innovative 'In The Light', all combined to create a truly credible musical landmark.

➤ Tracks: Custard Pie; The Rover; In My Time Of Dying; Houses Of The Holy; Trampled Under Foot; Kashmir; In The Light; Bron-Y-Aur; Down By The Seaside; Ten Years Gone; Night Flight; The Wanton Song; Boogie With Stu; Black Country Woman; Sick Again.

★ First released 1975
★ UK peak chart position: 1
★ USA peak chart position: 1
★ Previous Top 1000 position: 1998 (50): 1994 (258)

112 GARBAGE ↑
Garbage

An exceptional debut that buried the quality of the music behind the attention that focused on lead singer Shirley Manson. She was outspoken and provocative visually and verbally, and the hacks rushed to kneel before her. From the opening 'Supervixen', the pace is set; the split-second pauses during this track are a powerful hook and grab the attention of the listener. Heavy and melodic, the band sound like a seasoned unit, bass and drum mixed together brilliantly, and the lead guitar never stealing the show, only complementing Manson's dusky vocals. Although much of the album utilizes loops and computer technology, the overall sound is that of a real rock band.

➤ Tracks: Supervixen; Queer; Only Happy When It Rains; As Heaven Is Wide; Not My Idea; A Stroke Of Luck; Vow; Stupid Girl; Dog New Tricks; My Lover's Box; Fix Me Now; Milk.

★ First released 1995
★ UK peak chart position: 6
★ USA peak chart position: 20
★ Previous Top 1000 position: 1998 (198): 1994 (–)

113 DON'T SHOOT ME I'M ONLY THE PIANO PLAYER ↑ Elton John

In writing reviews it is impossible to refer to this artist as John; it fits for some, but this subject has to be Elton, which immediately endears him to the public. He is one of the best-liked personalities in the music business yet not tolerant of fools. This album contains several classic songs that bonds him to music fans, notably the happiness/sadness of 'Daniel', to which we can all relate, and the nostalgic sentiments of 'Teacher I Need You'. He rocks out and induces warmth with the irritatingly catchy 'Crocodile Rock' (the listener hates to love it), and on and on with 'Elderberry Wine'. Elton John is popularly seen as a paparazzi star, a view that sometimes clouds his huge talent as a musician and a music collector.

❱❱ Tracks: *Daniel; Teacher I Need You; Elderberry Wine; Blues For My Baby and Me; Midnight Creeper; Have Mercy On The Criminal; I'm Going To Be A Teenage Idol; Texan Love Song; Crocodile Rock; High Flying Bird.*

★ First released 1973
★ UK peak chart position: 1
★ USA peak chart position: 1
★ Previous Top 1000 position: 1998 (534): 1994 (182)

114 DOOLITTLE ↓ THE PIXIES

The album that brought the Pixies commercial acclaim in the UK did so without self-sacrifice. In their homeland they struggled to make it above cult status. A travesty because the hammered chords, twisting melodies and obtuse lyrics abound, and it was all pulled together and given new purpose by Gil Norton's incisive production. Black Francis and Kim Deal share the vocal spoils, imbuing the content with contrasting textures. The raw anger of 'Debaser' is offset by the aurally sweet 'Monkey Gone To Heaven', while elsewhere, dynamite tunes confirm a collective love of pop. Where later releases showed increasing schizophrenia, *Doolittle* fully captures the Pixies' unified zeal.

❱❱ Tracks: *Debaser; Tame; Wave Of Mutilation; I Bleed; Here Comes Your Man; Dead; Monkey Gone To Heaven; Mr. Grieves; Crackity Jones; La La Love You; No. 13 Baby; There Goes My Gun; Hey; Silver; Gouge Away.*

★ First released 1989
★ UK peak chart position: 8
★ USA peak chart position: 98
★ Previous Top 1000 position: 1998 (90): 1994 (511)

115 GREATEST HITS ↑ Abba

Everybody likes Abba, or at least no-one wishes to say anything against Sweden's greatest export since Volvo. Abba appeal to the widest section of music critics and this album spent two and a half years in the UK chart. Since their well-documented personal break-up and professional parting, Abba's reputation has continued to grow. Television comedy sketches, Abba lookalikes and a further reissued collection, which also went to number 1, enhanced their reputation. This is the famous cover that graced a zillion homes, but only now do we realize that 'Knowing Me Knowing You', 'Dancing Queen' and 'Take A Chance On Me' are contained on volume 2.

❱❱ Tracks: *SOS; He Is Your Brother; Ring Ring; Hasta Manana; Nina; Pretty Ballerina; Honey Honey; So Long; I Do I Do I Do; People Need Love; Bang A Boomerang; Another Town Another Train; Mamma Mia; Dance (While The Music Still Goes On); Waterloo; Fernando.*

★ First released 1976
★ UK peak chart position: 1
★ USA peak chart position: 48
★ Previous Top 1000 position: 1998 (431): 1994 (189)

116 COURT AND SPARK ↑ Joni Mitchell

This continued Mitchell's transition from folk-singer to sophisticated rock auteur. Crafted songs are bathed in a warm, textured backing, courtesy of Tom Scott's L.A. Express, a sinuous jazz-based combo. Her expressive voice weaves in and around engaging melodies that support and enhance the imagery suggested by evocative, personal lyrics. The title track alone is worth the price of admission, but the gorgeous lilt of 'Help Me' and the elegant sweep of 'Free Man In Paris' show an artist in firm control of her craft. Her attempt at covering the jazz standard 'Twisted' also demonstrated a possible new direction. This was confirmed in 2000 with *Both Sides Now*.

❱❱ Tracks: *Court and Spark; Help Me; Free Man In Paris; People's Parties; The Same Situation; Car On A Hill; Down To You; Just Like This Train; Raised On Robbery; Trouble Child; Twisted.*

★ First released 1974
★ UK peak chart position: 14
★ USA peak chart position: 2
★ Previous Top 1000 position: 1998 (224): 1994 (145)

117 HOUSES OF THE HOLY ↑
Led Zeppelin

Knowing that almost anything they did would reach the top, Led Zeppelin were at their most wilfully inventive. Displaying an eclectic irreverence for their recent history, they struck out with an assured astuteness that let them play what they felt. Consequently, the results were so genuinely original that the idea that they had any real musical contemporaries suddenly seemed absurd. 'The Crunge', played at funk rock years before the popular press had discovered and christened it, 'D'yer Mak'er' tossed reggae around for fun, while 'No Quarter' went on to be lifted wholesale by Pearl Jam predecessors, Mother Love Bone. At the heart of, and yet still ahead of, their time.

❯❯ Tracks: *The Song Remains The Same; The Rain Song; Over The Hills and Far Away; The Crunge; Dancing Days; D'yer Mak'er; No Quarter; The Ocean.*

★ First released 1973
★ UK peak chart position: 1
★ USA peak chart position: 1
★ Previous Top 1000 position: 1998 (310): 1994 (660)

118 AJA ↑
Steely Dan

This represents the pinnacle of Steely Dan's gradual transition from rock band to their own brand of jazz-influenced white soul. Guitars were replaced by keyboards, and saxophones became more common. Walter Becker and Donald Fagen were only interested in spending time in the recording studios, while fans pined and waited. The result set new standards in recorded excellence, and was regularly used as a hi-fi shop demonstration record. Its all a bit grown up and sensible but the music cannot be faulted. In addition to the ambitious title track, there are two overtly accessible tracks; 'Josie' and 'Peg'. And then there is that song we have to blame for Deacon Blue.

❯❯ Tracks: *Black Cow; Aja; Peg; Deacon Blues; Home At Last; I Got The News; Josie.*

★ First released 1977
★ UK peak chart position: 5
★ USA peak chart position: 3
★ Previous Top 1000 position: 1998 (287): 1994 (129)

119 HELP! ↑
The Beatles

Although *A Hard Day's Night* as a film captured more hearts than *Help*, both soundtrack albums are full of terrific songs. Half of this material was showcased in the movie. Who could forget the expertly filmed studio scene, as the boys record 'You're Going To Lose That Girl'. Prior to Ringo disappearing through the sawn-through floor with his drums, the engineer asks, 'boys are you buzzing?'. 'No thanks I've got the car', quips back John. The hit single 'Ticket To Ride' took on a new meaning as they skied down the mountain at night with flares. Beautiful, harmless stuff, and yet another album to testify to their enduring fabness.

❯❯ Tracks: *Help!; The Night Before; You've Got To Hide Your Love Away; I Need You; Another Girl; You're Going To Lose That Girl; Ticket To Ride; Act Naturally; It's Only Love; You Like Me Too Much; Tell Me What You See; I've Just Seen A Face; Yesterday; Dizzy Miss Lizzy.*

★ First released 1965
★ UK peak chart position: 1
★ USA peak chart position: 1
★ Previous Top 1000 position: 1998 (196): 1994 (69)

120 LIKE A PRAYER ↑
Madonna

Madonna's exquisite sense of the pop song, and suitably stylish aesthetic to match, was pushed to the hilt for 1989's *Like A Prayer*. Sporting a bare midriff and a stylishly dark bob, she immediately set the Moral Majority up in arms with the title track's video, depicting, among other things, a black Christ and a hillside of burning crosses. The song, however, was as strong and as dazzling as the images. Before deciding on utilizing a constant barrage of public sexuality over songs, Madonna made great records. Highlights here include the sexy bubble-gum of 'Cherish' and the delightful 'Express Yourself'. Great pop to go.

❯❯ Tracks: *Like A Prayer; Express Yourself; Love Song; Till Death Us Do Part; Promise To Try; Cherish; Dear Jessie; Oh Father; Keep It Together; Spanish Eyes; Act Of Contrition.*

★ First released 1989
★ UK peak chart position: 1
★ USA peak chart position: 1
★ Previous Top 1000 position: 1998 (237): 1994 (300)

121 BAT OUT OF HELL ↓
Meat Loaf

Pomp and circumstance of the grandest order for the multi-platinum Meat Loaf and his songwriting mentor, Jim Steinman. The grandiose intro to the title track was indication enough of the tone of the album, with songs stretching out over what at times seemed like musical infinity. Steinman set his songs in evocative wastelands populated by full orchestras and small-town weirdos; 'Paradise By The Dashboard Light', an entire two-handed play in itself, and 'Two Out Of Three Ain't Bad', an overblown symphony of regret and unrequited love. Between them, they pretty much provided the balance of the album. A huge commercial success only to be repeated by its follow-up in 1993.

» Tracks: *Bat Out Of Hell; You Took The Words Right Out Of My Mouth; Heaven Can Wait; All Revved Up With No Place To Go; Two Out Of Three Ain't Bad; Paradise By The Dashboard Light; For Cryin' Out Loud.*

★ First released 1977
★ UK peak chart position: 9
★ USA peak chart position: 14
★ Previous Top 1000 position: 1998 (77): 1994 (90)

122 WAR ↑
U2

U2's strident march into rock 'n' roll legend took its first true steps with this record. *Boy* and *October* had given them an audience of hardcore devotees, but *War* gave them the full and rapt ear of the world. Their case was made with a record of contrasting moments; it is interesting to note that the lyrics printed on the gatefold sleeve are done so selectively. When this record breaks the silence, it roars, U2's now familiar outcry making itself apparent through dogmatic, but insatiable appeal. At the same time, 'Drowning Man' hinted at the texture and depth of work they would later produce. They were well on the way with this.

» Tracks: *Sunday Bloody Sunday; Seconds; Like A Song; New Years Day; Two Hearts Beat As One; The Refugee; Drowning Man; Red Light; '40'; Surrender.*

★ First released 1983
★ UK peak chart position: 1
★ USA peak chart position: 12
★ Previous Top 1000 position: 1998 (273): 1994 (105)

123 HOT RATS ↑
Frank Zappa

Having temporarily disbanded the Mothers Of Invention, Zappa recorded this exceptional solo album. His group was renowned for musical satire, but here the artist opted to showcase his prowess on guitar. 'Willie The Pimp' apart, which features a cameo vocal by his old friend Captain Beefheart, the set is comprised of instrumentals. The players, who include Don 'Sugarcane' Harris, Jean-Luc Ponty and Ian Underwood, are uniformly excellent, combining to provide a solid jazz-rock platform for Zappa's always compulsive soloing. He relishes a freedom which, while acknowledging past achievements, prepared new territories for exploration. Still embarrassingly good, and still there are solos that have never managed to be copied.

» Tracks: *Peaches En Regalia; Willie The Pimp; Son Of Mr. Green Genes; Little Umbrellas; The Gumbo Variations; It Must Be A Camel.*

★ First released 1969
★ UK peak chart position: 9
★ USA peak chart position: 173
★ Previous Top 1000 position: 1998 (184): 1994 (195)

124 EVERYBODY KNOWS THIS IS NOWHERE ↑ Neil Young

Young's second solo album introduced his long-standing relationship with backing group Crazy Horse. The partnership allowed the singer greater musical flexibility and the understanding generated gave a unique synergy to his work. The combination could be concise, as on the chunky 'Cinnamon Girl', with its unusual timing and changes. The pivotal selections are the lengthy, guitar-based workouts, 'Down By The River' and especially 'Cowgirl In The Sand'. The group urge Young into textured, improvised playing, the appeal of which never palls. Elsewhere, the singer revisits his folk past and embraces country rock and pop, none better than the title track. For many, the best Young album ever.

» Tracks: *Cinnamon Girl; Everybody Knows This Is Nowhere; Round & Round (It Won't Be Long); Down By The River; The Losing End (When You're On); Running Dry (Requiem For The Rockets); Cowgirl In The Sand.*

★ First released 1969
★ UK peak chart position: did not chart
★ USA peak chart position: 34
★ Previous Top 1000 position: 1998 (151): 1994 (225)

125 FRANK SINATRA SINGS FOR ONLY THE LONELY ↑
Frank Sinatra

Asked to reveal the mood of this album prior to its release, Frank Sinatra (tongue-in-cheek) said: 'Put it this way – we discarded 'Gloomy Sunday' (the 'suicide' song) because it was too swingin'!' Bleak, it certainly is, but with the singer at the height of his powers singing a classy set of saloon songs, superbly arranged and conducted by Nelson Riddle, this is still the number 1 album of all time for many a Sinatra aficionado. Even in the 90s he was compelled to include one of the tracks, 'One For My Baby', complete with the distinctive piano introduction, in every concert performance. Even the album's cover, with its sad clown-face picture, won a Grammy Award.

» Tracks: *Only The Lonely; Angel Eyes; What's New?; It's A Lonesome Old Town; Willow Weep For Me; Good-bye; Blues In The Night; Guess I'll Hang My Tears Out To Dry; Ebb Tide; Spring Is Here; Gone With The Wind; One For My Baby.*

★ First released 1958
★ UK peak chart position: 5
★ USA peak chart position: 1
★ Previous Top 1000 position: 1998 (223); 1994 (290)

126 CLEAR SPOT ↑
Captain Beefheart and The Magic Band

After the bizarre *Trout Mask Replica*, Beefheart moved slowly to what we earth mortals would call music, very much like the stuff on *Safe As Milk*. His 'music from Venus' had never been quite so easy on the ear and *Clear Spot* was a hit album, of sorts. Nobody other than John Lennon has been able to twist the English language so brilliantly as this man. How can you resist 'My Head Is My Only House Unless It Rains' or 'Her Eyes Are A Blue Million Miles'? Beefheart can also fool us with a real love song, the sublime 'Too Much Time'. Oh how we miss this man's continuing genius on record.

» Tracks: *Low Yo Yo Stuff; Nowadays A Woman's Gotta Hit A Man; Too Much Time; Circumstances; My Head Is My Only House Unless It Rains; Sun Zoom Spark; Clear Spot; Crazy Little Thing; Long Neck Bottles; Her Eyes Are A Blue Million Miles; Big Eyed Beans From Venus; Golden Birdies.*

★ First released 1972
★ UK peak chart position: did not chart
★ USA peak chart position: 191
★ Previous Top 1000 position: 1998 (203); 1994 (–)

127 THE FREEWHEELIN' BOB DYLAN ↑
Bob Dylan

With this album Dylan emerged from the cloak of Woody Guthrie and proclaimed his own unique talent. No longer detached – the set was originally entitled 'Bob Dylan's Blues' – he personalized his songs, famously rejecting four from the final draft in favour of others reflecting his newer muse. Protest songs were given a wider resonance – the text of 'Masters Of War' remains as relevant some 30 years on – while his love songs are haunting, but universal, statements. His Bobness injected black humour into the talking blues and railed against injustice in all forms with a perception encompassing the anger of a generation. *Freewheelin'* is a landmark in the development of folk and pop music.

» Tracks: *Blowin' In The Wind; Girl From The North Country; Masters Of War; Down The Highway; Bob Dylan's Blues; Hard Rain's Gonna Fall; Don't Think Twice; Bob Dylan's Dream; Oxford Town; Talking World War III Blues; Corina Corina; Honey, Just Allow Me One More Chance; I Shall Be Free.*

★ First released 1964
★ UK peak chart position: 1
★ USA peak chart position: 22
★ Previous Top 1000 position: 1998 (193); 1994 (80)

128 IMAGINE ↓
John Lennon

John Lennon's solo debut, although powerful, did not have the universal commercial appeal of this album. Lennon veered from spitting anger in 'How Do You Sleep?', 'Give Me Some Truth' and cruel humour with 'Crippled Inside', yet the man was capable of intense romanticism as highlighted in 'Jealous Guy' and 'Oh My Love'. Those who resented Lennon for his part in the Beatles' break-up finally forgave him and began to love him again with this collection. The title-track will stand as a classic of popular song and one that should be made part of the national curriculum, if not the new national anthem.

» Tracks: *Imagine; Crippled Inside; Jealous Guy; It's So Hard; I Don't Want To Be A Soldier; Give Me Some Truth; Oh My Love; How Do You Sleep?; How?; Oh Yoko!.*

★ First released 1971
★ UK peak chart position: 1
★ USA peak chart position: 1
★ Previous Top 1000 position: 1998 (104); 1994 (66)

129 STEPHEN STILLS ↑
Stephen Stills

This outstanding solo debut came at a particularly successful and creative time for Stills. In the space of a couple of years he made two solo albums, released the superb Manassas double album and was part of Crosby, Stills, Nash and Young. He was also living in Surrey, England, which explains the appearance of many UK-based musicians, from Eric Clapton to Ringo Starr and even Jimi Hendrix. This varied set shows Stills to be precociously talented as he tackled Memphis soul, folk, blues, rock and goodtime pop with the still fresh-sounding 'Love The One You're With'. Equally arresting is 'Black Queen', allegedly recorded after Stills had downed a bottle of Jose Cuervo gold label, and was 'drunk as a skunk'.

» Tracks: Love The One You're With; Do For The Others; Church (Part Of Someone); Old Times, Good Times; Go Back Home; Sit Yourself Down; To A Flame; Black Queen; Cherokee; We Are Not Helpless.

★ First released 1970
★ UK peak chart position: 30
★ USA peak chart position: 3
★ Previous Top 1000 position: 1998 (192): 1994 (295)

130 CLOSE TO THE EDGE ↑
Yes

Taken as a musical whole, this three-part suite is very sound, but what does begin to jar are some of the lyrics. In the 90s, even with the hippie revival and new age travellers, lyrics such as 'my eyes convinced eclipsed with the younger moon attained with love' do make you shake your head and say out loud, 'whaaaat?!' Yes have been shabbily treated by the press over the years yet their continuing popularity is in some way a vindication of their immense talent as musicians. Steve Howe's guitar work sounds justly confident, Squire's bass wanders and thunks throughout, but what makes the album so good is the highly melodic theme that runs through everything.

» Tracks: Solid Time Of Change; Total Mass Retain; I Get Up, I Get Down; Seasons Of Man; And You and I; Cord Of Life; Eclipse; The Preacher; Teacher; Siberian Khatru.

★ First released 1972
★ UK peak chart position: 4
★ USA peak chart position: 3
★ Previous Top 1000 position: 1998 (263): 1994 (304)

131 PINK MOON ↑
Nick Drake

Drake arrived unannounced to drop the master tapes for this album into his record company's offices before disappearing back into self-imposed seclusion. Pink Moon can be listened to as a diary of its deeply troubled creator's state of mind, a defiantly stark and uncommercial record in marked contrast to the lush autumnal beauty of his first two albums. However, it is arguably Drake's most perfect musical expression. The eleven tracks achieve a haiku-like perfection, with only a piano overdub on the title track intruding on the exquisite stillness achieved by the razor-sharp recording of Drake's acoustic guitar and his delicate but clearly depressed voice. Sad but brilliant.

» Tracks: Pink Moon; Place To Be; Road; Which Will; Horn; Things Behind The Sun; Know; Parasite; Ride; Harvest Breed; From The Morning.

★ First released 1972
★ UK peak chart position: did not chart
★ USA peak chart position: did not chart
★ Previous Top 1000 position: 1998 (221): 1994 (–)

132 FUN HOUSE ↓
The Stooges

The Stooges' minimalist approach to rock erupted fully on this, their second album. Simple riffs and splattered chords echo primitive R&B and provide a basic framework over which vocalist Iggy Pop tore the notion of 'singer' apart. Impulsive yelps and orgasmic moans punctuate a delivery that thrills and surprises in equal measure. Conventional structure disintegrates as the set progresses, culminating in the mayhem of a cacophonous finale into which recent addition, saxophonist Steve Mackay, adds a stream of notes from Bedlam. Deranged yet free, Fun House destroyed preconceptions of 60s music and prepared a path for 70s punk.

» Tracks: Down On The Street; Loose; TV Eye; Dirt; 1970; Fun House; LA Blues.

★ First released 1970
★ UK peak chart position: did not chart
★ USA peak chart position: did not chart
★ Previous Top 1000 position: 1998 (128): 1994 (427)

133 ANOTHER SIDE OF BOB DYLAN ↑ Bob Dylan

On this album it was clear that the artist was becoming bored with straight folk. Although still acoustic, with a great deal more piano tinkling, his left-thinking devotees began to raise an eyebrow at subtle lyrical shifts. This album was to be raided time and again – particularly by the Byrds – in 1965's folk rock boom. There is much free-spirited music, as if Dylan was somehow aware of the acceptance that was around the corner, and here were the first signs of the trademark vocal so prevalent through the rest of the 60s. Take your pick: most of the offerings are striking. 'My Back Pages', 'All I Really Want To Do', a last nod to protest, 'Chimes Of Freedom' and the bleeding song of lost love 'Ballad in Plain D'.

» Tracks: *All I Really Want To Do; Black Crow Blues; Spanish Harlem Incident; Chimes Of Freedom; I Shall Be Free; To Ramona; Motorpsycho Nightmare; My Back Pages; I Don't Believe You; Ballad In Plain D; It Ain't Me Babe.*

★ First released 1964
★ UK peak chart position: 8
★ USA peak chart position: 43
★ Previous Top 1000 position: 1998 (635): 1994 (938)

134 MEAT IS MURDER ↑ The Smiths

The second Smiths album expanded upon the twin flight paths of its predecessor: singer Morrissey's unabashed solipsism and Johnny Marr's textured guitar playing. Opening with the plangent 'The Headmaster Ritual', *Meat Is Murder* brings both these facets into sharp focus with layers of sound supporting the singer's confessional, singsong style. Bittersweet humour and rampant profligacy mark the album's lyrical content, no more so than on the indignant, pro-vegetarian title track. The rhythm section of Andy Rourke and Mike Joyce provides a supple spine for the group's two central sparring partners, keeping both their potential excesses in check. Self-indulgent? Yes of course, but brilliantly so.

» Tracks: *The Headmaster Ritual; Rusholme Ruffians; I Want The One I Can't Have; What She Said; Nowhere Fast; That Joke Isn't Funny Anymore; Well I Wonder; Barbarism Begins At Home; Meat Is Murder.*

★ First released 1985
★ UK peak chart position: 1
★ USA peak chart position: 110
★ Previous Top 1000 position: 1998 (296): 1994 (378)

135 SCREAMADELICA ↓ Primal Scream

Primal Scream's understanding of rock's varied vistas is encapsulated on this release. At its core are a series of dance-oriented tracks that broach several musical barriers. Samples, tape loops, dub and plangent chords gel together over various grooves, at times uplifting, at others ambient. Mixmasters Terry Farley and Andy Weatherall add different perspectives to individual tracks, with gospel choirs, pumping brass and spaceward basslines bubbling around several selections. Former Rolling Stones producer Jimmy Miller generated the spirit of *Beggars Banquet* for the rousing 'Movin' On Up', while elsewhere the group imply acknowledgement to talismen the Beach Boys and Big Star. *Screamadelica* is the ultimate confluence of rock and dance music cultures.

» Tracks: *Movin' On Up; Slip Inside This House; Don't Fight It, Feel It; Higher Than The Sun; Inner Flight; Come Together; Loaded; Damaged; I'm Comin' Down; Higher Than The Sun (A Dub Symphony In Two Parts); Shine Like Stars.*

★ First released 1991
★ UK peak chart position: 8
★ USA peak chart position: did not chart
★ Previous Top 1000 position: 1998 (37): 1994 (200)

136 THE CHRONIC ↑ Dr. Dre

The Chronic, you should be warned, has some of the most puerile lyrics ever to park their sorry arse (to use the vernacular) on vinyl. Yet it remains a high watermark recording in rap's turbulent history. Why? Because, musically, it works beautifully. Dr. Dre is no rapper (he is helped out here by Snoop Doggy Dog). Instead he concentrates on what he's best at – engrossing, energized, multi-layered hip-hop. Pretty much the definitive soundtrack to the US urban environment of the early 90s, Dre's choppy soundclash mix-and-dash approach (and prodigious sampling of P-Funk era black music) founded a whole new genre, G-Funk. It also launched a few careers that should have been stillborn.

» Tracks: *The Chronic (Intro); Wit Dre Day (And Everybody's Celebratin'); Let Me Ride; The Day The Niggaz Took Over; Nuthin' But A 'G' Thang; Deeez Nuuuts; Lil' Ghetto Boy; A Nigga Witta Gun; Rat-Tat-Tat-Tat; The $20 Sack Pyramid; Lyrical Gangbang; High Powered; The Doctor's Office; Stranded On Death Row; The Roach (The Chronic Outro).*

★ First released 1993
★ UK peak chart position: did not chart
★ USA peak chart position: did not chart
★ Previous Top 1000 position: 1998 (503): 1994 (–)

137 APPETITE FOR DESTRUCTION ↓ Guns N'Roses

Already a legend in its own meagre lifetime, this startling debut shrouded itself in controversy, from its original Robert Williams artwork to Axl Rose's unblinking accounts of LA's underbelly. This mawkish storytelling, combined with a brattish collective swagger and a surprisingly mature approach to their songs, guaranteed Guns N'Roses a speedy notoriety that was to serve their legend brilliantly. From the laconic 'Paradise City' to the achingly beautiful 'Sweet Child O' Mine', or the furious 'Welcome To The Jungle', the record brims with a brutal integrity. An album they are now unlikely ever to surpass.

❯❯ Tracks: *Welcome To The Jungle; It's So Easy; Nightrain; Out Ta Get Me; Mr. Brownstone; Paradise City; My Michelle; Think About You; Sweet Child O' Mine; You're Crazy; Anything Goes; Rocket Queen.*

★ First released 1987
★ UK peak chart position: 5
★ USA peak chart position: 1
★ Previous Top 1000 position: 1998 (112): 1994 (206)

138 3 FEET HIGH AND RISING ↑ De La Soul

The closest the rap world would come to the cartoon quality of Madness, with a similar musical integrity lurking beneath, De La Soul were warmly embraced both by hip-hop fans and chart-followers for their infectious, uninhibited blend of laconic rhymes and buoyant humour. Posdnous, Trugoy and Pasemaster Mase emerged from Long Island with an entirely different slant on rap's place in the scheme of things, piecing together this 1989 debut around the concept of a game show. The vitality of the single, 'Me Myself and I', was merely an appetizer for a carefree creative feast. Daisy Age Soul (Da Inner Sound, Y'all) had arrived, and everybody liked it very much.

❯❯ Tracks: *Intro; The Magic Number; Change In Speak; Cool Breeze On The Rocks; Can You Keep A Secret; Jenifa (Taught Me); Ghetto Thang; Transmitting Live From Mars; Eye Know; Take It Off; A Little Bit Of Soap; Tread Water; Say No Go; Do As De La Does; Plug Tunin'; De La Orgee; Buddy; Description; Me Myself and I; This Is A Recording For Living In A Fulltime Era; I Can Do Anything; D.A.I.S.Y. Age; Potholes In My Lawn.*

★ First released 1989
★ UK peak chart position: 13
★ USA peak chart position: 24
★ Previous Top 1000 position: 1998 (433): 1994 (630)

139 GREEN ↑ R.E.M.

The LP that found the band sandwiched between being an important cult band on the verge of major success and being the world's most successful rock band of the 90s. A tricky situation, but this album made the breakthrough and mighty Warner Brothers were behind it. R.E.M. were able to get their folky mandolin material like 'You Are The Everything' accepted on an equal footing with great pop such as 'Stand' or 'Pop Song 89' (which could have been written by Jim Morrison and titled 'Hello I Love You'). 'Orange Crush' is already an FM radio favourite, and the rest is all recent history. Another must have R.E.M. album.

❯❯ Tracks: *Pop Song 89; Get Up; You Are The Everything; Stand; World Leader Pretend; The Wrong Child; Orange Crush; Turn You Inside Out; Hairshirt; I Remember California; Untitled.*

★ First released 1988
★ UK peak chart position: 27
★ USA peak chart position: 12
★ Previous Top 1000 position: 1998 (185): 1994 (193)

140 SLANTED AND ENCHANTED ↑ Pavement

The punk era had already posited the notion that limited production values and/or technique could exist in inverse proportion to good music. Pavement, then, were the first Americans of note to conceptualize the message as the medium, accentuating perceived shortcomings. This stance had several advantages – their stripped-and-raw aesthetic pushed the group's hooky songs to the forefront. Unlike their earlier recordings, which were too scattershot and tentative to be easily accessible, *Slanted and Enchanted* saw the recently expanded line-up at their best. 'Chesley's Little Wrists' and 'No Life Singed Her' are just two examples of the songwriting's high-quality threshold. America's answer to the Fall was a long time coming, but proved to be well worth the wait.

❯❯ Tracks: *Summer Babe (Winter Version); Trigger Cut; Wounded-Kite At: 17; No Life Singed Her; In The Mouth A Desert; Conduit For Sale!; Zurich Is Stained; Chesley's Little Wrists; Loretta's Scars; Here; Two States; Perfume-V; Flame Throwa; Jackals, False Grails: The Lonesome Era; Our Singer.*

★ First released 1991
★ UK peak chart position: 72
★ USA peak chart position: did not chart
★ Previous Top 1000 position: 1998 (897): 1994 (–)

141 THE KINKS ARE THE VILLAGE GREEN PRESERVATION SOCIETY
↑ The Kinks

Although *Tommy* is seen as the first rock opera, Ray Davies actually conceived the idea with *Arthur* and this album. Taking the theme of England and its quaint Englishness, *The Kinks Are The Village Green Preservation Society* addresses Dr. Beeching's barbaric railway closures with 'The Last Of The Steam Powered Trains', and nostalgia in the title track; 'god save Donald Duck, vaudeville and variety'. 'Picture Book' describes growing old and 'Animal Farm' is a wonderful plea for rural sanity. The commercial failure of the album was in not having one outstanding song, but as a concept the collection is an absolute classic. Who else could use a lyric like 'we are the custard pie appreciation consortium' and get away with it.

» Tracks: *The Village Green Preservation Society; Do You Remember Walter; Picture Book; Johnny Thunder; The Last Of The Steam-Powered Trains; Big Sky; Sitting By The Riverside; Animal Farm; Village Green; Starstruck; Phenomenal Cat; All My Friends Were There; Wicked Annabella; Monica; People Take Pictures Of Each Other.*
★ First released 1968
★ UK peak chart position: did not chart
★ USA peak chart position: did not chart
★ Previous Top 1000 position: 1998 (171): 1994 (367)

142 BLOOD SUGAR SEX MAGIK ↓
Red Hot Chili Peppers

With this they produced the defining moment of funk rock and the high point of their career. Raunchy and explicit from the first, the lyrical content was not for the easily offended and frequently strayed into misogyny. Musically, it straddled metal and funk with ease; in addition to the stomping, infectious rockers ('Give It Away', 'The Power Of Equality') and the downright funky ('Mellowship Slinky', 'Apache Rose Peacock'), all underpinned by Flea's virtuosic but unselfish basslines, the band also showed themselves capable of writing surprisingly melodic ballads, including 'Under The Bridge'. A cover version of this classic by the All Saints has kindled some belated mainstream interest. However, plagued by destructive drug problems and personnel changes, the Chilis have, sadly, never topped the achievements of this album.

» Tracks: *The Power Of Equality; If You Have To Ask; Breaking The Girl; Funky Monks; Suck My Kiss; I Could Have Lied; Mellowship Slinky; The Righteous & The Wicked; Give It Away; Blood Sugar Sex Magik; Under The Bridge; Naked In The Rain; Apache Rose Peacock; The Greeting Song; My Lovely Man; Sir Psycho Sexy; They're Red Hot.*
★ First released 1991
★ UK peak chart position: 25   ★ USA peak chart position: 3
★ Previous Top 1000 position: 1998 (114): 1994 (–)

143 INNERVISIONS ↓
Stevie Wonder

Uplifting and rolling continuing a sequence o outstanding albums, Stevie Wonder again stamped his seal of importance during the early 70s. More than twenty years later, 'Living For the City' does sound a bit crass, especially rhyming pollution with solution, but that is a small carp when placed against the magnificence of 'He's Misstra Know-It-All', the out-and-out cleverness of 'Too High' and the graceful 'Golden Lady'. Wonder has an amazing conception of what vision is, something we take for granted when listening to the lyrics of 'Golden Lady', for example. Quite uncanny, he sees more than the sighted and puts it to music.

» Tracks: *Too High; Visions; Living For The City; Golden Lady; Higher Ground; Jesus Children Of America; All In Love Is Fair; Don't You Worry 'Bout A Thing; He's Misstra Know-It-All.*

★ First released 1973
★ UK peak chart position: 8
★ USA peak chart position: 4
★ Previous Top 1000 position: 1998 (124): 1994 (479)

144 RUM, SODOMY & THE LASH
↑ The Pogues

The Elvis Costello-produced *Rum, Sodomy & The Lash*, a title apparently taken from Winston Churchill's description of life in the Royal Navy, was the creative apex of their lolling, folky output. Shane MacGowan's rolling lilt expounded upon the rich lyrical tinges of 'A Pair Of Brown Eyes' and 'Dirty Old Town', while the band's ragged glory, dipping from a whisper to a powerful roar, shone through with 'The Old Main Drag' and 'I'm A Man You Don't Meet Every Day', utilizing their sometime sumptuous rasp. A fiercely unique record alive with abandon and a carefree soul.

» Tracks: *The Sick Bed Of Cúchulainn; The Old Main Drag; Wild Cats Of Kilkenny; I'm A Man You Don't Meet Every Day; A Pair Of Brown Eyes; Sally Maclennane; Dirty Old Town; Jesse James; Navigator; Billy's Bones; The Gentleman Solder; And The Band Played Waltzing Matilda.*

★ First released 1985
★ UK peak chart position: 13
★ USA peak chart position: did not chart
★ Previous Top 1000 position: 1998 (332): 1994 (273)

145 ENTER THE WU-TANG (36 CHAMBERS) ↑ Wu-Tang Clan

Staten Island's Wu-Tang Clan made their 1993 debut with an album that single-handedly rectified regional imbalance in US rap. New York had given the world hip-hop but by the early 90s it was dominated by west coast artists, and Ice-T and Ice Cube, in particular. *Enter The Wu-Tang (36 Chambers)* introduced the world to Prince Rakeem – alongside Dr. Dre the most talented and prolific producer in hip-hop. On top of Rakeem's lovingly assembled collages of urban strife, the Wu-Tang's numerous retinue of rappers laid siege to the microphone. At times an achievement of head-spinning musical intensity (and language that is not so much bad as grievous), when the component pieces work coherently, the formula makes for spectacular listening.

» Tracks: *Bring Da Ruckus; Shame On A Nigga; Clan In Da Front; Wu-Tang: 7th Chamber; Can It Be All So Simple; Intermission; Da Mystery Of Chessboxin'; Wu-Tang Clan Ain't Nuthing Ta F' Wit; C.R.E.A.M.; Method Man; Protect Ya Neck; Tearz; Wu-Tang: 7th Chamber – Part II; Method Man (Remix) Skunk Mix.*

★ First released 1993
★ UK peak chart position: did not chart
★ USA peak chart position: 41
★ Previous Top 1000 position: 1998 (660): 1994 (–)

146 ALADDIN SANE ↑ David Bowie

Aladdin Sane was released as its creator's star was firmly ascending. A sprawling US tour inspired much of its content, particularly 'Drive In Saturday' and 'Panic In Detroit', but such images were infused with David Bowie's contemporary interest in science fiction-styled alter egos. Regular backing group the Spiders From Mars, which included guitarist Mick Ronson, fuelled the compositions with an intuitive punch, although the diverse nature of the material demonstrated Bowie's ever-present desire to challenge. Futuristic vistas are even harnessed to vintage R&B, as evinced on 'Jean Genie', which inspires comparisons with the Yardbirds, and a reworking of the Rolling Stones' 'Let's Spend The Night Together'. The singer disbanded his group following this album, and *Aladdin Sane* thus marks a watershed in his inventive career.

» Tracks: *Watch That Man; Aladdin Sane; Drive In Saturday; Panic In Detroit; Cracked Actor; Time; The Prettiest Star; Let's Spend The Night Together; Jean Genie; Lady Grinning Soul.*

★ First released 1973
★ UK peak chart position: 1
★ USA peak chart position: 17
★ Previous Top 1000 position: 1998 (367): 1994 (270)

147 AXIS: BOLD AS LOVE ↑ The Jimi Hendrix Experience

Live performances and the brilliant *Are You Experienced* established Jimi Hendrix as a guitarist nonpareil. This second set was largely less demonstrative, focusing on the artist's gifts as a songwriter. It included several reflective compositions, notably the haunting 'Little Wing'. This did not represent a radical change of emphasis – many of the tracks were actually recorded at sessions producing its predecessor – and the set simply offered another side to his talent. The guitarist's sonic creativity underscored 'If Six Was Nine' and 'Spanish Castle Magic' and although sometimes eclipsed by the albums issued on either side of it, *Axis: Bold As Love* brims with the same inventiveness. The 1997 MCA reissue is highly recommended.

» Tracks: *EXP; Up From The Skies; Spanish Castle Magic; Wait Until Tomorrow; Ain't No Telling; Little Wing; If Six Was Nine; You've Got Me Floating; Castles Made Of Sand; She's So Fine; One Rainy Wish; Little Miss Lover; Bold As Love.*

★ First released 1967
★ UK peak chart position: 5
★ USA peak chart position: 3
★ Previous Top 1000 position: 1998 (326): 1994 (198)

148 FOR THE ROSES ↑ Joni Mitchell

A gigantic leap from the frail folky to a major writer of breathtaking depth. Critics were unanimous in recognizing Joni Mitchell as the first icon of 70s singer-songwriters. Combining folk roots with pop sensibility and delicately laced with jazz (just listen to the soprano saxophone at the end of 'Cold Blue Steel and Sweet Fire' by Tom Scott), this marked the first in a series of classic albums from Mitchell. The outstanding use of metaphors in 'Electricity' comparing love to electricity has rarely been bettered. Using lines such as 'the masking tape tangles, it's sticky and black' and 'but the lines overloaded and the sparks started flying', Mitchell was on a roll. Similarly stunning was 'You Turn Me On I'm A Radio'.

» Tracks: *Banquet; Cold Blue Steel and Sweet Fire; Barangrill; Lesson In Survival; Let The Wind Carry Me; For The Roses; See You Sometime; Electricity; You Turn Me On I'm A Radio; Blonde In The Bleachers; Woman Of Heart and Mind; Judgement Of The Moon and Stars (Ludwig's Tune).*

★ First released 1972
★ UK peak chart position: did not chart
★ USA peak chart position: 11
★ Previous Top 1000 position: 1998 (813): 1994 (–)

149 SONGS OF LEONARD COHEN ↑ Leonard Cohen

Cohen's sombre debut encapsulated the performer's artistry. A successful poet and novelist, he came to music through the folk idiom and this set combines the aural simplicity and visual clarity of these two passions. Cohen's lugubrious voice brought an intensity to a haunting collection bound together by beautiful melodies and deeply personal lyrics. Members of Kaleidoscope joined producer John Simon in creating a delicate backdrop for some memorable love songs. Cohen's ability to be both intimate and universal is a rare gift and results in a body of work that is both timeless and enthralling, albeit a bit maudlin.

» Tracks: *Suzanne; Master Song; Winter Lady; The Stranger Song; Sisters Of Mercy; So Long, Marianne; Hey, That's No Way To Say Goodbye; Stories Of The Street Teachers; One Of Us Cannot Be Wrong.*

★ First released 1968
★ UK peak chart position: 13
★ USA peak chart position: 83
★ Previous Top 1000 position: 1998 (241): 1994 (52)

150 OLDER ↓ George Michael

After his agonizing litigation with Sony, George Michael could have gone under. He had put his recorded career on ice for some time, and pop is fickle and disloyal. *Older* was preceded by the single 'Jesus To A Child', which, although a substantial hit, disappointed. Over the past two years this track has grown as a song that has seeped into the consciousness. Together with the rest of the album, it has taken a while, but it is now seen as a very fine record. Michael is better at the slow ballads like 'Older' and 'To Be Forgiven', but 'Fastlove' brings back strong memories of that fresh-faced lad performing with whassisname in Wham! Michael is here for the long haul.

» Tracks: *Jesus To A Child; Fastlove; Older; Spinning The Wheel; It Doesn't Really Matter; The Strangest Thing; To Be Forgiven; Move On; Star People; You Have Been Loved; Free.*

★ First released 1996
★ UK peak chart position: 1
★ USA peak chart position: 6
★ Previous Top 1000 position: 1998 (94): 1994 (–)

151 PARADE ↑ Prince and The Revolution

Another soundtrack that fared more favourably than the movie, 'Under The Cherry Moon', from which it came, this was also the record that marked Prince's return to the live arena. The record itself came with a high camp video and guaranteed hit in the shape of 'Kiss' (which a collaboration of Tom Jones and the Art Of Noise would later cover), a delightfully funky little number around which the world threatened to dance. Elsewhere, both 'Girls and Boys' and 'Anotherloverholenyohead' charted. While the lilting strains of 'Sometimes It Snows In April' rounded off a wonderfully whole album, nothing could quite save the film.

» Tracks: *Christopher Tracey's Parade; New Position; I Wonder U; Under The Cherry Moon; Girls and Boys; Life Can Be So Nice; Venus De Milo; Mountains; Do U Lie; Kiss; Anotherloverholenyohead; Sometimes It Snows In April.*

★ First released 1986
★ UK peak chart position: 4
★ USA peak chart position: 3
★ Previous Top 1000 position: 1998 (377): 1994 (180)

152 THIS YEAR'S MODEL ↑ Elvis Costello

Yet another fine collection from Costello, surely the most prolific lyricist of the past two decades. This is a young, angry, and inexperienced Costello. He shouts and spits but always retains irresistible melody. 'Pump It Up' contains driving pop with a fine example of 'cheesy' organ, and is a high point. The Attractions sound like the best backing band in the world, and it is staggering to think that Costello had so much more bursting to get out when many of us would have been happy with this one album. Anyone who can rhyme Chelsea with Elsie and still sound cool has to be a bit special.

» Tracks: *No Action; This Year's Girl; The Beat; Pump It Up; Little Triggers; You Belong To Me; Hand In Hand; (I Don't Want To Go To) Chelsea; Lip Service; Living In Paradise; Lipstick Vogue; Night Rally.*

★ First released 1978
★ UK peak chart position: 4
★ USA peak chart position: 30
★ Previous Top 1000 position: 1998 (164): 1994 (67)

153 IN A SILENT WAY ↑
Miles Davis

Miles Davis' hushed masterpiece *In A Silent Way* was pieced together in the studio from a series of long stretches of quiet and intense collective improvisation. Masterfully demonstrating to the jazz world that rock's electric instruments were not necessarily harsh and noisy creatures, he again proved his creative and conceptual genius, fashioning the sound of fusion with the aid of Herbie Hancock, Chick Corea and Joe Zawinul on electric pianos and organ, John McLaughlin on electric guitar, Wayne Shorter on soprano saxophone, British bassist Dave Holland and drummer Tony Williams. This is a delicate and beautiful thing that has rarely been repeated.

❱❱ Tracks: *SHHH/Peaceful; In A Silent Way; It's About That Time.*

★ First released 1969
★ UK peak chart position: did not chart
★ USA peak chart position: 134
★ Previous Top 1000 position: 1998 (187): 1994 (464)

155 SKETCHES OF SPAIN ↑
Miles Davis

The third collaboration between Miles Davis and Gil Evans was another work of two men who were musically plugged into each other. The orchestral score by Evans is both haunting and breathtaking when it bursts into life, while the understated playing from Davis is the parmesan on the pasta. The 16-minute 'Concierto De Aranjuez' is a stunning opening track. Many people stop the record at this point because there is so much to take in, and often one track will suffice. It sounds somewhat insulting to say that this album is the perfect background music for a dinner party. Conversation can continue, but it is the magnificent music that really captures the ears of the guests.

❱❱ Tracks: *Concierto De Aranjuez; Will O' The Wisp; The Pan Piper; Saeta; Solea.*

★ First released 1960
★ UK peak chart position: did not chart
★ USA peak chart position: did not chart
★ Previous Top 1000 position: 1998 (240): 1994 (–)

154 QUADROPHENIA ↑
The Who

To write and record one successful 'rock opera' is an achievement but to attempt it all over again and succeed is credit to Pete Townshend's determination and deep talent. *Tommy* was a naïve storyline compared to this, a story of a frustrated and angry mod in 1964. The band play blindingly well throughout and the remastered version in 1996 is outstanding. The fact that there is a storyline is almost irrelevant on a double album of excellent songs. '5:15' was the lone hit single, a sign that the pop charts were no longer a priority for Townshend; he wanted to be an artist. The subsequent film with Phil Daniels merely reinforced Townshend's vision.

❱❱ Tracks: *I Am The Sea; The Real Me; Quadrophenia; Cut My Hair; The Punk and The Godfather; I'm One; The Dirty Jobs; Helpless Dancer; Is It In My Head?; I've Had Enough; 5:15; Sea and Sand; Drowned; Bell Boy; Doctor Jimmy; The Rock; Love Reign O'er Me.*

★ First released 1973
★ UK peak chart position: 2
★ USA peak chart position: 2
★ Previous Top 1000 position: 1998 (230): 1994 (–)

156 IF I COULD ONLY REMEMBER MY NAME ↓
David Crosby

Although this was a highly successful album, Crosby was accused of being self-indulgent by some critics in their hasty reviews. In recent years that opinion has reversed, acknowledging that the amount of space he allowed to fellow musicians, makes this a wholly unselfish record. The cream of San Francisco assembled, and in no particular order, there are Jerry Garcia, Phil Lesh, Jack Casady, Paul Kantner, Joni Mitchell and Grace Slick. Crosby moves from the humour in his modern-day Jesse James story, 'Cowboy Movie', to glorious spiritual voice excursions in 'I'd Swear There Was Somebody Here' and 'Tamalpais High'. The playing is faultless throughout and if you are not familiar with this miraculous record, please take the risk.

❱❱ Tracks: *Music Is Love; Cowboy Movie; Tamalpais High; Laughing; What Are Their Names; Traction In The Rain; Song With No Words (Tree With No Leaves); Orleans; I'd Swear There Was Somebody Here.*

★ First released 1971
★ UK peak chart position: 12
★ USA peak chart position: 12
★ Previous Top 1000 position: 1998 (143): 1994 (288)

157 1962-66 ↑
The Beatles

From the famous pair of red and blue, this one was always the poor relative, being one or two positions behind in the charts and selling one or two million fewer copies. Quite why will never be known, as the singles contained on this were bigger hits, and make for a better greatest hits package. The balance is now redressed. You cannot tamper with the general opinion of the record buying public. What would be easier is that every government throughout the world give every child a complete set of Beatles albums when they start school. The greatest popular 'beat combo' in the world. Some things are cast in stone.

» Tracks: *Love Me Do; Please Please Me; From Me To You; She Loves You; I Want To Hold Your Hand; All My Loving; Can't Buy Me Love; A Hard Day's Night; And I Love Her; Eight Days A Week; I Feel Fine; Ticket To Ride; Yesterday; Help; You've Got To Hide Your Love Away; We Can Work It Out; Day Tripper; Drive My Car; Norwegian Wood; Nowhere Man; Michelle; In My Life; Girl; Paperback Writer; Eleanor Rigby; Yellow Submarine.*

★ First released 1973
★ UK peak chart position: 3
★ USA peak chart position: 3
★ Previous Top 1000 position: 1998 (311): 1994 (147)

158 THE NOTORIOUS BYRD BROTHERS ↓ The Byrds

Building on the maturity of their previous masterpiece *Younger Than Yesterday*, the Byrds delivered a suite of songs that naturally flow into one another with uncanny ease. It is one of the few vinyl releases where both sides would always be played. 30 years later on CD it begs to be heard uninterrupted, because when played individually, the songs lose their power. This was an artistic triumph and a commercial disappointment, as the memory of David Crosby faded only to be replaced (allegedly) by a horse on the album sleeve. The Byrds moved on to their country phase and numerous line-ups but they were never to sound so happy or youthful again.

» Tracks: *Artificial Energy; Goin' Back; Natural Harmony; Draft Morning; Wasn't Born To Follow; Get To You; Change Is Now; Old John Robertson; Tribal Gathering; Dolphins' Smile; Space Odyssey.*

★ First released 1968
★ UK peak chart position: 12
★ USA peak chart position: 47
★ Previous Top 1000 position: 1998 (75): 1994 (133)

159 THE LEXICON OF LOVE ↓
ABC

ABC are frequently described as purveyors of high-quality pop music, but this undervalues the elegance and attention to detail of their work. Although they have failed to repeat the success of *Lexicon Of Love*, it nevertheless represents an achievement to which many other artists can only aspire. The maturity of Trevor Horn's production created a remarkable debut album, yielding hits in 'Tears Are Not Enough', 'Poison Arrow', 'The Look Of Love' and 'All Of My Heart', with Martin Fry's talent as songwriter and vocalist delivering the goods with consistent aplomb. Probably still the best ever example of 80s pop music.

» Tracks: *Show Me; Poison Arrow; Many Happy Returns; Tears Are Not Enough; Valentine's Day; The Look Of Love (Part 1); Date Stamp; All Of My Heart; 4 Ever 2 Gether; The Look Of Love.*

★ First released 1982
★ UK peak chart position: 1
★ USA peak chart position: 24
★ Previous Top 1000 position: 1998 (140): 1994 (253)

160 BORN IN THE USA ↑
Bruce Springsteen

Springsteen purists may well bemoan the overtly commercial stance taken on this record, but its catchiness, high toe-tapping factor and damn good songs cannot be denied. 'Darlington County' and 'Working On The Highway' are familiar Springsteen themes, but it is the incredible power of the title track's riff and the euphoria that 'Dancing In The Dark' still manages to convey over fifteen years later that make this album special. He hit a multi million peak with this LP although his credibility is still maintained. *Born In The USA* still delivers a mighty punch and above all, it still sounds like a great rock album.

» Tracks: *Born In The USA; Cover Me; Darlington County; Working On The Highway; Downbound Train; I'm On Fire; No Surrender; Bobby Jean; I'm Goin' Down; Glory Days; Dancing In The Dark; My Hometown.*

★ First released 1984
★ UK peak chart position: 1
★ USA peak chart position: 1
★ Previous Top 1000 position: 1998 (215): 1994 (70)

161 FRESH FRUIT FOR ROTTING VEGETABLES ↑ The Dead Kennedys

Where most American groups formed in the Sex Pistols' wake adopted their image but none of their substance, the Dead Kennedys brought a new perspective to punk's Sturm und Drang. Group leader Jello Biafra attacked hypocrisy with a series of virulent anthems and, by extension, fought a tireless campaign against censorship. Bitter sarcasm is unleashed on 'Kill The Poor' and 'Holiday In Cambodia' while 'California Uber Alles' savages the 'new age' politics of contemporary governor Jerry Brown. Furious tempos and gunshot guitar emphasize the album's anger and frustration, and set a pattern for the ensuing hardcore movement. A hugely influential set that continues to gain popularity.

» Tracks: Kill The Poor; Forward To Death; When Ya Get Drafted; Let's Lynch The Landlord; Drug Me; Your Emotions; Chemical Warfare; California Uber Alles; I Kill Children; Stealing People's Mail; Funland At The Beach; Ill In The Head; Holiday In Cambodia; Viva Las Vegas.

★ First released 1980
★ UK peak chart position: 33
★ USA peak chart position: did not chart
★ Previous Top 1000 position: 1998 (254): 1994 (799)

162 LIFES RICH PAGEANT ↑ R.E.M.

For the first time in four albums, Michael Stipe evidently wanted the 'happy throngs' of listeners to hear and absorb his lyrics. On Lifes Rich Pageant, the band confidently tackled political and environmental issues, a direction more fully explored on the later Document and Green. Defiant and celebratory returns to their punk influences ('Just A Touch', 'These Days') were balanced by laments about US environmental policy and the folk tradition of the American South ('Swan Swan H'). Mills' and Berry's harmonies shone through, particularly on 'Fall On Me', still one of the best songs in the vast R.E.M. catalogue. A curiously sensitive and affecting album, packed with crafted pop songs, it marked a watershed for a group on the brink of unimagined worldwide success.

» Tracks: Begin The Begin; These Days; Fall On Me; Cuyahoga; Hyena; Underneath The Bunker; The Flowers Of Guatemala; I Believe; What If We Give It Away?; Just A Touch; Swan Swan H; Superman.

★ First released 1986
★ UK peak chart position: 43
★ USA peak chart position: 21
★ Previous Top 1000 position: 1998 (348): 1994 (–)

163 THE PIPER AT THE GATES OF DAWN ↓ Pink Floyd

During the spring of 1967, while the Beatles were at Abbey Road finishing Sgt. Pepper's Lonely Hearts Club Band, Pink Floyd were upstairs recording an album that would have a similarly immeasurable effect on the development of psychedelic rock. Its name taken from A.A. Milne's The Wind in the Willows (one of guitarist Syd Barrett's favourite books), Piper At The Gates Of Dawn was a child's garden of acid, an album-length exposition on the effects of LSD on a troubled mind. One of the first 'head' albums, it was rumoured that the tracks contained sounds – conversations, even – that one could only hear while hallucinating. 'Bike', however, brought it all back to basics with such profound lyrics as 'I've got a mouse, and he lives in a house, I don't know why I call him Gerald'.

» Tracks: Astronomy Domine; Lucifer Sam; Matilda Mother; Flaming; Pow R. Toc H.; Take Up Thy Stethoscope and Walk; Interstellar Overdrive; Gnome; Chapter 24; Scarecrow; Bike.

★ First released 1967
★ UK peak chart position: 6
★ USA peak chart position: 131
★ Previous Top 1000 position: 1998 (138): 1994 (–)

164 AMERICANA ↑ The Offspring

Highly popular in the USA, the Offspring have yet to make more than a cultish dent elsewhere in the world. The signs are good, however, and this album will not disappoint those seeking some tough rock laced with a punk attitude. A little No Doubt with a sprinkle of Green Day this is steering wheel tapping stuff, and the perfect way to release tension after a sweaty day in the office. That remark, of course, wrongly assumes that Offspring fans are respectable suits. The closest they would ever have come would have been to have purchased and wooed their spouses with the original version of Morris Albert's insipid 'Feelings'; 'oh honey I'm home'.

» Tracks: Welcome; Have You Ever; Staring At The Sun; Pretty Fly (For A White Guy); The Kids Aren't Alright; Feelings; She's Got Issues; Walla Walla; The End Of The Line; No Brakes; Why Don't You Get A Job?; Americana; Pay The Man.

★ First released 1998
★ UK peak chart position: 10
★ USA peak chart position: 2
★ Previous Top 1000 position: 1998 (–): 1994 (–)

165 BUFFALO SPRINGFIELD AGAIN ↑ Buffalo Springfield

A few months after *Sgt. Pepper's Lonely Hearts Club Band* came America's potential answer, both in terms of the formidable talent within the band, including Stephen Stills, Richie Furay and Neil Young, and the varied content of folk, rock, country, soul and mild psychedelia. The strong egos within made their future together an impossibility, while the leaders went on to major success with CSNY and Poco. Hearing this record made David Crosby want to join them, while the UK rock cognoscenti prayed for them to stay together long enough to tour in the UK. It was not to be, but this was a document to their great potential. An amazingly creative record.

》 Tracks: *Mr. Soul; A Child's Claim To Fame; Everydays; Expecting To Fly; Bluebird; Hung Upside Down; Sad Memory; Good Time Boy; Rock 'N' Roll Woman; Broken Arrow.*

★ First released 1967
★ UK peak chart position: did not chart
★ USA peak chart position: 44
★ Previous Top 1000 position: 1998 (218): 1994 (227)

166 MACHINE HEAD ↑ Deep Purple

From the heady intro of 'Highway Star', written in a couple of hours on a bus between shows, to the lazy beat of 'Space Truckin'', *Machine Head* would have remained one of the classic line-up's (Roger Glover, Ian Paice, Ian Gillan, Ritchie Blackmore, Jon Lord) great albums. However, the hand of fate took them to Montreux at the same time as Frank Zappa's Mothers Of Invention. Their witnessing of the burning down of the Casino, immortalized in 'Smoke On The Water' with Blackmore's plaintive riff studied and dedicated to memory in a thousand guitar classes, and Gillan's simple retelling of events, elevated them and their record to legendary status. 'Da da da, dada dada, da da da, da da'.

》 Tracks: *Highway Star; Maybe I'm A Leo; Pictures Of Home; Never Before; Smoke On The Water; Lazy; Space Truckin'.*

★ First released 1972
★ UK peak chart position: 1
★ USA peak chart position: 7
★ Previous Top 1000 position: 1998 (454): 1994 (103)

167 DOG MAN STAR ↓ Suede

Although guitarist/ songwriter Bernard Butler quit midway through the making of this, Suede's second album, he co-wrote all the songs with singer Brett Anderson and remains a strong presence. Future Butlerless albums have lacked his sound. *Dog Man Star*, which in recent times has gained critical popularity, was not nearly as successful as the group's first album, *Suede*, but it boasts more continuity and, many would argue, more depth. The David Bowie influence, so prominent on *Suede*, is, if anything, more obvious, particularly on 'Heroine', with its pained analogies between women and drugs and 'The Wild Ones', which exudes the kind of hopeless romanticism not heard since Bowie's 'Heroes'.

》 Tracks: *Introducing The Band; We Are The Pigs; Heroine; The Wild Ones; Daddy's Speeding; The Power; New Generation; This Hollywood Life; The 2 Of Us; Black Or Blue; The Asphalt World; Still Life.*

★ First released 1994
★ UK peak chart position: 3
★ USA peak chart position: did not chart
★ Previous Top 1000 position: 1998 (62): 1994 (–)

168 SURFER ROSA ↑ Pixies

Now seen as an important alternative band of the 80s, it is a pity they were not more appreciated at the time. The Boston-based Pixies exploded into life with this abrasive selection. Produced by *enfant terrible* Steve Albini, the album emphasized the quartet's scratchy tension. A vicious drum sound underpins the group's uncanny blend of urgency and melody, where Black Francis's rabid intonation contrasts with Kim Deal's more gentle perspective. Obtuse lyrics and barely controlled guitar accentuate the Pixies' uncompromising visions and emphasize an approach that both excites and intrigues. Terse, exhilarating, unrelenting and single-minded, *Surfer Rosa* is an audacious collection.

》 Tracks: *Bone Machine; Break My Body; Something Against You; Broken Face; Gigantic; River Euphrates; Where Is My Mind?; Cactus; Tony's Theme; Oh My Golly!; Vamos; I'm Amazed; Brick Is Red.*

★ First released 1988
★ UK peak chart position: did not chart
★ USA peak chart position: did not chart
★ Previous Top 1000 position: 1998 (202): 1994 (391)

169 WHITE ON BLONDE ↓
Texas

Scottish guitar band Texas were generally felt to have peaked with their debut set, *Southside*. Their third album, *Rick's Road*, contained some strong material but their sales continued a downward spiral. This 1997 comeback, therefore, was a pleasant surprise, picking up awards everywhere and still selling in large quantities. For a band who might have been looking over their shoulders, this is a supremely confident album, full of good songs written by the band and, in particular, by Sharleen Spiteri and John McElhone (formerly of Altered Images). Respectable rock for the 90s, from the full production of tracks such as 'Halo' to the chiming tension created by 'Put Your Arms Around Me'.

❱❱ Tracks: *0.34; Say What You Want; Drawing Crazy Patterns; Halo; Put Your Arms Around Me; Insane; Black Eyed Boy; Polo Mint City; White On Blonde; Postcard; 0.28; Ticket To Lie; Good Advice; Breathless.*

★ First released 1997
★ UK peak chart position: 1
★ USA peak chart position: did not chart
★ Previous Top 1000 position: 1998 (144): 1994 (–)

170 STEVE MCQUEEN ↑
Prefab Sprout

While many felt that *Jordan: The Comeback* was their creative peak, this remains the most popular choice. Recorded before the band's creative force Paddy MacAloon was hyped as the next big thing, it stands as a truly great pop album with enough complexity to make it special. The hit single, 'When Love Breaks Down', opened doors to a wider market and 'Faron Young' reawakened interest in the country music star. The jury is still out on their long-term prospects after so much promise and we wait to see whether MacAloon can surpass the quality of *Steve McQueen*. For now this remains the Prefab industry standard.

❱❱ Tracks: *Faron Young; Bonny; Appetite; When Love Breaks Down; Goodbye Lucille #1; Hallelujah; Moving The River; Horsing Around; Desire As; Blueberry Pies; When The Angels.*

★ First released 1985
★ UK peak chart position: 21
★ USA peak chart position: 178
★ Previous Top 1000 position: 1998 (281): 1994 (433)

171 DUSTY IN MEMPHIS ↑
Dusty Springfield

Not only is this Dusty's finest work it is unanimously acknowledged as one of the great soul albums of all time. The secret is in the production; Jerry Wexler, Tom Dowd and Arif Mardin enlisted the Sweet Inspirations for vocal support and the best Memphis session boys. Her selection of material is exemplary, choosing songs by Randy Newman, Mann/Weill, Goffin/King and Bacharach/David. This should have made her an international megastar; instead it scraped into the US Top 100, failed to chart in the UK and marked the started of her slow decline. It is a faultless record on which we have, thankfully, now recognized that Dusty was far too ahead of her time for her own good.

❱❱ Tracks: *Just A Little Lovin'; So Much Love; Son Of A Preacher Man; I Don't Want To Hear It Anymore; Don't Forget About Me; Breakfast In Bed; Just One Smile; The Windmills Of Your Mind; In The Land Of Make Believe; No Easy Way Down; I Can't Make It Alone.*

★ First released 1969
★ UK peak chart position: did not chart
★ USA peak chart position: 99
★ Previous Top 1000 position: 1998 (227): 1994 (136)

172 SAFE AS MILK ↑
Captain Beefheart and The Magic Band

The cover depicts four clean-cut kids in suits and tie; one is even wearing his father's hat. Is this not the most paradoxically bizarre cover ever, in relation to the music within? This sounded like music from Saturn in 1967; now it just sounds remarkably good. Don van Vliet's Howlin' Wolf growl almost tears the speaker-cloth as he launches into 'Electricity'. Other marvellous excursions are 'Dropout Boogie', 'Plastic Factory' and 'Yellow Brick Road'. The latter should have opened the original album as the spoken 'the following tone is a reference tone' section sets the tone for this unforgettable album. An easy introduction to wayward genius.

❱❱ Tracks: *Sure 'Nuff 'N Yes I Do; Zig Zag Wanderer; Call On Me; Dropout Boogie; I'm Glad; Electricity; Yellow Brick Road; Abba Zaba; Plastic Factory; Where There's A Woman; Grown So Ugly; Autumn's Child.*

★ First released 1967
★ UK peak chart position: did not chart
★ USA peak chart position: did not chart
★ Previous Top 1000 position: 1998 (233): 1994 (–)

173 CAPTAIN FANTASTIC AND THE BROWN DIRT COWBOY
↑ Elton John

In the pre-punk era, where severely inflated egos and ludicrous concept albums were all over the place, Elton John and Bernie Taupin's account of their rise from struggling penury to the peak of superstardom is one of rock's better attempts at self-mythology. The original vinyl record was an elaborate package in itself, and the music within is on a suitably grandiose and self-indulgent scale. At times, Elton's music and Taupin's lyrics struggle to gel, but when they come together on tracks such as 'Someone Saved My Life Tonight' and 'Gotta Get A Meal Ticket', the concept is carried off with suitable aplomb. This album is much more appreciated in the USA.

» Tracks: *Captain Fantastic and The Brown Dirt Cowboy; Tower Of Babel; Bitter Fingers; Tell Me When The Whistle Blows; Someone Saved My Life Tonight; (Gotta Get A) Meal Ticket; Better Off Dead; Writing; We All Fall In Love Sometimes; Curtains.*

★ First released 1975
★ UK peak chart position: 2
★ USA peak chart position: 1
★ Previous Top 1000 position: 1998 (799): 1994 (–)

174 SURREALISTIC PILLOW ↑
Jefferson Airplane

One of a handful of albums epitomizing the 'Summer of Love', *Surrealistic Pillow's* strengths lie in a gorgeous cross-section of folk, blues and acid-rock. Vocalists Grace Slick and Marty Balin interwove over a seamless instrumental section in which Jack Casady (bass) and Jorma Kaukonen (guitar) enjoyed an almost telepathic understanding. The scope of the material is breathtaking, be it science fiction, Lewis Carroll or a succession of haunting, fragile love songs such as the exquisite 'Today'. Restrained when required, animated at others, but always challenging, the album succeeds through a collective determination. There is nothing remotely weird about this recording, which is why it has lasted so well.

» Tracks: *She Has Funny Cars; Somebody To Love; My Best Friend; Today; Comin' Back To Me; 3/5 Mile In 10 Seconds; D.C.B.A-25; How Do You Feel; White Rabbit; Plastic Fantastic Lover; Embryonic Journey.*

★ First released 1967
★ UK peak chart position: did not chart
★ USA peak chart position: 3
★ Previous Top 1000 position: 1998 (182): 1994 (131)

175 NEW YORK ↑
Lou Reed

In the world of contemporary Rock 'n' Roll, nobody has ever been able to sing about New York the way Reed can. Right from the decadent New York of the 60s with the Velvet Underground, Reed has had his finger on the nipple of what made it tick. He writes about the city as he views it from a dustbin. 'Romeo Had Juliette' has a great line, 'Manhattan's sinking like a rock into the filthy Hudson' and 'Halloween Parade' captures the downside of the glossy procession that takes place in Greenwich Village every year. It is no surprise that this album fared better outside the state of New York.

» Tracks: *Romeo Had Juliette; Halloween Parade; Dirty Blvd; Endless Cycle; There Is No Time; Last Great American Whale; Beginning Of A Great Adventure; Busload Of Faith; Sick Of You; Hold On; Good Evening Mr. Waldheim; Xmas In February; Strawman; Dime Store Mystery.*

★ First released 1989
★ UK peak chart position: 14
★ USA peak chart position: 40
★ Previous Top 1000 position: 1998 (370): 1994 (–)

176 DIG YOUR OWN HOLE ↓
Chemical Brothers

Proclaimed by some as the future of rock music, the Chemical Brothers broke out of clubland and into the mainstream with this album of electronica *extraordinaire*. Already kings of the funky breakbeat, infectious hook and imaginative sample, on *Dig Your Own Hole* Tom Rowlands and Ed Simons refined the formula to near-perfection. The Schoolly D-inspired 'Block Rockin' Beats' kicks off the whole in bold fashion; Oasis's Noel Gallagher does a star turn on the hypnotic 'Setting Sun'; the lovely 'Where Do I Begin?', featuring Beth Orton, brings down the mood; and the stunning 'Private Psychedelic Reel', layered with sitars and drum loops, ends the breathtaking journey. This album defied anyone not to get up and dance.

» Tracks: *Block Rockin' Beats; Dig Your Own Hole; Elektrobank; Piku; Setting Sun; It Doesn't Matter; Don't Stop The Rock; Get Up On It Like This; Lost In The K-Hole; Where Do I Begin?; Private Psychedelic Reel.*

★ First released 1997
★ UK peak position: 1
★ USA peak position: 14
★ Previous Top 1000 position: 1998 (86): 1994 (–)

177 TOYS IN THE ATTIC ↑
Aerosmith

A truly inventive Aerosmith album, still suffused with a gloriously raspy sense of the blues, but quietly evocative in its timbre and approach. It showed Tyler working out lyrics that were so much more than simple cars and girls fodder, 'Adam's Apple' theorizing that creation could quite possibly have occurred with an alien mothership landing on earth and setting the wheels of the human race in motion. 'Sweet Emotion' throbbed slowly into life, 'Big Ten Inch Record', a salty R&B work-out, while 'You See Me Crying' was heightened and given body by a warm orchestration. A clear steeple of great work amid a skyline of repeating successes.

➍ Tracks: *Toys In The Attic; Uncle Salty; Adam's Apple; Walk This Way; Big Ten Inch Record; Sweet Emotion; No More No More; Round and Round; You See Me Crying.*

★ First released 1975
★ UK peak chart position: did not chart
★ USA peak chart position: 11
★ Previous Top 1000 position: 1998 (479): 1994 (319)

178 NO OTHER ↓
Gene Clark

Clark' songwriting contribution to the early Byrds was a glorious asset that even they did not appreciate at the time. Many fans willed him to make this excellent album, if only to reinforce the respect and faith they had in his ability. Ill-health and booze kept him from repeating this solo effort and continuing his life as a songwriter. This paradoxical recording can be taken lightly (easy-on-the-ear songs) or as a heavy symbolic lyrical statement (deep stuff). More country rock than pop and like *Astral Weeks*, it has long-term hidden depths. The silk flares he wears on the cover have never been topped, by male or female. The music is similarly wide and flowing.

➍ Tracks: *Life's Greatest Fool; Silver Raven; No Other; Strength Of Strings; From A Silver Phial; Some Misunderstanding; The True One; Lady Of The North.*

★ First released 1974
★ UK peak chart position: did not chart
★ USA peak chart position: 144
★ Previous Top 1000 position: 1998 (136): 1994 (–)

179 LIVE! ↑
Bob Marley

Nobody who likes music could fail to be emotionally moved by this album, and not just because Marley is no longer with us. It was a special live treat before he died. The great thing about this record is the feeling that this is what it was like every night, unlike other live recordings which capture one or two gigs of a tour. Marley was extra special and a giant of popular music. Wallow in this vital record and listen to a man who had something to say and yet had fun while he said it. Most of the tracks you would want to be on the record are here, including the definitive version of 'No Woman No Cry' and a funky 'Lively Up Yourself'. And people who were at the Lyceum can still tell the tale.

➍ Tracks: *Trenchtown Rock; Burnin' and Lootin'; Them Belly Full (But We Hungry); Lively Up Yourself; No Woman No Cry; I Shot The Sheriff; Get Up, Stand Up.*

★ First released 1975
★ UK peak chart position: 38
★ USA peak chart position: 90
★ Previous Top 1000 position: 1998 (259): 1994 (64)

180 THE CLASH ↓
The Clash

The definitive punk statement, this album's power and authority have not diminished. It assails a variety of subjects; unemployment, imperialism and rebellion, deriding or lauding according to political stance. Joe Strummer's barking vocals expressed the anger of a disenfranchised generation, guitarist Mick Jones punctuating his ire with near telepathic precision. Almost every track is essential and in tackling Junior Murvin's 'Police and Thieves', the Clash show an empathy for reggae rarely heard in white rock. The added tracks to the original UK released LP include 'London's Burning' which still manages to evoke and attack 70s complacency in Britain, and is still relevant today.

➍ Tracks: *Janie Jones; Remote Control; I'm So Bored With The USA; White Riot; Hate and War; What's My Name; Deny; London's Burning; Career Opportunities; Cheat; Protex Blue; Police and Thieves; 48 Hours; Garageland.*

★ First released 1977
★ UK peak chart position: 12
★ USA peak chart position: 126
★ Previous Top 1000 position: 1998 (74): 1994 (214)

181 SETTING SONS ↑
The Jam

After the creative *tour de force* and career regeneration that was *All Mod Cons*, the Jam continued their commercial ascendancy with *Setting Sons*. While it is not the band's most cohesive album ('Girl On The Phone' and 'Heatwave' are throwaway efforts at best), it did reveal further progress in Paul Weller's songwriting. There has never been a better song written about English class division than 'Eton Rifles'. Its sense of humour and self-deprecation is unique within Weller's usually austere songbook. Bruce Foxton also makes his key contribution to the Jam's arsenal with his best song, 'Smithers-Jones'. Weller's 'Thick As Thieves' and 'Saturday's Kids' are the other obvious crowd-pleasers.

▶▶ Tracks: *Girl On The Phone; Thick As Thieves; Private Hell; Little Boy Soldiers; Wasteland; Burning Sky; Smithers-Jones; Saturday's Kids; The Eton Rifles; Heatwave*

★ First released 1979
★ UK peak chart position: 4
★ USA peak chart position: 137
★ Previous Top 1000 position: 1998 (328): 1994 (–)

182 DISRAELI GEARS ↓
Cream

This is the power trio's perfect studio album which captured the dayglo spirit of psychedelic London like no other record could. As their blues influences waned, the hippie lyrics of Pete Brown came to the fore, while the strident voice of Jack Bruce fused with Eric Clapton's stinging and milky guitar and Ginger Baker's polyrhythmic drums. 'Tales Of Brave Ulysses', 'SWLABR' and 'Strange Brew' remain classics of their era, while 'Sunshine Of Your Love' has become one of rock's most imitated opening riffs. The Martin Sharpe album sleeve completes the package and displays Eric Clapton with the finest perm of 1967, although I bet he regrets painting the guitar.

▶▶ Tracks: *Strange Brew; Sunshine Of Your Love; World Of Pain; Dance The Night Away; Blue Condition; Tales Of Brave Ulysses; SWLABR; We're Going Wrong; Outside Woman Blues; Take It Back; Mother's Lament.*

★ First released 1967
★ UK peak chart position: 5
★ USA peak chart position: 4
★ Previous Top 1000 position: 1998 (156): 1994 (65)

183 PORNOGRAPHY ↑
The Cure

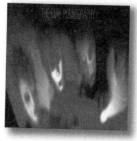

Before founder Robert Smith drew up his archetype for eccentric pop and a fresh sense of lament that turned his band into an arena act in the USA, the Cure's leanings were more darkly felt. *Pornography*, a beautifully still and deep record, is a room full of shadows. Ambient in part, and occasionally challenging, its vision, even down to the oddly distorted photo on the cover, was one darkly wrapped. Smith's yelp of a vocal rose and fell in and out of the light, while 'The Hanging Garden' hinted at his as yet untapped, but clearly commercial, bent. The Cure's present regeneration is due to their huge cult popularity in the USA, helped by appearances on *South Park*.

▶▶ Tracks: *Pornography; The Hanging Garden; One Hundred Years; Siamese Twins; Figurehead; A Strange Day; Cold; A Short Term Effect.*

★ First released 1982
★ UK peak chart position: 8
★ USA peak chart position: did not chart
★ Previous Top 1000 position: 1998 (565): 1994 (522)

184 FLEETWOOD MAC ↑
Fleetwood Mac

The loss of founding member Peter Green dealt a blow to Fleetwood Mac which it took them five years to assimilate. Numerous changes in personnel robbed them of focus until Californian singer-songwriters Stevie Nicks and Lindsay Buckingham joined the ranks. The duo introduced a new dynamism to the group, their bright, melodious compositions offsetting the earthier muse of pianist/vocalist Christine McVie. Buckingham's quicksilver guitarwork energized the group's pulsating rhythm section, regaining, at last, the sense of purpose marking early releases. Titling the album *Fleetwood Mac* suggested a new beginning, which indeed it was. This set saved the group from ignominy, and turned them into one of the world's leading rock bands.

▶▶ Tracks: *Monday Morning; Warm Always; Blue Letter; Rhiannon; Over My Head; Crystal; Say You Love Me; Landslide; I'm So Afraid; World Turning; Sugar Daddy.*

★ First released 1975
★ UK peak chart position: 23
★ USA peak chart position: 1
★ Previous Top 1000 position: 1998 (599): 1994 (213)

185 HEROES ↑
David Bowie

The Germanic feel of this album is not surprising, as Bowie recorded it in Berlin during his infatuation with the city. It was a much more lively affair than *Low* and has the benefit of a title track that remains one of his best ever songs (in addition to excellent contributions from Robert Fripp and Brian Eno). 'Beauty and The Beast' was difficult to accept as a single, yet it works as the album's opener. 'Sense Of Doubt' is the opposite of 'Heroes' – dark and moody, as is 'Neuköln'. Even through the doom and gloom, this is an important Bowie album, and one to which critics return time and time again. Depression seems to beat happiness every time.

❱❱ Tracks: *Beauty and The Beast; Joe The Lion; Heroes; Sons Of The Silent Age; Blackout; V-2 Schneider; Sense Of Doubt; Moss Garden; Neuköln; The Secret Life Of Arabia.*

★ First released 1977
★ UK peak chart position: 3
★ USA peak chart position: 35
★ Previous Top 1000 position: 1998 (464): 1994 (–)

186 NEW ADVENTURES IN HI-FI
↓ R.E.M.

The deeper you dig in a goldmine, the better the quality of the gold. This is R.E.M.'s secret gem, an album of rich songs that has been overlooked by the record-buying public at large. Low-key production, gentle themes and Michael Stipe's crystal-clear vocals grace great compositions such as 'E-Bow The Letter', 'Electrolite', 'So Fast, So Numb' and the simple but glorious 'Be Mine'. Like so much of the band's work, there was virtually nothing to fault, even if, equally, there was nothing that was truly innovative. The latter, irrelevant concern has arguably prejudiced critics against this album, which it is hoped will gain credibility as its true greatness is discovered.

❱❱ Tracks: *How The West Was Won and Where It Got Us; The Wake-Up Bomb; New Test Leper; Undertow; E-Bow The Letter; Leave; Departure; Bittersweet Me; Be Mine; Binky The Doormat; Zither; So Fast, So Numb; Low Desert; Electrolite.*

★ First released 1996
★ UK peak chart position: 1
★ USA peak chart position: 2
★ Previous Top 1000 position: 1998 (93): 1994 (–)

187 AVALON ↑
Roxy Music

Like the Police, Roxy Music never outstayed their welcome and retired while they were on top. Their farewell album leaves a good taste in the mouth when remembering the doyens of art rock. By the time of this album they had become immaculate smoothies: Bryan Ferry had taken to suits, Brian Eno was long gone and Andy Mackay had kept his quiff but had grown an extra chin. Appearances aside, this is an enduring record and it proved to be one of their most successful. 'More Than This' and 'Take A Chance With Me' were both hit singles, as was the title track, on which Ferry at his most seductive informs us 'now the party's over, I'm so tired'. A most agreeable exit.

❱❱ Tracks: *More Than This; The Space Between; Avalon; India; While My Heart Is Still Beating; Main Thing; Take A Chance With Me; To Turn You On; True To Life; Tara.*

★ First released 1982
★ UK peak chart position: 1
★ USA peak chart position: 53
★ Previous Top 1000 position: 1998 (213): 1994 (348)

188 #1 RECORD ↑
Big Star

In mid-60s America, a typical AM radio station featured every style of music that was on the charts. Big Star grew up with that wide-ranging buffet on their transistor radios and could not tolerate the barriers that had arisen between pop and rock. On the Memphis quartet's luminous debut, *#1 Record*, they channelled the Beatles and the Byrds via the Who, layering high-decibel guitars over delicate folk-rock tunes. There was also a hint of Memphis soul, not surprising since one of the group's songwriter/ guitarists, Alex Chilton, had led 60s hitmakers the Box Tops. While critics canonized it, poor distribution doomed it to the deletion bins. A great lost album.

❱❱ Tracks: *Feel; The Ballad Of El Goodo; In The Street; Thirteen; Don't Lie To Me; The India Song; When My Baby's Beside Me; My Life Is Right; Give Me Another Chance; Try Again; Watch The Sunrise; ST100/6.*

★ First released 1972
★ UK peak chart position: did not chart
★ US peak chart position: did not chart
★ Previous Top 1000 position: 1998 (190): 1994 (–)

189 BRINGING IT ALL BACK HOME ↓ Bob Dylan

Howls of rage greeted Bob Dylan as he presented the world with folk rock – he was roundly booed at both the Newport Folk Festival and the Royal Albert Hall. Yet here is one of those moments of cross-influence that changed the course of popular music. *Bringing It All Back Home* gave his Bobness an audience on a plate; it was a massive breakthrough. An album of two different sides, acoustic (his past) and electric (his future), the music – covered a thousandfold – has among it 'Maggie's Farm', 'Subterranean Homesick Blues', 'Mr. Tambourine Man', 'Love Minus Zero – No Limit', and the cosmopolitan political speak of 'It's Alright, Ma (I'm Only Bleeding)' You can debate the 'is it folk or is it rock' argument in a circle.

➤ Tracks: *Subterranean Homesick Blues; She Belongs To Me; Maggie's Farm; Love Minus Zero – No Limit; Outlaw Blues; On The Road Again; Bob Dylan's 115th Dream; Mr. Tambourine Man; Gates Of Eden; It's Alright Ma (I'm Only Bleeding); It's All Over Now, Baby Blue.*

★ First released 1965
★ UK peak chart position: 1
★ USA peak chart position: 6
★ Previous Top 1000 position: 1998 (91): 1994 (150)

190 SEPTEMBER OF MY YEARS ↑ Frank Sinatra

Released shortly before Sinatra's 50th birthday, this album predictably found the singer in a warm, melancholic and reflective mood. Conductor-arranger Gordon Jenkins provided a string-laden setting for a mixture of songs old and new, including Sammy Cahn and Jimmy Van Heusen's specially written title number. Released in the middle of the beat boom, it was awarded Grammys for album of the year and Sinatra's best male vocal performance on one of the tracks, 'It Was A Very Good Year' (Erwin Drake), and provided a great deal of musical comfort for many middle-aged, former 'Swingin' Lovers'. One of the essential six Sinatra albums to own.

➤ Tracks: *September Of My Years; How Old Am I; Don't Wait Too Long; It Gets Lonely Early; This Is All I Ask; Last Night When We Were Young; The Man In The Looking Glass; It Was A Very Good Year; When The Wind Was Green; Hello Young Lovers; I See It Now; Once Upon A Time; September Song.*

★ First released 1965
★ UK peak chart position: did not chart
★ USA peak chart position: 5
★ Previous Top 1000 position: 1998 (373): 1994 (256)

191 BOSTON ↑ Boston

If you can forget the silly flying saucers on the cover and pretend that those jackets and hairstyles never happened then the music from the leading AOR band of the 70s is pretty good. Opening with the classic radio favourite 'More Than A Feeling', every twiddle, every lick and every harmony are recorded to perfection. The project was masterminded by Tom Scholz who prepared the near perfect demos in his home. This is an unrelenting album with the vocals cemented together in wall-cracking harmony and the twin lead guitars melodic but never crunching. The Keith Emerson-inspired organ trills are also worth waiting for. This album went on to sell over 24 million copies worldwide.

➤ Tracks: *More Than A Feeling; Peace Of Mind; Foreplay/Long Time; Rock & Roll Band; Smokin'; Hitch A Ride; Something About You; Let Me Take You Home Tonight.*

★ First released 1976
★ UK peak chart position: 11
★ USA peak chart position: 3
★ Previous Top 1000 position: 1998 (611): 1994 (–)

192 HATFUL OF HOLLOW ↓ The Smiths

A composite of radio sessions and sundry early singles, *Hatful Of Hollow* provides an alternative snapshot of the Smiths' early career. Compiled in the wake of their debut album, it exhibited all of their considerable strengths, in particular Johnny Marr's ringing, expressive guitarwork. The riff he creates on 'How Soon Is Now' is thoroughly captivating. Vocalist Morrissey's distinctive croon and solipsistic lyrics are already unique and give the group its originality. At times ironic, at others wistful (as on 'Back To The Old House'), he takes the Smiths into new areas of expression and his contrasting visions are fully expressed herein.

➤ Tracks: *William, It Was Really Nothing; What Difference Does It Make?; These Things Take Time; This Charming Man; How Soon Is Now?; Handsome Devil; Still Ill; Heaven Knows I'm Miserable Now; This Night Has Opened My Eyes; You've Got Everything Now; Accept Yourself; Girl Afraid; Back To The Old House; Reel Around The Fountain; Please, Please, Please Let Me Get What I Want.*

★ First released 1984
★ UK peak chart position: 2
★ USA peak chart position: did not chart
★ Previous Top 1000 position: 1998 (125): 1994 (577)

193 IN THE COURT OF THE CRIMSON KING ↑ King Crimson

One of the pioneering works of art-rock, and a musical and lyrical signpost for the pomposity of early 70s progressive rock music, *In The Court Of The Crimson King* is of lasting interest mainly thanks to the superb musicianship of Greg Lake, Ian McDonald and Michael Giles, and the wonderfully inventive guitarwork of the masterful Robert Fripp. Subtitled 'An Observation By King Crimson', the album flounders on Pete Sinfield's dreadful lyrics and the stilted dynamics of the multi-part arrangements. Anyone wishing to investigate the roots of Yes and Emerson, Lake and Palmer, however, should refer to this album. It's a lot better.

» Tracks: *21st Century Schizoid Man; I Talk To The Wind; Epitaph; Moonchild; The Court Of The Crimson King.*

★ First Released 1969
★ UK peak chart position: 5 ★ USA peak chart position: 28
★ Previous Top 1000 position: 1998 (285): 1994 (–)

194 SANDINISTA! ↑ The Clash

Sprawling, self-important, yet strangely compelling, *Sandinista!* remains the most ambitious work by the group that deemed itself 'the only band that matters'. Although its broad scope left them open to criticisms of a lack of musical direction, no one could accuse them of having lost their political conviction. They made an agreement with their label, CBS Records, that they would relinquish their royalties on the first 200,000 copies sold if the label would release the triple album at the price of a double. Tackling a wide range of issues, from racism and unemployment to Cold War paranoia, the album's 36 songs include Clash classics such as 'Washington Bullets', 'The Magnificent Seven', and a witty remake of the Equals' 'Police On My Back'.

» Tracks: *The Magnificent Seven; Hitsville U.K.; Junco Partner; Ivan Meets G.I. Joe; The Leader; Something About England; Rebel Waltz; Look Here; The Crooked Beat; Somebody Got Murdered; One More Time; One More Dub; Lightning Strikes (Not Once But Twice); Up In Heaven (Not Only Here); Corner Soul; Let's Go Crazy; If Music Could Talk; The Sound Of The Sinners; Police On My Back; Midnight Log; The Equaliser; The Call Up; Washington Bullets; Broadway; Lose This Skin; Charlie Don't Surf; Mensforth Hill; Junkie Slip; Kingston Advice; The Street Parade; Version City; Living In Fame; Silicone On Sapphire; Version Pardner; Career Opportunities; Shepherds Delight.*

★ First released 1980
★ UK peak chart position: 19 ★ USA peak chart position: 24
★ Previous Top 1000 position: 1998 (277): 1994 (–)

195 ON THE BEACH ↑ Neil Young

Still no appearance of this album on CD, but it cannot be ignored because of Young's stubbornness. Sometimes the artist should be overruled. We don't care that Neil Young is unhappy with it, his public want it out and it is unfair to continue to deprive them. That said, this is one of Young's finest works, melodic, intense yet light, played exquisitely. Everything that some suggest *Harvest* lacks is present on this record. Young devotees read more into this album than the dark *Tonight's The Night*, such as the spectre of Charles Manson in 'Revolution Blues'. The real clincher is the autobiographical title track, with the simplistically powerful line 'the world is turning, I hope it don't turn away'.

» Tracks: *Walk On; See The Sky About To Rain; Revolution Blues; For The Turnstiles; Vampire Blues; On The Beach; Motion Pictures; Ambulance Blues.*

★ First released 1974
★ UK peak chart position: 42
★ USA peak chart position: 16
★ Previous Top 1000 position: 1998 (361): 1994 (–)

196 CHECK YOUR HEAD ↑ Beastie Boys

The Beastie Boys are the leading white rap act of their generation and it is inconceivable to think that they could be toppled from the podium unless they gave up tomorrow. Like so much of their output this is instant attention grabbing stuff. After their exciting and mildly dangerous debut and a highly original and influential follow-up, the trio returned to their thrash roots on this album, mixing the hip-hop beats with traditional instruments such as guitars and congas. I defy anybody not to love this, one of five essential Beastie Boys albums for your collection, even if they have problems admitting it. Check your head around 'Pass The Mic', the Santana-influenced 'Lighten Up', and see if you can spot the intro for Doris Day's rap classic from *Calamity Jane*, 'The Deadwood Stage'.

» Tracks: *Jimmy James; Funky Boss; Pass The Mic; Gratitude; Lighten Up; Finger Lickin' Good; So What'cha Want; The Biz-vs-The Nuge; Time For Livin'; Something's Got To Give; The Blue Nun; Stand Together; Pow!; The Maestro; Groove Holmes; Live At P.J.'s; Mark On The Bus; Professor Booty; In 3's; Namaste.*

★ First released 1992
★ UK peak chart position: did not chart
★ USA peak chart position: 10
★ Previous Top 1000 position: 1998 (–): 1994 (–)

197 YOUNGER THAN YESTERDAY ↓
The Byrds

With this album the Byrds proclaimed fully their musical genius. Distinctive three-part harmonies and chiming 12-string guitars affirmed the quartet's unique sound as a succession of superior compositions embraced folk, pop and country styles. Beguiling melodies nestled alongside experiment as the principals asserted an individuality while remaining aware of the strength of the whole. The acerbic wit of 'So You Wanna Be A Rock 'n' Roll Star' showed a group aware of commercial entrapment. On this set they rejected such advances and offered a beautiful altruism. Every individual song on this set has managed to grow in stature, especially those by David Crosby and Chris Hillman. Majestic and inventive.

» Tracks: *So You Want To Be A Rock 'N' Roll Star; Have You Seen Her Face; CTA-102; Renaissance Fair; Time Between; Everybody's Been Burned; Thoughts and Words; Mind Gardens; My Back Pages; The Girl With No Name; Why.*

★ First released 1967
★ UK peak chart position: 37
★ USA peak chart position: 24
★ Previous Top 1000 position: 1998 (95): 1994 (148)

198 DOOKIE ↑
Green Day

Green Day took all the good elements of grunge and mixed them with a fine blend of 70s power pop. That way, they managed to appeal to a wide range of listeners and it probably goes a long way to explain why they sell a damn sight more records than the Pleasers, the Shoes, Flamin' Groovies, Jane's Addiction and Sebadoh put together. *Dookie* has sold 10 million copies in their homeland, and probably half that again worldwide. Essentially they are a very good pop punkster band with catchy songs and some adrenalin-rush middle-eights. And 'Basket Case' is such a great burst of nonsense.

» Tracks: *Burnout; Having A Blast; Chump; Long View; Welcome To Paradise; Pulling Teeth; Basket Case; She; Sassafras Roots; When I Come Around; Coming Clean; Emenius Sleepus; In The End; F.O.D.*

★ First released 1994
★ UK peak chart position: 13
★ USA peak chart position: 2
★ Previous Top 1000 position: 1998 (708): 1994 (-)

199 EVERYTHING MUST GO ↓
Manic Street Preachers

The cathartic album title perfectly reflected not only its contents but the band itself: following the traumatic breakdown and disappearance of Richey Edwards, the other Manics were left to pick up the pieces – it was an extraordinary and unexpected recovery. Perhaps most striking was their new sober image – the make-up, military garb and much of the bravado were gone – and their characteristic disaffection seemed more pertinent and controlled. Despite losing a member, the Manic Street Preachers had discovered a new voice, delivering a collection of powerful and socially aware songs. Poignantly, Edwards' lyrics graced songs including 'Kevin Carter' and 'Small Black Flowers . . . ', all delivered in James Dean Bradfield's emotional tones.

» Tracks: *Elvis Impersonator: Blackpool Pier; Design For Life; Kevin Carter; Enola/Alone; Everything Must Go; Small Black Flowers That Grow In The Sky; Girl Who Wanted To Be God; Removables; Australia; Interiors (Song For Willem De Kooning); Further Away; No Surface All Feeling.*

★ First released 1996
★ UK peak position: 2
★ USA peak position: did not chart
★ Previous Top 1000 position: 1998 (41): 1994 (-)

200 FUMBLING TOWARDS ECSTASY ↑   Sarah McLachlan

Despite the hokey synthesized drumbeats that dot such tracks as 'Mary', *Fumbling Towards Ecstasy* confirmed Sarah McLachlan's status as an heir to the tradition of Canadian bedsitter singer-songwriters that includes Gordon Lightfoot and Joni Mitchell. This third album brought her to her widest audience yet, most notably in America, where it spent over a year on the charts and went gold. Written during a period of deep introspection brought on by a harrowing charity trip to Cambodia and Thailand, most of the lyrics are laced with pain. However, the overall tone is that of a survivor, as in the title track, where she repeats over and over, 'I will not talk in class', 'I will not fear love.'

» Tracks: *Possession; Wait; Plenty; Good Enough; Mary; Elsewhere; Circle; Ice; Hold On; Ice Cream; Fear; Fumbling Towards Ecstasy.*

★ First released 1994
★ UK peak chart position: did not chart
★ USA peak chart position: 50
★ Previous Top 1000 position: 1998 (322): 1994 (-)

201 RAY OF LIGHT ↑
Madonna

What a treat for old prog hippie Dave Curtiss to suddenly find his fairly obscure song 'Sepheryn' had been demoed for Madonna to adapt and record as the title track of her new album. Curtiss rightly benefited from a financial windfall and Madonna benefited by reaping a major hit. None of this would have been possible without the quite superb production from the darling of the dance scene, William Orbit. He gave Madonna's career a much-needed shot in the arm and made many wish he had become involved with the singer earlier. Never has she sounded so funky and rich, and dare I say it, contented.

❱ Tracks: *Drowned World/Substitute For Love; Swim; Ray Of Light; Candy Perfume Girl; Skin; Nothing Really Matters; Sky Fits Heaven; Shanti/Ashtangi; Frozen; The Power Of Good-bye; To Have And Not To Hold; Little Star; Mer Girl.*

★ First released 1998
★ UK peak chart position: 1
★ USA peak chart position: 2
★ Previous Top 1000 position: 1998 (–): 1994 (–)

202 ABRAXAS ↑
Santana

Santana has received unprecedented success over the past year, with an inferior record. Their initial quartet of albums still sound incredibly alive and exciting. *Abraxas* is the best of the four, imbuing the Latin fusion of their debut with smooth edges of *Caravanserai*. The relaxed opening elegantly slips into 'Black Magic Woman', the finest interpretation of a Peter Green song. 'Se A Cabo', 'El Nicoya' and the memorable 'Oye Como Va' give us our quota of Latin rock. The album's star turn is the beautifully erotic 'Samba Pa Ti', which features a superb guitar solo that oozes the sexuality blatantly depicted by the Mati cover illustration.

❱ Tracks: *Singing Winds, Crying Beasts; Black Magic Woman/Gypsy Queen; Oye Como Va; Incident At Neshabur; Se A Cabo; Mother's Daughter; Samba Pa Ti; Hope You're Feeling Better; El Nicoya.*

★ First released 1970
★ UK peak chart position: 7
★ USA peak chart position: 1
★ Previous Top 1000 position: 1998 (286): 1994 (120)

203 JOHN WESLEY HARDING ↑
Bob Dylan

Dylan's eighth album followed a lengthy hibernation in which the singer re-evaluated his art. He emerged with a set of stark simplicity and heartfelt intensity. Neither folk, nor rock, nor country, the selection boasts elements of all three, slipping into consciousness with a mesmerizing power belying its setting. A biblical purity encompasses the collection as Dylan paints graphic portraits of the disenfranchised – hobo, immigrant, drifter, messenger – articulating the uncertainty of the times. The mood lifts for the final track, a beautifully tender love song, suggesting that this is where salvation lies. *John Wesley Harding* repays repeated play with ever-unfolding metaphor and interpretation, including four hidden Beatles on the cover.

❱ Tracks: *John Wesley Harding; As I Went Out One Morning; I Dreamed I Saw St. Augustine; All Along The Watchtower; The Ballad Of Frankie Lee And Judas Priest; Drifter's Escape; Dear Landlord; I Am A Lonesome Hobo; I Pity The Poor Immigrant; The Wicked Messenger; Down Along The Cove; I'll Be Your Baby Tonight.*

★ First released 1968
★ UK peak chart position: 1
★ USA peak chart position: 2
★ Previous Top 1000 position: 1998 (252): 1994 (170)

204 BEATLES FOR SALE ↑
Beatles

Released at the end of an exhausting 12 months, the fab four were a little jaded when they recorded this. Still, the genius comes through, with some classic Lennon/McCartney songs such as 'Eight Days A Week', 'Baby's in Black' and Lennon's early hint at the trough he was in with 'I'm A Loser'. When he sang 'although I laugh and I act like a clown, beneath this mask I am wearing a frown', he was not just being flippant. McCartney delivered the beautifully compact 'I'll Follow the Sun' and brilliantly belted out Leiber and Stoller's 'Kansas City'. Even when they were a little off colour, they were better than the rest.

❱ Tracks: *No Reply; I'm A Loser; Baby's In Black; Rock And Roll Music; I'll Follow The Sun; Mr Moonlight; Kansas City; Hey Hey Hey Hey; Eight Days A Week; Words Of Love; Honey Don't Every Little Thing; I Don't Want To Spoil The Party; What You're Doing; Everybody's Trying To Be My Baby.*

★ First released 1964
★ UK peak chart position: 1
★ USA peak chart position: did not chart
★ Previous Top 1000 position: 1998 (789): 1994 (–)

205 STRANGE DAYS ↑
The Doors

The Doors' second album redefined their uncompromising art. The disturbing timbre of Ray Manzarek's organ work provided the musical cloak through which guitarist Robbie Kreiger and vocalist Jim Morrison projected. Few singers in rock possessed his authority, where every nuance and inflection bore an emotional intensity. *Strange Days* contains some of the quartet's finest work, from the apocalyptic vision of 'When The Music's Over' to the memorable quirkiness of 'People Are Strange' and 'Moonlight Drive'. The graphic 'Horse Latitudes', meanwhile, confirmed Morrison's wish to be viewed as a poet, a stance ensuring the Doors were always seen as more than just another rock band.

» Tracks: *Strange Days; You're Lost Little Girl; Love Me Two Times; Unhappy Girl; Horse Latitudes; Moonlight Drive; People Are Strange; My Eyes Have Seen You; I Can't See Your Face In My Mind; When The Music's Over.*

★ First released 1967
★ UK peak chart position: did not chart
★ USA peak chart position: 3
★ Previous Top 1000 position: 1998 (321): 1994 (224)

206 RECKONING ↑
R.E.M.

The murmuring continued with this, R.E.M.'s second album, recorded in only two weeks, and yet critical acclaim and a growing fanbase had not made the music any less elusive. From the cover depiction of a winding river/snake, the jangly music within was similarly ambiguous, drenched in alternately murky, then dazzlingly clear, images. The water theme predominates throughout side one's five-song suite, with talk of harbours, oceans and water towers, crowned by the sublime lament of 'So. Central Rain'. Later, the melancholic eulogy of 'Camera' sits comfortably beside the cod-country of '(Don't Go Back To) Rockville' and the brisk but disillusioned tour around 'Little America'. An astonishingly assured and uncommercial half-sibling to *Murmur*: File under water.

» Tracks: *Harborcoat; 7 Chinese Brothers; So. Central Rain; Pretty Persuasion; Time After Time (Annelise); Second Guessing; Letter Never Sent; Camera; (Don't Go Back To) Rockville; Little America.*

★ First released 1984
★ UK peak chart position: 91
★ USA peak chart position: 27
★ Previous Top 1000 position: 1998 (728): 1994 (–)

207 CAN'T BUY A THRILL ↓
Steely Dan

Even the debut from Becker and Fagen put them stylistically a cut above the others. Played alongside the Doobie Brothers and the Eagles on smooth FM radio, Steely Dan were linked immediately to the west coast music scene, a fact that was utterly wrong. This was and is, an east coast album; it also assured, laid-back and layered with the jazz and soul influences that made their special kind of rock. Jeff 'Skunk' Baxter added the metal and David Palmer added pop vocal – but, from this sparkling debut we can clearly see Becker and Fagen in immaculate control. 'Do It Again', the long version, is, of course, a diamond.

» Tracks: *Do It Again; Dirty Work; Kings; Midnite Cruiser; Only A Fool Would Say That; Reelin' In The Years; Fire In The Hole; Brooklyn (Owes The Charmer Under Me); Change Of The Guard; Turn That Heartbeat Over Again.*

★ First released 1972
★ UK peak chart position: 38
★ USA peak chart position: 17
★ Previous Top 1000 position: 1998 (152): 1994 (169)

208 ENDTRODUCING... ↑
DJ Shadow

The record-shop browser pictured on the cover of *Endtroducing...* offered fairly accurate indication of the contents: an obsessive and pointillistic amalgam of influences, ranging from hip-hop, through dance and jazz, to classical. A dark and brooding record, this album has quickly and quietly become a low-key classic. Subtly enveloping a core of old school hip-hop with layer upon layer of obscure samples, jazz vibes and moody instrumental and choral themes, Josh Davis's multitextured album attracted lavish critical praise and popular attention, and seemed a world away from the feisty rock of the more commercial dance artists.

» Tracks: *Best Foot Forward; Building Steam With A Grain Of Salt; The Number Song; Changeling; What Does Your Soul Look Like (Part 4); Stem/Long Stem; Mutual Slump; Organ Donor; Why Hip-hop Sucks In '96; Midnight In A Perfect World; Napalm Brain/Scatter Brain; What Does Your Soul Look Like (Part 1 – Blue Sky Revisit).*

★ First released 1996
★ UK peak position: did not chart
★ USA peak position: did not chart
★ Previous Top 1000 position: 1998 (345): 1994 (–)

209 DUBNOBASSWITHMYHEADMAN
↑ Underworld

Romford, Essex is not exactly the most interesting place in England. The street market was its biggest claim to fame prior to the rise of Underworld. This is their third, and some argue their best album, an eclectic masterpiece which helped lay the groundwork for the following year's 'Born Slippy', the classic track that gained Underworld mass exposure after featuring prominently on the soundtrack to *Trainspotting*. Subtle ambient undertones underpin the moody, funky beats, demonstrating a subtlety alien to most of today's dance acts. What do lines such as 'dogdirty numbangel in the doorway she was lipstickbeautifultears and all in space' mean? Formulate your own answer, the music is good enough. Maybe Marc Bolan could have explained.

➤ Tracks: *Dark & Long; Mmm Skyscraper I Love You; Surfboy; Spoonman; Tongue; Dirty Epic; Cowgirl; River Of Bass; M.E.*

★ First released 1993
★ UK peak chart position: 12
★ USA peak chart position: did not chart
★ Previous Top 1000 position: 1998 (–): 1994 (–)

210 WEST SIDE STORY ↑
Various

Electrifying on stage and screen – and just as exciting in superb stereo on this sensational album featuring Natalie Wood, Richard Beymer, Rita Moreno, Russ Tamblyn and George Chakiris. The singing voices of the first three of those artists were dubbed at various times by Marni Nixon, Jim Bryant and Betty Wand, respectively, and they more than lived up to the challenge of Leonard Bernstein and Stephen Sondheim's dynamic and breathtaking score. The figures are staggering – USA: 144 weeks in the Top 40, 54 of them at number 1; UK: 175 weeks in the Top 20, including 13 at number 1. Plus a US Grammy for best soundtrack album.

➤ Tracks: *West Side Story – Prologue; Jet Song; Something's Coming; Dance At The Gym (Blues Promenade Jump); Maria; Tonight; America; Cool; One Hand, One Heart; Tonight; The Rumble; I Feel Pretty; Somewhere; Gee Officer Krupke; A Boy Like That; I Have A Love; West Side Story – Finale.*

★ First released 1962
★ UK peak chart position: 1
★ USA peak chart position: 1
★ Previous Top 1000 position: 1998 (251): 1994 (55)

211 PROTECTION ↑
Massive Attack

The follow-up to the hugely influential *Blue Lines* was a long time coming. Had they spliffed themselves into oblivion? Not a chance, this is the critics' favourite, and blends familiar grooves with the wonderfully compatible voice of Tracy Thorn on the title track. 'Karmacoma' is still a favourite feature of their live act, and both became hit singles. 'Weather Storm' errs into Dave Grusin style slick jazz, but is nonetheless irresistible. Similarly derivative, but another gem, is the Lee Perry-influenced 'Spying Glass'. Trip-hop belongs to Bristol, England and Massive Attack should always reign as the standard to judge all others by.

➤ Tracks: *Protection; Karmacoma; Three; Weather Storm; Spying Glass; Better Things; Eurochild; Sly; Heat Miser; Light My Fire (Live).*

★ First released 1994
★ UK peak chart position: 4
★ USA peak chart position: did not chart
★ Previous Top 1000 position: 1998 (–): 1994 (–)

212 MURMUR ↑
R.E.M.

R.E.M.'s debut was a brilliant, original master-piece, blending punk, garage and folk influences with their own inspired musical vision, and in the process creating a perplexing and organic whole. Michael Stipe's muffled, mumbled vocals were the focus of attention, seemingly consisting of phonetic approximations of words rather than actual lyrics (significantly, 'conversation fear' was the only audible lyric in '9-9'). Peter Buck's insistent Rickenbacker dominates the melodies, and the echoing vocal harmonies are precise throughout. Providing alternative radio anthems ('Radio Free Europe') as well as understated R.E.M. classics ('Perfect Circle'), this remains one of the band's best albums, and one of the sharpest indie debuts in popular music history.

➤ Tracks: *Radio Free Europe; Pilgrimage; Laughing; Talk About The Passion; Moral Kiosk; Perfect Circle; Catapult; Sitting Still; 9-9; Shaking Through; We Walk; West Of The Fields.*

★ First released 1983
★ UK peak chart position: did not chart
★ USA peak chart position: 36
★ Previous Top 1000 position: 1998 (280): 1994 (–)

213 URBAN HYMNS ↓
The Verve

Although the band imploded in 1998, their standing has been maintained through this collection. This was a triumph of belief over adversity, after they had already called it a day once before. Richard Ashcroft and Nick McCabe finally managed to focus their wayward talents into a coherent whole, creating a sweeping modern psychedelic masterpiece in the process. 'Bitter Sweet Symphony' and 'The Drugs Don't Work' also broke the band in the singles chart, with the former's creepingly insistent string motif becoming one of the most recognizable sounds on UK radio in 1997. If some of Ashcroft's subsequent grandiose claims for his band grated, there was no denying that his belief in his band had been spectacularly vindicated.

》 Tracks: *Bitter Sweet Symphony; Sonnet; The Rolling People; The Drugs Don't Work; Catching The Butterfly; Neon Wilderness; Space And Time; Weeping Willow; Lucky Man; One Day; This Time; Velvet Morning; Come On.*

★ First released 1997
★ UK peak chart position: 1
★ USA peak chart position: 23
★ Previous Top 1000 position: 1998 (45): 1994 (–)

214 STATION TO STATION ↑
David Bowie

Earmarking a more experimental phase *Station To Station* provided a more angular take on dance rhythms (most obvious on this album through the sublime funk bass of George Murray). Preference herein was for a more chilly, alienated dynamic, percolated through Bowie's heavily stylised vocals and increased use of electronica. The title-track takes over three minutes to announce 'the return of the Thin White Duke', its initial minimalism eventually crystallising into high-camp rock splendour. Over 10 minutes long, it is an intimidating introduction to what has often been perceived as Bowie's most bemusing work. 'Golden Years' is more yielding and easier on the ear. 'TVC15' betrays a rockier edge, leaving the aching beauty of 'Wild Is The Wind' to finally steal the show.

》 Tracks: *Station To Station; Golden Years; Word On A Wing; TVC15; Stay; Wild Is The Wind; Word On A Wing (Live); Stay (Live).*

★ First released 1976
★ UK peak chart position: 5
★ USA peak chart position: 3
★ Previous Top 1000 position: 1998 (305): 1994 (–)

215 ROXY MUSIC ↑
Roxy Music

Totally original and a breath of bizarre air when released in 1972, it put the Bryan Ferry and Brian Eno at the forefront of the art-rock movement. Why Roxy are not held in higher esteem by masses is beyond explanation. The sheer style of the band gave rock music a powerful, brilliant injection after years of meandering British prog and American west coast lethargy. From the opening bars of 'Re-Make/Re-Model', and the bitter end of 'Bitters End', the album enthrals and holds the listener. You can almost believe that Ferry is sincere when he states, 'I would climb mountains, walk a thousand miles and put roses around our door'; almost, but not quite.

》 Tracks: *Bitters End; The Bob (Medley); Chance Meeting; If There Is Something; Ladytron; Re-Make/Re-Model; 2HB; Would You Believe?; Sea Breezes.*

★ First released 1972
★ UK peak chart position: 10
★ USA peak chart position: did not chart
★ Previous Top 1000 position: 1998 (283): 1994 (96)

216 DIFFERENT CLASS ↓
Pulp

Jarvis Cocker's lyrical masterpiece propelled Pulp into the major league of British pop music. In 12 breathtakingly melodic pop songs, Cocker expressed his fascination for modern Britain and its social and sexual mores, exposing the banalities of life through lyrics that flow as easily as conversation. The album's centrepiece, 'I Spy', features a malevolent, breathy Jarvis in a moment of high melodrama, spitting out the classic 'take your *Year In Provence* and shove it up your ass'. Elsewhere, there are delights in the pure pop of 'Common People' and 'Disco 2000', the touchingly simple 'Something Changed', and the wrenching pathos of 'Live Bed Show' ('something beautiful left town and she never even knew its name').

》 Tracks: *Mis-Shapes; Pencil Skirt; Common People; I Spy; Disco 2000; Live Bed Show; Something Changed; Sorted For E's & Wizz; F.E.E.L.I.N.G.C.A.L.L.E.D.L.O.V.E; Underwear; Monday Morning; Bar Italia.*

★ First released 1995
★ UK peak chart position: 1
★ USA peak chart position: did not chart
★ Previous Top 1000 position: 1998 (42): 1994 (–)

217 THE HISSING OF SUMMER LAWNS ↑ Joni Mitchell

A continuing move towards jazz was the most striking element of this record when first released. Larry Carlton and Robben Ford became the two names to bandy around in order to appear cool. Indeed, their guitar playing throughout is superlative. The real strength, however, is the way in which Joni Mitchell reached new plateaux with graceful ease. The remarkable 'The Jungle Line' features the drums of Burundi and must be played loud to fully appreciate its *avant garde* quality. The opening line, 'Rousseau walk on trumpet paths', has the listener reaching for the *Dictionary Of Art*. As understated and lyrically deep as anything she has recorded, it is a stunning piece of work.

▶ Tracks: *In France They Kiss On Main Street; The Jungle Line; Edith And The Kingpin; Don't Interrupt The Sorrow; Shades Of Scarlett Conquering; The Hissing Of Summer Lawns; The Boho Dance; Harry's House/Centerpiece; Sweet Bird; Shadows And Light.*

★ First released 1975
★ UK peak chart position: 14
★ USA peak chart position: 4
★ Previous Top 1000 position: 1998 (289): 1994 (–)

218 HEAVEN OR LAS VEGAS ↑ Cocteau Twins

A band who have had to endure the term 'ethereal' being bandied about around their name more than any other. With their soulful and quite blissful meanderings, their music has a sustainable beauty free of regard for contemporaries or peers. *Heaven Or Las Vegas* saw vocalist Elizabeth Fraser substituting the occasional obscure lyric in place of her uniquely visionary wall of sound, and the single, 'Ice Blink Luck', even had a near-recognizable structure and a very tempting hook. Their unearthly wealth of ideas remains undiminished even though Fraser has suffered greatly from problems with her voice in recent years.

▶ Tracks: *Cherry-coloured Funk; Pitch The Baby; Ice Blink Luck; Fifty-fifty Clown; Heaven Or Las Vegas; I Wear Your Ring; Fotzepolitic; Wolf In The Breast; River, Road And Rail; Frou-frou Foxes In Midsummer Fires.*

★ First released 1990
★ UK peak chart position: 7
★ USA peak chart position: 99
★ Previous Top 1000 position: 1998 (640): 1994 (582)

219 BROTHERS IN ARMS ↓ Dire Straits

The album many critics hate to love. Mark Knopfler's multi-million-seller was one of the success stories of the 80s in the same way that Pink Floyd's *Dark Side Of The Moon* was in the 70s. Those who doubt its greatness argue that it was not a patch on the debut album, *Love Over Gold* or even *Making Movies*. The public clearly disagreed. The dangerously overrated and overplayed 'Money For Nothing' and turgid 'Walk Of Life' were perfect songs for 80s mainstream formatted rock radio. Yet it was the undeniable beauty of Knopfler's playing on tracks such as 'Brothers In Arms' that give some credence to its phenomenal success.

▶ Tracks: *So Far Away; Money For Nothing; Walk Of Life; Your Latest Trick; Why Worry?; Ride Across The River; The Man's Too Strong; One World; Brothers In Arms.*

★ First released 1985
★ UK peak chart position: 1
★ USA peak chart position: 1
★ Previous Top 1000 position: 1998 (89): 1994 (68)

220 SUEDE ↓ Suede

Suede played intellectual high jinks with this, their debut album, employing provocative lyrics, a weighty, unknowing sexuality and the pointed angst of troubled teenagers the world over. The clever lure of their androgynous artwork combined tellingly with Brett Anderson's teasing flamboyance and dedicated (some might say studied) David Bowie air. However, they would have remained a one trick pony were it not for their stirring ability to put together some unashamedly great singles and adapt a host of subtle mood swings and arrangements that took Anderson's vocals to soaring new heights. Another bedsitter classic for indie lovers.

▶ Tracks: *So Young; Animal Nitrate; She's Not Dead; Moving; Pantomime Horse; The Drowners; Sleeping Pills; Breakdown; Metal Mickey; Animal Lover; The Next Life.*

★ First released 1992
★ UK peak chart position: 1
★ USA peak chart position: did not chart
★ Previous Top 1000 position: 1998 (96): 1994 (228)

221 TOUCH ↑
Eurythmics

This came at the end of 1983, a particularly prolific period for Stewart and Lennox – they had already spent most of the year in the chart with *Sweet Dreams*. This album shows less reliance on programmed instrumentation and a less 'Germanic' feel to the production. 'The First Cut' and 'Right By Your Side' indicate a loosening up and a more rootsy approach as Annie Lennox discovers she has a great R&B/soul voice. 'Here Comes The Rain Again' and 'Who's That Girl?' exemplify the more familiar haunting Eurythmics sound. Now that they are back together again and this album should find favour as they attract a new audience.

➤➤ Tracks: *Here Comes The Rain Again; Regrets; Right By Your Side; Cool Blue; Who's That Girl?; The First Cut; Aqua; No Fear, No Hate, No Pain (No Broken Hearts); Paint A Rumour.*

★ First released 1983
★ UK peak chart position: 1
★ USA peak chart position: 7
★ Previous Top 1000 position: 1998 (504): 1994 (226)

222 THE ORB'S ADVENTURES BEYOND THE ULTRAWORLD
↑ The Orb

The Orb lent new-found credibility to the concept album with the release of this impressively long debut in 1991. Having already pioneered ambient house music with the initial release of 'A Huge Ever Growing Pulsating Brain That Rules From The Centre Of The Ultraworld', Alex Patterson and his assorted collaborators constructed a whole double album's worth of blissed-out ambience that found favour with both the dance and rock communities. Based around the concept of a voyage to dimensions beyond normal consciousness, *Adventures Beyond The Ultraworld* was an almost perfect record for its time, providing an aural snapshot of acid house culture at its fleeting peak.

➤➤ Tracks: *Little Fluffy Clouds; Earth (Gaia); Supernova At The End Of The Universe; Back Side Of The Moon; Spanish Castles In Space; Perpetual Dawn; Into The Fourth Dimension; Outlands; Star 6 & 7 8 9; A Huge Ever Growing Pulsating Brain That Rules From The Centre Of The Ultraworld: Live Mix Mk 10.*

★ First released 1991
★ UK peak chart position: 29
★ USA peak chart position: did not chart
★ Previous Top 1000 position: 1998 (331): 1994 (–)

223 VIVA HATE ↑
Morrissey

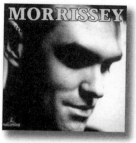

When internal strife killed off the Smiths, attention focused on ex-lead singer Morrissey. His response was a self-assured debut album in which echoes of his former group, notably on 'Suedehead', largely gave way to softer, orchestrated material. Aided by Durutti Column guitarist Vini Reilly and sometime Smiths producer Stephen Street, Morrissey crooned in now-accustomed fashion, toying with melody lines and articulating high-camp angst for a wan generation. The ambition of 'Late Night, Maudlin Street' is balanced by the crispness of 'Everyday Is Like Sunday' and for those worried that Morrissey would flounder without Smiths foil Johnny Marr, *Viva Hate* is a singularly confident riposte

➤➤ Tracks: *Alsatian Cousin; Little Man, What Now?; Everyday Is Like Sunday; Bengali In Platforms; Angel, Angel, Down We Go Together; Late Night, Maudlin Street; Suedehead; Break Up The Family; The Ordinary Boys; I Don't Mind If You Forget Me; Dial A Cliché; Margaret On The Guillotine.*

★ First released 1988
★ UK peak chart position: 1 ★ USA peak chart position: 48
★ Previous Top 1000 position: 1998 (723): 1994 (267)

224 ALL EYEZ ON ME ↑
2Pac

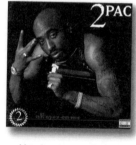

Having read the life story you can appreciate this man's work from a different perspective. He was no angel, that much is clear, but by isolating the music from the personal problems that led to his early death you become aware that you are listening to the work of a genius. His rapping was the best, his timing was the best, and his rhyming was the best. This sprawling double set is one of the most important albums in the troubled history of rap music. 'How many brothers fell victims to the street, rest in peace' he observes in 'Life Goes On' over the most evocative of melodies. 2Pac is to rap what Jimi Hendrix was to the electric guitar.

➤➤ Tracks: *Ambitionz Az A Ridah; All Bout U; Skandalouz; Got My Mind Made Up; How Do U Want It; 2 Of Amerikaz Most Wanted; No More Pain; Heartz Of Men; Life Goes On; Only God Can Judge Me; Tradin War Stories; California Love; I Ain't Mad At Cha; What'z Ya Phone #; Can't C Me; Shorty Wanna Be A Thug; Holla At Me; Wonda Why They Call U; When We Ride; Thug Passion; Picture Me Rollin'; Check Out Time; Ratha Be Ya; All Eyez On Me; Run Tha Streetz; Ain't Hard 2 Find; Heaven Ain't Hard 2 Find.*

★ First released 1996
★ UK peak chart position: 32 ★ USA peak chart position: 1
★ Previous Top 1000 position: 1998 (–): 1994 (–)

225 NOTHING'S SHOCKING ↑
Jane's Addiction

The instrumental track that opens the album reminds the listener of Randy California and his Spirit. Everything changes from then on; the lightness of Spirit gives way to harder stuff, much closer to Blue Cheer. Musically, it is easy to understand why the band were strongly tipped for great things; lyrically, there are some strange ramblings. 'Standing In The Shower' is a nice concept, but tells us nothing, and it is hard to agree with the paradox of 'Ted, Just Admit It' and just why 'sex is violent'. Maybe the art of enjoyment is to let the music wash over you at a high volume, because these chappies could certainly play.

» Tracks: *Up The Beach; Ocean Size; Had A Dad; Ted, Just Admit It; Standing In The Shower; Thinking; Summertime Rolls; Mountain Song; Idiot's Rule; Jane Says; Thank You Boys; Pigs In Zen.*

★ First released 1988
★ UK peak chart position: did not chart
★ USA peak chart position: 103
★ Previous Top 1000 position: 1998 (369): 1994 (–)

226 RAGE AGAINST THE MACHINE ↑ Rage Against The Machine

It is easy to be sniffy about west coast rock's political pretensions, but Rage Against The Machine are nothing if not sincere (from cover artwork through to personal activism). Their 1992 debut album also demonstrated an awareness of the inherent contradictions of their existence, which few of their many critics have ever acknowledged. The music lifts elements from hip-hop and funk, but the spinal column is Tom Moreno's full-blooded chord work, which locates the group firmly within the metal pantheon. And if some of Zack de la Rocha's more cerebral moments are lost between the bluster, that's a trade-off with which RATM seem happy.

» Tracks: *Bombtrack; Killing In The Name; Take The Power Back; Settle For Nothing; Bullet In The Head; Know Your Enemy; Wake Up; Fistful Of Steel; Township Rebellion; Freedom.*

★ First released 1993
★ UK peak chart position: 17
★ USA peak chart position: 45
★ Previous Top 1000 position: 1998 (984): 1994 (–)

227 REMAIN IN LIGHT ↑
Talking Heads

Led by the animated David Byrne and held together musically by a mathematically precise rhythm section of Tina Weymouth (bass) and Chris Frantz (drums), Talking Heads articulated America's post-60s cultural malaise. *Remain In Light*, their fourth album, consolidated a relationship with composer/producer Brian Eno, adding horns and guest performers to their intellectually based music. Compositions and styles are deconstructed then reassembled afresh, no more so than on the exquisite 'Once In A Lifetime', which suggests a pan-international sound without expressing it aurally. Post-modern alienation was never so danceable.

» Tracks: *Born Under Punches (The Heat Goes On); Crosseyed And Painless; The Great Curve; Once In A Lifetime; Houses In Motion; Seen And Not Seen; Listening Wind; The Overload.*

★ First released 1980
★ UK peak chart position: 21
★ USA peak chart position: 19
★ Previous Top 1000 position: 1998 (261): 1994 (135)

228 SWEET BABY JAMES ↑
James Taylor

James Taylor had already 'seen and been' enough by the time this album was released, having survived drug addiction, broken relationships and mental institutions by the age of 19. There was much for the listener to relate to during those heady days and this album made him a star, a status from which he tried to recoil. Two tracks from this album have been performed at every Taylor gig for 25 years – the irritating encore 'Steamroller' and his greatest song, 'Fire And Rain', which tells the story of his first 20 years in just over three minutes. Headphone and beanbag-friendly; remember to sit on the beanbag not the headphones.

» Tracks: *Sweet Baby James; Lo And Behold; Sunny Skies; Steamroller; Country Roads; Oh Susannah; Fire And Rain; Blossom; Anywhere Like Heaven; Oh Baby Don't You Lose Your Lip On Me; Suite For 20G.*

★ First released 1970
★ UK peak chart position: 7
★ USA peak chart position: 3
★ Previous Top 1000 position: 1998 (416): 1994 (280)

229 SWEETHEART OF THE RODEO ↑ The Byrds

Country music had always been an essential influence on the Byrds, but the decision to record an entire album in that style was controversial. Despite contemporary disquiet, *Sweetheart Of The Rodeo* has since become a landmark release, popularizing the notion of country rock. Traditional songs, standards, Bob Dylan compositions and original material were drawn together in a seamless whole, its continuity enhanced by crack Nashville session musicians. New group member Gram Parsons proved an adept catalyst; his departure soon after the album's release ensured it remained a one-off experiment. The Byrds moved elsewhere stylistically, but the influence of this recording remained immeasurable.

▶▶ Tracks: *You Ain't Goin' Nowhere; I Am A Pilgrim; The Christian Eye; You Don't Miss Your Water; You're Still On My Mind; Pretty Boy Floyd; Hickory Wind; One Hundred Years From Now; Blue Canadian Rockies; Life In Prison; Nothing Was Delivered.*

★ First released 1968
★ UK peak chart position: did not chart
★ USA peak chart position: 77
★ Previous Top 1000 position: 1998 (288): 1994 (832)

230 SURF'S UP ↓ The Beach Boys

This established the Beach Boys as an 'albums' band without sacrificing their individuality. The group's harmonies are as peerless as ever, their grasp of evocative melody unerring, particularly on Bruce Johnston's 'Disney Girls (1957)'. The ecological tenor of several tracks was politically shrewd and by opting to revive the title song from the unit's fabled *Smile* project, the Beach Boys reminded the outside world of their innovative past. Carl Wilson emerged as a fine composer ('Long Promised Road'), 'Till I Die' showed that Brian Wilson's gifts were just intact, and the result was an artistic triumph, enabling the group to progress unfettered by artistic preconceptions.

▶▶ Tracks: *Don't Go Near The Water; Long Promised Road; Take A Load Off Your Feet; Disney Girls (1957); Student Demonstration Time; Feel Flows; Lookin' At Tomorrow (A Welfare Song); A Day In The Life Of A Tree; 'Till I Die; Surf's Up.*

★ First released 1971
★ UK peak chart position: 15
★ USA peak chart position: 29
★ Previous Top 1000 position: 1998 (175): 1994 (179)

231 FABLES OF THE RECONSTRUCTION ↑ R.E.M.

Georgia's finest have been blessed in that they have retained both respect and affection throughout their lengthy career. This album is over 15 years old and although more recent recordings have eclipsed it in sales terms there really is little difference in the quality. It contains some superb songs including 'Feeling Gravity's Pull', the Gene Clark-tinged beauty 'Green Grow The Rushes', and the chiming 'Driver 8' and 'Auctioneer (Another Engine)'. This recording deserves a much higher profile outside of the R.E.M. cognoscenti. There is much to discover beyond *Automatic For The People* and *Out Of Time*, this album being a possible starting point.

▶▶ Tracks: *Feeling Gravitys Pull; Maps And Legends; Driver; Life And How To Live It; Old Man Kensey; Can't Get There From Here; Green Grow The Rushes; Kohoutek; Auctioneer (Another Engine); Good Advices; Wendell Gee.*

★ First released 1985
★ UK peak chart position: 35
★ USA peak chart position: 28
★ Previous Top 1000 position: 1998 (–): 1994 (–)

232 RAMONES ↓ The Ramones

Wuntoofreefore. Described alternately as minimalists or cartoon characters, the Ramones brought both elements to their métier. Drawing upon the undying appeal of simple 50s and 60s pop, the quartet reclaimed simplicity, adding to it a buzzsaw guitar and trash-culture values. Gore films, beach parties and solvent abuse are canonized in turn, but a sense of innocent self-deprecation prevents the charge of cheap sensationalism. Each track flirts around the two-minute watershed, the gaps between them barely discernible, the cumulative sense of fun and excitement as vital as ever. Over the years this formula has been acknowledged and loved and will continue to be passed down through recommendation. Wuntoofreefore.

▶▶ Tracks: *Blitzkrieg Bop; Beat On The Brat; Judy Is A Punk; I Wanna Be Your Boyfriend; Chain Saw; Now, I Wanna Sniff Some Glue; I Don't Wanna Go Down To The Basement; Loudmouth; Havana Affair; Listen To My Heart; Fifty Third And Third; Let's Dance; I Don't Wanna Walk Around With You; Today Your Love, Tomorrow The World.*

★ First released 1976
★ UK peak chart position: did not chart
★ USA peak chart position: 111
★ Previous Top 1000 position: 1998 (139): 1994 (340)

233 SOMETHING ELSE BY THE KINKS ↑ The Kinks

Often seen as the older-sister album to *The Village Green Preservation Society* and the one that saw the Kinks shift from being a raunchy beat combo to arty popsters. Ray Davies' notebook was bursting with observations of simple life and ordinary people at this particular time in his life. In addition to the monumental 'Waterloo Sunset', some of Davies' best songs are on this album. The recent remastered version is absolutely necessary, with the addition of eight tracks, including gems such as 'Act Nice And Gentle' and 'Autumn Almanac'. Dave Davies' excellent 'Susannah's Still Alive' is also included. These additions make an already perfect album just a bit more recommendable.

⟩⟩ Tracks: *David Watts; Death Of A Clown; Two Sisters; No Return; Harry Rag; Tin Soldier Man; Situation Vacant; Love Me Till The Sun Shines; Lazy Old Sun; Afternoon Tea; Funny Face; End Of The Season; Waterloo Sunset;* bonus Tracks: *Act Nice And Gentle; Autumn Almanac; Susannah's Still Alive; Wonderboy; Polly; Lincoln County; There's No Life Without Love; Lazy Old Sun (alternate).*

★ First released 1967
★ UK peak chart position: 35
★ USA peak chart position: 153
★ Previous Top 1000 position: 1998 (428): 1994 (–)

234 MECHANICAL ANIMALS ↑ Marilyn Manson

Underneath all the demonic bluster lurks a very fine rock album. Manson's antichrist persona connects in the same way as Bowie's glam alter ego Ziggy Stardust – even if you thought Ziggy was a pain in the neck you couldn't help liking his album a lot. Manson's words can be meaningful or meaningless depending on your attitude and age. Do drugs or don't do drugs, die or don't die, be from this planet or be an alien, be very weird or completely ignore the contrived weirdness. This should be of musical benefit to anyone with an open mind and a penchant for riff-heavy 70s glam rock.

⟩⟩ Tracks: *Great Big White World; The Dope Show; Mechanical Animals; Rock Is Dead; Disassociative; The Speed Of Pain; Posthuman; I Want To Disappear; I Don't Like The Drugs (But The Drugs Like Me); New Model No. 15; User Friendly; Fundamentally Loathsome; The Last Day On Earth; Coma White.*

★ First released 1998
★ UK peak chart position: 8
★ USA peak chart position: 1
★ Previous Top 1000 position: 1998 (–): 1994 (–)

235 OFF THE WALL ↓ Michael Jackson

The album that moved Jackson out of juvenile pop, even though the suit he wears on the cover belies his still tender years untouched by facial butchery. Is it really 20 years ago that, along with the Clash, Jackson was deemed OK? The Quincy Jones production was immaculate and totally sympathetic to the 90s sound. Virtually the whole album holds up, with a thumbs-down for 'Burn This Disco Down', but remember that this does contain the perfection of 'Rock With You', the angst of 'She's Out Of My Life', Paul McCartney's 'Girlfriend' and the abandon of 'Get On The Floor/Off The Wall'. Absolutely harmlessly brilliant and recommended to young children.

⟩⟩ Tracks: *Don't Stop 'Til You Get Enough; Rock With You; Working Day And Night; Get On The Floor/Off The Wall; Girlfriend; She's Out Of My Life; I Can't Help It; It's The Falling In Love; Burn This Disco Down.*

★ First released 1979
★ UK peak chart position: 5
★ USA peak chart position: 3
★ Previous Top 1000 position: 1998 (158): 1994 (92)

236 EVERY PICTURE TELLS A STORY ↓ Rod Stewart

Rod Stewart's third solo album brought the singer long-awaited commercial success. Its combination of strong, original songs and plum cover versions was finely judged as the artist paid tribute to mentors and declared his own craft. Members of Stewart's regular group, the Faces, provide intuitive support without the sense of compromise apparent on their own recordings. The singer's voice was rarely better; his interpretation of the Temptations' '(I Know I'm) Losing You' brought new dimensions to a Tamla/Motown Records classic. The highlight is, inevitably, 'Maggie May', one of the great pop anthems, but the remaining selections, such as 'Mandolin Wind' and Tim Hardin's beautiful 'Reason To Believe' contain a similar sense of purpose.

⟩⟩ Tracks: *Every Picture Tells A Story; Seems Like A Long Time; That's All Right; Tomorrow Is A Long Time; Maggie May; Mandolin Wind; (I Know I'm) Losing You; Reason To Believe.*

★ First released 1971
★ UK peak chart position: 1
★ USA peak chart position: 1
★ Previous Top 1000 position: 1998 (172): 1994 (320)

237 CROOKED RAIN, CROOKED RAIN ↑ Pavement

The wonderfully sloppy, distorted guitar on the opening track 'Silence Kid' provides an apt taster for this excellent album, on which Pavement's brand of lo-fi, rough edged alternative rock reached an early peak. There is method in the madness of Pavement's ramshackle sound, however. At times, such as on the highly commercial 'Cut Your Hair' and the chorus of 'Unfair', the playing and sound is worryingly slick. Fortunately the band stumbles back into magnificent disorder on 'Gold Soundz'. These are not the sort of chaps to tidy their bedrooms up after them, but you can't help liking them all the same.

>> Tracks: Silence Kid; Elevate Me Later (Ell Ess Two); Stop Breathin; Cut Your Hair; Newark Wilder; Unfair; Gold Soundz; 5-4 = Unity; Range Life; Heaven Is A Truck; Hit The Plane Down; Fillmore Jive.

★ First released 1994
★ UK peak chart position: 15
★ USA peak chart position: 121
★ Previous Top 1000 position: 1998 (–): 1994 (–)

238 L.A. WOMAN ↓ The Doors

The final Doors album to feature vocalist Jim Morrison reaffirmed the quartet's grasp of blues/rock. Beset by personal and professional problems, they retreated to a rehearsal room, cast such pressures aside and recorded several of their most memorable compositions. The musicianship is uniformly excellent, the interplay between guitarist Robbie Krieger and keyboard player Ray Manzarek exudes confidence and empathy, while the strength and nuances of Morrison's voice add an unmistakable resonance. His death within weeks of the album's completion inevitably casts a pall over its content, especially the eerie rain and the funereal electric piano of 'Riders On The Storm'.

>> Tracks: The Changeling; Love Her Madly; Been Down So Long; Cars Hiss By My Window; L.A. Woman; L'America; Hyacinth House; Crawling King Snake; The W.A.S.P. (Texas Radio And The Big Beat); Riders On The Storm.

★ First released 1971
★ UK peak chart position: 28
★ USA peak chart position: 9
★ Previous Top 1000 position: 1998 (177): 1994 (111)

239 1967-70 ↑ The Beatles

The famous red and blue double albums were finally released on CD in 1994 to a public outcry, with complaints that the price was too high. The record company argued that it was the high royalty negotiated with the artists that hiked up the price of a double CD. It made no difference whatsoever: both albums zoomed into the charts as everybody forked out over £20 for the pleasure of buying tracks they already owned in some other shape or form – such is the power of the greatest pop group that ever was and will ever be. No discussion of the tracks is necessary – they are already part of our national heritage, and should be sung in morning assembly in every school in every part of the world.

>> Tracks: Strawberry Fields Forever; Penny Lane; Sgt. Pepper's Lonely Hearts Club Band; With A Little Help From My Friends; Lucy In The Sky With Diamonds; A Day In The Life; All You Need Is Love; I Am The Walrus; Hello Goodbye; The Fool On The Hill; Magical Mystery Tour; Lady Madonna; Hey Jude; Revolution; Back In The USSR; While My Guitar Gently Weeps; Ob La Di Ob La Da; Get Back; Don't Let Me Down; Ballad Of John And Yoko; Old Brown Shoe; Here Comes The Sun; Come Together; Something; Octopus's Garden; Let It Be; Across The Universe; The Long And Winding Road.

★ First released 1973
★ UK peak chart position: 2 ★ USA peak chart position: 1
★ Previous Top 1000 position: 1998 (342): 1994 (77)

240 RUST NEVER SLEEPS ↓ Neil Young And Crazy Horse

Neil Young's lengthy recording career contains several landmark albums of which Rust Never Sleeps is one of the most vital. Half-acoustic, half-electric, it is bookended by contrasting versions of the same song which pays homage to Sex Pistols vocalist, Johnny Rotten. Long-time associates Crazy Horse support Young on the electric selections which exude white-noise power, marrying savage guitarwork with emphatic lyrics. The remaining selections offer a pastoral atmosphere. Part country, part folk, their gentle qualities invoke the atmosphere of Young's bestseller, Harvest. This was the record that placed Young on a hip pedestal by new wave the critics, a position ol' shakey has retained.

>> Tracks: My My, Hey Hey (Out Of The Blue); Thrasher; Ride My Llama; Pocahontas; Sail Away; Powder Finger; Welfare Mothers; Sedan Delivery; Hey Hey, My My (Into The Black).

★ First released 1979
★ UK peak chart position: 13
★ USA peak chart position: 8
★ Previous Top 1000 position: 1998 (189): 1994 (126)

241 INGÉNUE ↑
k.d. lang

Emerging from her ambivalent affair with country music, k.d. lang assembled a solid collection of material for this, her most commercially successful album. The opening lines: 'Save me/Save me from you/But pave me/The way to you', introduce a recurring theme – the agonizing conflict between the pain and the ecstasy of love. This is serious stuff; anthems of introspection and cries for honesty illuminated with startling imagery. There are lighter moments too, particularly in 'Miss Chatelaine', and the omnipresent Ben Mink ensures that the country influence is not totally abandoned. This will probably remain her best album, no matter how hard she tries.

➤ Tracks: *Save Me; The Mind Of Love; Miss Chatelaine; Wash Me Clean; So It Shall Be; Still Thrives This Love; Season Of Hollow Soul; Outside Myself; Tears Of Love Is Recall; Constant Craving.*

★ First released 1992
★ UK peak chart position: 3
★ USA peak chart position: 18
★ Previous Top 1000 position: 1998 (524): 1994 (360)

242 LIVE DEAD ↑
The Grateful Dead

As the archetypal west coast band, famed for lengthy improvisation, the Grateful Dead found it difficult to translate their in-concert fire onto record. The group addressed this dilemma by recording this partly live in the studio, allowing free rein for guitarist Jerry Garcia's liquid flights. The twin drumming of Mickey Hart and Bill Kreutzman provides an imaginative platform, bassist Phil Lesh takes his instrument into new dimensions, while organist Pigpen provides a distinctive swirling sound that envelops and enhances his colleagues' interplay. The last-named takes a vocal cameo on 'Turn On Your Lovelight', a performance showing the Dead's R&B roots, while 'Dark Star' exposes new levels of musical empathy. It ducks and dives and weaves, but keeps coming back to the root; Garcia's amazing fluidity.

➤ Tracks: *Dark Star; Death Don't Have No Mercy; Feedback; And We Bid You Goodnight; St. Stephen; Eleven; Turn On Your Lovelight.*

★ First released 1970
★ UK peak chart position: did not chart
★ USA peak chart position: 64
★ Previous Top 1000 position: 1998 (435): 1994 (700)

243 EXILE IN GUYVILLE ↓
Liz Phair

From Big Mama Thornton to Madonna, the sexually aggressive woman has always held a special fascination for pop fans. With *Exile In Guyville*, Liz Phair became the latest and by far the most foul-mouthed addition to the line. Her mission was to put a lacquered fingernail up the posterior of alternative rock's 'Guyville' establishment. Her model was the Rolling Stones' *Exile On Main Street* and its portrait of a lonely, nihilistic world. Phair's ingenuous voice, stripped-down arrangements, and catchy melodies made her sound like a female Jonathan Richman. However, it was her biting lyrics that drew the most attention, making *Exile In Guyville* one of the most critically acclaimed albums of 1993.

➤ Tracks: *Six Foot One; Help Me Mary; Glory; Dance Of The Seven Veils; Never Said; Soap Star Joe; Explain It To Me; Canary; Mesmerizing; Fuck And Run; Girls, Girls, Girls; Divorce Song; Shatter; Flatter; Flower; Johnny Sunshine; Gunshy; Stratford-On-Guy; Strange Loop.*

★ First released 1993
★ UK peak chart position: did not chart
★ USA peak chart position: 196
★ Previous Top 1000 position: 1998 (238): 1994 (–)

244 JOHN LENNON/PLASTIC ONO BAND ↓ John Lennon

Now referred to as the primal scream album, John Lennon allowed his tonsils and heart to bleed in a powerful exorcism of many of his demons. The plea for his lost mother in 'Mother' is as desperate as the realization expressed in 'I Found Out', with 'I've seen religion from Jesus to Paul'. His Yoko songs are also a reassurance that, throughout this therapy, his Yoko was always there, and history has shown that it was his Yoko that helped him make it through. 'Working Class Hero' is another equally powerful track, even though Lennon was not one. Essential listening for Beatles students with strong hearts and inquiring minds.

➤ Tracks: *Mother; Hold On; I Found Out; Working Class Hero; Isolation; Remember; Love; Well Well Well; Look At Me; God; My Mummy's Dead.*

★ First released 1970
★ UK peak chart position: 11
★ USA peak chart position: 10
★ Previous Top 1000 position: 1998 (146): 1994 (259)

245 SATURDAY NIGHT FEVER ↑
Various

The disco revival came in the mid-90s. White suits, gigantic shirt collars and trousers with such massive flares, the owners were in danger of flying off, were once again the order of the day. While this album's success and disco drove people mad as punk's greatest enemy in the late 70s, it is now seen as a great piece of musical history. The very high-voiced Bee Gees did write numerous meaningful songs on this, but there is further perfect disco soul from Yvonne Elliman ('If I Can't Have You'), Tavares and Kool And The Gang. This is one soundtrack that is better than the film.

» Tracks: *Stayin' Alive; How Deep Is Your Love; Night Fever; Jive Talkin'; You Should Be Dancing; More Than A Woman; Calypso Breakdown; If I Can't Have You; A Fifth Of Beethoven; Open Sesame; Boogie Shoes; MFSB; K. Jee; Disco Inferno; Manhattan Skyline; Night On Disco Mountain; Salsation.*

★ First released 1978
★ UK peak chart position: 1
★ USA peak chart position: 1
★ Previous Top 1000 position: 1998 (355): 1994 (293)

246 THE STRANGER ↑
Billy Joel

During the late 70s many bemoaned the fact that Billy Joel spent hours on our radios and years on the charts. UK comedian Alexei Sayle even used his name in vain on 'Hello John Got A New Motor'. Two of Joel's other albums, *An Innocent Man* and *52nd Street*, came close to greatness, but this monster of smooth AOR is the industry-standard Joel album that no comprehensive collection should be without. Layers of rich Fender Rhodes piano and crystal-clear vocals resulted in 16 million worldwide sales, even though Barry White recorded a better version of 'Just The Way You Are'.

» Tracks: *Movin' Out (Anthony's Song); The Stranger; Just The Way You Are; Scenes From An Italian Restaurant; Vienna; Only The Good Die Young; She's Always A Woman; Get It Right The First Time; Everybody Has A Dream.*

★ First released 1978
★ UK peak chart position: 25
★ USA peak chart position: 2
★ Previous Top 1000 position: 1998 (344): 1994 (79)

247 ZOOROPA ↓
U2

If you study the wild computer graphics on the sleeve you could be expecting something frantic and electric. In fact, this is the most relaxing U2 album to date, and one on which they sound content to cruise instead of sermonizing. Brian Eno's prescience no doubt added the ambient feel that is present on most of the tracks. Bono manages to sound like Roland Gift (Fine Young Cannibals) on 'Lemon', and The Edge like a monosyllabic Lou Reed on 'Numb'. U2 took risks with this album because it broke a familiar pattern by not sounding like a U2 record. They sailed through the audition.

» Tracks: *Zooropa; Babyface; Numb; Lemon; Stay (Faraway So Close); Daddy's Gonna Pay For Your Crashed Car; Some Days Are Better Than Others; The First Time; Dirty Day; The Wanderer.*

★ First released 1993
★ UK peak chart position: 1
★ USA peak chart position: 1
★ Previous Top 1000 position: 1998 (176): 1994 (–)

248 LIVE AT THE APOLLO VOL. 1
↓ James Brown

Superlatives abound when considering this seminal set. It has been called 'the greatest live album of all time' while James Brown's position as the Godfather of Soul is almost indisputable. The singer was largely unknown outside black music circles prior to the release of this million-seller which fully captured the power and intensity of Brown in concert. It contains the cream of his releases, each of which is injected with a passionate fervour. Brilliantly paced, the set grows in stature, as the famed Apollo audience responds to and, indeed, adds to the excitement. Brown towers majestically over the proceedings; pleading, extolling, proving himself the finest R&B singer of his generation. The actual recording is primitive, but still worth it for excitement.

» Tracks: *I'll Go Crazy; Try Me; Think; I Don't Mind; Lost Someone (Part 1); Lost Someone (Part 2); Please, Please, Please; You've Got The Power; I Found Someone; Why Do You Do Me Like You Do; I Want You So Bad; I Love You Yes I Do; Why Does Everything Happen To Me; Bewildered; Please Don't Go; Night Train.*

★ First released 1963
★ UK peak chart position: did not chart
★ USA peak chart position: 2
★ Previous Top 1000 position: 1998 (132): 1994 (36)

249 UNKNOWN PLEASURES ↓
Joy Division

Joy Division's music inhabits an eerie, twilight world. Decay and alienation envelop the late singer Ian Curtis, whose cavernous, but dispassionate, voice belied the intensity he brought to bear. Rolling drum patterns, thudding bass lines and uncluttered synthesizer combine to create a dank, brooding atmosphere, chillingly supporting the songs' bleak lyrics. Yet listening to *Unknown Pleasures* is not a depressing experience. The group generate a terse excitement, emphasizing individual strengths and avoiding unnecessary embellishment. Their sense of commitment is utterly convincing and few debut albums can boast such unremitting power.

» Tracks: *Disorder; Day Of The Lords; Candidate; Insight; New Dawn Fades; She's Lost Control; Shadow Play; Wilderness; Interzone; I Remember Nothing.*

★ First released 1979
★ UK peak chart position: 71
★ USA peak chart position: did not chart
★ Previous Top 1000 position: 1998 (111): 1994 (493)

250 PLACEBO ↓
Placebo

An interesting combination of a Swede, a Swiss and an American, meeting in Luxembourg and sounding very British, in a post-punk sort of way. The group were signed for a reputed large advance, partly owing to the marketable, androgynous Brian Molko. However, the quality of their songwriting was demonstrated on their excellent debut. 'Nancy Boy', a surprising hit single, is in fact one of the lesser tracks on the album. There is much more depth to be found in 'Bionic', 'Come Home' and 'I Know', the latter complete with didgeridoo. After such a sparkling debut the cynical jury is already out.

» Tracks: *Come Home; Teenage Angst; Bionic; 36 Degrees; Hang On To Your IQ; Nancy Boy; I Know; Bruise Pristine; Lady Of The Flowers; Swallow.*

★ First released 1996
★ UK peak chart position: 40
★ USA peak chart position: did not chart
★ Previous Top 1000 position: 1998 (154): 1994 (-)

251 ALL MOD CONS ↓
The Jam

Tagged punk by default, the Jam preferred 60s iconography, particularly the Mod movement, to the rattle of safety-pins. However, if the uniform was different, the sense of commitment was identical, and on *All Mod Cons*, the trio fused references and individuality. The spectres of the Who and the Kinks remained, but songwriter Paul Weller restructured such influences to proclaim his own voice. Thus, the cover version of 'David Watts' introduced a new edge to the original Ray Davies song. The entire album successfully explored several avenues postulated by the Jam's craft. Social comment, personal reflection and assured musicianship bind the collection into a cohesive whole and set down the contrasting areas of music Weller would follow.

» Tracks: *All Mod Cons; To Be Someone (Didn't We have A Nice Time); Mr. Clean; David Watts; English Rose; In The Crowd; Billy Hunt; It's Too Bad; Fly; The Place I Love; 'A' Bomb In Wardour Street; Down In The Tube Station At Midnight.*

★ First released 1978
★ UK peak chart position: 6
★ USA peak chart position: did not chart
★ Previous Top 1000 position: 1998 (109): 1994 (678)

252 HIS 'N' HERS ↓
Pulp

Pulp's breakthrough album arrived after an unbelievably long haul, and then Jarvis Cocker was suddenly sharing front pages of music magazines with Liam Gallagher and Damon Albarn. Here, the songs explored now-familiar Pulp territory, social class, seedy sexual encounters, voyeurism ('Babies'), bad sex ('you bought a toy that can reach the places he never goes'), good sex, and lots more sex, all blessed with Cocker's humorous, touching and, conversely, often innocent lyrical observations. Capable of writing almost unbearably tender love songs and laments for wasted lives ('your hair is a mess and your eyes are just holes in your face'), Cocker's honesty and insight were distilled to perfection in the wonderful 'Do You Remember The First Time?'.

» Tracks: *Joyriders; Lipgloss; Acrylic Afternoons; Have You Seen Her Lately?; Babies; She's A Lady; Happy Endings; Do You Remember The First Time?; Pink Glove; Someone Like The Moon; David's Last Summer.*

★ First released 1994
★ UK peak chart position: 9
★ USA peak chart position: did not chart
★ Previous Top 1000 position: 1998 (110): 1994 (-)

253 GREASE ↑
Various

Three of the first four tracks on this double album, 'Summer Nights', 'Hopelessly Devoted To You' and 'You're The One That I Want', all went on to become big hits in the USA and UK for the new disco sensation John Travolta and his co-star Olivia Newton-John. Frankie Valli also took the title song into the upper reaches of charts all over the world. As for this album, it lingered for 12 weeks at number 1 in America, and topped the British chart for a lucky 13. Even in the 90s several of these tracks are still guaranteed floor-fillers at many a party night, and once again it is showing at a cinema near you.

)) Tracks: *Grease; Summer Nights; Hopelessly Devoted To You; Sandy; Look At Me, I'm Sandra Dee; Greased Lightning; It's Raining On Prom Night; You're The One That I Want; Beauty School Dropout; Alone At The Drive In Movie; Blue Moon; Rock 'N' Roll Is Here To Stay; Those Magic Changes; Hound Dog; Born To Hand Jive; Tears On My Pillow; Mooning; Rock 'N' Roll Party Queen; Freddy My Love; There Are Worse Things I Could Do; Look At Me, I'm Sandra Dee (Reprise); We Go Together; Love Is A Many Splendoured Thing; Grease (Reprise).*

★ First released 1978
★ UK peak chart position: 1 ★ USA peak chart position: 1
★ Previous Top 1000 position: 1998 (862): 1994 (465)

254 LIEGE AND LIEF ↓
Fairport Convention

Where so much began. The advertisements ran: 'the first (literally) British folk rock LP ever.' It also represented a catharsis for the band, reconvening after a traumatic road accident that killed drummer Martin Lamble. Once again focused and with redoubtable folk fiddler Dave Swarbrick now permanently involved, they threw themselves into the electrification of ballads, myths and rollickin' jigs. The results were both innovative and stimulating. The union was blessed. If you sat down and tried to imagine a dream folk rock band, it still would not match the potential here. From the lusting pace of 'Matty Groves' to the tender cooing of 'Crazy Man Michael', Sandy Denny's voice is the perfect vehicle for this milestone. Imitated a thousand times, but never equalled.

)) Tracks: *Come All Ye; Reynardine; Matty Groves; Farewell Farewell; The Deserter; The Lark In The Morning; Tamlin; Crazy Man Michael; Rakish Paddy; Foxhunters Jigs; Toss The Feathers.*

★ First released 1970
★ UK peak chart position: 17
★ USA peak chart position: did not chart
★ Previous Top 1000 position: 1998 (149): 1994 (61)

255 MEDDLE ↑
Pink Floyd

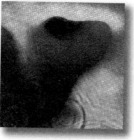

This famous 'inside the ear' cover is often put at the bottom of the Pink Floyd pile alongside the *More* album, in place of their many mega-selling others. *Meddle* is often remembered for the (admittedly impressive) 'Echoes', nearly 24 minutes of sweeping organ, building over clashing guitar. Equally good is the lilting 'A Pillow Of Winds', which is a delight, as is the easy-going 'Fearless', with some lovely chord changes. Roger Waters also sings well as the whole band sound relaxed and more together than at any stage in their turbulent career. *Meddle* deserves reappraisal as their most therapeutic and enjoyable album.

)) Tracks: *One Of These Days; A Pillow Of Winds; Fearless; San Tropez; Seamus; Echoes.*

★ First released 1971
★ UK peak chart position: 3
★ USA peak chart position: 70
★ Previous Top 1000 position: 1998 (260): 1994 (–)

256 KISS ME KISS ME KISS ME
↑ The Cure

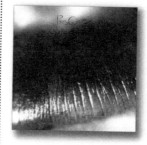

This hefty double album often sounds more like a compilation than a coherent whole, with musical ideas bouncing frantically back and forth. Nevertheless, in typical Cure style, *Kiss Me Kiss Me Kiss Me* successfully combined catchy pop with bitter despair. Through 17 immensely sensual songs, Robert Smith is at his most poetic ('strange as angels, dancing in the deepest ocean, twisting in the water, you're just like a dream') and vitriolic ('get your fucking voice out of my head . . . I never wanted any of this, I wish you were dead'). The joyous pop of 'Just Like Heaven' and 'The Perfect Girl' still delights, and the frisson provided by 'Shiver And Shake' reinforces the physical nature of this collection.

)) Tracks: *The Kiss; Catch; Torture; If Only Tonight We Could Sleep; Why Can't I Be You?; How Beautiful You Are; The Snakepit; Just Like Heaven; All I Want; Hot Hot Hot!!!; One More Time; Like Cockatoos; Icing Sugar; The Perfect Girl; A Thousand Hours; Shiver And Shake; Fight.*

★ First released 1987
★ UK peak chart position: 6
★ USA peak chart position: 35
★ Previous Top 1000 position: 1998 (615): 1994 (–)

257 SUPERUNKNOWN ↑
Soundgarden

Although the world has overdosed on negative 'feel my pain' and suicide lyrics, there is such a quality to the work of bands like Soundgarden it remains addictive. The overall sound and thick quality to *Superunknown* is rich beyond belief. It is possible merely to listen to the music and skip the lyrics, especially if it is a sunny happy day. Chris Cornell may have some internal demons and addictions from which to recover, but this has never clouded his ability to write some excellent music. Of course, if you are suicidal you might like to listen to this and contemplate living, just so that you can play it again and again.

» Tracks: *Let Me Drown; My Wave; Fell On Black Days; Mailman; Superunknown; Head Down; Black Hole Sun; Spoonman; Limo Wreck; The Day I Tried To Live; Kickstand; Fresh Tendrils; 4th Of July; Half; Like Suicide; She Likes Surprises.*

★ First released 1994
★ UK peak chart position: 4
★ USA peak chart position: 1
★ Previous Top 1000 position: 1998 (603): 1994 (–)

258 STARS ↓
Simply Red

Mick Hucknall is one of the most prodigious talents in the music business; anyone who disputes this statement need only listen without prejudice to *Stars*. His voice has a range, sensitivity and accuracy that puts others to shame, and enables him to journey between soul, hip-hop and jazz with alacrity. As if that were not enough, he has an almost Mozartian ability to compose melodies woven from the very essence of music. On *Stars* he left behind much of the narcissism of previous albums, gave the band high-quality material to develop and produced an enduring classic.

» Tracks: *Something Got Me Started; Stars; Thrill Me; Your Mirror; She's Got It Bad; For Your Babies; Model; Freedom; How Could I Fall; Wonderland.*

★ First released 1991
★ UK peak chart position: 1
★ USA peak chart position: 76
★ Previous Top 1000 position: 1998 (167): 1994 (50)

259 LADY SOUL ↓
Aretha Franklin

Aretha Franklin's position as soul music's premier female vocalist was consolidated by this album. Her strident reading of Don Covay's 'Chain Of Fools' set the tone for a collection on which the singer unveiled several stellar original compositions and reinterpreted a batch of classic songs. Franklin's gospel roots were clearly displayed on the anthem-like 'People Get Ready' while her interpretation of 'Natural Woman' showed both vulnerable and assertive qualities. *Lady Soul* captures a performer at the peak of her power, restating her ability to take material and make it uniquely her own. She still is the greatest female singer in the world.

» Tracks: *Chain Of Fools; Money Won't Change You; People Get Ready; Niki Hoeky; (You Make Me Feel Like) A Natural Woman; Since You've Been Gone (Sweet Sweet Baby); Good To Me As I Am To You; Come Back Baby; Groovin'; Ain't No Way.*

★ First released 1968
★ UK peak chart position: 25
★ USA peak chart position: 2
★ Previous Top 1000 position: 1998 (183): 1994 (85)

260 PYROMANIA ↑
Def Leppard

The album that elevated Def Leppard to their now familiar superstar status. The combination of Mutt Lange's lush vocal arrangements and Def Leppard's hard-bitten, riffing approach to their music, gave them an endearing and instantly accessible formula of sometimes furious rock/pop, best typified by the excellent 'Photograph' and the enigmatic 'Comin' Under Fire'. Vocalist Joe Elliot's lyricism was also developing, with the thematic Vietnam War backdrop for 'Die Hard The Hunter' and the effect on its veterans in 'Billy's Got A Gun' hinting at the band's burgeoning songwriting maturity. They were able to build on this with succeeding albums, and are now the UK's Metallica (i.e. very popular).

» Tracks: *Rock Rock ('Til You Drop); Photograph; Stagefright; Too Late For Love; Die Hard The Hunter; Foolin'; Rock Of Ages; Comin' Under Fire; Action Not Words; Billy's Got A Gun.*

★ First released 1983
★ UK peak chart position: 18
★ USA peak chart position: 2
★ Previous Top 1000 position: 1998 (578): 1994 (439)

261 MINGUS AH UM ↑
Charles Mingus

One of the six essential Charles Mingus albums to own, and even if you are not a jazz fan this is still worthy of being in any comprehensive collection. The opening track, 'Better Git It In Your Soul', rushes along at a furious pace and then there is a wonderful change of tempo into an *a cappella* and handclap pause. It rolls on, of course, but the nature of this track reflects the nature of Mingus who never failed to experiment (even though sometimes he failed). The personnel comprises John Handy III, Shafi Hadi and Booker Ervin (saxophones), Horace Parlan Jr (piano), Willie Dennis and James Knepper (trombones) and Charles Richmond (drums). Mingus whoops, shouts and holds it all together and then turns the pace majestically on numbers such as 'Goodbye Pork Pie Hat'.

» Tracks: *Better Git It In Your Soul; Goodbye Pork Pie Hat; Boogie Stop Shuffle; Self-Portrait In Three Colours; Open Letter To Duke; Bird Calls; Fables Of Faubus; Pussy Cat Dues; Jelly Roll*

★ First released 1960
★ UK peak chart position: did not chart
★ USA peak chart position: did not chart
★ Previous Top 1000 position: 1998 (698): 1994 (536)

262 THE VELVET UNDERGROUND
↓ The Velvet Underground

Astonishingly this did not chart. Now affectionately known as the 'the third album', it forms part of a catalogue that contains some of the most influential music of the rock era. Not even recouping its money when released, nor making the charts, it is astonishing how deeply this important band has seeped into our minds. Every track has huge merit, whether it is Maureen Tucker's innocent voice or Reed's drawl of sexuality on 'Some Kinda Love'; even the enthrallingly bizarre 'The Murder Mystery' still baffles. Like the cover, dark and decadent; like Lou Reed on the back cover, upside-down and out of his head.

» Tracks: *Candy Says; What Goes On; Some Kinda Love; Pale Blue Eyes; Jesus; Beginning To See The Light; I'm Set Free; That's The Story Of My Life; The Murder Mystery; After Hours.*

★ First released 1969
★ UK peak chart position: did not chart
★ USA peak chart position: did not chart
★ Previous Top 1000 position: 1998 (130): 1994 (202)

263 ESCAPE ↑
Journey

One of America's biggest rock bands of all time, Journey managed to achieve a perfect blend of spirited and soulful AOR that brought them both commercial and critical success. With Steve Perry's blistering vocal range and Neal Schon's colourful shading of sounds, they created an album that was neither understated or overblown. Their songwriting skill as a band was extraordinary, passing quickly from fond balladeering to hard rock in an assured instant. From the astounding 'Don't Stop Believing' to the quiet sanctity of 'Open Arms', their all-round musical ability still astounds even though their overall credibility appears low. Forgive them, they have stopped wearing flares.

» Tracks: *Don't Stop Believing; Stone In Love; Who's Crying Now; Keep On Running; Still They Ride; Escape; Lay It Down; Dead Or Alive; Mother, Father; Open Arms.*

★ First released 1981
★ UK peak chart position: 32
★ USA peak chart position: 1
★ Previous Top 1000 position: 1998 (783): 1994 (281)

264 ARMED FORCES ↑
Elvis Costello

Only recently has this album been reappraised favourably – this was, after all, his most commercial offering. Its political content should have given it credibility; lyrically, it is as powerful as anything Elvis Costello has ever written. Even the overtly radio-friendly 'Oliver's Army' delivered some pretty uncompromising words, and exemplifies Costello's great strength – his ability to dress up a statement under the guise of a pop song. 'Green Shirt', 'Accidents Will Happen' and 'Goon Squad' are all as important as a pop song can be. Costello rarely wastes a lyric, and this album is no exception. Even the non-original 'My Funny Valentine' seems to work. The reissued CD now has many bonus tracks.

» Tracks: *Accidents Will Happen; Senior Service; Oliver's Army; Big Boys; Green Shirt; Party Girl; Goon Squad; Busy Bodies; Sunday's Best; Chemistry Class; Two Little Hitlers; (What's So Funny Bout) Peace Love And Understanding; My Funny Valentine; Tiny Steps; Clean Money; Talking In The Dark; Wednesday Week; Accidents Will Happen (live); Alison (live); Watching The Detectives (live).*

★ First released 1979
★ UK peak chart position: 2
★ USA peak chart position: 10
★ Previous Top 1000 position: 1998 (309): 1994 (236)

265 HIGHWAY TO HELL ↑
AC/DC

It's a mystery how a grown man can spend his life wearing a school tie and short trousers and receive adulation from the heavy metal fraternity. He even played a guitar which at that time was painfully out of fashion; the Gibson SG. The sounds he got from it were universal however. Angus Young's riff-laden fills, combined with the tough vocals of the late Bon Scott, made AC/DC one of the genre's all-time leading lights. Bordering on the lighter side of metal, songs such as 'Love Hungry Man', 'Touch Too Much' and the title track will always delight. Actually its not heavy metal at all.

» Tracks: *Highway To Hell; Girl's Got Rhythm; Walk All Over You; Touch Too Much; Beating Around The Bush; Shot Down In Flames; Get It Hot; If You Want Blood (You've Got It); Love Hungry Man; Night Prowler.*

★ First released 1979
★ UK peak chart position: 8
★ USA peak chart position: 17
★ Previous Top 1000 position: 1998 (343): 1994 (–)

266 MY AIM IS TRUE ↓
Elvis Costello

'Oh I used to be disgusted, and now I try to be amused', sang a youngish Elvis Costello in 1977, as he opened what for many is his best album. The pent-up frustration of the first album was mixed with melancholy. 'Alison' is a beautiful song that could and should be covered by Tony Bennett and Barbra Streisand, and deserves to become a universal standard like Paul McCartney's 'Yesterday'. Elsewhere, the wonderful Attractions (Steve Nieve, Bruce Thomas, Pete Thomas) supported fine songs such as 'Mystery Dance', '(The Angels Wanna Wear My) Red Shoes' and the paradoxical 'I'm Not Angry'. I wonder whether Costello knew how significant both he and this album would eventually become?

» Tracks: *Welcome To The Working Week; Miracle Man; No Dancing; Blame It On Cain; Alison; Sneaky Feelings; (The Angels Wanna Wear My) Red Shoes; Less Than Zero; Mystery Dance; Pay It Back; I'm Not Angry; Waiting For The End Of The World.*

★ First released 1977
★ UK peak chart position: 14
★ USA peak chart position: 32
★ Previous Top 1000 position: 1998 (207): 1994 (46)

267 MR TAMBOURINE MAN ↑
The Byrds

The only other major group of the 60s, other than the Beatles (the fab four), to elicit such universal love and approval are the Byrds (the famous five). They were originally seen as copyists, and were certainly slammed when they first came to hostile England. The great Byrdologist Johnny Rogan and most of us lesser mortals now realise their massive influence on popular music since 1965. The Roger McGuinn 12-string Rickenbacker opening of the title track is still one of the greatest sounds in music! On this, Gene Clark showed us he was already a genius songwriter. The CD reissue with bonus tracks is as essential and dutiful as breathing and smiling. Just like David Crosby did in those days.

» Tracks: *Mr Tambourine Man; I'll Feel A Whole Lot Better; Spanish Harlem Incident; You Won't Have To Cry; Here Without You; The Bells Of Rhymney; All I Really Want To Do; I Knew I'd Want You; It's No Use; Don't Doubt Yourself Babe; Chimes Of Freedom; We'll Meet Again; She Has A Way; You And Me.*

★ First released 1965
★ UK peak chart position: 7
★ USA peak chart position: 6
★ Previous Top 1000 position: 1998 (178): 1994 (–)

268 LIKE A VIRGIN ↑
Madonna

The title track, which, combined with her overt sexuality, caused waves of controversy at the time, has now become part of movie folklore, with director Quentin Tarantino letting his brutish cast mull over the meaning of its lyrics for the opening sequence of the film *Reservoir Dogs*. It is somehow gratifying that the Madonna album that unleashed her on the world should have become a cultural icon and reference point for the 80s. A telling blend of lush pop songs and street suss – the snappy come-on of 'Into The Groove', the Marilyn Monroe pastiche of 'Material Girl' – the dancing went on all through the night. She turned out all right really.

» Tracks: *Material Girl; Shoo-bee-doo; Pretender; Stay; Angel; Like A Virgin; Over And Over; Love Don't Live Here Anymore; Into The Groove; Dress You Up.*

★ First released 1984
★ UK peak chart position: 6
★ USA peak chart position: 1
★ Previous Top 1000 position: 1998 (471): 1994 (102)

269 THE FAT OF THE LAND ↓
Prodigy

Dismissed by *real* dance fans as cartoon purveyors of techno-rock, mix-maestro Liam, Keith *et al.* conquered the world with this long-anticipated album. A merciless, seering blast of punk, hip-hop and dance beats, it did not so much demand your attention as hold you at gunpoint. Never ones to admit to selling out the dance crowd, the Prodigy followed two number 1 singles ('Firestarter' and 'Breathe') with the wilfully uncommercial 'Smack My Bitch Up', complete with a highly controversial video. They also helped to fuel the old school revival with the masterful rapping of Kool Keith on 'Diesel Power', and, somewhat incongruously, enlisted Kula Shaker's Crispian Mills and Republica's Saffron for vocals on 'Narayan' and 'Fuel My Fire', respectively.

» Tracks: *Smack My Bitch Up; Breathe; Diesel Power; Funky Shit; Serial Thrilla; Mindfields; Narayan; Firestarter; Climbatize; Fuel My Fire.*

★ First released 1997
★ UK peak position: 1 ★ USA peak position: 1
★ Previous Top 1000 position: 1998 (33): 1994 (–)

270 HISTORY PAST PRESENT AND FUTURE BOOK 1 ↑
Michael Jackson

Michael Jackson had a lot to do to regain his credibility at this point. He was canny in offering the listener an irresistible greatest hits collection on disc one, so as to remind us how damn good he was. On disc two he gave us some new songs, many with lyrics that were more biting than usual. Jackson was angry in 'They Don't Really Care About Us' and 'Money', while in 'Earth Song' he attempts, and succeeds with the epic song of anti-pollution, anti-war. Quietly hidden on this disc is 'Stranger In Moscow', one of his best ever compositions. For all his quirks and failings, Jackson is still a major force.

» Tracks: *Billie Jean; The Way You Make Me Feel; Black Or White; Rock With You; She's Out Of My Life; Bad; I Just Can't Stop Loving You; Man In The Mirror; Thriller; Beat It; The Girl Is Mine; Remember The Time; Don't Stop Til You Get Enough; Wanna Be Startin' Somethin'; Heal The World; Scream; They Don't Care About Us; Stranger In Moscow; This Time Around; Earth Song; D.S.; Money; Come Together; You Are Not Alone; Childhood (Theme From Free Willy); Tabloid Junkie; Bad; History; Little Susie; Smile.*

★ First released 1995
★ UK peak chart position: 1 ★ USA peak chart position: 1
★ Previous Top 1000 position: 1998 (290): 1994 (–)

271 BLUR ↓
Blur

Wisely escaping the Blur versus Oasis media hype, Damon Albarn and his band disappeared to Iceland to work on material for this, their fifth album. The result initially disappointed both critics and public, but subsequent investigation has deemed it a great piece of work. The coy sexiness of 'Beetlebum' and the tremendous, all-out thrash of 'Song 2' were light years away from the pub-chant of 'Parklife', and they and other tracks ('Country Sad Ballad Man') hinted at a new lo-fi influence, inspired by bands such as Pavement. *Blur* gave the band a magnificent chance to experiment and to cast off their chirpy image; in doing so, they reinforced their musical credibility while retaining their sense of humour.

» Tracks: *Beetlebum; Song 2; Country Sad Ballad Man; M.O.R.; On Your Own; Theme From Retro; You're So Great; Death Of A Party; Chinese Bombs; I'm Just A Killer For Your Love; Look Inside America; Strange News From Another Star; Movin' On; Essex Dogs.*

★ First released 1997
★ UK peak chart position: 1 ★ USA peak chart position: 61
★ Previous Top 1000 position: 1998 (57): 1994 (–)

272 THE HOLY BIBLE ↑
Manic Street Preachers

The tragic and unresolved disappearance of Richey Edwards looms larger than life every time this album is played. Just as they were being hailed as the potential 'next big thing', the band was thrown into disarray, and as a result, this credible album was somewhat overlooked while the world searched for Richey. Now that the dust has settled and people have accepted his likely demise, this album can at last be appreciated. Even though the spoken introduction 'Of Walking Abortion' is spookily prophetic, the understated quality of all the songs puts this album much closer to the gigantic *Everything Must Go* than its success would indicate. They are strangely absent in the USA.

» Tracks: *Yes; Ifwhiteamericatoldthetruthforonedayitsworld wouldfallapart; Of Walking Abortion; She Is Suffering; Archives Of Pain; Revol; 4st 7lb; Mausoleum; Faster; This Is Yesterday; Die In The Summertime; The Intense Humming Of Evil; P.C.P.*

★ First released 1994
★ UK peak chart position: 6
★ USA peak chart position: did not chart
★ Previous Top 1000 position: 1998 (56): 1994 (–)

273 TRACY CHAPMAN ↑
Tracy Chapman

Although she must be tired of the comparisons, Tracy Chapman did look like Joan Armatrading, and at times sounded like her. Even *Q Magazine* sneakily substituted her pen picture once. She also debuted with an impressive album. Her career was given an unexpected shot in the arm when she appeared at the Nelson Mandela concert. Her solo spot was extended at short notice because Stevie Wonder was unable to come on. She won over the crowd, who loved her brave vulnerability, and rose to the occasion, playing an immaculate and memorable set. This album leaped into the charts the following day and refused to be budged for many months.

➤ Tracks: *Talkin' 'Bout A Revolution; Fast Car; Across The Lines; Behind The Wall; Baby Can I Hold You; Mountains O' Things; She's Got Her Ticket; Why?; For My Lover; If Not Now...; For You.*

★ First released 1988
★ UK peak chart position: 1
★ USA peak chart position: 1
★ Previous Top 1000 position: 1998 (393): 1994 (381)

274 MUSIC FOR THE JILTED GENERATION ↓ Prodigy

The band who stand to give the much maligned English county of Essex a 'good' reputation, Prodigy succeed where Ian Dury And The Blockheads and Brian Poole And The Tremeloes failed, i.e., achieving worldwide acceptance and success. Braintree worked where Billericay and Dagenham failed. Their aggressive, original and extraordinarily exciting style of dance music has created a thousand imitators. Although this record has since been overshadowed by the international success of *The Fat Of The Land*, it is still a vital record for students of 90s techno/dance. Prodigy lead their pack by a mile. fat and nasty dance music with real 'kick yer 'ead in attitude'.

➤ Tracks: *Intro; Break & Enter; Their Law; Full Throttle; Voodoo People; Speedway; The Heat (The Energy); Poison; No Good (Start The Dance); One Love: The Narcotic Suite; 3 Kilos; Skylines; Claustrophobic Sting.*

★ First released 1994
★ UK peak chart position: 1
★ USA peak chart position: did not chart
★ Previous Top 1000 position: 1998 (64): 1994 (–)

275 WITH THE BEATLES ↓
The Beatles

Released as its creators evolved from pop group to phenomenon, this both affirmed promise and proclaimed genius. A slew of memorable Lennon/McCartney compositions embraced pop at its most multi-faceted; robust, melancholic, excited and wistful. Their grasp of melody and harmony startled, yet for every unusual chord sequence employed, the Beatles' vigour and sense of purpose remained true. Influences and mentors were acknowledged by a handful of cover versions, but the strength of the album lies in the group's own creations. It freed artists to record their own material, and the course of pop was irrevocably changed. Ringo's ride cymbal work is hypnotic, and Lennon proved his point with the ripping vocal on 'Money'.

➤ Tracks: *It Won't Be Long; All I've Got To Do; All My Loving; Don't Bother Me; Little Child; Till There Was You; Please Mister Postman; Roll Over Beethoven; Hold Me Tight; You Really Got A Hold On Me; I Wanna Be Your Man; (There's A) Devil In Her Heart; Not A Second Time; Money (That's What I Want).*

★ First released 1964
★ UK peak chart position: 1 ★ USA peak chart position: 1
★ Previous Top 1000 position: 1998 (168): 1994 (99)

276 VERSION 2.0 ↑
Garbage

A few doubters thought that Shirley Manson and her band would not be able to match the success of their debut album. As with all decent software *Version 2.0* was a refinement and a slight improvement of the original winner. Even though the opening track 'Temptation Waits' has the listener thinking the record company has dropped a Chrissie Hynde CD in the box, the album is a lively and, for the most part, happy excursion. The development has already been considerable and having to follow up wonderful singles such as 'I Think I'm Paranoid' is not to be envied. They must skip Version 2.1 and go straight to a full upgrade 3.0.

➤ Tracks: *Temptation Waits; I Think I'm Paranoid; When I Grow Up; Medication; Special; Hammering In My Head; Push It; The Trick Is To Keep Breathing; Dumb; Sleep Together; Wicked Ways; You Look So Fine.*

★ First released 1998
★ UK peak chart position: 1
★ USA peak chart position: 13
★ Previous Top 1000 position: 1998 (–): 1994 (–)

277 IN UTERO ↓
Nirvana

Following his final act of self-destruction, Kurt Cobain will probably assume Jim Morrison-like status, which is a little out of balance since the band have only three proper albums under their belt compared with the Doors' output. Taken as a rock band, they were the phenomenon of the 90s, both important and successful. Their penchant for romanticizing death is being followed with Pied Piper regularity. Their ability to shock was far better than any of the new wave followers. It was only the troubled Cobain who could write songs such as 'Rape Me' (an anti-rape song!) and 'Heart-Shaped Box' with real conviction.

» Tracks: *Serve The Servants; Scentless Apprentice; Heart-Shaped Box; Rape Me; Frances Farmer Will Have Her Revenge On Seattle; Dumb; Very Ape; Milk It; Pennyroyal Tea; Radio Friendly Unit Shifter; Tourette's; All Apologies; Gallons Of Rubbing Alcohol Flow Through The Strip.*

★ First released 1993
★ UK peak chart position: 1
★ USA peak chart position: 1
★ Previous Top 1000 position: 1998 (84): 1994 (83)

278 DIRT ↑
Alice In Chains

Brutal and hard but at the same time exciting and surprisingly melodic, *Dirt* made Alice In Chains national stars in 1992 after being around the Seattle alternative rock scene for many years. They produce a blindingly together sound, with the bass of Mike Starr able to switch between following the bass drum beat and cloning Layne Staley's guitar note for note, albeit a few octaves lower. They have such polish that they are often reminiscent of the heyday of Led Zeppelin. Lyrically they plow the familiar angst furrow with tracks such as 'Junkhead', 'Sickman' and 'God Smack'. Equally satisfying are 'Them Bones' and 'Rooster', which saw them start in a direction that led to the magnificent *Jar Of Flies* two years later.

» Tracks: *Them Bones; Dam That River; Rain When I Die; Down In A Hole; Sickman; Rooster; Junkhead; Dirt; God Smack; Hate To Feel; Angry Chair; Would?*

★ First released 1992
★ UK peak chart position: 4
★ USA peak chart position: 42
★ Previous Top 1000 position: 1998 (663): 1994 (–)

279 CLOSER ↓
Joy Division

The news of singer Ian Curtis' suicide still hung in the air when this album was released. Given the deep introspective nature of Joy Division's music, his death invested *Closer* with an even greater pessimism. Yet there is a fragile beauty in its content and if Curtis' voice seems more distant, it complements the sparse textures created by mesmerizing synthesizer lines and occasional, highly effective, piano. Slow, hypnotic tempos increase the sense of brooding mystery and if the few faster songs provide musical relief, their lyrics prove equally tortured. Eerie, yet compulsive, *Closer* confirmed Joy Division's pre-eminent place in on the alternative darkside of pop.

» Tracks: *Atrocity Exhibition; Isolation; Passover; Colony; A Means To An End; Heart And Soul; Twenty Four Hours; The Eternal; Decades.*

★ First released 1980
★ UK peak chart position: 6
★ USA peak chart position: did not chart
★ Previous Top 1000 position: 1998 (68): 1994 (266)

280 VIOLATOR ↑
Depeche Mode

Following a lengthy gap between this and the last album *Music For The Masses*, the band had now become a huge attraction in the USA, playing to huge audiences at large stadiums. They were the only group to take what was very much European music, to the Americans. The synthesizers and keyboards still dominated the sound but there was a greater depth to the lyrics, or at least more was read into them. Religion, that red rag to a rock 'n' roller, had taken over. Additionally, Gahan was heading down a dark path of drugs, as Martin Gore attempted to hold the band together. Their unresolved problems permeated this dramatic album.

» Tracks: *World In My Eyes; Sweetest Perfection; Personal Jesus; Halo; Waiting For The Night; Enjoy The Silence; Policy Of Truth; Blue Dress; Clean.*

★ First released 1990
★ UK peak chart position: 2
★ USA peak chart position: 7
★ Previous Top 1000 position: 1998 (908): 1994 (–)

281 WHAT WE DID ON OUR HOLIDAYS ↑ Fairport Convention

An album that revels in an embarrassment of influences which the band blend together, making it entirely their own. This was the Fairport Convention that ran with the psychedelic underground scene, flexing their muscles, a slumbering entity about to wake. This was their beatnik phase, producing such evergreens as Sandy Denny's beautiful 'Fotheringay', the first tangible examples of electrified trad in 'Nottamun Town' and 'She Moves Through The Fair' – neither song, incidentally, British. More significantly, Richard Thompson began to move in his own mysterious way, proffering 'Meet On The Ledge' which has since become their signature tune. Variety, as they say, is the spice of life and this collection adroitly exploits just that.

❱❱ Tracks: Fotheringay; Mr. Lacey; Book Song; The Lord Is In His Place; No Man's Land; I'll Keep It With Mine; Eastern Rain; Nottamun Town; Tale In Hard Time; She Moves Through The Fair; Meet On The Ledge; End Of A Holiday.

★ First released 1969
★ UK peak chart position: did not chart
★ USA peak chart position: did not chart
★ Previous Top 1000 position: 1998 (301): 1994 (379)

282 BEGGARS BANQUET ↓ The Rolling Stones

The Rolling Stones emerged into the post-flower power age with this declamatory selection. Producer Jimmy Miller was instrumental in rekindling a musical power that possessed renewed forcefulness and focus. R&B remained rooted at the group's core – their reading of Robert Wilkins' 'Prodigal Son' is enthralling – while menace and anger ooze from what remain some of their finest compositions. Lascivious, malevolent, even politically impotent, they articulate a group freed from indecision and assured of direction. Their career as 'the world's greatest rock 'n' roll band' properly began with this release. Worth it alone for the strumming of electric chords, that is the unforgettable intro to 'Street Fighting Man' when Charlie's drums come in on the off-beat.

❱❱ Tracks: Sympathy For The Devil; No Expectations; Dear Doctor; Parachute Woman; Jig-Saw Puzzle; Street Fighting Man; Prodigal Son; Stray Cat Blues; Factory Girl; Salt Of The Earth.

★ First released 1968
★ UK peak chart position: 3
★ USA peak chart position: 5
★ Previous Top 1000 position: 1998 (106): 1994 (24)

283 THE BLANTON-WEBSTER YEARS ↓ Duke Ellington

A special kind of magic surrounds the Duke Ellington band that featured Ben Webster and Jimmy Blanton; the former's tenor solos, breathily romantic or fiercely swinging, the latter changing the role of the bass in jazz. Yet these two were far from being the only stars. Not least among others were the liquid beauty of Johnny Hodges' alto and Cootie Williams' plangent trumpet. In addition, there was always the arranging-composing skills of Billy Strayhorn, another new arrival, and the maestro himself. Together, they brought to eternal life masterpieces such as 'Just A-Settin' And A-Rockin', 'Ko-Ko', 'Jack The Bear', 'Cotton Tail' and 'Concerto For Cootie'.

❱❱ Tracks: You, You Darlin'; Jack The Bear; Ko Ko; Morning Glory; So Far, So Good; Conga Brava; Concerto For Cootie (Do Nothin' Till You Hear From Me); Me And You; Cotton Tail; Never No Lament; Dusk; Bojangles; A Portrait Of Bert Williams; Blue Goose; Harlem Air Shaft; At A Dixie Roadside Diner; All Too Soon; Rumpus In Richmond; My Greatest Mistake; Sepia Panorama; There Shall Be No Night; In A Mellotone; Five O'Clock Whistle; Warm Valley; The Flaming Sword; Jumpin' Punkins; Across The Track Blues; John Hardy's Wife; Blue Serge; After All; Chloe; Bakiff; Are You Sticking?; I Never Felt This Way Before; Just A-Settin' And A-Rockin'; The Giddybug Gallop; The Sidewalks Of New York; Chocolate Shake; Flamingo; I Got It Bad (And That Ain't Good); Clementine; Brown Skin Gal; The Girl In My Dreams Tries To Look Like You; Jump For Joy; Moon Over Cuba; Take The 'A' Train; Five O'clock Drag; Rocks In My Bed; Blip Blip; Chelsea Bridge; Raincheck; What Good Would It Do?; I Don't Mind; Someone; My Little Brown Book; Main Stem; Johnny Come Lately; Hayfoot Strawfoot; Sentimental Lady; A Sip Of The Lip (Can Sink A Ship); Sherman Shuffle.

★ First released 1987 (1940-1942 recordings)
★ UK peak chart position: did not chart
★ USA peak chart position: did not chart
★ Previous Top 1000 position: 1998 (204): 1994 (31)

284 BAD ↓ Michael Jackson

Michael Jackson's domination of the world record market continued following Thriller, although by comparison it was an almighty flop, with only 12 million sales. As Pink Floyd and Dire Straits have proved, one album can go completely haywire without necessarily being any better. The title track and the gorgeous 'Man In The Mirror' were substantial hits, but high-quality material such as 'Dirty Diana' and 'Liberian Girl' bolster a strong album. At the time, Jackson also seemed to have found the romance he was seeking in 'I Just Can't Stop Loving You' and 'The Way You Make Me Feel'. Regardless of his eccentricity, he has made a lot of people very, very happy.

❱❱ Tracks: Bad; The Way You Make Me Feel; Speed Demon; Liberian Girl; Just Good Friends; Another Part Of Me; Man In The Mirror; I Just Can't Stop Loving You; Dirty Diana; Smooth Criminal.

★ First released 1987
★ UK peak chart position: 1 ★ USA peak chart position: 1
★ Previous Top 1000 position: 1998 (117): 1994 (23)

285 CATCH A FIRE ↓
The Wailers

One of the biggest drawbacks of the CD age is the lack of potential for the covers. The original issue of this pivotal album came in the shape of a Zippo lighter, which opened with a riveted flip-top (eventually) to reveal the cut-out flame. Beyond the flame was the real fire: a superb collection of songs that stand up to repeated play over 20 years later. Even with the subsequent huge commercial success that Bob Marley enjoyed with big-selling albums, the Wailers' followers and critics come back to this superb record time and time again. The first proper reggae album for any new collector of the genre.

» Tracks: *Concrete Jungle; Slave Driver; 400 Years; Stop That Train; Rock It Baby; Stir It Up; Kinky Reggae; No More Trouble; Midnight Ravers.*

★ First released 1972
★ UK peak chart position: did not chart
★ USA peak chart position: 171
★ Previous Top 1000 position: 1998 (200): 1994 (141)

286 PRETTY HATE MACHINE ↑
Nine Inch Nails

There are lyrics on Nine Inch Nails' 1989 debut album which you wouldn't want your children to recite and Trent Reznor, good looks notwithstanding, is hardly the sort you'd invite round to meet your parents. On this Reznor's despair, self-loathing and anxiety are animated by a fearful barrage of bone-crunching industrial noise. Parts of 'Something I Can Never Have', for example, could teach Motorhead a thing or two about the power riff. It's not all jet-propelled hate and fury, however, with varied producers (Flood, Adrian Sherwood, Keith LeBlanc) all bringing something new to the table. And if Reznor's nihilism clouds proceedings, his vitriol nevertheless produces some spectacular moments – 'Head Like A Hole', 'Sin' and 'Ring Finger' being prime examples.

» Tracks: *Head Like A Hole; Terrible Lie; Down In It; Sanctified; Something I Can Never Have; Kinda I Want To; Sin; That's What I Get; The Only Time; Ring Finger.*

★ First released 1989
★ UK peak chart position: 67
★ USA peak chart position: 75
★ Previous Top 1000 position: 1998 (588): 1994 (–)

287 LAYLA AND OTHER ASSORTED LOVE SONGS ↓
Derek And The Dominos

Studying the photographs inside the fold-out sleeve makes you question how such a wrecked bunch of musos could make such a great record. Excess was obviously the order of the day, yet excel was what they did. Everybody knows that 'Layla' is one of the best rock songs ever written, but here is the chance to strike a blow for Duane Allman's consistent guitar, especially on lost gems such as 'Anyday' and 'Key To The Highway'. Did anybody also notice how good Jim Gordon's drumming was? And the CD age means we can skip past the wimpish and certainly dreadful 'Thorn Tree In The Garden'.

» Tracks: *I Looked Away; Bell Bottom Blues; Keep On Growing; Nobody Knows You; I Am Yours; Anyday; Key To The Highway; Tell The Truth; Why Does Love Got To Be So Sad; Have You Ever Loved A Woman; Little Sing; It's Too Late; Thorn Tree In The Garden; Layla.*

★ First released 1970
★ UK peak chart position: did not chart
★ USA peak chart position: 16
★ Previous Top 1000 position: 1998 (161): 1994 (138)

288 THE NIGHTFLY ↓
Donald Fagen

Quality will out. There was no need to put a great big 'he is the bloke from Steely Dan' sticker on this smooth little number, the radio programmers took care of that. Not surprisingly it sounded like another excellent album from the dildo duo. No tracks jar, each has a big-smile middle eight and although it may be just too slick for some people's taste, mostly it is a tremendous solo album. 'I.G.Y. (International Geophical Year)', 'New Frontier' and the title track are gloriously easy on the ear. The cover version of Leiber And Stoller's 'Ruby Baby' is so good it sounds like a Donald Fagen original.

» Tracks: *I.G.Y.; Green Flower Street; Ruby Baby; Maxine; New Frontier; The Nightfly/Goodbye Look/Walk Between The Raindrops.*

★ First released 1982
★ UK peak chart position: 44
★ USA peak chart position: 11
★ Previous Top 1000 position: 1998 (191): 1994 (–)

289 A NORTHERN SOUL ↓
The Verve

Although a fine album in its own right, the popularity of *A Northern Soul* probably owed much to the huge success of *Urban Hymns* in 1997/8. A collection of swirling, grand epics and expansive landscapes, it is more sprawling, and, many fans would argue, more inspired than its tighter, commercial successor. Richard Ashcroft's lyrics are undoubtedly less oblique than on the group's debut, *A Storm In Heaven*. The album's highlight is 'History', with its fluid guitar and crafted strings. A worthy, if rambling, record, it is significant both musically and as an indication of the group's imminent dissolution, prior to their triumphant return two years later.

❱❱ Tracks: *New Decade; This Is Music; On Your Own; So It Goes; Northern Soul; Brainstorm; Interlude; Drive You Home; History; No Knock On My Door; Life's An Ocean; Stormy Clouds; Reprise.*

★ First released 1995
★ UK peak position: 13
★ USA peak position: did not chart
★ Previous Top 1000 position: 1998 (81): 1994 (–)

290 FIFTH DIMENSION ↓
Byrds

Now seen as an album that was as far ahead as the Beatles' *Revolver*, released the same year. Roger McGuinn's flirtation with space rock peaked on stunning tracks such as 'What's Happening?!?!' and the brilliant 'I See You'. The ultimate, however, is 'Eight Miles High', which over 30 years later constantly causes a shiver. The guitar solo is still a remarkable experience. Their mass market popularity had already peaked by the release of this album, and it has been left to the likes of biographer Johnny Rogan to re-emphasize their greatness over the years. The remastered CD is unmissable, as the original single version of 'Why' is also included.

❱❱ Tracks: *5D (Fifth Dimension); Wild Mountain Thyme; Mr. Spaceman; I See You; What's Happening?!?!; I Come And Stand At Every Door; Eight Miles High; Hey Joe (Where You Gonna Go); Captain Soul; John Riley; 2-4-2 Fox Trot (The Lear Jet Song); Why (single version); I Know My Rider (I Know You Rider); Psychodrama City; Eight Miles High (alternate); Why (alternate); John Riley (instrumental).*

★ First released 1966
★ UK peak chart position: 27
★ USA peak chart position: 24
★ Previous Top 1000 position: 1998 (225): 1994 (406)

291 HORSES ↓
Patti Smith

Poet/playwright Patti Smith embraced rock as a critic and performer during New York punk's formative era. These different elements gelled to startling effect on *Horses*, which attacked pre-conceptions and declared innovation to great effect. Her untutored voice provides raw realism while a refusal to compromise took music into uncharted territory. Smith's splicing together of her own 'Horses' to the standard 'Land Of 1000 Dances' simultaneously declared pop history and its future. John Cale's production inevitably suggests comparisons with the Velvet Underground, but despite a sense of shared commitment, Smith's music is powerful and exciting on its own terms. Few debut albums are as intense or as fully formed.

❱❱ Tracks: *Gloria (In Excelsis Deo); Redondo Beach; Birdland; Free Money; Kimberly; Break It Up; Land: Horses – Land Of A 1000 Dances – La Mer; Elegie.*

★ First released 1975
★ UK peak chart position: did not chart
★ USA peak chart position: 47
★ Previous Top 1000 position: 1998 (88): 1994 (805)

292 PRETZEL LOGIC ↓
Steely Dan

Donald Fagen and Walter Becker were session musicians and staff songwriters prior to founding the magnificent Steely Dan in 1972. Their highly inventive music relied on a synthesis of styles, heard to perfection on this, their third album. Jazz, bayou-based R&B and sumptuous west coast pop were fused together to create a sound greater than the sum of its parts and one that was uniquely 'Steely Dan'. Crafted session musicians brought a technical excellence to the set, but the strength of the duo's vision ensured that sterility did not supplant inspiration. Even though they nicked Horace Silver's intro from' The Jody Grind' in 'Rikki Don't Lose That Number'.

❱❱ Tracks: *Rikki Don't Lose That Number; Night By Night; Any Major Dude Will Tell You; Barrytown; East St. Louis Toodle-o; Parker's Band; Through With Buzz; Pretzel Logic; With A Gun; Charlie Freak; Monkey In Your Soul.*

★ First released 1974
★ UK peak chart position: 37
★ USA peak chart position: 8
★ Previous Top 1000 position: 1998 (250): 1994 (110)

293 BITCHES BREW ↓
Miles Davis

A thoroughly unsaintly concoction of jazz experimentation and rock psychedelia, *Bitches Brew* took the loose, exploratory, collective improvisation and rock beat approach that Miles Davis had developed on *In A Silent Way*, and painted it a slightly harsher and more sinister hue. This is a long work, sold as a double album, with a mesmerizing feel to its collection of strange funk-rock grooves. Benny Maupin's bass clarinet adds an unnerving dimension to the group's sound, creaking threateningly from deep within, while Davis himself plays lean, but fragmented, trumpet lines. An inspired and intense work, *Bitches Brew* dramatically influenced the course of jazz history, and ushered in the fusion movement.

➤ Tracks: *Pharaoh's Dance; Bitches Brew; Spanish Key; John McLaughlin; Miles Runs The Voodoo Down; Sanctuary.*

★ First released 1970
★ UK peak chart position: 71
★ USA peak position: 35
★ Previous Top 1000 position: 1998 (253): 1994 (523)

294 BREAKFAST IN AMERICA ↑
Supertramp

Supertramp are often forgotten, and when prompted to be remembered, it is usually for the often tedious, but huge-selling, *Crime Of The Century*. This record cuts away the pomp and keeps it comparatively simple with some memorable songs and lyrics; for example, in the title track a simple statement, 'take a look at my girlfriend, she's the only one I've got', or the ridiculously simple rhymes in 'The Logical Song', and the painful truth of 'Goodbye Stranger' and 'Take The Long Way Home', which are further irritatingly catchy songs. Sadly Supertramp were not able to build on this excellent collection. More pop than prog.

➤ Tracks: *Gone Hollywood; The Logical Song; Goodbye Stranger; Breakfast In America; Oh Darling; Take The Long Way Home; Lord Is It Mine; Just Another Nervous Wreck; Casual Conversation; Child Of Vision.*

★ First released 1979
★ UK peak chart position: 3
★ USA peak position: 1
★ Previous Top 1000 position: 1998 (553): 1994 (343)

295 LOADED ↓
The Velvet Underground

The Velvet Underground were never ones to follow the crowd. In 1966, when catchy, lucid, three-minute pop tunes were the rule, they recorded their first album, which was dominated by dark celebrations of drug use. By 1970, when they recorded their fourth album, the vogue was for unwieldy drug anthems. Therefore, they made *Loaded*, an album dominated by catchy, lucid three-minute pop tunes. Their record label, expecting a wild, Warholesque romp, did not know what to make of the album, and it died a commercial death. Since then, it has gained respect from both fans and critics as the source of many of Lou Reed's best compositions, including bona fide classics such as 'Rock And Roll' and 'Sweet Jane'.

➤ Tracks: *Who Loves The Sun; Sweet Jane; Rock And Roll; Cool It Down; New Age; Head Held High; Lonesome Cowboy Bill; I Found A Reason; Train Round The Bend; Oh! Sweet Nuthin'.*

★ First released 1970.
★ UK peak chart position: did not chart
★ USA peak chart position: did not chart
★ Previous Top 1000 position: 1998 (274): 1994 (–)

296 MAXINQUAYE ↓
Tricky

Tricky made a low-key entrance onto the music scene as a guest vocalist on Massive Attack's 1991 classic *Blue Lines*. There was little indication that he would resurface four years later with an album as powerfully unsettling as *Maxinquaye*. Accompanied by the sweet-voiced Martine, Tricky takes the listener on a tour of the dark corridors of his mind, dealing exclusively in paranoia and obsession. The striking rhythms of stand-out tracks 'Overcome', 'Hell Is Round The Corner' and 'Suffocated Love' merge seamlessly with a hard-rock reworking of Public Enemy's 'Black Steel In The Hour Of Chaos' and the warped soul of 'Abbaon Fat Tracks' to create one of the 90s' most compellingly atmospheric records.

➤ Tracks: *Overcome; Ponderosa; Black Steel; Hell Is Round The Corner; Pumpkin; Aftermath; Abbaon Fat Tracks; Brand New You're Retro; Suffocated Love; You Don't; Strugglin'; Feed Me.*

★ First released 1995
★ UK peak chart position: 3
★ USA peak chart position: did not chart
★ Previous Top 1000 position: 1998 (129): 1994 (–)

297 NATTY DREAD ↓
Bob Marley

Out on his own following the defection of Bunny Wailer and Peter Tosh, this album saw Bob Marley utilizing the talents of the I-Threes for the first time. There was still a nod to his past in the inclusion of a cover version of a Wailers tune, 'Lively Up Yourself', but elsewhere he revelled in his new found freedom, on 'Revolution' and most particularly, 'No Woman, No Cry', which has practically become a Jamaican national anthem since its release. If that song had an instantly universal appeal, Rasta themes were also brilliantly conveyed via 'Them Belly Full (But We Hungry)' and 'Rebel Music (Three O'Clock Roadblock)'. Marley had unintentionally announced himself as one of the icons of modern music.

» Tracks: *Lively Up Yourself; No Woman No Cry; Them Belly Full (But We Hungry); Rebel Music (3 O'Clock Roadblock); So Jah Seh; Natty Dread; Bend Down Low; Talkin' Blues; Revolution.*

★ First released 1975
★ UK peak chart position: 75
★ USA peak chart position: 28
★ Previous Top 1000 position: 1998 (255): 1994 (510)

298 GET HAPPY!! ↓
Elvis Costello

This album highlights the fine line between Elvis Costello's pop/punk and R&B and soul. The impression is that he wrote, recorded and produced this album while on a creative roll, creating a set of short, snappy, simple songs that go straight to the heart. Both he and the Attractions played with fiery energy without losing their great sense of melody. The contrasts are great, from the lyrical ingenuity of 'New Amsterdam' to the pace of 'I Stand Accused' and 'High Fidelity'. A record to which one should lie down and rest after digestion. Quite magnificent and even better with the extra tracks on the CD reissue.

» Tracks: *Love For Tender; Opportunity; The Imposter; Secondary Modern; King Horse; Possession; Man Called Uncle; Clowntime Is Over; New Amsterdam; High Fidelity; I Can't Stand Up For Falling Down; Black And White World; Five Gears In Reverse; B Movie; Motel Matches; Human Touch; Beaten To The Punch; Temptation; I Stand Accused; Riot Act.*

★ First released 1980
★ UK peak chart position: 2
★ USA peak chart position: 11
★ Previous Top 1000 position: 1998 (246): 1994 (187)

299 RAIN DOGS ↓
Tom Waits

Tom Waits discarded his bohemian sage persona with the radical *Swordfishtrombones*, and this follow-up release synthesized and developed themes from that groundbreaking album. Ever-shifting percussive textures are supported, where applicable, by horns or Farfisa organ and several guest musicians, including Rolling Stone Keith Richards, contribute to its mélange. Waits' bourbon-laced voice is as riveting as ever, intoning lyrics that are, at various times, touching, evocative, sly or simply funny. His off-kilter perceptions encompass country, polkas and heart-rending ballads, each of which he expresses with consummate ease. *Rain Dogs* is yet another strong statement from this highly innovative artist.

» Tracks: *Singapore; Clap Hands; Cemetery Polka; Jockey Full Of Bourbon; Tango Till They're Sore; Big Black Maria; Diamonds And Gold; Hang Down Your Head; Time; Rain Dogs; Midtown; Ninth And Headpin; Gun Street Girl; Union Square; Blind Love; Walking Spanish; Downtown Train; Bride Of Raindog; Anywhere I Lay My Head.*

★ First released 1985
★ UK peak chart position: 29 ★ USA peak chart position: 181
★ Previous Top 1000 position: 1998 (186): 1994 (292)

300 SOME GIRLS ↑
The Rolling Stones

One of the few latter period Rolling Stones albums that stands up to any real scrutiny in the light of their magnificent catalogue. Strolling out as the 70s were diminishing and punk was beginning to inflict a stranglehold and cultivate a disdain for anything over 30, the Stones once more enlivened their audience with the ability to surprise. Disregarding the contemporary mood and discarding their earlier R&B leanings, which they would later readopt, for funkier ground, irresistible undercurrents of rock 'n' roll patiently rumbled on, and 'Miss You', the particularly excellent 'Beast Of Burden' and the furious drum beat of 'Respectable' or, repectabowwwwl as Jagger sings.

» Tracks: *Miss You; When The Whip Comes Down; Just My Imagination; Some Girls; Lies; Faraway Eyes; Respectable; Before They Make Me Run; Beast Of Burden; Shattered.*

★ First released 1978
★ UK peak chart position: 2
★ USA peak chart position: 1
★ Previous Top 1000 position: 1998 (327): 1994 (314)

301 PABLO HONEY ↓
Radiohead

Before the breakthrough that was *The Bends* and the colossal *OK Computer*, there was the quietly magnificent *Pablo Honey*. 'Creep' was the surprise hit single in the UK, but even that song's lyric gave scant indication of how 'fuckin' special' this band would become. Benefiting from a raw production, the debut was undoubtedly less slick and accomplished than subsequent work, although Thom Yorke's vulnerable but impressive vocal styling was already in place on songs such as 'Stop Whispering'. Many of the compositions were somewhat simplistic, but in terms of musical maturity Radiohead were years ahead of their time. An indispensable album, it should not be parted from its two big sisters.

➡ Tracks: *You; Creep; How Do You?; Stop Whispering; Thinking About You; Anyone Can Play Guitar; Ripcord; Vegetable; Prove Yourself; I Can't; Lurgee; Blow Out.*

★ First released 1993
★ UK peak chart position: 25
★ USA peak chart position: 32
★ Previous Top 1000 position: 1998 (100): 1994 (–)

302 RAW POWER ←
Iggy And The Stooges

After Iggy Pop remixed *Raw Power* for CD release, he said that he believed the album held its own against the work of modern-day acts such as Smashing Pumpkins and Nirvana. Although he was referring to the album's unrelenting assault of loud, distorted guitars and gut-wrenching vocals, *Raw Power* has another quality that surpasses its modern-day emulators: melody. For all its noise, the album is surprisingly catchy, and tracks such as 'Search And Destroy' and the title track became singalong anthems for the punk generation. In light of the commercialization of alternative rock, *Raw Power's* combination of rebellion and accessibility fits in far better with today's alternative rock giants than it did in the somnolent past.

➡ Tracks: *Search And Destroy; Gimme Danger; Your Pretty Face Is Going To Hell; Penetration; Raw Power; I Need Somebody; Shake Appeal; Death Trip.*

★ First released 1973
★ UK peak chart position: 44
★ USA peak chart position: 182
★ Previous Top 1000 position: 1998 (302): 1994 (–)

303 GET A GRIP ↑
Aerosmith

On the opening track, 'Eat The Rich', Steven Tyler sounds like he is enjoying putting down the wealthy, even though there must be some element of ironic humour. Tyler and his band have certainly done their share of 'eating rich'. Elsewhere, there are plenty of similar moments of excess; 'Gotta Love It' has a psychedelic sandwich and 'Flesh' extols the virtues of pure, unadulterated sex. Aerosmith do nothing by halves; Tyler sings exactly what he thinks, good and bad. His mood is matched exactly by the energy of some excellent complementary guitar from Joe Perry. Not for those of a nervous disposition.

➡ Tracks: *Intro; Eat The Rich; Get A Grip; Fever; Livin' On The Edge; Flesh; Walk On Down; Shut Up And Dance; Cryin'; Gotta Love It; Crazy; Line Up; Can't Stop Messin'; Amazing; Boogie Man.*

★ First released 1993
★ UK peak chart position: 2
★ USA peak chart position: 1
★ Previous Top 1000 position: 1998 (605): 1994 (–)

304 USE YOUR ILLUSION II ↑
Guns N' Roses

A better collection than its sister album, although the margin is small. 'Civil War' is, for all its bluster and profundity, a damn good song. Similarly powerful, but for all the wrong reasons, is 'Pretty Tied Up', a song much more in keeping with the band's reputation. Even though it became an anthem at their live gigs, 'Knockin' On Heavens Door', or 'dohwer' as Axl Rose sings, still fails to convince. Everything is thrown at this track, girl singers, crunching guitar solo, wall of sound production, and still in the last minute Bob Dylan comes down the wing and crosses the ball into the net, to take the points.

➡ Tracks: *Civil War; 14 Years; Yesterdays; Knockin' On Heaven's Door; Get In The Ring; Shotgun Blues; Breakdown; Pretty Tied Up; Locomotive; So Fine; Estranged; You Could Be Mine; Don't Cry; My World.*

★ First released 1991
★ UK peak chart position: 1
★ USA peak chart position: 1
★ Previous Top 1000 position: 1998 (–): 1994 (–)

305 ANIMALS ↑
Nick Drake → Pink Floyd

Equally famous for its ambitious cover, featuring the inflatable pig and Battersea Power Station, *Animals* was a much more successful album than people now recall. Part of its invisibility is in not having a named single song. The album is divided into five parts and needs to be played as a whole; CD technology aids appreciation. 'Pigs (Three Different Ones)' is the most accessible song, even though the vitriolic lyrics aim to shock. UK censorship queen Mary Whitehouse comes in for some ridicule from Roger Waters in the last verse. Among other things, she is described as a 'house proud town mouse'.

➤➤ Tracks: *Pigs On The Wing 1; Dogs; Pigs (Three Different Ones); Sheep; Pigs On The Wing 2.*

★ First released 1992
★ UK peak chart position: 2
★ USA peak chart position: 3
★ Previous Top 1000 position: 1998 (508): 1994 (–)

306 BRYTER LAYTER ↓
Nick Drake

This is the late Nick Drake's most fully realized album, a beautifully melancholic and moving collection of songs featuring elegantly understated backing from the likes of Richard Thompson and John Cale. Although at times a deeply disturbing record, particularly on 'Hazey Jane II' and 'Fly', the album evokes an air of wistful calm with three delicate instrumentals framing the wry wit of 'Poor Boy', the studied isolation of 'At The Chime Of A City Clock' and the aching beauty of the matchless 'Northern Sky'. Over thirty years after it was first released, *Bryter Layter* retains its beauty and freshness. Of its kind, it has no rivals, anywhere.

➤➤ Tracks: *Introduction; Hazey Jane II; At The Chime Of A City Clock; One Of These Things First; Hazey Jane I; Bryter Layter; Fly; Poor Boy; Northern Sky; Sunday.*

★ First released 1970
★ UK peak chart position: did not chart
★ USA peak chart position: did not chart
★ Previous Top 1000 position: 1998 (118): 1994 (–)

307 COUNTDOWN TO ECSTASY ↓
Steely Dan

Steely Dan were on a roll by the time this, their second album, was released. Already, they were the most critically favoured band of the 70s, and their star has never once dimmed. Prolific they were not, and quality not quantity was the order of the day. Jeff 'Skunk' Baxter added some tough meat to their smooth vegetables. This is never better demonstrated than on 'My Old School'. This track has a series of almost-false guitar endings that the listener begs not to finish, even though he/she was probably smoking funny cigarettes at the time. Similarly gorgeous are 'The Boston Rag' and 'King Of The World'. And just who are those loveable gloops on the album cover?

➤➤ Tracks: *Bodhisattva; Razor Boy; The Boston Rag; Your Gold Teeth; Show Biz Kids; My Old School; Pearl Of The Quarter; King Of The World.*

★ First released 1973
★ UK peak chart position: did not chart
★ USA peak chart position: 35
★ Previous Top 1000 position: 1998 (135): 1994 (–)

308 TEN SUMMONERS TALES ↑
Sting

Mr 'Sheer Profundity' delivered a stunning fourth solo album and probably surprised himself as well as the critics, who were prepared to watch his fall from grace after the seeming failure of the intense *The Soul Cages*. Right from the opener, 'If I Ever Lose My Faith In You', the album holds its pace. That track will be seen as a classic in years to come, as will the beautiful 'Fields Of Gold' and 'Shape Of My Heart'. Sting is established as a major artist with a solo career that has now eclipsed his former supergroup. Anything he produces in the future will be compared against this outstanding LP.

➤➤ Tracks: *Prologue (If I Ever Lose My Faith In You); Love Is Stronger Than Justice (The Munificent Seven); Fields Of Gold; Heavy Cloud No Rain; She's Too Good For Me; Seven Days; Saint Augustine In Hell; It's Probably Me; Everybody Laughed But You; Shape Of My Heart; Something The Boy Said; Epilogue (Nothing 'Bout Me).*

★ First released 1993
★ UK peak chart position: 2
★ USA peak chart position: 2
★ Previous Top 1000 position: 1998 (400): 1994 (672)

309 WHITE LIGHT/WHITE HEAT ↓
The Velvet Underground

The difficult second album from one of rock's greatest influences was dusted off with little regard for trying to sell records. Blissfully unaware of how important this band was to become, their label Verve Records must have torn out their hair when presented with John Cale telling the story of Waldo over a guitar backdrop, on the eight minute plus 'The Gift', or 17 minutes of chunking and distorted heaven with 'Sister Ray', and Lou Reed innocently extolling the virtues of 'searching for his mainline' or 'oh man I haven't got the time time, too busy sucking on his ding dong'.

» Tracks: *White Light; White Heat; The Gift; Lady Godiva's Operation; Here She Comes Now; I Heard Her Call My Name; Sister Ray.*

★ First released 1968
★ UK peak chart position: did not chart
★ USA peak chart position: 171
★ Previous Top 1000 position: 1998 (282): 1994 (239)

310 PIECES OF YOU ↑
Jewel

An extraordinary debut, both in terms of maturity and sales. Produced by ex-Neil Young cohort Ben Keith, the album, subtitled *What We Call Human Nature In Actuality Is Human Habit*, was one of the standout albums of 1997. Lyrically between Suzanne Vega and Beth Orton, the album is full of surprises on the ear, not all of them sweet. The title-track is meant to hurt with its ironic cruelty. Jewel has the range of Joni Mitchell, Joan Baez and Emmylou Harris in a contemporary setting. She is definitely a major new talent, providing there are more stories like these ones to tell, even if she makes up the new ones.

» Tracks: *Who Will Save Your Soul; Pieces Of You; Little Sister; Foolish Games; Near You Always; Painters; Morning Song; Adrian; I'm Sensitive; You Were Meant For Me; Don't; Daddy; Angel Standing By; Amen; Foolish Games.*

★ First released 1997
★ UK peak chart position: did not chart
★ USA peak chart position: 4
★ Previous Top 1000 position: 1998 (891): 1994 (–)

311 THROWING COPPER ↑
Live

Live sound like a cross between Nirvana and Counting Crows, with a lead vocalist (Ed Kowalczyk) who has definite shades of Michael Stipe (he even gets a credit on the sleeve). This album was one of the most successful of the year in the USA, where it approached sales of seven million copies. Although lyrically they were standard-fare 'angst' rock, one song managed to upset their home-town of York, in Pennsylvania. The song 'Shit Towne' did little to see the boys welcomed home after their success. They mostly succeed, however, and tracks such as 'All Over You' have no controversial content and are simply high-standard rock.

» Tracks: *The Dam At Otter Creek; Selling The Drama; I Alone; Iris; Lightning Crashes; Top; All Over You; Shit Towne; T.B.D.; Stage; Waitress; Pillar Of Davidson; White Discussion.*

★ First released 1994
★ UK peak chart position: 37
★ USA peak chart position: 1
★ Previous Top 1000 position: 1998 (585): 1994 (–)

312 TRAFFIC ↑
Traffic

On their second album the cottage dwellers from Berkshire refined their hippie pop into a looser and vastly mature work. Evocative tales of nonsense in the beautiful '40,000 Headmen', joyful malarkey with Dave Mason's 'You Can All Join In' and 'Feelin Alright', which was a signpost to Mason's imminent departure. Throughout the record Jim Capaldi's understated yet steady drums demonstrate just what a great rock drummer should do, and Chris Wood's sound is everywhere, with trills on flute and blasts on saxophone. Traffic's greatness is bought to the fore with the recent expanded and remastered version of this winner.

» Tracks: *You Can All Join In; Pearly Queen; Don't Be Sad; Who Knows What Tomorrow May Bring; Feelin Alright; Vagabond Virgin; 40,000 Headmen; Cryin' To Be Heard; No Time To Live; Means To An End.*

★ First released 1968
★ UK peak chart position: 9
★ USA peak chart position: 17
★ Previous Top 1000 position: 1998 (501): 1994 (146)

313 TUESDAY NIGHT MUSIC CLUB ↑ Sheryl Crow

Sheryl Crow's previous credentials included working with Eric Clapton. Then suddenly she stepped forward and delivered an album of such breathtaking maturity that it sounded as though she had been making albums forever. Furthermore, she also sounds like we have been listening to her for 20 years. However, this debut album has tended to be overplayed on mainstream rock radio. The full-bodied anguish of 'Run, Baby, Run' complements the cutesy Ricky Lee Jones voice on 'All I Wanna Do'; her lyrics are honest, original and never dull, and are wrapped around immediate songs. An album to go back to occasionally.

▶▶ Tracks: Run, Baby, Run; Leaving Las Vegas; Strong Enough; Can't Cry Anymore; Solidify; No One Said It Would Be Easy; What I Can Do For You; All I Wanna Do; We Do What We Can; I Shall Believe.

★ First released 1994
★ UK peak chart position: 8
★ USA peak chart position: 3
★ Previous Top 1000 position: 1998 (759): 1994 (738)

314 BERLIN ↑ Lou Reed

This album missed the bus in the USA but was his most successful album in the UK. One theory is that his association with David Bowie kicked it into action. Another is that the overtly European theme appealed to more people outside the USA. Over the years this has all changed; Berlin is now viewed as a tremendous work, and second only to his albatross, Transformer. Reed's rich patina vocal may be flat but on tracks such as 'Caroline Says II' and 'Sad Song', it benefits the song. The darkness of the album is best exemplified by the powerful suicide of 'The Bed'. Reed is at his most moribund, yet sings with a childlike skip in his voice.

▶▶ Tracks: Berlin; Lady Day; Men Of Good Fortune; Caroline Says I; How Do You Think It Feels; Oh Jim; Caroline Says II; The Kids; The Bed; Sad Song.

★ First released 1973
★ UK peak chart position: 7
★ USA peak chart position: 98
★ Previous Top 1000 position: 1998 (621): 1994 (–)

315 FREAK OUT! ↑ Frank Zappa/The Mothers Of Invention

Led by the irascible Frank Zappa, The Mothers Of Invention were outsiders, even on this, their debut album. Older than most of their contemporaries, they brought a cynicism to their work that celebrated joys without recourse to nostalgia. Telling parodies of pop forms were as engaging as those upon which they drew, while experimental pieces, drawn from avant garde compositions by Edgar Varese and Stravinsky, took the notion of 'rock' into uncharted territory. Zappa's overview allowed such contrasting elements to function without disengagement, his skills as musician and engineer ensuring the innovative nature of this creation. It is also still great fun to listen to.

▶▶ Tracks: Hungry Freaks, Daddy; I Ain't Got No Heat; Who Are The Brain Police?; Go Cry On Somebody Else's Shoulder; Motherly Love; How Could I Be Such A Fool; Wowie Zowie; You Didn't Try To Call Me; Any Way The Wind Blows; I'm Not Satisfied; You're Probably Wondering Why I'm Here; Trouble Every Day; Help, I'm A Rock; The Return Of The Son Of Monster Magnet.

★ First released 1967 ★ UK peak chart position: did not chart
★ USA peak chart position: 130
★ Previous Top 1000 position: 1998 (351): 1994 (221)

316 MTV UNPLUGGED IN NEW YORK ↓ Nirvana

Recorded in November 1993, Kurt Cobain was dead by the time this beautiful record was released, shooting himself into notoriety as rock music's most significant casualty since John Lennon. MTV Unplugged is the acoustic antithesis of Nirvana's studio albums, casting the net wide to take in cover versions of songs by Lead Belly, David Bowie, the Meat Puppets and the Vaselines, alongside eloquent readings of songs from all three Nirvana albums. Though Cobain's voice struggles on several of the tracks, the overall atmosphere is of an intimate and wonderfully human recording, offering little indication of the tragedy that was to follow.

▶▶ Tracks: About A Girl; Come As You Are; Jesus Doesn't Want Me For A Sunbeam; The Man Who Sold The World; Pennyroyal Tea; Dumb; Polly; On A Plain; Something In The Way; Plateau; Oh Me; Lake Of Fire; All Apologies; Where Did You Sleep Last Night.

★ First released 1994
★ UK peak chart position: 1
★ USA peak chart position: 1
★ Previous Top 1000 position: 1998 (119): 1994 (–)

317 THE YES ALBUM ↑
Yes

OK, so much of Yes' output was pretentious, overblown and over-long. However, that does not detract from the volume of adventurous and technically brilliant work that lies buried beneath the less enduring (and endearing) stuff. *The Yes Album* benefits from having been recorded before Jon Anderson's lyrics became embarrassingly obtuse, and before the producers lost the use of their fader fingers. The album opens with a storming 'Yours Is No Disgrace', Steve Howe excels on 'The Clap', the band take 'Starship Trooper' into orbit, and we all sing along to 'I've Seen All Good People'. It's really not all that proggy after all, and those bits are pretty clever.

▶▶ Tracks: *Yours Is No Disgrace; The Clap; Starship Trooper; Life Seeker; Disillusion; Wurm; I've Seen All Good People; Your Move; All Good People; A Venture; Perpetual Change.*

★ First released 1971
★ UK peak chart position: 7
★ USA peak chart position: 40
★ Previous Top 1000 position: 1998 (356): 1994 (382)

318 MADONNA ↑
Madonna

Now manufactured as *The First Album*, this marked the debut of the biggest new female pop star of the 80s, and one that will be remembered throughout her life, regardless of any new music. Madonna was *the* female pop icon that the world had always sought. As for the music, this is a credible debut of familiar-sounding pop that broke no barriers. Today, the 80s drum machine and synths sound stodgy and dated. More significant was the clear signal that here was a major new artist in the making. Not only was Madonna outspoken and outrageously confident but she wrote all her own songs, and it is the songs that stand out regardless of the production.

▶▶ Tracks: *Lucky Star; Borderline; Burning Up; I Know It; Holiday; Think Of Me; Physical Attraction; Everybody.*

★ First released 1982
★ UK peak chart position: 6
★ USA peak chart position: 8
★ Previous Top 1000 position: 1998 (871): 1994 (-)

319 RADIO CITY ↓
Big Star

Big Star's level of influence is inversely proportionate to their sales. *Radio City*, the second album by the band from Memphis, Tennessee, is the greatest example of this phenomenon. When it was first released, practically the only people who knew about it were rock critics. Today, it is universally recognized as a major inspiration for the indie and alternative rock movements, influencing everyone from R.E.M. to Teenage Fanclub. Although the term 'power pop' had been kicking around for a while, *Radio City* defined the genre. Best-known (or least-obscure) of its tracks is the sparkling 'September Gurls', which has been covered by many artists, including the Bangles and the late-model Searchers. Still very modern in sound, it is a landmark of the second pop era.

▶▶ Tracks: *O My Soul; Life Is White; Way Out West; What's Goin Ahn; You Get What You Deserve; Mod Lang; Back Of A Car; Daisy Glaze; She's A Mover; September Gurls; Morpha Too; I'm In Love With A Girl.*

★ First released 1974
★ UK peak chart position: did not chart
★ US peak chart position: did not chart
★ Previous Top 1000 position: 1998 (211): 1994 (-)

320 STRAIGHT OUTTA COMPTON
↑ NWA

They might have lacked Chuck D's dexterity, but when Ice Cube, Dr Dre, MC Ren, Eazy-E, *et al.* arrived on the scene in 1988 they did so with irresistible force. The intensity of the music, the brutality of the rhymes and the explicit violence of the lyrics single-handedly triggered gangsta rap. There had been historical precedents, notably Schooly-D, but we have *Straight Outta Compton* to blame for everything from the Geto Boys to Snoop Doggy Dogg (whom Dre would produce). Unlike Public Enemy, NWA were unable to maintain the momentum, and after this album their influence would dissipate with the defection of chief lyricist Cube. However, this album even provoked the interest of the FBI.

▶▶ Tracks: *Straight Outta Compton; Fu** The Police; Gangsta Gangsta; If It Ain't Rough It Ain't Me; Parental Discretion Is Advised; Express Yourself; I Ain't The One; Dopeman; Compton's In The House; 8 Ball.*

★ First released 1989
★ UK peak chart position: 41
★ USA peak chart position: 37
★ Previous Top 1000 position: 1998 (682): 1994 (561)

321   IMPERIAL BEDROOM ↓
Elvis Costello

Costello clearly had a lot to get off his chest on this album, dealing with emotional turmoil, a lot related to his own circumstances. While much of its lyrical brilliance deals with his own thoughts, a small percentage slipped through with which we mortals could empathize. Now, having shown us he can tackle humour, politics and romance like no other, *Imperial Bedroom* was his most substantial album, as the issues covered will always be relevant and important. Chris Difford pitched in with one composition, 'Boy With A Problem'; perhaps Costello found it too painful to write so directly about himself? Every track is powerful, simply follow the lyrics. A gigantic record.

» Tracks: *Beyond Belief; Tears Before Bedtime; Shabby Doll; The Long Honeymoon; Man Out Of Time; Almost Blue; And In Every Home; The Loved Ones; Human Hands; Kid About It; Little Savage; Boy With A Problem; Pidgin English; You Little Fool; Town Crier.*

★ First released 1982
★ UK peak chart position: 6
★ USA peak chart position: 30
★ Previous Top 1000 position: 1998 (147): 1994 (37)

322   TALKING BOOK ↓
Stevie Wonder

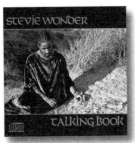

An even more mature album from the artist who confirmed everything promised on *Music Of My Mind*. Although he came dangerously close to AOR the quality of the songs and the remarkable choice of running order makes this an all-important Wonder album. Even if you choose to skip the MOR first track 'You Are The Sunshine Of My Life', the beautifully relaxing sound will eventually force you to admit your romantic vulnerability. Jeff Beck sneaks in some subtle guitar on 'Lookin' For Another True Love' and Wonder plays some innovative Arp and Moog Synthesizers throughout. One of the most memorable albums of the 70s.

» Tracks: *You Are The Sunshine Of My Life; Maybe Your Baby; You And I (We Can Conquer The World); Tuesday Heartbreak; You've Got It Bad Girl; Superstition; Big Brother; Blame It On The Sun; Lookin' For Another Pure Love; I Believe (When I Fall In Love It Will Be Forever).*

★ First released 1972
★ UK peak chart position: 16
★ USA peak chart position: 3
★ Previous Top 1000 position: 1998 (159): 1994 (51)

323   BAD COMPANY ↑
Bad Company

This is not heavy metal, this is not rock, this is heavy rock. There is a subtle difference and Bad Company embodied it. Coming out of the blues-based band Free, Paul Rodgers immediately found good company with the talented guitarist Mick Ralphs who had recently baled out of Mott The Hoople. Although subsequent albums reworked the same basic theme, this is the standard by which Bad Company should be judged. Tightly structured songs, driving beat, immaculate guitar and, of course, the definitive vocals of Rodgers. Just replay 'Can't Get Enough', 'Bad Company' and 'Ready For Love' as a reminder, and finish with the gentle 'Seagull', one of Rodgers/Ralphs' finest compositions.

» Tracks: *Can't Get Enough; Rock Steady; Ready For Love; Don't Let Me Down; Bad Company; The Way I Choose; Movin' On; Seagull.*

★ First released 1974
★ UK peak chart position: 3
★ USA peak chart position: 1
★ Previous Top 1000 position: 1998 (740): 1994 (297)

324   GRIEVOUS ANGEL ↓
Gram Parsons

Parsons' short life had already ended by the time his second album was released. An inevitable poignancy colours its content, but the singer's work was always charged with atmosphere. His subject matter followed accustomed country music precepts – broken hearts, stolen love and mortality – but Parsons' grasp of melody and lyrical intensity showed remarkable insight and ensured the lasting quality of his work. His duets with Emmylou Harris possess a heartfelt vulnerability and stand among the finest popular music has produced. Parsons' articulation of naked emotion is his final legacy. His status now is neither overblown or undeserved, he was a pioneer of the west. This CD is now packaged with the follow -up *GP* – a fantastic bargain.

» Tracks: *Return Of The Grievous Angel; Hearts On Fire; I Can't Dance; Brass Buttons; $1000 Dollar Wedding; Medley Live From Northern Quebec: a) Cash On The Barrelhead, b) Hickory Wind; Love Hurts; Las Vegas; In My Hour Of Darkness.*

★ First released 1974
★ UK peak chart position: did not chart
★ USA peak chart position: 195
★ Previous Top 1000 position: 1998 (141): 1994 (770)

325 DANGEROUS ↑
Michael Jackson

After a lengthy gap of nearly five years, Michael Jackson had to pull something out of the bag. *Bad* was, after all, a difficult act to follow, and the press were trying to prove he was bonkers. This was a pretty decent attempt and fell in with the hard dance beat of the early 90s. 'Heal The World' was much like the old melodic Jackson, and it became a major hit. 'Black Or White' was the best of the rest, a well-constructed song in which he attempted to repeat 'Ebony And Ivory' in the context of 90s dance music. All was well until he jarred when he rhymed 'nations' with 'relations'. Yucccch!

» Tracks: *Jam; Why You Wanna Trip On Me; In The Closet; She Drives Me Wild; Remember The Time; Can't Let Her Get Away; Heal The World; Black Or White; Who Is It; Give In To Me; Will You Be There; Keep The Faith; Gone Too Soon; Dangerous.*

★ First released 1991
★ UK peak chart position: 1
★ USA peak chart position: 1
★ Previous Top 1000 position: 1998 (721): 1994 (–)

326 THE WHO SELL OUT ↓
The Who

One of the most memorable album cover images of the 60s is of baby-faced Roger Daltrey really sitting in a bath of cold baked beans. Apart from the cover, the music encapsulates London in the swinging 60s. The segments of pirate Radio London and the corny Rotosound strings are priceless. This album was and still is much more appreciated in the USA; maybe they saw something we failed to see. The CD reissue with extra tracks certainly proves the point. The track order and editing is faultless; 'Armenia City In The Sky' is followed by the sensational acoustic guitar of 'Mary Anne With The Shaky Hand' and the stinging opening bass note of 'I Can See For Miles' is still euphoric.

» Tracks: *Armenia City In The Sky; Heinz Baked Beans; Mary Anne With The Shaky Hand; Odorono; Tattoo; Our Love Was; I Can See For Miles; I Can't Reach You; Medac; Relax; Silas Stingy; Sunrise; Rael 1; Rael 2; Glittering Girl; Melancholia; Someone's Coming; Jaguar; Early Morning Cold Taxi; Hall Of The Mountain King; Girl's Eyes; Mary Anne With The Shaky Hand (Alternate); Glow Girl.*

★ First released 1967
★ UK peak chart position: 13
★ USA peak chart position: 48
★ Previous Top 1000 position: 1998 (121): 1994 (–)

327 GRACE & DANGER ↓
John Martyn

Martyn shared the break-up of his marriage to Beverly with us, by tearing open his heart and exposing all his emotions on record. Those listeners who were experiencing similar problems found it torturously compelling. The three emotional killers run consecutively – 'Sweet Little Mystery', 'Hurt In Your Heart' and 'Baby Please Come Home'. Each one pleads, begs and reasons and inevitably you ask, how on earth could she ever leave him? The answer is in the penultimate track where he announces, 'I saved some for me' and 'I didn't give it all'. If you survived this album you can survive anything in later life, as our John seems to have done.

» Tracks: *Some People Are Crazy; Grace And Danger; Lookin' On; Johnny Too Bad; Sweet Little Mystery; Hurt In Your Heart; Baby Please Come Home; Save Some For Me; Our Love.*

★ First released 1980
★ UK peak chart position: 54
★ USA peak chart position: did not chart
★ Previous Top 1000 position: 1998 (313): 1994 (435)

328 TUNNEL OF LOVE ↓
Bruce Springsteen

Popular music as an art form has attained some of its greatest peaks when dealing with the thorny material of relationships. Bruce Springsteen's *Tunnel Of Love*, a powerful meditation on his own disintegrating marriage, represents a classic of its type. Predominantly an intimate solo recording the songs convey the gamut of emotions experienced in a long-term relationship, from desire ('Ain't Got You') through disquiet and deceit ('Tunnel Of Love' and 'Brilliant Disguise') to despair ('When You're Alone'), ending on a note of cautious optimism ('Valentine's Day'). Springsteen would never again be as nakedly emotional as he was on this beautiful and honest album.

» Tracks: *Ain't Got You; Tougher Than The Rest; All That Heaven Will Allow; Spare Parts; Cautious Man; Walk Like A Man; Tunnel Of Love; Two Faces; Brilliant Disguise; One Step Up; When You're Alone; Valentine's Day.*

★ First released 1987
★ UK peak chart position: 1
★ USA peak chart position: 1
★ Previous Top 1000 position: 1998 (145): 1994 (–)

329   FACE VALUE ↑
Phil Collins

The risk that Phil Collins took in displaying painful lyrics at an obviously harrowing time could have been taken as self-indulgence, but almost 20 years on this album is still seen as his best and most assured. The Genesis drummer displayed dynamic arrangements ('In The Air Tonight'), melancholy piano ('You Know What I Mean') and Philadelphia soul ('I Missed Again'), and wrapped up with a cover of 'Tomorrow Never Knows' at which even John Lennon would have tipped his hat. After *Face Value* Collins embarked on an extraordinarily busy career that included a rejuvenated Genesis, film roles and huge solo success, but this will always be the album closest to his heart, with the paint pot on the piano, to shame the decorator.

» Tracks: *In The Air Tonight; This Must Be Love; Behind The Lines; Roof Is Leaking; Droned; Hand In Hand; I Missed Again; You Know What I Mean; I'm Not Moving; If Leaving Me Is Easy; Tomorrow Never Knows; Thunder And Lightning.*

★ First released 1981
★ UK peak chart position: 1
★ USA peak chart position: 7
★ Previous Top 1000 position: 1998 (347): 1994 (71)

330   RATTLE AND HUM ↑
U2

The album of the movie, or the movie of the album? U2's trip into the America of myths and legends took them into the musical heartland of their heroes. Jamming and recording with both B.B. King and Bob Dylan in Sun Studios, the Irish four-piece doffed their metaphorical hats in respect and not some little awe. Jimi Hendrix's 'The Star Spangled Banner' stood alone, quietly dignified, towards the end of the set. It now seems a long way from Mephisto's Zoo TV antics, and perhaps, in retrospect, that is not such a bad thing. They sound important and grand, and that, any artist will tell you is fifty one percent of the battle.

» Tracks: *Helter Skelter; Hawkmoon 269; Van Dieman's Land; Desire; Angel Of Harlem; I Still Haven't Found What I'm Looking For; When Love Comes To Town; God Part II; Bullet The Blue Sky; Silver And Gold; Love Rescue Me; Heartland; The Star Spangled Banner; All I Want Is You; Freedom For My People; All Along The Watchtower; Pride (In The Name Of Love).*

★ First released 1988
★ UK peak chart position: 1
★ USA peak chart position: 1
★ Previous Top 1000 position: 1998 (731): 1994 (257)

331   DA CAPO ↓
Love

Although *Forever Changes* is *the* Love album, there are enough beautiful songs on *Da Capo* to make it a worthy second. 'Orange Skies' and 'She Comes In Colours' are both radiant songs, but they are dwarfed by the unusual changes and acoustic beauty of 'The Castle', probably their greatest song. 'Seven & Seven Is' is also a stand-out; the energy put into this track is phenomenal, climaxing with a nuclear ending that has been imitated but never bettered. The second side of the old vinyl album is now of course sequenced for CD. What has to be done is to program only tracks 1 to 6. Track 7 is the 18-minute 'Revelation'. What should be revealed is that your CD player never need know about it. It is a self-indulgent dog of a track that does not know when to finish.

» Tracks: *Stephanie Knows Who; Orange Skies; Que Vida!; Seven & Seven Is; The Castle; She Comes In Colours; Revelation.*

★ First released 1967
★ UK peak chart position: did not chart
★ USA peak chart position: 80
★ Previous Top 1000 position: 1998 (294): 1994 (–)

332   TWELVE DREAMS OF DR SARDONICUS ↓   Spirit

The charismatic and legendary Randy California starred alongside his stepfather Ed Cassidy with the bare-chested and handsome Jay Ferguson. Together with Mark Andes and pianist John Locke this west coast band were one of the finest to come out of the late 60s movement. This is such an excellent album it is hard to imagine that Spirit were not a more successful band. They hit a peak with this suite of songs right from the word go; 'Nothing To Hide' informs us that 'we're married to the same bride', then on to 'Nature's Way', an early ecological song, where the listener is told that something is wrong with the planet. This is a masterful concept album from which nobody ever really understood what the concept was.

» Tracks: *Prelude-Nothing To Hide; Nature's Way; Animal Zoo; Love Has Found A Way; Why Can't I Be Free; Mr. Skin; Space Child; When I Touch You; Street Worm; Life Has Just Begun; Morning Will Come; Soldier.*

★ First released 1970
★ UK peak chart position: did not chart
★ USA peak chart position: 63
★ Previous Top 1000 position: 1998 (236): 1994 (330)

333 BLUES AND THE ABSTRACT TRUTH ↓
Oliver Nelson

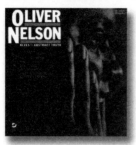

Beautifully recorded and easily the best album of Oliver Nelson's varied career, which, early on, had included stints with Louis Jordan and Quincy Jones, and conducting and arranging for Jimmy Smith (notably 'Walk On The Wild Side'). The line-up on this record is formidable and probably enhances the album's high standing – Eric Dolphy (alto and flute), Bill Evans (piano), Roy Haynes (drums), Freddie Hubbard (trumpet), George Barrow (baritone) and Nelson (alto, tenor and writer/arranger). It is hard to imagine that the man wholly behind this exceptional album was responsible for the *Six Million Dollar Man* television series theme. The sublime 'Stolen Moments' deserves to be a jazz classic.

» Tracks: *Stolen Moments; Hoe Down; Cascades; Yearnin'; Butch And Butch; Teenie's Blues.*

★ First released 1961
★ UK peak chart position: did not chart
★ USA peak chart position: did not chart
★ Previous Top 1000 position: 1998 (325): 1994 (540)

334 MAGICAL MYSTERY TOUR ↑
The Beatles

The Americans saw the sense in making this an album, with a few extra tracks. In the UK it was released as a double EP, highly original, but a pain to keep turning over four sides. The CD stopped all that, and we can universally benefit from some high-quality Beatles music. This album deserves better appreciation because it does contain three of John Lennon's finest – the swirling 'Baby You're A Rich Man', the staggering lyrics of 'I Am The Walrus' and the pinnacle, 'Strawberry Fields Forever'. The film may have disappointed but there is enough great material here to keep any dissenter quiet. America at least, appreciates it.

» Tracks: *Magical Mystery Tour; The Fool On The Hill; Flying; Blue Jay Way; Your Mother Should Know; I Am The Walrus; Hello Goodbye; Strawberry Fields Forever; Penny Lane; Baby You're A Rich Man; All You Need Is Love.*

★ First released 1967
★ UK peak chart position: 31
★ USA peak chart position: 1
★ Previous Top 1000 position: 1998 (926): 1994 (–)

335 LAZER GUIDED MELODIES ↓
Spiritualized

Since *Lazer Guided Melodies* Spiritualized have had to endure the vagaries of indie credibility, but their musical blueprint has altered little from this powerful debut. Picking up where his former band Spaceman 3 had left off, Jason Pierce refined his exploration of trance-rock with elaborate arrangements and more sympathetic production values. The up-tempo 'Run' and 'Angel Sigh' hinted at the band's awesome live sound, but the album's true heart is found in the blissed-out nirvana of tracks such as 'Symphony Space', 'Sway' and '200 Bars'. This record virtually requires the listener be in a transcendental state while it is being played.

» Tracks: *You Know It's True; If I Were With Her Now; I Want You; Run; Smiles; Step Into The Breeze; Symphony Space; Take Your Time; Shine A Light; Angel Sigh; Sway; 200 Bars.*

★ First released 1992
★ UK peak chart position: 27
★ USA peak chart position: did not chart
★ Previous Top 1000 position: 1998 (304): 1994 (–)

336 EVERYBODY ELSE IS DOING IT, SO WHY CAN'T WE ↑
The Cranberries

It is impossible to be indifferent about the Cranberries. Dolores O'Riordan has a voice that either irritates like mad, or charms you into hopeless submission. Mixing her expressive yodelling against a chiming U2 guitar sound, the band could not fail. Strong folk elements remain, because of O'Riordan's dreamlike Celtic warbling. In the USA, where Irish music always finds a strong favour, they were huge, before the British public really caught on. This album spent 130 weeks in the US chart and sold over five million copies there. Perfect songs that roll off the CD player, the only thing lacking is a lyric sheet.

» Tracks: *I Still Do; Dreams; Sunday; Pretty; Waltzing Back; Not Sorry; Linger; Wanted; Still Can't; I Will Always; How; Put Me Down.*

★ First released 1993
★ UK peak chart position: 1
★ USA peak chart position: 18
★ Previous Top 1000 position: 1998 (613): 1994 (–)

337 OGDENS' NUT GONE FLAKE
↓ The Small Faces

Having begun their career as the archetypal Mod band, the Small Faces latterly embraced traces of flower-power's whimsy. Astute enough not to sacrifice their identity, the quartet retained a distinctive perspective, as evinced by a string of superb pop singles, including 'Here Comes The Nice' and 'Itchycoo Park'. A sense of pop melody and adventurism culminated on this album which encompassed tongue-in-cheek fun ('Lazy Sunday') and passionate love songs ('Afterglow'). Steve Marriott's voice remains completely self-assured and the group's characteristic organ-based swell is often enhanced by P.P. Arnold's emotional backing vocals. Eccentric comedian Stanley Unwin narrates the concept suite 'Hapiness Stan', but the music is strong enough to withstand the novelty tag. This was the Small Faces' swan-song, at least until an ill-starred reunion, but it proved a fitting end to a golden era.

» Tracks: *Ogdens' Nut Gone Flake; Afterglow; Long Agos And Worlds Apart; Rene; Song Of A Baker; Lazy Sunday; Hapiness Stan; Rollin' Over; The Hungry Intruder; The Journey; Mad John; Happy Days Toy Town; Tin Soldier (live).*

★ First released 1967
★ UK peak chart position: 1 ★ USA peak chart position: 159
★ Previous Top 1000 position: 1998 (306): 1994 (366)

338 BOOKENDS ↑
Simon And Garfunkel

Over the years the overblown acclaim of *Bridge Over Troubled Water* has lessened as the credibility of *Bookends* has grown. The gap has slightly narrowed in succeeding years as listeners discover some of Paul Simon's most entertaining lyrics in 'Fakin' It', 'Punky's Dilemma' and 'Save The Life Of My Child', not to forget, for God's sake, 'Mrs Robinson' and the evocative 'America'. 'Toss me a cigarette, I think there's one in my raincoat', simple but immensely powerful stuff. Sadly, there is nothing to be done about still having to sit through the dreadful 'Voices Of Old People'. although CD technology makes this less painful. *Bookends* dwarfs that other album. There, its been said.

» Tracks: *Bookends; Save The Life Of My Child; America; Overs; Voices Of Old People; Old Friends; Fakin' It; Punky's Dilemma; Hazy Shade Of Winter; At The Zoo; Mrs. Robinson.*

★ First released 1968
★ UK peak chart position: 1
★ USA peak chart position: 1
★ Previous Top 1000 position: 1998 (389): 1994 (160)

339 BLUE TRAIN ↓
John Coltrane

Although it would seem that Alfred Lion's Blue Note label would have been the perfect home for a Bluetrane, this is his only record for the label as a leader. Notwithstanding, this 1957 recording shows a confident John Coltrane before he became a giant in the field. The opening track is the leader; although a straightforward blues, it is a warming and familiar song. He is supported adequately by Lee 'Sidewinder' Morgan (trumpet), Kenny Drew (piano), Paul Chambers (bass), Curtis Fuller (trombone) and Philly Joe Jones (drums). For those fearing Coltrane is over their head, this one is an accessible treat. Coltrane may have made more important albums, but none swung as effectively as this one.

» Tracks: *Blue Train; Moments Notice; The Locomotion; I'm Old Fashioned; Lazy Bird.*

★ First released 1957
★ UK peak chart position: did not chart
★ USA peak chart position: did not chart
★ Previous Top 1000 position: 1998 (329): 1994 (717)

340 EROTICA ↑
Madonna

Madonna set out to shock and outrage and she absolutely succeeded. She pushed the obscenity law to the limit, with the stage act and with the photographs in the book that was published at the same time. The music, however, was pretty tame and was mainly innuendo, and nowhere near as overtly sexual as, say, Jen Tryin or PJ Harvey. *Erotica* succeeded when combined with Madonna's blush-inducing live show. Her version of Peggy Lee's classic 'Fever' is warm compared to the original breathy version, but the remaining material is highly charged disco pop. 'Where Life Begins' does challenge the listener to 'go down where it's warm inside', but the songs succeed on their own, without the contrived sex.

» Tracks: *Erotica; Fever; Bye Bye Baby; Deeper And Deeper; Where Life Begins; Bad Girl; Waiting; Thief Of Hearts; Words; Rain; Why's It So Hard; In This Life; Secret Garden.*

★ First released 1992
★ UK peak chart position: 2
★ USA peak chart position: 2
★ Previous Top 1000 position: 1998 (544): 1994 (–)

341 FAITH ↑
George Michael

Before *Faith* George Michael was, to the record buyer, one half (or more) of Wham!, with its trite pop material and sexy pina colada teen image. *Faith* was crafted to establish him as a mature artist and serious lyricist, and it accomplished exactly that. Having had two years in gestation, it sold over 10 million copies and launched Michael's new personal and artistic image. 'I Want Your Sex' was a guaranteed number 1 hit after being widely banned, and was followed by five more hit singles. Although now seeming dated by its club-style production and spoilt by some embarrassing lyrics, it nevertheless marked the emergence of a major pop talent for the 90s.

➤ Tracks: *Faith; Father Figure; I Want Your Sex, Pt. 1 & 2; One More Try; Hard Day; Hand To Mouth; Look At Your Hands; Monkey; Kissing A Fool; Hard Day; Last Request (I Want Your Sex, Pt. 3).*

★ First Released 1987
★ UK peak chart position: 1
★ USA peak chart position: 1
★ Previous Top 1000 position: 1998 (376): 1994 (–)

342 TEA FOR THE TILLERMAN ↑
Cat Stevens

The series of albums Yusuf Islam (formerly Cat Stevens) made following this magnificent introspective set were all of similar but gradually declining quality. What was totally original became less so, even though his voice retained its sad quality and his acoustic guitar was as wooden as ever. This record has been played so many hundreds of times that the running order seems automatic: the long intro on 'Where Do The Children Play', into 'Hard Headed Woman', and then on track 3 wait for the middle eight – 'oh baby baby it's a wild world'. Turn it over and you still have 'Father And Son' yet to come. The CD makes life easier.

➤ Tracks: *Where Do The Children Play; Hard Headed Woman; Wild World; Sad Lisa; Miles From Nowhere; But I Might Die Tonight; Longer Boats; Into White; On The Road To Find Out; Father And Son; Tea For The Tillerman.*

★ First released 1970
★ UK peak chart position: 20
★ USA peak chart position: 8
★ Previous Top 1000 position: 1998 (744): 1994 (298)

343 WE'RE ONLY IN IT FOR THE MONEY ↓
Frank Zappa/Mothers Of Invention

The early Frank Zappa albums were treasured by the few and totally misunderstood by the majority. The brilliant satire of the *Sgt. Pepper* cover should have garnered extra sales, but no. Zappa's scathing wit homed in on modern middle-class America and the west coast hippies. Nineteen vignettes of *avant garde*, doo-wop, some regular pop music and a lot of hilarious dialogue, which was so hip it has never dated. Zappa made us confront the obvious, and the results were alarming. These issues are best demonstrated on 'What's The Ugliest Part Of Your Body', 'Bow Tie Daddy' and 'The Idiot Bastard Son'.

➤ Tracks: *Are You Hung Up; Who Needs The Peace Corps; Concentration Moon; Mom & Dad; Telephone Conversation; Bow Tie Daddy; Harry, You're A Beast; What's The Ugliest Part Of Your Body; Absolutely Free; Flower Punk; Hot Poop; Nasal Retentive Calliope Music; Let's Make The Water Turn Black; The Idiot Bastard Son; Lonely Little Girl; Take Your Clothes Off When You Dance; What's The Ugliest Part Of Your Body; Mother People; The Chrome Plated Megaphone Of Destiny.*

★ First released 1967 ★ UK peak chart position: did not chart
★ USA peak chart position: 30
★ Previous Top 1000 position: 1998 (205): 1994 (–)

344 LIFE AFTER DEATH ↑
The Notorious B.I.G.

Fabulous arrangements, thoughtful samples and production by Sean 'Puffy' Combs make this ambitious double CD easy on the ear. Notorious B.I.G. had a hip-hop voice that never grated; in fact, he had the ability to lapse into smooth soul so easily, he could have been Luther Vandross. Rap has come a long way since the angry shouters, and this takes the genre to a peak of perfection; listeners who feel that rap is not for them should start with this as a sampler. The sermonizing is there, and much of it is relevant, but there is so much cool soul that the record is easy on the ear. Tragically, in the light of his later murder, B.I.G. posed for the album cover standing beside a hearse.

➤ Tracks: *Life After Death Intro; Somebody's Gotta Die; Hypnotize; Kick In The Door; !@ You Tonight; Last Day; I Love The Dough; What's Beef; B.I.G. Interlude; Mo Money Mo Problems; Niggas Bleed; I Got A Story To Tell; Notorious Thugs; Miss U; Another; Going Back To Cali; Ten Crack Commandments; Playa Hater; Nasty Boy; Sky's The Limit; The World Is Filled; My Downfall; Long Kiss Goodnight; You're Nobody (Til Somebody Kills You).*

★ First released 1997
★ UK peak chart position: 23 ★ USA peak chart position: 1
★ Previous Top 1000 position: 1998 (816): 1994 (–)

345 HATS ↑
The Blue Nile

Finding a category into which critics can slot this excellent Scottish group has been a problem. File under 'very good quality pop' no longer exists on the record label. For the uninitiated, they have the soulful, wandering nature of John Martyn, mixed with some anthemic U2, plus a tolerable dose of Deacon Blue/Simply Red. A strong 80s synthesizer backdrop may deter, but the lush arrangements are truly pleasing. Paul Buchanan has an emotive voice that is well suited to his melancholic material. Three albums in nearly 15 years is hardly prolific, but they are all critically acclaimed and quality is always better than quantity.

❯❯ Tracks: *Over The Hillside; The Downtown Lights; Let's Go Out Tonight; Headlights On The Parade; From A Late Night Train; Seven A.M.; Saturday Night.*

★ First released 1989
★ UK peak chart position: 12
★ USA peak chart position: 108
★ Previous Top 1000 position: 1998 (402): 1994 (–)

346 OUT OF THE BLUE ↑
Electric Light Orchestra

Leader Jeff Lynne took his Lennon/Beatles sound to the extreme by releasing a double album of Beatlesque pop. Hit after hit followed and it is arguable that radio overplay made us sick of the sound of the Electric Light Orchestra and their subsequent fall from credibility. However, this would be unfair since Lynne is a master songwriter and this album is crammed full of great melodies and 'interesting twiddly bits'. Rather than recall the flogged hits, let us recall other corkers; 'Jungle', 'Standing In The Rain' and 'Birmingham Blues'. Who will own up to building the impossible cardboard cut-out space ship that came with the original, and how many still exist?

❯❯ Tracks: *Turn To Stone; It's Over; Sweet Talkin' Woman; Across The Border; Night In The City; Starlight; Jungle; Believe Me Now; Steppin' Out; Standing In The Rain; Summer And Lightning; Mr. Blue Sky; Sweet Is The Night; The Whale; Wild West Hero; Birmingham Blues.*

★ First released 1977
★ UK peak chart position: 4
★ USA peak chart position: 4
★ Previous Top 1000 position: 1998 (434): 1994 (219)

347 SLIPPERY WHEN WET ↓
Bon Jovi

Bon Jovi took a few faltering steps with their promising self-titled debut album and its shoddy *7800 Degrees Fahrenheit* follow-up. However, it was with this third record, a mixture of New Jersey storytelling and songwriter/collaborator Desmond Child's keen awareness of commercial appeal, that the perfect equation of songs and suss was established. The almost noble 'Wanted Dead Or Alive' spawned a thousand copycat monochrome, on-the-road videos, while the sure-fire snap of 'Livin' On A Prayer' and 'You Give Love A Bad Name' simply elevated the banner much higher. Jon Bon is a consummate professional desperately trying to be a bit bad. He can't, he was born to be good.

❯❯ Tracks: *Let It Rock; You Give Love A Bad Name; Livin' On A Prayer; Social Disease; Wanted Dead Or Alive; Raise Your Hands; Without Love; I'd Die For You; Never Say Goodbye; Wild In The Streets.*

★ First released 1986
★ UK peak chart position: 6
★ USA peak chart position: 1
★ Previous Top 1000 position: 1998 (312): 1994 (119)

348 PARANOID ↑
Black Sabbath

The murderous riff on which the title track hinges set the tone for this bruising album. Doom, death and destruction are Black Sabbath's staple diet, which they devour with numbing intensity. Repetition is at the heart of the album, sustained chords and ponderous bass often slowing tempos to crawling pace until, on 'War Pigs', they groan with suffocation. Guitarist Tony Iommi punctuates the sound with simple but lengthy solos, leaving vocalist Ozzy Osbourne to inject a sly cockiness. Pretenders have often grasped at their crown, but *Paranoid* shows that Black Sabbath remain the quintessential heavy metal band. Thirty years on and the old vinyl is being replaced by CD, just to see how good 'Paranoid' sounds.

❯❯ Tracks: *Paranoid; War Pigs; Planet Caravan; Iron Man; Electric Funeral; Hand Of Doom; Rat Salad; Fairies Wear Boots; Wicked World.*

★ First released 1970
★ UK peak chart position: 1
★ USA peak chart position: 12
★ Previous Top 1000 position: 1998 (375): 1994 (94)

349 BIRTH OF THE COOL ↓
Miles Davis

Although this album is credited to Miles Davis, the importance of Gerry Mulligan's playing and, especially, his stellar compositions 'Jeru', 'Rocker' and the gorgeous 'Venus De Milo', make this 1956 album special. Although it is generally considered to be less accomplished than *Kind Of Blue*, this collection is, in some ways more important. It would be churlish to say this was the birth of the cool, but the songs recorded by the legendary nonet and collected together here certainly mark the birth of something significant. Hearing all the tracks on the newly available CD version makes it more complete, and therefore, more necessary than ever. It is an indispensable album, now superseded by the *Complete Birth Of The Cool*.

» Tracks: *Move; Jeru; Moon Dreams; Venus De Milo; Budo; Deception; Godchild; Boplicity; Rocker; Israel; Rouge.*

★ First released 1950
★ UK peak chart position: did not chart
★ USA peak chart position: did not chart
★ Previous Top 1000 position: 1998 (234): 1994 (42)

350 MUSIC FOR THE MASSES ↑
Depeche Mode

Not only one of the bands which dominated the charts for most of the 80s, but one which typified the music that is now looked back on as the sound of that decade. Their Germanic electronic pop became softer on this album. They were becoming more of a band and they were beginning to rock, just a little. Keyboards still dominated but the melody seemed less regimented. Vocalist Dave Gahan excelled, as his voice grew in power. In a year or two they would become stadium rock stars, and change forever. The reissued CD has a number of excellent bonus tracks including some interesting remixed material.

» Tracks: *Never Let Me Down Again; The Things You Said; Strangelove; Sacred; Little 15; Behind The Wheel; I Want You Now; To Have And To Hold; Nothing; Pimpf; Agent Orange; Never Let Me Down Again (Aggro Mix); To Have And To Hold (Spanish Taster); Pleasure Little Treasure (Glitter Mix).*

★ First released 1987
★ UK peak chart position: 10
★ USA peak chart position: 35
★ Previous Top 1000 position: 1998 (797): 1994 (–)

351 THE NUMBER OF THE BEAST
↑ Iron Maiden

A creative zenith for Iron Maiden. Capitalizing on new vocalist Bruce Dickinson and his rapturous wail, along with a keen eye for songwriting detail, *The Number Of The Beast* is an uncompromising, though surprisingly subtle, great hard rock record. Subject matter includes *The Prisoner* television series as well as the plight of the native American in the Old West. They combine arch arrangements with a telling use of melody that, after the initial assault, lingers brilliantly in the mind. Dickinson has recently returned to the fold, after a few years in solo land. A rejuvenated Maiden can now use most of this album's material with a fresh eye.

» Tracks: *The Invaders; Children Of The Damned; The Prisoner; 22, Acacia Avenue; The Number Of The Beast; Run To The Hills; Gangland; Hallowed Be Thy Name.*

★ First released 1982
★ UK peak chart position: 1
★ USA peak chart position: 33
★ Previous Top 1000 position: 1998 (363): 1994 (229)

352 I NEVER LOVED A MAN THE WAY I LOVE YOU ↓
Aretha Franklin

Following her signing to Atlantic, Aretha emerged from years of often inappropriate recordings with Columbia Records. The Jerry Wexler-produced masterpiece 'I Never Loved A Man', is still one of soul music's definitive moments. The song's simple, uncluttered arrangement allowed the singer free expression and her sense of artistic relief is palpable. The attendant album captured all of Franklin's gifts as she brings gospel fervour and individuality to a peerless collection of songs. Material drawn from Sam Cooke, Otis Redding and Ray Charles is infused with a rampant spirituality and given new perspectives when sung by this woman. The set also provides a showcase for Franklin's own compositional skills, as well as her propulsive piano playing. This album unleashed her to become the world's greatest female singer.

» Tracks: *Respect; Drown In My Own Tears; I Never Loved A Man (The Way I Love You); Soul Serenade; Don't Let Me Lose This Dream; Baby, Baby, Baby; Dr. Feelgood (Love Is A Serious Business); Good Times; Do Right Woman Do Right Man; Save Me; A Change Is Gonna Come.*

★ First released 1967
★ UK peak chart position: 36
★ USA peak chart position: 2
★ Previous Top 1000 position: 1998 (320): 1994 (553)

353 SAILOR ↑
Steve Miller Band

Long before Miller discovered the art of writing great short pop songs with infectious guitar licks and four chords, he had a fabulous blues band that featured Boz Scaggs. This incandescent transitional album was their last together and for the vast majority of Miller followers it remains the pinnacle. Sandwiched in-between their love for the blues and R&B with 'Gangster Of Love' and 'You're So Fine', are great rock tracks such as 'Living In The USA' and 'Dime-A-Dance Romance'. The desert island choice, however, is the imaginative instrumental 'Song For Our Ancestors'; close your eyes and you can actually hear ferry boats entering San Francisco the harbour, without needing those funny cigarettes.

❯❯ Tracks: *Song For Our Ancestors; Dear Mary; My Friend; Living In The USA; Quicksilver Girl; Lucky Man; Gangster Of Love; You're So Fine; Overdrive; Dime-A-Dance Romance.*

★ First released 1968
★ UK peak chart position: did not chart
★ USA peak chart position: 24
★ Previous Top 1000 position: 1998 (463): 1994 (303)

354 COME ON OVER ↑
Shania Twain

Opinion is divided among country music aficionados over Shania Twain. Some think she has sold out and betrayed her country roots. Others think that her move towards pop has given country a shot in the arm and will ultimately lead people towards the purer stuff. The artist observes this with a big smile and a beautiful bank statement. Twain is probably the most popular female singer at the dawn of 2000 and not without reason; this is an irresistible corker of a record. Not one weak moment and enough niggling choruses to hum in your head all day. Elitists avoid, this is for wide open ears only.

❯❯ Tracks: *Man! I Feel Like A Woman!; I'm Holdin' On To Love (To Save My Life); Love Gets Me Every Time; Don't Be Stupid (You Know I Love You); From This Moment On; Come On Over; When; Whatever You Do! Don't!; If You Wanna Touch Her, Ask!; You're Still The One; Honey, I'm Home; That Don't Impress Me Much; Black Eyes, Blue Tears; I Won't Leave You Lonely; Rock This Country!; You've Got A Way.*

★ First released 1997
★ UK peak chart position: 1
★ USA peak chart position: 2
★ Previous Top 1000 position: 1998 (–): 1994 (–)

355 ELIMINATOR ↑
Z.Z. Top

1983 was the year Z.Z. Top went from being everyone's favourite bar-room boogie band to international superstars. Graced with mind-boggling and incredibly photogenic beards, a very neat trilogy of sexist but harmless videos and a collective ear for a quite distinct and highly stylized, if somewhat grizzled, blues/pop, the sudden enormity of their success seems in retrospect like no real surprise. MTV had never quite seen the like and the attention given to the excellent 'Gimme All Your Lovin' single was quickly repeated for both 'Sharp-Dressed Man' and the quite irreverent 'Legs'. It still sounds fresh, innovative and fun today, in the wake of many imitators.

❯❯ Tracks: *Gimme All Your Lovin'; Got Me Under Pressure; Sharp-dressed Man; I Need You Tonight; I Got The Six; Legs; Thug; TV Dinners; Dirty Dog; If I Could Only Flag Her Down; Bad Girl.*

★ First released 1983
★ UK peak chart position: 3
★ USA peak chart position: 9
★ Previous Top 1000 position: 1998 (865): 1994 (409)

356 LIVE AT LEEDS ↓
The Who

The Who forged their reputation as an exciting live attraction and elected to issue this set in the wake of the highly successful *Tommy*. Selections from that ground-breaking rock opera formed the core of this concert, but the group used the opportunity equally to restate past glories and acknowledge influences. Rock 'n' roll star Eddie Cochran had inspired Pete Townshend; the former's 'Summertime Blues' exploded with new fury within. 'Young Man Blues', first recorded by jazz singer Mose Allison, was given a new dimension through power chords, pulsating drumming and Roger Daltrey's expressive vocal. The CD remastered reissue with bonus tracks is outstanding. Oh to have gone to Leeds University in 1970.

❯❯ Tracks: *Heaven And Hell; I Can't Explain; Fortune Teller; Tattoo; Young Man Blues; Substitute; Happy Jack; I'm A Boy; A Quick One (While He's Away); Amazing Journey; Sparks; Summertime Blues; Shakin' All Over; My Generation; Magic Bus.*

★ First released 1970
★ UK peak chart position: 3
★ USA peak chart position: 4
★ Previous Top 1000 position: 1998 (317): 1994 (490)

357 THE KÖLN CONCERT ↑
Keith Jarrett

Album that sell vast quantities are not always to be recommended. This exceptional example of solo piano is the biggest selling record in the 25 year history of the pioneering jazz label ECM Records. It is an almost perfect recording of the art of piano dynamics, full of emotion, and throughout the hour or so duration the listener is never bored. Jarrett has repeated his concerts of improvisation hundreds of times. Many have been recorded, and presumably, many routes of his spontaneity have led to blind alleys of jazz doodling. This and the Bremen concerts are the best recorded example of this art. A jazz record to recommend and pass on without any qualms.

➤ Tracks: *Part I; Part II a; Part II b; Part II c.*

★ First released 1975
★ UK peak chart position: did not chart
★ USA peak chart position: did not chart
★ Previous Top 1000 position: 1998 (592): 1994 (212)

358 THE WILD, THE INNOCENT & THE E STREET SHUFFLE
↑ Bruce Springsteen

Although Bruce Springsteen's world domination has cooled in recent years, he does have a back-catalogue of considerable power. This early sleeper contains at least two Springsteen classics in the shape of the lovely '4th Of July, Asbury Park (Sandy)' and the powerful concert encore 'Rosalita (Come Out Tonight)', on which saxophonist Clarence Clemons demonstrated what an asset he is to Springsteen's sound. The album failed to chart when released in 1973, and made the lists during his breakthrough year of 1975. That year, *Born To Run* turned him into a superstar, and the down-home friendliness that this record had was lost forever. The album's title summed up everything.

➤ Tracks: *The E Street Shuffle; 4th Of July, Asbury Park (Sandy); Kitty's Back; Wild Billy's Circus Story; Incident On 57th Street; Rosalita (Come Out Tonight); New York City Serenade.*

★ First released 1973
★ UK peak chart position: 33
★ USA peak chart position: 59
★ Previous Top 1000 position: 1998 (883): 1994 (–)

359 IN THE WEE SMALL HOURS ↓
Frank Sinatra

As ever, Sinatra's collaboration with his best arranger, Nelson Riddle is wholly successful, this time a magnificent statement in understated orchestration. Emotional and romantic Sinatra gently eases himself through another 16 classics of great American popular song. Although he fails to swing he never ceases to move the listener, and images of comfy sofas, scotch on the rocks and hi-fi radiograms spring to mind as the listener wallows in songs by Duke Ellington, Rodgers and Hart, Van Heusen, Arlen and Harburg, and Cole Porter. Mellow, rich and pure, and now universally acclaimed as one of the best albums Sinatra ever recorded. Top the glass up before your tears melt the ice.

➤ Tracks: *In the Wee Small Hours Of The Morning; Mood Indigo; Glad To Be Unhappy; I Get Along Without You Very Well; Deep In A Dream; I See Your Face Before Me; Can't We Be Friends?; When Your Lover Has Gone; What Is This Thing Called Love; Last Night When We Were Young; I'll Be Around; Ill Wind; It Never Entered My Mind; Dancing On The Ceiling; I'll Never Be The Same; This Love Of Mine.*

★ First released 1955 ★ UK peak chart position: did not chart
★ USA peak chart position: 2
★ Previous Top 1000 position: 1998 (222): 1994 (199)

360 GENIUS + SOUL = JAZZ ↓
Ray Charles

This is a difficult album to categorize. It is big band swing, jazz, soul, R&B, pop and blues, but mostly it is 'the genius' at work. This giant has managed to stay hip for succeeding generations and also appeal to middle-class white America. This superb recording was made in 1961 shortly before he hit his commercial peak. Do not be put off by the big band: it is dynamic stuff, for example, 'Moanin'' and 'Strike Up The Band'. The CD reissue adds three live tracks from his *Genius Hits The Road* album to make this even more necessary and vital. Regularly referring to this man as 'the genius' is not overblown.

➤ Tracks: *Mister C; From The Heart; I've Got News For You; Moanin'; Let's Go; One Mint Julep; I'm Gonna Move To The Outskirts Of Town; Stompin' Room Only; Mister; Strike Up The Band; Birth Of The Blues; Golden Boy; Booty-Butt; This Here; I Remember Clifford; Sidewinder; Bluesette; Pas-Se-O-Ne Blues; Zig Zag; Angel City; Señor Blues.*

★ First released 1961
★ UK peak chart position: did not chart
★ USA peak chart position: 4
★ Previous Top 1000 position: 1998 (339): 1994 (76)

361 LED ZEPPELIN III ↓
Led Zeppelin

They could do no wrong for many years, both in Britain and America. At the point of this album they were humungous, and, therefore, if they had gone into a recording studio and recited Milly Molly Mandy stories, they would have topped the charts. *Led Zeppelin III* was only a good album by their standards, great by most of their imitators. It was a forerunner to the peerless *IV*, and remains overshadowed by it. Hints of acoustic material to follow came with 'Gallows Pole', first rehearsed with others at Bron-Y-Aur Stomp, the idyllic 'cottage in the country'. This is followed by the fat 12-string opening sound of 'Hats Off To (Roy) Harper', a composition by the mysterious Charles Obscure.

» Tracks: *Immigrant Song; Friends; Celebration Day; Since I've Been Loving You; Out On The Tiles; Gallows Pole; Tangerine; That's The Way; Bron-Y-Aur Stomp; Hats Off To (Roy) Harper.*

★ First released 1970
★ UK peak chart position: 1
★ USA peak chart position: 1
★ Previous Top 1000 position: 1998 (346): 1994 (–)

362 LIVE AT FILLMORE EAST/ THE FILLMORE CONCERTS ↑
The Allman Brothers Band

The original *Fillmore East* album is one of the finest live documents of the rock era, capturing the original line-up of one of the 70s tightest outfits before they were cruelly robbed of Duane Allman and Berry Oakley. Taken from five 1971 performances at New York's fabled Fillmore East, the extended and effortlessly melodic workouts of 'In Memory Of Elizabeth Reed' and 'Whipping Post' remain definitive recordings. The dual guitar interplay of Duane Allman and Dickey Betts glides effortlessly over the propulsive rhythm section of Oakley and twin drummers Jaimoe and Butch Trucks, while Greg Allman's powerful blues voice and melodic keyboard work provides the icing on the cake. The expanded *Fillmore Concerts* CD adds more tracks and digital clarity.

» Tracks: *Statesboro Blues; Trouble No More; Don't Keep Me Wonderin'; In Memory Of Elizabeth Reed; One Way Out; Done Somebody Wrong; Stormy Monday; You Don't Love Me; Hot 'Lanta; Whipping Post; Mountain Jam; Drunken Hearted Boy.*

★ First Released 1971
★ UK peak chart position: did not chart
★ USA peak chart position: 13
★ Previous Top 1000 position: 1998 (406): 1994 (–)

363 GENERATION TERRORISTS ↓
Manic Street Preachers

Those fans that discovered this album when it was first released deserve to feel ever so slightly smug. It took most of the rest of the world until *Everything Must Go* before this album was fully appreciated. Sounding like a cross between metal and punk, the energy and melody never lets up for one second. After the first three tracks are over, a quick lie-down is in order before you tackle the sentiment of 'Motorcycle Emptiness'. Lyrically, the Manic Street Preachers are giants; it is a great pity that their statements of ironic values of the 80s and 90s are not listened to more. Thank goodness this album was finally discovered (except in America).

» Tracks: *Slash N' Burn; Nat West, Barclays, Midlands, Lloyds; Born To End; Motorcycle Emptiness; You Love Us; Love's Sweet Exile; Little Baby Nothing; Repeat (Stars And Stripes); Tennessee; Another Invented Disease; Stay Beautiful; So Dead; Repeat -; Spectators Of Suicide; Damn Dog; Crucifix Kiss; Methadone Pretty; Condemned To Rock N' Roll.*

★ First released 1992
★ UK peak chart position: 13
★ USA peak chart position: did not chart
★ Previous Top 1000 position: 1998 (210): 1994 (–)

364 LET'S GET IT ON ↓
Marvin Gaye

Relishing the artistic freedom afforded by the success of *What's Goin' On*, Gaye recorded this sultry paean to sex. Where its predecessor relied on complex arrangements, the straightforward sound of this focused attention on its tight rhythms, strong melodies and his expressive singing. Either celebratory, as on the explicit title track, or reflective ('Distant Lover'), he explores a range of emotions with equal ease and intensity. Seductive sound matches seductive lyrics and attitudes at a time when Al Green, Barry White and Isaac Hayes laid claim to the lover man sobriquet. *Let's Get It On* showed Marvin Gaye to be its undoubted master. Just listen to the way he delivers 'there's nothing wrong with me' on the amazing title track.

» Tracks: *Let's Get It On; Please Don't Stay (Once You Go Away); If I Should Die Tonight; Keep Gettin' It On; Come Get To This; Distant Lover; You Sure Know How To Ball; Just To Keep You Satisfied.*

★ First released 1973
★ UK peak chart position: 39
★ USA peak chart position: 2
★ Previous Top 1000 position: 1998 (271): 1994 (597)

365 THE DREAMING ↑
Kate Bush

Before *The Dreaming* Kate Bush had released three eccentric but likeable albums, yet was still widely seen as a mainstream pop artist. Writing with the aid of a drum machine and producing herself for the first time, Bush let her imagination run wild with this album's dense, convoluted arrangements, premiered by the defiantly uncommercial single 'Sat In Your Lap'. Lyrically she shed her kooky image with songs inspired by Vietnam ('Pull Out The Pin'), Aboriginal culture ('The Dreaming') and film ('Get Out Of My House'). Even though it was a commercial failure, *The Dreaming* was a blueprint album for other studio-based artists in the 80s. A pity she dozed off in the 90s.

» Tracks: *Sat In Your Lap; There Goes A Tenner; Pull Out The Pin; Suspended In Gaffa; Leave It Open; The Dreaming; Night Of The Swallow; All The Love; Houdini; Get Out Of My House.*

★ First Released 1982
★ UK peak chart position: 3
★ USA peak chart position: 157
★ Previous Top 1000 position: 1998 (542): 1994 (–)

366 BOYS FOR PELE ↑
Tori Amos

The artist challenges the listener to work out the hidden depths to this powerful album. The double entendre and sexual imagery of the lyrics are as much to do with the listener's imagination as with Amos' intention. This makes it work in so far as both male and female perspectives can be construed. If animals could read, they too would find this an agreeable record. The harpsichord and piano offer dramatic and sometimes brutally stark backgrounds, but for once the lyrics rule the song and the music becomes secondary. A special-edition CD features the Armand's Star mix of 'Professional Widow', the lightest moment of an intense but excellent record.

» Tracks: *Horses; Blood Roses; Father Lucifer; Professional Widow; Professional Widow (Armand's Star Trunk Funkin' Mix); Mr Zebra; Marianne; Caught A Lite Sneeze; Muhammad My Friend; Hey Jupiter; Way Down; Little Amsterdam; Talula (The Tornado Mix); Not The Red Baron; Agent Orange; Doughnut Song; Putting The Damage On; Twinkle.*

★ First released 1996
★ UK peak chart position: 39
★ USA peak chart position: 2
★ Previous Top 1000 position: 1998 (921): 1994 (–)

367 SAVAGE ↑
Eurythmics

Annie Lennox, the visual chameleon puts on another face; this time she is a blonde Barbie. Under the covers she is very much the familiar voice that became one of the most listened to throughout the 80s. This came towards the end, and as such is not the usual greatest hits package that many of their regular albums sounded like. Dave Stewart was beginning to experiment with electronic sound (again) as Lennox seemed to want to sing more. In 'I Need A Man', she sings of the type of man she does not want, in 'Shame' she mourns nostalgia, while in 'Savage' there is sadness, bitterness and anger. This sounds like it was a difficult album to make.

» Tracks: *Beethoven (I Love To Listen To); I've Got A Lover (Back In Japan); Do You Want To Break Up?; You Have Placed A Chill In My Heart; Shame; Savage; I Need A Man; Put The Blame On Me; Heaven; Wide Eyed Girl; I Need You; Brand New Day.*

★ First released 1987
★ UK peak chart position: 7
★ USA peak chart position: 41
★ Previous Top 1000 position: 1998 (868): 1994 (–)

368 SWING EASY! ↓
Frank Sinatra

For a number of Sinatra devotees this remains the best album above the populist *Songs For Swingin' Lovers!*. They discovered he could swing before we did. Sinatra swang on this collection, albeit in a more relaxed mode akin to 40s dance bands rather than brassy 50s orchestration. Nelson Riddle is present here, adding golden touches to Cole Porter's 'Just One Of Those Things', in addition to high-quality songs chosen with care. Everybody knew Sinatra could sing, he just needed to find the right songs and the right arranger. This album, together with its sister, *Songs For Young Lovers* (included on the CD version), started it all.

» Tracks: *Jeepers Creepers; Taking A Chance On Love; Wrap Your Troubles In Dreams; Lean Baby; I Love You; I'm Gonna Sit Right Down And Write Myself A Letter; Get Happy; All Of Me; Why Should I Cry Over You; Sunday; Just One Of Those Things.*

★ First released 1960
★ UK peak chart position: 5
★ USA peak chart position: did not chart
★ Previous Top 1000 position: 1998 (229): 1994 (56)

369 JOHN BARLEYCORN MUST DIE ↑ Traffic

This was intended to be *Mad Shadows*, the first Steve Winwood solo album following the stop-start-stop career of Traffic as a working unit. Jim Capaldi and Chris Wood were drafted in as session musicians. This logic sounds ridiculous now, as of course we always knew they would re-form. *Melody Maker* proclaimed 'TRAFFIC TO ROAR AGAIN'. The rest did them good, both physically and musically with two new Traffic standards added to their catalogue, the instrumental 'Glad' and 'Empty Pages'. The late Wood was an exceptional flute player, never hogging the limelight. The subtlety of his playing excels on the title track. They held it together for four more years after this.

» Tracks: *Glad; Freedom Rider; Empty Pages; Stranger To Himself; John Barleycorn; Every Mother's Son.*

★ First released 1970
★ UK peak chart position: 11
★ USA peak chart position: 5
★ Previous Top 1000 position: 1998 (512); 1994 (–)

370 THE DREAM OF THE BLUE TURTLES ↑ Sting

Disbanding the Police at the height of their success was a bold move, but with a set of striking cheekbones, spikey hair and a McCartneyesque ear for melody Sting was always on to a winner with his solo career. Parts of his debut album came dangerously close to scuppering his pop kudos, as Sting and his all-star jazz sessionmen backing band (Branford Marsalis, Kenny Kirkland) dabbled in vapid jazz-rock fusion. The sublime, soulful pop of 'If You Love Somebody Set Them Free' and 'Fortress Around Your Heart' indicated a more profitable and appealing direction, one that Sting would pursue to great effect on 1993's *Ten Summoner's Tales*.

» Tracks: *If You Love Somebody Set Them Free; Love Is The Seventh Wave; Russians; Children's Crusade; Shadows In The Rain; We Work The Black Seam; Consider Me Gone; The Dream Of The Blue Turtles; Moon Over Bourbon Street; Fortress Around Your Heart.*

★ First Released 1985
★ UK peak chart position: 3
★ USA peak chart position: 2
★ Previous Top 1000 position: 1998 (552); 1994 (–)

371 WORKINGMAN'S DEAD ↓ Grateful Dead

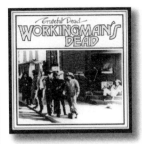

Nobody who had experienced the Grateful Dead's previous albums or live performances could have believed that they could go soft. In fact, they did it in such style that people hardly noticed. This folky gem is heavily influenced by Crosby, Stills & Nash and was their first major commercial success. Robert Hunter's lyrics dominate and suit the style and old-fashioned themes the record conjures up. Prior to this album the Dead could only jam. After this they were respected as also being able to sing, harmonize and play. A wonderfully rootsy album that is as American as the Band's self-titled record and equally as good.

» Tracks: *Uncle John's Band; High Time; Dire Wolf; New Speedway Boogie; Cumberland Blues; Black Peter; Easy Wind; Casey Jones.*

★ First released 1970
★ UK peak chart position: did not chart
★ USA peak chart position: 80
★ Previous Top 1000 position: 1998 (299); 1994 (–)

372 BRING IT ON ↑ Gomez

An exceptionally mature debut, sounding like a bunch of experienced musicians with an amazing breadth of influences and ideas. The band are a true co-operative sharing songwriting and vocal duties with shirt-changing ease. Their blend of Americana, pop, funk, soul, and blues influences creates a refreshingly original and hard to define sound. For once clever inventive music got out of the cult box and into the heart and soul of the record buying public. The excellent hit single 'Whippin' Piccadilly' alluded to the way they breezed out of Manchester and conquered the world. And still had time to catch the bus back home.

» Tracks: *Get Miles; Whippin' Piccadilly; Make No Sound; 78 Stone Wobble; Tijuana Lady; Here Comes The Breeze; Love Is Better Than A Warm Trombone; Get Myself Arrested; Free To Run; Bubble Gum Years; Rie's Wagon; The Comeback.*

★ First released 1998
★ UK peak chart position: 11
★ USA peak chart position: did not chart
★ Previous Top 1000 position: 1998 (–); 1994 (–)

373 ELTON JOHN ↑
Elton John

Still learning his craft as a songwriter, this is the album that really made the critics take notice of Elton John. Although recording techniques now make this (even on CD) sound dated, the quality of the songs and the mood they convey still have the ability to move us all. 'Your Song' will perennially be in the top 100 singles of all time. 'Border Song' and 'No Shoestrings On Louise' continue to show that Bernie Taupin should have been born in the Midwest, and romantics will still see the painful logic of 'I Need You To Turn To'. This is a remarkably mature album that often gets overlooked.

▶ Tracks: Your Song; I Need You To Turn To; Take Me To The Pilot; No Shoestrings On Louise; First Episode At Heinton; 60 Years On; Border Song; Greatest Discovery; The Cage; The King Must Die.

★ First released 1970
★ UK peak chart position: 11
★ USA peak chart position: 4
★ Previous Top 1000 position: 1998 (465); 1994 (101)

374 SWORDFISHTROMBONES ↓
Tom Waits

Tom Waits' early recordings cast him as a bohemian sage. Part Kerouac, part Bukowski, he infused beat culture with the sweep of Hollywood movie soundtracks and the precision of a Tin Pan Alley songsmith. Aware of a stylistic straitjacket, he cast it aside and produced this challenging album. Eschewing a traditional back-up group, Waits opted for a percussive sound based around marimbas, woodblocks and ever-shifting rhythm patterns. Elements of Captain Beefheart and *avant garde* composer Harry Partch can be heard as the singer roars, barks and growls through a series of adventurous compositions reliant on impression and suggestion for effect. Uncompromising and exciting, *Swordfishtrombones* is a remarkable achievement from an already unconventional sculptor.

▶ Tracks: Underground; Shore Leave; Dave The Butcher; Johnsburg, Illinois; 16 Shells From A 30.6; Town With No Cheer; In The Neighbourhood; Just Another Sucker On The Vine; Frank's Wild Years; Swordfishtrombones; Down, Down, Down; Soldier's Things; Gin Soaked Boy; Trouble's Braids; Rainbirds.

★ First released 1983
★ UK peak chart position: 62
★ USA peak chart position: 167
★ Previous Top 1000 position: 1998 (244); 1994 (174)

375 OUTLANDOS D'AMOUR ↑
The Police

It is hard to imagine, after the sophistication of *Synchronicity* and Sting's excellent solo work, together with the new age/prog direction that Andy Summers has taken, that the Police debut is a bit punky. This writer saw one of their first gigs supporting hippie darlings Spirit. They were energetic and raw but when they played 'So Lonely', 'Next To You' and 'Roxanne', you realized the potential of something really special. This album is under produced and raw but it retains a quality that cannot be quantified. These are the real inventors of white reggae-flavoured punk pop. Derivative but innovative.

▶ Tracks: Next To You; So Lonely; Roxanne; Hole In My Life; Peanuts; Can't Stand Losing You; Truth Hits Everybody; Born In The 50s; Be My Girl – Sally; Masoko Tanga.

★ First released 1979
★ UK peak chart position: 6
★ USA peak chart position: 23
★ Previous Top 1000 position: 1998 (438); 1994 (151)

376 ANTHEM OF THE SUN ↓
Grateful Dead

Although much of this seminal record was taken from 15 live gigs it counts as a studio album because of the studio content and the remarkable tape splicing that removes any audience participation. 'The Faster We Go, The Rounder We Get' is one track, and 'the older we grow the easier it gets', is how we now view this work. Quite why it works is perplexing but there is incredible depth in the instrumentation, which reveals new facets after hundreds of plays. There is also a haunting beauty about the overall sound. It is an astonishingly good record that demands concentration.

▶ Tracks: That's It For The Other One; Cryptical Envelopment; Quadlibet; For Tender Feet; The Faster We Go, The Rounder We Get; We Leave The Castle; Alligator; Caution (Do Not Stop On The Tracks).

★ First released 1968
★ UK peak chart position: did not chart
★ USA peak chart position: 87
★ Previous Top 1000 position: 1998 (340); 1994 (432)

377 HERE COME THE WARM JETS ↓ Brian Eno

Having left Roxy Music, Brian Eno began his solo career with this idiosyncratic album. Robert Fripp, Paul Thompson and Phil Manzanera are among those appearing on a set of songs exhibiting a mischievous love of pure pop music. Macabre lyrics constantly subvert the quirky melodies, a feature fully expressed on 'Baby's On Fire', while the singer's cheeky vocals exaggerate the ambiguity. Savage guitar lines, erratic synthesizer and pounding drums provide exciting textures on a collection as beguiling as it is invigorating.

» Tracks: *Needles In A Camel's Eye; The Paw Paw Negro Blowtorch; Baby's On Fire; Cindy Tells Me; Driving Me Backwards; On Some Faraway Beach; Blank Frank; Dead Finks Don't Talk; Some Of Them Are Old; Here Come The Warm Jets.*

★ First released 1974
★ UK peak chart position: 26
★ USA peak chart position: 151
★ Previous Top 1000 position: 1998 (206): 1994 (413)

378 THE TIMES THEY ARE A-CHANGIN' ↓ Bob Dylan

On his third album Dylan both redefined and expanded his musical palate. Fêted as a protest singer, a nomenclature he rejected, he brought new insight to the genre, particularly with 'Only A Pawn In Their Game', in which he paints a wider canvas relating to the murder of civil rights leader Medgar Evers. Dylan's love songs herein are particularly poignant, their stark, acoustic setting enhancing a graphic lyricism. The title song boasts a wonderful ambiguity, managing to be political and personal, the latter aspect suggesting the changes Dylan would bring to his music. The last album as a folk artist *per se*, *The Times They Are A-Changin'* is yet another essential Dylan collection.

» Tracks: *Times They Are A Changin'; The Ballad Of Hollis Brown; With God On Our Side; One Too Many Mornings; North Country Blues; Only A Pawn In Their Game; Boots Of Spanish Leather; When The Ship Comes In; Lonesome Death Of Hattie Carroll; Restless Farewell.*

★ First released 1964
★ UK peak chart position: 4
★ USA peak chart position: 20
★ Previous Top 1000 position: 1998 (256): 1994 (41)

379 ON HOW LIFE IS ↑ Macy Gray

A stunning debut that is still selling like hot doughnuts. Macy Gray has a unique voice somewhere between Eartha Kitt and Lisa out of the Simpsons. Awards have followed since its release, but it was the slowburn success of the single 'I Try' that promoted the album into the top division. The album's subtle blend of hip-hop and urban R&B provides the perfect backing for Gray's mature voice. There is nothing sweet about Macy's singing, merely a delicious twist of lemon, and it keeps her apart from the saccharine soul Barbie doll divas. Strong Al Green chord changes ('Why Didn't You Call Me') and Aretha Franklin timings ('A Moment To Myself') give credibility to a brand new star.

» Tracks: *Why Didn't You Call Me; Do Something; Caligula; I Try; Sex O Matic Venus Freak; I Can't Wait To Meetchu; Still; I've Committed Murder; A Moment To Myself; The Letter.*

★ First released 1999
★ UK peak chart position: 3
★ USA peak chart position: 4
★ Previous Top 1000 position: 1998 (–): 1994 (–)

380 SWEET DREAMS ↑ Eurythmics

Still finding their way after a disjointed debut album following the break-up of the Tourists, Annie Lennox and David A. Stewart found commercial success with this, their 'programmed' album. The electronic drums and keyboards fit well into the eerie and mysterious qualities of the songs (Edward de Bono is thanked on the sleeve). For those who thought synthesizer pop was the answer during the lull of the 80s, then the Eurythmics embodied it, and did it better than most. It will be good to see these songs performed by a live band when they eventually reform, perhaps in the 21st century.

» Tracks: *Love Is A Stranger; I've Got An Angel; Wrap It Up; I Could Give You (A Mirror); The Walk; Sweet Dreams (Are Made Of This); Jennifer; This Is The House; Somebody Told Me; This City Never Sleeps.*

★ First released 1983
★ UK peak chart position: 3
★ USA peak chart position: 15
★ Previous Top 1000 position: 1998 (639): 1994 (352)

381 PSYCHOCANDY ↓
Jesus And Mary Chain

A love of classic pop songs and sonic terrorism conspire on this euphoric collection. Fuzz guitar, distortion and feedback drench almost every track, but beneath this assertive noise lies a gift for melody inspired by the Beach Boys and girl-group genre. The contrast is beguiling and if the constituent parts are not original, the audacity of such a combination is. Understated voices and nihilistic lyrics belie the intensity forged within. Created by passionate adherents of pop culture, *Psychocandy* is one of the 80s' landmark releases, inspiring some to follow a similar course, while others took similar influences to forge a quite different perspective.

» Tracks: *Just Like Honey; The Living End; Taste The Floor; Hardest Walk; Cut Dead; In A Hole; Taste Of Cindy; Never Understand; Inside Me; Sowing Seeds; My Little Underground; You Trip Me Up; Something's Wrong; It's So Hard.*

★ First released 1985
★ UK peak chart position: 31
★ USA peak chart position: 188
★ Previous Top 1000 position: 1998 (272): 1994 (74)

382 ROCK 'N' ROLL ANIMAL ↑
Lou Reed

Reed turned from the minimalist fuelled on anger and betrayal to full-blown, heavy metal rock superstar for this album, producing a gloriously live revamping and work-out of his older hits, filled with a strutting confidence that his audience had never fully experienced before. Ferocity was at a premium with tough reworkings of 'White Light', 'White Heat', 'Sweet Jane' and 'Lady Day', among others, all recorded as part of a set at New York's Academy Of Music. Purists may have been galled by his approach, but *Rock 'N' Roll Animal* went on to earn Reed his first gold disc.

» Tracks: *Intro; Sweet Jane; White Light; White Heat; Heroin; Lady Day; Rock And Roll.*

★ First released 1974
★ UK peak chart position: 26
★ USA peak chart position: 45
★ Previous Top 1000 position: 1998 (765): 1994 (276)

383 BURNIN' ↓
Bob Marley And The Wailers

Catch A Fire launched Jamaica's Wailers into international prominence with a brilliant cross of reggae and rock. Purists did fault its emphasis on the latter, a criticism answered with the earthier *Burnin'*. Stripped of session musicians, the group's frontline harmonies were supported by the sinewy Barrett brothers rhythm section which provided a dry counterpoint. Although Bob Marley was fully in control, the support of Bunny Livingston and Peter Tosh was crucial to the overall sound. Their vocal interplay mirrored that of the Impressions, but lyrically the Wailers proclaimed a vibrant militancy instantly heard on 'Get Up Stand Up'. Eric Clapton helped to popularize 'I Shot The Sherrif', but this album is noteworthy for its uncompromising blend of polemics and tough melodies.

» Tracks: *Get Up Stand Up; Hallelujah Time; I Shot The Sheriff; Burnin' And Lootin'; Put It On; Small Axe; Pass It On; Duppy Conqueror; One Foundation; Rastaman Chant.*

★ First released 1975
★ UK peak chart position: did not chart
★ USA peak chart position: 151
★ Previous Top 1000 position: 1998 (276): 1994 (262)

384 THE CARS ↑
The Cars

This ranks as one of the best debut albums from a rock band. The Cars are filed under rock, but they are closer to power pop than any other genre. Ric Ocasek sounded like a cross between the Raspberries and Television, punk sound with a pop attitude. The giveaway was the irresistible harmony-ridden hooks in just about every one of his songs. Listen again to 'You're All I've Got Tonight', 'Just What I Needed' or 'My Best Friend's Girl' and be thrilled. Lots of chunk chunk chunk chunk guitar and Mamas And Papas harmonies, and rarely a dull moment. They only managed six albums in 20 years, but they never bettered this.

» Tracks: *Good Times Roll; My Best Friend's Girl; Just What I Needed; I'm In Touch With Your World; Don't Cha Stop; You're All I've Got Tonight; Bye Bye Love; Moving In Stereo; All Mixed Up.*

★ First released 1978
★ UK peak chart position: 29
★ USA peak chart position: 18
★ Previous Top 1000 position: 1998 (563): 1994 (–)

385 SEAL ↑
Seal

A fantastic debut album from an artist who had much to do with the commercial acceptance of UK dance music in the early 90s. Wisely signed up by Trevor Horn this debut album could not have been timed better. 'The Beginning' tells us to 'hold on to the love', enriched with Gamble And Huff style strings. Seal is blessed with a naturally expressive voice which he ably demonstrates, in the best possible way, on this album. On the hit single 'Crazy' he sounds as if he has reserve strength in his lungs, but his effortless flow on the gentle 'Whirlpool' is equally impressive.

▶ Tracks: *The Beginning; Deep Water; Crazy; Killer; Whirlpool; Future Love Paradise; Wild; Show Me; Violet.*

★ First released 1991
★ UK peak chart position: 1
★ USA peak chart position: 24
★ Previous Top 1000 position: 1998 (473): 1994 (–)

386 BANDWAGONESQUE ↓
Teenage Fanclub

Teenage Fanclub emerged from a fraternal milieu centred on the Scottish town of Bellshill. A common love of pop tradition bound the quartet together and elements of their mentors abound on this collection. Neil Young, the Byrds and Big Star are obvious reference points, but the band are not merely copyists. Dizzy melodies, long-hair guitar and unpretentiousness abound, the set's attraction ultimately residing in its cumulative, carefree charm. An impishness enhances the entire proceedings; only the churlish can resist its obvious attractions. Highly derivative, but they are forgiven because of the pedigree of their mentors. Also, a band not shy to put Status Quo in a lyric and mean the band.

▶ Tracks: *The Concept; Satan; December; What You Do To Me; I Don't Know; Star Sign; Metal Baby; Pet Rock; Sidewinder; Alcoholiday; Guiding Star; Is This Music?*

★ First released 1991
★ UK peak chart position: 22
★ USA peak chart position: 137
★ Previous Top 1000 position: 1998 (334): 1994 (448)

387 AFTERMATH ↓
The Rolling Stones

The fourth Rolling Stones LP was the first to consist solely of Jagger/Richard compositions. As such, it reflected a switch from pure R&B, although the group's roots are still to the fore, particularly in Brian Jones' slide guitarwork. The same musician was also responsible for introducing exotica to the quintet's overall sound, marimbas, dulcimer, harpsichord and sitar being added at his behest. The result is a selection of unrivalled scope, where the Knightsbridge chic of 'Lady Jane' sits beside C&W ('High And Dry') and improvised workouts ('Goin' Home'). The desultory 'Under My Thumb' would, meanwhile, remain an integral part of the Stones' lexicon throughout the subsequent two decades. *Aftermath* confirmed that the directions suggested by 'The Last Time' and 'Satisfaction' could be successfully sustained.

▶ Tracks: *Mother's Little Helper; Stupid Girl; Lady Jane; Under My Thumb; Doncha Bother Me; Goin' Home; Flight 505; High And Dry; Out Of Time; It's Not Easy; I Am Waiting; Take It Or Leave It; Think; What To Do.*

★ First released 1966
★ UK peak chart position: 1 ★ USA peak chart position: 2
★ Previous Top 1000 position: 1998 (295): 1994 (250)

388 1984 ↑
Van Halen

Vocalist David Lee Roth's final record for the band and as such, the album stands as a testament of worth somewhere between high camp and high class. Eddie Van Halen's venerable, rolling guitar pulled immaculately into place, while his new-found love of the keyboard gave them their first international smash with 'Jump'. However, it is the quite demented rush of 'Panama', and the hilarious 'Hot For Teacher' with Roth exuding a droll litany of school-yard fantasies over a thunderous Alex Van Halen backbeat, which give ultimate credence to the rock 'n' roll party that was the Roth/Van Halen partnership.

▶ Tracks: *Jump; Panama; Top Jimmy; Drop Dead Legs; Hot For Teacher; I'll Wait; Girl Gone Bad; House Of Pain.*

★ First released 1984
★ UK peak chart position: 15
★ USA peak chart position: 2
★ Previous Top 1000 position: 1998 (554): 1994 (535)

389 ONCE UPON A TIME ↓
Simple Minds

Simple Minds gained belated US chart success with '(Don't You) Forget About Me' and a distinctly transatlantic burr covered this ensuing album. Producers Jimmy Iovine and Bob Clearmountain sculpted an unambiguous sound where crowd-pleasing anthems invoked real excitement. Loud, forthright and shorn of subtlety, *Once Upon A Time* shows the group's core trio – Jim Kerr (vocals), Charlie Burchill (guitar) and Mick McNeil (keyboards) – working together with genuine empathy, while a revamped rhythm section underpins the material with sinewy precision. They combine to create what many consider to be Simple Minds' most exciting and exhilarating release.

» Tracks: *Once Upon A Time; All The Things She Said; Ghostdancing; Alive And Kicking; Oh Jungleland; I Wish You Were Here; Sanctify Yourself; Come A Long Way.*

★ First released 1985
★ UK peak chart position: 1
★ USA peak chart position: 10
★ Previous Top 1000 position: 1998 (378): 1994 (88)

390 THE GENIUS OF RAY CHARLES ↓
Ray Charles

Neither pop nor jazz, once again Ray Charles is hard to categorize even though many of the musicians have strong jazz credentials; Paul Gonsalves, Clark Terry, Zoot Sims and Bob Brookmeyer, for example. The album's strength (in addition to Brother Ray) lies in the choice of classic songs matched with lush orchestration. Ray's soulful voice will break hearts on 'Don't Let The Sun Catch You Cryin'', 'Just For A Thrill' and the ultimate song for hopeless romantics, Johnny Mercer and Harold Arlen's starry-eyed 'Come Rain Or Come Shine'. The excellent recording, particularly with Ray's up-front vocals, is the work of Jerry Wexler, Tom Dowd and Bill Schwartau.

» Tracks: *Let The Good Times Roll; It Had To Be You; Alexander's Ragtime Band;. Two Years Of Torture; When Your Lover Has Gone; Deed I Do; Just For A Thrill; You Won't Let Me Go; Tell Me You'll Wait For Me; Don't Let The Sun Catch You Cryin'; Am I Blue; Come Rain Or Come Shine.*

★ First released 1959
★ UK peak chart position: did not chart
★ USA peak chart position: 17
★ Previous Top 1000 position: 1998 (371): 1994 (87)

391 BLUESBREAKERS WITH ERIC CLAPTON ↓
John Mayall

The principals may have regarded the famous *Beano* cover album merely as a representation of their live work, but this album had as much to do with the British invasion of America's musical dominance as the Beatles or the Rolling Stones. John Mayall willingly assumed the mantle of British blues from Alexis Korner. Eric Clapton, however, was a blues purist who discovered other demons to drive his ambition, even if he could only emulate originals such as Freddie King, Buddy Guy, Otis Rush and Jimi Hendrix. Some maintain that he has never played as well since, notwithstanding his current godlike status. Mayall has since pursued a notable and satisfying career, confident that this early achievement has never been bettered.

» Tracks: *All Your Love; Hideaway; Little Girl; Another Man; Double Crossin' Time; What'd I Say; Key To Love; Parchman Farm; Have You Heard; Ramblin' On My Mind; Steppin' Out; It Ain't Right.*

★ First released 1966
★ UK peak chart position: 6
★ USA peak chart position: did not chart
★ Previous Top 1000 position: 1998 (364): 1994 (210)

392 MY FAVORITE THINGS ↑
John Coltrane

One of John Coltrane's many extraordinary talents was his ability to transcend drastically the material he chose to play, and often infuse the trivial or frivolous with something altogether profound. Under the spell of the quartet (with pianist McCoy Tyner, temporary bassist Steve Davis and drummer Elvin Jones), 'My Favorite Things' becomes an almost religious celebration of life, brought to a series of ecstatic climaxes by Coltrane's nasal, Eastern-sounding soprano saxophone and Jones's propulsive, 6/8 clatter. This popular album also contains 'But Not For Me', a breakneck version of 'Summertime' and a beautiful 'Every Time We Say Goodbye'.

» Tracks: *My Favorite Things; Every Time We Say Goodbye; Summertime; But Not For Me.*

★ First released 1960
★ UK peak chart position: did not chart
★ USA peak chart position: did not chart
★ Previous Top 1000 position: 1998 (841): 1994 (333)

393 TUMBLEWEED CONNECTION
↑ Elton John

Even though the atmospheric photograph of the old railway station that graces the cover is obviously English, the overwhelming theme of this album is Americana. Bernie Taupin's western lyrics complement Elton John's bar-room piano perfectly on the more lively tracks such as 'Son Of Your Father', 'Burn Down The Mission' and 'Country Comfort'. The peaks, however, centre on two beautiful songs, 'Come Down In Time', with a brilliant string arrangement and the gentle acoustic duet with Lesley Duncan on 'Love Song', which she also wrote. Elton had not yet discovered the excesses of superstardom and this album retains little glamour and a lot of simple honesty.

❱❱ Tracks: *Ballad Of A Well-Known Gun; Come Down In Time; Country Comfort; Son Of Your Father; My Father's Gun; Where To Now St. Peter?; Love Song; Amoreena; Talking Old Soldiers; Burn Down The Mission; Into The Old Man's Shoes; Madman Across The Water (original version).*

★ First released 1970
★ UK peak chart position: 6
★ USA peak chart position: 4
★ Previous Top 1000 position: 1998 (455): 1994 (–)

394 STOP MAKING SENSE ↑
Talking Heads

A live album made for the film of the same name, and one that deserves to survive, as it is one of the finest 'rock' concert recordings ever made. The quality remastering is such that the listener can be lulled into forgetting it is live; only the up-front and raw drums give the game away. Elsewhere, David Byrne performs majestically, giving new life to old masters. Both 'Psycho Killer' and' Once In A Lifetime' benefit from fresher versions, and the hypnotic, lengthy finale, 'Take Me To The River', is guaranteed to stay in your head for days. Talking Heads sound better on this than they do on record, if you get my drift.

❱❱ Tracks: *Psycho Killer; Swamp; Slippery People; Burning Down The House; Girlfriend Is Better; Once In A Lifetime; What A Day That Was; Life During Wartime; Take Me To The River.*

★ First released 1984
★ UK peak chart position: 37
★ USA peak chart position: 41
★ Previous Top 1000 position: 1998 (823): 1994 (327)

395 WRECKING BALL ↑
Emmylou Harris

It says a lot for the originality of a record producer when a good ear can immediately recognise their work. Such is the talent of Daniel Lanois. He did it with Bob Dylan, and now he's done it with Emmylou Harris. Lanois makes good songs great and enhances the artist's reputation, even though Harris has never suffered from a negative press. This is a fantastic record for a number of reasons. The aforementioned production is perfect. The choice of songs is inspired, with contributions from Steve Earle, Neil Young, Dylan, Jimi Hendrix, Gillian Welch, and Lucinda Willliams. And finally Harris sings better than at any time in her career. Is that enough?

❱❱ Tracks: *Where Will I Be; Goodbye; All My Tears; Wrecking Ball; Goin' Back To Harlan; Deeper Well; Every Grain Of Sand; Sweet Old World; May This Be Love; Orphan Girl; Blackhawk; Waltz Across Texas Tonight.*

★ First released 1995
★ UK peak chart position: 46
★ USA peak chart position: 94
★ Previous Top 1000 position: 1998 (–): 1994 (–)

396 TALKING HEADS 77 ↑
Talking Heads

The first album from this hard-to-categorize quartet has been constantly available since release. They bucked the trend of American rock bands by sounding different and strangely British. This hybrid sound, with a mix of punk, reggae and funk, induced curiosity, and ultimately they became one of the most influential bands of the latter part of the decade, even though their own sound was itself derivative. Twenty years on, this sounds a little vapid compared to their later work, although the power of some songs is retained. 'Psycho Killer', 'The Book I Read' and the ironic lyrical jollity of 'Don't Worry About The Government' still have the ability to sting.

❱❱ Tracks: *Uh-Oh Love Comes To Town; New Feeling; Tentative Decisions; Happy Day; Who Is It?; No Compassion; The Book I Read; Don't Worry About The Government; First Week/Last Week, Carefree; Psycho Killer; Pulled Up.*

★ First released 1977
★ UK peak chart position: 60
★ USA peak chart position: 97
★ Previous Top 1000 position: 1998 (658): 1994 (–)

397 DOGGYSTYLE ↑
Snoop Doggy Dogg

As newer converts to rap go back to acquire a comprehensive collection of essential albums this should be in their top ten. Snoop is a real bad motherfucker, probably the baddest, who set a standard for hardcore rap that has rarely been bettered. His off microphone activity has tended to distract potential listeners from the quality of his music, brilliantly produced by the omnipresent Dr. Dre. This grooves along as a single suite, with untitled tracks alongside glorious highlights such as 'Serial Killa' and 'Doggy Dogg World'. Along with 2Pac, Snoop took hard edged lyrics and smoothed them out with a gorgeous groove.

)) Tracks: *Bathtub; G Funk Intro; Gin And Juice; That Shiznit; Lodi Dodi; Murder Was The Case (Death After Visualizing Eternity); Serial Killa; Who Am I (What's My Name)?; For All My Niggaz & Bitches; Aint No Fun (If My Homies Can't Have None); Doggy Dogg World; GZ And Hustlas; Pump Pump.*

★ First released 1993
★ UK peak chart position: 38
★ USA peak chart position: 1
★ Previous Top 1000 position: 1998 (–): 1994 (–)

398 REGGATTA DE BLANC ↓
The Police

The career of the Police was planned, controlled and timed to perfection. The three talented individuals probably always knew that they would attempt to conquer the world and then disappear to pursue their own musical interests. This is the second of their five albums and contains two number 1 hits. Both are interesting little vignettes from the mind of Sting; 'Walking On The Moon', where he pleads 'I hope my legs don't break', and 'Message In A Bottle', which has a similarly desperate theme, with Sting observing 'seems I'm not alone in being alone, 100 billion castaways looking for a home'. Sting's theories do still hold water.

)) Tracks: *Message In A Bottle; Reggatta De Blanc; It's Alright For You; Bring On The Night; Deathwish; Walking On The Moon; On Any Other Day; The Bed's Too Big Without You; Contact; Does Everybody Stare; No Time This Time.*

★ First released 1979
★ UK peak chart position: 1
★ USA peak chart position: 25
★ Previous Top 1000 position: 1998 (392): 1994 (242)

399 MILES SMILES ↑
Miles Davis

This was the last Miles Davis album before his next plateau (or his next album), an occurrence that happened throughout his career. This is the quintet that moved into electronic music with *Bitches Brew*, Herbie Hancock, Wayne Shorter, Tony Williams, Ron Carter, an astonishing line-up and surely Miles' best post-Coltrane group. This is like music for the last supper; they all knew that Fender Rhodes pianos and Precision basses were coming and this is a superb farewell to acoustic jazz. All six tracks are rewarding, all different, yet the sound is the same. Much more appreciated today than when it was first released.

)) Tracks: *Orbits; Circle; Footprints; Dolores; Freedom Jazz Dance; Ginger Bread Boy.*

★ First released 1966
★ UK peak chart position: did not chart
★ USA peak chart position: did not chart
★ Previous Top 1000 position: 1998 (437): 1994 (104)

400 FLY LIKE AN EAGLE ↑
Steve Miller Band

Miller forsook his love of the blues for this and its sister project *Book Of Dreams*. In turning to mainstream pop/rock he became a huge star and developed the knack of delivering high-quality three-minute songs that were perfect for FM radio. The album is linked by Miller's fascination with electronic sounds, sandwiched between the irresistible title track, the Bonnie and Clyde tale of 'Take The Money And Run', the irritatingly simple 'Rock 'n' Me' and the subdued 'The Window', with its quirky lyric 'ask my baby what she wants to be, she says a monkey in a tree'. His baby replies 'there's nothing greater than love', true enough. After all, it was Miller who rhymed 'northern California' with 'girls are warm yeah'.

)) Tracks: *Blue Odyssey; Dance, Dance, Dance; Fly Like An Eagle; Mercury Blues; Rock 'n' Me; Serenade; 2001; Sweet Marie; Take The Money And Run; Wild Mountain Honey; The Window; You Send Me.*

★ First released 1976
★ UK peak chart position: 11
★ USA peak chart position: 3
★ Previous Top 1000 position: 1998 (487): 1994 (144)

401 FOO FIGHTERS ↑
Foo Fighters

Formed by ex-Nirvana drummer Dave Grohl, this was a much better album than anybody expected outside of the band circle. Much lighter than the oppressive direction grunge was taking, it contained some fabulous moments. Sounding like a cross between Sugar and the Pixies, Grohl moved to guitar and blossomed as a songwriter, mixing heavy riffs over classic 60s pop chord changes, such as the stunning 'I'll Stick Around'. The legacy of his former famous past has already been eclipsed by the success of this band and, in particular, by the way he acted fast and redirected the media's attention. A remarkable debut.

» Tracks: *This Is A Call; I'll Stick Around; Big Me; Alone + Easy Target; Good Grief; Floaty; Weenie Beenie; Oh, George; For All The Cows; X-Static; Watershed; Exhausted.*

★ First released 1995
★ UK peak chart position: 3
★ USA peak chart position: 23
★ Previous Top 1000 position: 1998 (837): 1994 (–)

402 THE BUDDY HOLLY STORY ↓
Buddy Holly

Few artists had exercised such a profound influence in such a short space of time. Buddy Holly's untimely death robbed pop of a performer adept as a solo act and as leader of his group, the Crickets. He wrote, or co-wrote, most of his own material at a time when many singers relied on outside material, and his sparse, but effective, guitar style proved highly influential, particularly on British beat groups. *The Buddy Holly Story* abounds with songs now indisputably pop classics and confirms Holly's status as a major figure. The Beatles, Tex-Mex music and the singer-songwriter genre each owe Holly a debt, which is itself a lasting tribute to the quality of his work.

» Tracks: *Raining In My Heart; Early In The Morning; Peggy Sue; Maybe Baby; Everyday; Rave On; That'll Be The Day; Heartbeat; Think It Over; Oh Boy; It's So Easy; It Doesn't Matter Any More.*

★ First released 1959
★ UK peak chart position: 2
★ USA peak chart position: 11
★ Previous Top 1000 position: 1998 (357): 1994 (190)

403 PRETENDERS II ↑
The Pretenders

The young band look magnificent on the cover as they pose with make-up or heavily retouched faces. They look confident, knowing that their follow-up is almost as good as the sparkling debut. Two members of this excellent quartet were to die tragically young. The album drives and dives, pausing for the ballad 'I Go To Sleep', an old Kinks song. By coincidence Chrissie Hynde and Ray Davies were stepping out at this time, hence the opening track, 'The Adultress', as Hynde whispers her confession over a furious wall of sound, to be immediately followed by her reminder that 'Bad Boys Get Spanked'. If only Chrissie, if only.

» Tracks: *The Adultress; Bad Boys Get Spanked; Messages Of Love; I Go To Sleep; Birds Of Paradise; Talk Of The Town; Pack It Up; Waste Not, Want Not; Day After Day; Jealous Dogs; English Rose; Louie Louie.*

★ First released 1981
★ UK peak chart position: 7
★ USA peak chart position: 10
★ Previous Top 1000 position: 1998 (439): 1994 (217)

404 GENIUS OF MODERN MUSIC VOLS. 1 & 2 ↓
Thelonious Monk

Taken as a body of work these are two of the most important jazz albums of all time. Over the years Thelonious Monk's importance grows, yet when these sessions were recorded his reputation was of cult status only. Monk has given us some outstanding compositions, and many are contained here. Naturally, the most recorded jazz song of all time, 'Round Midnight', is present, but so is the evergreen 'Ruby My Dear' and 'Monk's Mood'. And so on and so on; it reads like a greatest hits package. The CD versions are indispensable as there are many additional alternate takes.

» Tracks: *Volume 1 – Humph; Evonce (outtake); Evonce; Suburban Eyes; Suburban Eyes (outtake); Thelonious; Nice Work If You Can Get It (outtake) Nice Work If You Can Get It; Ruby My Dear (outtake); Ruby My Dear; Well You Needn't; Well You Needn't (outtake); April In Paris (outtake); April In Paris; Off Minor; Introspection; In Walked Bud; Monk's Head; Who Knows; Round Midnight; Who Knows (outtake). Volume 2 – Four In One; Four In One (outtake); Criss Cross; Criss Cross (outake); Ask Me Now; Willow Weep For Me; Skippy; Skippy (outtake); Hornin' In (outtake); Hornin' In; Sixteen (1st take), Sixteen (2nd take); Carolina Moon; Let's Cool One; I'll Follow You.*

★ First Released (1947-1952 recordings)
★ UK peak chart position: did not chart
★ USA peak chart position: did not chart
★ Previous Top 1000 position: 1998 (358): 1994 (91)

405 SAXOPHONE COLOSSUS ↑
Sonny Rollins

A truly flawless album representing bop at its best, *Saxophone Colossus* is a quartet recording from 1956 led by the great Sonny Rollins on tenor saxophone and featuring pianist Tommy Flanagan, bassist Doug Watkins and drummer Max Roach. The record opens with the original, catchy and rousing version of Rollins' much-loved Caribbean-flavoured standard, 'St. Thomas', and includes a richly emotional 'You Don't Know What Love Is' and a superbly angular, side-long blues entitled 'Blue Seven'. Few musicians ever spoke the bebop language with such consistent inspiration and flair, and we are lucky enough to have Rollins still with us and still playing like a demon.

》 Tracks: *Moritat; Blue Seven; Strode Rode; St. Thomas; You Don't Know What Love Is.*

★ First released 1956
★ UK peak chart position: did not chart
★ USA peak chart position: did not chart
★ Previous Top 1000 position: 1998 (441): 1994 (425)

406 THE HANGMAN'S BEAUTIFUL DAUGHTER ↑   Incredible String Band

Although it sounds élitist, 'you had to be there to really appreciate it'. Seeing them perform in 1968 and 1969 was a bizarre and rewarding sight. Medieval costumes, dancing maidens and an unbelievable array of instruments. They anticipated the 'new age traveller' and as such are highly influential, and sadly under-appreciated. Thirty years later, their challenging folk music has not become any easier. Hearing the epic 13-minute 'A Very Cellular Song', with its many changes and parts, is still pretty formidable. Easy to poke fun at, like Mike Leigh's Keith and Candice-Marie, but they were absolutely sincere, and very good at it.

》 Tracks: *Koeeaddi There; The Minotaur's Song; Witches Hat; A Very Cellular Song; Mercy I Cry City; Waltz Of The New Moon; The Water Song; Three Is A Green Crown; Swift As The Wind; Nightfall.*

★ First released 1968
★ UK peak chart position: 5
★ USA peak chart position: 161
★ Previous Top 1000 position: 1998 (408): 1994 (–)

407 A WALK ACROSS THE ROOFTOPS ↑   The Blue Nile

This tremendous debut album from the enigmatic Blue Nile received tremendous reviews, yet barely scraped the chart. The promise was there, and it took shape on the second album *Hats*. Paul Buchanan's pleading voice is made for late-night listening in a cosy bedsitting room. Mulling over love lost, love found, happy times, sad times and kitchen sinks (I lied about the last bit, but you get the picture), a beautiful landscape of evocative music soaks in rather than hitting you first time. Blue Nile can be played over and over again, which is why they have only felt the need to put out three records in 15 years!

》 Tracks: *A Walk Across The Rooftops; Tinseltown In The Rain; From Rags To Riches; Stay; Easter Parade; Heatwave; Automobile Noise.*

★ First released 1983
★ UK peak chart position: 80
★ USA peak chart position: did not chart
★ Previous Top 1000 position: 1998 (432): 1994 (–)

408 MY OWN PRISON ↑
Creed

Creed's songwriters, vocalist Scott Stapp and guitarist Mark Tremonti, craft alternative metal anthems that have placed them at the forefront of America's post-Pearl Jam rock scene. Even if the prevailingly doom-laden lyrics do become a tad boring, leaving the listener to want the sun to shine through the closed curtains, this is a *tour de force* of a record. Even though Stapp does have a similar voice to Eddie Vedder. The dynamics of the band are excellent, and a sign of committed musician's at work. Creed play with a venom and confidence that never lets their songs get buried by the ferocity of their sound.

》 Tracks: *Torn; Ode; My Own Prison; Pity For A Dime; In America; Illusion; Unforgiven; Sister; What's This Life For; One.*

★ First released 1997
★ UK peak chart position: did not chart
★ USA peak chart position: 22
★ Previous Top 1000 position: 1998 (–): 1994 (–)

409 ... AND JUSTICE FOR ALL ↑
Metallica

It cannot be stated enough that Metallica is the most consistently innovative heavy metal band of the past two decades. In the quest for the cleanest, chunkiest, hardest sound, Metallica are the undisputed leaders and, like Led Zeppelin a decade before them, they remain an inspiration to other, lesser bands. Listeners cannot fail to be impressed by the precise way the bass and drums lock into the twin lead guitars. The title track and the hit single 'One' are prime examples. So tight are the instruments that James Hetfield's vocals are almost irrelevant.

» Tracks: Blackened; ... And Justice For All; Eye Of The Beholder; One; The Shortest Straw; Harvester Of Sorrow; The Frayed Ends Of Sanity; To Live Is To Die; Dyers Eve.

★ First released 1988
★ UK peak chart position: 4
★ USA peak chart position: 6
★ Previous Top 1000 position: 1998 (–): 1994 (–)

410 ZUMA ↓
Neil Young and Crazy Horse

Released to universally favourable reviews, Zuma has lasted as a favourite Neil Young album. On this, he pleased guitar devotees by at last attempting to sound and play like he did on stage. The tone and volume he achieves on his old Gibson throughout this record is perfection. 'Drive Back' is a shining example of the style, played over a shuffling and changing tempo. Similarly evocative are 'Danger Bird' and 'Stupid Girl', but the album's tour de force is 'Cortez The Killer', a lengthy song that builds, noodles and droops but is never boring. Crosby, Stills And Nash make a cursory appearance at the end with 'Through My Sails'.

» Tracks: Don't Cry No Tears; Danger Bird; Pardon My Heart; Lookin' For A Love; Barstool Blues; Stupid Girl; Drive Back; Cortez The Killer; Through My Sails.

★ First released 1975
★ UK peak chart position: 25
★ USA peak chart position: 44
★ Previous Top 1000 position: 1998 (398): 1994 (–)

411 ATOMIC BASIE ↓
Count Basie

An inspired collaboration that worked so well, it is surprising that Count Basie and Neal Hefti did not form a long-term Sinatra/Riddle partnership. Hefti later found solace in writing musical opuses such as 'The Batman Theme'! Great for his bank balance, but little aid to his credibility. This, however, is a magnificent record that should always be played in its entirety. Basie rarely sounded so fresh and crisp. For a 1958 album, this is a staggering record. 'Splanky', in particular, spits out with an incredible force and their reading of 'Li'l Darlin' is definitive. The original engineer Bob Arnold deserves a special mention. The CD remastering is fabulous and comes with five bonus tracks.

» Tracks: The Kid From Red Bank; Duet; After Supper; Flight Of The Foo Birds; Double-O; Teddy The Toad; Whirly-Bird; Midnite Blue; Splanky; Fantail; Li'l Darlin'; Silks And Satins; Sleepwalker's Serenade; Sleepwalker's Serenade (alternate take); The Late Late Show; The Late Late Show (vocal version).

★ First released 1958
★ UK peak chart position: did not chart
★ USA peak chart position: did not chart
★ Previous Top 1000 position: 1998 (372): 1994 (–)

412 COPPERHEAD ROAD ↓
Steve Earle

Earle is one of the hip recent stars who have given new country music acceptance with non-honky tonkers. Earle is a renegade who has been married almost as many times as the number of albums he has released. His songs are new country-Springsteen and he is not frightened to rock (the Pogues give great support on this memorable album). His career has faltered commercially since this release as his music has taken on a harder edge. The title track is a highlight, featuring some fine mandolin over an infectious beat; similar fare is 'You Belong To Me' and 'Back To The Wall'. Country purists may balk, but this album is destined to have a wider appeal beyond the core.

» Tracks: Copperhead Road; Snake Oil; Back To The Wall; The Devil's Right Hand; Johnny Come Lately; Even When I'm Blue; You Belong To Me; Waiting On You; Once You Love; Nothing But A Child

★ First released 1988
★ UK peak chart position: 44
★ USA peak chart position: 56
★ Previous Top 1000 position: 1998 (379): 1994 (860)

413 FULFILLINGNESS' FIRST FINALE ↑ Stevie Wonder

Having to follow *Talking Book* and *Innervisions* was a massive task, and yet a year later, with hardly a pause Stevie Wonder did it. This period of his career is the most prolific and most fertile in terms of ideas. Overall this is a beautifully mellow album. Tracks such as 'Smile Please' and 'It Ain't No Use' are wonderfully understated and relaxed. The anti-Nixon 'You Haven't Done Nothing' is dangerously similar in sound to 'Superstition', but Wonder can be forgiven for such a small lapse. He ends with a pleading love song 'Please Don't Go', with yet another great middle hook. He finds more ebony and ivory notes on the piano than anybody else.

» Tracks: *Smile Please; Heaven Is 10 Zillion Light Years Away; Too Shy To Say; Boogie On Reggae Woman; Creepin'; You Haven't Done Nothin'; It Ain't No Use; They Won't Go When I Go; Bird Of Beauty; Please Don't Go.*

★ First released 1974
★ UK peak chart position: 5
★ USA peak chart position: 1
★ Previous Top 1000 position: 1998 (627): 1994 (–)

414 THE LOW-END THEORY ↑ A Tribe Called Quest

With their second album in 1991, they became serious contenders for Public Enemy's (until then) undisputed crown as hip-hop's cultural leaders. However, where their debut was propelled by a disparate array of samples, *The Low-End Theory* was built on a stricter musical doctrine – its spine provided by bebop jazz. Though jazz-rap crossover would become a staple of popular music in the mid-90s (Gang Starr, Jazzmatazz, etc.), this album played a substantial part in breaking down barriers between genres. Phife Dog and Q-Tip are on great form too, making the most of Quest's energetic production with cool asides and insightful observations ('The Infamous Date Rape', 'Showbusiness').

» Tracks: *Excursions; Buggin' Out; Rap Promoter; Butter; Verses From The Abstract; Showbusiness; Vibes And Stuff; The Infamous Date Rape; Check The Rhime; Everything Is Fair; Jazz (We've Got); Skypager; What?; Scenario.*

★ First released 1991
★ UK peak chart position: 58
★ USA peak chart position: 45
★ Previous Top 1000 position: 1998 (912): 1994 (–)

415 SMILEY SMILE ↓ Beach Boys

The aborted *Smile* project was replaced with this gentle yet perplexing release that lost the band some of their surf and hot-rod fans, but endeared them to people who smoked those funny cigarettes. Rumour has it that the band were so high they had to stay low, and recorded much of this album lying on the floor. Van Dyke Parks wove his wackiness around 'Heroes And Villains', 'Vegetables' and 'She's Goin' Bald'. The monumental 'Good Vibrations' was thrown in for good measure in glorious stereophonic sound. Now regarded as a minor classic of understated beauty, and the album from which Brian Wilson has never quite been the same man again.

» Tracks: *Heroes And Villains; Vegetables; Fall Breaks And Back To Winter (W. Woodpecker Symphony, Instrumental); She's Goin' Bald; Little Pad; Good Vibrations; With Me Tonight; Wind Chimes; Gettin' Hungry; Wonderful; Whistle In.*

★ First released 1967
★ UK peak chart position: 9
★ USA peak chart position: 41
★ Previous Top 1000 position: 1998 (396): 1994 (251)

416 VS ↑ Pearl Jam

The second album from Pearl Jam saw them attempt to establish their own identity – previously they had trailed in the wake of Nirvana as 'Seattle's other band'. If *Ten* had seen them arrive from nowhere, then by the advent of this follow-up everyone knew who they were. The album entered the US chart at number 1, and recorded the highest one-week sales total in history – after which a critical commentary on the merits or otherwise of the album is rendered utterly irrelevant. It was, however, another rock-solid performance, substituting *Ten's* verve for greater coherence. The opening track 'Go' should convince after approximately 57 seconds.

» Tracks: *Go; Animal; Daughter; Glorified G; Dissident; WMA; Blood; Rearviewmirror; Rats; Elderly Woman Behind The Counter In A Small Town; Leash; Indifference.*

★ First released 1993
★ UK peak chart position: 2
★ USA peak chart position: 1
★ Previous Top 1000 position: 1998 (725): 1994 (495)

417 THE COMPLETE SAVOY SESSIONS ↓ Charlie Parker

Although they do not contain the number of classic sides found within the Dial collection, the importance of Charlie Parker's Savoy recordings is more than justified by the involvement of bebop piano genius Bud Powell (perhaps the only other true bebopper playing with the level of invention and profundity of Parker himself) and the fascinating play-off between a young and troubled Miles Davis and his own hero Dizzy Gillespie. The Savoy records include the legendary 'KoKo' (a breakneck torrent of improvisation based around the tricky 'Cherokee' chord sequence), and two classic blues in F major: 'Billie's Bounce' and 'Now's The Time'.

» Tracks: including – Billie's Bounce; Now's The Time i; Now's The Time ii; Thriving On A Riff i; Thriving On A Riff ii; Meandering; KoKo; Dizzy Boogie i; Dizzy Boogie ii; Flat Foot Floogie i; Flat Foot Floogie ii; Popity Pop; Slim's Jam.

★ First released 1982
★ UK peak chart position: did not chart
★ USA peak chart position: did not chart
★ Previous Top 1000 position: 1998 (411): 1994 (237)

418 THE ROLLING STONES ↑ The Rolling Stones

This was, is and will always be a great white rhythm and blues record. Recorded swiftly and simply it smells of the London club scene of 1963. Although admittedly crude by the Stones' later high standards, it is still a vital and historically important album. They attempt Muddy Waters, 'I Just Want To Make Love To You', at a fast pace, and slow down Jimmy Reed, 'Honest I Do', a frantic Chuck Berry, 'Carol', and even Marvin Gaye's 'Can I Get A Witness'. They even improve on Rufus Thomas's whistle on 'Walking The Dog'. Fantastic bass on 'I'm A King Bee' (or kang bye in Jaggerspeak). Primitive but dazzling.

» Tracks: Route 66; I Just Want To Make Love To You; Honest I Do; I Need You Baby; Now I've Got A Witness; Little By Little; I'm King Bee; Carol; Tell Me (You're Coming Back); Can I Get A Witness; You Can Make It If You Really Try; Walking The Dog.

★ First released 1964
★ UK peak chart position: 1
★ USA peak chart position: 11
★ Previous Top 1000 position: 1998 (427): 1994 (395)

419 SPIRIT OF EDEN ↑ Talk Talk

As the album opens, you almost think that you have put on a Miles Davis album by mistake. The strains of UK jazz trumpeter Henry Lowther are highly convincing. Mark Hollis and his band moved on from the New Romantic tag and certainly produced a much more varied and ambitious album. 'The Rainbow' is a startling opener, and after Lowther's trumpet solo is a spooky harmonica solo from ex-Nine Below Zero ace, Mark Feltham. Other cameos convince the listener that Talk Talk have grown. The choice of musicians such as Nigel Kennedy, and the marvellous string bassist Danny Thompson, can do nothing but enhance their reputation. The City of Chelmsford choir are the icing on the cake.

» Tracks: The Rainbow; Eden; Desire; Inheritance; I Believe In You; Wealth.

★ First released 1988
★ UK peak chart position: 19
★ USA peak chart position: did not chart
★ Previous Top 1000 position: 1998 (442): 1994 (–)

420 KICK ↑ INXS

Probably the one INXS album to own, for those who feel the need to own one. By the time of Michael Hutchence's tragic death in 1997 the band had fallen out of favour – musical fashion has a cruel way of dumping former press darlings. Kick gave INXS a lot of commercial momentum, and certainly their live performances around the time were not to be missed. Hutchence was a charismatic frontman and many of these tracks, in particular 'New Sensation' and 'Need You Tonight', became highlights of their stage act. Hutchence would sing lines such as 'slide over here and give me a moment' directly to the female fans. Certainly, the girls would chorus.

» Tracks: Guns In The Sky; New Sensation; Devil Inside; Need You Tonight; Mediate; The Loved One; Wild Life; Never Tear Us Apart; Mystify; Kick; Calling All Nations; Tiny Daggers.

★ First released 1987
★ UK peak chart position: 9
★ USA peak chart position: 3
★ Previous Top 1000 position: 1998 (–): 1994 (–)

421 THERE GOES RHYMIN' SIMON ↑ Paul Simon

Was it really the tail-end of the 60s when Simon gave us this continuation of *Bookends*, an album with a similar feel? After he parted from Art Garfunkel, Simon wrote songs without having to consider two-part harmonies, and this in turn gave his music a freer, less folk rock flavour. 'American Tune' remains one of his greatest compositions and would make a better alternative to 'America The Beautiful' as the national anthem. Simon had to wait a long time before he topped this record artistically, but he did it in style with *Graceland*. This is the other Paul Simon album to own.

» Tracks: *Kodachrome; Tenderness; Take Me To The Mardi Gras; Something So Right; One Man's Ceiling Is Another Man's Floor; American Tune; Was A Sunny Day; Learn How To Fall; St. Judy's Comet; Loves Me Like A Rock.*

★ First released 1973
★ UK peak chart position: 4
★ USA peak chart position: 2
★ Previous Top 1000 position: 1998 (451): 1994 (197)

422 SHOOT OUT THE LIGHTS ↑ Richard And Linda Thompson

Probably the world's most underrated songwriter, although Richard Thompson must tire of hearing it so often. Together with his ex-wife Linda they made a series of quite brilliant albums that garnered heaps of praise and minimal sales. This is another slice of perfection that veers from the whimsical fun of 'Wall Of Death' to the desperate emotions of 'Shoot Out The Lights', the latter featuring the definitive Thompson guitar solo. Critics have often been accused of hyping artists, but try as they may, they can't do it with this one. Time will tell, but this album deserves, more than most, to be in many more homes.

» Tracks: *Don't Renege On Our Love; Walking On A Wire; Man In Need; Just The Motion; Shoot Out The Lights; Back Street Slide; Did She Jump Or Was She Pushed?; Wall Of Death.*

★ First released 1982
★ UK peak chart position: did not chart
★ USA peak chart position: did not chart
★ Previous Top 1000 position: 1998 (452): 1994 (334)

423 I WANT YOU ↑ Marvin Gaye

Another in a series of superb wandering groove albums from the premier sweet soul singer. Marvin Gaye took the standard three-minute pop soul song and expanded the format. It is Gaye that is responsible for today's smooching urban R&B; he was for much of his career many years ahead of the game. This has been described as his 'oral sex' album, not that the others were not; this has the erotic edge. Built around the title track, the album is a theme album and as such should be played as a whole. There is nothing like 'Too Busy Thinking About My Baby' on this; it is a much more challenging but satisfying work.

» Tracks: *I Want You (Vocal); Come Live With Me Angel; After The Dance (Instrumental); Feel All My Love Inside; I Wanna Be Where You Are; I Want You (Intro Jam); All The Way Round; Since I Had You; Soon I'll Be Loving You Again; I Want You (Intro Jam); After The Dance (Vocal).*

★ First released 1976
★ UK peak chart position: 22
★ USA peak chart position: 4
★ Previous Top 1000 position: 1998 (458): 1994 (–)

424 THE HEALER ↑ John Lee Hooker

When popular culture embraced John Lee Hooker, purists turned up their noses. They should have been pleased that the world's greatest living Delta bluesman was going to make some money before he turned up his toes. Teaming up with Carlos Santana, Bonnie Raitt, Los Lobos, Canned Heat (not for the first time) and others, lent Hooker's blues a contemporary gloss. It took the album to the upper reaches of the album charts around the world, brought him a number of Grammy awards and a new career in advertising. The blues is not only a healer, it drinks brandy and wears jeans. The Carlos Santana guitar solo on the title track is breathtaking and Hooker is the coolest senior citizen in the world.

» Tracks: *The Healer; I'm In The Mood; Baby Lee; Cuttin' Out; Think Twice Before You Go; Los Lobos; Sally Mae; That's Alright; Rockin' Chair; My Dream; No Substitute.*

★ First released 1989
★ UK peak chart position: 63
★ USA peak chart position: 62
★ Previous Top 1000 position: 1998 (474): 1994 (116)

425 NEBRASKA ↑
Bruce Springsteen

Dispensing with his famous E Street Band, Springsteen sat with only his guitar and a tape recorder (albeit a pretty good one). He recorded a series of barren songs, adding only a spooky harmonica and some reverb. This was the most atmospheric and naked album of the decade, and may have inspired the unplugged phenomenon of the 90s. He sounds like an 80s version of Johnny Cash, both in sound and in theme/content, although 'Used Cars' reveals his great weakness. It is impossible for the Boss to get through any album without making a reference to cars. It did however, do wonders for the acoustic guitar industry.

» Tracks: *Nebraska; Atlantic City; Mansion On The Hill; Johnny 99; Highway Patrolman; State Trooper; Used Cars; Open All Night; My Father's House; Reason To Believe.*

★ First released 1982
★ UK peak chart position: 3
★ USA peak chart position: 3
★ Previous Top 1000 position: 1998 (480): 1994 (–)

426 THE BLACK SAINT AND THE SINNER LADY ↑ Charles Mingus

In many ways the essential Mingus album, more than *Ah Um. The Black Saint And The Sinner Lady* is a rich and powerful suite, embracing in one work the elements of blues, gospel, funk and Latin music that infused Mingus' sound and made it what it was. As well as featuring some of the best group arrangement outside the work of Duke Ellington, it boasts superb contributions by pianist Jaki Byard and alto saxophonist Charlie Mariano. This album is also revealing for its early use (in jazz) of studio dubbing, heard on the occasions when Mariano can be identified in the ensemble at the same time as he is soloing.

» Tracks: *Solo Dancer (Stop! Look! And Listen, Sinner Jim Whitney); Duet Solo Dancers (Heart's Beat And Shades In Physical Embraces); Group Dancers ([Soul Fusion] Freewoman); Trio And Group Dancers (Stop! Look! And Sing Songs Of Revolutions!); Single Solos And Group Dance (Saint And Sinner Join In Merriment On Battle Front); Group And Solo Dance (Of Love, Pain, And Passioned Revolt, Then Farewell, My Beloved).*

★ First released 1963
★ UK peak chart position: did not chart
★ USA peak chart position: did not chart
★ Previous Top 1000 position: 1998 (489): 1994 (178)

427 NO MORE HEROES ↑
The Stranglers

Punk's *parents terribles*, the Stranglers courted controversy throughout their early career. Caustic lyrics brought charges of misogyny, although the group suggested that outrage was merely part of the genre's tenet. They answered such criticism of their debut album with the even more uncompromising *No More Heroes*, a vengeful collection echoing the nihilism of its title. Role-playing apart, there was no denying a musical prowess compressing savage guitar, throbbing bass and swirling organ into vicious, driving sound. Hugh Cornwell's sneering intonation matched the aggression of his accompaniment, but the album also offered indications of the lighter pop style that the quartet would later follow.

» Tracks: *I Feel Like A Wog; Bitching; Dead Ringer; Dagenham Dave; Bring On The Nubiles; Something Better Change; No More Heroes; Peasant In The Big Shitty; Burning Up Time; English Towns; School Mam; In The Shadows.*

★ First released 1977
★ UK peak chart position: 2
★ USA peak chart position: did not chart
★ Previous Top 1000 position: 1998 (526): 1994 (569)

428 SAUCERFUL OF SECRETS ↑
Pink Floyd

Hearing this played live in 1967 must have been quite an experience. Nobody was doing material like this, quite like this; although there were a quite a few purple kandy chocolate bicycle mushrooms around. The original audience was probably as out of it as the band, yet this album still holds a nostalgic charm for the listener. Pink Floyd have since stretched recording technique to perfection and this recording now sounds lame in terms of production. The songs, however, maintain great character of times past; Rick Wright's 'Remember A Day' still provokes a hum and 'Set The Controls For The Heart Of The Sun' evokes those dodgy light shows.

» Tracks: *Let There Be More Light; Remember A Day; Set The Controls For The Heart Of The Sun; Corporal Clegg; A Saucerful Of Secrets; See-saw; Jugband Blues.*

★ First released 1968
★ UK peak chart position: 9
★ USA peak chart position: did not chart
★ Previous Top 1000 position: 1998 (887): 1994 (–)

429 BOSSANOVA ↑
Pixies

With a keen sense of the absurd, Black Francis's (now Frank Black) Pixies were the consummate darlings of the UK press – no surprise, with their refreshing mix of overblown guitars, discreet nods to the surreal and a vibrant grasp of pure pop that offered a luscious blow to the senses on execution. 'Cecilia Ann' stood somewhere between spandex metal and 'Beach Blanket Bingo', while the deranged singalong of 'Is She Weird' sat alongside the first single, 'Velouria', underlining their ability to write timeless singles that filled the head and sent toes tapping incessantly out of time. Re-formation now!

» Tracks: Cecilia Ann; Velouria; Is She Weird; All Over The World; Down To The Well; Blown Away; Stormy Weather; Rock Music; Allison; Ana; Dig For Fire; The Happening; Hang Wire; Havalina.

★ First released 1990
★ UK peak chart position: 3
★ USA peak chart position: 70
★ Previous Top 1000 position: 1998 (686): 1994 (462)

430 TIM HARDIN 2 ↑
Tim Hardin

Tim Hardin's beguiling brand of jazz/folk, unveiled on his debut album, is equally prevalent on its follow-up. Although many of its songs last less than two minutes, they each possess a resonant beauty enhanced by the singer's smoky intonation. Always an introspective composer, Hardin takes the opportunity to extol pleasures discovered through family life, and few writers can expose such emotions without resorting to cliché. Sweet melodies and tinkling accompaniment reinforce the songs' fragility, underscoring the aura of gracefulness Hardin's best work generates. The CD reissue couples Tim Hardin 1 as a marvellous bonus.

» Tracks: Don't Make Promises; Green Rocky Road; Smugglin' Man; How Long; While You're On Your Way; It'll Never Happen Again; Reason To Believe; Never Too Far; Part Of The Wind; Ain't Gonna Do Without; Misty Roses; How Can We Hang On To A Dream; If I Were A Carpenter; Red Balloon; Black Sheep Boy; Lady Came From Baltimore; Baby Close It's Eyes; You Upset The Grace Of Living When You Lie; Speak Like A Child; See Where You Are And Get Out; It's Hard To Believe In Love For Long; Tribute To Hank Williams.

★ First released 1967
★ UK peak chart position: did not chart
★ USA peak chart position: did not chart
★ Previous Top 1000 position: 1998 (527): 1994 (407)

431 VEEDON FLEECE ↑
Van Morrison

One of many Van Morrison albums to feature interesting but pointless covers, the besuited singer with country mansion and two large dogs gives no indication of the emotion and intensity contained on this album. Veedon Fleece is sadly ignored by all but the cognoscenti, even though the gap between this and Astral Weeks is not that great. 'Fair Play' is a magnificent, lilting opener, but the following 'Linden Arden Stole The Highlights' is a masterpiece, and a song that cries for another ten verses and five minutes length – a strange omission when you consider the many lengthy odes he has written. Exposure is all it needs (and, some would say, a decent cover).

» Tracks: Fair Play; Linden Arden Stole The Highlights; Who Was That Masked Man; Streets Of Arklow; You Don't Pull No Punches, But You Don't Push The River; Bulbs; Cul De Sac; Comfort You; Come Here My Love; Country Fair.

★ First released 1974
★ UK peak chart position: 41
★ USA peak chart position: 53
★ Previous Top 1000 position: 1998 (475): 1994 (–)

432 RISQUÉ ↑
Chic

They made two great albums, yet for some reason this one comes out on top over C'est Chic. They represented the pinnacle of late 70s disco music, with a brand of slick soul that was made for the dancefloor. Nile Rodgers and the late Bernard Edwards were the Babyfaces of their day. Their compositions, record production and sparing musicianship (guitar and bass, respectively) made Chic such a classy unit. Hard to imagine listening to this in a normal home environment as the fantasy of white suits and exotic cocktails is just too much to bear. 90s urban R&B owes everything to Chic.

» Tracks: Good Times; A Warm Summer Night; My Feet Keep Dancing; My Forbidden Lover; Can't Stand To Love You; Will You Cry (When You Hear This Song); What About Me.

★ First released 1979
★ UK peak chart position: 29
★ USA peak chart position: 5
★ Previous Top 1000 position: 1998 (446): 1994 (–)

433 BE YOURSELF TONIGHT ↑
Eurythmics

This album replays like a greatest hits package, such is the content of its full-blown memorable pop songs. The list is almost endless as this album is a chilling reminder of how good pop can be and how well Annie Lennox and David A. Stewart worked together. Even without the legendary Aretha Franklin on 'Sisters Are Doing It For Themselves', there is the pace and guts of 'I Love You Like A Ball And Chain' or the numerous confessional 'I'll be's' of 'It's Alright (Baby's Coming Back)'. This album stands up to repeated plays and will continue to improve with age. What perfection.

❯❯ Tracks: It's Alright (Baby's Coming Back); Would I Lie To You; There Must Be An Angel (Playing With My Heart); I Love You Like A Ball And Chain; Sisters Are Doing It For Themselves; Conditioned Soul; Adrian; Here Comes That Sinking Feeling; Better To Have Lost In Love Than Never To Have Loved At All.

★ First released 1985
★ UK peak chart position: 3
★ USA peak chart position: 9
★ Previous Top 1000 position: 1998 (477): 1994 (118)

434 MAIDEN VOYAGE ↑
Herbie Hancock

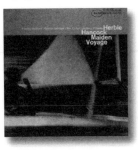

Probably the best in Herbie Hancock's series of fine Blue Note albums from the 60s, Maiden Voyage finds him in what is basically the Miles Davis band of the time, with Davis replaced by the young Freddie Hubbard. Hancock has always been a fine composer, but Maiden Voyage contains two classic compositions in particular – the beautiful 'Dolphin Dance', and the atmospheric and popular title track. Saxophonist George Coleman, bassist Ron Carter and drummer Tony Williams play as well as they have ever played throughout, and the whole record is marked with a timeless freshness and sense of creative tension.

❯❯ Tracks: Maiden Voyage; The Eye Of The Hurricane; Little One; Survival Of The Fittest; Dolphin Dance.

★ First released 1964
★ UK peak chart position: did not chart
★ USA peak chart position: did not chart
★ Previous Top 1000 position: 1998 (491): 1994 (732)

435 PETER GREEN'S FLEETWOOD MAC ↑ Fleetwood Mac

Now known as the 'dustbin' album, after its evocative cover, it is hard to believe that such an out-and-out blues album could have remained in the album charts for almost a year; but that is what this one achieved. The blues was on the crest of a wave in 1968; Eric Clapton had left John Mayall for Cream, but never really lost sight of the blues, and his successor, Peter Green, put together his ideal band with John McVie and Mick Fleetwood. Completing the band was the diminutive slide guitarist Jeremy Spencer. The album reflected their live appearances, with the 12 tracks shared between the two vocalists. At this remove, it is plain that Spencer's Elmore James imitations, while uncannily accurate, would quickly date. What has not dated are the sensitive songwriting and performances by the most accomplished blues guitarist Britain has ever produced.

❯❯ Tracks: My Heart Beat Like A Hammer; Merry Go Round; Long Grey Mare; Shake Your Moneymaker; Looking For Somebody; No Place To Go; My Baby's Good To Me; I Loved Another Woman; Cold Black Night; The World Keep On Turning; Got To Move.

★ First released 1968
★ UK peak chart position: 4 ★ USA peak chart position: 198
★ Previous Top 1000 position: 1998 (533): 1994 (880)

436 TRAGIC KINGDOM ↑
No Doubt

The distinctive lead vocals of the stunning Gwen Stefani and the punchy musical backing made this one of 1995's most pleasant surprises. Tom Dumont chunka chunka chunkas on his guitar and Tony Kanal doesn't hit his drums, he crisply smacks them. Sandwiched between the Cars and Blondie, No Doubt mix impeccable studio production with a knack for writing infectious hooklines. 'Happy Now' and 'Just A Girl' burst out of the speakers in a joyful pop frenzy, while 'Don't Speak' is a beautifully mature and clever song that silenced critics who tagged them airhead popsters.

❯❯ Tracks: Spiderwebs; Excuse Me Mr.; Just A Girl; Happy Now?; Different People; Hey You; The Climb; Sixteen; Sunday Morning; Don't Speak; You Can Do It; World Go Round; End It On This; Tragic Kingdom.

★ First released 1995
★ UK peak chart position: 3
★ USA peak chart position: 4
★ Previous Top 1000 position: 1998 (–): 1994 (–)

437 BLIND FAITH ↑
Blind Faith

One magnificent supergroup, one tasteless cover, one album, one tour; that's all folks. Contrary to popular myth, they were very, very good; Eric Clapton and Steve Winwood found corners of the stage in which they could hide as they tried to shun the spotlight under which Cream and Traffic had put them. And that is why the fans rebelled. They wanted lots of Clapton guitar solos and another 'Dear Mr Fantasy'. What they got was a collection that improves with age; a delightfully ramshackle 'Well All Right', a great Clapton song, 'In The Presence Of The Lord', and a sparse but powerful Winwood on 'Can't Find My Way Home'. The CD reissue includes two bonus tracks.

➠ Tracks: *Had To Cry Today; Can't Find My Way Home; Well All Right; Presence Of The Lord; Sea Of Joy; Do What You Like; Exchange And Mart; Spending All My Days.*

★ First released 1969
★ UK peak chart position: 1
★ USA peak chart position: 1
★ Previous Top 1000 position: 1998 (885): 1994 (–)

438 OH MERCY ↑
Bob Dylan

Dylan has been written off many times, and yet he has and will always come back and surprise us with another tremendous album. Much credit is given to producer Daniel Lanois, but don't forget, a producer cannot do much with pencil shavings. Some of Dylan's most cryptic statements are on this album. He was always better as a romantic than as a protest folky, and the less obscure his lyrics become, the more he opens his heart. Take, for example, the simple 'Where Teardrops Fall'. Alternatively, the brilliant twist in the tail of the love song, 'Most Of The Time', is the deepest: 'Don't even remember what her lips felt like on mine, most of the time'.

➠ Tracks: *Political World; Where Teardrops Fall; Everything Is Broken; Ring Them; Man In The Long Black Coat; Most Of The Time; What Good Am I?; Disease Of Conceit; What Was It You Wanted; Shooting Star.*

★ First released 1989
★ UK peak chart position: 6
★ USA peak chart position: 30
★ Previous Top 1000 position: 1998 (595): 1994 (–)

439 BUENA VISTA SOCIAL CLUB
↑ Ry Cooder and The Buena Vista Social Club

Ry Cooder produced and played with a loose conglomeration of Cuban musicians, some of them elderly veterans, on this 1996 album, recorded in Havana. However, unlike other cultural tourists (Paul Simon on *Graceland*, David Byrne on *Rei Momo*) who appropriate foreign musical styles and fashion their own songs around them, Cooder wants the Cubans to play their own material. Is this, nevertheless, a Ry Cooder album? Debatable. Regardless, it is a lovely, often stirring collection, encompassing various styles. The musicologist in Cooder would be gratified to have made the point that Cuban music is far more than a single entity.

➠ Tracks: *Chan: De Camino A La Vereda; El Cuarto De Tula; Pueblo Nuevo; Dos Gardenias; Y Tu Que Has Hecho?; Veinte Anos; El Carretero; Candela; Amor De Loca Juventad; Orgullecida; Murmullo; Buena Vista Social Club; La Batamesa.*

★ First Released 1997
★ UK peak chart position: did not chart
★ USA peak chart position: 178
★ Previous Top 1000 position: 1998 (820): 1994 (–)

440 REVENGE ↑
Eurythmics

Having made the transition into a full-blooded band that rocked, Lennox and Stewart could then do no wrong and must be seen as one of the musical highlights of the 80s. To maintain such a high standard through six albums in four years takes some doing, yet here they go again, each time growing musically and adding that little extra, for example, the meaty harmonica opening on 'Missionary Man', the harder drum sound on all tracks, and finally Stewart back to playing lots of guitar and sounding as though he is having fun. Hypnotic, bouncy music that never threatens. The long break they took was well earned and desperately needed.

➠ Tracks: *Let's Go; Take Your Pain Away; A Little Of You; Thorn In My Side; In This Town; I Remember You; Missionary Man; The Last Time; When Tomorrow Comes; The Miracle Of Love.*

★ First released 1986
★ UK peak chart position: 3
★ USA peak chart position: 12
★ Previous Top 1000 position: 1998 (580): 1994 (203)

441 THIS NATION'S SAVING GRACE ↑ The Fall

As stubbornly maverick as ever, the Fall's tenth album hinges on their now-accustomed dissonance, into which a tighter, commercial edge was introduced. New guitarist Brix Smith, wife of leader Mark E., added a partly melodious sheen that brought an air of 60s subculture to the group's post-industrial rattle. Nothing was sacrificed in the process and while 'Bombast' hurtles with a vicious power, talismen Can were acknowledged in 'I Am Damo Suzuki', the name of the German band's Japan-born singer. Mark E. Smith towers over the proceedings, his voice prowling about the music, enhancing its intensity. This album shows the Fall extending stylistic barriers without sacrificing their individuality.

❱❱ Tracks: *Mansion; Bombast; Barmy; What You Need; Spoilt Victorian Child; LA; Vixen; Couldn't Get Ahead; Gut Of The Quantifier; My New House; Paintwork; I Am Damo Suzuki; To NK Roachment: Yarbles; Petty (Thief) Lout; Rollin' Danyy; Cruisers Creek.*

★ First released 1985 ★ UK peak chart position: 54
★ USA peak chart position: did not chart
★ Previous Top 1000 position: 1998 (569): 1994 (468)

442 DRESSED TO KILL ↑ Kiss

As outrageous as they looked, Kiss were pretty tame by today's Marilyn Manson standards. *Dressed To Kill* was the first album that found them being taken seriously as a commercial proposition. The clunky stack heels and the face paint undermined their ability as a straight-ahead heavy rock band. Basically, it's sex, drugs and glam rock 'n' roll. Similar happy-go-lucky themes are explored in 'Room Service' and the line 'baby I could use a meal', or in 'Ladies In Waiting' with 'and the meat looks good tonight'. Or, as they repeat at the end, 'I wanna rock and roll all nite and party every day'. Crank it up loud, it kicks ass.

❱❱ Tracks: *Room Service; Two Timer; Ladies In Waiting; Getaway; Rock Bottom; C'mon And Love Me; Anything For My Baby; She; Love Her All I Can; Rock And Roll All Nite.*

★ First released 1975
★ UK peak chart position: did not chart
★ USA peak chart position: 32
★ Previous Top 1000 position: 1998 (584): 1994 (–)

443 FOR EVERYMAN ↑ Jackson Browne

Browne had already been critically applauded for his songwriting skills, but this was the album that consolidated his position as a singer after his debut album. This also showcases the finest band of LA musicians including Sneaky Pete, Russ Kunkel, Jim Keltner, Craig Doerge and Lee Sklar. Add to this harmony vocals from Bonnie Raitt, David Crosby, Don Henley and finally, the guitar of the exceptional David Lindley. All these stars embellish rather than steal the show and Browne's gentle happy/sad lyrics shine through on a solid album. Things toughened up on later works, but this has innocent charm of a singer songwriter feeling his way.

❱❱ Tracks: *Take It Easy; Our Lady Of The Well; Colors Of The Sun; I Thought I Was A Child; These Days; Red Neck Friend; The Times You've Come; Ready Or Not; Sing My Songs To Me; For Everyman.*

★ First released 1973
★ UK peak chart position: did not chart
★ USA peak chart position: 43
★ Previous Top 1000 position: 1998 (582): 1994 (–)

444 THE DOWNWARD SPIRAL ↑ Nine Inch Nails

Once you embark upon *The Downward Spiral* you must be prepared to get sucked into an unrelenting hour's worth of Trent Reznor exploring themes of death, suicide, sex, drugs and violence. The opening 'Mr Self Destruct' repeats over and over 'I control you', and throughout the lyrics are uncompromising, disturbing and, by the closing track 'Hurt', hold out little hope. The multi-layered blend of synthesizers and raging guitars provides the perfect backdrop for Reznor to wrestle with his personal demons. Not for those of a nervous disposition, those used to lyrics of a more upbeat nature, potential suicide cases or sunshine pop fans.

❱❱ Tracks: *Mr Self Destruct; Piggy; Heresy; March Of The Pigs; Closer; Ruiner; The Becoming; I Do Not Want This; Big Man With A Gun; A Warm Place; Eraser; Reptile; The Downward Spiral; Hurt.*

★ First released 1994
★ UK peak chart position: 9
★ USA peak chart position: 2
★ Previous Top 1000 position: 1998 (–): 1994 (–)

445 CLUB CLASSICS VOL. ONE ↑
Soul II Soul

Where previous UK translations of classic US black music styles had been hit and miss affairs, Jazzie B revolutionised contemporary soul music on both sides of the channel with the sublime *Club Classics*. Caron Wheeler's emotive performance on the opening track, 'Keep On Movin'' (the album's title in the USA) set the tone of the album. It's not flawless – Jazzie B, producer and all-round music man, may be many things, but a rapper he is not. And a second great single, 'Back To Life', is included here only in *a cappella* form. When Jazzie and Nellee Hooper's ideas and musical instincts coalesce, the results boast a positive feel.

» Tracks: *Keep On Movin'; Fairplay; Holdin' On; Feeling Free; African Dance; Dance; Feel Free; Happiness; Back To Life; Jazzie's Groove.*

★ First released 1989
★ UK peak chart position: 1
★ USA peak chart position: did not chart
★ Previous Top 1000 position: 1998 (550): 1994 (–)

446 FEAR OF MUSIC ↓
Talking Heads

If there is any warning before The Bomb drops, you know that every radio is going to be blaring 'Life During Wartime', the best-known track on *Fear Of Music*, which was produced by Brian Eno, already well versed in the apocalypse through his work on David Bowie's *Low*. Talking Heads' third album showed them straying ever further from their roots in New York's CBGB's vehemently anti-disco scene, as they experimented with dance beats and African rhythms. Its black, industrial-looking cover reflected the bleak subject matter, with a high proportion of minor-key songs. David Byrne's cynical lyrics took a dim view of the effects of technology on humans, despite the group's increasing reliance on studio gadgetry.

» Tracks: *I Zimbra; Mind; Paper; Cities; Life During Wartime; Memories Can't Wait; Air; Heaven; Animals; Electric Guitar; Drugs.*

★ First released 1979
★ UK peak chart position: 33
★ USA peak chart position: 21
★ Previous Top 1000 position: 1998 (410): 1994 (–)

447 RASTAMAN VIBRATION ↑
Bob Marley and The Wailers

The overwhelming sadness of the song 'Johnny Was' seems to cling to the entire album like a sore. The power of Marley consoling a mother after her son has been pointlessly murdered is hard to forget, especially the lyric 'shot down in the street and died just because of the system'. Marley went some way to improving things by later getting the warring leaders Manley and Seaga at least to meet and hold hands. After that bold move he was seen as a cultural icon as much as a musician and Jamaica's finest songwriter. This is Marley's deepest album and one that shows his compassion.

» Tracks: *Positive Vibration; Roots, Rock, Reggae; Johnny Was; Cry To Me; Want More; Crazy Baldhead; Who The Cap Fits; Night Shift; War; Rat Race.*

★ First released 1976
★ UK peak chart position: 15
★ USA peak chart position: 8
★ Previous Top 1000 position: 1998 (576): 1994 (–)

448 GERRY MULLIGAN MEETS BEN WEBSTER ↑
Gerry Mulligan and Ben Webster

This album combines the talents of two jazz giants. Saxophonist Ben Webster was one of the instrument's most influential exponents, primarily through his work with Duke Ellington. Gerry Mulligan, meanwhile, was an integral part of the 50s west coast movement and this set represents the confluence of two different generations. The featured quintet includes drummer Mel Lewis and bassist Leroy Vinnegar (who later played on the Doors' *The Soft Parade*), but the six tracks are noteworthy for the splendid empathy struck by Mulligan (baritone) and Webster (tenor). One of several collaborations between the former and notable guest artists, *Gerry Mulligan Meets Ben Webster* is a fine example of how two seemingly disparate musicians can perform together superbly.

» Tracks: *Chelsea Bridge; Cat Walk; Sunday; Who's Got Rhythm?; Tell Me When; Go Home.*

★ First released 1960
★ UK peak chart position: 15
★ USA peak chart position: did not chart
★ Previous Top 1000 position: 1998 (555): 1994 (196)

449 SUNFLOWER ↑
The Beach Boys

Ah, if only the thousands who love *Pet Sounds* would discover this beautiful hidden gem. Its sales and chart position are an insult – this is a sublime record of gigantic proportion. Try out the harmonic power of 'This Whole World', shed a tear at the beauty of 'Add Some Music To Your Day', be impressed with their early new-age discovery of 'Cool Cool Water', and be surprised that they can rock on 'Got To Know The Woman'. Brian Wilson is the acknowledged genius, but this album contains one of their greatest songs, written by the fast developing Dennis Wilson: 'Forever' will make you melt, assuming you do have a romantic bone in your body.

❱❱ Tracks: *Slip On Through; This Whole World; Add Some Music To Your Day; Got To Know The Woman; Deirdre; It's About Time; Tears In The Morning; All I Wanna Do; Forever; Our Sweet Love; At My Window; Cool Cool Water.*

★ First released 1970
★ UK peak chart position: 29
★ USA peak chart position: 151
★ Previous Top 1000 position: 1998 (594): 1994 (–)

450 PAID IN FULL ↑
Eric B. & Rakim

The New York duo of DJ Eric Barrier and William Griffin Jr were early pioneers of rap. This was a highly influential album when first released, although nowadays it seems slightly tame. 'Eric B. Is President' created a stir when first issued and it was followed by the heavily remixed 'Paid in Full' (numerous versions were issued). Their sampling and scratching inspired a host of imitators. The use of funk backing caused James Brown to object, although in reality it rejuvenated Brown's career. They revelled in the plagiarism of other material, but in the light of what has happened since, they were angelicly innocent.

❱❱ Tracks: *I Ain't No Joke; Eric B. Is On The Cut; My Melody; I Know You Got Soul; Move The Crowd; Paid In Full; As The Rhythm Goes On; Chinese Arithmetic; Eric B. Is President; Extended Beat.*

★ First released 1987
★ UK peak chart position: 85
★ USA peak chart position: 58
★ Previous Top 1000 position: 1998 (579): 1994 (–)

451 THE GENIUS HITS THE ROAD
↑ Ray Charles

Contrary to the misleading title, this is not a live album. It is a journey through America with the titles acting as a travelogue. Many of the tracks are familiar, but it is Ray Charles' unique touch that indelibly stamps every song he attempts. The best example is his golden touch on Hoagy Carmichael's gem 'Georgia'. Charles has made this his own with an emotional performance. Other credible covers are 'Moonlight In Vermont' and 'Basin Street Blues'. The 50th anniversary reissue CD contains some excellent bonus tracks, including the gritty and fittingly titled 'Hit The Road Jack'. This is an essential 'Brother Ray' album to own.

❱❱ Tracks: *Alabamy Bound; Georgia On My Mind; Basin Street Blues; Mississippi Mud; Moonlight In Vermont; New York's My Home; California, Here I Come; Moon Over Miami; Deep In The Heart Of Texas; Carry Me Back To Old Virginny; Blue Hawaii; Chattanooga Choo-Choo. Sentimental Journey; Hit The Road Jack; Blue Moon Of Kentucky (Swingova); Rainy Night In Georgia; I'm Movin' On; Swanee River Rock (Talkin' Bout That River); Lonely Avenue.*

★ First released 1960 ★ UK peak chart position: did not chart
★ USA peak chart position: 9
★ Previous Top 1000 position: 1998 (572): 1994 (–)

452 MUSIC FROM BIG PINK ↓
The Band

The Band emerged from months of seclusion with this enthralling debut album. It followed a lengthy spell accompanying Bob Dylan, which culminated in sessions known as *The Basement Tapes*. Three songs herein were revived from those recordings, and the remainder showed a similar pastoral spirit. Where contemporaries sought expression in progressive music, the Band were largely reflective, creating atmosphere from traditional forms and distilling the results in an economic style. Their ensemble playing and rural voices were best captured on 'The Weight', an elliptical composition which displayed their craft to perfection. Americana of every hue can be gleaned from this collection, the depth of which left a marked impression on audiences and musicians alike.

❱❱ Tracks: *Tears Of Rage; To Kingdom Come; In A Station; Caledonia Mission; The Weight; We Can Talk; Long Black Veil; Chest Fever; Lonesome Suzie; Wheels On Fire; I Shall Be Released.*

★ First released 1968 ★ UK peak chart position: did not chart
★ USA peak chart position: 30
★ Previous Top 1000 position: 1998 (258): 1994 (163)

453 THE PATSY CLINE SHOWCASE ↑ Patsy Cline

Astonishingly, only three albums were released during Patsy Cline's lifetime, this being the best one. Although she was a competent up-tempo performer, she excelled with tear-jerking ballads like 'I Fall To Pieces' and Willie Nelson's 'Crazy'. Producer Owen Bradley bathed her throbbing vocals with echo, added a vocal group (the Jordanaires) and a gentle beat, sweetened by strings. Thus, they created the template for country music of the 60s. Cline's male counterpart was Jim Reeves and in 1981, their versions of 'Have You Ever Been Lonely?' and 'I Fall To Pieces' were merged for duet recordings. LeAnn Rimes would not be singing today if it were not for the voice of Patsy Cline.

》 Tracks: I Fall To Pieces; Foolin' Round; The Wayward Wind; South Of The Border; I Love You So Much It Hurts; Seven Lonely Days; Crazy; San Antonio Rose; True Love; Walking After Midnight; A Poor Man's Roses.

★ First released 1963 ★ UK peak chart position: did not chart
★ USA peak chart position: 74
★ Previous Top 1000 position: 1998 (684): 1994 (864)

454 THE MAN AND HIS MUSIC ↑ Sam Cooke

This collection demonstrates Sam Cooke's enormous catalogue of sweet soul music. The age of CD gave listeners a selection which is unbeatable in choice, ranging from his early days of gospel right through to the period before he was tragically killed. The fresh-faced man on the cover looks exactly as you imagine his music to sound; his voice was like cream in coffee. Most of the songs have been covered dozens of time by artists such as Cat Stevens, Rod Stewart, Aretha Franklin, Steve Miller and Otis Redding, but none has succeeded in interpreting any Cooke song as anything more than a humble tribute. Rod Stewart would be the first to admit this. Cooke is the perfect bridge between the soul of Otis Redding and Marvin Gaye.

》 Tracks: Touch The Hem Of His Garment; That's Heaven To Me; I'll Come Running Back To You; You Send Me; Win Your Love For Me; Just For You; Chain Gang; When A Boy Falls In Love; Only Sixteen; Wonderful World; Cupid; Nothing Can Change This Love; Rome Wasn't Built In A Day; Love Will Find A Way; Everybody Loves To Cha Cha Cha; Another Saturday Night; Meet Me At Mary's Place; Having A Party; Good Times; Twistin' The Night Away; Shake; Somebody Have Mercy; Sad Mood; Ain't That Good News; Bring It On Home To Me; Soothe Me; That's Where It's At; A Change Is Gonna Come.
★ First released 1986
★ UK peak chart position: 8 ★ USA peak chart position: 175
★ Previous Top 1000 position: 1998 (538): 1994 (514)

455 ARC OF A DIVER ↑ Steve Winwood

With a glorious voice that sounds as if he has just swallowed a terminally sticky jar of toffee, Steve Winwood has the advantage of instant recognition; add to this a musicianship that has been employed in sessions for most major recording artists, and the result is a prodigious talent that runs like a vein of gold through rock music since the mid-60s. Arc Of A Diver, released at the end of 1980 after a long period of self-imposed retreat, is a triumphant resurgence. With lyrical contributions by Vivian Stanshall (the rich imagery of the title-track) and Will Jennings, Winwood never falls into the trap of shaming the music with sub-standard words. Another musical genius, taking a nap at the moment.

》 Tracks: While You See A Chance; Second Hand Woman; Slowdown Sunset; Spanish Dancer; Night Train; Dust; Arc Of A Diver.

★ First released 1980
★ UK peak chart position: 13
★ USA peak chart position: 3
★ Previous Top 1000 position: 1998 (730): 1994 (278)

456 I'M ALIVE ↑ Jackson Browne

An album that saw Browne return to high-quality songs brought about by the familiar chestnut 'relationship problems'. Much media attention was given to his break-up with actress Darryl Hannah, and Browne seemed to come off worse. However, he deserves the last laugh because it prompted stellar songs such as the title track, 'My Problem Is You' and the light reggae beat of 'Everywhere I Go'. Few contemporary songwriters can analyse and discuss their own problems and failings through songs as openly and, apparently honestly, as Jackson Browne. Anybody that wrote him off as one of 'those 70s singer songwriters' should lend an ear to this album, especially those with marital problems.

》 Tracks: I'm Alive; My Problem Is You; Everywhere I Go; I'll Do Anything; Miles Away; Too Many Angels; Take This Rain; Two Of Me, Two Of You; Sky Blue And Black; All Good Things.

★ First released 1993
★ UK peak chart position: 35
★ USA peak chart position: 40
★ Previous Top 1000 position: 1998 (645): 1994 (–)

457 THESE DAYS ↑
Bon Jovi

One of the best hard rock bands currently working, Bon Jovi have every ingredient in their music for customer satisfaction – softer than the hardest metal, but tougher than your standard AOR. Richie Sambora is a modern-day guitar hero, and certainly on a par with the 60s dinosaurs – the Jeff Beck, Jimmy Page and Ritchie Blackmore crowd. He can play unobtrusively, as on 'These Days', or he can tear out your insides, like the solo on 'Damned'. High standards delivered seemingly with ease. If they decide to call it a day, Bon Jovi, with his drop-dead good looks, can make it as a movie star.

❱❱ Tracks: *Hey God; Something For The Pain; This Ain't A Love Song; These Days; Lie To Me; Damned; My Guitar Lies Bleeding In My Arms; It's Hard Letting You Go; Hearts Breaking Even; Something To Believe In; If That's What It Takes; Diamond Ring; All I Want Is Everything; Bitter Wine.*

★ First released 1995
★ UK peak chart position: 1
★ USA peak chart position: 9
★ Previous Top 1000 position: 1998 (609): 1994 (–)

458 UP ↑
R.E.M.

The first album following the departure of the irreplaceable Bill Berry received mixed reviews upon release. It also stalled slightly in the sales department, not because of the loss of Berry but because it was a deeper and more challenging collection. They have to be admired in pushing forward and trying something different, and that is why R.E.M. are probably the most respected band in the world at this time. The contrasting music styles are exciting, ranging from the moody opener 'Airportman' through the angry 'Lotus' and back to the lethargic 'Suspicion'. Even though they occasionally miss the mark Stipe, Mills and Buck always remain interesting.

❱❱ Tracks: *Airportman; Lotus; Suspicion; Hope; At My Most Beautiful; The Apologist; Sad Professor; You're In The Air; Walk Unafraid; Why Not Smile; Daysleeper; Diminished; Parakeet; Falls To Climb.*

★ First released 1998
★ UK peak chart position: 2
★ USA peak chart position: 3
★ Previous Top 1000 position: 1998 (–): 1994 (–)

459 BE HERE NOW ↓
Oasis

A year on, and undoubtedly overshadowed by its superior predecessors, *Be Here Now* represented more of the same at a time when Oasis could do no wrong. The fact that their third Beatles-derived album showed negligible musical progression did not dent its sales, nor affect the initially warm critical reception. Tailor-made for stadium audience singalongs, even the better tracks – 'Stand By Me', 'It's Gettin' Better (Man!!)', 'D'You Know What I Mean?' and the title track – struggled in comparison with the band's earlier work. The popular backlash was quick in coming, the tumble followed. *Be Here Now* is now slammed by the critics and disowned by many fans, in addition to its own creators.

❱❱ Tracks: *D'You Know What I Mean?; My Big Mouth; Magic Pie; Stand By Me; I Hope, I Think, I Know; The Girl In The Dirty Shirt; Fade In-Out; Don't Go Away; Be Here Now; All Around The World; It's Gettin' Better (Man!!); All Around The World (Reprise).*

★ First released 1997
★ UK peak position: 1
★ USA peak position: 2
★ Previous Top 1000 position: 1998 (36): 1994 (–)

460 AT NEWPORT ↑
Duke Ellington

This concert marked the so-called rebirth of Duke Ellington. Of course, it was the jazz audience that had lost sight of the band. However, *At Newport* saw the end of his temporary obscurity. Irritated by the place on the programme and his musicians' habitual tardiness, Ellington began the second set in a do-or-die mood. They did not die. Wonderful solos by Clark Terry, Johnny Hodges and Paul Gonsalves links the two parts of 'Diminuendo In Blue' and 'Crescendo In Blue', and makes this an evening that will live forever in the annals of jazz. Ellington had obviously intended to blow the audience away with the set. He succeeded beyond his wildest dreams.

❱❱ Tracks: *Newport Jazz Festival Suite – a) Festival Junction b) Blues To Be There c) Newport Up; Jeep's Blues; Diminuendo And Crescendo In Blue.*

★ First released 1957
★ UK peak chart position: did not chart
★ USA peak chart position: 14
★ Previous Top 1000 position: 1998 (672): 1994 (247)

461 SINATRA AT THE SANDS ↑
Frank Sinatra

Very few live albums equal the original recording, and generally live albums do not capture the performance. This one does. You can sense immediately that Frank Sinatra was in a good mood the minute he stepped on the stage. His patter is spot on and he is able to move from great humour into classy love songs (such as 'The Shadow Of Your Smile') with great ease. The Quincy Jones arrangements and the Count Basie orchestra are both faultless. Although critics have suggested he was past his peak by 1966, there is little to prove their case on this album. The tinkling whiskey glasses and smokers coughs are also a bonus.

» Tracks: *Come Fly With Me; I've Got A Crush On You; I've Got You Under My Skin; The Shadow Of Your Smile; Street Of Dreams; One For My Baby (And One More For The Road); Fly Me To The Moon; One O'Clock Jump; Monologue; You Make Me Feel So Young; All Of Me; The September Of My Years; Get Me To The Church On Time; It Was A Very Good Year; Don't Worry Bout Me; Makin' Whoopee!; Where Or When; Angel Eyes; My Kind Of Time; Monologue; My Kind Of Town (Reprise).*

★ First released 1966
★ UK peak chart position: 7 ★ USA peak chart position: 9
★ Previous Top 1000 position: 1998 (642); 1994 (–)

462 THE KICK INSIDE ↑
Kate Bush

Discovered and nurtured by Pink Floyd's Dave Gilmour, Kate Bush burst into an unsuspecting world with the dramatic 'Wuthering Heights'. The ambitiousness of this startling single was carried over into the singer's debut album where already imaginative compositions were enriched by her evocative falsetto. Bush's intonation expressed a variety of emotions. Alternately coy, playful and sensual, she uses her voice to swoop and glide around the material, enhancing the imagery posed by graphic lyrics. Sympathetic accompaniment added weight to a collection in which the artist's single-mindedness was already apparent.

» Tracks: *Moving; Saxophone Song; Strange Phenomena; Kite; The Man With The Child In His Eyes; Wuthering Heights; James And The Cold Gun; Feel It; Oh To Be In Love; L'Amour Looks Something Like You; Them Heavy People; Room For The Life; The Kick Inside.*

★ First released 1978
★ UK peak chart position: 3
★ USA peak chart position: did not chart
★ Previous Top 1000 position: 1998 (675); 1994 (275)

463 TROUBLE MAN ↑
Marvin Gaye

Tenuous though it is, history books list it as a Marvin Gaye album. Those who did not see the film (from which this is a soundtrack) might unsuspectingly think Gaye might sing on it. In fact he does on one track, the title song. The film was another low-budget blaxploitation detective movie that fell short of both *Superfly* (Curtis Mayfield) and *Shaft* (Isaac Hayes). Musically, however, the remaining instrumental music is hard to fault, even though it sounds very much of its era. Approach with some degree of caution, but expect to be pleasantly surprised. Avoid the trap of treating this as background music.

» Tracks: *Main Theme From Trouble Man; T Plays It Cool; Poor Abbey Walsh; The Break In (Police Shoot Big); Cleo's Apartment; Trouble Man; Theme From Trouble Man; T Stands For Trouble; Main Theme From Trouble Man; Life Is A Gamble; Deep-In-It.*

★ First released 1972
★ UK peak chart position: did not chart
★ USA peak chart position: 14
★ Previous Top 1000 position: 1998 (651); 1994 (–)

464 YIELD ↑
Pearl Jam

The second most famous and popular band to come out of Seattle, Pearl Jam have reached such a level of consistency that even the critics have given up expecting a poor album. *Yield* is their fifth album and, after the experimental *No Code*, marked a return to their traditional sound, with enough slightly different chord permutations to keep the fans happy. Eddie Vedder's fragile, melodic vocals make a refreshing change from the full-throated, barechested roar usually expected from the singer of a heavy alternative rock band. This in turn makes Pearl Jam a bit special, and alongside R.E.M. and Nirvana they represent the best of the commercially successful US alternative rock groups of the 90s.

» Tracks: *Brain Of J; Faithful; No Way; Given To Fly; Wishlist; Pilate; Do the Evolution; ·; MFC; Low Light; In Hiding; Push Me, Pull Me; All Those Yesterdays.*

★ First released 1998
★ UK peak chart position: 7
★ USA peak chart position: 2
★ Previous Top 1000 position: 1998 (–); 1994 (–)

465 WALTZ FOR DEBBY ↑
Bill Evans

Recorded on the same night as *Sunday At The Village Vanguard*, *Waltz For Debby* captures one of the most important and well-integrated piano trios in the history of jazz, working on a superbly inspired night. It is clear, listening to this record, that bassist Scott La Faro had a very special rapport with Evans, and drummer Paul Motian's subtle, improvised accompaniments and eccentric, quirkily quiet swing was the perfect engine for this subtle, impressionistic pianist. Check out the lovely, gentle 'My Foolish Heart', and the lively 'Milestones' and, of course, 'Waltz For Debby'.

》 Tracks: *My Foolish Heart; Waltz For Debby; Detour Ahead; My Romance; Some Other Time; Milestones.*

★ First released 1961
★ UK peak chart position: did not chart
★ USA peak chart position: did not chart
★ Previous Top 1000 position: 1998 (664): 1994 (580)

466 BIG WILLIE STYLE ↑
Will Smith

This immensely talented artist can do no wrong at the moment. Quite apart from his hugely successful acting career, Smith cornered the bubblegum rap market with smooth pop-rap confections such as 'Gettin' Jiggy Wit It' and the title track of the movie *Men In Black*. The huge success of the latter helped propel Smith headlong into the pre-teen market, and this album is therefore free from a parental guidance sticker. Smith's innuendo-laden lyrics are so clever, nonetheless, that he gets away with blue murder. This is an irresistible record that will effortlessly lift your spirits on a gloomy day.

》 Tracks: *Intro; Y'All Know; Gettin' Jiggy Wit It; Candy; Chasing Forever; Keith B-Real I (Interlude); Don't Say Nothin'; Miami; Yes Yes Y'All; I Loved You; Keith B-Real II (Interlude); It's All Good; Just The Two Of Us; Keith B-Real III (Interlude); Big Willie Style; Men In Black.*

★ First released 1997
★ UK peak chart position: 11
★ USA peak chart position: 8
★ Previous Top 1000 position: 1998 (–): 1994 (–)

467 AFRICAN HERBSMAN ↑
Bob Marley and The Wailers

Prior to the universal success that Bob Marley later experienced, he was already a giant at home. Having worked with all the legendary producers, he still could not find the key to expand his territory. This album represents his work with Lee Perry at the end of the 60s and up to *Catch A Fire*. Many of the songs he later re-recorded, and the latter versions are the familiar ones. These, however, have authenticity; they are less polished but sound Jamaican. 'Lively Up Yourself', '400 Years' and 'Kaya' sound smoother than their famous relatives. The bass is rounder and Marley's vocals are mixed in, rather than up-front. Historically indispensable.

》 Tracks: *Lively Up Yourself; Small Axe; Duppy Conquerer; Trench Town Rock; African Herbsman; Keep On Moving; Fussing And Fighting; Stand Alone; All In One; Don't Rock The Boat; Put It On; Sun Is Shining; Kaya; Riding High; Brain Washing; 400 Years.*

★ First released 1974
★ UK peak chart position: did not chart
★ USA peak chart position: did not chart
★ Previous Top 1000 position: 1998 (694): 1994 (–)

468 LITTLE CRIMINALS ↑
Randy Newman

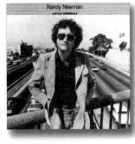

Newman's most commercially successful album opens with his misunderstood masterpiece, 'Short People'. Of course he is not being derogatory towards people of restricted growth, that's just the way it seems. Those who understand Newman's brilliant pathos and irony know he has a heart of gold. After all, what heart of stone could write evocative material such as 'Baltimore' and 'I'll Be Home'. It is widely known that Newman is one of America's greatest ever songwriters – if only his music could be more widely known and appreciated, and not have to rely on the 'helping hands' of the Eagles to escalate its US sales and chart position.

》 Tracks: *Short People; You Can't Fool The Fat Man; Little Criminals; Texas Girl At The Funeral Of Her Father; Jolly Coppers On Parade; In Germany Before The War; Sigmund Freud's Impersonation Of Albert Einstein In America; Baltimore; I'll Be Home; Rider In The Rain; Kathleen (Catholicism Made Easier); Old Man On The Farm.*

★ First released 1977
★ UK peak chart position: did not chart
★ USA peak chart position: 9
★ Previous Top 1000 position: 1998 (729): 1994 (–)

469 SAILIN' SHOES ↑
Little Feat

A band that received nothing but praise and is rightly remembered with great affection. The re-formed version of the 90s with Craig Fuller does not come near the magical unit led by the late Lowell George. Most of their albums are recommended. 'Easy To Slip' opens with George smacking chords from his acoustic guitar as his partners fall in line, loose yet totally together. Little Feat were one of the finest bands of the 70s – only now do we really appreciate just how great they were. And yes, this is the one that has the best version of 'Willin' on it.

▶▶ Tracks: *Easy To Slip; Cold Cold Cold; Trouble; Tripe Face Boogie; Willin'; A Apolitical Blues; Sailin' Shoes; Teenage Nervous Breakdown; Got No Shadow; Cat Fever; Texas Rose Cafe.*

★ First released 1972
★ UK peak chart position: did not chart
★ USA peak chart position: did not chart
★ Previous Top 1000 position: 1998 (718): 1994 (264)

470 MY FUNNY VALENTINE ↑
Miles Davis

One of the finest live albums in the history of jazz, *My Funny Valentine* presents the Miles Davis Quintet live at the Lincoln Centre's Philharmonic Hall in 1964. Surrounded by the vibrant and youthful rhythm section of Herbie Hancock (piano), Ron Carter (bass) and Tony Williams (drums), Davis was enjoying a strong new surge of creativity, and played with a stunning level of invention and passion throughout. The resonance of the long title track – one of those flawless performances that happens only very occasionally – dominates the record. Front-line partner George Coleman (tenor saxophone) chose a good evening to play some of the most beautiful solos of his life.

▶▶ Tracks: *My Funny Valentine; All Of You; Stella By Starlight; All Blues; I Thought About You.*

★ First released 1964
★ UK peak chart position: did not chart
★ USA peak chart position: 138
★ Previous Top 1000 position: 1998 (768): 1994 (788)

471 SIXTEEN STONE ↑
Bush

The success of this album is not so much a fluke, more a question of the marketing department being aware that this is an American alternative rock classic. The fact that it was written and performed by lads from London should not spoil anybody's enjoyment. Their canny record label shifted millions of units in a US market desperate for bands who sounded like Pearl Jam and Soundgarden. In contrast, Bush is at best a cult act in their native country despite repeated attempts to break them in the UK market. The music on this debut album is unrelentingly passionate, no more so than on the first single 'Everything Zen'. Seek out the limited edition 2-CD set that features an excellent acoustic version of 'Come Down'.

▶▶ Tracks: *Everything Zen; Swim; Bomb; Little Things; Comedown; Body; Machinehead; Testosterone; Monkey; Glycerine; Alien; X-Girlfriend.*

★ First released 1994
★ UK peak chart position: 42
★ USA peak chart position: 4
★ Previous Top 1000 position: 1998 (–): 1994 (–)

472 OLIVER! ↑
Various

Ron Moody recreates his magnificent stage performance as Fagin on this soundtrack album of what must be the best British musical film ever. Shani Wallis replaced Georgia Brown as Nancy, and, together with Mark Lester (Oliver), Jack Wild (Artful Dodger) and Oliver Reed (the sinister Bill Sikes), gives Lionel Bart's marvellous score the full treatment. Highlights are impossible to select; Oliver's tender 'Where Is Love' and Fagin's 'You've Got To Pick A Pocket Or Two' linger in the memory, but the complete set is as fresh now as when it was released over 25 years ago. In those pre-Andrew Lloyd Webber days, musicals had lots of strong songs, not just one.

▶▶ Tracks: *Overture; Food Glorious Food; Boy For Sale; Where Is Love?; You've Got To Pick A Pocket Or Two; Consider Yourself; I'd Do Anything; Be Back Soon; As Long As He Needs Me; Who Will Buy; It's A Fine Life; Reviewing The Situation; Oom Pah Pah; Finale.*

★ First released 1968
★ UK peak chart position: 4
★ USA peak chart position: 20
★ Previous Top 1000 position: 1998 (776): 1994 (309)

473 ELLA FITZGERALD SINGS THE GEORGE AND IRA GERSHWIN SONGBOOK ↑
Ella Fitzgerald

The paradox of Ella Fitzgerald's prominence in the history of jazz singing and her lack of emotional intensity is much less apparent on this album. George Gershwin's affinity with jazz, and the corresponding delight jazz musicians take in performing his material, allow the singer to fly with the music. As for brother Ira's lyrics, they receive their due as cheerful, tender and always delightful examples of the lyricist's art. The Songbook series remains one of Ella Fitzgerald's major contributions – among many – to American popular music and this in particular is one of the best of the sizeable bunch.

》 Tracks: *Including – Sam And Delilah; But Not For Me; My One And Only; Let's Call The Whole Thing Off; I've Got Beginners Luck; Lady Be Good; Nice Work If You Can Get It; Things Are Looking Up; Just Another Rhumba; How Long Has This Been Going On; S'wonderful; Man I Love; That Certain Feeling; By Strauss; Who Cares; Someone To Watch Over Me; Real American Folk Song; They All Laughed; Looking For A Boy; My Cousin From Milwaukee; Somebody From Somewhere; Foggy Day; Clap Yo' Hands; For You, For Me, Forever More; Stiff Upper Lip; Strike Up The Band; Soon; I've Got A Crush On You; Bidin' My Time; Aren't You Kind Of Glad We Did; Of Thee I Sing; Half It Dearie Blues; I Was Doing It Right; He Loves And She Loves; Love Is Sweeping The Country; Treat Me Rough; Love Is Here To Stay; Slap That Bass; Isn't It A Pity; Shall We Dance.*

★ First released 1959   ★ UK peak chart position: did not chart
★ USA peak chart position: 111
★ Previous Top 1000 position: 1998 (749); 1994 (696)

474 GOODBYE JUMBO ↑
World Party

This is a fine album that paradoxically owes much of its originality to its up-front eclecticism. Karl Wallinger's undoubted talent and experience (musical director of *The Rocky Horror Show*, ex-Waterboys) are applied to create a powerful tribute to his 60s influences. The opening 'Is It Too Late' is reminiscent of Them's 'Baby Please Don't Go', and is followed by 'Way Down Now', complete with 'Sympathy For The Devil'-style 'woo-woos'. It is difficult to keep track of all the styles cleverly woven into the fabric, but the Beatles abound – Wallinger even had his studio built to reproduce the Abbey Road sound for the follow-up, *Bang!*

》 Tracks: *Is It Too Late; Way Down Now; When The Rainbow Comes; Put The Message In The Box; Ain't Gonna Come Till I'm Ready; And I Fell Back Alone; Take It Up; God On My Side; Show Me To The Top; Love Street; Sweet Soul Dream; Thank You World.*

★ First Released 1990
★ UK peak chart position: 36
★ USA peak chart position: 73
★ Previous Top 1000 position: 1998 (778); 1994 (–)

475 BLOOD AND CHOCOLATE ↑
Elvis Costello

On this album the Attractions were reunited with Elvis Costello (aka Napoleon Dynamite), and the result was another powerful stream of angst, emotion and vitriol. Costello has so much lyrical frustration, he should be commissioned to write the entire Top 40. 'I Want You' is one of the most intense songs he has ever written; he really does open up his soul, and makes a public statement set over a simple melody, accompanied by Nick Lowe on acoustic guitar. The album is similar in feel to *Imperial Bedroom* and a record that needs the lyric sheet to be read, digested and acted upon. Costello might yet end up working for Relate.

》 Tracks: *Uncomplicated; I Hope You're Happy Now; Tokyo Storm Warning; Home Is Anywhere You Hang Your Head; I Want You; Honey Are You Straight Or Are You Blind; Blue Chair; Battered Old Bird; Crimes Of Paris; Poor Napoleon; Next Time Round.*

★ First released 1986
★ UK peak chart position: 16
★ USA peak chart position: 84
★ Previous Top 1000 position: 1998 (750); 1994 (285)

476 LONELY AT THE TOP ↑
Randy Newman

A criminally underrated man who has been writing poetical songs about American life for four decades. This is Randy Newman's greatest hits offering with the reality being that he only hit once with the misunderstood 'Short People'. Many of his early songs recorded by the likes of Dusty Springfield and Gene Pitney are still overlooked on this compilation, but we do have heartfelt ramblings and powerful understatements. To think that Newman can move us to tears of emotion with a lyric that merely states 'I think it's going to rain today' is remarkable. Astonishing to think that such a collection did not make the charts.

》 Tracks: *Love Story; Living Without You; I Think It's Going To Rain Today; Mama Told Me Not To Come; Sail Away; Simon Smith And The Amazing Dancing Bear; Political Science; God's Song; Rednecks; Birmingham; Louisiana 1927; Marie; Baltimore; Jolly Coppers On Parade; Rider In The Rain; Short People; I Love L.A.; Lonely At The Top.*

★ First released 1987
★ UK peak chart position: did not chart
★ USA peak chart position: did not chart
★ Previous Top 1000 position: 1998 (509); 1994 (458)

477 MILESTONES ↑
Miles Davis

An album that has matured with age, and becomes more popular as it is handed down to younger students of Miles. Featuring the classic sextet with the personnel of John Coltrane, Cannonball Adderley, Red Garland, Philly Joe Jones and Paul Chambers, it hints at what was to come with the phenomenal *Kind Of Blue* the following year. The modal jazz period was germinated here, particularly with 'Sid's Ahead', featuring one of Davis's finest solos, a tribute to late-night New York disc jockey Symphony Sid. Elsewhere the pace is swing and cool, with a unique drum sound on 'Billy Boy'. It closes with a superior reading of Thelonious Monk's 'Straight No Chaser'.

▶▶ Tracks: *Doctor Jekyll; Sid's Ahead; Two Bass Hits; Miles; Billy Boy; Straight No Chaser.*

★ First released 1958
★ UK peak chart position: did not chart
★ USA peak chart position: did not chart
★ Previous Top 1000 position: 1998 (506): 1994 (158)

478 MIDNIGHT LOVE ↑
Marvin Gaye

Leaving the safety and familiarity of Tamla/Motown has seen many artists take a flight to obscurity. Marvin Gaye turned it on its head and made his most successful album for over ten years. The pivotal track is 'Sexual Healing', an idea given to him by his biographer David Ritz and co-written with Odell Brown. This track alone is worth the price of the album (even though it was a single). It oozes greatness with every second and was the last great Marvin Gaye song. And for the record, he played drums, piano, organ, bells, synths and bongos. A premier voice lost to the world.

▶▶ Tracks: *Midnight Lady; Sexual Healing; Rockin' After Midnight; 'Til Tomorrow; Turn On Some Music; Third World Girl; Joy; My Love Is Waiting.*

★ First released 1982
★ UK peak chart position: 10
★ USA peak chart position: 7
★ Previous Top 1000 position: 1998 (784): 1994 (–)

479 NUGGETS – ORIGINAL ARTYFACTS FROM THE FIRST PSYCHEDELIC ERA 1965-1968 ↑
Various Artists

A compilation that actually *defined* a genre, this sent out musical ripples that influenced innumerable bands, from the Damned to R.E.M. Compiler Lenny Kaye even gave the genre a name: punk. Although the music was later better known as 'garage', Kaye – himself about to pioneer 70s punk as Patti Smith's guitarist – was onto something when he asserted that America's aggressive teen bands of the mid-60s were the original punks. To prove that this was not an isolated, parochial movement, Kaye included not only hits such as the Castaways' 'Liar, Liar' and the Count Five's 'Psychotic Reaction', but also buried treasures like the Remains' classic 'Don't Look Back' and the Chocolate Watch Band's 'Let's Talk About Girls'. Superseded by the amazing expanded CD box set.

▶▶ Tracks: *I Had Too Much To Dream (Last Night); Dirty Water; Night Time; Lies; Respect; A Public Execution; No Time Like The Right Time; Oh Yeah; Pushin' Too Hard; Moulty; Don't Look Back; Invitation To Cry; Liar, Liar; You're Gonna Miss Me; Psychotic Reaction; Hey Joe; Just Like Romeo And Juliet; Sugar And Spice; Baby Please Don't Go; Tobacco Road; Let's Talk About Girls; Sit Down I Think I Love You; Run Run Run; My World Fell Down; Open My Eyes; Farmer John; It's-A-Happening.*

★ First released: 1972 ★ UK peak chart position: did not chart
★ USA peak chart position: did not chart
★ Previous Top 1000 position: 1998 (515): 1994 (–)

480 BODY AND SOUL ↑
Coleman Hawkins

This 1958 release features Coleman Hawkins' definitive interpretation of the title track. Although he did not write 'Body And Soul', he managed to engrave his own soul into it, and on the strength of this recording, should be entitled to claim it as his own. Regardless of recording techniques and location, the sparse, breathy tone produced by Hawkins is breathtaking. Without denigrating the other tracks on this record, the title track alone justifies its importance (as significant as *Kind Of Blue*) in any comprehensive record collection. Beautifully preserved from 10-inch disc and recorded in 1939, also included on this album is the 1956 recording, on which even the subtle clicks of the saxophone keys are discernible.

▶▶ Tracks: *Meet Doctor Foo; Fine Dinner; She's Funny That Way; Body And Soul; When Day Is Done; The Sheik Of Araby; My Blue Heaven; Bouncing With Bean; Say It Isn't So; Spotlight; April In Paris; How Strange; Half Step Down Please; Jumping For Jane; I Love You; There Will Never Be Another You; Little Girl Blue; Dinner For One, Please James; I Never Knew; His Very Own Blues; Thirty Nine Inches; Bean Stalks Again; I'm Shooting High; Have You Met Miss Jones?; The Day You Came Along; The Essence Of You.*

★ First released 1958 ★ UK peak chart position: did not chart
★ USA peak chart position: did not chart
★ Previous Top 1000 position: 1998 (520): 1994 (161)

481 YOUNG AMERICANS ↑
David Bowie

David Bowie abandoned the glam/sci-fi personae of *Ziggy Stardust*, *Aladdin Sane* and *Diamond Dogs* with this radical departure. Recorded at Sigma Sound Studios, the home of Philadelphia International Records, it featured the label's crack house band and, as a result, confirmed the singer's growing love of soul and R&B. Pulsating dance grooves abound, in particular on the disco-influenced 'Fame', which topped the US singles chart. The song was co-written with John Lennon, a compliment Bowie repaid by reinventing the Beatles' 'Across The Universe' as a dancefloor classic. Such self-confidence abounds throughout this album which shows the singer firmly in command of yet another musical direction.

▶ Tracks: *Young Americans; Win; Fascination; Right; Somebody Up There Likes Me; Across The Universe; Can You Hear Me; Fame.*

★ First released 1975
★ UK peak chart position: 2
★ USA peak chart position: 9
★ Previous Top 1000 position: 1998 (521): 1994 (260)

482 PERMANENT VACATION ↑
Aerosmith

Their second release for Geffen Records, and the album that saw them crawl out of the indifferent route they had been following for a few years. Aerosmith's rise from the ashes is a great tale of rock 'n' roll excess, and one for which Geffen must thank their lucky stars. This album has the sparkle and energy of *Rocks* and the chorus of *Toys in The Attic*. 'Magic Touch' climbs and soars, the crude beat of 'Rag Doll' creeps under the skin and 'Dude (Looks Like A Lady)' is a reworked tale of the Kinks' 'Lola'. Career-wise they have not looked back since this album.

▶ Tracks: *Heart's Done Time; Magic Touch; Rag Doll; Simoriah; Dude (Looks Like A Lady); St. John; Hangman Jury; Girl Keeps Coming Apart; Angel; Permanent Vacation; I'm Down; The Movie.*

★ First released 1987
★ UK peak chart position: 37
★ USA peak chart position: 11
★ Previous Top 1000 position: 1998 (629): 1994 (–)

483 THE FABULOUS ↑
Little Richard

Little Richard's third album captured a singer building on his acknowledged style. He had forged a reputation based on undiluted R&B, typified on such expressive recordings as 'Tutti Frutti', 'Long Tall Sally' and 'Good Golly Miss Molly'. *The Fabulous* offered a wider musical perspective, although there was no denying the frantic fervour surrounding his readings of 'Kansas City' and 'Whole Lotta Shakin' Goin' On'. Such performances contrast with the more conciliatory 'Directly From My Heart', but the opportunity to broaden musical horizons suggested by this set was never fully taken up. In 1957 Richard denounced his work and joined the church, but although he later reversed that decision, this album closes his most creative period.

▶ Tracks: *Shake A Hand; Chicken Little Baby; All Night Long; The Most I Can Offer; Lonesome And Blue; Wonderin'; Whole Lotta Shakin' Goin' On; She Knows How To Rock; Kansas City; Directly From My Heart; Maybe I'm Right; Early One Morning; I'm Just A Lonely Guy.*

★ First released 1958
★ UK peak chart position: did not chart
★ USA peak chart position: did not chart
★ Previous Top 1000 position: 1998 (536): 1994 (185)

484 COUNTRY LIFE ↑
Roxy Music

The sleeve proclaims 'the fourth Roxy Music album' and although it is the poor relative to the famous three, there is enough substance to merit a place in any collection. Guitarist Phil Manzanera is particularly inspired throughout; listen to his solo on 'Out Of The Blue'. Bryan Ferry makes his mark with expert delivery on the hit single 'All I Want Is You' and the heavily germanic 'Bitter Sweet'. The closing track is 'Prairie Rose', leaving one to ponder where should they have gone from here? Ferry could have been Engelbert Humperdinck if he had not got into such a boring funk groove on his later albums.

▶ Tracks: *The Thrill Of It All; Three And Nine; All I Want Is You; Out Of The Blue; If It Takes All Night; Bitter Sweet; Triptych; Casanova; A Really Good Time; Prairie Rose.*

★ First released 1974
★ UK peak chart position: 3
★ USA peak chart position: 37
★ Previous Top 1000 position: 1998 (537): 1994 (–)

485 HEAVEN UP HERE ↑
Echo And The Bunnymen

On their debut album this Liverpool quartet unveiled a sound crossing post-punk with psychedelic pop. Rather than repeat the formula, the group teased out the constituent parts of their sound to create *Heaven Up Here*. Alternately dreamlike and melancholically fragile, the set is marked by Ian McCulloch's arresting vocals which sweep across the textured sound with awesome confidence. The album exudes a cumulative power, building in atmosphere as it progresses, with Will Sergeant's plangent guitar emphasizing and supporting the drift of the singer's nuances. It is the icing on an exquisite collection.

▶▶ Tracks: *Show Of Strength; With A Hip; Over The Wall; It Was A Pleasure; A Promise; Heaven Up Here; The Disease; All My Colours; No Dark Things; Turquoise Days; All I Want.*

★ First released 1981
★ UK peak chart position: 10
★ USA peak chart position: 184
★ Previous Top 1000 position: 1998 (540): 1994 (589)

486 KICK OUT THE JAMS ↑
The MC5

A true explosion of a record. Unfeasibly heady in its approach and delivery, it still stands today as one of the great, unabashed roars of bare, musical energy. Vocalist Rob Tyner crawls from a whisper to a scream, the tunnel of sound constructed around him both desperate and admirable. The title track is a manifestation of sound threatening to stumble and fall in on itself, and on the simply great 'Motor City Is Burning', the appropriately monikered guitarist, Fred 'Sonic' Smith, proves the power of his well-chosen nickname. Meanwhile, the eager sentiment of 'I Want You Right Now' speaks volumes about the tone of the album. One that will blow away your speaker covers, if you have not already removed them by now.

▶▶ Tracks: *Ramblin' Rose; Kick Out The Jams; Come Together; Rocket Reducer No. 62 (Rama Lama Fa Fa Fa); Borderline; Motor City Is Burning; I Want You Right Now; Starship.*

★ First released 1969
★ UK peak chart position: did not chart
★ USA peak chart position: 30
★ Previous Top 1000 position: 1998 (545): 1994 (816)

487 AVALON SUNSET ↑
Van Morrison

One of Van Morrison's more commercially successful albums. Maybe a few extra sales were made by having Cliff Richard as co-vocalist on the overtly Christian 'Whenever God Shines His Light'. The overall themes are the same; the songs have that glorious quality of melancholy and Morrison sings as well as ever. The religion and spiritualism that have become a strong part of his work are here in large doses. The real success is behind the lyrics, where the private man reveals a bit more about himself. 'Have I Told You Lately' has to be one the best ever statements of unconditional love.

▶▶ Tracks: *Whenever God Shines His Light; Contacting My Angel; I'd Love To Write Another Song; Have I Told You Lately; Coney Island; I'm Tired Joey Boy; When Will I Ever Learn To Live In God; Orangefield; Daring Night; These Are The Days.*

★ First released 1989
★ UK peak chart position: 13
★ USA peak chart position: 91
★ Previous Top 1000 position: 1998 (559): 1994 (205)

488 COMPLETE & UNBELIEVABLE... THE DICTIONARY OF SOUL ↑
Otis Redding

Soul giant Otis Redding crossed over into the pop charts with a version of the Temptations' 'My Girl'. This album followed that achievement and showed him bringing a wider perspective to R&B. Working in tandem with guitarist Steve Cropper, Redding tore up the blueprints of Beatles songs and standards, making them as much his own as the original songs the pair contributed. Never a subtle singer, Otis possessed a raw intensity, charging the material through the force of his personality. *Dictionary Of Soul* was the last album issued before the singer's untimely death; the artistic challenges it posed were sadly left unrealized.

▶▶ Tracks: *Fa-Fa-Fa-Fa-Fa (Sad Song); I'm Sick Y'all; Tennessee Waltz; Sweet Lorene; Try A Little Tenderness; Day Tripper; My Lover; Prayer; She Put The Hurt On Me; Ton Of Joy; You're Still My Baby; Hang For You; Love Have Mercy.*

★ First released 1966
★ UK peak chart position: 23
★ USA peak chart position: 73
★ Previous Top 1000 position: 1998 (558): 1994 (274)

489 KEEP THE FAITH ↑
Bon Jovi

This bunch of soft hard rockers was beginning to fade into rock history prior to the release of this comeback album. Nearly four years had passed since *New Jersey* dominated the charts, and newer and nastier pretenders to the commercial rock crown were appearing. *Keep The Faith* knocked everyone sideways with its quality and helped spur a Bon Jovi revival that put them affectionately in the 'pending dinosaur status' folder. Every track was a winner, with future stadium favourites including the title track, 'I'll Sleep When I'm Dead' and 'Blame It On The Love Of Rock & Roll'. Arguably their finest album.

▶▶ Tracks: *I Believe; Keep The Faith; I'll Sleep When I'm Dead; In These Arms; Bed Of Roses; If I Was Your Mother; Dry County; Woman In Love; Fear; I Want You; Blame It On The Love Of Rock & Roll; Little Bit Of Soul.*

★ First released 1992
★ UK peak chart position: 5
★ USA peak chart position: 5
★ Previous Top 1000 position: 1998 (–); 1994 (–)

490 ELLA FITZGERALD SINGS THE COLE PORTER SONGBOOK ↑
Ella Fitzgerald

One of Ella Fitzgerald's great assets was also, paradoxically, one of her failings as a jazz singer. Throughout her long career her voice was that of an innocent girl. This immaturity of sound, allied as it was to consummate musical mastery, weakened her jazz performances, especially in the blues where emotional intensity is of paramount importance. As if sensing this, Norman Granz heard in Fitzgerald's voice the ideal vehicle for a selection of readings from the Great American Songbook. Her coolly detached approach to lyrics is nowhere better displayed than on this album of songs by one of the most sophisticated American songwriters.

▶▶ Tracks: *All Through The Night; Anything Goes; Miss Otis Regrets; Too Darn Hot; In The Still Of The Night; I Get A Kick Out Of You; Do I Love You; Always True To You In My Fashion; Let's Do It; Just One Of Those Things; Every Time We Say Goodbye; All Of You; Begin The Beguine; Get Out Of Turn; I Am In Love; From This Moment On; I Love Paris; Do I Love You; Riding High; Easy To Love; It's Alright With Me; Why Can't You Behave; What Is This Thing Called Love; You're The Top; Love For Sale; It's D'Lovely; Night And Day; Ace In The Hole; So In Love; I've Got You Under My Skin; I Concentrate On You; Don't Fence Me In.*

★ First released 1956 ★ UK peak chart position: did not chart
★ USA peak chart position: 15
★ Previous Top 1000 position: 1998 (567); 1994 (643)

491 MINGUS MINGUS MINGUS MINGUS MINGUS ↑
Charles Mingus

While Charles Mingus is rightly revered by the jazz world, he is yet to receive the universal blessing of the rock audience in the way that John Coltrane and Miles Davis have. This album is perfect for a Mingus primer. It is fat, gorgeous, accessible and often breathtaking. Suddenly, the swinging orchestra will pause its riff completely and a few notes of Mingus' growling bass will sneak in. For once the sleeve-note is right: 'he jolts with the unexpected'. 'II B.S.' is a stunning opener and from then on the listener can settle into a comfortable half-hour. A brilliant record.

▶▶ Tracks: *II B.S.; I X Love; Celia; Mood Indigo; Better Get Hit In Yo' Soul; Theme For Lester Young; Hora Decubitus.*

★ First released 1963
★ UK peak chart position: did not chart
★ USA peak chart position: did not chart
★ Previous Top 1000 position: 1998 (564); 1994 (–)

492 SHEER HEART ATTACK ↑
Queen

Although Queen's first and second albums both made the upper half of *Billboard's* Top 200, *Sheer Heart Attack* was the one that broke them in America. It included their first US Top 40 single, 'Killer Queen', a melodramatic *tour de force* of multilayered harmonies, Nöel Coward-style lyrics, wilfully erratic guitar crunches, and psychedelic phasing that laid the groundwork for such future hits as 'Bohemian Rhapsody'. Despite the album's Stateside success, it retained the quintessentially English sound and attitude that had marked the group's earlier efforts. And Freddie made a brilliant 'Stormtrooper in Stilettoes'.

▶▶ Tracks: *Brighton Rock; Killer Queen; Tenement Funster; Flick Of The Wrist; Lily Of The Valley; Now I'm Here; In The Lap Of the Gods; Stone Cold Crazy; Dear Friends; Misfire; Bring Back That Leroy Brown; She Makes Me (Stormtrooper In Stilettoes); In The Lap Of The Gods ... Revisited.*

★ First released 1974
★ UK peak chart position: 2
★ USA peak chart position: 12
★ Previous Top 1000 position: 1998 (602); 1994 (–)

493 SPICE ↓
Spice Girls

If the column inches of Spice Girls press were placed end to end, they would encircle the world 18,000 times. Such was their power, and their ability to capture most people's attention, and many of their hearts. This album of pure pop harks back to the days when children, grannies, milkmen and window-cleaners were all singing the Beatles' 'She Loves You'. This group of feisty women brought about girl power, but mostly they brought a smile back to angst-ridden pop music. 'Wannabe' and '2 Become 1' are classics of the art. Don't hold your breath for them to top this though.

➤ Tracks: Wannabe; Say You'll Be There; 2 Become 1; Love Thing; Last Time Lover; Mama; Who Do Think You Are; Something Kinda Funny; Naked; If U Can't Dance.

★ First released 1996
★ UK peak chart position: 1
★ USA peak chart position: 1
★ Previous Top 1000 position: 1998 (101): 1994 (–)

494 WAITING FOR THE SUN ↑
The Doors

The Doors' third album is one of contrast, capturing brash commerciality and political militancy. It survives the artistic dilemma this poses through a succession of excellent songs and many of singer Jim Morrison's most explicit lyrics. 'The Unknown Soldier' and 'Five To One' capture the Doors at their most politically strident, wherein music and image complement each other perfectly. Other selections show the quartet playful ('Hello I Love You'), wistful ('Summer's Almost Gone') or even peculiar ('My Wild Love'), but in each case the Doors proved themselves as intriguing as ever.

➤ Tracks: Hello I Love You; Love Street; Not To Touch; The Earth; Summer's Almost Gone; Winter Time Love; The Unknown Soldier; Spanish Caravan; My Wild Love; We Could Be So Good Together; Yes, The River Knows; Five To One.

★ First released 1968
★ UK peak chart position: 16
★ USA peak chart position: 1
★ Previous Top 1000 position: 1998 (597): 1994 (208)

495 I'M YOUR MAN ↑
Leonard Cohen

A strange juxtaposition of biting lyrics, haunting melodies, world-weary vocals, and dinky production, I'm Your Man was Leonard Cohen's best-received album in years, making the UK Top 50 and earning kudos from critics across the globe. The lead-off track, 'First We Take Manhattan', immediately sets the mood, as Cohen intones sinisterly, 'They sentenced me to twenty years of boredom' but then, to borrow from Lou Reed, the coloured girls sing, and we're in Las Vegas. However, despite Cohen's dodgy self-production, the songs, and his unmistakable delivery, quickly take centre-stage. One standout is 'Everybody Knows', a love-gone-wrong tune full of angst.

➤ Tracks: First We Take Manhattan; Ain't No Cure For Love; Everybody Knows; I'm Your Man; Take This Waltz; Jazz Police; I Can't Forget; Tower Of Song.

★ First released 1988
★ UK peak chart position: 48
★ USA peak chart position: did not chart
★ Previous Top 1000 position: 1998 (620): 1994 (–)

496 KAYA ↑
Bob Marley & The Wailers

Bob Marley is in a mellow and happy mood as the album opens with 'excuse me while I light my spliff' on 'Easy Skanking' and maintains the feeling throughout. 'Kaya' has one of the best bass riffs of any Marley song (played by the wonderful Aston Family Man Barrett). The hit single 'Is This Love' is included and he sounds upbeat singing 'She's Gone', although the subject is that his lover has just left him. Nothing fazed him; he was able to address political and emotional subjects with the same degree of feeling and his manner was truly saintly. Kaya is one of his finest moments of the studio albums.

➤ Tracks: Easy Skanking; Kaya; Is This Love; Sun Is Shining; Satisfy My Soul; She's Gone; Misty Morning; Crisis; Running Away; Time Will Tell.

★ First released 1978
★ UK peak chart position: 4
★ USA peak chart position: 50
★ Previous Top 1000 position: 1998 (608): 1994 (–)

497 NIGHT AND DAY ↑
Joe Jackson

Joe Jackson's great New York album, full of atmosphere, high-quality musicianship and mature arrangements, put him way beyond the pop of his first two albums. The cosmopolitan flavour is captured on the Latin-styled 'Cancer', Jackson's romantic nature is exposed on the beautiful 'Would You Be My Number Two' and the album's headliner is the modern classic 'Steppin' Out', with its unforgettable bass and piano intro. This album should have been a platform to make Jackson an international artist, but for some reason his career faltered and he was eventually dropped by his record company. Repeated radio play of 'Steppin' Out' should keep this album in print.

▶ Tracks: *Another World; Chinatown; TV Age; Target; Would You Be My Number Two; Steppin' Out; Breaking Us In Two; Cancer; Real Men; Slow Song.*

★ First released 1982
★ UK peak chart position: 3
★ USA peak chart position: 4
★ Previous Top 1000 position: 1998 (646): 1994 (310)

498 HERE MY DEAR ↑
Marvin Gaye

A concept album of some magnitude, although the subject matter could hardly have been comfortable listening for Anna, Marvin Gaye's ex-wife. She was the subject of Gaye's public 'divorce album'. The illustration on the sleeve depicts love, marriage, pain and divorce, in addition to the balanced scales of justice. This lengthy album (originally a double vinyl) was poorly received by the critics, although now it has grown in stature, and it really does have considerable depth and melody. Let's face it, if Gaye sang a gardening seed catalogue from cover to cover it would be acceptable.

▶ Tracks: *Here, My Dear; I Met A Little Girl; When Did You Stop Loving Me, When Did I Stop Loving You; Anger; Is That Enough; Everybody Needs Love; Time To Get It Together; Sparrow; Anna's Song; When Did You Stop Loving Me, When Did I Stop Loving You (Instrumental); A Funky Space Reincarnation; You Can Leave, But It's Going To Cost You; Falling In Love Again; When Did You Stop Loving Me, When Did I Stop Loving You (Reprise).*

★ First released 1978 ★ UK peak chart position: did not chart
★ USA peak chart position: 26
★ Previous Top 1000 position: 1998 (720): 1994 (–)

499 WORKERS PLAYTIME ↑
Billy Bragg

Few singers in recent history have the honesty to sing as they sound. There is no false American twang, no hip angst vocals and no lo-fi intensity. Billy Bragg sings like a geezer from Barking, Essex, which is exactly what he is. He is, however, blessed with a knack for writing powerful political songs of lyrical truth and romantic ballads of heart-rending openness. Long after Bragg has hung up his Burns guitar, other people with twangy American accents and plenty of angst will record songs such as 'She's Got A New Spell' and 'The Price I Pay', and they will have huge hits with them.

▶ Tracks: *She's Got A New Spell; Must I Paint You A Picture; Tender Comrade; The Price I Pay; Little Time Bomb; Rotting On Remand; Valentine's Day Is Over; Life With The Lions; The Only One; The Short Answer; Waiting For The Great Leap Forwards.*

★ First released 1988
★ UK peak chart position: 17
★ USA peak chart position: 198
★ Previous Top 1000 position: 1998 (631): 1994 (–)

500 SONGS OF LOVE AND HATE ↑
Leonard Cohen

Leonard Cohen was already established as a denizen of 'bedsitter music' by the time this third album was issued. Deftly balanced between newly written material and older songs, it contains several of the singer's most graphic and literate compositions. Allegory vies with personal recollection to create a set of unparalleled depth while Cohen's grasp of melody stays as secure as ever. His unconventional voice remains fixedly morose, but its individuality ensures a bewitching resonance on 'Famous Blue Raincoat' and 'Joan Of Arc'. Cohen's poetic imagery was never as striking or as moving.

▶ Tracks: *Avalanche; Last Year's Man; Dress Rehearsal Rag; Diamonds In The Mine Field; Love Calls You By Your Name; Famous Blue Raincoat; Sing Another Song, Boys; Joan Of Arc.*

★ First released 1971
★ UK peak chart position: 4
★ USA peak chart position: 145
★ Previous Top 1000 position: 1998 (676): 1994 (789)

501 TRES HOMBRES ↑
ZZ Top

Few bands have endeared themselves to the public by maintaining a sound that has barely changed over a quarter of a century. ZZ Top didn't even bother to trim their beards. The Rolling Stones, the Bee Gees and even Genesis all changed. ZZ Top have been successfully stubborn, they have merely refined, as more recording tracks have become available in the studio. This is a superb heavy rock/boogie album, better than most of the competition in 1973, and because of their refusal to change, it sounds great in the 90s. Try this in addition to *Eliminator*.

➤ Tracks: *Waitin' For The Bus; Jesus Just Left Chicago; Beer Drinkers & Hell Raisers; Master Of Sparks; Hot, Blue and Righteous; Move Me On Down The Line; Precious and Grace; La Grange; Shiek; Have You Heard.*

★ First released 1973
★ UK peak chart position: did not chart
★ USA peak chart position: 8
★ Previous Top 1000 position: 1998 (530): 1994 (–)

502 IN SEARCH OF THE LOST CHORD ↑ Moody Blues

After the success of *Days Of Future Passed*, the Mark II Moody Blues knew that they had hit upon a winning formula. Once again, mellotrons swirled around each member's contributions, a truly democratic band at this stage. 'Voices In The Sky' became a hit single, but here it is one part of a trilogy that includes 'Visions Of Paradise' and the hypnotic 'The Best Way To Travel'. Whatever 'beep' they created to simulate a spaceship travelling through the cosmos, it works. The throwaway 'Dr Livingstone I Presume' does not, but can be programmed out in the CD age. 'Ride My See-Saw' proved that they had not gone completely soft, and could still rock.

➤ Tracks: *Departure; Ride My See-Saw; Dr. Livingstone I Presume; House Of Four Doors; Legend Of A Mind; House Of Four Doors (Part Two); Voices In The Sky; The Best Way To Travel; Visions Of Paradise; The Actor; The Word; Om.*

★ First released 1968
★ UK peak chart position: 5
★ USA peak chart position: 23
★ Previous Top 1000 position: 1998 (722): 1994 (–)

503 EDEN ↑
Everything But The Girl

Tracey Thorn and Ben Watt decided to step forward with this album and shed the twee 'not quite in tune' indie image that permeated much of their early work. Using tasteful arrangements and some excellent session players, *Eden* was an important transitional record. Peter King, Nigel Nash and Dick Pearce added some fine reed and brass that made good songs such as 'Tender Blue' and the bossa nova 'Each And Every One' sound positively great. The stand-out track is 'Another Bridge', which has a gentle Hammond organ doodling over a fat acoustic G chord throughout. They became chart stars long after this album.

➤ Tracks: *Each And Every One; Bittersweet; Tender Blue; Another Bridge; The Spice Of Life; The Dustbowl; Crabwalk; Even So; Frost And Fire; Fascination; I Must Confess; Soft Touch.*

★ First released 1984
★ UK peak chart position: 14
★ USA peak chart position: did not chart
★ Previous Top 1000 position: 1998 (752): 1994 (–)

504 GAUCHO ↑
Steely Dan

Probably the most critically revered band of the 70s, Steely Dan's brand of slick pop with a dose of jazz/funk left a meagre but vital catalogue to cling on to. This was their last gasp at the onset of the 80s. Perhaps they were aware of the fact that they were too 70s for the 80s. This was their least accessible and most mature album (no criticism is intended), as the content washes over the listener like a warm shower. 'Hey Nineteen' is the hit single from this set, a radio-friendly nostalgic look at 1967, impeccable in production and with evocative lyrics. Lots of echoey Fender Rhodes and sensitive brass. This is a sanitized record that cannot be faulted.

➤ Tracks: *Babylon Sisters; Hey Nineteen; Glamour Profession; Gaucho; Time Out Of Mind; My Rival; Third World Man.*

★ First released 1980
★ UK peak chart position: 27
★ USA peak chart position: 9
★ Previous Top 1000 position: 1998 (774): 1994 (–)

505 LAST TIME AROUND ↑
Buffalo Springfield

Although this album is effectively the potato peelings of a delicious meal, the fragmentation of the band is no longer apparent thirty years later. Reappraising this record puts it still behind *Buffalo Springfield Again*, but there is a gentle quality about the whole record. As Jim Messina and Richie Furay took control, the album develops a country rock feel. Neil Young's premier contribution is 'I Am A Child' and the prolific Stephen Stills hits the button with four gems: the plea for world unity, 'Uno Mundo', the song of a fugitive, 'Four Days Gone', 'Special Care' and the original 'Questions'. A much better album than we could have expected from this outstanding group.

» Tracks: *On The Way Home; It's So Hard To Wait; Pretty Girl Why; Four Days Gone; Carefree Country Day; Special Care; The Hour Of Not Quite Rain; Questions; I Am A Child; Merry-Go-Round; Uno Mundo; Kind Woman.*

★ First released 1968
★ UK peak chart position: did not chart
★ USA peak chart position: 42
★ Previous Top 1000 position: 1998 (667): 1994 (–)

506 HYPOCRISY IS THE GREATEST LUXURY ↑
Disposable Heroes Of Hiphoprisy

Often berated as the group that it is OK for non-rap fans to like, the Disposable Heroes' solitary album proper represents much more than that might imply. Shades of Michael Franti and Rono Tse's previous incarnation, as part of the beatnigs, resurface in the collision of samples, noise and breakbeats. Tse's technique is exemplary. However, it is Franti's fiercely intelligent narratives that carry the day. Where bombast and finger-pointing had been the order of the day in hip-hop, Franti includes his own inadequacies (notably calling himself a 'jerk' in 'Music and Politics') in his diagnosis of the problem.

» Tracks: *Satanic Reverses; Famous and Dandy (Like Amos 'N' Andy); Television, The Drug Of The Nation; Language Of Violence; The Winter Of The Long Hot Summer; Hypocrisy Is The Greatest Luxury; Everyday Life Has Become A Health Risk; Ins Greencard A-19 191 500; Socio-Genetic Experiment; Music and Politics; Financial Leprosy; California Über Alles; Water Pistol Man.*

★ First released 1992
★ UK peak chart position: 40
★ USA peak chart position: did not chart
★ Previous Top 1000 position: 1998 (748): 1994 (527)

507 STARSAILOR ↓
Tim Buckley

Tim Buckley's work was always challenging, developing from that of a superior folk-singer to one encompassing many forms of expression. A growing jazz influence came to full fruition on *Starsailor*, which embraced the radical *avant garde* aspects of John Coltrane and Ornette Coleman. On several tracks the singer largely eschewed melody, giving full rein to his astonishing range, turning his voice into another instrument. Yet there were equal moments of gorgeous melancholia, no more so than on 'Song To The Siren', later popularized by This Mortal Coil. Supported only by muted electric guitar and eerie sound effects, Buckley sings with heartfelt emotion, resulting in one of his finest ever performances. The contrast between its ethereal atmosphere and the dense textures elsewhere result in an enthralling, intense collection.

» Tracks: *Come Here Woman; I Woke Up; Monterey; Moulin Rouge; Song To The Siren; Jungle Fire; Starsailor; The Healing Festival; Down By The Borderline.*

★ First released 1970
★ UK peak chart position: did not chart
★ USA peak chart position: did not chart
★ Previous Top 1000 position: 1998 (284): 1994 (403)

508 NEW BOOTS AND PANTIES!!
Ian Dury and The Blockheads

Good evening, I'm from Essex. The late Ian Dury's greatest album, rarely has a musical artist been so loved and respected. Dury portrayed the Essex man long before Essex man was conceived. He brilliantly satirized it in 'Billericay Dickie' and 'Clevor Trever'. It is hard to imagine Dury the softie, but there is a romantic soul in 'Wake Up and Make Love To Me' and 'I'm Partial To Your Abracadabra'; there is also sadness and regret in the beautiful 'My Old Man'. He should be remembered for his dynamite band the Blockheads and this necessary album – not his gold radio station albatross 'Hit Me With Your Rhythm Stick'.

» Tracks: *Sweet Gene Vincent; Wake Up and Make Love To Me; I'm Partial To Your Abracadabra; My Old Man; Billericay Dickie; Clevor Trever; If I Was With A Woman; Plaistow Patricia; Blockheads; Blackmail Man.*

★ First released 1977
★ UK peak chart position: 5
★ USA peak chart position: 168
★ Previous Top 1000 position: 1998 (188): 1994 (53)

509 THE PRETENDER ↑
Jackson Browne

Jackson Browne's literate Californian music reached a creative peak with this exceptional release. A pensive, introspective songwriter, he combines a poetic perceptiveness with subtle melodies, resulting in an engaging music reliant on suggestion, rather than power. *The Pretender* contains several of his finest songs, particularly the lengthy title track and the melancholic 'Here Come Those Tears Again'. Superb support from guitarist David Lindley emphasizes the nuances in Browne's work, gently adding to its poignancy. Recorded following the suicide of the singer's wife, *The Pretender* provided Browne with an artistic catharsis that never slips into self-pity.

▶ Tracks: *The Fuse; Your Bright Baby Blues; Linda Paloma; Here Comes Those Tears Again; Only Child; Daddy's Tune; Sleep's Dark and Silent Gate; The Pretender.*

★ First released 1976
★ UK peak chart position: 26
★ USA peak chart position: 5
★ Previous Top 1000 position: 1998 (760): 1994 (287)

510 OAR ↓
Alexander 'Skip' Spence

This is the product of a mad, tortured genius who took too many chemicals and lost it. Moby Grape had so much potential and Spence was a major figure in the band. This stark, disjointed collection is a classic 'cult' album, and will remain so as long as Syd Barrett, Roky Erickson, Peter Green and Spence continue to be written about. This is a challenging, brilliant, odd, loveable album that comes highly recommended. The Sony reissue in 1991 contains five bonus tracks. When Spence delivered this to Columbia Records, imagine the record executive listening to it, sitting back in his chair and saying, 'gee . . . I don't hear a hit single'.

▶ Tracks: *Little Hands; Cripple Creek; Diana; Margaret-Tiger Rug; Weighted Down (The Prison Song); War In Peace; Broken Heart; All Come To Meet Her; Book Of Moses; Dixie Peach Promenade; Lawrence Of Euphoria; Grey/Afro; This Time He Has Come; It's The Best Thing For You; Keep Everything Under Your Hat; Halo Of Gold; Doodle.*

★ First released 1969
★ UK peak chart position: did not chart
★ USA peak chart position: did not chart
★ Previous Top 1000 position: 1998 (461): 1994 (–)

511 CAN'T SLOW DOWN ↓
Lionel Richie

Richie's brand of silky-smooth macho soul was the butt of some critics during the early 80s. A plethora of handsome studs with great voices, whopping great medallions, who just wanted to love all night long followed Richie. Yet another album crammed with hit singles, it was one of the 80s' sales phenomena both in the USA and the UK – as was 'Hello' when released as a single. This album is corny but unashamedly romantic, and consequently more couples have danced to his 'All Night Long (All Night)' than any other – and 16 million couples went out and bought it. A lot of children were born nine months later.

▶ Tracks: *Can't Slow Down; All Night Long (All Night); Penny Lover; Stuck On You; Love Will Find A Way; The Only One; Running With The Night; Hello.*

★ First released 1983
★ UK peak chart position: 1
★ USA peak chart position: 1
★ Previous Top 1000 position: 1998 (291): 1994 (60)

512 THE SKY IS CRYING ↑
Stevie Ray Vaughan and Double Trouble

Vaughan's death on 27 August 1990 brought to a tragic end the surging wave of his popularity. The album he had made with his brother Jimmie, *Family Style*, had just been released and this album, prepared by Jimmie from the various album sessions, was not expected to amount to much. In fact, this was at least as good as any of them – and better than *Live Alive*. 'Little Wing' was perhaps his best adaptation of a Jimi Hendrix song. His take on the Elmore James title song was also a fitting tribute to both the writer and the performer. There are bound to be further compilations and live recordings released, but these studio recordings are testimony to Stevie Ray Vaughan's devotion to his craft.

▶ Tracks: *Boot Hill; The Sky Is Crying; Empty Arms; Little Wing; Wham; May I Have A Talk With You; Close To You; Chittlins Con Carne; So Excited; Life By The Drop.*

★ First released 1991
★ UK peak chart position: did not chart
★ USA peak chart position: 10
★ Previous Top 1000 position: 1998 (781): 1994 (456)

513 STAND UP ↓
Jethro Tull

The vinyl sleeve reveals four cute little Tulls, who pop up to greet the listener; sadly, CD does not have this luxury. The music, however, is still as good. On *Stand Up*, Jethro Tull reached a peak of heavy rock that was slowly to fade with subsequent albums as Ian Anderson discovered the acoustic guitar. This featured 'new' guitarist Martin Barre and he plays like a demon on powerful tracks such as 'A New Day Yesterday' and 'Nothing Is Easy'. The band have never sounded so together as they attempted Bach on the joyous, flute-led 'Bouree' and sprinkled some rustic humour with the acoustic 'Fat Man'.

» Tracks: *A New Day Yesterday; Jeffrey Goes To Leicester Square; Bouree; Back To The Family; Look Into The Sun; Nothing Is Easy; Fat Man; We Used To Know; Reasons For Waiting; For A Thousand Mothers.*

★ First released 1969
★ UK peak chart position: 1
★ USA peak chart position: 20
★ Previous Top 1000 position: 1998 (413): 1994 (–)

514 WHAT'S THE 411? ↑
Mary J. Blige

The opening track 'Leave A Message' is an immediately intriguing hook for the listener. A series of answerphone messages over a funky drum beat does not fail, even though most callers insist on saying 'peace' instead of 'goodbye' at the end of every call. The artist first appears on track two, and stays in control throughout an album of high-quality urban R&B/soul. Highly commercial, yet it never sinks to the blandness of some other 90s female pop acts. Tracks such as 'Real Love' lend more to the best of Aretha Franklin pop flirtations than to 90s R&B. Mary J. Blige is Franklin's heir apparent.

» Tracks: *Leave A Message; Reminisce; Real Love; You Remind Me; Intro Talk; Sweet Thing; Love No Limit; I Don't Want To Do Anything; Slow Down; My Love; Changes I've Been Going Through; What's The 411?*

★ First released 1992
★ UK peak chart position: 53
★ USA peak chart position: 6
★ Previous Top 1000 position: 1998 (766): 1994 (–)

515 BAND ON THE RUN ↓
Wings

McCartney's immediate solo career was largely viewed as lightweight. This album restated artistic strengths missing from earlier releases, reclaiming the his grasp of pop's dynamics and hooklines. From the pulsating abandonment of 'Jet' to the measured control of 'Let Me Roll It', *Band On The Run* is a tight, disciplined collection, full of contrast and commitment. McCartney's unfettered self-confidence permeates a selection that not only forced commentators to revise their views, but also asserted the band and the singer's individual identity, rather than solely that of ex-Beatle.

» Tracks: *Band On The Run; Jet; Bluebird; Mrs. Vandebilt; Let Me Roll It; Mamunia; No Words; Picasso's Last Words (Drink To Me); Nineteen Hundred and Eighty Five.*

★ First released 1973
★ UK peak chart position: 1
★ USA peak chart position: 1
★ Previous Top 1000 position: 1998 (500): 1994 (311)

516 GOODBYE AND HELLO ↓
Tim Buckley

Initially a folk-singer, Tim Buckley quickly defied stylistic categorization. *Goodbye and Hello* offers a rich musical vocabulary, from plaintive love song to free-form expressionism, with its core the artist's remarkable voice. Buckley glides and swoops around the melodies, colouring his material with raw emotion. His range is startling, from sonorous baritone to wild falsetto, but the intonation is never gratuitous. The beautiful 'Morning Glory' is on this record. He integrates with the song and musicians, most of whom were steeped in modern jazz. The haunting beauty of Tim Buckley's work is caught to perfection herein and continues to influence.

» Tracks: *No Man Can Find The War; Carnival Song; Pleasant Street; Hallucinations; I Never Asked To Be Your Mountain; Once I Was; Phantasmagoria In Two; Knight-Errant; Goodbye and Hello; Morning Glory.*

★ First released 1967
★ UK peak chart position: did not chart
★ USA peak chart position: 171
★ Previous Top 1000 position: 1998 (318): 1994 (444)

517 MR FANTASY ↑
Traffic

Released at the height of 60s flower power, Traffic were originally the perfect 'dayglo candy coloured chrysanth-emum' group. Dave Mason's hippie dipsy ditties blended with Steve Winwood's more ambitious musical aspirations. Although they were given the same title, the US and UK albums had different track-listings. The US version has the edge because it includes the hit singles 'Hole In My Shoe' and 'Paper Sun' as well as 'Smiling Phases', which was covered by Blood, Sweat & Tears. The UK version has 'Utterly Simple' and 'Hope I Never Find Me There' in their place. Mercifully, both versions include the magnificent title-track with the definitive Winwood guitar solo (or was it Mason?).

» Tracks: *Paper Sun; Dealer; Coloured Rain; Hole In My Shoe; No Face, No Name, No Number; Heaven Is In Your Mind; House For Everyone; Berkshire Poppies; Giving To You; Smiling Phases; Dear Mr Fantasy.*

★ First released 1967
★ UK peak chart position: 8
★ USA peak chart position: 88
★ Previous Top 1000 position: 1998 (860): 1994 (–)

518 BEDTIME STORIES ↑
Madonna

Madonna changed her image from sex and erotica to looking like a cross between Marilyn Monroe and Barbara Cartland. Musically, she was growing and expanding her sound, and this album was her classiest to date. Less pop and more soul, resulting in wholly satisfying tracks such as 'Secret' and 'I'd Rather Be Your Lover'. The co-opted writers/producers no doubt helped in giving the songs and production greater depth, notably Dallas Austin, Dave Hall and, especially, Babyface, with the excellent 'Forbidden Love' and 'Take A Bow'. A wonderfully rich and creamy album that should stand as one of her best achievements.

» Tracks: *Survival; Secret; I'd Rather Be Your Lover; Don't Stop; Inside Of Me; Human Nature; Forbidden Love; Love Tried To Welcome Me; Sanctuary; Bedtime Story; Take A Bow.*

★ First released 1994
★ UK peak chart position: 2
★ USA peak chart position: 3
★ Previous Top 1000 position: 1998 (894): 1994 (–)

519 THE "CHIRPING" CRICKETS ↓
The Crickets

Another great classic that failed to chart on both sides of the Atlantic; perhaps the name Crickets on the cover deterred purchasers who did not realize that this featured Buddy Holly. The tracks speak for themselves, timeless pop-flavoured rock 'n' roll songs that still take some beating; 'Maybe Baby', 'That'll Be The Day' and 'Oh Boy' were the main hit singles, but the inclusion of 'Not Fade Away', 'It's Too Late' and 'Send Me Some Lovin'' make this collection essential. The cover is a priceless timepiece from the days before real graphic designers were used, where a wonderful false sky has been dropped in behind four men who look like senior citizens, posing uncomfortably with guitars.

» Tracks: *Oh Boy; Not Fade Away; You've Got Love; Maybe Baby; It's Too Late; Tell Me How; That'll Be The Day; I'm Looking For Someone To Love; An Empty Cup (And A Broken Date); Send Me Some Lovin'; Last Night; Rock Me My Baby.*

★ First released 1958
★ UK peak chart position: did not chart
★ USA peak chart position: did not chart
★ Previous Top 1000 position: 1998 (502): 1994 (762)

520 SONGS FROM THE WOOD ↑
Jethro Tull

Ian Anderson's folk leanings had always crept into Jethro Tull's work. The progressive instrumental sections of albums such as *Benefit* and *Aqualung* were more medieval folk than heavy rock. On this excellent album, flute and acoustic guitar had never sounded more fitting, and there was just enough grit in Anderson's voice ('Jack-In-The-Green') to remind listeners that he was a rock 'n' roller after all. They sound like they looked on the cover of *This Was*, which was the album on which they looked like they sound on this. Sort of progressive Wurzels. An undeniably earthy record from a fertile soul.

» Tracks: *Songs From The Wood; Jack-In-The-Green; Cup Of Wonder; Hunting Girl; Ring Out, Solstice Bells; Velvet Green; The Whistler; Pibroch (Cap In Hand); Fire At Midnight.*

★ First released 1977
★ UK peak chart position: 13
★ USA peak chart position: 8
★ Previous Top 1000 position: 1998 (943): 1994 (–)

521 IN THE DARK ↑
Grateful Dead

The great comeback album, or at least an album that no deadhead expected at this stage in their career. Jerry Garcia had been seriously ill for some time, and was not expected to recover. Suddenly, a new studio album was announced, as a seemingly fit Garcia started to tour and was reportedly appalled when they had a huge hit single with the autobiographical 'Touch Of Grey'. Other strong tracks are Bob Weir's 'Hell In A Bucket' and the magnificent 'Black Muddy River' written by Garcia and Robert Hunter. With such a strong bunch of songs it is amazing that the underwhelming 'Tons Of Steel', by the late Brent Mydland, was even considered.

» Tracks: *Touch Of Grey; Hell In A Bucket; When Push Comes To Shove; West L.A. Fadeaway; Tons Of Steel; Throwing Stones; Black Muddy River.*

★ First released 1987
★ UK peak chart position: 57
★ USA peak chart position: 6
★ Previous Top 1000 position: 1998 (840): 1994 (–)

522 REGGAE GREATS ↑
Toots and The Maytals

Second only to the Wailers, the Maytals were rumoured to have been the band that Chris Blackwell wanted to sign in preference to the Wailers. True or false, they are a magnificent band and this album confirms their standing as a pivotal influence on 'reggay', as they spelt it. '54-46 That's My Number' is still the best rocksteady track ever released and is a natural choice for any reggae compilation. Equally effective are the soulful 'Just Like That' and probably the best treatment of John Denver's 'Take Me Home Country Roads'. Toots has one of the best voices to come out of Jamaica, bar none.

» Tracks: *54-46 (That's My Number); Reggae Got Soul; Monkey Man; Just Like That; Kunky Kingston; Sweet & Dandy; Take Me Home Country Roads; Time Tough; Spiritual Healing; Pressure Drop; Peace Perfect Peace; Bam Bam.*

★ First released 1988
★ UK peak chart position: did not chart
★ USA peak chart position: did not chart
★ Previous Top 1000 position: 1998 (859): 1994 (–)

523 THE SINGLES 1969-1973 ↓
Carpenters

A most difficult album to admit to liking. Abba sounded positively hardcore punk compared to Karen and Richard Carpenter, and yet just look at the sales and the position it gained. This album's popularity is represented by public opinion as well as reviewers and music biz types. The Carpenters' success was extraordinary and without explanation. The reissued/re-compiled CD also had incredible success when released. This will continue selling for as long as the record company keeps it in print. The lead guitar solo on 'Goodbye To Love' is still amazing though.

» Tracks: *We've Only Just Begun; Top Of The World; Ticket To Ride; Superstar; Rainy Days and Mondays; Goodbye To Love; Yesterday Once More; It's Going To Take Some Time; Sing; For All We Know; Hurting Each Other; (They Long To Be) Close To You.*

★ First released 1974
★ UK peak chart position: 1
★ USA peak chart position: 1
★ Previous Top 1000 position: 1998 (488): 1994 (305)

524 THE RIVER ↓
Bruce Springsteen

Only Bruce Springsteen could have got away with releasing a double album with 19 tracks of what was basically the same song. Such was his standing that he did, and it worked like a dream. Almost all the tracks hit you in the stomach, with burning saxophone from Clarence Clemons and piercing wurlitzer organ. Springsteen, meanwhile, sings of cars and girls and girls and cars, but at no stage does he forget that this is rock 'n' roll. With this release Springsteen completed a rite of passage. Described as 'the new Dylan' early in his career, the singer proved this tag a fallacy, drawing on Dansette pop – Phil Spector, Gary US Bonds, Mitch Ryder – rather than the folk tradition. The singer articulated the dilemmas of America's blue-collar workforce, encapsulating a generation trapped in a post-60s malaise. He does so with sumptuous melodies which draw in rather than confront the listener, and show Springsteen not just as a magnetic showman but as a pensive, literate songwriter.

» Tracks: *The Ties That Bind; Sherry Darling; Jackson Cage; Two Hearts; Independence Day; Hungry Heart; Out In The Street; Crush On You; You Can Look (But You Better Not Touch); I Wanna Marry You; The River; Point Blank; Cadillac Ranch; I'm A Rocker; Fade Away; Stolen Car; Ramrod; The Price You Pay; Drive All Night; Wreck On The Highway.*

★ First released 1980
★ UK peak chart position: 2 ★ USA peak chart position: 1
★ Previous Top 1000 position: 1998 (275): 1994 (139)

525 HERE'S LITTLE RICHARD ↓
Little Richard

The enigmatic Little Richard turned rock 'n' roll inside-out with a succession of highly expressive recordings during the mid-50s. Fuelled by an unfettered New Orleans backbeat, he combined gospel fervour and orgasmic delight in equal doses, singing without recourse to convention, hammering the piano keys with barely checked passion. *Here's Little Richard* abounds with essential performances that define an era and few collections offer such unremitting excitement. The pace barely relents, while almost every track has become an integral part of pop history, either in their own right, or through the countless cover versions they have inspired. It is an exceptional album from an exceptional legend.

» Tracks: *Tutti Frutti; True, Fine Mama; Ready Teddy; Baby; Slippin' and Slidin'; Long Tall Sally; Miss Ann; Oh Why?; Rip It Up; Jenny Jenny; She's Got It; Can't Believe You Wanna Leave.*

★ First released 1957
★ UK peak chart position: did not chart
★ USA peak chart position: 13
★ Previous Top 1000 position: 1998 (493): 1994 (134)

526 ROUND ABOUT MIDNIGHT ↑
Miles Davis

An important album that saw Miles Davis and his best ever quintet (John Coltrane, Red Garland, Philly Joe Jones and Paul Chambers) move to the mighty Columbia Records. It was while at Columbia that he grew to be the biggest name in jazz, and with their marketing, even made the pop chart. This debut is also musically very fine; with production by George Avakian, the quintet breeze through six tracks that include excellent readings of 'Tadd's Delight' and, from his Charlie Parker apprenticeship, the familiar 'Ah-Leu-Cha'. The title track is just a shade too dry, but nevertheless credible. This album started a 30-year relationship with Columbia.

» Tracks: *Round Midnight; Ah-Leu-Cha; All Of You; Bye Bye Blackbird; Tadd's Delight; Dear Old Stockholm.*

★ First released 1957
★ UK peak chart position: did not chart
★ USA peak chart position: did not chart
★ Previous Top 1000 position: 1998 (846): 1994 (–)

527 LADY IN AUTUMN ↓
Billie Holiday

Without question the greatest jazz singer there has ever been (or will ever be), Billie Holiday's unmistakable sound, her inimitable phrasing, her faultless sense of what was right, helped mould an artist unique in the history of popular music. In the early years her joyous, youthful voice was backed by soloists of the calibre of Buck Clayton, her close friend Lester Young, and her ideal arranger, pianist Teddy Wilson. Towards the end of her life her voice was a flaking, fractured caricature of itself but her commanding artistry and musical integrity lent dignity and poignancy to her recordings.

» Tracks: *Body and Soul; Strange Fruit; Trav'lin' Light; All Of Me; (There Is) No Greater Love; I Cover The Waterfront; These Foolish Things (Remind Me Of You); Tenderly; Autumn In New York; My Man; Stormy Weather; Yesterdays; (I Got A Man, Crazy For Me) He's Funny That Way; What A Little Moonlight Can Do; I Cried For You (Now It's Your Turn To Cry Over Me); Too Marvelous For Words; I Wished On The Moon; I Don't Want To Cry Anymore; Prelude To A Kiss; Nice Work If You Can Get It; Come Rain Or Come Shine; What's New?; God Bless The Child; Do Nothin' Till You Hear From Me; April In Paris; Lady Sings The Blues; Don't Explain; Fine and Mellow; I Didn't Know What Time It Was; Stars Fell On Alabama; One For My Baby (And One More For The Road); Gee Baby, Ain't I Good To You; Lover Man (Oh, Where Can You Be?); All The Way; Don't Worry 'bout Me.*

★ First released 1973
★ UK peak chart position: did not chart
★ USA peak chart position: did not chart
★ Previous Top 1000 position: 1998 (374): 1994 (86)

528 ONE OF THESE NIGHTS ↑
The Eagles

This marked the transition from a nifty country rock band to a rock combo with the potential for world domination. The music was a tad sweeter and less ironic, a morsel rockier with Top 40 friendliness. Tracks such as 'Take It To The Limit' and 'Lyin' Eyes' have been played far too much on the radio. They need to be rested in place of Bernie Leadon's unusual instrumental, 'Journey Of The Sorcerer' (used as the theme to BBC Television's *Hitchhiker's Guide To The Galaxy*), or the other great Leadon song, 'I Wish You Peace'. Financially, the Eagles never looked back after this, but the critical snipers were out in force.

» Tracks: *One Of These Nights; Too Many Hands; Hollywood Waltz; Journey Of The Sorcerer; Lyin' Eyes; Take It To The Limit; Visions; After The Thrill Is Gone; I Wish You Peace.*

★ First released 1975
★ UK peak chart position: 8
★ USA peak chart position: 1
★ Previous Top 1000 position: 1998 (867): 1994 (–)

529 BAND OF GYPSIES ↑
Jimi Hendrix

No sooner had the Experience imploded than Jimi Hendrix was playing in another trio, this time with bassist Billy Cox and the very large ex-Electric Flag drummer Buddy Miles. This is the result of a live performance on New Year's Eve 1969, and although live albums are hard to recommend, this is an exception to the rule. Although the band seem under-rehearsed and a little stodgy (especially Cox), the quality of Hendrix's playing is exceptional. Maybe the fact that he could rely on Miles for most of the vocals enabled him to concentrate purely on guitar. He is fluid and clear and the remastered CD issued in 1997 is excellent.

》 Tracks: *Who Knows; Machine Gun; Changes; Power To Love; Message To Love; We Gotta Live Together.*

★ First released 1970
★ UK peak chart position: 6
★ USA peak chart position: 5
★ Previous Top 1000 position: 1998 (556): 1994 (–)

530 ONE STEP BEYOND ↑
Madness

Madness were at the forefront of the UK ska scene at the end of the 70s, which was very much a regional revival. Madness were very London and they soon shed the two-tone image and became one of the most consistent UK chart groups of the following decade. This debut shows both sides, from the excellent blue beat signature tune 'Chipmunks Are Go!' and a first class cover of Prince Buster's 'One Step Beyond' to their own masterful pop, and in particular the highly polished 'My Girl'. What Lindisfarne are to Newcastle, and Fairport Convention are to Cropredy, Madness are to Finsbury Park.

》 Tracks: *One Step Beyond; My Girl; Night Boat To Cairo; Believe Me; Land Of Hope and Glory; The Prince; Tarzan's Nuts; In The Middle Of The Night; Bed & Breakfast; Razor Blade Alley; Swan Lake; Rockin' In A Flat; Mummy's Boy; Chipmunks Are Go!*

★ First released 1979
★ UK peak chart position: 2
★ USA peak chart position: 128
★ Previous Top 1000 position: 1998 (874): 1994 (–)

531 MONEY JUNGLE ↑
Duke Ellington

Although this excellent album is listed as a Duke Ellington recording, equal billing should be given to the participation of Charles Mingus and Max Roach. The remastered CD is outstanding, having been cleaned up from the original master tape. The CD also has the addition of six extra tracks, including four unheard Ellington originals: 'Very Special', 'Rem Blues', 'Switch Blade' and 'Backward Country Boy Blues'. He is as at home in the setting of a trio as he is with a wailing big-band, and as usual, he allows the other musicians to play. The trio version of 'Caravan' is exceptional, raucous and swinging.

》 Tracks: *Very Special; A Little Max (Parfait); A Little Max (Parfait) Alternate Take; Fleurette Africaine (African Flower); Rem Blues; Wig Wise; Switch Blade; Caravan; Money Jungle; Solitude (Alternate Take); Solitude; Warm Valley; Backward Country Boy Blues.*

★ First released 1963
★ UK peak chart position: did not chart
★ USA peak chart position: did not chart
★ Previous Top 1000 position: 1998 (616): 1994 (–)

532 JANET ↑
Janet Jackson

Although Janet Jackson's sleeve note dedication to her fans, 'who made me what I am', might seem a little over the top, those fans responded by buying millions of copies. Although there are 27 listed tracks, many merely constitute a few-second segue. Nevertheless, the album showed increasing confidence aligned with a desire to explore a wider variety of styles, not always successfully – perfect production, good voice, but somehow lacking in heart and soul. Can 10 million fans be wrong? Perhaps the promise of an album is greater than the content. Oh, and Janet, the top button and zip on your Levi's have inadvertently come undone.

》 Tracks: *Morning; That's The Way Love Goes; You Know; You Want This; Be A Good Boy; If; Back; This Time; Go On Miss Janet; Throb; What'll I Do; The Lounge; Funky Big Band; Racism; New Agenda; Love pt 2; Because Of Love; Wind; Again; Another Lover; Where Are You Now; Hold On Baby; The Body That Loves You; Rain; Any Time Any Place; Are You Still Up; Sweet Dreams.*

★ First released 1993
★ UK peak chart position: 1 ★ USA peak chart position: 1
★ Previous Top 1000 position: 1998 (780): 1994 (–)

533 BURN ↑
Deep Purple

The first Deep Purple album to feature Glenn Hughes and David Coverdale, and as such it is a much more bluesy effort all round. Coverdale's throaty roar, combined with Hughes' soaring vocal, made for a heartfelt, rootsy record. 'Might Just Take Your Life' was a hit single, and the album featured a series of extended jams, which worked most spectacularly with the elongated 'Mistreated', later resurrected by Coverdale as a live favourite with Whitesnake. The title track and 'Lay Down, Stay Down' gave vent to their more familiar refrains and emphasized the strength of their songwriting.

» Tracks: *Burn; Might Just Take Your Life; Lay Down, Stay Down; Sail Away; You Fool No-one; What's Goin' On Here?; Mistreated; 'A' Zoo.*

★ First released 1974
★ UK peak chart position: 3
★ USA peak chart position: 9
★ Previous Top 1000 position: 1998 (875): 1994 (342)

534 FULL MOON FEVER ↑
Tom Petty

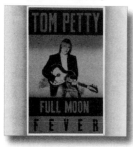

This album is just damn good fun – a great collection of easy-going rock songs, not crafted to change the world, but certainly to make it just a little brighter. Tom Petty's first solo project (without the Heartbreakers), *Full Moon Fever* shares the goodtime feel of the Traveling Wilburys' contemporary 'Handle With Care'. This is not altogether surprising; Jeff Lynne co-produced and George Harrison and Roy Orbison guest. The only non-Petty composition is a version of Gene Clark's 'Feel A Whole Lot Better', while 'Zombie Zoo', a bewildered parent's diatribe on the kids of today, comes perilously close to social commentary.

» Tracks: *Free Fallin'; I Won't Back Down; Love Is A Long Road; A Face In The Crowd; Runnin' Down A Dream; Feel A Whole Lot Better; Yer So Bad; Depending On You; The Apartment Song; Alright For Now; A Mind With A Heart Of It's Own; Zombie Zoo.*

★ First released 1989
★ UK peak chart position: 8
★ USA peak chart position: 3
★ Previous Top 1000 position: 1998 (858): 1994 (338)

535 PINK FLAG ↑
Wire

Wire's furious interpretation of punk was encapsulated on this primitive, minimalist debut. Abrasive and disjointed, these 21 tracks exude a fury impossible to ignore and one enhanced by their very brevity. Tracks halt, sometimes abruptly, when the point has been made, creating an ever-changing mélange of sound and texture. While generally aggressive, *Pink Flag* also boasts two wonderful pop songs ('Ex-Lion Tamer' and 'Mannequin'), suggesting that Wire would not be constrained by stylistic expectations. The album's mixture of polemics and pointedness would influence several US groups, including R.E.M., who later covered 'Strange'. Its perceptive urgency grows with time.

» Tracks: *Reuters; Field Day For The Sundays; Three Girl Rhumba; Ex Lion Tamer; Lowdown; Start To Move; Brazil; It's So Obvious; Surgeon's Girl; Pink Flag; The Commercial; Straight Line; 106 Beats That; Mr. Suit; Strange; Fragile; Mannequin; Different To Me; Champs; Feeling Called Love; 12 X U.*

★ First released 1977
★ UK peak chart position: did not chart
★ USA peak chart position: did not chart
★ Previous Top 1000 position: 1998 (735): 1994 (496)

536 BLACK AND BLUE ↑
The Rolling Stones

One in a series of their 70s 'groove' albums, and one of the best, even though they had obviously been listening to far too many James Brown albums judging by the opening track, 'Hot Stuff'. More traditionally Stones-sounding is 'Hand Of Fate', full of Keef's chiming barred chords. 'Cherry Oh Baby' could have been skipped in favour of more riff. 'Memory Road' comes close to AOR but 'Fool To Cry' is a gem, demonstrating how far from Dartford their music and Mick Jagger's accent have travelled. Even when they are coasting, and they seem to be doing so on this, they still knocked out most of the opposition. And they still do.

» Tracks: *Hot Stuff; Hand Of Fate; Cherry Oh Baby; Memory Motel; Hey Negrita; Melody; Fool To Cry; Crazy Mama.*

★ First released 1976
★ UK peak chart position: 2
★ USA peak chart position: 1
★ Previous Top 1000 position: 1998 (656): 1994 (–)

537 DAMN THE TORPEDOES ↓
Tom Petty and The Heartbreakers

It is encouraging to note that in compiling the superlative recent *Greatest Hits*, four tracks from this blinder of an album are included, more than from any other. This is the ideal starting point for Tom Petty students, and then you can acquire all his other albums. For those unfamiliar, he is a rock 'n' roll Roger McGuinn, complete Rickenbacker and voice. Those who are already aware of him will know that he has the knack of writing some of the best middle eight hooks ever heard, and that he has an addictive voice and a knock-out supporting band. Hard to pick this out from any of his albums.

➤➤ Tracks: *Refugee; Here Comes The Girl; Even The Losers; Century City; Don't Do Me Like That; What Are You Doin' In My Life?; Louisiana Rain.*

★ First released 1979
★ UK peak chart position: 57
★ USA peak chart position: 2
★ Previous Top 1000 position: 1998 (528): 1994 (172)

538 ROCKS ↑
Aerosmith

One of the reasons why Aerosmith, after a number of creatively lean years, are still given legendary credence and an eager ear with each new release, *Rocks* encapsulated the very essence of rock 'n' roll. They may have been the target of detractors who still pinned them as nothing more than a poor man's Rolling Stones, but *Rocks* pioneered a strength and swagger and real depth that remains very nearly unsurpassed. From the slowly escalating 'Back In The Saddle' to the dying strains of 'Home Tonight', this album held the full spirit and soul of Aerosmith in both hands.

➤➤ Tracks: *Back In The Saddle; Last Child; Rats In The Cellar; Combination; Sick As A Dog; Nobody's Fault; Get The Lead Out; Lick and A Promise; Home Tonight.*

★ First released 1976
★ UK peak chart position: did not chart
★ USA peak chart position: 3
★ Previous Top 1000 position: 1998 (662): 1994 (370)

539 TEASER AND THE FIRECAT ↑
Cat Stevens

Following in the tradition of his previous effort, with a similar cover design and feel, Cat Stevens continued his painful journey through life. Even then, there was a sadness linked to his happy songs such as 'Moonshadow', 'How Can I Tell You' and 'Tuesday's Dead'. Our favourite school hymn was also given the treatment – how did he manage to make such a happy verse sound so sad? The answer, as we have all seen, was in himself; he was a rare songwriter but he was mostly a very troubled soul, something he seems to have resolved through his conversion to the Muslim faith. He won, we lost him. At least he now acknowledges this past.

➤➤ Tracks: *The Wind; Rubylove; If I Laugh; Changes IV; How Can I Tell You; Tuesday's Dead; Morning Has Broken; Bitterblue; Moonshadow; Peace Train.*

★ First released 1971
★ UK peak chart position: 3
★ USA peak chart position: 2
★ Previous Top 1000 position: 1998 (697): 1994 (595)

540 KING OF AMERICA ↓
Elvis Costello

Costello's first album without the Attractions in tow also proved to be one of his best since 1980's *Get Happy*. A varied selection of musicians appear on the album, including legendary session veterans James Burton and Jerry Scheff, lending Costello's songs a distinctly American roots-rock feel. The songs, in turn, were some of the strongest he had ever written, from the finely observed character studies of 'American Without Tears' and 'Sleep Of The Just', to the scathing rants of 'Glitter Gulch' and 'Little Palaces'. On 'Our Little Angel', Costello sings about 'a chainsaw running through a dictionary', an apt description of the endlessly inventive lyricism that characterizes *King Of America*.

➤➤ Tracks: *Brilliant Mistake; Lovable; Our Little Angel; Don't Let Me Be Understood; Glitter Gulch; Indoor Fireworks; Little Palaces; I'll Wear It Proudly; American Without Tears; Eisenhower Blues; Poisoned Rose; The Big Light; Jack Of All Parades; Suit Of Lights; Sleep Of The Just.*

★ First released 1986
★ UK peak chart position: 11
★ USA peak chart position: 39
★ Previous Top 1000 position: 1998 (401): 1994 (–)

541 DARKNESS ON THE EDGE OF TOWN ↓ Bruce Springsteen

This album seems to get passed over in favour of *Born To Run* and *Tunnel of Love*. This was after all, after the famous but pretentious Jon Landau statement ('I saw rock 'n' roll future, and its name is Bruce Springsteen') came to pass, and although there are still many references to cars and girls it is a blistering album. It has a similar energy that was later to be found on *The River*. He states in 'Something In The Night', 'soon as you've got something they send someone to try and take it away'. He repeated the themes again and again, and we loved it; maybe his fall from grace is because we ultimately only need one song about cars and girls.

▶ Tracks: *Badlands; Adam Raised A Cain; Something In The Night; Candy's Room; Racing In The Street; The Promised Land; Factory; Streets Of Fire; Prove It All Night; Darkness On The Edge Of Town.*

★ First released 1978
★ UK peak chart position: 16
★ USA peak chart position: 5
★ Previous Top 1000 position: 1998 (181): 1994 (235)

542 BADUIZM ↑ Erykah Badu

In describing Erykah Badu's voice as sensational, there is no exaggeration. It is effortless, smooth and expressive, and she is stunning live. This album was one of 1997's surprises and nearly topped the US album chart. Described as African R&B, she veers from light hip-hop ('On & On') to sweet soul ('Otherside Of The Game'). She has such an expressive style that she could attempt blues, jazz, soul, rap, even pop and still wipe the floor. The only negative side is the corny spoken dialogue, which just sticks in the back of the throat. That aside, a sensational debut that needs a follow-up.

▶ Tracks: *Rimshot (Intro); On & On; Appletree; Otherside Of The Game; Sometimes (Mix #9); Next Lifetime; Afro (Freestyle Skit); Certainly; 4 Leaf Clover; No Love; Drama; Sometimes; Certainly (Flipped It); Rimshot (Outro).*

★ First released 1997
★ UK peak chart position: 18
★ USA peak chart position: 2
★ Previous Top 1000 position: 1998 (835): 1994 (–)

543 COLLECTIVE SOUL ↑ Collective Soul

The second and, so far, easily the best album from this Georgia, USA-based act pays homage to the stop/start heavy riffing style that was so common in Led Zeppelin's later work. Like the latter they never descend into heavy metal cliché, and the delicious snippets of pop harmony that creep into some of their material (the 'I just believe in you' hook in 'Untitled', for instance) shows a band willing to experiment. On 'The World I Know' they refreshingly introduce strings and acoustic guitar. Collective Soul know that if they turned up the volume they could wipe the floor with the heaviest metal bands around; it is highly encouraging that they don't feel the need to.

▶ Tracks: *Simple; Untitled; The World I Know; Smashing Young Man; December; Where The River Flows; Gel; She Gathers Rain; When The Water Falls; Collection Of Goods; Bleed; Reunion.*

★ First released 1995
★ UK peak chart position: did not chart
★ USA peak chart position: 23
★ Previous Top 1000 position: 1998 (–): 1994 (–)

544 UNLEASHED IN THE EAST ↑ Judas Priest

The first real transatlantic breakthrough for Judas Priest came with this most unforgiving of live albums. Playing on their early success in the Far East, Judas Priest recorded a handful of shows in Tokyo on the back of their *Hell Bent For Leather* album. Their magnanimous success there made for a brutal and excited showing of live favourites that translated as a riotous success with the Japanese. Their inspired cover versions of Joan Baez's 'Diamonds and Rust' and Fleetwood Mac's 'Green Manalishi', as well as such gruelling standards as 'Exciter' and 'Ripper', made for a convincing sweatpit of a show. One to raise your hands to.

▶ Tracks: *Exciter; Running Wild; Sinner; Ripper; Green Manalishi (With The Two-Pronged Crown); Diamonds and Rust; Victim Of Changes; Genocide; Tyrant.*

★ First released 1979
★ UK peak chart position: 10
★ USA peak chart position: 70
★ Previous Top 1000 position: 1998 (583): 1994 (194)

545 NICE 'N' EASY ↓
Frank Sinatra

The perfect Sinatra album, which bridged both swing and gentle ballads, and yet another immaculate collaboration with Nelson Riddle and producer David Cavanaugh at Capitol Records. It is remarkable that ol' Blue Eyes continued to find exquisite songs to fill an album and not have to resort to any fillers that might have occurred when deadlines loomed. The title track sets the mood and he tackles 'Fools Rush In', 'Try A Little Tenderness' and Johnny Mercer's 'Dream'. Many of these songs were previously recorded when Sinatra was contracted with Columbia as he prepared to depart to form his own record company Reprise.

▶ Tracks: *Nice 'n' Easy; That Old Feeling; How Deep Is The Ocean; I've Got A Crush On You; You Go To My Head; Fools Rush In; Nevertheless (I'm In Love With You); She's Funny That Way; Try A Little Tenderness; Embraceable You; Mam'selle; Dream.*

★ First released 1960
★ UK peak chart position: 4
★ USA peak chart position: 1
★ Previous Top 1000 position: 1998 (350): 1994 (191)

546 REPUBLIC ↑
New Order

Their cult years behind them, 1993 saw New Order put their best commercial foot forward with this, their major label debut. By this time they were an act geared to mainstream appetites, and the lighter tone and preponderance of upbeat synthesizer hooks on *Republic* suggested a group who had identified their strengths and weaknesses in the four-year interval since their last album. The vibrant tunesmithery that has always been the group's trademark was augmented by a typically polished Stephen Hague production. 'Regret' duly became their first major US radio hit. Other effective tracks include set-closer 'Avalanche', and 'World', the record's most feisty interlude.

▶ Tracks: *Regret; World; Ruined In A Day; Spooky; Everyone Everywhere; Young Offender; Liar; Chemical; Times Change; Special; Avalanche.*

★ First released 1993
★ UK peak chart position: 1
★ USA peak chart position: 11
★ Previous Top 1000 position: 1998 (624): 1994 (–)

547 STRANDED ↓
Roxy Music

Roxy Music subverted a jaded progressive rock scene with an original blend of science fiction imagery, art-school nonce and eccentric music. Vocalist Bryan Ferry sang in a camp-styled croon, part Noël Coward, part Lou Reed, and having dismissed leadership rival Brian Eno, assumed full control of artistic direction for the group's third album. *Stranded* introduced violinist Eddie Jobson, whose contributions slotted in perfectly alongside reed player Andy Mackay and guitarist Phil Manzanera. A sense of cohesion permeates the set. Group members contribute lyrically, but there was no denying that Roxy Music here represent Ferry's vision. Melodically strong, the album provides an ideal structure for his quirky intonation, resulting in a heady mix of experimentation and commercial acumen.

▶ Tracks: *Street Life; Just Like You; Amazon; Psalm; Serenade; Song For Europe; Mother Of Pearl; Sunset.*

★ First released 1973
★ UK peak chart position: 1
★ USA peak chart position: 186
★ Previous Top 1000 position: 1998 (399): 1994 (308)

548 ELLINGTON INDIGOS ↑
Duke Ellington

An extraordinary man, with an equally extraordinary small group. Among the other masterful musicians are Harry Carney, Jimmy Hamilton, Johnny Hodges, Paul Gonsalves, Shorty Baker, Clark Terry and Ray Nance. This was probably his finest band since the Jimmy Blanton-Ben Webster days. They play with relaxed beauty on numbers that many of them knew how to play in their sleep. The Gonsalves solo on 'Where Or When' is beautiful, and the balance the band strike on 'Mood Indigo' is exemplary. The reissued CD comes with two additional tracks, both superb; Cole Porter's 'Night and Day' and Oscar Hammerstein and Jerome Kern's 'All The Things You Are'.

▶ Tracks: *Solitude; Where Or When; Mood Indigo; Night and Day; Prelude To A Kiss; All The Things You Are; Willow Weep For Me; Tenderly; Dancing In The Dark; Autumn Leaves; The Sky Fell Down.*

★ First released 1958
★ UK peak chart position: did not chart
★ USA peak chart position: did not chart
★ Previous Top 1000 position: 1998 (638): 1994 (–)

549 KATE & ANNA McGARRIGLE
↓   Kate & Anna McGarrigle

These Canadian sisters unsuspectingly recorded this album, which is a huge critics' favourite yet deserves much wider acceptance. Spotted and recorded by the canny Joe Boyd it is an album brimming with melancholy. Kate McGarrigle was formerly the wife of Loudon Wainwright, and the excellent 'Swimming Song' was written by him. Elsewhere, the evocative and anthemic '(Talk To Me Of) Mendocino' is a total joy and completely captures a feeling of being resigned to homesickness. Those who have not yet discovered this album will not be disappointed with this strong recommendation. Another quiet critic's classic of great depth.

» Tracks: *Kiss and Say Goodbye; My Town; Blues In D; Heart Like A Wheel; Foolish You; (Talk To Me Of) Mendocino; Complainte Pour Ste-Catherine; Tell My Sister; Swimming Song; Jigsaw Puzzle Of Life; Go Leave; Travellin' On For Jesus.*

★ First released 1975
★ UK peak chart position: did not chart
★ USA peak chart position: did not chart
★ Previous Top 1000 position: 1998 (265): 1994 (149)

550 MODERN SOUNDS IN COUNTRY AND WESTERN MUSIC ↑
Ray Charles

Ray Charles had dabbled with country music at Atlantic Records, notably 'I'm Movin' On', but the move to ABC-Paramount prompted him to record a full album. His version of Don Gibson's 'I Can't Stop Loving You' was a transatlantic number 1 and not far behind his bittersweet performance of Eddy Arnold's 'You Don't Know Me'. Charles's own favourite was 'I Love You So Much It Hurts'. The album was so successful that he recorded a second volume and had hits with 'Take These Chains From My Heart' and 'Cryin' Time'. Although the album showed that black soul and white country could be merged, Ray Charles later lost his momentum, tending to cruise along on the same theme.

» Tracks: *Bye Bye Love; You Don't Know Me; Half As Much; I Love You So Much It Hurts; Just A Little Lovin'; Born To Lose; Worried Mind; It Makes No Difference Now; You Win Again; Careless Love; I Can't Stop Loving You; Hey Good Lookin'.*

★ First released 1962
★ UK peak chart position: 6
★ USA peak chart position: 1
★ Previous Top 1000 position: 1998 (955): 1994 (875)

551 WILD WOOD ↑
Paul Weller

Even though Paul Weller had already given us dozens of great songs with both the Jam and the much-derided Style Council his endless supply showed no signs of drying up on this formidable album. *Wild Wood* followed his rather shaky debut and restored Weller to favour in the monthly music magazines. It opens with 'Sunflower', featuring blistering guitar work and a soulful vocal chorus ('and I miss you so') that sounds reassuringly familiar. In fact much of this album has a late 60s prog pop feel which is particularly reminiscent of mid-period Traffic. The title track, a gentle acoustic ballad with an ominous lyric, remains one of Weller's finest compositions.

» Tracks: *Sunflower; Can You Heal Us (Holy Man); Wild Wood; Instrumental One (Part 1); All The Pictures On The Wall; Has My Fire Really Gone Out?; Country; Instrumental Two; 5th Season; The Weaver; Instrumental One (Part 2); Foot Of The Mountain; Shadow Of The Sun; Holy Man (Reprise); Moon On Your Pyjamas; Hung Up.*

★ First released 1993
★ UK peak chart position: 2
★ USA peak chart position: did not chart
★ Previous Top 1000 position: 1998 (–): 1994 (–)

552 DAMNED DAMNED DAMNED
↑   The Damned

The first British punk band to release a single ('New Rose'), the Damned followed this achievement with the genre's debut album. *Damned Damned Damned* captured its furious rattle of basic chords and angry sentiments, delivered at amphetamine-like speed. Producer Nick Lowe ensured the quartet's primal scream was not modified by prevailing attitudes of musical correctness and the set's success is as much due to his detached overview as to the group's fevered nihilism. Their energy is exciting, the sense of freedom and mischief unrelenting. *Damned Damned Damned* defined punk both aurally and philosophically.

» Tracks: *Neat Neat Neat; Fan Club; I Fall; Born To Kill; Stab Your Back; Feel The Pain; New Rose; Fish; See Her Tonite; 1 Of The 2; So Messed Up; I Feel Alright.*

★ First released 1977
★ UK peak chart position: 36
★ USA peak chart position: did not chart
★ Previous Top 1000 position: 1998 (747): 1994 (289)

553 HAPPY TRAILS ↓
Quicksilver Messenger Service

If the quintessential San Francisco Sound is defined by lengthy improvised guitarwork and near-telepathic interplay, then *Happy Trails* crystallizes the genre on record. Taking cues from two Bo Diddley songs, the quartet introduce new realms of expression to rock music. Guitarists John Cipollina and Gary Duncan offer contrasting textures and sound, goading each other to greater heights. Largely recorded live in concert, *Happy Trails* encapsulates an era of experimentation, employing images that embodied the outlaw chic of the hippie subculture. Its strengths are not, however, bound to that era; the album's mesmerizing power remains as true as ever. The famous George Hunter cover painting is also indispensable.

» Tracks: *Who Do You Love (Part One); When You Love; Where You Love; How Do You Love; Which Do You Love; Who Do You Love (Part Two); Mona; Maiden Of The Cancer Moon; Calvary; Happy Trails.*

★ First released 1968
★ UK peak chart position: did not chart
★ USA peak chart position: 27
★ Previous Top 1000 position: 1998 (365): 1994 (765)

554 FACE TO FACE ↓
The Kinks

Sadly, the long and magnificent career of one of the finest songwriters of our age, Ray Davies, is not truly represented on any one album, other than greatest hits packages. Many Kinks albums have appeared but the absolute five star gem was never made. So many albums, so prolific with the butter spread thinly. This record summed up swinging London in the 60s and like its great successor, *Something Else*, contained Ray's observations of ordinary people and situations. The album is strengthened by the classic 'Sunny Afternoon' but perceptive tracks such as 'Fancy', 'Dandy', 'Session Man' and 'Most Exclusive Residence For Sale' are gentle satires that give the record its heart.

» Tracks: *Party Line; Rosy Won't You Please Come Home; Dandy; Too Much On My Mind; Session Man; Rainy Day In June; House In The Country; Holiday In Waikiki; Most Exclusive Residence For Sale; Fancy; Little Miss Queen Of Darkness; You're Looking Fine; Sunny Afternoon; I'll Remember.*

★ First released 1967
★ UK peak chart position: 12
★ USA peak chart position: 135
★ Previous Top 1000 position: 1998 (249): 1994 (356)

555 THE LAST RECORD ALBUM ↑
Little Feat

Many remember their Little Feat albums by which wonderful Neon Park illustration was on the cover. The famous giant jelly graces this one. The music within is equally delectable, with the horizontal mambo on 'Romance Dance' and 'All That You Dream', as they celebrate by singing 'I've Been Down But Not Like This Before'. The album's star is the tear-jerking, beautiful ballad 'Long Distance Love'. Very probably Lowell George's greatest song, its gentle understatement and simplicity is pure genius; 'ah her toes were so pretty, and her life so sweet'. An essential Little Feat album. The CD reissue contains two extra tracks from the live album *Waiting For Columbus*.

» Tracks: *Romance Dance; All That You Dream; Long Distance Love; Day Or Night; One Love; Down Below The Borderline; Somebody's Leavin'; Mercenary Territory.*

★ First released 1975
★ UK peak chart position: 36
★ USA peak chart position: 36
★ Previous Top 1000 position: 1998 (650): 1994 (261)

556 FROM THE MARS HOTEL ↑
Grateful Dead

Set off by the beautiful Kelly/Mouse cover with the lonely hotel and the indecipherable lettering – that is until somebody has the wacky idea of holding the album up against a mirror so you can read the lettering back to front. Some of their long-standing live favourites are on this exemplary record. The highly commercial bounce of 'Scarlet Begonias' and infectiously loose 'Loose Lucy' are both here. The beautiful 'Ship Of Fools' is only bettered by the jazzy 'Unbroken Chain'. A mellow and beautifully articulate record that still retains shades of the Crosby, Stills and Nash influence left over from *American Beauty*.

» Tracks: *U.S. Blues; China Doll; Unbroken Chain; Loose Lucy; Scarlet Begonias; Pride Of Cucamonga; Money Money; Ship Of Fools.*

★ First released 1974
★ UK peak chart position: 47
★ USA peak chart position: 16
★ Previous Top 1000 position: 1998 (756): 1994 (–)

557 BELLYBUTTON ↑
Jellyfish

History has shown that there will always be a market for McCartneyesque popsters, such as World Party and Crowded House. However, it has also shown that said market does not chartbusters make. And so it went, when San Francisco's Jellyfish landed on the beach in 1990 with *Bellybutton*, eliciting raves from pop-starved critics and enjoying an MTV hit with 'The King Is Half-Undressed', but failing to reach the grunge-caked upper reaches of the US charts. Although writers compared them with 60s artists such as the Beatles and the Beach Boys, their hearts were in the 70s, as evidenced by their overt Queen references and their choice of Albhy Galuten, who had worked with the disco-era Bee Gees, as their producer.

▶ Tracks: *The Man I Used To Be; That Is Why; The King Is Half-Undressed; I Wanna Stay Home; She Still Loves Him; All I Want Is Everything; Now She Knows She's Wrong; Bedspring Kiss; Baby's Coming Back; Calling Sarah.*

★ First released 1990
★ UK peak chart position: did not chart
★ USA peak chart position: 124
★ Previous Top 1000 position: 1998 (959): 1994 (–)

558 ARETHA NOW ↑
Aretha Franklin

This opens with the explosive 'Think', an ecstatic performance propelled by the singer's gospel-like fervour and punchy piano playing. It set the tone for yet another self-assured selection, in which Aretha Franklin brought her expressive voice to bear on a series of excellent songs. She brings new authority to material first recorded by Sam Cooke ('You Send Me'), Don Covay ('See-Saw') and Dionne Warwick ('I Say A Little Prayer'), investing each with a ferocious pride and zeal. The original songs are equally strong, resulting in one of the most accomplished soul albums of the 60s. Recorded at the height of Atlantic soul's golden age.

▶ Tracks: *Think; I Say A Little Prayer; See-Saw; Night Time Is The Right Time; You Send Me; You're A Sweet Sweet Man; I Take What I Want; Hello Sunshine; A Change; I Can't See Myself Leaving You.*

★ First released 1968
★ UK peak chart position: 6
★ USA peak chart position: 3
★ Previous Top 1000 position: 1998 (828): 1994 (374)

559 MY FAIR LADY ↑
Original Broadway Cast

By the early 90s this unforgettable album of what some still consider to be the most perfect stage musical ever, had spent a record-breaking 292 weeks in the US Top 40 – 15 of them at number 1. It also stayed in the upper reaches of the UK chart for 129 weeks. The album was recorded in mono. Alan Jay Lerner and Frederick Loewe's wonderful score, with a cast headed by Rex Harrison, Julie Andrews and Stanley Holloway, were not nearly so effective in the subsequent stereo version. Just 10 years after its initial release sales were estimated to be well over six million, and the album was inducted into the NARAS Hall of Fame in 1977.

▶ Tracks: *Overture; Why Can't The English; Wouldn't It Be Loverly?; With A Little Bit Of Luck; I'm An Ordinary Man; Just You Wait; The Rain In Spain; I Could Have Danced All Night; Ascot Gavotte; On The Street Where You Live; You Did It; Show Me; Get Me To The Church On Time; Hymn To Him; Without You; I've Grown Accustomed To Her Face.*

★ First released 1956
★ UK peak chart position: 2
★ USA peak chart position: 1
★ Previous Top 1000 position: 1998 (683): 1994 (246)

560 ORGAN GRINDER SWING ↑
Jimmy Smith

Using the monicker 'Incredible' was no flash banner, it was true. Smith defined the Hammond organ as a jazz instrument and milked and bled it to its limit. The sub-credit for guitarist Kenny Burrell and drummer Grady Tate is also well deserved. This is the ultimate groovy, smokey jazz trio record that Smith made. The title track has been used for countless radio trailers over the years, while the often covered Duke Ellington classic, 'Satin Doll', is given extra special effort. Burrell has worked with Smith more than any other musician. His mellow tone and Smith's treble notes blend like cucumber and salmon. Back in fashion due to a television car advertisement using the title track.

▶ Tracks: *The Organ Grinder's Swing; Oh, No, Babe; Blues For J; Greensleeves; I'll Close My Eyes; Satin Doll.*

★ First released 1965
★ UK peak chart position: did not chart
★ USA peak chart position: 15
★ Previous Top 1000 position: 1998 (812): 1994 (693)

561 PIECES OF THE SKY ↑
Emmylou Harris

The title of Emmylou Harris's first major-label solo album comes from a line in one of its songs, 'Before Believing': 'How would you feel if the world was falling all apart all around you?'. She knew how it felt. Two years earlier, she had been devastated by the death of her partner Gram Parsons. Nine of its ten songs are cover versions, with the lone original, 'Boulder To Birmingham', standing as a poignant tribute to Parsons (it has become her signature tune). One track, a cover of the Louvin Brothers' 'If I Could Only Win Your Love', became the first of Harris's many US country hits.

» Tracks: *Bluebird Wine; Too Far Gone; If I Could Only Win Your Love; Boulder To Birmingham; Before Believing; Bottle Let Me Down; Sleepless Nights; Coat Of Many Colours; For No One; Queen Of The Silver Dollar.*

★ First released 1975
★ UK peak chart position: did not chart
★ USA peak chart position: 45
★ Previous Top 1000 position: 1998 (801): 1994 (–)

562 HELLO, I MUST BE GOING! ↑
Phil Collins

The ubiquitous Phil took two years to follow *Face Value*, which cynics believed to be a fluke and fans willed him to repeat. This album rocketed him back to the top, together with a number 1 single, 'You Can't Hurry Love', and a superb video featuring him in triplicate with a tonic mohair suit and Blues Brother shades. The rest is in a similar vein to his debut, albeit with a happier theme running throughout. The album's finale is the touching 'Why Can't It Wait 'Til Morning', a sentence we have all used in the same way at some time in our lives. He doesn't have to write songs like this anymore.

» Tracks: *I Don't Care Anymore; I Cannot Believe It's True; Like China; Do You Know, Do You Care?; You Can't Hurry Love; It Don't Matter To Me; Thru' These Walls; Don't Let Him Steal His Heart Away; The West Side; Why Can't It Wait 'Til Morning.*

★ First released 1982
★ UK peak chart position: 2
★ USA peak chart position: 8
★ Previous Top 1000 position: 1998 (727): 1994 (252)

563 DIXIE CHICKEN ↑
Little Feat

Yet another great Neon Parks album cover, which were anticipated almost as much as the next collection from Little Feat, the band with which his work became inextricably linked. *Dixie Chicken* found them at a musical peak as a stellar 70s rock band who had oodles of swamp blues and funk, with a loose shambling style that came with confidence not sloppiness. The late Lowell George was singing better than ever on this collection, notably with the sublime 'Roll Um Easy' where his voice was chillingly expressive. Bill Payne and Richie Haywood play their respective keyboard and drums with calm and precision. There are no weak tracks here, and this is another vital album, in keeping with all recordings with which George was involved.

» Tracks: *Dixie Chicken; Two Trains; Roll Um Easy; On Your Way Down; Kiss It Off; Fool Yourself; Walkin All Night; Fat Man In The Bathtub; Juliette; Lafayette Railroad.*

★ First released 1973
★ UK peak chart position: did not chart
★ USA peak chart position: did not chart
★ Previous Top 1000 position: 1998 (844): 1994 (–)

564 SONNY ROLLINS VOL. 2 ↑
Sonny Rollins

The famous Harold Feinstein cover borrowed by Joe Jackson ('how dare he', said the jazz purists) for *Body And Soul* also announces 'Monaural' Sonny Rollins. Did we ever have a 'Stereophonic' Charlie Parker; do we care? This is a blisteringly good album that never once loses pace. The formidable line-up is Jay Jay Johnson (trombone), Horace Silver (piano), Art Blakey (drums) and Paul Chambers (bass). Wonderful versions of Thelonious Monk's 'Misterioso' and 'Reflections' are included, plus Rollins' own 'Why Don't I' and 'Wail March'. The finest 'monaural' record Rollins ever made.

» Tracks: *Why Don't I; Wail March; Misterioso; Reflections; You Stepped Out Of A Dream; Poor Butterfly.*

★ First released 1957
★ UK peak chart position: did not chart
★ USA peak chart position: did not chart
★ Previous Top 1000 position: 1998 (854): 1994 (354)

565 SHIFT WORK ↑
The Fall

Shift Work is divided into two parts, both exhuming the doom that was prevalent for the unprivileged during Thatcher's reign. Mark Smith illuminates his feelings with some of his finest sneering and slurred vocals. Part 1, 'Earth's Impossible Day' and Part 2, 'Notebooks Out Plagiarists', are both essential listening. The Fall churn out great albums, quickly and quietly – they need to be noisy so that the rest of the world can catch up with an incredible band who should stand alongside the Smiths as giants of thinking people's irreverent music. Mark E. Smith's time will surely come, even though he is leaving it rather late.

▶ Tracks: *"Earths Impossible Day"*: So What About It?; Idiot Joy Showland; Edinburgh Man; Pittsville Direkt; The Book Of Lies; High Tension Line; The War Against Intelligence; *"Notebooks Out Plagiarists"*: Shift-Work; You Haven't Found It Yet; The Mixer; White Lightning; A Lot Of Wind; Rose; Sinister Waltz.

★ First released 1991
★ UK peak chart position: 17
★ USA peak chart position: did not chart
★ Previous Top 1000 position: 1998 (702): 1994 (488)

566 BARE WIRES ↑
John Mayall

One of John Mayall's bravest and best changes of style and line-ups. He enlisted some of the cream of the British jazz movement (Henry Lowther, Dick Heckstall Smith, Chris Mercer) who, together with drummer Jon Hiseman, made a formidable, brassy album. Mayall's lyrics, although often obscured by the great musicianship, were also notable, as this was a highly reflective time in his life. The album is best enjoyed complete, as the links between songs are vital to its enjoyment, especially the 'Bare Wires Suite' containing the sad but beautiful 'I Know Now'. Guitarist Mick Taylor added the obligatory but indispensable lead breaks. Very possibly his finest album.

▶ Tracks: Bare Wires Suite; Where Did I Belong; Start Walking; Open A New Door; Fire; I Know How; Look In The Mirror; I'm A Stranger; No Reply; Hartley Quits; Killing Time; She's Too Young; Sandy.

★ First released 1968
★ UK peak chart position: 3
★ USA peak chart position: 59
★ Previous Top 1000 position: 1998 (972): 1994 (661)

567 VAN HALEN II ↑
Van Halen

Dismissed as the poor relation to their thrilling debut on its release, it has only been with the passage of time that *Van Halen II* has been afforded any kind of classic stature. David Lee Roth's impertinent, sly humour is still in place, but it is Eddie Van Halen's easy experimentation that takes this record to another level. His daring and frantic switches in styles set him aside as the most versatile of players. He still worked the effusive pop for 'Dance The Night Away', but his brush strokes, particularly within 'DOA' and 'You're No Good', were now much more adventurous and wide.

▶ Tracks: You're No Good; Dance The Night Away; Somebody Get Me A Doctor; Bottoms Up; Outta Love Again; Light Up The Sky; DOA; Women In Love; Spanish Fly; Beautiful Girls.

★ First released 1979
★ UK peak chart position: 23
★ USA peak chart position: 6
★ Previous Top 1000 position: 1998 (861): 1994 (341)

568 STEEL WHEELS ↑
The Rolling Stones

The *Steel Wheels* tour of 1989 was the biggest-grossing in the USA, and was noteworthy for this fact rather than for the quality of the material on offer. *Steel Wheels* represented the Rolling Stones' response to persistent rumours of their demise. After a well-publicized spat, both Mick Jagger and Keith Richard had released solo albums, and some reassurance was clearly needed. The opening riff of 'Sad Sad Sad' provided it; unmistakable Stones stuff, as is the rest of the album. A critical and radio success, *Steel Wheels* yielded a few minor hits in 'Mixed Emotions', 'Rock and A Hard Place' and 'Almost Hear You Sigh'.

▶ Tracks: Sad Sad Sad; Mixed Emotions; Terrifying; Hold On To Your Hat; Hearst For Sale; Blinded By Love; Rock and A Hard Place; Can't Be Seen; Almost Hear You Sigh; Continental Drift; Break The Spell; Slipping Away.

★ First Released 1989
★ UK peak chart position: 2
★ USA peak chart position: 3
★ Previous Top 1000 position: 1998 (851): 1994 (–)

569 THE SOUL ALBUM ↑
Otis Redding

The Soul Album is often overlooked when examining Otis Redding's output. No singles were culled from its content, but this does not diminish the quality of the excellent songs it contains. The original material reveals the strength of the singer's partnership with guitarist Steve Cropper, and the cover versions show Redding's gift for reinterpretation. Sam Cooke, the Temptations and Wilson Pickett are each acknowledged in turn, while Redding also takes shots at two contemporary hits, Roy Head's 'Treat Her Right' and Slim Harpo's 'Scratch My Back'. The Soul Album is as strong as any other records issued by the singer during his short lifetime, and deserves attention.

» Tracks: Just One More Day; It's Growing; Cigarettes and Coffee; Chain Gang; Nobody Knows You (When You're Down and Out); Good To Me; Scratch My Back; Treat Her Right; Everybody Makes A Mistake; Any Ole Way; 634-5789.

★ First released 1966
★ UK peak chart position: 22
★ USA peak chart position: 54
★ Previous Top 1000 position: 1998 (818): 1994 (656)

570 TRAVELS ↑
Pat Metheny Group

A double album that flirts with rock, folk, country and Latin – but is emphatically a jazz album. Pat Metheny is equipped with probably his best ever live group; Steve Rodby, Danny Gottlieb, Nana Vasconcelos, and his right arm, keyboard virtuoso Lyle Mays. The recording exudes warmth, and often improves on tracks already issued in studio albums; for example, 'Phase Dance' is played with more verve and 'Song For Bilbao' sounds more passionate in a live context. The diamond in the mine, however, is the shortest piece, and recorded at a low level – the glorious and delicate title track – worth the price of the album alone.

» Tracks: Are You Going With Me?; The Fields, The Sky; Goodbye; Phase Dance; Straight On Red; Farmer's Trust; Extradition; Goin' Ahead; As Falls Wichita, So Falls Wichita Falls; Travels; Song For Bilbao; San Lorenzo.

★ First released 1983
★ UK peak chart position: did not chart
★ USA peak chart position: 62
★ Previous Top 1000 position: 1998 (848): 1994 (328)

571 VIVID ↑
Living Colour

One of the most innovative and exciting live acts ever to emerge from New York City, Living Colour vaulted into the spotlight with this debut recording. Critically acclaimed and embraced by fans, Vivid defies categorization even 10 years after its release. It transcends genres and fuses disparate musical formats while providing a solid rhythmic foundation for Vernon Reid's impressive guitar work. 'Broken Hearts' is an inventive fusion of hip-hop with a country twang. 'Funny Vibe' juxtaposes hardcore with funk and a biting commentary. 'Cult Of Personality' and 'Which Way To America' are both relentless rockers that provide a compelling backdrop (complete with media sound bites) for Reid's often amazing guitar solos.

» Tracks: Cult Of Personality; I Want To Know; Middle Man; Desperate People; Open Letter (To A Land Lord); Funny Vibe; Memories Can't Wait; Broken Hearts; Glamour Boys; What's Your Favorite Color? (Theme Song); Which Way To America.

★ First released 1988
★ UK peak chart position: did not chart
★ USA peak chart position: 6
★ Previous Top 1000 position: 1998 (719): 1994 (–)

572 OUR MAN IN PARIS ↑
Dexter Gordon

One of the most successful of Blue Note Records' 'blue' period and an album that remains Dexter Gordon's finest work. Although his tenor sax occasionally grates, this is a brilliant example of late bebop. Supported by Bud Powell (piano), Kenny Clarke (drums) and Pierre Michelot (bass), the simple quartet sound coolly in control. 'Willow Weep For Me' is played with great beauty and 'A Night in Tunisia' is yet another well-crafted version. The bonus of 'Our Love Is Here To Stay' and 'Like Someone In Love' (from Powell's Alternate Takes) on the CD reissue emphasises the importance of this maverick album.

» Tracks: Scrapple From The Apple; Willow Weep For Me; Stairway To The Stars; A Night In Tunisia; Our Love Is Here To Stay; Like Someone In Love; Broadway.

★ First released 1963
★ UK peak chart position: did not chart
★ USA peak chart position: did not chart
★ Previous Top 1000 position: 1998 (798): 1994 (318)

573 HOT BUTTERED SOUL ↑
Isaac Hayes

A staff songwriter with the legendary Stax Records label, Isaac Hayes, with partner David Porter, composed material for many of the company's artists, including Sam and Dave, Carla Thomas and Johnnie Taylor. Frustrated with this backroom role, he began recording in his own right, and with *Hot Buttered Soul*, redefined the notion of soul music. Although the tracks were lengthy, there was no sense of self-indulgence, each one evolving over sensual rhythms and taut arrangements. Hayes' vocal anticipated the 'rap' genre of Barry White and Millie Jackson without slipping into self-parody. Hayes has a revitalized career thanks to his cartoon part as Chef on *South Park*.

》 Tracks: *Walk On By; Hyperbolicsyllabiscesquedalymistic; One Woman; By The Time I Got To Phoenix.*

★ First released 1969
★ UK peak chart position: did not chart
★ USA peak chart position: 8
★ Previous Top 1000 position: 1998 (809): 1994 (749)

574 THIS WAS ↑
Jethro Tull

A debut of incredible maturity that fitted in nicely between blues and prog. Mick Abrahams was the darling of the clubs, and for a brief moment held a candle to Eric Clapton, especially with his showpiece 'Cat's Squirrel'. Abrahams soon left to form Blodwyn Pig. Ian Anderson, Jethro Tull's undisputed leader, wore a great coat, played flute and stood like a pretty flamingo. Live they were tremendous, and on record they got even better than this. 'Song For Jeffrey' was the choice single. Other interesting tracks are the flute-led 'Serenade For a Cuckoo' (written by Roland Kirk) and 'Dharma For One', with a drum solo that for once is not boring.

》 Tracks: *My Sunday Feeling; Some Day The Sun Won't Shine For You; Beggar's Farm; Move On Alone; Serenade To A Cuckoo; Dharma For One; It's Breaking Me Up; Cat's Squirrel; A Song For Jeffrey; Round.*

★ First released 1968
★ UK peak chart position: 10
★ USA peak chart position: 62
★ Previous Top 1000 position: 1998 (878): 1994 (–)

575 THE FAMILY THAT PLAYS TOGETHER ↑ Spirit

Still overlooked, the magnificent Spirit, under their guiding light Randy California, released many albums. It is their Columbia/Ode work that contains the golden age. This and *The Twelve Dreams Of Doctor Sardonicus* are the first ones to own. Here the band sound united and in full flow as the tracks blend like an opera. John Locke's piano is particularly rewarding, but then so are the songs; the jazzy summer-day feel of 'It Shall Be', the epic build-up of 'It's All The Same', the guitar-laden finale of 'Aren't You Glad' and the winsome 'Darlin' If'. The excellent CD reissue has five bonus tracks to savour.

》 Tracks: *I Got A Line On You; It Shall Be; Poor Richard; Silky Sam; Drunkard; Darlin' If; It's All The Same; Jewish; Dream Within A Dream; She Smiles; Aren't You Glad; Fog; So Little To Say; Mellow Fellow; Now Or Anywhere; Space Chile.*

★ First released 1968
★ UK peak chart position: did not chart
★ USA peak chart position: 22
★ Previous Top 1000 position: 1998 (951): 1994 (–)

576 KILL 'EM ALL ↑
Metallica

Occasionally one album can be pinpointed as the turning point in a musical genre. *Kill 'Em All* is one such album and, boy, did the heavy metal genre need a transfusion of new blood. Herein trad metal was stripped of its late-70s pomposity and reduced to its base element of brutal sonic force. The rhythm section of Burton and Ulrich do a masterful job, as does rhythm guitar ace and vocalist James Hetfield, on a set that owes a debt to punk as much as to Iron Maiden and Judas Priest. The phantasmagorical allusions are still there in the lyrics, as some long-winded guitar solos, but otherwise *Kill 'Em All* promised a creative rebirth for hard rock.

》 Tracks: *Hit The Lights; The Four Horsemen; Motorbreath; Jump In The Fire; (Anesthesia) – Pulling Teeth; Whiplash; Phantom Lord; No Remorse; Seek & Destroy; Metal Militia.*

★ First released 1983
★ UK peak chart position: did not chart
★ USA peak chart position: 155
★ Previous Top 1000 position: 1998 (967): 1994 (–)

577 TOGETHER ALONE ↑
Crowded House

The mainstream success that the pride and joy of New Zealand enjoyed with the highly commercial *Woodface* would have driven many lesser artists to panic about following it up. Not these chaps, instead they delivered a humble laid back album, that although not as strong as its predecessor has quiet charm and subtle depth on its side. 'Pineapple Head' and 'Nails In My Feet' certainly rank as classic Crowded House, the latter a particularly poignant tale of love. Elsewhere, they sound dangerously like a rock 'n' roll band on the Split Enz-influenced 'Black & White Boy' and the 70s glam rock soundalike 'In My Command'.

» Tracks: *Kare Kare; In My Command; Nails In My Feet; Black & White Boy; Fingers Of Love; Pineapple Head; Locked Out; Private Universe; Walking On The Spot; Distant Sun; Catherine Wheel; Skin Feeling; Together Alone.*

★ First released 1993
★ UK peak chart position: 4
★ USA peak chart position: 73
★ Previous Top 1000 position: 1998 (–): 1994 (–)

578 NO NEED TO ARGUE ↑
The Cranberries

Few listeners can be indifferent about Dolores O'Riordan's voice, which will either charm or irritate depending on one's point of view. She warbles and yodels her way through this album, sounding as proud as ever to put an emphasis on words that bring her intoxicating Irish accent to the fore. This is an admirable record that saw the band knuckling down and refusing to be overawed by the phenomenal success of their debut *Everybody Else Is Doing It, So Why Can't We?* 'Zombie', an angry summation of the continuing madness in Northern Ireland, is the album's key song. O'Riordan's strident vocal and the threatening bass and fuzz guitar conjure up the smell of smoke clearing in the aftermath.

» Tracks: *Ode To My Family; I Can't Be With You; Twenty One; Zombie; Empty; Everything I Said; The Icicle Melts; Disappointment; Ridiculous Thoughts; Dreaming My Dreams; Yeat's Grave; Daffodil Lament; No Need To Argue.*

★ First released 1994
★ UK peak chart position: 2
★ USA peak chart position: 6
★ Previous Top 1000 position: 1998 (–): 1994 (–)

579 NASHVILLE SKYLINE ↑
Bob Dylan

It is hard to recall now how deeply unfashionable country music was in 1969 – Dylan's label, Columbia, dismayed at his apparent retrogression, begged him to remove the word 'Nashville' from the album's title. However, as usual, he proved ahead of the game; his embrace of country ushered in Gram Parsons, the Flying Burrito Brothers and scores of subsequent artists under the Americana banner. Prescient too was his nod to Johnny Cash, with whom he duets on the gorgeous 'Girl From The North Country'. Most tracks are pleasant and enduring; the chart hit 'Lay Lady Lay' remains the Dylan song of choice for radio programmers.

» Tracks: *Girl From The North Country; Nashville Skyline Rag; To Be Alone With You; I Threw It All Away; Peggy Day; Lay Lady Lay; One More Night; Tell Me That It Isn't True; Country Pie; Tonight I'll Be Staying Here With You.*

★ First Released 1969
★ UK peak chart position: 1
★ USA peak chart position: 3
★ Previous Top 1000 position: 1998 (886): 1994 (–)

580 OPERATION RADICATION ↑
Yellowman

Originally released on vinyl only, this vital CD reissue covers the early part of Winston Foster's career. The tall, imposing figure of a black albino is now seen as a sex-symbol; in his school-days he was often an outcast as people found it hard to come to terms with the way he looked. Sly and Robbie give all the tracks here the edge of professionalism, although the secret of being able to appreciate *Yellowman* is the depth of his humour. Subtly hidden, his humour, often very rude, is a joy to discover. Take 'Even Tide Fire' as a perfect example. Highly rewarding, and makes a change from Bob Marley's reggae domination.

» Tracks: *11 + 11; Shorties; Morning Ride; Even Tide Fire; Operation Radication; Couchie; Out A Hand; Mad Over Me; Lovers Corner; Bim & Bam; Badness; My Possie.*

★ First released 1980
★ UK peak chart position: did not chart
★ USA peak chart position: did not chart
★ Previous Top 1000 position: 1998 (782): 1994 (–)

581 YOUR ARSENAL ↑
Morrissey

Produced by the late Mick Ronson, this record has incredible tension, long before the overblown and unnecessary Morrissey/ Johnny Rogan feud started. Beat group echoes, doom-laden lyrics and a full atmosphere that conjures up memories of Johnny Kidd and The Pirates, the Ventures and the Pretenders. Solo artists often mellow out and mature, but on this superlative recording, Morrissey paradoxically rocks more than ever and shows further creative maturity. 'You're Gonna Need Someone On Your Side' and 'Glamorous Glue' are only two reasons to buy this album. How many more lyrical odes does he have left?

» Tracks: *You're Gonna Need Someone On Your Side; Glamorous Glue; We'll Let You Know; The National Front Disco; Certain People I Know; We Hate It When Our Friends Become Successful; You're The One For Me, Fatty; Seasick, Yet Still Docked; I Know It's Gonna Happen Someday.*

★ First released 1993
★ UK peak chart position: 4
★ USA peak chart position: 21
★ Previous Top 1000 position: 1998 (922): 1994 (501)

582 SAIL AWAY ↑
Randy Newman

On *Sail Away* Newman returned to the lush orchestration of his debut album, but here the strings framed a more substantial collection of songs. *Sail Away* opens with the now infamous title track, where Newman voices the pitch of a slave trader to his cargo of slaves over one of his most beautiful melodies. Elsewhere on the album, the targets of 'Political Science', 'Burn On' and 'God's Song' may have been easy pickings for a satirist of Newman's stature, but the winning character sketches of 'Simon Smith and His Dancing Bear', 'Lonely At The Top' and 'Dayton, Ohio – 1903' showcased a songwriter close to his peak.

» Tracks: *Sail Away; Lonely At The Top; He Gives Us All His Love; Last Night I Had A Dream; Simon Smith and The Amazing Dancing Bear; Old Man; Political Science; Burn On; Memo To My Son; Dayton, Ohio – 1903; You Can Leave Your Hat On; God's Song (That's Why I Love Mankind).*

★ First released 1972
★ UK peak chart position: did not chart
★ USA peak chart position: 163
★ Previous Top 1000 position: 1998 (916): 1994 (–)

583 E. 1999 ETERNAL ↑
Bone Thugs'N'Harmony

By the time Bone Thugs-N-Harmony released their 1994 debut, *Creepin On Ah Come Up*, gangsta rap was rapidly becoming an embarrassing cliché. With their much more considered follow-up, the quintet worked within the considerations to produce something fresh, resonant and invigorating. Drawing on hip-hop's old school conventions, the group weld lyrical and vocal gymnastics (at times akin to scat jazz) to samples and restrained beats. Take the opening track, where the scene is set with constant rainfall, or 'Budsmokers Only', where DJ U-Neek employs an old Earth, Wind and Fire sample to propel their advocacy of 'weed'. Or try '1st Of Tha Month', which showcases their ability to shift gears between classic R&B high harmonies and an authentic contemporary rap aesthetic.

» Tracks: *Da Introduction; East 1999 Eternal; Crept and We Came; Down 71 (The Getaway); Mr Bill Collector; Budsmokers Only; Crossroad; Me Killa; Land Of That Heartless; No Shorts, No Loses; 1st Of That Month; Buddah Lovaz; Die Die Die; Mr Ouija 2; Mo' Murda; Shotz To Tha Double Glock; Tha Crossroads (DJ U-Neek's Mo Thug Remix).*

★ First released 1995
★ UK peak chart position: did not chart
★ USA peak chart position: 1
★ Previous Top 1000 position: 1998 (915): 1994 (–)

584 THE SIDEWINDER ↓
Lee Morgan

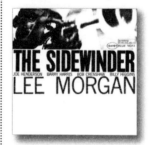

Simple and direct and somewhat of a runt album in the history of jazz. The solo on Art Blakey's recording of Bobby Timmons' 'Moanin' is by Lee Morgan, as is that on 'A Night In Tunisia'. By the time he came to record this album he had simplified his style, which appealed to the soul/jazz lovers of the 60s. To use the ultimate cliché, this is groovin' music; it rolls, it bops, it makes you feel good and its success is that it is refreshingly uncomplicated. Supported by Joe Henderson (tenor), Billy Higgins (drums), Barry Harris (piano) and Bob Cranshaw (bass). The title track is still one of the most played tracks on popular jazz radio.

» Tracks: *The Sidewinder; Totem Pole; Gary's Notebook; Boy, What A Night!; Hocus Pocus.*

★ First released 1964
★ UK peak chart position: did not chart
★ USA peak chart position: 25
★ Previous Top 1000 position: 1998 (570): 1994 (554)

585 I DO NOT WANT WHAT I HAVEN'T GOT ↑ Sinéad O'Connor

A beautiful follow-up to *The Lion and The Cobra*, and without question O'Connor's best work to date. Unfortunately the artist could not let her music do the talking and became untidily embroiled in a number of political and religious arguments. Her clumsy actions did not affect sales, and in the USA, where she appeared to court bad press, the album was a huge hit. The album, of course, also includes her transatlantic chart-topping version of Prince's 'Nothing Compares 2 U'. Also noted is the thank you to Shane MacGowan and the Pogues, a friendship that has recently gone bad after she allegedly shopped the singer.

❱❱ Tracks: *Feel So Different; I Am Stretched On Your Grave; Three Babies; The Emperor's New Clothes; Black Boys On Mopeds; Nothing Compares 2 U; Jump In The River; You Cause As Much Sorrow; The Last Day Of Our Acquaintance; I Do Not Want What I Haven't Got.*

★ First released 1990
★ UK peak chart position: 1
★ USA peak chart position: 1
★ Previous Top 1000 position: 1998 (–): 1994 (–)

586 LIVE AT THE REGAL ↑ B.B. King

No matter how good the studio sessions were, B.B. King was at his best on stage in front of an appreciative, if not ecstatic, crowd. This set, recorded at Chicago's premier black theatre on 21 November 1964, delivered just that. Despite the less than perfect recording conditions, at a time when technology had yet to catch up with the demands placed upon it, the King of the Blues delivers a definitive performance in a programme that includes his then most recent single, 'Help The Poor', and a clutch of songs that were responsible for much of his success, 'Everyday I Have The Blues', 'Sweet Little Angel', 'It's My Own Fault', 'You Upset Me Baby' and 'Woke Up This Morning', among them. The band, including tenorman Johnny Board and organist Duke Jethro, is lean but tight, providing King with a springboard from which to leap into flights of immaculate guitar playing and singing.

❱❱ Tracks: *Everyday I Have The Blues; Sweet Little Angel; It's My Own Fault; How Blue Can You Get; Please Love Me; You Upset Me Baby; Worry, Worry; Woke Up This Morning; You Done Lost Your Good Thing Now; Help The Poor.*

★ First released 1965
★ UK peak chart position: did not chart
★ USA peak chart position: 78
★ Previous Top 1000 position: 1998 (593): 1994 (483)

587 THE SONG REMAINS THE SAME ↑ Led Zeppelin

No one can doubt their pedigree and, like the Beatles and Rolling Stones, Led Zeppelin's catalogue will sell and sell forever. Heavy rock has and will never have any greater role models; they defined it and they own it. That said, there is a touch of the Emperor's new clothes about this recording. They did have their off nights, and this mammoth live set caught them slightly off colour as regular Zep concert goers will testify and confirm. However no one should argue with any concert that opens with 'Rock and Roll' and ends with 'Whole Lotta Love'. And yes, no worries, the one you all want, it's there, CD2 track 2.

❱❱ Tracks: *Rock and Roll; Celebration Day; The Song Remains The Same; Rain Song; Dazed and Confused; No Quarter; Stairway To Heaven; Moby Dick; Whole Lotta Love.*

★ First released 1976
★ UK peak chart position: 1
★ USA peak chart position: 2
★ Previous Top 1000 position: 1998 (–): 1994 (–)

588 BIG ONES ↓ Aerosmith

A collection that can stand on its own as a bona fide album, *Big Ones* is a celebration of the survival of a rock band who have lived on the edge for many years. In the late 90s Steven Tyler even manages to look more weathered than Keith Richard, and that must be the ultimate compliment. More than the Rolling Stones, more than Led Zeppelin, Aerosmith epitomize the attitude, lifestyle and sound of hard rock 'n' roll. This is the best introduction to Aerosmith and will no doubt lead to debauchery, non-stop partying and the rest of their outrageously great catalogue.

❱❱ Tracks: *Walk On Water; Love In An Elevator; Rag Doll; What It Takes; Dude (Looks Like A Lady); Janie's Got A Gun; Cryin'; Amazing; Blind Man; Deuces Are Wild; The Other Side; Crazy; Eat The Rich; Angel; Livin' On The Edge; Dude (Looks Like A Lady) Live.*

★ First released 1994
★ UK peak chart position: 7
★ USA peak chart position: 6
★ Previous Top 1000 position: 1998 (574): 1994 (–)

589 STANLEY ROAD ↓
Paul Weller

Named after a street in Paul Weller's home-town of Woking in Surrey, this album was greeted with universal approval by critics and fans. The brilliant Peter Blake collage that runs throughout the package portrays much greater nostalgia than is contained in the lyrics. The family snapshots and the Green Line bus picture serve only to fool the listener. The title track is about the terraced houses that have now given way to 90s starter apartments, but the more personal content of tracks such as 'You Do Something To Me' and 'Out Of The Sinking' is where Weller truly bares his soul. It would appear that before recording *Stanley Road*, Weller listened to many Traffic albums.

» Tracks: *The Changingman; Porcelain Gods; I Walk On Gilded Splinters; You Do Something To Me; Woodcutters Son; Time Passes; Stanley Road; Broken Stones; Out Of The Sinking; Pink On White Walls; Whirlpools End; Wings Of Speed.*

★ First released 1995
★ UK peak chart position: 1
★ USA peak chart position: did not chart
★ Previous Top 1000 position: 1998 (66): 1994 (–)

590 BETWEEN THE LINES ↑
Janis Ian

A breakthrough album of considerable stature, Janis Ian joined the bedsitter songwriter set with a collection of powerful and beautiful songs with beautifully understated arrangements. 'At Seventeen' was the hit single, a magnificent, mature song about the pains of growing up. Elsewhere, similar sentiments of elusive love are offered with 'When The Party's Over' and the promise of a one-night stand with 'The Come-On'. There were no veiled obscure lyrics here; Ian spoke out loudly and clearly to an audience that could closely relate to at least one of the songs. This album still retains that great quality.

» Tracks: *When The Party's Over; At Seventeen; From Me To You; Bright Lights and Promises; In The Winter; Water Colors; Between The Lines; The Come On; Light A Light; Tea & Sympathy; Lover's Lullaby.*

★ First released 1975
★ UK peak chart position: did not chart
★ USA peak chart position: 1
★ Previous Top 1000 position: 1998 (710): 1994 (–)

591 CROWN OF CREATION ↑
Jefferson Airplane

A rich and varied collection showing off the different talents of the main songwriters. Their major breakthrough was still to come with *Volunteers* a year or so later; this is most certainly their *Revolver*. Among the many memorable moments are Grace Slick's beautiful vocal on 'Lather', the band's sensitive cover version of David Crosby's 'Triad' and Jorma Kaukonen's stunning wah-wah solo on 'If You Feel'. Add to this the intense lyrics, such as the drug problems of the subject in 'Greasy Heart', and Marty Balin and Paul Kantner's consistently strong vocals throughout. Finally, although under-recorded compared to his Hot Tuna work, Jack Casady shows his remarkable dexterity on bass.

» Tracks: *Lather; In Time; Triad; Star Track; Share A Little Joke; Chushingura; If You Feel; Crown Of Creation; Ice Cream Phoenix; Greasy Heart; The House At Pooneil Corners.*

★ First released 1968
★ UK peak chart position: did not chart
★ USA peak chart position: 6
★ Previous Top 1000 position: 1998 (711): 1994 (–)

592 BONE MACHINE ↑
Tom Waits

Well into his career Tom Waits released this album to probably his best ever set of reviews, and that includes *Swordfishtrombones*. It also captured a wider audience, indicating that at last the rest of the world was catching on to this genius musical poet. Featuring Waits' trademark vocal croak, somewhere between Captain Beefheart and Robbie Robertson, this is not a bundle of laughs and it will kill your dinner party stone dead. Those seeking further evidence of Waits unique talent should look no further than dark tales such as 'Murder In The Red Barn', 'Black Wings', and 'That Feel', the latter co-written with Keith Richards. Spookily disturbing.

» Tracks: *Earth Died Screaming; Dirt In The Ground; Such A Scream; All Stripped Down; Who Are You; The Ocean Doesn't Want Me; Jesus Gonna Be Here; A Little Rain; In The Colosseum; Goin' Out West; Murder In The Red Barn; Black Wings; Whistle Down The Wind; I Don't Wanna Grow Up; Let Me Get Up On It; That Feel.*

★ First released 1992
★ UK peak chart position: 26
★ USA peak chart position: 176
★ Previous Top 1000 position: 1998 (–): 1994 (–)

593 X ↑
INXS

The album opens with 'Suicide Blonde', a creepy title in view of the fact that this was recorded three years before lead singer Michael Hutchence embarked on his much publicized, and ultimately tragic romance with Paula Yates. By 1990, INXS were enjoying huge commercial success throughout the world, and *X* maintained the sales momentum generated by its predecessor *Kick*. This time around a little more pop was the order of the day, and the band sounds bored on plain ordinary tracks such as 'The Stairs' and 'By My Side'. 'Lately' has some punch, but right through to the last track 'Hear That Sound' they struggle to get into the comfort of fifth gear.

)) Tracks: *Suicide Blonde; Disappear; The Stairs; Faith In Each Other; By My Side; Lately; Who Pays The Price; Know The Difference; Bitter Tears; On My Way; Hear That Sound.*

★ First released 1990
★ UK peak chart position: 2
★ USA peak chart position: 5
★ Previous Top 1000 position: 1998 (–): 1994 (–)

594 LATE FOR THE SKY ↓
Jackson Browne

Jackson Browne's early career was inextricably linked to the singer-songwriter movement of the 70s, and *Late For The Sky* has proved to be one of the era's strongest and most enduring albums. Browne's reflective songwriting style attained a new level of maturity on songs such as 'Fountain Of Sorrow' and 'For A Dancer', the latter a strikingly literate meditation on death. *Late For The Sky* is overshadowed by the title track and 'Before The Deluge', two brooding songs of personal and social apocalypse that book-end the album and serve as a textbook definition of the Californian lethargic mindset of the 70s.

)) Tracks: *Late For The Sky; Fountain Of Sorrow; Farther On; The Late Show; The Road and The Sky; For A Dancer; Walking Slow; Before The Deluge.*

★ First released 1974
★ UK peak chart position: did not chart
★ USA peak chart position: 14
★ Previous Top 1000 position: 1998 (366): 1994 (–)

595 AFTER BATHING AT BAXTER'S ↓ Jefferson Airplane

Always appreciated more in its homeland, *After Bathing At Baxter's* is a loose and challenging record. Transitional, as they left behind the folkiness of *Surrealistic Pillow* on their way to the surreal acidity of *Crown Of Creation*, it does have great charm. Love or hate the indulgence of Jack Casady and Jorma Kaukonen's 'Spare Chaynge', it does sound good coming through large speakers. Paul Kantner's 'Won't You Try' was his earliest anthem and set the pattern of much of his future work. This album is full of stoned innocence, the key being in the jumbled 'A Small Package Of Value Will Come To You Shortly'. It may have been self-indulgent, but they never came close to sounding this loose and experimental again.

)) Tracks: *Streetmasse: i The Ballad Of You & Me & Pooneil; ii A Small Package Of Value Will Come To You Shortly; iii Young Girl Sunday Blues; The War Is Over: i Martha; ii Wild Tyme; Hymn To An Older Generation: i The Last Wall Of The Castle; ii Rejoyce; How Suite It Is: i Watch Her Ride; ii Spare Chaynge; Shizoforest Love Suite: i Two Heads; ii Won't You Try/Saturday Afternoon.*

★ First released 1967
★ UK peak chart position: did not chart
★ USA peak chart position: 17
★ Previous Top 1000 position: 1998 (352): 1994 (–)

596 ONE SIZE FITS ALL ↑
Frank Zappa/The Mothers Of Invention

Unusual for a Zappa album to open with the star turn; he usually waits until midway. 'Inca Road' is a superb piece that reaffirms, should it be necessary, that Zappa was an astonishingly great lead guitarist. The quality of the guitar solo is matched throughout by some skilful keyboards from George Duke. Having said that, the solo on 'Po-Jama People' is also pretty nifty. This was a high-charting album for Zappa (in the USA), and for once justice was done, as other similarly great Zappa albums failed completely. This is but one of 71 necessary Frank Zappa/Mothers albums to covet.

)) Tracks: *Inca Roads; Can't Afford No Shoes; Sofa No 1; Po-Jama People; Florentine Pogen; Evelyn, A Modified Dog; San Ber'dino; Andy; Sofa No. 2.*

★ First released 1975
★ UK peak chart position: did not chart
★ USA peak chart position: 26
★ Previous Top 1000 position: 1998 (673): 1994 (–)

597 WORD GETS AROUND ↑
Stereophonics

An excellent debut, without the anticipation that their second album would be even better. The Stereophonics were at the forefront of the Welsh invasion of the late 90s, alongside bands such as the Manic Street Preachers, Catatonia and the Super Furry Animals. 'A Thousand Trees' opens, with its 'Like A Rolling Stone' chord progression allowing the confident Kelly Jones to immediately stamp his vocal authority on the album. Voice and guitar are evenly matched in tone, both gritty and dirty. Even a lightweight pop song such as 'More Life In A Tramps Vest' is transformed into a tough sermon by the band's energetic delivery. And what about the fabulous melody in 'Local Boy In The Photograph'. Bloody marvelous, boyo.

» Tracks: *A Thousand Trees; Looks Like Chaplin; More Life In A Tramps Vest; Local Boy In The Photograph; Traffic; Not Up To You; Check My Eyelids For Holes; Same Size Feet; Last Of The Big Time Drinkers; Goldfish Bowl; Too Many Sandwiches; Billy Daveys Daughter.*

★ First released 1997
★ UK peak chart position: 6
★ USA peak chart position: did not chart
★ Previous Top 1000 position: 1998 (–): 1994 (–)

598 DREADLOCKS DREAD ↓
Big Youth

This is the perfect Big Youth album and as close to pop has he could get without losing credibility. Gone is the thundering sparse bass and echoing dub. In its place is a more orchestrated effort with shades of Bob Marley and Burning Spear. 'Lightning Flash (Weak Heart Drop)' is sensational, while the happy-go-lucky 'Some Like It Dread' should have been a national hit. His recorded output in recent years is meagre but this album and the even more powerful *Screaming Target* should keep Youth's name alive long after any reggae boom has faded. He was after all the biggest name of 1973 (in Jamaica).

» Tracks: *Train To Rhodesia; House Of Dreadlocks; Lightning Flash (Weak Heart Drop); Natty Dread She Want; Some Like It Dread; Marcus Garvey; Big Youth Special; Dread Organ; Blackman Message; You Don't Care; Moving Away.*

★ First released 1975
★ UK peak chart position: did not chart
★ USA peak chart position: did not chart
★ Previous Top 1000 position: 1998 (486): 1994 (704)

599 MAKING MOVIES ↓
Dire Straits

The last album of their career that sounded as if they were trying to play, instead of going through the motions. David Knopfler had already departed from the band and brother Mark had a free rein, clear from any sibling rivalry. Every song stands up, apart from the dreadful 'Les Boys', hardly one of their show-stoppers. 'Solid Rock', 'Tunnel Of Love', 'Romeo and Juliet' and 'Skateaway' would be on any decent greatest hits package. Following this artistic triumph they proceeded to release *Love Over Gold*, and we all know what overrated album followed after that, don't we? Ho hum.

» Tracks: *Tunnel Of Love; Romeo and Juliet; Skateaway; Expresso Love; Hand In Hand; Solid Rock; Les Boys.*

★ First released 1980
★ UK peak chart position: 4
★ USA peak chart position: 19
★ Previous Top 1000 position: 1998 (337): 1994 (128)

600 SUBSTANCE ↑
New Order

NEW
ORDER
——
SUBSTANCE
1987

Career retrospectives are usually shoddy affairs, ignored by weary bands with little concern for the integrity of their discography, and overseen instead by haphazard record company execs trying to wring the last penny from their fading stars. *Substance* deflects both potential criticisms – the music is overwhelmingly strong and the presentation superior. Listening to this collection of singles and b-sides, it is impossible not to admire both the continuity and consistency of New Order's sound. Every fan will have their own favourites, from the group's sublime debut single through to the mature synth-pop of 'True Faith', but it is hard to identify a single dud a-side, and some of the flip-sides included on the second CD are also pretty remarkable.

» Tracks: *Ceremony; Everything's Gone Green; Temptation; Blue Monday; Confusion; Thieves Like Us; Perfect Kiss; Subculture; Shellshock; State Of The Nation; Bizarre Love Triangle; True Faith; In A Lonely Place; Procession; Mesh; Hurt; The Beach; Confused Instrumental; Lonesome Tonight; Murder; Thieves Like Us Instrumental; Kiss Of Death; Shame Of The Nation; 1963.*

★ First released 1987
★ UK peak chart position: 3
★ USA peak chart position: 36
★ Previous Top 1000 position: 1998 (681): 1994 (–)

601 STRANGEWAYS, HERE WE COME ↑ The Smiths

So just how important are the most acclaimed band of the eighties now? Well, judging by the fact that this, their final studio album, was not regarded as one of the band's best at the time, the quality of the music still knocks a lot of their supposed rivals into the gutter. Johnny Marr had officially left the partnership by the time this was released and his guitar is often buried too deep in the mix. Marr had seemingly lost interest as the newer songs left less space for his improvisation. Morrissey's lyrical edge is as sharp as ever. He does not fail to satisfy, conjuring up magnificent couplets throughout.

▶ Tracks: *A Rush and A Push and The Land Is Ours; I Started Something I Couldn't Finish; Death Of A Disco Dancer; Girlfriend In A Coma; Stop Me If You Think You've Heard This One Before; Last Night I Dreamt That Somebody Loved Me; Unhappy Birthday; Paint A Vulgar Picture; Death At One's Elbow; I Won't Share You.*

★ First released 1987
★ UK peak chart position: 2
★ USA peak chart position: 55
★ Previous Top 1000 position: 1998 (–): 1994 (–)

602 FOR THOSE ABOUT TO ROCK WE SALUTE YOU ↑ AC/DC

FOR THOSE ABOUT TO ROCK

Brian Johnson's second album as AC/DC's frontman following the death of Bon Scott, and as such he helped them create a phenomenal commercial success, with the singles 'Let's Get It Up' and the title track charting on both sides of the Atlantic. The album went on to sell over a million copies worldwide and the title track became an immediate live favourite, complete with a cannon-fire salute stage show that became instant encore material. Elsewhere, their familiar rattle remained intact, with 'Night Of The Long Knives' and 'Breaking The Rules' forging a familiar piece of metal.

▶ Tracks: *For Those About To Rock (We Salute You); Put The Finger On You; Let's Get It Up; Inject The Venom; Snowballad; Evil Walk; COD; Breaking The Rules; Night Of The Long Knives; Spellbound.*

★ First released 1981
★ UK peak chart position: 3
★ USA peak chart position: 1
★ Previous Top 1000 position: 1998 (738): 1994 (283)

603 FOR YOUR PLEASURE ↓ Roxy Music

The second album from the purveyors of art rock and glamour. Three out of five members appear to be left-handed, according to the inner sleeve. This put them way out of balance with the rest of the world, and for a while their wondrously inventive music put them out of step with the music being fed to us. The energy of tracks such as 'Editions Of You' still incites the need to dance. And how many times did you wait patiently for Bryan Ferry to get to the 'but you blew my mind' part of 'In Every Dream Home A Heartache', just so you could hear Phil Manzanera's excellent phased guitar?

▶ Tracks: *Do The Strand; Beauty Queen; Strictly Confidential; Editions Of You; In Every Dream Home A Heartache; The Bogus Man; Grey Lagoons; For Your Pleasure.*

★ First released 1973
★ UK peak chart position: 4
★ USA peak chart position: 193
★ Previous Top 1000 position: 1998 (160): 1994 (271)

604 HOKEY POKEY ↑ Richard and Linda Thompson

A brave follow-up to their masterful *I Want To See The Bright Lights Tonight*, this attempts to encapsulate various British working-class musical styles – folk, brass band, playground songs and pub singalongs – much as the Band did for indigenous American genres. The Thompsons do not always succeed; *Hokey Pokey* sometimes feels like a theoretical exercise. Nevertheless, the tension between the songs' jaunty surfaces and the neurotic undercurrent of Richard's blistering guitar is beguiling. The one undeniably great song (other than the upbeat title track) is 'A Heart Needs A Home', sung by Linda with grave beauty and authority.

▶ Tracks: *Hokey Pokey; I'll Regret It In The Morning; Smiffy's Glass Eye; The Egypt Room; Never Again; Georgie On A Spree; Old Man Inside A Young Man; The Sun Never Shines On The Poor; A Heart Needs A Home; Mole In A Hole.*

★ First released 1975
★ UK peak chart position: did not chart
★ USA peak chart position: did not chart
★ Previous Top 1000 position: 1998 (850): 1994 (–)

605 APOSTROPHE ↑
Frank Zappa

Quite why this remains the most commercially successful album in Frank Zappa's massive catalogue is a mystery. He employed the same brilliantly irreverent humour, chose familiarly wacky titles, and, as always, played like a demon. I would put forward the motion that once you have a serious taste for Zappa, you will want to investigate the whole back catalogue. For most listeners he is still the last undiscovered genius of modern music. For now you can marvel at his playing on the title track, laugh out loud at 'Stink-Foot', and take heed of the sensible warning on 'Don't Eat The Yellow Snow'.

▶▶ Tracks: *Don't Eat The Yellow Snow; Nanook Rubs It; St. Alfonzo's Pancake Breakfast; Father O'Blivion; Cosmik Debris; Excentrifugal Forz; Apostrophe'; Uncle Remus; Stink-Foot.*

★ First released 1974
★ UK peak chart position: did not chart
★ USA peak chart position: 10
★ Previous Top 1000 position: 1998 (–): 1994 (–)

606 MUSIC IN A DOLL'S HOUSE ↑
Family

From the opening Jim King falsetto on 'The Chase' to the quirky 'God Save The Queen' ending, *Music From A Doll's House* never flags. In 1968 King's saxophone and Ric Grech's violin were imaginative additions to the standard band profile, and their playing was skin-tight. With the strangled vibrato of Roger Chapman's vocals – still one of rock's most astonishing performers – Family created a power that has rarely been matched. 'Old Songs New Songs' is a great rocker in anyone's book (why fade it in mid-flight?), and 'Voyage' presents a classic slice of psychedelia. Over-produced (by Dave Mason) it may be, but as a debut album there are few equals of its time.

▶▶ Tracks: *The Chase; Mellowing Grey; Never Like This; Me My Friend; Variation On A Theme Of Hey Mr Policeman; Winter; Old Songs New Songs; Variation On A Theme Of The Breeze; Hey Mr. Policeman; See Through Windows; Variation On A Theme Of Me My Friend; Peace Of Mind; Voyage; Breeze; 3 X Time.*

★ First Released 1968
★ UK peak chart position: 35
★ USA peak chart position: did not chart
★ Previous Top 1000 position: 1998 (753): 1994 (–)

607 VOLUNTEERS ↓
Jefferson Airplane

The album that made relations with the then ultra-conservative RCA Records a little tense. Knowing that they had potentially one of America's biggest bands, the label had to let them use the 'f' word (on 'We Can Be Together'). A bigger problem was their left-of-centre political stance at that time. *Volunteers* is a fat album, full of great ideas but with a surplus of gastric juice. 'The Farm' doodles just half a minute too long, their version of 'Wooden Ships' just misses the mark and the Stephen Stills organ on 'Meadowlands' is a waste. However, 'Eskimo Blue Day' and 'Good Shepherd' succeed, as does the blatant sexuality of 'Hey Frederick' when Grace Slick sings 'either go away or go all the way in, look at what you hold'.

▶▶ Tracks: *We Can Be Together; Good Shepherd; The Farm; Hey Frederick; Turn My Life Down; Wooden Ships; Eskimo Blue Day; A Song For All Seasons; Meadowlands; Volunteers.*

★ First released 1969
★ UK peak chart position: 34
★ USA peak chart position: 13
★ Previous Top 1000 position: 1998 (449): 1994 (–)

608 SONG FOR MY FATHER ↓
Horace Silver Quintet

Yet another jazz steal; this time, Steely Dan borrowed the title track for 'Rikki Don't Lose That Number'. Horace Silver should take heart, this is his most successful album and one that finds its way onto many recommended lists, not just for the jazz fraternity. Its strength is its accessibility and, in keeping with many piano leader albums, Silver does not seek to dominate. The quintet is completed by Carmell Jones (trumpet), Joe Henderson (tenor), Teddy Smith (bass) and Roger Humphries (drums). The reissued CD version contains four extra tracks from the same 1963/1964 sessions. This and *The Jody Grind* are essential Silver albums.

▶▶ Tracks: *Song For My Father; The Natives Are Restless Tonight; Calcutta Cutie; Que Pasa; Kicker; Lonely Woman.*

★ First released 1965
★ UK peak chart position: did not chart
★ USA peak chart position: 95
★ Previous Top 1000 position: 1998 (600): 1994 (734)

609 CARAVANSERAI ↑
Santana

The recent unprecedented commercial success of *Supernatural* and the cupboard full of Grammy Awards it reaped for the guitarist raises the question; yeah, but what about the first four Santana albums? *Caravanserai* was the fourth and most ambitious of these. Written as one long suite the album really needs to be listened to in one sitting to do it justice. Carlos stays way above the twelfth fret throughout, leaving even the listener with blisters on their fingers. No one track deserves an extra mention as all contribute to make this a stupendous piece of music. The bit on track 6 where organ and guitar flow into the 'I don't really care about tomorrow' does make the hairs stand up a bit more though.

》 Tracks: *Eternal Caravan Of Reincarnation; Waves Within; Look Up (To See What's Coming Down); Just In Time To See The Sun; Song Of The Wind; All The Love Of The Universe; Future Primitive; Stone Flower; La Fuente Del Ritmo; Every Step Of The Way.*

★ First released 1972
★ UK peak chart position: 6
★ USA peak chart position: 8
★ Previous Top 1000 position: 1998 (–): 1994 (–)

610 NINE LIVES ↑
Aerosmith

Just like the Doctor Seuss-styled top hat that Steven Tyler pops out of on stage, Aerosmith conjured up an unexpectedly great album. Sounding rejuvenated, there are enough strong new songs to add permanently to their (still) magnetic stage show. Standard Aerosmith rock comes in the shape of the excellent title track, and the album's first hit single, 'Falling In Love'. Equally good, but more interesting, are the mantic-styled 'Taste Of India' and the cheeky sexual innuendo in the many shades of 'Pink'. Lyrics such as 'pink as the bing on your cherry' show that Tyler still has a sense of humour.

》 Tracks: *Nine Lives; Falling In Love; Hole In My Soul; Taste Of India; Full Circle; Something's Gotta Give; Ain't That A Bitch; The Farm; Crash; 10; Pink; Falling Off; Attitude Adjustment; Fallen Angels.*

★ First released 1997
★ UK peak chart position: 4
★ USA peak chart position: 1
★ Previous Top 1000 position: 1998 (739): 1994 (–)

611 CRACKED REAR VIEW ↑
Hootie and The Blowfish

This album was phenomenally successful in the USA where Hootie and The Blowfish were adopted by settled 30 somethings (or late twenty somethings if their cameo appearance in the TV series *Friends* is anything to go by). That they cornered the mainstream intelligent rock market was in no small part thanks to lead singer Darius Rucker being blessed with an exceptionally natural and distinctive voice. Quality oozes through on tracks such as 'Hold My Hand', with its 'La Bamba'/'Twist and Shout' chords, or the anthemic 'Let Her Cry' (imagine the waving scarves and lighted matches). It's all good accessible stuff, undemanding and as deep as you want it to be.

》 Tracks: *Hannah Jane; Hold My Hand; Let Her Cry; Only Wanna Be With You; Running From An Angel; I'm Goin' Home; Drowning; Time; Look Away; Not Even The Trees; Goodbye.*

★ First released 1994
★ UK peak chart position: 12
★ USA peak chart position: 1
★ Previous Top 1000 position: 1998 (–): 1994 (–)

612 STUTTER ↓
James

Yet another product of Manchester's impressive scene, James offered this brash, folk-styled pop selection as their debut album following acclaimed singles for the Factory label. Produced by former Patti Smith Group guitarist Lenny Kaye, it opened with the eccentric 'Skullduggery' and proceeded in a quirky, unconventional manner. Complex arrangements and unorthodox lyrics abound, while vocalist Tim Booth accentuates the loose arrangements with highly stylized vocals that demand attention. An expanded line-up would gain commercial success with a very different sound, but *Stutter* captures James during their formative, experimental era.

》 Tracks: *Skullduggery; Scarecrow; So Many Ways; Just Hipper; John Yen; Summer Songs; Really Hard; Billy's Shirts; Why So Close; Withdrawn; Black Hole.*

★ First released 1986
★ UK peak chart position: 68
★ USA peak chart position: did not chart
★ Previous Top 1000 position: 1998 (505): 1994 (414)

613 THE SCREAM ↑
Siouxsie and The Banshees

Despite evolving from a group of Sex Pistols fans, Siouxsie and The Banshees eschewed the clichés of punk, offering instead an austere and bleak creation. Bassist Steve Severin and drummer Kenny Morris provide simple, Teutonic-style patterns over which Siouxsie Sioux wails in the manner of former Velvet Underground chanteuse Nico. Unremitting original songs are joined by a version of the Beatles' 'Helter Skelter', which the Banshees interpret with the full knowledge of its inspiration for Charles Manson. *The Scream* is an apt title for such desolate music.

» Tracks: *Pure; Jigsaw Feeling; Overground; Carcass; Helter Skelter; Mirage; Metal Postcard; Nicotine Stain; Suburban Relapse; Switch.*

★ First released 1978
★ UK peak chart position: 12
★ USA peak chart position: did not chart
★ Previous Top 1000 position: 1998 (920): 1994 (679)

614 EAST SIDE STORY ↑
Squeeze

In one of the smartest free transfer deals ever, Squeeze were able to plug the massive midfield gap left by the departing Jools Holland with the nimble-fingered Paul Carrack. They gained an extra vocalist in the process, but there seems to have been little room for Carrack's underrated and expressive voice. For many, the album's best track was 'Tempted', with Carrack taking lead vocal (with help from producer Elvis Costello). Close behind in the queue is 'Someone Else's Bell', 'Is That Love', 'In Quintessence' – in fact the whole set, except possibly the uncomfortable chord/key change of 'F-hole', which leads back to the hypnotically great 'Tempted'.

» Tracks: *In Quintessence; Someone Else's Heart; Tempted; Piccadilly; There's No Tomorrow; A Woman's World; Is That Love; F-hole; Labelled With Love; Someone Else's Bell; Mumbo Jumbo; Vanity Fair; Messed Around.*

★ First released 1981
★ UK peak chart position: 19
★ USA peak chart position: 44
★ Previous Top 1000 position: 1998 (855): 1994 (363)

615 NICK OF TIME ↑
Bonnie Raitt

Although famed primarily for her interpretation of compositions by the likes of Joni Mitchell, John Hiatt, James Taylor and Paul Brady, *Nick Of Time* includes two fine Raitt-penned songs. 'The Road's My Middle Name' is an up-tempo blues number, harking back to her early career performing alongside Son House and Mississippi Fred McDowell. The title track is one of her best, a sensitive examination of the traumas of ageing. Throughout the album her voice is haunting and controlled, bringing new meaning and depth to a varied range of material. Having been dropped by her former label, Bonnie turned 40 gracefully with this album and it gave her unexpected massive success just in the nick of time.

» Tracks: *Nick Of Time; A Thing Called Love; Love Letters; Cry On My Shoulder; Real Man; Nobody's Girl; Have A Heart; Too Soon To Tell; I Will Not Be Denied; I Ain't Gonna Let You Break My Heart Again; The Road's My Middle Name.*

★ First released 1989
★ UK peak chart position: 51
★ USA peak chart position: 1
★ Previous Top 1000 position: 1998 (742): 1994 (420)

616 COME FLY WITH ME ↓
Frank Sinatra

A mildly conceptual album that has lasted, with a choice of songs that takes the listener around the world in 45 minutes. Some of Frank Sinatra's finest moments are on this album, notably with Sammy Cahn and Jimmy Van Heusen's uplifting 'Come Fly With Me' and 'It's Nice To Go Trav'ling'. This was Sinatra's first album arranged and conducted by Billy May, a relationship that produced further classic orchestrations. Once again the CD purchaser will greatly benefit from three bonus tracks with Nelson Riddle in charge; 'Chicago', 'South Of The Border' and 'I Love Paris'. Happy-go-lucky fare that we all need an infusion of from time to time.

» Tracks: *Come Fly With Me; Around The World; Isle Of Capri; Moonlight In Vermont; Autumn In New York; On The Road To Madalay; Let's Get Away From It All; April In Paris; London By Night; Brazil; Blue Hawaii; It's Nice To Go Trav'ling.*

★ First released 1958
★ UK peak chart position: 2
★ USA peak chart position: 1
★ Previous Top 1000 position: 1998 (245): 1994 (107)

617 FEAR OF A BLACK PLANET
↓ Public Enemy

If Public Enemy's two previous albums had ruffled feathers, *Fear Of A Black Planet* set out its stall to exploit mainstream fears. Again, the title spoke volumes. This time they raged just as hard, but their political consciousness had grown. Professor Griff had been ejected from the band for his anti-Semitic stance, and much of the album's atmosphere is created by the bunker mentality of resultant clashes with the press. The siege mentality only underscores the group's hard-nosed, cut-and-paste sample technique and the eloquence of Chuck D. 'Fight The Power' still bites harder than just about any other track in rap's history.

)) Tracks: *Contract On The World Love Jam; Brothers Gonna Work It Out; 911 Is A Joke; Incident At 66.6 FM; Welcome To The Terrordome; Meet The G That Killed Me; Pollywanacraka; Anti-nigger Machine; Burn Hollywood Burn; Power To The People; Who Stole The Soul; Fear Of A Black Planet; Revolutionary Generation; Can't Do Nuttin' For Ya Man; Reggie Jax; Leave This Off Your F***in' Charts; B Side Wins Again; War At Thirty Three and A Third; Final Count Of The Collision Between Us and Them.*

★ First released 1990
★ UK peak chart position: 4 ★ USA peak chart position: 10
★ Previous Top 1000 position: 1998 (278): 1994 (509)

618 BEING THERE ↑
Wilco

back musical approach brings out old fans of Neil Young and the Band who had stopped buying records years ago. Ex-Uncle Tupelo member Jeff Tweedy has clearly found his spiritual home in the comfort of this band. All of the songs on this ambitious double album were written by him, and he covers both melancholia ('Say You Miss Me') and straight bouncy pop ('Outtasite (Outta Mind)') with equal panache and worldly confidence. The reprise on disc two ('Outta Mind (Outta Site)') is not quite as good, but there is the compensation of the tears in your beer track 'Someone Else's Song' (Hank Williams, I think).

)) Tracks: *Misunderstood; Far, Far Away; Monday; Outtasite (Outta Mind); Forget The Flowers; Red-Eyed and Blue; I Got You (At The End Of The Century); What's The World Got In Store; Hotel Arizona; Say You Miss Me; Sunken Treasure; Someday Soon; Outta Mind (Outta Sight); Someone Else's Song; Kingpin; (Was I) In Your Dreams; Why Would You Wanna Live; The Lonely 1; Dreamer In My Dreams.*

★ First released 1996
★ UK peak chart position: did not chart
★ USA peak chart position: did not chart
★ Previous Top 1000 position: 1998 (–): 1994 (–)

619 ELVIS PRESLEY ↓
Elvis Presley

Although five tracks remained from the Sun cellar this is usually known as Elvis Presley's first RCA album, and what a lucky company they were, probably unaware that they had signed the greatest ever donor to their company pension scheme. No rock aficionado should be unaware of the tracks, although the album has long been replaced with compilations. It still is nominated by the majority of the cognoscenti who are old enough to remember this album plopping down on their Dansettes. It was a vitally important album although now doomed by the age of CD, as there are much better compilations with many more tracks.

)) Tracks: *Blue Suede Shoes; I Love You Because; Tutti Frutti; I'll Never Let You Go; Money Honey; I'm Counting On You; I Got A Woman; One-Sided Love Affair; Just Because; Tryin' To Get To You; I'm Gonna Sit Right Down and Cry Over You; Blue Moon.*

★ First released 1956
★ UK peak chart position: did not chart
★ USA peak chart position: 1
★ Previous Top 1000 position: 1998 (228): 1994 (49)

620 THE GILDED PALACE OF SIN
↓ Flying Burrito Brothers

This great debut allowed two former Byrds, Gram Parsons and Chris Hillman, fully to explore country music. Several selections, notably 'Christine's Tune' and 'Wheels', succeeded in capturing the joys of Nashville-inspired rock, but the group proved equally adept at interpreting southern soul standards. Parsons' aching vocal on Dan Penn's 'Dark End Of The Street' articulated the dilemmas of infidelity, while on his own composition, 'Hot Burrito No. 1', he revealed a vulnerability unusual in a male singer. 'Sneaky' Pete Kleinow explored the sonic possibilities of the pedal steel guitar, rather than employ orthodox embellishments, and this desire to question preconceptions gives this album its unique qualities.

)) Tracks: *Christine's Tune; Sin City; Do Right Woman, Do Right Man; Dark End Of The Street; My Uncle; Wheels; Juanita; Hot Burrito No. 1; Hot Burrito No. 2; Do You Know How It Feels; Hippie Boy.*

★ First released 1969
★ UK peak chart position: did not chart
★ USA peak chart position: 164
★ Previous Top 1000 position: 1998 (173): 1994 (849)

621 52ND STREET ↑
Billy Joel

Although never referred to as a 'loveable queen', singer-songwriter Joel has musical qualities similar to Elton John. Both have experienced such mainstream success that their talent is sometimes overshadowed by their public lives, and both are better piano players than the public are aware of. The multi-million-selling *52nd Street* contains a clutch of great songs which happen to be very radio-friendly. Both 'Honesty' and 'My Life' have been played to death, but they are undeniably good songs with powerful lyrics. The cryptical 'Stiletto' is either a perky tale about obsessive love or an allegory for intravenous drug use. Either way they are both bad for you.

▶ Tracks: *Big Shot; Honesty; My Life; Zanzibar; Stiletto; Rosalinda's Eyes; Half A Mile Away; Until The Night; 52nd Street.*

★ First released 1978
★ UK peak chart position: 10
★ USA peak chart position: 1
★ Previous Top 1000 position: 1998 (–): 1994 (–)

622 PLEASE PLEASE ME ↓
The Beatles

Recorded in between a cup of tea and a cigarette, this album is raw yet dazzling. Here were four lads, highly experienced on stage, but with little or no idea of what a recording studio was like. They were subtly marshalled by the much respected George Martin to deliver an entire album that was exactly what the fans wanted, but was still a surprise. Things were never as simple as this again, yet the genius is there – for example, Lennon's unmatchable rasping on 'Twist and Shout', McCartney's graceful ease in singing 'I Saw Her Standing There', Harrison's sparse but definite Gretsch chords and Starr's ace vocal on 'Boys'.

▶ Tracks: *I Saw Her Standing There; Misery; Anna (Go To Him); Chains; Boys; Ask Me Why; Please Please Me; Love Me Do; P.S. I Love You; Baby Its You; Do You Want To Know A Secret; A Taste Of Honey; There's A Place; Twist and Shout.*

★ First released 1963
★ UK peak chart position: 1
★ USA peak chart position: record never released
★ Previous Top 1000 position: 1998 (333): 1994 (–)

623 DOCUMENT ↓
R.E.M.

R.E.M.'s later albums have sold by the container load, but they had to make albums like this to build a fan-base that brought them to notice. A number of critics place this record as their best. The band sound as though they are having to work to be heard; there is significant energy in 'Finest Worksong' and the Byrds-like 'Welcome To The Occupation'. It has been some time since Michael Stipe had as many words to say as he did in 'It's the End Of The World As We Know It', and 'The One I Love' has to be one of their best songs of all time.

▶ Tracks: *Finest Worksong; Welcome To The Occupation; Exhuming McCarthy; Disturbance At The Heron House; Strange; It's The End Of The World As We Know It (And I Feel Fine); The One I Love; Fireplace; Lightnin' Hopkins; King Of Birds; Oddfellows Local 151.*

★ First released 1987
★ UK peak chart position: 28
★ USA peak chart position: 10
★ Previous Top 1000 position: 1998 (307): 1994 (245)

624 GRAND PRIX ↓
Teenage Fanclub

The adorable Fannies are in danger of becoming a 'much-loved institution' like the Kinks and XTC: great for warm-hearted feelings, but lousy for record sales. *Grand Prix* breaks the band's Byrdsian mould slightly, but there are enough jangly G chords to satisfy everyone. Virtually every song is a flawless gem, complete with the most precise harmonies; each rolls into the next with love and care, played, sung and produced with supreme clarity. With the fantastic boon of possessing three talented songwriters, Teenage Fanclub offer plenty of variety; in particular, Gerard Love's irresistible 'Sparky's Dream' achieves classic pop song status, and his 'Don't Look Back' is this accomplished album's highlight.

▶ Tracks: *About You; Sparky's Dream; Mellow Doubt; Don't Look Back; Verisimilitude; Neil Jung; Tears; Discolite; Say No; Going Places; I'll Make It Clear; I Gotta Know; Hardcore/Ballad.*

★ First released 1995
★ UK peak chart position: 7
★ USA peak chart position: did not chart
★ Previous Top 1000 position: 1998 (353): 1994 (–)

625 THE LOW SPARK OF HIGH HEELED BOYS ↓ Traffic

The wandering jazzy music into which Traffic gradually flowed, hit a peak with this exceptional recording. The title track, with its perplexing lyrics, reaches numerous musical heights during its 12 minutes of life as it repeatedly comes back to Steve Winwood's accomplished vocal. Equally impressive, although shorter, is 'Hidden Treasure', highlighting what a good musician the late Chris Wood was. Finally, the band's loyal anchor, 'Gentleman' Jim Capaldi, takes lead on the cheeky (and sexist) 'Light Up Or Leave Me Alone'. The power of Traffic was in the atmosphere and space they created; this captures it.

» Tracks: Hidden Treasure; The Low Spark Of High Heeled Boys; Light Up Or Leave Me Alone; Rock 'N' Roll Stew; Many A Mile To Freedom; Rainmaker.

★ First released 1971
★ UK peak chart position: did not chart
★ USA peak chart position: 7
★ Previous Top 1000 position: 1998 (338): 1994 (184)

626 DREAD IN A BABYLON ↓ U-Roy

Along with Big Youth, U-Roy held the crown for Jamaica's greatest 'DJ's'. They were arguably the voices of the early 70s, and in their homeland were heard as often as Bob Marley. Repetitive though the DJ style is, it is nonetheless unforgettable and often hypnotic. U-Roy has a voice that could recite the side of a cornflakes packet and still make it sound appealing. This is a more polished album than his earlier work, produced by Prince Tony, with the bass a little mixed down. The usual lyrics, however, sing out loud and clear; 'as I will say, good gosh, as I will tell you now'.

» Tracks: Runaway Girl; Chalice In The Palace; I Can't Love Another; Dreadlocks Dread; The Great Psalms; Natty Don't Fear; African Message; Silver Bird; Listen To The Teacher; Trench Town Rock.

★ First released 1975
★ UK peak chart position: did not chart
★ USA peak chart position: did not chart
★ Previous Top 1000 position: 1998 (573): 1994 (-)

627 PILLS 'N' THRILLS AND BELLYACHES ↑ Happy Mondays

The sound of Madchester baggydom could be heard going to the wall with this album, which represented a creative peak for the whole scene and the Happy Mondays especially. Shaun Ryder's laconic vocal dips created some real ambience and body for their swaying and almost graceful dancing backdrops. It was his clever, almost punning wordplay and sometimes wonderfully obscure vocal and lyrical chatter, combined with Mark Day's surprisingly credible guitarwork, that helped create a stylish, if loose-fitting album. 'Kinky Afro', 'Step On', 'Holiday', were all charming and charmed, long before anyone could see them falling away.

» Tracks: Kinky Afro; God's Cop; Donovan; Grandbag's Funeral; Loose Fit; Dennis and Lois; Bob's Yer Uncle; Step On; Holiday; Harmony.

★ First released 1990
★ UK peak chart position: 4
★ USA peak chart position: 89
★ Previous Top 1000 position: 1998 (758): 1994 (364)

628 PERMANENT WAVES ↓ Rush

Falling somewhere in between heavy metal and AOR, Rush were one of the success stories of the period from 1976 to 1986 – all the more surprising because few Canadians manage to break out from the land of the maple leaf in this area of music. Much of their following idolized Alex Lifeson, who was a guitar hero with the technical ability of a Jimmy Page or a Jeff Beck. Occasionally Neil Peart's lyrics leave a little to be desired: 'the shifting shafts of shining, weave the fabric of their dreams . . .' Jon Anderson from Yes was afflicted with the same deadly condition of pretentiolyricitus. That aside, the music is faultless.

» Tracks: The Spirit Of Radio; Freewill; Jacob's Ladder; Entre Nous; Different Strings; Natural Science.

★ First released 1980
★ UK peak chart position: 3
★ USA peak chart position: 4
★ Previous Top 1000 position: 1998 (549): 1994 (-)

629 KING OF THE DELTA BLUES SINGERS ↓ Robert Johnson

A vitally important record. If you are a mountain climber you tackle Everest; if you are a blues lover you get to know this album very well. Very few had heard Robert Johnson's music when this milestone album was first released in 1962, but it was evident that this was a body of work of fundamental importance to the development of post-war Chicago blues and blues in general. Little known in his lifetime, Johnson synthesized traditions represented by men like Charley Patton, Son House, Lonnie Johnson and Leroy Carr, and refined them through his unique interpretative skills. An accomplished guitarist with finger and slide, Johnson matched his virtuosity with a tortured vocal style that added deeper resonance to his words.

» Tracks: *Crossroads Blues; Terraplane Blues; Come On In My Kitchen; Walking Blues; Last Fair Deal Gone Down; 32-20 Blues; Kindhearted Woman Blues; If I Had Possession Over Judgement Day; Preaching Blues; When You Got A Good Friend; Rambling On My Mind; Stones In My Passway; Traveling Riverside Blues; Milkcow's Calf Blues; Me and The Devil Blues; Hellhound On My Trail*

★ First released 1962
★ UK peak chart position: did not chart
★ USA peak chart position: did not chart
★ Previous Top 1000 position: 1998 (270): 1994 (168)

630 HIS BAND AND THE STREET CHOIR ↑ Van Morrison

Those unaware of the power and glory of Van Morrison's recorded output would be making a mistake to start with this album. Coming after two miraculous albums (*Astral Weeks* and *Moondance*) it is something of a soggy roman candle. Everything seems in place, Morrison's voice sounds good and is well recorded, and his musicians play what they are supposed to play. 'Domino' is a catchy opening track, 'I've Been Working' hints at soulful greatness, and 'I'll Be Your Lover, Too' is a fine bluesy ballad. In fact, ignore what I said previously, this is a damn fine record which only just misses out on being truly exceptional.

» Tracks: *Domino; Crazy Face; Give Me A Kiss; I've Been Working; Call Me Up In Dreamland; I'll Be Your Lover, Too; Blue Money; Virgo Clowns; Gypsy Queen; Sweet Jannie; If I Ever Needed Someone; Street Choir.*

★ First released 1970
★ UK peak chart position: did not chart
★ USA peak chart position: 32
★ Previous Top 1000 position: 1998 (–): 1994 (–)

631 DESPERADO ↓ The Eagles

Drawing from their previous experience as hired musicians, the Eagles quickly became one of America's leading country rock attractions. *Desperado*, their second release, was an ambitious concept album wherein the outlaw was used as a metaphor for the rock performer. Recorded in London under the aegis of Glyn Johns, the set was marked by the quartet's highly measured playing and distinctive harmonies. Described at their inception as the 'new Buffalo Springfield', the Eagles certainly drew on Californian musical heritage, but on this album they proclaimed an original identity. *Desperado* is their most complete, and for many, their best album. It deserves at least equal billing with *Hotel California*.

» Tracks: *Doolin Dalton; 21; Out Of Control; Tequila Sunrise; Desperado; Certain Kind Of Fool; Outlaw Man; Saturday Night; Bitter Creek.*

★ First released 1973
★ UK peak chart position: 39
★ USA peak chart position: 41
★ Previous Top 1000 position: 1998 (444): 1994 (192)

632 PEARL ↓ Band

Released posthumously in 1971, *Pearl* is a startling, multi-coloured portrait of a major artist bestriding her material with consummate ease. From the chugging 'Move Over' to the portentous 'Get It While You Can', the power never wavers. 'Me and Bobby McGee' leaves all other versions at the starting blocks (it was a number 1 in the USA), while the a cappella 'Mercedes Benz' demonstrates that she only needed the Full Tilt Boogie Band to add colour, not depth. The balance is perfect on 'Half Moon', which sounds like Little Feat backing Grace Slick with laryngitis. If only there was more.

» Tracks: *Move Over; Cry Baby; A Woman Left Lonely; Half Moon; Buried Alive In The Blues; Me and Bobby McGee; Mercedes Benz; Get It While You Can; Trust Me.*

★ First released 1971
★ UK peak chart position: 50
★ USA peak chart position: 1
★ Previous Top 1000 position: 1998 (470): 1994 (302)

633 THE CROSS OF CHANGES ↑
Enigma

Enigma's creator Michael Cretu mixes the music of his Romanian homeland with Peruvian instruments, African rhythms and Gregorian chants. The result is ambitious in construction, enchanting to listen to, and impossible to categorise. Imagine the orchestral bits of the Moody Blues crossed with a North American Enya, mixed with a snippet of Rick Wakeman and Mike Oldfield's keyboards. Those four examples could act as a deterrent for the listener. Rest assured, this is a stunning piece of music meant to be played loud whether or not, as the title track states, 'you understand or you don't, if you believe or if you doubt.'

》 Tracks: *Second Chapter; The Eyes Of Truth; Return To Innocence; I Love You ... I'll Kill You; Silent Warrior; The Dream Of The Dolphin; Age Of Loneliness (Carly's Song); Out From The Deep; The Cross Of Changes.*

★ First released 1993
★ UK peak chart position: 1
★ USA peak chart position: 9
★ Previous Top 1000 position: 1998 (–): 1994 (–)

634 SECRETS ↓
Toni Braxton

Braxton has the voice, Babyface has the words, and together they equal hot steamy sex – that is, if you happen to have the lyric sheet in front of you. If not, the intonation cleverly disguises the erotic content of songs such as 'You're Makin' Me High'. That aside, this is an overwhelmingly melancholic album, even though some of the songs are 'up' love songs, for example, 'Let It Flow'. Breaking hearts, love and sex, infidelity, 'how can I love again', and Kenny G are all present. Very much the way life has to be, for better or worse – apart from the horrible Kenny G bit, that is.

》 Tracks: *Come On Over Here; You're Makin Me High; There's No Me Without You; Un-Break My Heart; Talking In His Sleep; How Could An Angel Break My Heart; Find Me A Man; Let It Flow; Why Should I Care; I Don't Want To; I Love Me Some Him; In The Late Of Night.*

★ First released 1996
★ UK peak chart position: 4
★ USA peak chart position: 2
★ Previous Top 1000 position: 1998 (170): 1994 (–)

635 PURPLE ↑
Stone Temple Pilots

The *Let It Bleed*-style cake on the back cover of the Stone Temple Pilots' second album announces '12 Gracious Melodies'. Gracious is not a word normally associated with the band, but the icing is as thick as the grunge within. Beefy, muscular, call it what you will, this band remain one of the leaders of the genre. Scott Weiland's drug intake had reached ridiculous heights by the time this was released, and his subsequent run-ins with the authorities hindered the band's progress. This is a great pity, as this album marks a tremendous development over their debut. A fabulous slab of melodic meat.

》 Tracks: *Meat Plow; Vasoline; Lounge Fly; Interstate Love Song; Still Remains; Pretty Penny; Silvergun Superman; Big Emty; "Unglued"; Army Ants; Kitchen Ware & Candybars.*

★ First released 1994
★ UK peak chart position: 10
★ USA peak chart position: 1
★ Previous Top 1000 position: 1998 (–): 1994 (–)

636 ELLA AND LOUIS ↑
Ella Fitzgerald and Louis Armstrong

An inspired collaboration, masterminded by producer Norman Granz. Both artists were riding high at this stage in their careers. Granz assembled a stellar quartet of Oscar Peterson (piano), Buddy Rich (drums), Herb Ellis (guitar) and Ray Brown (bass). Equally inspired was the choice of material, with the gruffness of Armstrong's voice blending like magic with Fitzgerald's stunningly silky delivery. Outstanding are Irving Berlin's 'Cheek To Cheek' and 'Isn't This A Lovely Day', and everything else works like a dream, with the gold star going to Ira and George Gershwin's 'They Can't Take That Away From Me'. Gentle and sincere, this is deserving of a place in every home.

》 Tracks: *Can't We Be Friends; Isn't This A Lovely Day; Moonlight In Vermont; They Can't Take That Away From Me; Under A Blanket Of Blue; Tenderly; A Foggy Day; Stars Fell On Alabama; Cheek To Cheek; The Nearness Of You; April In Paris.*

★ First released 1957
★ UK peak chart position: did not chart
★ USA peak chart position: 12
★ Previous Top 1000 position: 1998 (971): 1994 (–)

637 ODESSEY & ORACLE ↓
The Zombies

Reappraised, and now widely accepted as a masterpiece of late 60s pop, this is as timeless as it is faultless. Swirling Mellotron over Colin Blunstone's emotive voice and every track to be cherished, it was a major success in the USA where the Zombies were appreciated. 'Time of The Season' reached near to the top of the charts. The UK gave up on them after 'She's Not There'. Rod Argent went on to great success with Argent, Blunstone became a solo singer, but they have never forgotten their first love. The five Zombies are all alive and well, and are now basking in the much-deserved praise this album now receives.

» Tracks: Care Of Cell 44; A Rose For Emily; Maybe After He's Gone; Beechwood Park; Brief Candles; Hung Up On A Dream; Changes; I Want Her She Wants Me; This Will Be Our Year; Butchers Tale (Western Front 1914); Friends Of Mine; Time Of The Season.

★ First released 1968
★ UK peak chart position: did not chart
★ USA peak chart position: 95
★ Previous Top 1000 position: 1998 (381): 1994 (–)

638 A HARD ROAD ↑
John Mayall and The Bluesbreakers

Following Eric Clapton's departure after the magnificent Bluesbreakers album, John Mayall plugged the gap with Peter Green. Little did anyone know (except Green) that he would almost equal Clapton in the minds of fans and the cognoscenti. Two instrumentals on this 1967 collection, Freddie King's 'The Stumble' and Green's 'The Super-Natural', clearly demonstrate the clean and sparse sound of his Gibson Les Paul. The line-up was completed by bassist John McVie and Aynsley Dunbar on drums. Ex-commercial artist Mayall also designed and painted the cover, which itself is a fine piece of art-work and is probably rotting in some printer's basement, long forgotten. The remastered CD reissue is quite superb.

» Tracks: A Hard Road; It's Over; You Don't Love Me; The Stumble; Another Kinda Love; Hit The Highway; Leaping Christine; Dust My Blues; There's Always Work; The Same Way; The Super-Natural; Top Of The Hill; Someday After A While (You'll Be Sorry), Living Alone.

★ First released 1967
★ UK peak chart position: 10
★ USA peak chart position: did not chart
★ Previous Top 1000 position: 1998 (762): 1994 (576)

639 WITH A LITTLE HELP FROM MY FRIENDS ↓   Joe Cocker

Cocker's debut built on the promise of the title track, a hit single the previous year, which had introduced the world to the singer's astonishing blues rasp of a voice and remains to this day one of the finest Beatles cover versions ever recorded. The vocal pyrotechnics of that song are muted on this album, with Cocker demonstrating his fine handling of more subtle material such as Bob Dylan's 'Just Like A Woman' and 'I Shall Be Released'. Backed by his own seasoned Grease Band and stellar session players Jimmy Page and Steve Winwood, Cocker sings with a soulful intensity that shone all too briefly during his early career.

» Tracks: Feeling Alright; Bye Bye Blackbird; Change In Louise; Marjorine; Just Like A Woman; Do I Still Figure In Your Life; Sandpaper Cadillac; Don't Let Me Be Misunderstood; With A Little Help From My Friends; I Shall Be Released.

★ First Released 1969
★ UK peak chart position: did not chart
★ USA peak chart position: 35
★ Previous Top 1000 position: 1998 (404): 1994 (–)

640 DARE! ↓
The Human League

This is the acceptable face of computerized pop. Four out of six band members were playing nasty synthesizers. Dare! was a commercial one-off and apart from one or two further excellent singles, the Human League never came near to equalling such a collection of instantly recognizable melodies. Their later hits such as 'Mirror Man' and 'Human' were classy songs, but every track on this album will make you dance and sing along. This was one of Martin Rushent's finest productions and it is a pity that the Human League are not on our turntables any more. Maybe the fear of having to give up all those synthesizers for guitars was too scary.

» Tracks: Things That Dreams Are Made Of; Open Your Heart; The Sound Of The Crowd; Darkness; Do Or Die; Get Carter; I Am The Law; Seconds; Love Action (I Believe In Love); Don't You Want Me.

★ First released 1981
★ UK peak chart position: 1
★ USA peak chart position: 3
★ Previous Top 1000 position: 1998 (397): 1994 (395)

641 EQUAL RIGHTS ↑
Peter Tosh

Tosh was the second lieutenant to Bob Marley in the Wailers, and knew that to establish himself, he had to break loose from the greatest band in the history of reggae. *Legalize It* was his first major move, and this follow-up is equally strong; in particular, it contains his superb composition 'Get Up, Stand Up', surely one of the greatest anthems of Jamaican music, and Tosh's personal anthem 'Stepping Razor'. The album's weight is bolstered from the excellent support throughout of Bunny Wailer, and the peerless session men, Sly and Robbie. Tosh's hard-edged protest was curtailed when he was tragically gunned down in 1987.

» Tracks: *Get Up, Stand Up; Downpressor Man; I Am That I Am; Stepping Razor; Equal Rights; African; Jah Guide; Apartheid.*

★ First released 1977
★ UK peak chart position: did not chart
★ USA peak chart position: did not chart
★ Previous Top 1000 position: 1998 (772): 1994 (–)

642 ELLA FITZGERALD SINGS THE RODGERS AND HART SONGBOOK ↑
Ella Fitzgerald

Richard Rodgers' tuneful music and Lorenz Hart's wittily amusing lyrics form a very special part of American popular music. So too does Ella Fitzgerald, and their meeting – under the benign influence of Norman Granz – is a high-water mark in the story of popular singing. The singer's unworldly and ingenuous charm suits the material and transports the listener to times without care; until, that is, the occasional tartness of a Hart lyric reminds us that life is not always a song. Along with the rest of the Songbook series, this is popular vocal music at its best and sets standards never previously attained.

» Tracks: *Have You Met Miss Jones?; You Took Advantage Of Me; Ship Without A Sail; To Keep My Love Alive; Dancing On The Ceiling; The Lady Is A Tramp; With A Song In My Heart; Manhattan; Johnny One Note; I Wish I Were In Love Again; Spring Is Here; It Never Entered My Mind; This Can't Be Love; Thou Swell; My Romance; Where Or When; Little Girl Blue; Give It Back To The Indians; Ten Cents A Dance; There's A Small Hotel; I Don't Know What Time It Was; Everything I've Got; I Could Write A Book; Blue Room; My Funny Valentine; Bewitched; Mountain Greenery; Wait Till You See Her; Lover; Isn't It Romantic?; Here In My Arms; Blue Moon; My Heart Stood Still; I've Got Five Dollars.*

★ First released 1957
★ UK peak chart position: did not chart
★ USA peak chart position: 11
★ Previous Top 1000 position: 1998 (977): 1994 (668)

643 THE GREAT OTIS REDDING SINGS SOUL BALLADS ↑
Otis Redding

Redding epitomized 60s soul, proving equally adept at up-tempo styles and reflective ballads. By devoting an entire album to the latter mode, the singer created a measured, inspirational collection. Burning versions of songs from R&B's past are adapted and infused with elegant intensity, in particular his hypnotic reading of O.V. Wright's 'That's How Strong My Love Is'. 'Mr. Pitiful', co-written with guitarist Steve Cropper, offers Redding a slightly faster perspective without breaking the mood of reflection. Together with *Otis Blue*, *Soul Ballads* is an emotional highpoint in the singer's sadly foreshortened career.

» Tracks: *That's How Strong My Love Is; Chained and Bound; A Woman, A Lover, A Friend; Your One and Only Man; Nothing Can Change This Love; It's Too Late; For Your Precious Love; I Want To Thank You; Come To Me; Home In Your Heart; Keep Your Arms Around Me; Mr. Pitiful.*

★ First released 1965
★ UK peak chart position: 30
★ USA peak chart position: 147
★ Previous Top 1000 position: 1998 (978): 1994 (785)

644 IN MY TRIBE ↓
10,000 Maniacs

Natalie Merchant is one of those writers with an uncanny ability to portray the minutiae of life with pinpoint accuracy and detached humour. The songs on *In My Tribe* cover the difficulty of getting up in the morning ('Like The Weather'), her sister's wedding ('My Sister Rose') and childhood holidays ('Verdi Cries'), as well as relationships, drinking, corporal punishment and soldiering. Merchant writes free-flowing prose songs and performs them impeccably, ably assisted on this record by the other Maniacs and the production of Peter Asher. All slightly off-the-wall, but none the worse for that.

» Tracks: *What's The Matter Here?; Hey Jack Kerouac; Like The Weather; Cherry Tree; Painted Desert; Don't Talk; Peace Train; Gun Shy; My Sister Rose; A Campfire Song; City Of Angels; Verdi Cries.*

★ First released 1987
★ UK peak chart position: did not chart
★ USA peak chart position: 37
★ Previous Top 1000 position: 1998 (330): 1994 (284)

645 MUSIC OF MY MIND ↑
Stevie Wonder

The three albums that followed this hidden gem propelled 'little thunder' into the super league. They sold in millions while this sold in thousands. His dalliance with synclavier and vocoder started here, beautifully introduced on the uplifting opener 'Love Having You Around'. The 8 minute epic 'Superwoman (Where Were You When I Needed You)' is one of his best compositions that leaves the later, better known 'Sir Duke' standing. The track gently weaves for three minutes until a synth break, after which it becomes a different but equally brilliant song. Just as there is no excuse not to own *Talking Book*, no discerning music lover should lack awareness of the quality of this record.

▶ Tracks: *Love Having You Around; Superwoman (Where Were You When I Needed You); I Love Every Little Thing About You; Sweet Little Girl; Happier Than The Morning Sun; Girl Blue; Seems So Long; Keep On Running; Evil.*

★ First released 1972
★ UK peak chart position: did not chart
★ USA peak chart position: 21
★ Previous Top 1000 position: 1998 (–): 1994 (–)

646 WISH ↑
The Cure

Undoubtedly more commercial than previous albums, *Wish* nevertheless represented the Cure doing what they do best, oblivious to prevailing musical trends. Once again, Robert Smith tore out his innards and offered them to the listener (the wrenching and chilling 'Apart'), spitting bile in 'Cut' and effectively evoking the feeling of wretched, helpless drunkenness in 'Open'. Amid the darkness, there is still time for a couple of classic pop songs, particularly the catchy 'Friday I'm In Love', and the customary obsessive love odes. Although frequently dismissed by hardcore Cure fans as too pop-orientated, *Wish* managed to strike a balance between the extremes of utter despair and intoxicating joy.

▶ Tracks: *Open; High; Apart; From The Edge Of The Deep Green Sea; Wendy Time; Doing The Unstuck; Friday I'm In Love; Trust; Letter To Elise; Cut; To Wish Impossible Things; End.*

★ First released 1992
★ UK peak position: 1
★ USA peak position: 2
★ Previous Top 1000 position: 1998 (981): 1994 (–)

647 SMASH ↑
Offspring

When America rediscovered punk rock in the early 90s, Offspring and Green Day were the two most obvious beneficiaries. Nostalgics they might have been, but of the two bands the Offspring always sounded more authentic, truer to the original spirit. *Smash* has some terrific, high-velocity/melodic songs. After the spoken-word pastiche 'Time To Relax', the album hits its stride with 'Nitro (Youth Energy)', a kinetic trad punk slammer with Dexter Holland doing a fearfully good imitation of the Damned's Dave Vanian. The run of songs from 'Something To Believe In' (old-style hardcore), 'Come Out and Play' (featuring cute work by Noodles) and 'Self Esteem' is pure punk rock Valhalla.

▶ Tracks: *Time To Relax; Nitro (Youth Energy); Bad Habit; Gotta Get Away; Genocide; Something To Believe In; Come Out and Play; Self Esteem; It'll Be A Long Time; Killboy Powerhead; What Happened To You?; So Alone; Not The One; Smash.*

★ First released 1994
★ UK peak chart position: 21
★ USA peak chart position: 4
★ Previous Top 1000 position: 1998 (945): 1994 (–)

648 HOLLAND ↓
The Beach Boys

Having finally rid themselves of a dated stripe-shirt image with the masterful *Surf's Up*, the Beach Boys continued the process with this ambitious album. The entire group had decamped to the Nederlands to record much of its content, a decision adding an emotional fission to its 'California Saga' trilogy. Although Brian Wilson's contribution was limited to two excellent songs, siblings Dennis and Carl rose to the occasion, with the latter's particularly impressive 'Trader'. The group's harmonies remain as distinctive as ever, while two recent additions to the line-up, Blondie Chaplin and Ricky Fataar, increased the vocal range and added new instrumental muscle. This became their best-selling album for six years, and prepared the way for the Beach Boys' 70s comeback.

▶ Tracks: *Sail On Sailor; Steamboat; California Saga: Big Sur, The Beaks Of Eagles, California; Trader; Leaving This Town; Only With You; Funky Pretty; Mount Vernon and Fairway (A Fairy Tale).*

★ First released 1973
★ UK peak chart position: 20
★ USA peak chart position: 36
★ Previous Top 1000 position: 1998 (417): 1994 (365)

649 BERT JANSCH ↑
Bert Jansch

The enigmatic Jansch was the figurehead of the British 60s folk movement. An excellent composer and influential guitarist, he brought an earthy, blues-based perspective to the genre which took it out of the traditional circuit without sacrificing its strengths to commerciality. This album is little short of breathtaking. Jansch combines an arresting technique, as displayed on Davey Graham's 'Angie', with a gift for graphic lyricism, chillingly exhibited on 'Needle Of Death'. Artists as diverse as Jimmy Page and Donovan (who recorded 'Do You Hear Me Now?') cited Jansch as an influence. *Bert Jansch* proves why.

》 Tracks: *Strolling Down The Highway; Smokey River; Oh How Your Love Is Strong; I Have No Time; Finches; Rambling's Gonna Be The Death Of Me; Veronica; Needle Of Death; Do You Hear Me Now?; Alice's Wonderland; Running From Home; Courting Blues; Casbah; Dreams Of Love; Angie.*

★ First released 1965
★ UK peak chart position: did not chart
★ USA peak chart position: did not chart
★ Previous Top 1000 position: 1998 (956): 1994 (460)

650 THE SLIM SHADY LP ↑
Eminem

Modern day white boy rap artist Eminem makes a plausible stab at sounding convincing. Once you get your head around the fact that this ain't no gangsta out of Compton, and therefore the similar social and political issues addressed by Eminem are the same all over, it is a highly packed album. The ironic humour never once clouds the importance of this artist. Don't be fooled by the gratuitous swearing either, Eminem's partnership with Dr Dre and Marky and Jeff Bass has plenty of substance and raises some disturbing social and moral issues. Mostly it is compelling listening, very funny and a highly entertaining record. Make sure to get your ear into it, it deserves your concentration.

》 Tracks: *Public Service Announcement; My Name Is; Guilty Conscience; Brain Damage; Paul; If I Had; 97' Bonnie & Clyde; Bitch; Role Model; Lounge; My Fault; Ken Kaniff; Cum On Everybody; Rock Bottom; Just Don't Give A Fuck; Soap; As The World Turns; I'm Shady; Bad Meets Evil; Still Don't Give A Fuck.*

★ First released 1999
★ UK peak chart position: 12
★ USA peak chart position: 2
★ Previous Top 1000 position: 1998 (–): 1994 (–)

651 GREETINGS FROM ASBURY PARK N.J. ↑ Bruce Springsteen

Compared to the mighty *Born To Run* this is a pretty weak album, but even in the light of Springsteen's remarkable contribution to popular music it remains a credible debut. In re-appraising this album it becomes even more obvious than at the time that the flat production and limp arrangements are to blame, rather than the actual quality of the material. This probably explains why Manfred Mann was able to score a big hit with a glossed up cover version of 'Blinded By The Light'. Those who have seen Springsteen perform these songs live know exactly how good they can sound performed properly. For Springsteen completists only.

》 Tracks: *Blinded By The Light; Growin' Up; Mary Queen Of Arkansas; Does This Bus Stop At 82nd Street?; Lost In The Flood; The Angel; For You; Spirit In The Night; It's Hard To Be A Saint In The City.*

★ First released 1973
★ UK peak chart position: 41
★ USA peak chart position: 60
★ Previous Top 1000 position: 1998 (–): 1994 (–)

652 TIME OUT OF MIND ↑
Bob Dylan

Few would have put money on Sir Bob producing another classic at this stage in his career. Yet here it is, a brilliant, emotive, funereal record containing some of his finest material for many, many years. This is Dylan now, not a rehash of his timeless 60s classics – old and wise, disenchanted and forlorn, and, at various moments, incredibly sad. Getting straight to the point Dylan tells us on the opening 'Love Sick' how much he is sick of romance, but by 'Make You Feel My Love' he is stating 'no, there's nothing that I wouldn't do, to make you feel my love'. There he goes again, wonderfully erratic.

》 Tracks: *Love Sick; Dirt Road Blues; Standing In The Doorway; Million Miles; Tryin' To Get To Heaven; 'Til I Fell In Love With You; Not Dark Yet; Cold Irons Bound; Make You Feel My Love; Can't Wait; Highlands.*

★ First released 1997
★ UK peak chart position: 10
★ USA peak chart position: 80
★ Previous Top 1000 position: 1998 (–): 1994 (–)

653 THE LA'S ↓
The La's

The perpetually disenchanted Liverpudlians grumbled their way through most of their interviews. Scathingly perfectionist, they dismissed most of their output with a metaphorical wave of the hand, compliments bounced off them in all directions, but for the La's, it was never enough. It is hard now to see why they were so dissatisfied; *The La's* is a graceful, sweeping and rather grand pop record, utterly charming and filled with a meek beauty typified by the wonderful 'There She Goes' single, the sincere 'I Can't Sleep' and the shining 'Timeless Melody'. Great moments with only a couple of duds.

» Tracks: *Son Of A Gun; I Can't Sleep; Timeless Melody; Liberty Ship; There She Goes; Doledrum; Feeling; Way Out; IOU; Freedom Song; Failure; Lookin' Glass.*

★ First released 1990
★ UK peak chart position: 30
★ USA peak chart position: 196
★ Previous Top 1000 position: 1998 (485): 1994 (851)

654 THE BOY WITH THE ARAB STRAP ↑
Belle and Sebastian

More refined and confident than the excellent *If You're Feeling Sinister*, but still sounding like a delightful happy Nick Drake. This album won a BRIT Award in 1999 against all odds. Many people shook their heads as the award was announced not because Belle and Sebastian did not deserve it, but because few people in the audience had heard of them. Great credit to all concerned at Jeepster Recordings for sneaking out this minor gem, which allows worthy songs such as 'Sleep The Clock Around' to be appreciated by a mass audience usually fed on a diet of Cher. Lo-fi pop such as this is the perfect antidote.

» Tracks: *It Could Have Been A Brilliant Career; Sleep The Clock Around; Is It Wicked Not To Care?; Ease Your Feet In The Sea; A Summer Wasting; Seymour Stein; A Space Boy Dream; Dirty Dream Number Two; The Boy With The Arab Strap; Chickfactor; Simple Things; The Rollercoaster Ride.*

★ First released 1998
★ UK peak chart position: 12
★ USA peak chart position: did not chart
★ Previous Top 1000 position: 1998 (–): 1994 (–)

655 ONE FOR ALL ↑
Brand Nubian

From the Bronx, New York, and led by Grand Puba Maxwell, Brand Nubian's debut album was as cool and classy as anything in the genre. Backed by Lord Jamar, Sadat X and DJ Alamo, Puba kicked out reams of Muslim-influenced thinking, backed by steals from some of the great moments of soul music. Despite the creed of the Five Percent Nation, which was so manifest within its grooves, it was by no means humourless (highlighted by name-checks for people such as Engelbert Humperdinck), while samples of James Brown and Roy Ayers spiced up the backing tracks. In 1991 Puba left to go solo, taking DJ Alamo with him, and although Brand Nubian have persevered with a new line-up and recorded two well-received albums, they have yet to match this achievement.

» Tracks: *All For One; Feels So Good; Concerto In X Minor; Ragtime; To The Right; Dance To My Ministry; Drop The Bomb; Wake Up; Step To The Rear; Slow Down; Try To Do Me; Who Can Get Busy Like This Man; Grand Puba, Positive and LG; Brand Nubian; Wake Up; Dedication.*

★ First released 1991
★ UK peak chart position: did not chart
★ USA peak chart position: 130
★ Previous Top 1000 position: 1998 (791): 1994 (586)

656 NEW JERSEY ↑
Bon Jovi

The tremendous 'Lay Your Hands On Me' comes in like an anthemic encore, a bold move with which to open their fourth album. Bon Jovi embraced the hard rock fraternity but seemed to keep from falling into the debauchery that almost ruined Aerosmith. Jon Bon Jovi has looked after his body too well, and Richie Sambora was too interested in his status as the first real guitar hero since the days of Jimmy Page, Ritchie Blackmore and Jeff Beck. At the time *New Jersey* delivered everything the fans wanted, and a dozen years later it is still a highly popular album in their back catalogue. Shortly after the release of this album they took a break, adding fuel to the rumours that Jon would become a full-time actor, solo singer and all round clean living sex-god.

» Tracks: *Lay Your Hands On Me; Bad Medicine; Born To Be My Baby; Living In Sin; Blood On Blood; Homebound Train; Wild Is The Wind; Ride Cowboy Ride; Stick To Your Guns; I'll Be There For You; 99 In The Shade; Love For Sale.*

★ First released 1988
★ UK peak chart position: 1
★ USA peak chart position: 1
★ Previous Top 1000 position: 1998 (–): 1994 (–)

657 PHAEDRA ↑
Tangerine Dream

Very much at the forefront of Virgin Records' progressive/ krautrock catalogue in the first half of the 70s, Tangerine Dream have maintained a loyal following for many years. Unfashionable with the masses for so long they have now enjoyed a rebirth thanks to the popularity of contemporary ambient dance music. Although the four tracks should be listened to as a whole, particularly memorable is 'Mysterious Semblance At The Stand Of Nightmares'. To use the word challenging is usually a smokescreen for a subtle put down, so I will use the term beautifully challenging. Alternatively, if you like the tape loop intro to the Who's 'Baba O'Riley' then this is your bowl of satsumas.

» Tracks: *Phaedra; Mysterious Semblance At The Stand Of Nightmares; Movements Of A Visionary; Sequent C.*

★ First released 1974
★ UK peak chart position: 15
★ USA peak chart position: 196
★ Previous Top 1000 position: 1998 (–): 1994 (–)

658 SPIRIT ↑
Spirit

How cool their own logo lettering looked, how the composite head cover stood out from the crowd of badly painted, dayglo, rubbish album sleeves in the late 60s. Spirit were just a bit more classy, not just because they were jazzy and had a drummer who was in his 40s, but because they had some vision of how to fuse psych/jazz/rock. The use of strings and rock guitar is quite breathtaking; Randy California was a precocious guitarist and Jay Ferguson's lead vocals are immaculate. The CD reissue has four bonus tracks. As the opening track, 'Fresh Garbage', states, you should 'look beneath your lid some morning'.

» Tracks: *Fresh Garbage; Uncle Jack; Mechanical World; Taurus; Girl In Your Eye; Straight Arrow; Topanga Windows; Gramophone Man; Water Woman; The Great Canyon Fire In General; Elijah; Veruska; Free Spirit; If I Had A Woman; Elijah (alternate take).*

★ First released 1968
★ UK peak chart position: did not chart
★ USA peak chart position: 31
★ Previous Top 1000 position: 1998 (985): 1994 (–)

659 I STILL BELIEVE IN YOU ↑
Vince Gill

Gill wrote this album with eight songwriting partners, yet it still has a consistency and fluidity of its own. This is a truly great collection of love songs performed by a country singer with a beautiful tenor voice. Every track could make you weep but extra tissues are needed for 'One More Last Chance', 'I Still Believe In You' and 'Tryin' To Get Over You'. The care and attention lavished on this album is evident in every note, where nothing has been left to chance. The excellent musicians include Delbert McClinton, who played harmonica on Bruce Channel's 'Hey! Baby'.

» Tracks: *Don't Let Our Love Start Slipping Away; No Future In The Past; Nothing Like A Woman; Tryin' To Get Over You; Say Hello; One More Last Chance; Under These Conditions; Pretty Words; Love Never Broke Anyone's Heart; I Still Believe In You.*

★ First released 1992
★ UK peak chart position: did not chart
★ USA peak chart position: 10
★ Previous Top 1000 position: 1998 (986): 1994 (836)

660 BLOOD, SWEAT & TEARS ↓
Blood, Sweat and Tears

Their finest moment and a testimony to the best of the jazz/rock movement. Created by the legendary Al Kooper, the band was one of the major attractions throughout 1969. The album is bold, brassy and adventurous. Interpretations of Eric Satie music are followed by Traffic's 'Smiling Phases'. Hit singles galore were culled from this record – 'Spinning Wheel', 'You've Made Me So Very Happy', and 'And When I Die', not to forget a superb rendition of Billie Holiday's 'God Bless The Child'. And where is the superb beefy voice of David Clayton-Thomas to be found today?

» Tracks: *Variations On A Theme By Eric Satie (1st & 2nd Movement); Smiling Phases; Sometimes In Winter; More and More; And When I Die; God Bless The Child; Spinning Wheel; You've Made Me So Very Happy/Blues Part II; Variations On A Theme By Eric Satie (1st Movement).*

★ First released 1969
★ UK peak chart position: 15
★ USA peak chart position: 1
★ Previous Top 1000 position: 1998 (248): 1994 (359)

661 STRICTLY PERSONAL ↓
Captain Beefheart and His Magic Band

Raw yet accessible, like no other Captain Beefheart album. It is his real blues album, and the closest any white boy came to the Mississippi without falling in. 'Gimme Dat Harp Boy' is pure Howlin' Wolf, with Beefheart's voice and harmonica virtually cloning the Wolf. As usual there is great lyrical malarky at work, especially on 'Ah Feel Like Ahcid' and the ludicrous but brilliant 'Beatle Bones 'N' Smokin' Stones'. Much debate ensued about the merits of the phased or unphased versions; the former has finally won the day. This album should have been a commercial monster but it merely highlighted the sad fact that the world was not ready for such genius.

▶▶ Tracks: *Ah Feel Like Ahcid; Safe As Milk; Trust Us; Son Of Mirror Man – Mere Man; On Tomorrow; Beatle Bones 'N' Smokin' Stones; Gimme Dat Harp Boy; Kandy Korn.*

★ First released 1968
★ UK peak chart position: did not chart
★ USA peak chart position: did not chart
★ Previous Top 1000 position: 1998 (596): 1994 (–)

662 FRIENDS ↑
The Beach Boys

Before *Pet Sounds* became so universally loved Brian Wilson always said that his favourite Beach Boys album was this one. This is the shortest album of their career, and very much a series of vignettes rather than songs. Nonetheless, it is a sheer delight, and one that the High Llamas tried to emulate with *Hawaii*. Dennis Wilson became noticed as a songwriter of note with 'Little Bird' and the beautiful 'Be Still'. Brian sang lead on 'Busy Doin' Nothin'', the most accurate song of his life in which he actually directs you to his home. *Friends* passed a lot of people by, because it is so understated.

▶▶ Tracks: *Meant For You; Friends; Wake The World; Be Here In The Morning; When A Man Needs A Woman; Passing By; Anna Lee, The Healer; Little Bird; Be Still; Busy Doin' Nothin'; Diamond Head; Transcendental Meditation.*

★ First released 1968
★ UK peak chart position: 13
★ USA peak chart position: 126
★ Previous Top 1000 position: 1998 (987): 1994 (–)

663 THE COMPLETE LIVE AT THE PLUGGED NICKEL 1965 ↑
Miles Davis

With Wayne Shorter on sax, Herbie Hancock on piano, Ron Carter on bass and Tony Williams (just 20 years old) on drums, this is regarded as Miles Davis's most creative line-up. *Plugged Nickel* covers seven sets over two days and is an important historical document, not least in demonstrating how the chemistry between five strong musical personalities changes between sessions. To those unable to see him live, Davis' studio albums created a relatively mainstream impression. It was only when this live material started to emerge in 1975 that his groundbreaking work in applying chromatic techniques to classic compositions became widely appreciated.

▶▶ Tracks: i) *If I Were A Bell; Stella By Starlight; Walkin'; I Fall In Love Too Easily; The Theme* ii) *My Funny Valentine; Four; When I Fall In Love* iii) *Agitation; 'Round About Midnight; Milestones; The Theme* iv) *All Of You; Oleo; I Fall In Love Too Easily; No Blues; I Thought About You; The Theme* v) *If I Were A Bell; Stella By Starlight; Walkin'; I Fall In Love Too Easily; The Theme* vi) *All Of You; Agitation; My Funny Valentine; On Green Dolphin Street; So What; The Theme* vii) *When I Fall In Love; Milestones; Autumn Leaves; I Fall In Love Too Easily; No Blues; The Theme* viii) *Stella By Starlight; All Blues; Yesterdays; The Theme.*

★ First Released 1997
★ UK peak chart position: did not chart
★ USA peak chart position: chart
★ Previous Top 1000 position: 1998 (990): 1994 (–)

664 LOVE CHRONICLES ↑
Al Stewart

Al Stewart was part of the late 60s bedsitter folkies who went electric scene. John Martyn, Ralph McTell and Michael Chapman are others who spring to mind. Stewart was a credible songwriter with a hint of a camp lisp in his voice. Women loved it, men clearly felt threatened by it. Years before 'Year of The Cat', Stewart recorded his mammoth track 'Love Chronicles', a sort of up-tempo 'Sad Eyed Lady Of The Lowlands'. Even better was the woeful tale of a young girl falling into prostitution through a series of unlucky circumstances – 'Old Compton Street Blues' is a superb song, well worth your attention as 'the circle it turns and turns and turns so mad little girl'.

▶▶ Tracks: *In Brooklyn; Old Compton Street Blues; Ballad Of Mary Foster; Life and Life Only; You Should Have Listened To Al; Love Chronicles.*

★ First released 1969
★ UK peak chart position: did not chart
★ USA peak chart position: did not chart
★ Previous Top 1000 position: 1998 (942): 1994 (–)

665 RUMOR AND SIGH ↑
Richard Thompson

Thompson's albums with Mitchell Froom in the producer's chair tended to be hit-or-miss affairs, and at times on *Rumor and Sigh* the singer's distinctive English vocal inflections and biting guitarwork are lost in Froom's kitchen-sink approach to production. Part of Froom's problem must have been coping with Thompson's own wild stylistic approach, ranging from acoustic ballads ('1952 Vincent Black Lightning'), through radio-friendly tunes ('Keep Your Distance', 'You Dream Too Much'), to demonic rock 'n' rollers ('I Feel So Good', 'Mother Knows Best'). *Rumor and Sigh* also showcases Thompson's lyrical extremes, from the intense ('I Misunderstood', 'Mystery Wind') to the throwaway ('Don't Sit On My Jimmy Shands', 'Psycho Street'), via the wonderful narrative approach of '1952 Vincent Black Lightning'.

❱❱ Tracks: *Read About Love; I Feel So Good; I Misunderstood; Grey Walls; You Dream Too Much; Why Must I Plead; 1952 Vincent Black Lightning; Backlash Love Affair; Mystery Wind; Don't Sit On My Jimmy Shands; Keep Your Distance; Mother Knows Best; God Loves A Drunk; Psycho Street.*

★ First Released 1991
★ UK peak chart position: 32
★ USA peak chart position: did not chart
★ Previous Top 1000 position: 1998 (992): 1994 (–)

666 BEAUTIFUL FREAK ↑
Eels

Even though lead singer 'E' does not exactly look like your typical rock star he does have a highly original and attractive voice. Eels are one of the most interesting alternative rock bands to come out of America in recent times, and this debut album turned a few heads when it was released. Their eclectic style is heard to great effect on the stop/start structure of 'Susan's House' and the glorious middle eight of 'Novocaine For The Soul', songs which lull the listener into a relaxed state before bursting into glorious life. 'E' clearly has a lot on his mind for such a young man, and the songs are all the better for his honesty.

❱❱ Tracks: *Novocaine For The Soul; Susan's House; Rags To Rags; Beautiful Freak; Not Ready Yet; My Beloved Monster; Flower; Guest List; Mental; Spunky; Your Lucky Day In Hell; Manchild.*

★ First released 1996
★ UK peak chart position: 5
★ USA peak chart position: 124
★ Previous Top 1000 position: 1998 (–): 1994 (–)

667 TELL MAMA ↑
Etta James

Having already been an established leading soul singer for 13 years and having 18 R&B hits to her name, in 1967 Etta James went to record in Alabama at the legendary Muscle Shoals studio. The result was her most accomplished album, on which her voice had been mixed to perfection, allowing her to sound strong on the previously distorted high notes. James was rightly seen in a different light as one of the great soul voices of all time as she belted out powerful tracks such as 'The Love Of My Man' and 'Watch Dog'. Her slower numbers were equally arresting, including the wonderful 'I'd Rather Go Blind'.

❱❱ Tracks: *Tell Mama; I'd Rather Go Blind; Watch Dog; The Love Of My Man; I'm Gonna Take What He's Got; The Same Rope; Security; Steal Away; My Mother-In-Law; Don't Lose Your Good Thing; It Hurts Me So Much; Just A Little Bit.*

★ First released 1968
★ UK peak chart position: did not chart
★ USA peak chart position: 82
★ Previous Top 1000 position: 1998 (701): 1994 (473)

668 ON THE THRESHOLD OF A DREAM ↑ Moody Blues

If you disregard the precious sleeve-note introduction written by friend of the band Lionel Bart, and ignore the spoken-word 'therefore I am' twaddle at the beginning, this is arguably their best album. The band are oozing ideas and the contrast between Ray Thomas' songs and Justin Hayward's is as refreshing as the difference between Mike Pinder's 'So Deep Within You' and John Lodge's 'To Share Our Love'. The last segment is the album's peak; Pinder's sensitive 'Have You Heard' and 'The Voyage' sum up the whole album. Never had the Mellotron been used so well and it is a great pity they became so unfashionable.

❱❱ Tracks: *In The Beginning; Lovely To See You; Dear Diary; Send Me No Wine; To Share Our Love; So Deep Within You; Never Comes The Day; Lazy Day; Are You Sitting Comfortably; The Dream; Have You Heard Part 1; The Voyage; Have You Heard Part 2.*

★ First released 1969
★ UK peak chart position: 1
★ USA peak chart position: 20
★ Previous Top 1000 position: 1998 (923): 1994 (–)

669 OFFRAMP ↑
The Pat Metheny Group

Opening with some beautiful synclavier and Lyle Mays' exquisite soaring synths on 'Barcarole', this is an atmosphere album. It moves from delicacy to beauty and is arguably the most complete album of his incredible career. The delightful 'James' (a tribute to James Taylor, listen to the guitar inflections) is complemented by the awesome 'Au Lait'; and if that was not enough, this contains surely Pat Metheny's finest moment, 'Are You Going With Me', a song that builds and builds over the most fabulous rhythm, and even after nearly nine minutes it leaves you begging for more. A stunning piece of music that is neither jazz nor rock.

» Tracks: *Barcarole; Are You Going With Me?; Au Lait; Eighteen; Offramp; James; The Bat Part II.*

★ First released 1983
★ UK peak chart position: did not chart
★ USA peak chart position: 50
★ Previous Top 1000 position: 1998 (993): 1994 (565)

670 THE SOUTHERN HARMONY AND MUSICAL COMPANION ↑
The Black Crowes

Given the sub- Rolling Stones boogie of their debut, *Shake Your Money Maker*, *The Southern Harmony* came as a quietly accomplished body of work, apparently way beyond their relative youth and experience. The *Exile On Main Street* references were still intact, but the predominant swagger and sashay had been abandoned in favour of a soulful interpretation of their roots, rather than a parody of their influences. Chris Robinson's Jagger pastiche was replaced by a more gutsy, honest strut, while brother Rich plays with an aplomb and spirit that struck darkly at the heart of their songs.

» Tracks: *Sting Me; Remedy; Thorn In My Pride; Bad Luck Blue Eyes Goodbye; Sometimes Salvation; Hotel Illness; Black Moon Creepin'; No Speak, No Slave; My Morning Song; Time Will Tell.*

★ First released 1992
★ UK peak chart position: did not chart
★ USA peak chart position: 1
★ Previous Top 1000 position: 1998 (935): 1994 (404)

671 I'VE BEEN EXPECTING YOU
↑ Robbie Williams

Irresistible (even blokes own up to thinking he's great), cheeky, ambitious with oodles of new-found talent – and to think Williams was the one dancing next to Gary Barlow in Take That! This, his second album, contains enough quality material to last him for years. 'Strong' has a great opening line, referring to his post Take That binge: 'my breath smells of a thousand fags, and when I get drunk I dance like my dad'. Luckily for the public Williams cleaned his act up and decided to pay attention to his career. Other stars are the carefully timed 'Millennium' single and a tremendous cover version of Karl Wallinger's 'She's The One'.

» Tracks: *Strong; No Regrets; Millennium; Phoenix From The Flames; Win Some Lose Some; Grace; Jesus In A Camper Van; Heaven From Here; Karma Killer; She's The One; Man Machine; These Dreams.*

★ First released 1998
★ UK peak chart position: 1
★ USA peak chart position: did not chart
★ Previous Top 1000 position: 1998 (–): 1994 (–)

672 ANOTHER GREEN WORLD ↑
Brian Eno

The brilliant Mr. Brian Peter George St. Baptiste de la Salle Eno has become better known for his King Midas production touch on countless recordings by other artists. In between playing with the original Roxy Music and production work, however, he made a number of beautifully crafted progressive albums that remain a joy to listen to. *Here Come The Warm Jets* and this are probably the two essential items to own. The title track is well known, having been used for many years as the theme for BBC Television's arts programme *Arena*. Supporting musicians include John Cale, the great underrated bassist Percy Jones and Phil Collins, happy here just to play. It is mostly easy going and gentle, more tea on the lawn than bottled water in a nightclub.

» Tracks: *Sky Saw; Over Fire Island; St. Elmo's Fire; In Dark Trees; The Big Ship; I'll Come Running; Another Green World; Sombre Reptiles; Little Fishes; Golden Hours; Becalmed; Zawinul/Lava; Everything Merges With The Night; Spirits Drifting.*

★ First released 1975
★ UK peak chart position: did not chart
★ USA peak chart position: did not chart
★ Previous Top 1000 position: 1998 (–): 1994 (–)

673 JAILBREAK ↑
Thin Lizzy

Not true heavy metal perpetrators, more out-and-out rockers, with a feeling for pop. The late Phil Lynott has a growing core of younger fans, as word is passed down that even though he had his demons he was an outstanding performer. This is their best studio album and it contains two classics; 'The Boys Are Back In Town' and the title track. Both spit and crackle, bass and lead guitar bursting out of the speaker at loud volume, and throughout, the gentle, laconic voice of Lynott delivers his poetry. Don't allow his death to see Thin Lizzy fade from the memory.

▶▶ Tracks: *Angel From The Coast; The Boys Are Back In Town; Cowboy Song; Emerald; Fight Or Jail; Jailbreak; Romeo and The Lonely Girl; Running Back; Warriors.*

★ First released 1976
★ UK peak chart position: 10
★ USA peak chart position: 18
★ Previous Top 1000 position: 1998 (913): 1994 (386)

674 AOXOMOXOA ↑
Grateful Dead

For a Grateful Dead album to contain so many of their regular stage numbers, it is surprising that it has sold so poorly over the years – magnificent classics such as 'St Stephen', where you can feast your ears on Phil Lesh's incredible bass playing, or the early Robert Hunter tales by listening to the story of 'Dupree's Diamond Blues'. 'High ho the carrion crow fol de roll de riddle', sings Jerry Garcia on 'Mountains Of The Moon' (hardly acid rockers) and you can feel the tremendous build-up as they start 'Cosmic Charlie', with Bob Weir and Garcia meshing guitars. You can be forgiven for skipping 'What Becomes Of The Baby', however; most people do.

▶▶ Tracks: *St Stephen; Dupree's Diamond Blues; Rosemary; Doin' That Rag; Mountains Of The Moon; China Cat Sunflower; What's Becomes Of The Baby; Cosmic Charlie.*

★ First released 1969
★ UK peak chart position: did not chart
★ USA peak chart position: 73
★ Previous Top 1000 position: 1998 (994): 1994 (–)

675 154 ↑
Wire

A highly creative band who democratically shared songwriting duties on a superb series of albums, of which *154* is one of the best. Wire were always a bit too clever to be considered part of the brash world of punk, and as a result were treated with caution by diehards who wanted lots of gob and minimal chords. Twenty years on this album, here in expanded form, remains a rich and imaginative listening experience. All of which begs the question; why were Wire not as successful as the Stranglers or the other creative punk bands? If you missed out on them first time around, like I did, I urge you to investigate this, *Chairs Missing* and *Pink Flag* with some degree of urgency.

▶▶ Tracks: *I Should Have Known Better; Two People In A Room; The 15th; The Other Window; Single K.O.; A Touching Display; On Returning; A Mutual Friend; Blessed State; Once Is Enough; Map Ref. 41ºN 93ºW; Indirect Enquiries; 40 Versions; Song I; Get Down (Parts I & II); Let's Panic Later; Small Electric Piece.*

★ First released 1979 ★ UK peak chart position: 39
★ USA peak chart position: did not chart
★ Previous Top 1000 position: 1998 (–): 1994 (–)

676 BRAVE NEW WORLD ↑
The Steve Miller Band

Although Steve Miller no longer sells in vast quantities he does have a massive back catalogue of high-quality albums. This was during his first musical peak and followed the landmark *Sailor*. There are no weak tracks, and many are now classics. He was able to move from anthemic pop with 'Kow Kow' (who had himself a pet alligator) to the acoustic 12-string simplicity of 'Seasons'. 'My Dark Hour' features an illicit cameo from Paul McCartney, a favour Miller returned nearly 30 years later on *Flaming Pie*. A memorable, foot-tapping, happy album, with some great, short, slick guitar breaks. It is a pity the space cowboy lost his knack.

▶▶ Tracks: *Brave New World; Celebration Song; Can't You Hear Your Daddy's Heartbeat; Got Love 'Cause You Need It; Kow Kow; Seasons; Space Cowboy; LT's Midnight Dream; My Dark Hour.*

★ First released 1969
★ UK peak chart position: did not chart
★ USA peak chart position: 22
★ Previous Top 1000 position: 1998 (937): 1994 (–)

677 JOHNNY CASH AT FOLSOM PRISON ↓ Johnny Cash

Appearing at Glastonbury in 1994, it was clear that Johnny Cash has become an icon for the current generation. One reason is his alleged background of crime, although, in reality, Cash has only spent three days in jail – one of them for picking flowers. He is more like an old-time preacher, often finding his audiences in prisons. This classic album, which he had wanted to make for some years, brought out the best in his music. There is the gallows humour of 'Twenty-Five Minutes To Go', the whimsy of 'Dirty Old Egg-Sucking Dog', a song written by one of the prisoners, 'Greystone Chapel', and a duet of 'Jackson' with June Carter. But the real star of the record is the audience: Johnny Cash has recorded in other prisons, but this album is special.

➤ Tracks: *Folsom Prison Blues; Dark As A Dungeon; I Still Miss Someone; Cocaine Blues; 25 Minutes To Go; Orange Blossom Special; The Long Black Veil; Send A Picture Of Mother; The Wall; Dirty Old Egg-Sucking Dog; Flushed From The Bathroom Of Your Heart; Jackson; Give My Love To Rose; I Got Stripes; Green Green Grass Of Home; Greystone Chapel.*

★ First released 1968
★ UK peak chart position: 8
★ USA peak chart position: 13
★ Previous Top 1000 position: 1998 (535): 1994 (604)

678 EAGLES ↑ The Eagles

Their least commercially successful record still retains qualities that make it one of their best. Their classic reading of Jackson Browne and Glenn Frey's 'Take It Easy' never drags, and Henley's sex-charged vocal on 'Witchy Woman' still sounds convincing. Other delights are Leadon and Gene Clark's 'Train Leaves Here This Morning' and Jack Tempchin's memorable 'Peaceful Easy Feeling'. This was rock/country, as opposed to Poco and the Flying Burritos' country/rock. Nothing would be as simple and uncomplicated for the Eagles ever again, and this album retains a great charm and innocence that soon disappeared from their career. A very impressive debut album.

➤ Tracks: *Take It Easy; Witchy Woman; Chug All Night; Most Of Us Are Sad; Nightingale; Train Leaves Here This Morning; Take The Devil; Earlybird; Peaceful Easy Feeling; Tryin'.*

★ First released 1972
★ UK peak chart position: did not chart
★ USA peak chart position: 22
★ Previous Top 1000 position: 1998 (889): 1994 (–)

679 GOT MY MOJO WORKIN' ↑ Jimmy Smith

Nobody, but nobody, has ever made the Hammond organ work so hard as Jimmy Smith. He is the undisputed king of jazz organ, and defined the sound of 'soul jazz' throughout the 60s. His work with arrangers such as *Oliver Nelson* represents the commercial peak of his long career. As with many other albums on the Verve Records label, this record tucked under your arm automatically awarded you, the owner, with cool. Smooth cover versions of 'C-Jam Blues', '(I Can't Get No) Satisfaction' and 'Hi-Heel Sneakers' are fascinating re-interpretations. The CD reissue has the complete *Hoochie Coochie Man* as an excellent bonus. By the way 60s organ jazz is cool again.

➤ Tracks: *Hi-Heel Sneakers; (I Can't Get No) Satisfaction; 1-2-3; Mustard Greens; Got My Mojo Workin'; Johnny Come Lately; C-Jam Blues; Hobson's Hop; I'm Your Hoochie Coochie Man; One Mint Julep; Ain't That Just Like A Woman; Boom Boom; Blues and The Abstract Truth; TNT; (I Can't Get No) Satisfaction (alternate take).*

★ First released 1966
★ UK peak chart position: 19
★ USA peak chart position: 28
★ Previous Top 1000 position: 1998 (1000): 1994 (–)

680 EAT A PEACH ↑ The Allman Brothers Band

This was started before but completed after the tragic motorcycle accident that killed the band's immensely talented guitarist, Duane Allman. Ironically it shot into the US Top 5, even though from an artistic point of view it did not match the effortless flow of the previous live album documenting their Fillmore concerts. That said, there have only really been two top-notch jamming bands in the world and the Allmans are one of them (the other being the Grateful Dead, of course). The thirty minute-plus 'Mountain Jam', featuring Duane's slide guitar, is exactly what the fans wanted. In fact all the live tracks work a lot better than the insipid studio recordings.

➤ Tracks: *Ain't Wastin' Time No More; Les Brers In A Minor; Melissa; Mountain Jam; One Way Out; Trouble No More; Stand Back; Blue Sky; Little Martha.*

★ First released 1972
★ UK peak chart position: did not chart
★ USA peak chart position: 4
★ Previous Top 1000 position: 1998 (–): 1994 (–)

681 DUKE ↑
Genesis

Genesis still have a credibility problem which at present just trails the present standing of ex-drummer/vocalist Phil Collins. *Duke* was the record that shed their 'heavy prog' image and saw them beginning to loosen up and write some inventive pop songs. Collins had grown in confidence following Peter Gabriel's departure, and had stepped out from behind the drums. The band immediately became much tighter musically. In addition to the hit singles 'Duchess', the buoyant 'Turn It On Again', there is the painful honesty of 'Misunderstanding' and 'Please Don't Ask'. There have been many bigger Genesis albums, but none have anywhere near as much heart.

❯❯ Tracks: *Behind The Lines; Duchess; Guide Vocal; Man Of Our Times; Misunderstanding; Heathaze; Turn It On Again; Alone Tonight; Cul-de-sac; Please Don't Ask; Duke's Travels; Duke's End.*

★ First released 1980
★ UK peak chart position: 1
★ USA peak chart position: 11
★ Previous Top 1000 position: 1998 (870): 1994 (347)

682 EVE6 ↑
Eve6

Thicker than Green Day, thinner than Goo Goo Dolls, but equally appealing Eve6 burst onto college radio after a successful tour with Third Eye Blind. This debut album subsequently became a substantial hit on the national *Billboard* chart. Clever lyrics are sprinkled throughout, while the catchy 'Inside Out' manages to rhyme 'gotten stale' with 'ginger ale' and still not sound trite. Furthermore the whole caper is brimming with countless middle eights that raise the hairs on the arm, and some fairly uncomplicated but gorgeously chunky fat chords. Eve6 do have that special something that makes them stand out from the brat rock pack.

❯❯ Tracks: *How Much Longer; Inside Out; Leech; Showerhead; Open Road Song; Jesus Nitelite; Superhero Girl; Tongue Tied; Saturday Night; There's A Face; Small Town Trap.*

★ First released 1998
★ UK peak chart position: did not chart
★ USA peak chart position: 33
★ Previous Top 1000 position: 1998 (–): 1994 (–)

683 THE MISEDUCATION OF LAURYN HILL ↑ Lauryn Hill

Four years ago the Fugees surprised the world with the highly original and hugely successful *The Score*. Rather than follow it up immediately they fragmented into solo projects. Usually this is commercial and artistic suicide but Hill bucked the trend by making an even better and equally successful album. The mixture of funky hip-hop rhythms and soulful vocals appealed to a wide-ranging audience. The hit single 'Doo Wop (That Thing)' is an obvious highlight, but equally impressive are 'Superstar' and the seemingly autobiographical 'Every Ghetto, Every City'. The title track comes over like an old Stevie Wonder ballad (1973 period), complete with deliberate vinyl scratches throughout. A remarkably assured and mature album that should age well.

❯❯ Tracks: *Intro; Lost Ones; Ex-Factor; To Zion; Doo Wop (That Thing); Superstar; Final Hour; When It Hurts So Bad; I Used To Love Him; Forgive Them Father; Every Ghetto, Every City; Nothing Even Matters; Everything Is Everything; The Miseducation Of Lauryn Hill.*

★ First released 1998
★ UK peak chart position: 2
★ USA peak chart position: 1
★ Previous Top 1000 position: 1998 (–): 1994 (–)

684 BLESS THE WEATHER ↑
John Martyn

Idiosyncratic, difficult, loveable genius. Many other plaudits have been laid at the feet of this enigmatic giant. *Bless The Weather* was a gorgeous transitional record from folk to jazzier material, and features, among others, Richard Thompson and the mercurial Danny Thompson, arguably Martyn's greatest sparring partner. In addition to the hopelessly romantic title track and 'Head and Heart', there is a wonderful interpretation of 'Singin' In The Rain'. The experimental 'Glistening Glyndebourne' showed that John Martyn's developing interest in the 'echoplex' sound in which he was to immerse himself over the next few years. Other words that spring to mind are wayward, boozer, cheeky, passionate and, once more, genius.

❯❯ Tracks: *Go Easy; Bless The Weather; Sugar Lump; Walk On The Water; Just Now; Head and Heart; Let The Good Things Come; Back Down The River; Glistening Glyndebourne; Singin' In The Rain.*

★ First released 1971
★ UK peak chart position: did not chart
★ USA peak chart position: did not chart
★ Previous Top 1000 position: 1998 (877): 1994 (–)

685 THE GRAND ILLUSION ↑
Styx

The blossoming of adult rock bands in the mid-to-late 70s was anathema to the fast developing new wave scene. US pomp rockers Styx fared worse than most as their blend of soft harmonies and rock guitars seemed especially out of sync with what was happening. Twenty or so years later we are all so very forgiving. *The Grand Illusion* shifted over 3 million copies in America as fans rushed to hear twiddly church organs and complicated guitar bits with unusual time changes. In 2000, it all sounds unremarkable even though there is no denying the band's instrumental and vocal capabilities.

》 Tracks: *The Grand Illusion; Fooling Yourself (The Angry Young Man); Superstars; Come Sail Away; Miss America; Man In The Wilderness; Castle Walls; The Grand Finale.*

★ First released 1977
★ UK peak chart position: did not chart
★ USA peak chart position: 6
★ Previous Top 1000 position: 1998 (–): 1994 (–)

686 IN ROCK ↓
Deep Purple

Formed by discontented pop musicians, Deep Purple embraced progressive rock through judicious cover versions that drew acclaim at the expense of original material. Sensing a stylistic blind alley, Jon Lord (keyboards) and Ritchie Blackmore (guitar) brought new vocalist Ian Gillan into the line-up, a decision that irrevocably changed their fortunes. *In Rock* is one of the genre's definitive albums, combining hard-edged riffs with virtuoso technique, topped by Gillan's full-throated roar. Few singers could survive the instrumental power beneath him, but this he does with room to spare, reacting to and emphasizing his colleagues' musical prowess. Chock-full of material destined to become Deep Purple anthems, later releases were evaluated against this trail-blazing, heavy rock collection.

》 Tracks: *Speed King; Blood Sucker; Child In Time; Flight Of The Rat; Into The Fire; Living Wreck; Hard Lovin' Man.*

★ First released 1970
★ UK peak chart position: 4
★ USA peak chart position: 143
★ Previous Top 1000 position: 1998 (422): 1994 (117)

687 IMPRESSIONS ↑
John Coltrane

So this is the source of the Byrds' 'Eight Miles High'? (Yes, listen to 'India'.) John Coltrane continued to influence and break barriers both within his own highly fickle cognoscenti and outside in the rock world during the mid-60s, as his contemporaries cited his massive influence. Four exquisite excursions with McCoy Tyner (piano), Jimmy Garrison and Reggie Workman (bass), Elvin Jones and Roy Haynes (drums) and Eric Dolphy playing some extraordinary bass clarinet on the aforementioned 'India'. The other *tour de force* is the similarly explorative 'Impressions'. Not an easy record to digest but absolutely worthwhile. Maybe headphones are the answer.

》 Tracks: *India; Up Against The Wall; Impressions; After The Rain.*

★ First released 1963
★ UK peak chart position: did not chart
★ USA peak chart position: did not chart
★ Previous Top 1000 position: 1998 (924): 1994 (412)

688 UNHALFBRICKING ↓
Fairport Convention

The transitional album before Fairport Convention invented folk rock with *Liege and Lief*, on this album they stretch out on longer numbers and introduce Dave Swarbrick, who plays some particularly fine fiddle on the lengthy 'A Sailor's Life'. Richard Thompson continued to mature with 'Genesis Hall' and 'Cajun Woman'. Equally impressive is Sandy Denny's beautiful voice on her stellar composition 'Who Knows Where The Time Goes'. Bob Dylan abounds with three songs and 'Percy's Song' is a highlight. To round it up, a UK hit single, shock horror, with Dylan's 'Si Tu Dois Partir'. Also a bold move for a little-known band was not having their name on the album sleeve.

》 Tracks: *Genesis Hall; Si Tu Dois Partir; Autopsy; A Sailor's Life; Cajun Woman; Who Knows Where The Time Goes; Percy's Song; Million Dollar Bash.*

★ First released 1969
★ UK peak chart position: 12
★ USA peak chart position: did not chart
★ Previous Top 1000 position: 1998 (341): 1994 (480)

689 FORREST GUMP ↑
Soundtrack

Some various artist soundtracks seem to really hit the nail on the head. The choice of songs here seems on paper to be a fairly average list, with a few interesting selections at best. In the context of the movie the choice becomes quite inspiring. Presumably clearance for the Jimi Hendrix track could not be obtained, which is a great pity because its placement in the movie is highly evocative. Fortunately, several other excellent juxtapositions of film and music are included here. Who, in particular, could fail to be moved by the sickening explosion as Stephen Stills gets to the 'stop, hey what's that sound' segment of the marvelous 'For What It's Worth'.

» Tracks: *Hound Dog (Elvis Presley); Rebel Rouser (Duane Eddy); (I Don't Know Why) But I Do (Clarence 'Frogman' Henry); Walk Right In (The Rooftop Singers); Land Of 1000 Dances (Wilson Pickett); Blowin' In the Wind (Joan Baez); Fortunate Son (Creedence Clearwater Revival); I Can't Help Myself (Sugar Pie Honey Bunch) (The Four Tops); Respect (Aretha Franklin); Rainy Day Women #12 & #35 (Bob Dylan); Sloop John B (The Beach Boys); California Dreamin' (The Mamas and The Papas); For What It's Worth (Buffalo Springfield); What The World Needs Now Is Love (Jackie DeShannon); Break On Through (To The Other Side) (The Doors); Mrs. Robinson (Simon and Garfunkel); Volunteers (Jefferson Airplane); Let's Get Together (The Youngbloods); San Francisco (Be Sure To Wear Some Flowers In Your Hair) (Scott McKenzie); Turn! Turn! Turn! (The Byrds); Medley: Aquarius/Let The Sunshine In (The Fifth Dimension); Everybody's Talkin' (Harry Nilsson); Joy To The World (Three Dog Night); Stoned Love (The Supremes); Raindrops Keep Falling On My Head (B. J. Thomas); Mr. President (Have Pity On The Working Man) (Randy Newman); Sweet Home Alabama (Lynyrd Skynyrd); It Keeps You Runnin' (The Doobie Brothers); I've Got To Use My Imagination (Gladys Knight and The Pips); On The Road Again (Willie Nelson); Against The Wind (Bob Seger and The Silver Bullet Band); The Forrest Gump Suite (Alan Silvestri).*

★ First released 1994 ★ UK peak chart position: 5 ★ USA peak chart position: 2
★ Previous Top 1000 position: 1998 (–): 1994 (–)

690 MORE SONGS ABOUT BUILDINGS AND FOOD ↓
Talking Heads

Even though this was recorded at the beautiful Compass Point studio in the Caribbean, this album manages to retain the concrete urbanism of the American city, the subject of many of David Byrne's songs. Again produced by the mercurial Brian Eno; he and Byrne did work particularly well together. Eno's elaborate arrangements never once clouded the clarity of some of those simple pop riffs (especially some of those guitar trills on 'With Our Love'). Talking Heads seemed arty and complex at the time. More than twenty years later they seem less awesome but much more accessible and enjoyable. This album, in particular, holds up well.

» Tracks: *Thank You For Sending Me An Angel; With Our Love; The Good Thing; Warning Sign; The Girls Want To Be With The Girls; Found A Job; Artists Only; I'm Not In Love; Stay Hungry; Take Me To The River; The Big Country.*

★ First released 1978
★ UK peak chart position: 21★ USA peak chart position: 29
★ Previous Top 1000 position: 1998 (–): 1994 (–)

691 12 SONGS ↓
Randy Newman

Randy Newman began his career as a contract songwriter, before embarking on a recording career renowned for sardonic wit. On this, his second album, the singer opted for simple accompaniment, his ragged voice and stylized piano supported largely by a crisp backing group that included Byrds guitarist Clarence White. Superb melodies were matched by an intense lyricism that embraced sometimes disquieting images previously unheard of in rock. Cynicism, bitterness and sexual perversion are unleashed in turn as Newman adopts different roles and personae. His dispassionate delivery demands decisions from the listener, an interaction that is as compulsive as it is disquieting.

» Tracks: *Have You Seen My Baby?; Let's Burn Down The Cornfield; Mama Told Me Not To Come; Suzanne; Lover's Prayer; Lucinda; Underneath The Harlem Moon; Yellow Man; Old Kentucky Home; Rosemary; If You Need Oil; Uncle Bob's Midnight Blues.*

★ First released 1970
★ UK peak chart position: did not chart
★ USA peak chart position: did not chart
★ Previous Top 1000 position: 1998 (513): 1994 (373)

692 EUPHORIA ↑
Def Leppard

A credible if surprisingly dated sounding record which lends credence to the belief that Sheffield's finest heavy rock band were born a dozen years too late. Various influences creep in throughout this record. The soft rock harmonies on 'Demolition Man' work well, but the Gary Glitter-style 'Back In Your Face' is just too close to be comfortable with in light of recent events. The heavy metal seems to have been pushed aside throughout in favour of a 70s AOR sound that is more Los Angeles than Yorkshire, although the anthemic 'Goodbye' and 'All Night' are particularly enjoyable. They sing their socks off, but next time a little more gut wrenching guitar please.

» Tracks: *Demolition Man; Promises; Back In Your Face; Goodbye; All Night; Paper Sun; It's Only Love; 21st Century Sha La La La Girl; To Be Alive; Disintegrate; Guilty; Day After Day; Kings Of Oblivion.*

★ First released 1999
★ UK peak chart position: 6
★ USA peak chart position: 11
★ Previous Top 1000 position: 1998 (–): 1994 (–)

693 IT'S TOO LATE TO STOP NOW ↓ Van Morrison

Having completed a sequence of peerless studio albums, Van Morrison embarked on an expansive tour with this searing live set. Drawing sterling support from the Caledonia Soul Orchestra, the singer performs some of his most popular songs, acknowledges influences and even pays homage to his hit group, Them, with a medley of their two most successful singles. Not content with simply recreating material, Morrison uses his instinctive gifts to change inflections and bring new emphasis, reshaping each piece according to the moment's mood, rather than relying on previously recorded versions. His sense of timing on tracks such as the penultimate 'Caravan', is amazing; just to snap your finger and know the band can follow must be a great feeling.

▶▶ Tracks: *Ain't Nothing You Can Do; Warm Love; Into The Mystic; These Dreams Of You; I Believe To My Soul; I've Been Working; Help Me; Wild Children; Domino; I Just Wanna Make Love To You; Bring It On Home; Saint Dominic's Preview; Take Your Hand Out Of My Pocket; Listen To The Lion; Here Comes The Night; Gloria; Caravan; Cypress Avenue.*

★ First released 1974
★ UK peak chart position: did not chart
★ USA peak chart position: 53
★ Previous Top 1000 position: 1998 (214): 1994 (340)

694 JOAN ARMATRADING ↑ Joan Armatrading

The anchor hymn for this album is the compelling 'Love and Affection', a song that never fails to capture the heart even with regular radio play three decades later. Equally confessional is 'Down To Zero'. Armatrading exposes her inner self with a collection of desperately honest tracks that never lapse into sentimentality. Great musicians compliment the album; B.J. Cole, Jerry Donahue and both Dave Mattacks and Kenny Jones share drums. Her naturally bass-inflected voice is a match made in heaven for her acoustic guitar – the combination is like gin and tonic, especially on 'Water With The Wine'. This may explain why her later rock guitar-based albums are of average quality.

▶▶ Tracks: *Down To Zero; Help Yourself; Water With The Wine; Love and Affection; Save Me; Join The Boys; People; Somebody Who Loves You; Like Fire; Tall In The Saddle.*

★ First released 1976
★ UK peak chart position: 12
★ USA peak chart position: 67
★ Previous Top 1000 position: 1998 (–): 1994 (609)

695 COMING UP ↓ Suede

Suede's third album, and their first without main songwriter Bernard Butler, lacked none of their trademark glam rock and catchy melodies, but, crucially, it discarded the pomposity and indulgence that marred *Dog Man Star*. Instead, boosted by Richard Oakes' inventive guitarwork and the arrival of Neil Codling on keyboards, they presented a sparsely produced collection of Bowie-tinged pop songs. Brett Anderson's favourite lyrical themes – bored youth, casual sex, seedy urban life ('peepshows and freakshows') and escape from it – enjoyed free rein, but were predominantly framed within raunchy rockers rather than gloomy ballads. With the likes of 'Trash', 'Filmstar' and 'She', Suede firmly established themselves as the godfathers of indie glam and offered some classic pop into the bargain.

▶▶ Tracks: *Trash; Filmstar; Lazy; By The Sea; She; Beautiful Ones; Starcrazy; Picnic By The Motorway; The Chemistry Between Us; Saturday Night.*

★ First released 1996
★ UK peak position: 1
★ USA peak position: did not chart
★ Previous Top 1000 position: 1998 (195): 1994 (–)

696 AQUALUNG ↑ Jethro Tull

After the disappointing *Benefit* this recording came as a great relief to followers who had watched Jethro Tull mutate from a heavy blues band into a lighter progressive rock-orientated unit. They pursued the concept album path with great success, especially in the US, where *Aqualung* remains their most loved and commercially successful record. The concept, was based around the odious title character, very loosely explores organised religion. If you ignore the mumbo jumbo it is actually a pretty good rock record. Us simpletons will also bless the CD age for the six bonus tracks including some live BBC recordings.

▶▶ Tracks: *Aqualung; Cross-Eyed Mary; Cheap Day Return; Mother Goose; Wond'ring Aloud; Up To Me; My God; Hymn 43; Slipstream; Locomotive Breath; Wind-Up; Lick Your Fingers Clean; Wind Up (Quad Version); Excerpts From The Ian Anderson Interview; Song For Jeffrey; Fat Man; Bouree.*

★ First released 1971
★ UK peak chart position: 4
★ USA peak chart position: 7
★ Previous Top 1000 position: 1998 (–): 1994 (–)

697 DAYDREAM NATION ↓
Sonic Youth

The double album that brought Sonic Youth to the attention of a wider audience and prompted the eager interest of a handful of major labels. *Daydream Nation*, with its sleepy single candle flickering silently on the gatefold cover, harnessed their reckless live favourite, 'Teenage Riot', while they ran gloriously roughshod over 'Rain King' and 'Silver Rocket', and offered the overtly camp glee of 'Trilogy', which came with parts a, b and z. Their assured ascension to festival billing and the giant Geffen label came as no surprise to anyone who had heard this album.

❱❱ Tracks: *Teen Age Riot; Silver Rocket; The Sprawl; 'Cross The Breeze; Eric's Trip; Total Trash; Hey Joni; Providence; ?; Rain King; Kissability; Trilogy: a) The Wonder b) Hyperstation z) Eliminator Jr.*

★ First released 1988
★ UK peak chart position: 99
★ USA peak chart position: did not chart
★ Previous Top 1000 position: 1998 (349): 1994 (478)

698 SPACE ODDITY ↑
David Bowie

Apart from the twee and patchy Decca material, this really was the beginning of the long and winding road undertaken by everyone's favourite chameleon. The surprise hit single 'Space Oddity' spawned an album that felt its way rather than blazed a trail. Bowie sings like an angel and his acoustic 12-string guitar rings loud and clear, but unfortunately the lyrics are very much of the times and not unlike some of the jargon employed by Jon Anderson of Yes. Bowie has made many better albums, but such is his charm and importance it is hard to be unkind to a collection of songs that he passionately believed in at the time. His affection for Major Tom has been demonstrated by the number of times he has returned to the character over the course of his career.

❱❱ Tracks: *Space Oddity; Unwashed and Somewhat Slightly Dazed; Don't Sit Down; Letter To Hermione; Cygnet Committee; Janine; An Occasional Dream; Wild Eyed Boy From Freecloud; God Knows I'm Good; Memory Of A Free Festival.*

★ First released 1969
★ UK peak chart position: 17
★ USA peak chart position: 16
★ Previous Top 1000 position: 1998 (–): 1994 (–)

699 COPPER BLUE ↓
Sugar

Having disbanded the hugely influential Hüsker Dü, guitarist/vocalist Bob Mould embarked on a solo career during which he completed two contrasting albums. He then founded this power-packed trio, which resurrected the tone of his earlier group. *Copper Blue* sees Mould still firmly in control of his art, his barking voice enveloped by loud, crushing guitar and a succession of exhilarating hooklines. The album possesses power and drive, but beyond the speed and distortion lies an understanding of the mechanics of classic pop songs, short, sharp and highly memorable. Mould is a crafted composer; 'Changes' is an awesome piece of hard pop.

❱❱ Tracks: *The Act We Act; A Good Idea; Changes; Helpless; Hoover Dam; The Slim; If I Can't Change Your Mind; Fortune Teller; Slick; Man On The Moon.*

★ First released 1992
★ UK peak chart position: 10
★ USA peak chart position: did not chart
★ Previous Top 1000 position: 1998 (308): 1994 (332)

700 DAMN RIGHT, I'VE GOT THE BLUES ↓ Buddy Guy

And in 1991, he had good reason. At that point, Buddy Guy had not made a studio album for a decade. The fact that Eric Clapton, who made sure that Guy was a regular guest on his Albert Hall Blues Nights, had called him the world's greatest guitarist still had not gained him a recording contract. Silvertone put that right with sessions that included the best session men from Britain and America, with guest appearances by Clapton, Jeff Beck and Mark Knopfler. The album showed all sides of Guy's talent, the blues singer, the soul man and the extravagantly gifted guitarist. A reluctant star, he has nevertheless taken full advantage of his new-found status as the uncrowned King of Chicago Blues.

❱❱ Tracks: *Damn Right I Got The Blues; Where Is The Next One Coming From; Five Long Years; Missing Sally; There Is Something On Your Mind; Early In The Morning; Too Broke To Spend The Night; Let Me Love You Baby; Rememberin' Stevie.*

★ First released 1991
★ UK peak chart position: 43
★ USA peak chart position: 136
★ Previous Top 1000 position: 1998 (696): 1994 (507)

701 NIMROD ↑
Green Day

Own up. How many out there thought that *Dookie* was a flash in the pan, and Green Day would go down the Spin Doctors' toilet? Not so, they succeeded magnificently by masterfully cornering the pop/punk market while retaining their credibility in the alternative genre. In addition to their more familiar material they perform a 60s surf pastiche 'Last Ride In' with a cheeky confidence that would have the Ventures doffing their caps. Their acoustic encore, 'Good Riddance (Time Of Your Life)', is one of the great stage finales. After your heads have been blasted with sound it makes for an emotional ending.

» Tracks: *Nice Guys Finish Last; Hitchin' A Ride; The Grouch; Redundant; Scattered; All The Time; Worry Rock; Platypus (I Hate You); Uptight; Last Ride In; Jinx; Haushinka; Walking Alone; Reject; Take Back; King For A Day; Good Riddance (Time Of Your Life); Prosthetic Head.*

★ First released 1997
★ UK peak chart position: 11
★ USA peak chart position: 10
★ Previous Top 1000 position: 1998 (–): 1994 (–)

702 DIRE STRAITS ↓
Dire Straits

They do look happy and innocent on the back of the sleeve, blissfully unaware of the mantle they would be thrown and of the millions of fans they would be expected to please. This, for many, is the only Dire Straits album to own, yet it sold only moderately and was dwarfed by the subsequent *Brothers In Arms*. Knopfler sounded like he meant it on 'Sultans Of Swing' and who can forget the cheek of his lyric in the melancholic 'Wild West End'? 'I saw you walking out Shaftesbury Avenue, excuse me talking, I wanna marry you'. Hopefully Mark Knopfler has not forgotten this album.

» Tracks: *Down To The Waterline; Water Of Love; Setting Me Up; Six Blade Knife; Southbound Again; Sultans Of Swing; In The Gallery; Wild West End; Lions.*

★ First released 1978
★ UK peak chart position: 5
★ USA peak chart position: 2
★ Previous Top 1000 position: 1998 (522): 1994 (286)

703 THE MADCAP LAUGHS ↑
Syd Barrett

Poor Syd some say, he fried his brain with too much acid. Lucky Syd some say, he got out before the madness of the 70s took hold. Surely he would have hated to have been part of the *Dark Side Of The Moon* mega-stardom trip. There is still a devoted core of Pink Floyd fans who believe he was the heart and soul of the band. Syd spottings are rarer than UFO sightings these days, both are out there somewhere in a world known only to themselves. He produced one masterpiece before he went off to tend his garden, and this is it. Six extra tracks to lap up on this CD reissue.

» Tracks: *Terrapin; No Good Trying; Love You; No Man's Land; Dark Globe; Here I Go; Octopus; Golden Hair; Long Gone; She Took A Long Cold Look; Feel; If It's In You; Late Night; Octopus (Takes 1 & 2); It's No Good Trying (Take 5); Love You (Take 1); Love You (Take 3); She Took A Long Cold Look At Me (Take 4); Golden Hair (Take 5).*

★ First released 1970
★ UK peak chart position: 40
★ USA peak chart position: 163
★ Previous Top 1000 position: 1998 (–): 1994 (–)

704 STAGE FRIGHT ↓
The Band

The third Band album reflected their transformation from studio ensemble to live act. Several selections, notably the title track, articulated the disquiet this engendered. The set still offered the quintet's mesmerizing cross-section of American music – soul, country R&B and pop – but where previous releases took a historical perspective, this collection brought together the past and present. The ribald, carnival atmosphere of 'W.S. Walcott Medicine Show' is set against 'The Rumor', in which songwriter Robbie Robertson sculpts a chilling portrait of the Nixon era. This ambitious panorama yielded a pivotal early 70s release.

» Tracks: *Strawberry Wine; Sleeping; Time To Kill; Just Another Whistle Stop; All La Glory; The Shape I'm In; W.S. Walcott Medicine Show; Daniel and The Sacred Harp; Stage Fright; The Rumor.*

★ First released 1970
★ UK peak chart position: 15
★ USA peak chart position: 5
★ Previous Top 1000 position: 1998 (532): 1994 (230)

705 UNDER THE PINK ↑
Tori Amos

Bolstered by two important hit singles, 'Pretty Good Year' and the highly commercial 'Cornflake Girl', this album confirmed Amos as a major new female singer-songwriter. Confessional and tragic, but much angrier than her spiritual predecessor Joni Mitchell, Amos comes across like a rather offbeat Dory Previn in places. Spiky guitar work bolsters several tracks, and is especially complementary on 'God'. Amos' intensely personal tales of romantic suffering set her up as the new beacon for damaged women to find a safe haven – until the next time of course. Some people never learn.

» Tracks: *Pretty Good Year; God; Bells For Her; Past The Mission; Baker Baker; The Wrong Band; The Waitress; Cornflake Girl; Icicle; Cloud On My Tongue; Space Dog; Yes, Anastasia.*

★ First released 1994
★ UK peak chart position: 1
★ USA peak chart position: 12
★ Previous Top 1000 position: 1998 (–): 1994 (–)

707 DIAMOND LIFE ↓
Sade

Sade crept up on the music world when it was least expecting it. Her debut single, 'Your Love Is King', was a surprise hit and a very mature record for the mid-80s pop market, and one that opened the door for smooth soul-based pop acts. This album proved that Sade was no fluke, and it became one of the most acclaimed debuts of all time. 'Smooth Operator' put her back in the pop charts, but it was the class and confidence of the whole album that earned her the good reviews. Her version of Timmy Thomas's 'Why Can't We Live Together' is a particular highlight.

» Tracks: *Smooth Operator; Your Love Is King; Hang On To Your Love; When Am I Gonna Make A Living; Frankie's First Affair; Cherry Pie; Sally; I Will Be Your Friend; Why Can't We Live Together.*

★ First released 1984
★ UK peak chart position: 2
★ USA peak chart position: 5
★ Previous Top 1000 position: 1998 (262): 1994 (156)

706 OUR FAVOURITE SHOP ↑
Style Council

The fact that Paul Weller now admits that the Style Council went badly wrong should damn this record. In contrast, the passing of time seems to reveal hidden depths, such as the Jimmy McGriff acid jazz organ on the title track and the Blood, Sweat and Tears brass on 'All Gone Away'. Those who fondly remember the latter and are prepared to imbibe some Georgie Fame touches (*circa* 1966's *Sound Venture*) will be thoroughly delighted. It became hip to trash this band, but this is an undeniably great soulful record with barely a lapse. And Mick Talbot really did have a fantastic organ (sound).

» Tracks: *Homebrakers; All Gone Away; Come To Milton Keynes; Internationalists; A Stones Throw Away; The Stand Up Comic's Instructions; Boy Who Cried Wolf; A Man Of Great Promise; Down In The Seine; The Lodgers; Luck; With Everything To Lose; Our Favourite Shop; Walls Come Tumbling Down; Shout To The Top.*

★ First released 1985
★ UK peak chart position: 1
★ USA peak chart position: did not chart
★ Previous Top 1000 position: 1998 (–): 1994 (–)

708 TRUST ↓
Elvis Costello

Some of Elvis Costello's best songs are on this sometimes forgotten gem of a record. *This Year's Model* and *My Aim Is True* are usually favoured by fans and critics, but who could fault the special middle-eight of 'You'll Never Be A Man', the great riff of 'Clubland', the smouldering 'Watch Your Step', the tragic 'Shot With His Own Gun' and the sheer pop simplicity of 'From A Whisper To Scream'. Lyrically, he packs them in ten to a dozen, leaving the literate listener's wide-open ears aching. A request that prolific writers should be forced to include lyric sheets with the CD is made. A blinder of an album.

» Tracks: *Clubland; Lover's Walk; You'll Never Be A Man; Pretty Words; Strict Time; Luxembourg; Watch Your Step; New Lace Sleeves; From A Whisper To A Scream; Different Finger; White Knuckles; Shot With His Own Gun; Fish 'N' Chip Paper; Big Sister's Clothes.*

★ First released 1981
★ UK peak chart position: 9
★ USA peak chart position: 28
★ Previous Top 1000 position: 1998 (568): 1994 (–)

709 WIDE OPEN SPACES ↑
Dixie Chicks

In the past year or so this trio has become the most successful female country act of all time, although that in itself does not put them up against much opposition. *Wide Open Spaces*, their fourth and best album, has reached sales of close to 12 million copies thanks to a bouncy, uncomplicated country rock formula that has tremendous crossover appeal in the pop world. Their material is well chosen, using classy writers including Bonnie Raitt, Maria McKee and Radney Foster. There are enough touches of traditional bluegrass, however, to demonstrate the trio's real love for the genre. This should convince country purists that they are serious about their music. They can't help the way they look.

» Tracks: *I Can Love You Better; Wide Open Spaces; Loving Arms; There's Your Trouble; You Were Mine; Never Say Die; Tonight The Heartache's On Me; Let 'Er Rip; Once You've Loved Somebody; I'll Take Care Of You; Am I The Only One (Who's Ever Felt This Way); Give It Up Or Let Me Go.*

★ First released 1998
★ UK peak chart position: 29
★ USA peak chart position: 4
★ Previous Top 1000 position: 1998 (–): 1994 (–)

710 TALKING WITH THE TAXMAN ABOUT POETRY ↑   Billy Bragg

Agitpop's aggrieved and finely humoured singer-songwriter, Billy Bragg gave vent to his impassioned view of the world with the excellent *Talking With The Taxman About Poetry*. Less fully blown in execution than *Brewing Up*, or his mini-album *Life's A Riot With Spy Vs Spy*, his finely honed angst nevertheless remained intact, with his pungent and almost always topical material sitting comfortably alongside a new and instantly more accessible batch of songs. The wonderfully poignant 'Greetings To The New Brunette' and the uplifting 'Levi Stubbs Tears' were indicative of Bragg's rapidly developing craft.

» Tracks: *Greetings To The New Brunette; Train Train; The Marriage; Ideology; Levi Stubbs Tears; Honey I'm A Big Boy Now; There Is Power In A Union; Help Save The Youth Of America; Wishing The Days Away; The Passion; The Warmest Room; The Home Front.*

★ First released 1986
★ UK peak chart position: 8
★ USA peak chart position: did not chart
★ Previous Top 1000 position: 1998 (911): 1994 (357)

711 TIM HARDIN 1 ↑
Tim Hardin

Normally classed as a folk-singer, Tim Hardin brought a jazz/blues perspective to the genre. His relaxed, languid voice mirrored the ease of his stylish compositions, the strongest of which showcased a highly original talent. Fragile lyrics, romanticism, tender melodies and haunting instrumentation combine to perfection on a collection of enchanting songs, several of which have become pop standards, notably 'Reason To Believe'. Although known for wistful ballads, Hardin was equally adept with up-tempo material, a combination fully exploited herein. His highly personal reflections left their mark on a whole generation of singer-songwriters. The reissue comes with *Tim Hardin 2*.

» Tracks: *Don't Make Promises; Green Rocky Road; Smugglin' Man; How Long; While You're On Your Way; It'll Never Happen Again; Reason To Believe; Never Too Far; Part Of The Wind; Ain't Gonna Do Without; Misty Roses; How Can We Hang On To A Dream.*

★ First released 1966 ★ UK peak chart position: did not chart
★ USA peak chart position: did not chart
★ Previous Top 1000 position: 1998 (824): 1994 (780)

712 THE WOMAN IN ME ↑
Shania Twain

This artist had already given country music the biggest shake-up it had received for many a year. Her next target was the pop chart which she assaulted with ridiculous ease. After that there was only one way to go, upwards and popwards, saying goodbye to country with a fond look over her shoulder. This transitional album will be seen as her last proper country collection. All of the songs are written by Twain or co-written with producer and husband Mutt Lange, meaning for once the beautiful country ballad relates directly to the artist and not to contract writers holed up in Nashville. Twain can kick hoedown ass as well, as demonstrated by the invigorating 'Any Man Of Mine'.

» Tracks: *Home Ain't Where His Heart Is (Anymore); Any Man Of Mine; Whose Bed Have Your Boots Been Under?; (If You're Not In It For Love) I'm Outta Here!; The Woman In Me (Needs The Man In You); Is There Life After Love?; If It Don't Take Two; You Win My Love; Raining On Our Love; Leaving Is The Only Way Out; No One Needs To Know; God Bless The Child.*

★ First released 1995
★ UK peak chart position: 7
★ USA peak chart position: 5
★ Previous Top 1000 position: 1998 (–): 1994 (–)

713 THE CAT ↑
Jimmy Smith

'It all comes round again', sang Fairport Convention in 1968, and indeed the 'Incredible' Jimmy Smith's time has come again. Hammond organ jazz went so far out of fashion at one point that the chances of this album ever being made available again seemed remote. Smith is the genre's greatest exponent and recorded dozens of albums in the 60s. Now his songs are used to soundtrack television advertisements and he is actively recording again. The Cat is one of his best outings for Verve Records, and features a full orchestra brilliantly arranged by Lalo Schifrin. Bernstein's theme from the movie The Carpetbaggers and Schifrin's 'The Cat' are two naggingly familiar tunes that listeners don't realise they know. This is timeless, groovy music that has no equal.

❱❱ Tracks: Theme From 'Joy House'; The Cat; Basin Street Blues; Main Title From 'The Carpetbaggers'; Chicago Serenade; St. Louis Blues; Delon's Blues; Blues In The Night.

★ First released 1964
★ UK peak chart position: did not chart
★ USA peak chart position: 12
★ Previous Top 1000 position: 1998 (–): 1994 (–)

714 JOE'S GARAGE ↓
Frank Zappa

The superlative repackaging and remastering undertaken by Rykodisc Records has put the original three-part, two-record set of this magnificent nonsense tale together for the first time. This is back to the madness of Freak Out!, with more pop and doo-wop bursting through all the complicated stuff, letting you know that Frank Zappa could write a hit single, if he could be bothered to do so. Joe's Garage is a hoot and harmlessly pornographic. The sleeve-note states that it is 'a stupid story about how the government is trying to do away with music'. It is absolutely no coincidence that throughout, the listener mistakes the 'scrutinizer' as the 'scrotumizer'. Zappa was that rude, and that funny.

❱❱ Tracks: The Central Scrutinizer; Joe's Garage; Catholic Girls; Crew Slut; Fembot In A Wet T-Shirt; On The Bus; Why Does It Hurt When I Pee?; Lucille Has Messed My Mind Up; Scrutinizer Postlude; A Token Of My Extreme; Stick It Out; Sy Borg; Dong Work For Yuda; Keep It Greasy; Outside Now; He Used To Cut The Grass; Packard Goose; Watermelon In Easter Hay; A Little Green Rosetta.

★ First released 1979
★ UK peak chart position: 62 & 75
★ USA peak chart position: 27 & 53
★ Previous Top 1000 position: 1998 (457): 1994 (–)

715 VOLUME TWO ↑
The Soft Machine

Kevin Ayers had departed the fold by the time Volume Two was released, but drummer Robert Wyatt easily filled the gap. His cockney narration effortlessly fitted into the complex organ dominated sound explored on this album, although the jazz influence had yet to creep in and Elton Dean's avant garde phase was still to come. It is surprising that the band was able to build a substantial career as radio play was minimal. Only John Peel in the UK, and some of the FM stations on the west coast (notably Tom Donahue at KYA) would give them airplay. The Soft Machine gave progressive rock a good name, it is a pity that so many cosmic monkeys came along and spoilt it all.

❱❱ Tracks: Pataphysical Introduction, Part 1; A Concise British Alphabet, Part 1; Hibou Anenome and Bear; A Concise British Alphabet, Part 2; Hullo Der; Dada Was Here; Thank You Pierrot Lunaire; Have You Ever Bean Grean?; Pataphysical Introduction, Part 2; Out Of Tunes; As Long As He Lies Perfectly Still; Dedicated To You But You Weren't Listening; Fire Engine Passing With Bells Clanging; Pig; Orange Skin Food; A Door Opens and Closes; 10:30 Returns To The Bedroom.

★ First released 1969 ★ UK peak chart position: did not chart
★ USA peak chart position: did not chart
★ Previous Top 1000 position: 1998 (–): 1994 (–)

716 RANDY NEWMAN ↑
Randy Newman

Although the back cover of Randy Newman boasted 'Randy Newman Creates Something New Under the Sun', his songwriting talent was nothing new to the music industry who had long admired him. Unfortunately, even with the release of this, his debut, it would still be some time before the secret would become known to the record-buying public. Its commercial failure is astonishing in light of how many of its songs went on to become classics; 'Living Without You', 'So Long Dad', 'Love Story', and especially the heartbreaking 'I Think It's Going To Rain Today'. Vocally, too, Randy Newman is at the top of his game, bending notes as only he can and demonstrating the strong influence of his New Orleans home-town.

❱❱ Tracks: Love Story; Bet No One Ever Hurt This Bad; Living Without You; So Long Dad; I Think He's Hiding; Linda; Laughing Boy; Cowboy; The Beehive State; I Think It's Going To Rain Today; Davy The Fat Boy.

★ First released 1968 ★ UK peak chart position: did not chart
★ USA peak chart position: 191
★ Previous Top 1000 position: 1998 (773): 1994 (–)

717 VITALOGY ↑
Pearl Jam

This album is packaged in a nicely designed cardboard sleeve, but forget it if you are foolish enough to want it on your CD shelf alongside the rest of the collection – it is half an inch too deep. That aside, Pearl Jam's third album is par for the course but certainly not one of their best. At times they sound uninspired, with too many tracks built around lesser repetitions of past riffs. However, if boredom should creep in, the text contained in the booklet is fascinating, informing the listener that early mankind lived to be 500 to 900 years old. Ahem, maybe you should stick to the music after all.

»» Tracks: *Last Exit; Spin The Black Circle; Not For You; Tremor Christ; Nothingman; Whipping; Pry, To; Corduroy; Bugs; Satan's Bed; Better Man; Aye Davanita; Immortality; Hey Foxymophandlemama, That's Me.*

★ First released 1994
★ UK peak chart position: 1
★ USA peak chart position: 1
★ Previous Top 1000 position: 1998 (–): 1994 (–)

719 THE DIVISION BELL ↓
Pink Floyd

At last, Dave Gilmour and company rose majestically out of the sticky mire that had entrapped them and Roger Waters for years. It buried the ghost and enabled the new Floyd to be appraised separately, and, generally, very favourably. Gilmour had sharpened his singing almost to match his 'epic' guitar sound. 'What Do You Want From Me' had every necessary Pink Floyd ingredient, without digging up the past. A cynic would analyze the lyrics of 'Poles Apart' and interpret them as a snide dig at Waters, with lines such as 'why did we tell you then you were always the golden boy then'.

»» Tracks: *Cluster One; What Do You Want From Me; Poles Apart; Marooned; A Great Day For Freedom; Wearing The Inside Out; Take It Back; Coming Back To Life; Keep Talking; Lost For Words; High Hopes.*

★ First released 1994
★ UK peak chart position: 1
★ USA peak chart position: 1
★ Previous Top 1000 position: 1998 (495): 1994 (–)

718 FEATS DON'T FAIL ME NOW
↓ Little Feat

If albums could be rolled and smoked, this would be one to keep for a special occasion, passed from friend to friend in a grin-inducing haze of contentment. Everything, from the Neon Park artwork to the sleeve notes, is goodtime. The line-up of the band on *Feats Don't Fail Me Now* works equally well on composition and playing. The songs, from the rhythmically chunky 'Rock and Roll Doctor' to the sprawling and energetic 'Cold Cold Cold/Tripe Face Boogie', roll along without looking to left or right, and the arrangements are so tight you couldn't slide a Rizla in sideways. Country funk at its best, just remember not to inhale.

»» Tracks: *Rock and Roll Doctor; Oh Atlanta; Skin It Back; Down The Road; Spanish Moon; Feats Don't Fail Me Now; The Fan; Cold Cold Cold/Tripe Face Boogie.*

★ First released 1974
★ UK peak chart position: did not chart
★ USA peak chart position: 36
★ Previous Top 1000 position: 1998 (314): 1994 (243)

720 SPARKLE AND FADE ↑
Everclear

Everclear's major label debut immediately broadened their fanbase and put them high in the US alternative rock chart. They produce a remarkably full sound for a trio. The title track is just one thunking great riff-laden dollop of joy, punk like Green Day, heavy like Nirvana, but with a boyish charm that is hard to dislike. Why is it that the same old chords never fail to get the hairs to raise? 'Strawberry' is unbridled noise with a great chord sequence reminiscent of Bob Mould's Sugar. If this is modern day rock 'n' roll, then the 80s were almost worth living through. A spiffing 42 minutes full of glorious riffs.

»» Tracks: *Electra Made Me Blind; Heroin Girl; You Make Me Feel Like A Whore; Santa Monica; Summerland; Strawberry; Heartspark Dollarsign; The Twistinside; Her Brand New Skin; Nehalem; Queen Of The Air; Pale Green Stars; Chemical Smile; My Sexual Life.*

★ First released 1995
★ UK peak chart position: did not chart
★ USA peak chart position: 25
★ Previous Top 1000 position: 1998 (–): 1994 (–)

721 MEZZANINE ↑
Massive Attack

A long time coming and, for most people, well worth the wait. Accepted, it falls short of the previous two classics, but there is still the familiar warm glow reserved for hearing new material from one of the most important and vital bands of the 90s. The opening 'Angel' rumbles and builds in spectacular fashion and bleeds without pause into the ominous 'Risingson', featuring a snatch of the Velvet Underground. The listener is kept alert throughout the album by other samples, which including snippets lifted from the Cure and Isaac Hayes. Even with the recent personnel upheaval and their snails pace recording, it will be worth the wait for the next one.

» Tracks: *Angel; Risingson; Teardrop; Inertia Creeps; Exchange; Dissolved Girl; Man Next Door; Black Milk; Mezzanine; Group Four; (Exchange).*

★ First released 1998
★ UK peak chart position: 1
★ USA peak chart position: 60
★ Previous Top 1000 position: 1998 (–): 1994 (–)

722 PRETENDERS ↓
The Pretenders

Former NME rock critic Chrissie Hynde launched the Pretenders with an engaging, yet passive, version of the Kinks' 'Stop Your Sobbing'. She unveiled her own persona fully on *The Pretenders*, which contains a series of excellent compositions marked by her sensual vocals and brilliant sense of dynamics. An understanding of pop's structures allowed Hynde to exploit them to her own ends while sympathetic support, particularly that of guitarist James Honeyman-Scott, used the excitement of rock without reference to its clichés. Tough and opinionated, Chrissie Hynde's first declaration of independence established the formula she proceeded to follow.

» Tracks: *Precious; The Phone Call; Up The Neck; Tattooed Love Boys; Space Invader; The Wait; Stop Your Sobbing; Kid; Private Life; Brass In Pocket; Lovers Of Today; Mystery Achievement.*

★ First released 1980
★ UK peak chart position: 1
★ USA peak chart position: 9
★ Previous Top 1000 position: 1998 (319): 1994 (137)

723 ADORE ↑
The Smashing Pumpkins

Billy Corgan had a real problem on his hands attempting to match the brilliant *Mellon Collie and The Infinite Sadness*, not least of which was having to summon up the energy to write a new batch of songs after that exhausting double set. Apart from the occasional grunge flirtation (especially the excellent 'Ava Adore'), Corgan scaled down his aspirations on a lighter, looser and more acoustic outing. Guitarist James Iha even managed to turn his guitar down from eleven. That said, the quality remains even and Corgan's delivery of 'Shame' and 'To Sheila' makes the appreciative listener look forward to an all acoustic album at that stage in his career when the Pumpkins are pulp.

» Tracks: *To Sheila; Ava Adore; Perfect; Daphne Descends; Once Upon A Time; Tear; Crestfallen; Appels + Oranjes; Pug; The Tale Of Dusty and Pistol Pete; Annie-Dog; Shame; Behold! The Night Mare; For Martha; Blank Page; 17.*

★ First released 1998
★ UK peak chart position: 5
★ USA peak chart position: 2
★ Previous Top 1000 position: 1998 (–): 1994 (–)

724 ANTICHRIST SUPERSTAR ↑
Marilyn Manson

Yes Marilyn, I know you are very popular, but I just need clarification on some of the lyrics. 'I'd sell your suicide... I've got abortions in my eyes ... I am the animal who will not be himself, fuck it'. Well the last bit made sense, because that is exactly what I was thinking when I glanced over the lyric booklet while enjoying a salmon and cucumber sandwich and a pot of Earl Grey. But musically this is riveting, exciting, thoroughly decadent, and Manson does have a great voice. So where does this leave us? Maybe, just popping it on to liven up the dinner party.

» Tracks: *Irresponsible Hate Anthem; The Beautiful People; Dried Up, Tied and Dead To The World; Tourniquet; Little Horn; Cryptorchid; Deformography; Wormboy; Mister Superstar; Angel With The Scabbed Wings; Kinderfeld; Antichrist Superstar; 1996; Minute Of Decay; The Reflecting God; Man That You Fear.*

★ First released 1996
★ UK peak chart position: 73
★ USA peak chart position: 3
★ Previous Top 1000 position: 1998 (–): 1994 (–)

725 THE GREAT ESCAPE ↑
Blur

Blur were riding on the crest of a commercial wave at this point in their career. There was also immense pressure on them to follow the acclaimed *Parklife*, and to make matters worse the press decided to invent a sparring match between them and Oasis. Ultimately they had the last laugh even though the album sold less than its predecessor did. Damon Albarn's pseudo-Cockney vocal style reached its peak on perky songs such as 'Country House' and 'Stereotypes', but throughout this album it is easy to sense a band desperate to grow and move on. They have quite magnificently, and this album is the perfect snapshot of Blur in transition to becoming probably the UK's greatest pop band.

» Tracks: *Stereotypes; Country House; Best Days; Charmless Man; Fade Away; Top Man; The Universal; Mr. Robinsons' Quango; He Thought Of Cars; It Could Be You; Ernold Same; Globe Alone; Dan Abnormal; Entertain Me; Yuko & Hiro.*

★ First released 1995
★ UK peak chart position: 1
★ USA peak chart position: 150
★ Previous Top 1000 position: 1998 (–): 1994 (–)

726 CRAZY SEXY COOL ↓
TLC

Worldwide sales exceed 15 million copies at the time of writing, remarkable by any standards. TLC (tender loving care) are a female urban R&B trio, Chilli, Left Eye and T-Boz, who mixed in some funk and hip-hop over their graceful and effortless voices. When they sing smooth soul they are unbeatable; take, for example, 'Red Light Special', 'Diggin' On You' and the hugely successful single 'Waterfalls', in which they warn 'don't go chasing waterfalls, please stick to the rivers and lakes that you're used to'. Highly commercial, slick, immaculately produced and, ultimately, impossible to fault.

» Tracks: *Intro-lude; Creep; Kick Your Game; Diggin' On You; Case Of The Fake People; CrazySexyCool; Interlude; Red Light Special; Waterfalls; Intermission-lude; Let's Do It Again; If I Was Your Girlfriend; Sexy – Interlude; Take Our Time; Can I Get A Witness; Switch; Sumthin' Wicked This Way Comes.*

★ First released 1994
★ UK peak chart position: 4
★ USA peak chart position: 3
★ Previous Top 1000 position: 1998 (415): 1994 (–)

727 CELEBRITY SKIN ↑
Hole

The theme of this album, according to the sleeve, seems to concern the Los Angeles water department. Studying the lyrics, unless there is some double entendre intended, there seems to be absolutely no link with the real theme, Courtney Love's self-conscious, navel gazing exploration of her own superstar status. A lot less abrasive and more pop-orientated than *Live Through This*, this is first class, high-energy power rock. Courtney Love does seem to get better, the happier she becomes, and her band is now adding peerless support akin to Tom Petty and The Heartbreakers. There are similarities, and the excellent 'Hit So Hard' has definite Petty shades. 'Malibu' is another one of those songs that becomes instantly recognisable once the chorus arrives.

» Tracks: *Celebrity Skin; Awful; Hit So Hard; Malibu; Reasons To Be Beautiful; Dying; Use Once & Destroy; Northern Star; Boys On The Radio; Heaven Tonight; Playing Your Song; Petals.*

★ First released 1998
★ UK peak chart position: 11
★ USA peak chart position: 9
★ Previous Top 1000 position: 1998 (–): 1994 (–)

728 HERGEST RIDGE ↑
Mike Oldfield

A cynic might suggest that *Hergest Ridge* was only released to cash in on the success of its multi-million selling predecessor, *Tubular Bells*. Love it or hate it, that album was unique and the problem that this and any other Mike Oldfield album suffers from is that it is impossible to listen objectively without the gigantic spectre of *Tubular Bells* making its presence felt. Unless, of course, there is still someone in the world who has not heard *Tubular Bells*. Similar themes, similar sounds, lots of instruments, very clever. Anyway, this is pleasant and unremarkable, and ultimately nowhere near as good as *that* album.

» Tracks: *Hergest Ridge, Part One; Hergest Ridge, Part Two.*

★ First released 1974
★ UK peak chart position: 1
★ USA peak chart position: 8
★ Previous Top 1000 position: 1998 (–): 1994 (–)

729 FOLLOW THE LEADER ↑
Korn

I was stupid enough to return this CD as I thought it had a defect. Watch it skip through twelve tracks of silence. Be prepared to wait for track 13, which is of course the beginning. Once this is sorted, you can wallow in the sheer, unadulterated cacophony of sound generated by the current leaders of hardcore metal. Korn's third album was a massive commercial success, spurred on by the hit single 'Got The Life' (track 15, not 3). Percussive delights await on 'B.B.K.' as the drums threaten to bounce the speakers off the stands, and the guitars are as thick as girders. No comment on the lyrics, they are for most part indecipherable. Guaranteed excitement.

➤ Tracks: It's On!; Freak On A Leash; Got The Life; Dead Bodies Everywhere; Children Of The Korn; B.B.K.; Pretty; All In The Family; Reclaim My Place; Justin; Seed; Cameltosis; My Gift To You.

★ First released 1998
★ UK peak chart position: 5
★ USA peak chart position: 1
★ Previous Top 1000 position: 1998 (–): 1994 (–)

730 WHATEVER AND EVER AMEN ↑ Ben Folds Five

One of the most unique sounding rock acts currently performing thanks to the fact they use a piano as the lead instrument and don't possess a guitarist. Songwriter Ben Folds pours out his highly literate lyrics while tinkling away in a style located somewhere between Jools Holland and Bruce Hornsby. Although every song has merit, 'Song For The Dumped' stands out for the razor sharp line, 'give me back my money you bitch, and don't forget to give me back my black T-shirt'. The single 'The Battle Of Who Could Care Less' also raises a wry smile, and 'why don't we pitch it to the Franklin fuckin' Mint' is another great line on an album full of them.

➤ Tracks: One Angry Dwarf and 200 Solemn Faces; Fair; Brick; Song For The Dumped; Selfless, Cold and Composed; Kate; Smoke; Cigarette; Steven's Last Night In Town; The Battle Of Who Could Care Less; Missing The War; Evaporated.

★ First released 1997
★ UK peak chart position: 30
★ USA peak chart position: 42
★ Previous Top 1000 position: 1998 (–): 1994 (–)

731 LADIES OF THE CANYON ↓
Joni Mitchell

No longer the wistful folkie, Joni Mitchell had by now joined the late 60s rock fraternity through her association with David Crosby who led to Graham Nash. Her lyrics had acquired an originality, which she expanded on Blue and For The Roses, but it was the quality of the songs that made them classics of the era. 'For Free' was recorded by David Crosby and the re-formed Byrds, and Crosby, Stills, Nash and Young turned 'Woodstock' into a full-blown rock number. Mitchell's own definitive stamp remains on the much-covered 'The Circle Game', the ecology-conscious 'Big Yellow Taxi' and 'Willy', her song for her former 'old man' Nash.

➤ Tracks: Morning Morgantown; For Free; Conversation; Ladies Of The Canyon; Willy; The Arrangement; Rainy Night House; The Priest; Blue Boy; Big Yellow Taxi; My Old Man; Woodstock; The Circle Game.

★ First released 1970
★ UK peak chart position: 8
★ USA peak chart position: 27
★ Previous Top 1000 position: 1998 (484): 1994 (764)

732 HELLO NASTY ↑
The Beastie Boys

A splendid return to form after the hugely disappointing stop gap collection The In Sound From Way Out!. Some felt that the Beastie Boys day had passed, but the restless originality of the band is hard to resist. The choice sampling harks back to the groundbreaking Paul's Boutique, yet there is a fresh approach on some tracks demonstrating the trio's own need to expand their horizons. A sensitive drum and bass track drives 'Flowin' Prose', while 'I Don't Know' is, of all things, an acoustic ballad. They are perfectly poised to tackle anything, and it appears that their audience is happy to follow them on the evidence of this album.

➤ Tracks: Super Disco Breakin'; The Move; Remote Control; Song For The Man; Just A Test; Body Movin'; Intergalactic; Sneakin' Out The Hospital; Putting Shame In Your Game; Flowin' Prose; And Me; Three MC's and One DJ; Grasshopper Unit (Keep Movin'); Song For Junior; I Don't Know; The Negotiation Limerick File; Electrify; Picture This; Unite; Dedication; Dr. Lee, PhD; Instant Death.

★ First released 1998
★ UK peak chart position: 1
★ USA peak chart position: 1
★ Previous Top 1000 position: 1998 (–): 1994 (–)

733 THIRD/SISTER LOVERS ↓
Big Star

After Big Star released *Radio City*, they fell apart, leaving Alex Chilton to record in 1975 what was later released as their Third (aka *Sister Lovers*). The album is strikingly different from everything Chilton has done before or since. With pained outpourings such as the haunting 'Holocaust', it holds its own against rock's greatest monuments to existential angst, from *Tonight's The Night* to *Bryter Layter*. It also ranks alongside the Beach Boys' *Smile* as perhaps the only 'classic' album with no set sequence. Chilton never bothered to sequence it because, upon its completion, no label wanted to release it. It finally came out four years later, and since then, while it has appeared on several labels, no two have used the same track order.

» Tracks: *Stroke It Noel; For You; Kizza Me; You Can't Have Me; Nightime; Blue Moon; Take Care; Jesus Christ; Femme Fatale; O; Dana; Big Black Car; Holocaust; Kangaroo; Thank You Friends.*

★ First released 1978
★ UK peak chart position: did not chart
★ USA peak chart position: did not chart
★ Previous Top 1000 position: 1998 (157): 1994 (–)

734 THE SCORE ↑
Fugees

Combining traditional hip-hop with melodic soul, the Fugees were one of the most refreshing surprises of 1996. Released with little fanfare, the album succeeded on its merit alone, and picked up many awards in addition to several million sales. The success of the singles 'Ready Or Not' and their excellent version of Bob Marley's 'No Woman No Cry' helped to change the general public's previous negative reaction to rap. Joining the mainstream was further aided with the even more successful interpretation of Roberta Flack's 'Killing Me Softly'. A superb version over a steady, slow snare drum beat, it became a major hit all over the world. The clever use of sampling and overall 'good vibe' feel made for a formidable record.

» Tracks: *Red Intro; How Many Mics; Ready Or Not; Zealots; The Beast; Fu-Gee-La; Family Business; Killing Me Softly; The Score; The Mask; Cowboys; No Woman, No Cry; Manifest/Outro; Fu-Gee-La; Fu-Gee-La; Mista Mista; Fu-Gee-La*

★ First released 1996
★ UK peak chart position: 3
★ USA peak chart position: 1
★ Previous Top 1000 position: 1998 (754): 1994 (–)

735 MANASSAS ↓
Manassas/Stephen Stills

Originally a double album of four distinct sides, it was a well-planned package. Stills was bursting with ideas during his most prolific period (1970-72), and this supergroup was its real culmination. Ex-Byrd Chris Hillman added the occasional co-write, but this was sweet Stephen blue-eyes' show. Showing he could write, sing and play country, blues, rock and pop, this is a rich and varied collection. Dallas Taylor, Paul Harris, Fuzzy Samuels, Jo Lala and Al Perkins completed the band, who were as great live as they were on record. It lasted only a few rockin' months until Stills went back to Crosby, Stills and Nash, and took a nap for the next twenty-five years.

» Tracks: *The Raven: Song Of Love; Rock & Roll Crazies; Cuban Bluegrass; Jet Set (Sigh); Anyway; Both Of Us (Bound To Lose); Fallen Eagle; Jesus Gave Love Away For Free; Colorado; So Begins The Task; Hide It So Deep; Don't Look At My Shadow; It Doesn't Matter; Johnny's Garden; Bound To Fall; How Far; Move Around; The Love Gangster; What To Do; Right Now; The Treasure (Take One); Blues Man.*

★ First released 1972
★ UK peak chart position: 30
★ USA peak chart position: 4
★ Previous Top 1000 position: 1998 (426): 1994 (–)

736 READY TO DIE ↓
Notorious B.I.G.

There can have been few more prophetic album titles in the history of music than the one that accompanied Notorious B.I.G.'s 1994 debut. The larger-than-life Brooklyn denizen had turned to hip-hop after making a dodgy living on the streets – a fact celebrated in many of his lyrics. The tone is resolutely grim throughout street narratives such as 'Gimme The Loot', though most hip-hop fans came to Notorious through his cruder, lewder material ('Big Poppa', 'Me & My Bitch'). The album-closer, 'Suicidal Thoughts', in light of his subsequent murder, is an awe-inspiring exercise in fatalistic social realism – 'When I die, I want to go to hell/'Cos I'm a piece of shit, it ain't hard to fuckin' tell'.

» Tracks: *Intro; Things Done Changed; Gimme The Loot; Machine Gun Funk; Warning; Ready To Die; One More Chance; Fuck Me (Interlude); The What -; Juicy; Everyday Struggle; Me & My Bitch; Big Poppa; Respect; Friend Of Mine; Unbelievable; Suicidal Thoughts.*

★ First released 1994
★ UK peak chart position: did not chart
★ USA peak chart position: 15
★ Previous Top 1000 position: 1998 (625): 1994 (–)

737 VULGAR DISPLAY OF POWER ↑ Pantera

This Texan four-piece's instrumental sound is incredible, but for me, the moment Phil Anselmo starts to growl, the focus is immediately taken off the musicians. It is clear that a band such as Pantera need a lead singer with a brick in his throat – Colin Blunstone just would not do. The latter would probably struggle with a lyric such as 'got shit on, pissed on, spit on, stepped on, fucked with' (from 'A New Level'). I wouldn't diss this man either, in print or elsewhere. Pantera have a huge following and their playing is formidable, but give me Roger Chapman's strangulated vocals any day.

» Tracks: *Mouth For War; A New Level; Walk; Fucking Hostile; This Love; Rise; No Good (Attack The Radical); Live In A Hole; Regular People (Conceit); By Demons Be Driven; Hollow.*

★ First released 1992
★ UK peak chart position: 64
★ USA peak chart position: 44
★ Previous Top 1000 position: 1998 (–): 1994 (637)

738 2112 ↑ Rush

Much has changed in the 25 years since *2112* was recorded, and bands such as Rush and Yes should now be judged on musical merit alone. This album boasts lots of very good guitar complete with interesting stops and starts that were almost requisite in heavy prog rock's finest hour. At some stage lyrics will creep into the proceedings and may spoil things for the new listener, unless he or she has parents who still wear patchouli and say 'wow, cosmic' a lot. Older listeners who are familiar with this classic should ignore these facetious remarks and continue to enjoy it.

» Tracks: *'2112': Overture/ The Temples Of Syrinx/ Discovery/ Presentation/Oracle: The Dream/ Soliloquy/ Grand Finale; A Passage To Bangkok; The Twilight Zone; Lessons; Tears; Something For Nothing.*

★ First released 1976
★ UK peak chart position: did not chart
★ USA peak chart position: 61
★ Previous Top 1000 position: 1998 (–): 1994 (–)

739 NO FENCES ↑ Garth Brooks

The second album from new country's shining star. Since the release of this 1990 collection Garth Brooks has gone on to become the biggest-selling US solo recording artist of all time, an incredible achievement that has helped country music cross over into the mainstream. Brooks is a phenomenon and power-house tracks such as 'The Thunder Rolls' and 'Friends In Low Places' demonstrate just why. With this album Brooks made country acceptable to a mass audience and opened the door for countless others in the 90s. A considerable pat on the back is deserved.

» Tracks: *The Thunder Rolls; New Way To Fly; Two Of A Kind, Workin' On A Full House; Victim Of The Game; Friends In Low Places; Wild Horses; Unanswered Prayers; Same Old Story; Mr. Blue; Wolves.*

★ First released 1990
★ UK peak chart position: did not chart
★ USA peak chart position: 3
★ Previous Top 1000 position: 1998 (–): 1994 (–)

740 WHITNEY HOUSTON ↑ Whitney Houston

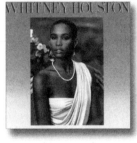

Although she has now been eclipsed by younger urban R&B female stars, Houston will stand as the first to bring this type of clean soul music to the world. In the USA alone, this record stayed in the charts for four years, sold fifteen million copies and spent fourteen weeks on top of the charts. It would be churlish to offer any criticism when most of the world would disagree. The immaculate production is by Jermaine Jackson, bank manager is Clive Davis, and even the bathing suit on the back cover gets a credit. It is however, with all its slickness, an indispensable soul album.

» Tracks: *You Give Good Love; Thinking About You; Someone For Me; Saving All My Love For You; Nobody Loves Me Like You Do; How Will I Know; All At Once; Take Good Care Of My Heart; Greatest Love Of All; Hold Me.*

★ First released 1985
★ UK peak chart position: 2
★ USA peak chart position: 1
★ Previous Top 1000 position: 1998 (863): 1994 (–)

741 CROSS ROAD ↓
Bon Jovi

Laid out side by side, track after track, the Bon Jovi catalogue is pretty formidable. Although this is a compilation, it is such a well-chosen selection, it sounds like a regular album. Lighter-sounding tracks such as 'Someday I'll Be Saturday Night' complement the rock anthem sound of 'Livin' On A Prayer'. Or how about the wonderful lyric of 'shot through the heart, and you're to blame, you give love a bad name'? How many thousands of spurned males and females have gone home and played that one very loud? The most highly accessible rock band currently around: loud, varied, melodic and great fun.

» Tracks: *Livin' On A Prayer; Keep The Faith; Someday I'll Be Saturday Night; Always; Wanted Dead Or Alive; Lay Your Hands On Me; You Give Love A Bad Name; Bed Of Roses; Blaze Of Glory; In These Arms; Bad Medicine; I'll Be There For You; In and Out Of Love; Runaway; Never Say Goodbye.*

★ First released 1994
★ UK peak chart position: 1
★ USA peak chart position: 8
★ Previous Top 1000 position: 1998 (577): 1994 (–)

742 LOVE IS THE THING ↓
Nat 'King' Cole

Released in the days when albums were not promoted by extracting individual tracks and issuing them as singles, this was the first opportunity that young record-buyers had of hearing Nat 'King' Cole sing 'When I Fall In Love' and 'Stardust', songs with which he would forever be identified. Composer Hoagy Carmichael, who wrote 'Stardust' with Mitchell Parish, always maintained that this version, complete with the lovely verse, was his personal favourite. Of all the singer's varied albums – jazz, 'soft' country, easy listening – *Love Is The Thing*, which spent 55 weeks in the US Top 40, was the only one that went to number 1, where it stayed for eight weeks.

» Tracks: *When I Fall In Love; The End Of A Love Affair; Stardust; Stay As Sweet As You Are; Where Can I Go Without You; Maybe It's Because I Love You Too Much; Love Letters; Ain't Misbehavin'; I Thought About Marie; At Last; It's All In The Game; When Sunny Gets Blue; Love Is The Thing.*

★ First released 1957
★ UK peak chart position: did not chart
★ USA peak chart position: 1
★ Previous Top 1000 position: 1998 (494): 1994 (132)

743 SPIRIT ↑
Jewel

After the major US success of Jewel's 1995 debut, *Pieces Of You*, her eagerly anticipated follow-up failed to attract a wider audience but at least gave her now deeply committed fans exactly what they wanted. Even though she became a best-selling poet at the same time, the saturation coverage in the media was at last dying down leaving the singer free to concentrate on her lyrics and music. This is a more finely tuned album that bodes well for Jewel's long-term recording career. She has a voice that occasionally threatens to burst into full Dolly Parton mode (especially on 'Hands'), but thankfully resists the temptation and stays in Joni Mitchell territory instead.

» Tracks: *Deep Water; What's Simple Is True; Hands; Kiss The Flame; Down So Long; Innocence Maintained; Jupiter; Fat Boy; Enter From The East; Barcelona; Life Uncommon; Do You; Absence Of Fear.*

★ First released 1998
★ UK peak chart position: 54
★ USA peak chart position: 3
★ Previous Top 1000 position: 1998 (–): 1994 (–)

744 PUMP ↑
Aerosmith

Sounding revitalized after a two year break following *Permanent Vacation*, America's favourite hard rock band launched into the opener 'Young Lust' like a bunch of hungry teenagers. The fact that Tyler and his cronies survived every excess imaginable never fails to amaze. As 'Young Lust' closes, drummer Joey Kramer refuses to stop and finishes with a furious flurry. 'F.I.N.E.' keeps up the incredible pace, and such is the energy generated by this album that it is difficult to believe it took several months to record. 'Love In An Elevator' is another reason for choosing *Pump* as your desert island Aerosmith album.

» Tracks: *Young Lust; F.I.N.E.; Going Down/Love In An Elevator; Monkey On My Back; Water Song/Janie's Got A Gun; Dulcimer Stomp/The Other Side; My Girl; Don't Get Mad, Get Even; Hoodoo/Voodoo Medicine Man; What It Takes.*

★ First released 1989
★ UK peak chart position: 3
★ USA peak chart position: 5
★ Previous Top 1000 position: 1998 (–): 1994 (–)

745 DESTROYER ↑
Kiss

At a time when many heavy rock bands were getting too pretentious for words Kiss managed to rise above it all by never once taking themselves seriously. Their glam-rock make-up and ridiculous stack heel boots would make that impossible anyway. This endearing quality means that Kiss, like Queen, have managed to retain their street cred with fickle rock fans. Somehow they can get away with lyrics such as 'everybody's gonna move their feet, everybody's gonna leave their seat', whereas REO Speedwagon would be dead in the water. 'Shout It Out Loud' shows Kiss at their barred chord/repeat chorus best. Just skip the daft lyrics.

❱❱ Tracks: *Detroit Rock City; King Of The Night Time World; God Of Thunder; Great Expectations; Flaming Youth; Sweet Pain; Shout It Out Loud; Beth; Do You Love Me?.*

★ First released 1976
★ UK peak chart position: 22
★ USA peak chart position: 11
★ Previous Top 1000 position: 1998 (–): 1994 (–)

746 THE B-52'S ↑
The B'52's

Formed in Athens, Georgia, the B-52's emerged from this nominal outback with 'Rock Lobster', a quirky pop song that drew critical praise and engendered a major recording contract. *The B-52's* maintained the originality of that debut single, with staccato voices, vox guitar and surreal lyrics. Drawing on 60s kitsch ephemera, both aurally and visually, the quintet created a unified image, but one reflecting post-modernism rather than nostalgia. A cracked sense of humour lay at the core of this album, but the group's infectious joy and sense of purpose blend with danceable rhythms to ensure a quality more enduring than mere wackiness.

❱❱ Tracks: *Planet Claire; 52 Girls; Dance This Mess Around; Rock Lobster; Lava; There's A Moon In The Sky (Called Moon); Hero Worship; 6060-842; Downtown.*

★ First released 1979
★ UK peak chart position: 22
★ USA peak chart position: 59
★ Previous Top 1000 position: 1998 (940): 1994 (383)

747 SOLO MONK ↑
Thelonious Monk

This was recorded at a time when Monk had fallen out of favour with jazz critics who felt his work had become predictable and stale. His record company had no such problem with their artist. The album sold well and was nominated for an Art Director's Club award (for the excellent Paul Davis cover). Musically it is a simple joy, with Monk gracefully plonking and smacking his way through an interesting selection of originals and standards. Two highlights are 'Ruby, My Dear' and 'These Foolish Things (Remind Me Of You)' both played with Monk's characteristic halted timing. There are stronger Monk sets, but none as charming.

❱❱ Tracks: *Dinah; I Surrender, Dear; Sweet and Lovely; North Of The Sunset; Ruby, My Dear; I'm Confessin' (That I Love You); I Hadn't Anyone Till You; Everything Happens To Me; Monk's Point; I Should Care; Ask Me Now; These Foolish Things (Remind Me Of You); Introspection.*

★ First released 1965
★ UK peak chart position: did not chart
★ USA peak chart position: did not chart
★ Previous Top 1000 position: 1998 (–): 1994 (–)

748 BURGERS ↑
Hot Tuna

The magnificent, though sometimes top-heavy, splinter group formed by Jack Casady and Jorma Kaukonen from the Jefferson Airplane, Hot Tuna allowed two exceptional musicians to stretch out and explore their love of old blues. It also stopped them becoming bored while Grace Slick and Paul Kantner gazed at the ocean. A strong feature of this Tuna album was the violin of Papa John Creach. They successfully mixed beautifully evocative instrumentals such as 'Highway Song' with traditional numbers like 'True Religion'. Their own blues sounded authentic, notably with the most agreeable 'Keep On Truckin'. Make a note of its tongue-in-cheek fishy lyrics, which only a Hot Tuna could sing.

❱❱ Tracks: *True Religion; Highway Song; 99 Year Blues; Sea Child; Keep On Truckin'; Water Song; Ode For Billy Dean; Let Us Get Together Right Down Here; Sunny Day Strut.*

★ First released 1972
★ UK peak chart position: did not chart
★ USA peak chart position: 68
★ Previous Top 1000 position: 1998 (976): 1994 (–)

749 A DAY AT THE RACES ↓
Queen

A Day At The Races, released in 1976, celebrated Queen's diversity and colourfully flamboyant sense of the unreal. Stylistically, the adoption of any one musical form over the other was simply beneath them. They flirted with a passion, dipping and whimsical with 'Good Old Fashioned Lover Boy', grand, entranced and eloquent with 'Somebody To Love', while 'Tie Your Mother Down', with its sense of mischief, scathing wit and a shrill, delighted laugh, put its foot through the floor and a fist through the ceiling. To paraphrase The Times, a work of sheer bloody poetry. I would not go quite that far, it is rock 'n' roll after all.

» Tracks: Long Away; The Millionaire Waltz; You and I; Somebody To Love; White Man; Good Old Fashioned Lover Boy; Drowse; Teo Torriate (Let Us Cling Together); Tie Your Mother Down; You Take My Breath Away.

★ First Released 1976
★ UK peak chart position: 1
★ USA peak chart position: 5
★ Previous Top 1000 position: 1998 (687): 1994 (238)

750 ILL COMMUNICATION ↑
The Beastie Boys

'Can blue men sing the whites?', sang the Bonzo Dog Band in the late 60s. Today's parallel is 'can white boys sing the rap?' and of course the answer is yes, as good as anybody, black, white or blue. These middle-class college boys spoke out for a generation of tense youth. Don't be fooled by the bluster, this is intelligent stuff with rhyming stanzas that no song hack could top. How about 'I do the Patty Duke in case you don't remember, I freak a funky beat like the shit was in a blender'. And on and on, great couplets, bad language, profound language, it's all from the same pie.

» Tracks: Sure Shot; Tough Guy; B-Boys Makin' With The Freak Freak; Bobo On The Corner; Root Down; Sabotage; Get It Together; Sabrosa; The Update; Futterman's Rule; Alright Hear This; Eugene's Lament; Flute Loop; Do It; Ricky's Theme; Heart Attack Man; The Scoop; Shambala; Bodhisattva Vow; Transitions.

★ First released 1994
★ UK peak chart position: 10
★ USA peak chart position: 1
★ Previous Top 1000 position: 1998 (–): 1994 (–)

751 PROMENADE ↑
The Divine Comedy

The Divine Comedy is the brainchild of Neil Hannon, a Scott Walker for the 90s, with a welcome side-order of arch humour thrown in. Promenade remains his most satisfying work, a concept album loosely based around a day in the life of two young lovers. With arrangements inspired by Michael Nyman and lyrics that quote freely from literature and film, Promenade continually borders on the pretentious. However, when Hannon's lush orchestral pop reaches its grand peaks on 'The Summerhouse' and the closing segue of 'Ten Seconds To Midnight' and 'Tonight We Fly', his overreaching ambition is spectacularly justified.

» Tracks: Bath; Going Downhill Fast; The Booklovers; A Seafood Song; Geronimo; Don't Look Down; When The Lights Go Out All Over Europe; The Summerhouse; Neptunes Daughter; A Drinking Song; Ten Seconds To Midnight; Tonight We Fly.

★ First released 1994
★ UK peak chart position: did not chart
★ USA peak chart position: did not chart
★ Previous Top 1000 position: 1998 (939): 1994 (–)

752 MELLOW GOLD ↑
Beck

Beck's breakthrough in the 90s from lo-fi singer-songwriter to something so original that classification became impossible saw hip-hop, country, rock, dance, blues, and metal filtered through his unique vision as part of a process that would eventually culminate with 1996's hugely acclaimed Odelay. Mellow Gold deserves serious attention as an important stepping stone, and in reality is only a rat's whisker behind Odelay in terms of quality. 'Pay No Mind (Snoozer)' and 'Truckdrivin Neighbors Downstairs' at least proves that somebody else listened to Skip Spence's Oar, and that Neil Diamond chords ('Fuckin' With My Head (Mountain Dew Rock)') have finally found a credible home. In other words, this is totally derivative and yet highly original. Another of his 'very important' albums.

» Tracks: Loser; Pay No Mind (Snoozer); Fuckin' With My Head (Mountain Dew Rock); Whiskeyclone, Hotel City 1997; Soul Suckin Jerk; Truckdrivin Neighbors Downstairs; Sweet Sunshine; Beercan; Steal My Body Home; Nitemare Hippy Girl; Mutherf..er; Blackhole.

★ First released 1994
★ UK peak chart position: 41 ★ USA peak chart position: 13
★ Previous Top 1000 position: 1998 (–): 1994 (–)

753 NO CODE ↑
Pearl Jam

The fourth album from the veteran grunge act is an experimental mixture of different styles and textures. A lot more acoustic based material appears alongside the usual stuff expected from Pearl Jam. The opening 'Sometimes' is a sombre affair followed by 'Hail, Hail' which opens with vocalist Eddie Vedder sounding uncannily like Johnny Rotten singing 'Holidays In The Sun'. The change in style has no alarming effect on the band's reputation, even though some of the more reflective tracks are much less exciting than the in-your-face rockers. *No Code* is a bold album that demonstrates Pearl Jam's confidence and determination to move forward.

❱❱ Tracks: *Sometimes; Hail, Hail; Who You Are; In My Tree; Smile; Off He Goes; Habit; Red Mosquito; Lukin; Present Tense; Mankind; I'm Open; Around The Bend.*

★ First released 1996
★ UK peak chart position: 3
★ USA peak chart position: 1
★ Previous Top 1000 position: 1998 (–): 1994 (–)

754 BACK STABBERS ↓
The O'Jays

With its in-house staff and recognizable sound, the Philadelphia International label was an early 70s equivalent of 60s Tamla/Motown. Flagship harmony act the O'Jays revelled in its sumptuous arrangements and flowing rhythms, as this excellent album testifies. Producers and songwriters Gamble and Huff sculpted brilliant scenarios for the group; cautionary tales, in the case of the exhilarating title track, or clarion calls for universal brotherhood, as exemplified in 'Love Train'. The O'Jays brought many years of experience to these recordings, and on *Back Stabbers* found a spiritual home for their considerable talents.

❱❱ Tracks: *When The World's At Peace; Back Stabbers; Who Am I; (They Call Me) Mr. Lucky; Time To Get Down; 992 Arguments; Listen To The Clock On The Wall; Shiftless, Shady, Jealous Kind Of People; Sunshine; Love Train.*

★ First released 1972
★ UK peak chart position: did not chart
★ USA peak chart position: 10
★ Previous Top 1000 position: 1998 (557): 1994 (741)

755 HARVEST MOON ↑
Neil Young

Q: How is it that old grumpy can get away with an opening line like 'she used to work in a diner, never saw a woman finer'? A: Because he is Neil Young, a man who could come out in support of Ronald Reagan and still not lose his credibility. As the title suggests this is essentially *Harvest* revisited, and it proved to be almost as much of a critical and commercial success as the earlier album. Ben Keith's steel guitar adds to the melancholic atmosphere on this thoroughly beautiful record. True to form (he has recorded seven diverse albums since) it did not mark a slide into easy nostalgia by a man approaching his late 40s.

❱❱ Tracks: *Unknown Legend; From Hank To Hendrix; You and Me; Harvest Moon; War Of Man; One Of These Days; Such A Woman; Old King; Dreamin' Man; Natural Beauty.*

★ First released 1992
★ UK peak chart position: 9
★ USA peak chart position: 16
★ Previous Top 1000 position: 1998 (–): 1994 (–)

756 DREAM LETTER (LIVE IN LONDON 1968) ↑ Tim Buckley

Tim Buckley's London debut was recorded shortly after the release of the pivotal *Happy Sad*, on which he had broken away from folk music and embraced a more expressive, jazz-based style. The respectful audience at the Queen Elizabeth Hall reserve their warmest applause for standard singer-songwriter fare like 'Morning Glory' and 'Once I Was', but Buckley himself seems more at ease on lengthier vocal workouts such as 'Love From Room 109/Strange Feeling' and 'Carnival Song/Hi Lily, Hi Lo', enjoying the new-found freedom of expression afforded his remarkable multi-octave voice. The musical accompaniment is superb, Buckley's 12-string backed by guitar, vibes and bass. The only mystery is why this recording did not gain an official release until 1990.

❱❱ Tracks: *Introduction; Buzzin' Fly; Phantasmagoria In Two; Morning Glory; Dolphins; I've Been Out Walking; The Earth Is Broken; Who Do You Love; Pleasant Street/You Keep Me Hanging On; Love From Room 109/Strange Feelin'; Carnival Song/Hi Lily, Hi Lo; Hallucinations; Troubadour; Dream Letter/Happy Time; Wayfaring Stranger/You Got Me Runnin'; Once I Was.*

★ First released 1990
★ UK peak chart position: did not chart
★ USA peak chart position: did not chart
★ Previous Top 1000 position: 1998 (775): 1994 (–)

757 WHEELS OF FIRE ↓
Cream

Wheels Of Fire solved Cream's artistic dilemma whereby studio work was largely concise but live appearances centred on improvisation. This double set successfully offered both facets and captured the trio at their most ambitious. The in-concert section, in particular 'Crossroads', showed remarkable musical empathy, especially the dexterity of Jack Bruce and the fluidity of Eric Clapton. Pop songs and blues standards nestled together while cellos, viola and trumpet embellished certain selections as the group, in tandem with producer Felix Pappalardi, expanded Cream's oeuvre. Lyricist Pete Brown enhanced this experimental vision which defined the unit's creative peak.

» Tracks: *White Room; Sitting On Top Of The World; Passing The Time; As You Said; Pressed Rat and Warthog; Politician; Those Were The Days; Born Under A Bad Sign; Deserted Cities Of The Heart; Crossroads; Spoonful; Train Time; Toad.*

★ First released 1968
★ UK peak chart position: 3
★ USA peak chart position: 1
★ Previous Top 1000 position: 1998 (279): 1994 (526)

758 ROPIN' THE WIND ↑
Garth Brooks

It's hard to believe that Garth Brooks is already the biggest selling solo singer in American music history. This means that the likes of Presley, Sinatra, Elton John and Skip Spence are dwarfed in comparison. Brooks is one of a few younger artists who makes country music OK to own up to liking. He has a marvellous slipnote in his voice, in the style of Floyd Cramer's unforgettable piano style. He seamlessly mixes his own material with songs by Billy Joel ('Shameless'), and Larry Bastian ('Rodeo') and surrounds himself with the finest Nashville sidemen. A hard to fault recording with some notable highlights in 'What She's Doing Now' and 'In Lonesome Dove'.

» Tracks: *Against The Grain; Rodeo; What She's Doing Now; Burning Bridges; Papa Loved Mama; Shameless; Cold Shoulder; We Bury The Hatchet; In Lonesome Dove; The River; Alabama Clay; Everytime That It Rains; Nobody Gets Off In This Town; Cowboy Bill.*

★ First released 1991
★ UK peak chart position: 41
★ USA peak chart position: 1
★ Previous Top 1000 position: 1998 (–): 1994 (–)

759 TATTOO YOU ↑
The Rolling Stones

Not a Stones album that rolls readily off the tongue when discussing their back catalogue over a vat of wine, but its benefits become clear once you can be bothered to put it in the CD player in preference to *Let It Bleed* or *Exile On Main Street*. From the first three chords the listener knows something special is about to burst out of the speakers, and indeed 'Start Me Up' is arguably the best ever opening track of a Stones album. The pace doesn't relent with 'Hang Fire' and 'Slave', the latter boasting a 'Honky Tonk Women' intro and sounding a little bit like Little Feat. A highly recommended album that finishes up nicely with the quite delightful 'Waiting On A Friend'.

» Tracks: *Start Me Up; Hang Fire; Slave; Little T&A; Black Limousine; Neighbours; Worried About You; Tops; Heaven; No Use In Crying; Waiting On A Friend.*

★ First released 1981
★ UK peak chart position: 2
★ USA peak chart position: 1
★ Previous Top 1000 position: 1998 (–): 1994 (–)

760 SCOTT 4 ↑
Scott Walker

This album was released at the tail end of the 60s when Walker was completely out of step with musical fashion. Consequently its sales were disastrous, it failed to chart and was soon deleted. Thirty years later it is viewed as a small masterpiece by a critical *cognoscenti* whose numbers still would not make it chart. Walker has one of the greatest voices in popular music, and that is not a flippant statement. Like his choice of material or not, the voice is omnipresent. The orchestral accompaniment perfectly complements Walker's ten beautiful compositions, especially 'Boy Child' and 'Angels Of Ashes', which are expertly conducted by Angela Morley (who used to be Wally Stott).

» Tracks: *The Seventh Seal; On Your Own Again; The World's Strongest Man; Angels Of Ashes; Boy Child; Hero Of The War; The Old Man's Back Again; Duchess; Get Behind Me; Rhymes Of Goodbye.*

★ First released 1969
★ UK peak chart position: did not chart
★ USA peak chart position: did not chart
★ Previous Top 1000 position: 1998 (–): 1994 (–)

761 DESIRE ↑
Bob Dylan

This album was the product of another great creative burst in the long and winding career of the twentieth century's leading musical poet. 'Hurricane', which angrily relates the story of unjustly imprisoned boxer Rubin Carter, and 'Joey' marked a rare return to topical politics. Dylan really shines on the album's personal songs, however, returning to the muse of 'Sad Eyed Lady Of The Lowlands' on the aching 'Sara' and the spiky 'Isis'. In addition to Dylan's excellent singing the album features some formidable playing from violinist Scarlet Rivera, and is a solid work from a man who had by then been there and done that many times.

》 Tracks: *Hurricane; Isis; Mozambique; One More Cup Of Coffee; Oh, Sister; Joey; Romance In Durango; Black Diamond Bay; Sara.*

★ First released 1976
★ UK peak chart position: 3
★ USA peak chart position: 1
★ Previous Top 1000 position: 1998 (–): 1994 (–)

762 HEAVY SOUL ↓
Paul Weller

As Paul Weller gets better, so his critics start coming out of the woodwork. *Heavy Soul* received black and white reviews, none were grey. Prolonged listening draws out more from the material. It continues his late 60s flirtation that developed on *Stanley Road*. This time the guitar is heavier, although it never clouds the obvious quality of songs such as 'Peacock Suit' and the title track. Weller reveals the pitfalls of neglecting a relationship in the beautiful 'I Should Have Been There To Inspire You'. Further revelatory lyrics can be found in 'Science' with 'I've got a pick in my pocket does that make me a player?'. That is for the listener to make up his or her mind.

》 Tracks: *Heavy Soul Pt 1; Peacock Suit; Up In Suzes' Room; Brushed; Driving Nowhere; I Should Have Been There To Inspire You; Heavy Soul Pt 2; Friday Street; Science; Golden Sands; As You Lean Into The Light; Mermaids.*

★ First released 1997
★ UK peak chart position: 2
★ USA peak chart position: did not chart
★ Previous Top 1000 position: 1998 (685): 1994 (–)

763 LOAD ↑
Metallica

Tremendous stuff, even for the most committed metal hater. Metallica are one of the few who even the most bigoted will grudgingly admit to liking. The line-up of James Hetfield, Lars Ulrich, Jason Newsted and Kirk Hammett, together since 1986, had by this time developed a phenomenally tight and streamlined sound. *Load* came after a lengthy recording hiatus following the unprecedented success of 1991's self-titled 'black' album. Nothing had changed in the interim except maybe one or two hairlines receding an inch or so. The two opening tracks 'Ain't My Bitch' and '2 X 4' burn as strongly as anything on *Metallica*, and this album is highly recommended to non-believers.

》 Tracks: *Ain't My Bitch; 2 X 4; The House Jack Built; Until It Sleeps; King Nothing; Hero Of The Day; Bleeding Me; Cure; Poor Twisted Me; Wasting My Hate; Mama Said; Thorn Within; Ronnie; The Outlaw Torn.*

★ First released 1996
★ UK peak chart position: 1
★ USA peak chart position: 1
★ Previous Top 1000 position: 1998 (–): 1994 (–)

764 GIANT STEPS ↓
John Coltrane

As influential upon contemporaries and successors as were Louis Armstrong and Charlie Parker, John Coltrane divided critical comment. For his supporters he was both high priest of contemporary jazz and prophet of what was yet to come. The ultimate statement of Coltrane's early obsession with chord progressions, this album marks the moment before he changed direction. *Giant Steps* is a vibrant demonstration of his inventive, dazzling and relentless playing of bop. Hereafter, Coltrane sought and found an avenue for his restless exploratory zeal in modal jazz. The album is therefore both a landmark and turning point and is still a textbook for many young musicians.

》 Tracks: *Giant Steps; Cousin Mary; Countdown; Spiral; Syeeda's Song Flute; Mr. P.C.; Naima.*

★ First released 1959
★ UK peak chart position: did not chart
★ USA peak chart position: did not chart
★ Previous Top 1000 position: 1998 (412): 1994 (240)

765 RID OF ME ↑
PJ Harvey

The album opens with a moodily strummed guitar that builds to a climax. Over and over she repeats 'Lick my lips I'm on fire' making the male listener squirm. This is highly charged sexuality, yet each time the title track is played, its shocking power never fails. PJ Harvey is an artist who takes absolutely no prisoners, a black widow of lyricism that threatens and makes you blush with painful honesty. Similar themes are explored with 'Legs' and 'Rub 'Til It Bleeds'. The only odd choice is a poor cover of Dylan's 'Highway 61 Revisited'. Johnny Winter tried and failed as well.

》 Tracks: *Rid Of Me; Missed; Legs; Rub 'Til It Bleeds; Hook; Man-Size Sextet; Highway '61 Revisited; 50ft Queenie; Yuri-G; Man-Size; Dry; Me-Jane; Snake; Ecstasy.*

★ First released 1993
★ UK peak chart position: 3
★ USA peak chart position: 158
★ Previous Top 1000 position: 1998 (964): 1994 (–)

766 RATTUS NORVEGICUS ↓
The Stranglers

Probably the most underrated of the new wave/punk bands, these non-too youthful Guildford brutes simply did not count, according to pundits such as Jon Savage, though that view may have been tempered by the fact that Jean Jaques Burnel gave him a kicking after a hostile review. The Stranglers combined a dark view of human nature with a musical legacy that stretched far beyond the year zero philosophy of others. *Rattus Norvegicus* offers a blend of cynicism, menace and antagonism unheard of since the Stooges (frequent comparisons to the Doors were misleading – they both had prominent keyboards). Stand-out tracks include the utterly venomous 'Ugly', the stage standard 'Hanging Around' and the elegiac 'Down In The Sewer'.

》 Tracks: *Sometimes; Goodbye Toulouse; London Lady; Princess Of The Streets; Hanging Around; Peaches; Get A Grip On Yourself; Ugly; Down In The Sewer: Falling; Down In The Sewer: Trying To Get Out Again; Rats Rally.*

★ First released 1977
★ UK peak chart position: 4
★ USA peak chart position: did not chart
★ Previous Top 1000 position: 1998 (231): 1994 (186)

767 DAYDREAM ↓
The Lovin' Spoonful

Even though their hits catalogue has been plundered, at least one album from this stellar New York pop band should be in every record collection. John Sebastian was a lyrical craftsman and master of short, humorous love songs. Lengthy titles said exactly what they meant, with 'Didn't Want To Have To Do It' or 'You Didn't Have To Be So Nice' (an unforgettable intro), both glorious. Sebastian, Boone, Yanovsky and Butler were no slouches at goodtime blues either on 'Bald Headed Lena' and 'Jug Band Music'. It is, however, the title track that brings the biggest smiles and happiest memories. As indispensable and timeless as the Beatles, and Sebastian's creative touch is greatly missed today.

》 Tracks: *Daydream; There She Is; It's Not Time Now; Warm Baby; Day Blues; Let The Boy Rock & Roll; Jug Band Music; Didn't Want To Have To Do It; You Didn't Have To Be So Nice; Bald Headed Lena; Butchie's Tune; Big Noise From Speonk.*

★ First released 1966
★ UK peak chart position: 8
★ USA peak chart position: 10
★ Previous Top 1000 position: 1998 (677): 1994 (306)

768 ACTUALLY ↓
Pet Shop Boys

Reappraisal is always revealing, whether for good or bad. In the case of this album, the great revelation is the magnificent orchestration, even though it is created by fairlights and keyboards. 'One More Chance' is blissfully symphonic and the favourite hits are still irritatingly effective. The production is shared between Julian Mendelsohn, David Jacob, Shep Pettibone and Stephen Hague and is mixed to digital perfection. Ultimately this album succeeds in delivering 'pop' exactly as it should be, but played too often it will begin to grate on your friends, as you will end up humming it all day and drive them to despair. One play through every six months is perfect.

》 Tracks: *One More Chance; Shopping; Rent; Hit Music; What Have I Done To Deserve This?; It Couldn't Happen Here; It's A Sin; I Want To Wake Up; Heart; King's Cross.*

★ First released 1987
★ UK peak chart position: 2
★ USA peak chart position: 25
★ Previous Top 1000 position: 1998 (226): 1994 (207)

769 EVERYWHERE ↑
Tim McGraw

How could anybody in their right mind not find this style of country music totally uplifting. Well you'd be surprised, in a world where the C&W tag has long gone there are still bigots and doubters. McGraw is probably the current male leader (over and above Garth Brooks and Vince Gill), of new country, and his wife Faith Hill probably leads the female field after Shania Twain. What a great life, discussing over breakfast who is going to pay the cheque in for today's record sales. This is a blinder of an album that opens up with three exemplary tracks. The third of these, 'It's Your Love', is performed with his breakfast partner.

⏭ Tracks: Where The Green Grass Grows; For A Little While; It's Your Love; Ain't That The Way It Always Ends; I Do But I Don't; One Of These Days; Hard On The Ticker; Everywhere; Just To See You Smile; You Just Get Better All The Time; You Turn Me On.

★ First released 1997
★ UK peak chart position: did not chart
★ USA peak chart position: 2
★ Previous Top 1000 position: 1998 (–): 1994 (–)

770 STILL CRAZY AFTER ALL THESE YEARS ↑   Paul Simon

Hardly prolific over the past thirty years, Paul Simon at least works on quality rather than quantity. This has its flaws, but as with every one of his records there are at least two or three absolute gems that will outlive us all. The title track is a perfect example, delivered with his intelligent, sweet charm – he could be telling us that he was just going outside to empty the bin and it would sound beautiful. Similarly 'Some Folks' Lives Roll Easy' and 'Have A Good Time' are still reminders to us all as to how we carry out our lives. Simon may have been speaking for himself in these songs, but they are charitably given to the listener to use.

⏭ Tracks: Still Crazy After All These years; My Little Town; I Do It For Your Love; 50 Ways To Leave Your Lover; Night Game; Gone At Last; Some Folks' Lives Roll Easy; Have A Good Time; You're Kind; Silent Eyes.

★ First released 1975
★ UK peak chart position: 6
★ USA peak chart position: 1
★ Previous Top 1000 position: 1998 (–): 1994 (–)

771 TO BRING YOU MY LOVE ↑
PJ Harvey

For such a waif-like figure, Polly Harvey has an attitude and voice which is sufficient to scare the pants off most men. On 'Meet Ze Monsta', the fear that her voice and the dirty buzzing guitars instil would certainly make anyone want to hide under the bed. The album simmers with a threatening, disquieting atmosphere, reaching the height of tension when the pace slows down to a crawl and Harvey's voice is reduced to a whisper, notably on 'Working For The Man' and 'Down By The Water'. Guitarist John Parish is Harvey's equal here, veering creepy acoustic strums to just plain evil electricity. Few albums can conjure up such a sinister ambience.

⏭ Tracks: To Bring You My Love; Meet Ze Monsta; Working For The Man; C'mon Billy; Teclo; Long Snake Moan; Down By The Water; I Think I'm A Mother; Send His Love To Me; The Dancer.

★ First released 1995
★ UK peak chart position: 12
★ USA peak chart position: 40
★ Previous Top 1000 position: 1998 (–): 1994 (–)

772 EPONYMOUS ↑
R.E.M.

This can be discounted as a proper compilation because of the alternate recordings and the inclusion of 'Romance', which appeared in the movie Made In Heaven. This is an excellent starting point to discover the joys of R.E.M. prior to their achieving rock stardom and becoming contemporary dinosaurs. The songs are drawn from a selection of albums beginning with Chronic Town and ending with Document, the album on which their sound began to thicken out and the songs became less whimsical. The Byrds-like 12-string guitar sound is in full chime throughout this selection, which includes their first classic pop single, 'The One I Love'. And try to get your head around the torrent of words on 'It's The End Of The World As We Know It (And I Feel Fine)'. In actual fact, the world was just beginning for R.E.M.

⏭ Tracks: Radio Free Europe; Gardening At Night; Talk About The Passion; So. Central Rain; (Don't Go Back To) Rockville; Can't Get There From Here; Driver 8; Romance; Fall On Me; The One I Love; Finest Worksong; It's The End Of The World As We Know It (And I Feel Fine).

★ First released 1988
★ UK peak chart position: 69 ★ USA peak chart position: 44
★ Previous Top 1000 position: 1998 (–): 1994 (–)

773 13 ↑
Blur

Following the release of *The Great Escape,* Blur watched from the sidelines while Oasis drowned in the rapidly stagnating Britpop pool. The cheeky Colchester chappies stealthily evolved into an inventive and mature unit and had the last laugh by effortlessly upping the creative stakes. Producer William Orbit works well with the often dramatic changes in style from song to song on *13.* 'Tender' is a sweetly sung and deceptively simple gospel-inflected ballad informed by Damon Albarn's recent split from Justine Frischmann, but the singer is just as convincing on experimental tracks such as 'Bugman' and 'B.L.U.R.E.M.I.'. Already way past worrying about commercial success, Blur now seems hell bent on being as different as possible. As such, *13* works a treat.

» Tracks: *Tender; Bugman; Coffee & TV; Swap Song; 1992; B.L.U.R.E.M.I.; Battle; Mellow Song; Trailerpark; Caramel; Trimm Trabb; No Distance Left To Run; Optigan 1.*

★ First released 1999
★ UK peak chart position: 1
★ USA peak chart position: did not chart
★ Previous Top 1000 position: 1998 (–): 1994 (–)

774 YOU'VE COME A LONG WAY, BABY ↑ Fatboy Slim

The album on which Norman Cook and mixer Simon Thornton put it all together and crossed over into the mainstream. *You've Come A Long Way, Baby* is a collection littered with outstanding tracks that helped put big beat music into the lives of everyday people. 'The Rockafeller Skank' was one of the year's most ubiquitous singles, no doubt thanks to the irresistibly singalong 'check it out now, the funk soul brother' vocal line. Almost as popular at slipping off the tongue at bath time were 'Right Here, Right Now', 'Gangster Tripping' ('its wot we're doing when the fat boys trippin'), and the magnificent 'Praise You'. A very clever chap, and one of 1998's highlights.

» Tracks: *Right Here, Right Now; The Rockafeller Skank; In Heaven; Gangster Tripping; Build It Up – Tear It Down; Kalifornia; Soul Surfing; You're Not From Brighton; Praise You; Love Island; Acid 8000.*

★ First released 1998
★ UK peak chart position: 1
★ USA peak chart position: 34
★ Previous Top 1000 position: 1998 (–): 1994 (–)

775 BOYS DON'T CRY ↑
The Cure

The endearing Cure have been with us for over 20 years, and although Robert Smith's wonderfully pleading voice has changed little, their sound has gradually become louder and beefier. This album recalls those early days when they were not quite punk, not quite new romantic, but definitely new wave. Labels aside, they were highly original and have maintained their own distinctive style ever since. Tinny guitar and wobbly bass complement each other, leaving a gap down the centre for Smith's vocals. Shades of Velvet Underground sneak in occasionally, but that is rather like saying that most drug addicts start out by drinking milk. A highly entertaining album.

» Tracks: *Boys Don't Cry ; Plastic Passion; 10.15 Saturday Night; Accuracy; So What; Jumping Someone Else's Train; Subway Song; Killing An Arab; Fire In Cairo; Another Day; Grinding Halt; Three Imaginary Boys.*

★ First released 1979
★ UK peak chart position: 71
★ USA peak chart position: did not chart
★ Previous Top 1000 position: 1998 (–): 1994 (–)

776 HEJIRA ↓
Joni Mitchell

Joni Mitchell draws freely on her heroes and influences, and in her turn inspires and informs the work of countless others; thus are the genes of our musical heritage passed on to new generations. The love of jazz glimpsed in *Court and Spark* and *The Hissing Of Summer Lawns* is wanton in *Hejira.* The arrangements are loose and the melodies seductively free-flowing. The lyrics, too, have broken free of rigid verse and rhyme structures and tend towards prose poetry. The cloak of introspection that weighs down on much of her work is lighter here; though far from mainstream. The chiming flanged guitar throughout, is inspired.

» Tracks: *Coyote; Amelia; Furry Sings The Blues; Strange Boy; Hejira; Song For Sharon; Black Crow; Blue Motel Room; Refuge Of The Road.*

★ First released 1976
★ UK peak chart position: 11
★ USA peak chart position: 13
★ Previous Top 1000 position: 1998 (201): 1994 (438)

777 BLEACH ↑
Nirvana

It should never be forgotten that this pre-*Nevermind* debut cost a monumental $600 to record. It should also be pointed out that the difference between the two records is not as wide as sales figures would indicate. The sound is sparser even though an additional guitarist, Jason Everman, was working with the band at the time. His name and photograph appear on the album, even though the guitar is pure Cobain. All the marvelous hooks, licks and riffs that made *Nevermind* so accessible are here in seed trays. In your personal quest for Nirvana this is an important and vital album.

» Tracks: *Blew; Floyd The Barber; About A Girl; School; Love Buzz; Paper Cuts; Negative Creep; Scoff; Swap Meet; Mr. Moustache; Sifting; Big Cheese; Downer.*

★ First released 1989
★ UK peak chart position: 33
★ USA peak chart position: 89
★ Previous Top 1000 position: 1998 (–): 1994 (–)

778 ... BABY ONE MORE TIME ↑
Britney Spears

There is a formula here: take the young hopeful, groom her, give her some catchy pop songs, and keep her shiny. It often fails, but with Britney Spears it has worked magically well. Britney is the great white hope for young girls, and a sweetheart for big boys. This album has already sold millions on the back of Spears' squeaky-clean reputation, which started on American TV with *The Mickey Mouse Club* and has been enhanced by her supposed vow of celibacy. The only surprise is the inclusion of Sonny and Cher's 'The Beat Goes On', with an 'interesting' new arrangement. Surely she does not need to emulate Cher?. Only time will tell.

» Tracks: *... Baby One More Time; (You Drive Me) Crazy; Sometimes; Soda Pop; Born To Make You Happy; From The Bottom Of My Broken Heart; I Will Be There; I Will Still Love You; Thinkin' About You; E-Mail My Heart; The Beat Goes On.*

★ First released 1998
★ UK peak chart position: 1
★ USA peak chart position: 1
★ Previous Top 1000 position: 1998 (–): 1994 (–)

779 LET'S STAY TOGETHER ↓
Al Green

The evocative title track that opens this glorious record sets a paradox. Al Green's remarkable voice, one that is hidden in the back of his throat, makes you constantly feel good. The subject matter of many of the songs on this album, however, is of sadness, lost love, frustration and confusion. Green was to popular soul in the 70s what Otis Redding was in the 60s; it was refreshing to see him performing and recording again in the early 90s. Perhaps the good reverend already knew in 1972 that he would be called to the church, because this collection has amazing healing powers.

» Tracks: *Let's Stay Together; La-La For You; So You're Leaving; What Is This Feeling; Old Time Lovin'; I've Never Found A Girl; How Can You Mend A Broken Heart; Judy; It Ain't No Fun To Me.*

★ First released 1972
★ UK peak chart position: did not chart
★ USA peak chart position: 8
★ Previous Top 1000 position: 1998 (335): 1994 (608)

780 CRASH ↑
Dave Matthews Band

A greatly anticipated follow-up to the big breakthrough *Under The Table and Dreaming*, this album widened the Dave Matthews Band's appeal and proved that they were not another repeat of the Spin Doctors. *Crash* contains a similarly eclectic mix of styles, with Matthews' now distinctive lead vocal lending the collection continuity and familiarity. Instruments usually unfamiliar in a rock context are tastefully employed, notably baritone saxophone, flute, mandolin and violin. 'Crash Into Me' builds beautifully over an acoustic riff, seemingly soft but in reality full of guts, while funky brass sneaks into the soulful 'Too Much'. Don't sneer, this is quite superb.

» Tracks: *So Much To Say; Two Step; Crash Into Me; Too Much; #41; Say Goodbye; Drive In Drive Out; Let You Down; Lie In Our Graves; Cry Freedom; Tripping Billies; Proudest Monkey.*

★ First released 1996
★ UK peak chart position: did not chart
★ USA peak chart position: 2
★ Previous Top 1000 position: 1998 (–): 1994 (–)

781 SONGS OF FAITH AND DEVOTION LIVE ↑ Depeche Mode

Fittingly enough this ambitious live set, released only eight months after the original studio album, does not feature any tracks recorded in their native England. Depeche Mode's early days in Basildon, Essex seems far away from the stadium rock sound they had adopted by the early 90s. America in particular, took them to their hearts, although their new-found popularity forced the band to work so long and play so hard it almost took the life of singer Dave Gahan. This is a powerful record, demonstrating how fat and rich their sound had become, and in particular how grand Gahan's voice had become. This is a poison chalice record; a reminder of a great, lucrative tour, but a chilling nudge towards excess and near death.

» Tracks: *I Feel You; Walking In My Shoes; Condemnation; Mercy In You; Judas; In Your Room; Get Right With Me; Rush; One Caress; Higher Love.*

★ First released 1993
★ UK peak chart position: 1
★ USA peak chart position: 1
★ Previous Top 1000 position: 1998 (–): 1994 (–)

782 PLAY ↑ Moby

If any one artist can cross the barrier from dance music into the mainstream, Moby has the best credentials. He has been sitting in his bedroom for months, noodling around, and absorbing all kinds of music from the past seventy years (not just post rock 'n' roll). His use of Alan Lomax field recordings of early American folk blues is staggering. The way he has melded 21st century electronica with primitive sound from a simple tape recorder, deserves a medal. And for those of you who find dance too clinical, Moby gets up on stage, straps a guitar and sings along with his samples. For a moment you can believe this is rock 'n' roll.

» Tracks: *Honey; Find My Baby; Porcelain; Why Does My Heart Feel So Bad?; South Side; Rushing; Bodyrock; Natural Blues; Machete; 7; Run On; Down Slow; If Things Were Perfect; Everloving; Inside; Guitar Flute & String; The Sky Is Broken.*

★ First released 1999
★ UK peak chart position: 1
★ USA peak chart position: 48
★ Previous Top 1000 position: 1998 (–): 1994 (–)

783 IN-A-GADDA-DA-VIDA ↑ Iron Butterfly

For many years this late 60s prog rock extravaganza was the biggest-selling record in Atlantic Records' history. The main reason was the title-track, a memorable but ponderous 17-minute slice of self-indulgence. It is all here: long drum solo (takka takka, ding ding, ba boom boom), the guitar solo sounds like it's played with a tenon saw, and finally an overlong church organ solo, that needed the beef of a Hammond instead of the tinny Vox Farfisa sound. The vocals are great, and indeed, in a strange sort of way, so is the whole album. Often put down, but glorious stuff, especially the Rhino Records reissue with the extra tracks and the fluttering butterfly cover.

» Tracks: *Most Anything You Want; My Mirage; Termination; Are You Happy; In-A-Gadda-Da-Vida; Flowers and Beads; In-A-Gadda-Da-Vida (Live Version); In-A-Gadda-Da-Vida (Single Version).*

★ First released 1968
★ UK peak chart position: did not chart
★ USA peak chart position: 4
★ Previous Top 1000 position: 1998 (996): 1994 (984)

784 SURFACING ↑ Sarah McLachlan

One of the best discoveries of the 90s, McLachlan often harvests a strip between Neil Young and Joni Mitchell. She borrows Neil's chords ('Building A Mystery') and hires Joni's themes and high yodels ('Angel'), but maybe all Canadian's are allowed this artistic licence. Clearly she has been through the emotional mill, but still seems to want to go back for more ('Do What You Have To Do'). Her songs like Mitchell's seems to thrive on romantic turmoil, heaven help her songwriting career if she should find true happiness. This McLachlan recognises everything is really black and white ('Black and White'), there really is no grey world in between.

» Tracks: *Building A Mystery; I Love You; Sweet Surrender; Adia; Do What You Have To Do; Witness; Angel; Black & White; Full Of Grace; Last Dance.*

★ First released 1997
★ UK peak chart position: 47
★ USA peak chart position: 2
★ Previous Top 1000 position: 1998 (–): 1994 (–)

785 PORGY AND BESS ↑
Miles Davis

Taking George and Ira Gershwin's great musical, and steadily working through each song was a brave and ambitious venture. Cherry-picking the stand-outs such as 'Summertime' or 'It Ain't Necessarily So' would have been the easy option for most. Not Miles, or the brilliant Gil Evans for that matter. They pushed the boundaries of jazz further and tested their own abilities to the full. Every single note of every track works like a dream, the arrangements are immaculate, and the playing is faultless, with Miles' trumpet allowed the space and time it richly deserved. A five star album, and unquestionably one of the trumpeter's finest achievements.

➤ Tracks: *The Buzzard Song; Bess, You Is My Woman Now; Gone; Gone, Gone, Gone; Summertime; Oh Bess, Oh Where's My Bess?; Prayer (Oh Doctor Jesus); Fishermen, Strawberry and Devil Crab; My Man's Gone Now; It Ain't Necessarily So; Here Come De Honey Man; I Loves You, Porgy; There's A Boat That's Leaving Soon For New York.*

★ First released 1958
★ UK peak chart position: did not chart
★ USA peak chart position: did not chart
★ Previous Top 1000 position: 1998 (–): 1994 (–)

786 MONSTER ↑
R.E.M.

Although not the chart monster the record company expected, this album nevertheless contained enough hit singles to satisfy. There was a self-consciously harder edge to the recording, although the trademark melodies and haunting hooks were present in small doses. 'Crush With Eyeliner' was the commercial highlight, and tracks such as 'Star 69' harked back to the punk feel of the early R.E.M. albums. The tremelo tone of Peter Buck's guitar is constant throughout, irritating some, but also reflecting the band's desire to move as far as possible from the mandolin-dominated ballads of their most recent work. Michael Stipe's vocals were also mixed down, a perplexing move for what the band had planned as their all-out rock album.

➤ Tracks: *What's The Frequency, Kenneth?; Crush With Eyeliner; King Of Comedy; I Don't Sleep, I Dream; Star 69; Strange Currencies; Tongue; Bang and Blame; I Took Your Name; Let Me In; Circus Envy; You.*

★ First released 1994
★ UK peak chart position: 1
★ USA peak chart position: 1
★ Previous Top 1000 position: 1998 (918): 1994 (–)

787 DON'T LOOK BACK ↑
Boston

The difference between this album and Boston's phenomenally successful debut is a mere 14 million copies. The same flying saucer graces the cover and musically there is nothing to choose between the two albums. Presumably many people took the view that maybe you only need one AOR classic in your collection, and this one was passed over by a few million. *Don't Look Back* is a exercise in unbelievably perfect rock music played with slick conviction, although you suspect their might have been a few studio retakes. It might lack real passion, and Grateful Dead fans will shake their heads in dismay, but this is the pinnacle of gut wrenching, in your face FM rock. If you like that sort of thing.

➤ Tracks: *Don't Look Back; The Journey; It's Easy; A Man I'll Never Be; Feeling' Satisfied; Party; Used To Bad News; Don't Be Afraid.*

★ First released 1978
★ UK peak chart position: 9
★ USA peak chart position: 1
★ Previous Top 1000 position: 1998 (–): 1994 (–)

788 UNPLUGGED ↑
Eric Clapton

Of all the MTV Unplugged sessions that saturated the market during the 90s this is the best as it represents the format in its truest sense. This is an extremely honest and original album from an artist who we don't normally associate with unplugged guitars. The accompanying acoustic guitar from Andy Fairweather-Low works particularly well, and Clapton clearly relishes the opportunity at having a go at some of his favourite blues songs. You can feel the joy in 'San Francisco Bay Blues' and 'Before You Accuse Me'. Equally moving are the Will Jennings poem for Clapton's late son Connor, 'Tears In Heaven', and a fresh arrangement of 'Layla'.

➤ Tracks: *Signe; Before You Accuse Me; Hey Hey; Tears In Heaven; Lonely Stranger; Nobody Knows You When You're Down and Out; Layla; Running On Faith; Walkin' Blues; Alberta; San Francisco Bay Blues; Malted Milk; Old Love; Rollin' & Tumblin'.*

★ First released 1992
★ UK peak chart position: 2
★ USA peak chart position: 2
★ Previous Top 1000 position: 1998 (834): 1994 (336)

789 A MOMENTARY LAPSE OF REASON ↑ Pink Floyd

Pink Floyd could hardly be accused of being paparazzi lovers as their photographs rarely appear on their album sleeves. A cynic might suggest that Dave Gilmour and Nick Mason are wearing smug smiles on the sleeve photograph of this late 80s comeback album. They had just won their legal battle with Roger Waters, allowing A Momentary Lapse Of Reason to be released under the Pink Floyd name. As it turned out this was a much better collection than Waters' swan song The Final Cut. As much as it may hurt (and Waters does have our sympathy) his absence is not missed. There is not a single track that his presence would have improved.

▶ Tracks: Signs Of Life; Learning To Fly; The Dogs Of War; One Slip; On The Turning Away; Yet Another Movie; Round and Around; A New Machine Part 1; Terminal Frost; A New Machine Part 2; Sorrow.

★ First released 1987
★ UK peak chart position: 3
★ USA peak chart position: 3
★ Previous Top 1000 position: 1998 (–): 1994 (–)

790 THE GLOBE SESSIONS ↑ Sheryl Crow

Just as some of you were beginning to think Ms Crow was on the way out after her disappointing second album she popped up with this storming collection. Even though she no longer sells as many units as Alanis Morissette, Crow has seemingly dug herself in for the long haul as a quality singer-songwriter. What better way to open the album than with 'My Favorite Mistake', a clever track that features just the right amount of dirty guitar to avoid falling into AOR slickness. The rock pace rarely changes throughout, although the additional brass vignettes (including the great Bobby Keys) and the strings on 'Riverwide' are quite noteworthy.

▶ Tracks: My Favorite Mistake; There Goes The Neighborhood; Riverwide; It Don't Hurt; Maybe That's Something; Am I Getting Through (Part I & II); Anything But Down; The Difficult Kind; Mississippi; Members Only; Crash and Burn.

★ First released 1998
★ UK peak chart position: 2
★ USA peak chart position: 5
★ Previous Top 1000 position: 1998 (–): 1994 (–)

791 THE DOCK OF THE BAY ↓ Otis Redding

Compiled in the wake of Redding's premature death, The Dock Of The Bay is a suitable testimony to a gigantic performer. The melancholic title track suggested a new musical blueprint and elements of the previously unissued 'Open The Door' show a similarly muted perspective. Tracks culled from Otis Blue and The Soul Album sit beside the playful 'Tramp', which represents the singer's brief partnership with Carla Thomas. The remaining material is drawn from various sources, including flip-sides and compilations and, taken as a whole, the album provides a précis of Redding's past, as well as intimating what was so sadly lost.

▶ Tracks: Shake; Mr. Pitiful; Respect; Love Man; (I Can't Get No) Satisfaction; I Can't Turn You Loose; Hard To Handle; Fa-Fa-Fa-Fa-Fa (Sad Song); My Girl; I've Been Loving You Too Long; Try A Little Tenderness; My Lover's Prayer; That's How Strong My Love Is; Pain In My Heart; A Change Is Gonna Come; (Sittin' On) The Dock Of The Bay.

★ First released 1968
★ UK peak chart position: 1
★ USA peak chart position: 4
★ Previous Top 1000 position: 1998 (601): 1994 (218)

792 UNDER THE TABLE AND DREAMING ↑ Dave Matthews Band

This album made the Dave Matthews Band a huge attraction in the USA and has since sold millions of copies. Their record company immediately sent the band over to the UK for a low key promo gig at London's Marquee club. Polite reviews. Since then there has been little action outside the USA where they remain one of the most popular bands in recent years. Producer Steve Lillywhite fashions a solid European sound with great bursts of violin and saxophone that is at odds with the perceived image of the Dave Matthews Band as a parochial attraction. They are not your run of the mill rock band and have enough quirks and twists to merit attention outside the USA.

▶ Tracks: The Best Of What's Around; What Would You Say; Satellite; Rhyme and Reason; Typical Situation; Dancing Nancies; Ants Marching; Lover Lay Down; Jimi Thing; Warehouse; Pay For What You Get; #34.

★ First released 1994
★ UK peak chart position: did not chart
★ USA peak chart position: 11
★ Previous Top 1000 position: 1998 (–): 1994 (–)

793 BEN FOLDS FIVE ↑
Ben Folds Five

What a breath of fresh air Mr. Folds and his two cohorts are. What other rock group (and Ben Folds Five are rock, not pop) could so successfully use piano as the lead instrument. It really is quite refreshing to get through nearly fifty minutes of music without a guitar solo or an acoustic strum. The songs pull in all kinds of directions like a modern day 10cc, with clever key changes led by Folds' wayward piano and lyrics which never fail to intrigue. Long may Ben Folds Five be able to continue without feeling the need to add that six-stringed electric instrumentation. Strings might be the answer.

» Tracks: *Jackson Cannery; Philosophy; Julianne; Where's Summer B.?; Alice Childress; Underground; Sports & Wine; Uncle Walter; Best Imitation Of Myself; Video; The Last Polka; Boxing.*

★ First released 1995
★ UK peak chart position: did not chart
★ USA peak chart position: did not chart
★ Previous Top 1000 position: 1998 (–): 1994 (–)

794 FULL MOON, DIRTY HEARTS ↑ INXS

It seemed that INXS were trying to capture the excitement of their live performances on this album, a much more spontaneous and tougher sounding collection of material than previous efforts. The blistering 'The Gift' was one of their strongest songs in many a long year, and the album's opener 'Days Of Rust' is equally arresting. The excellent growling bass from Garry Beers on 'Make Your Peace' is reminiscent of Jack Bruce in Cream, and the sombre and chillingly prophetic 'Kill The Pain' benefits greatly from the vocal presence of Chrissie Hynde. Rarely had INXS sounded as though they were enjoying their music so much as on this excellent album.

» Tracks: *Days Of Rust; The Gift; Make Your Peace; Time; I'm Only Looking; Please (You Got That ...); Full Moon, Dirty Hearts; Freedom Deep; Kill The Pain; Cut Your Roses Down; The Messenger; Viking Juice.*

★ First released 1993
★ UK peak chart position: 3
★ USA peak chart position: 53
★ Previous Top 1000 position: 1998 (–): 1994 (–)

795 PIANO MAN ↑
Billy Joel

The first album to bring Billy Joel international attention, it set down principles that marked his later career: clarity of production, annoyingly memorable tunes and some distinctly suspect lyrics – like Steve Miller, Joel is not above inverting 'gin and tonic' to 'tonic and gin' for the purposes of rhyming. His vocal style was blustery even back in 1975: it is as if he bullies listeners into going along for the ride. Still, he has undeniable skill as pianist and romantic commentator – *Piano Man* is easier to admire than to love, but few other artists ploughing the AOR furrow deliver the goods as effectively.

» Tracks: *Travelin' Prayer; Piano Man; Ain't No Crime; You're My Home; Ballad Of Billy The Kid; Worse Comes To Worst; Stop In Nevada; If Only I Had The Words (To Tell You); Somewhere Along The Line; Captain Jack.*

★ First Released 1973
★ UK peak chart position: 98
★ USA peak chart position: 27
★ Previous Top 1000 position: 1998 (936): 1994 (–)

796 SO MUCH FOR THE AFTERGLOW ↑ Everclear

A clever opening leads you to believe you are about to savor a Brian Wilson *a cappella* song before the title track bursts into life, taking you on a journey that is closer to Green Day than the Nirvana comparisons that continually plague the band. Great harmonies, chunky riffs and a general up attitude fill the record, even though their philosophy seems to be 'I don't want to be normal like you' (in 'Normal Like You'). Among a glut of strong tracks 'Sunflowers', which has a guitar track that sounds like a dozen Roger McGuinns playing their Rickenbackers simultaneously, is a particular stand-out. A stonking album.

» Tracks: *So Much For The Afterglow; Everything To Everyone; Ataraxia; Normal Like You; I Will Buy You A New Life; Father Of Mine; One Hit Wonder; El Distorto De Melodica; Amphetamine; White Men In Black Suits; Sunflowers; Why I Don't Believe In God; Like A California King.*

★ First released 1997
★ UK peak chart position: 63
★ USA peak chart position: 33
★ Previous Top 1000 position: 1998 (–): 1994 (–)

797 SOMETHING/ANYTHING ↓
Todd Rundgren

On only his third solo album, Todd Rundgren confirmed his status as the new Brian Wilson with a superb collection of miniature pop masterpieces. The first three sides of this double album feature Rundgren alone in the studio tackling pure pop ('I Saw The Light', 'One More Day (No Words)'), power pop ('Couldn't I Just Tell You'), ballads ('Cold Morning Light', 'Sweeter Memories') and pop pastiche ('Wolfman Jack', 'I Went To The Mirror') with effortless skill and an unimpeachable grasp of melody. The fourth side is also wonderful, with Rundgren's most successful single, 'Hello It's Me', thrown nonchalantly in among the sounds of a band jerking around in the studio.

▶▶ Tracks: *I Saw The Light; It Wouldn't Have Made Any Difference; Wolfman Jack; Cold Morning Light; It Takes Two To Tango (This Is For The Girls); Sweeter Memories; Intro; Breathless; The Night The Carousel Burned Down; Saving Grace; Marlene; Song Of The Viking; I Went To The Mirror; Black Maria; One More Day (No Words); Couldn't I Just Tell You; Torch Song; Little Red Lights; Overture – My Roots: Money (That's What I Want)/Messin' With The Kid; Dust In The Wind; Piss Aaron; Hello It's Me; Some Folks Is Even Whiter Than Me; You Left Me Sore; Slut.*

★ First released 1972 ★ UK peak chart position: did not chart
★ USA peak chart position: 29
★ Previous Top 1000 position: 1998 (268): 1994 (–)

798 SUZANNE VEGA ↑
Suzanne Vega

A latecomer to the art of bedsitter albums, especially as Vega was probably one of those American girls crying over James Taylor or Leonard Cohen. This is an assured debut that lends itself to the populist market. Suzanne Vega crafted the lyrics over a period of time and delivered a very controlled series of songs while managing to make herself sound totally vulnerable and insecure, especially in 'Cracking' and 'Small Blue Thing'. The mood is briefly broken by the slightly up-tempo 'Marlene On The Wall' but it's back to the cracks in the ceiling and broken kettle for 'Undertow' and 'Some Journey'.

▶▶ Tracks: *Cracking; Freeze Tag; Marlene On The Wall; Small Blue Thing; Straight Lines; Undertow; Some Journey; The Queen and The Soldier; Night Movies; Neighborhood Girls.*

★ First released 1985
★ UK peak chart position: 11
★ USA peak chart position: 91
★ Previous Top 1000 position: 1998 (–): 1994 (772)

799 RECKLESS ↓
Bryan Adams

Bryan Adams was played a great deal on the radio in 1984/5; his music was the most radio-friendly rock to have been heard in a long time. Revisiting this album more than a decade later still confirms this; if anything, hearing him less makes you like him more. The hit singles still sound consistently good – 'Somebody', 'Summer Of '69' and 'Run To You' – but although these have a clearly recognizable style and sound, all the other tracks sound fresh. Adams never needs to top this record as there is enough grist on this to keep him playing live forever. Assuming he still has an audience that is.

▶▶ Tracks: *The Only One; Take Me Back; This Time; Straight From The Heart; Cuts Like A Knife; I'm Ready; What's It Gonna Be; Don't Leave Me Lonely; The Best Was Yet To Come; One Night Love Affair; She's Only Happy When She's Dancin'; Run To You; Heaven; Somebody; Summer Of '69; Kids Wanna Rock; It's Only Love; Long Gone; Ain't Gonna Cry.*

★ First released 1984
★ UK peak chart position: 7
★ USA peak chart position: 1
★ Previous Top 1000 position: 1998 (666): 1994 (244)

800 AENIMA ↑
Tool

Their most assured album to date comes without a parental advice sticker. And these chaps sound angry, not just swearing for the sake of it. They are angry about everything; their love life, the system, the government. As they state on the sleeve 'beliefs are dangerous, beliefs allow the mind to stop functioning, a non-functioning mind is clinically dead, believe in nothing'. Strong views, but complete tosh as a philosophy. Better listen to Tony Hancock and 'it are not raining in Tokyo'. The quality of the sound however is glorious. The guitars sound like a squadron of fighter planes zooming in for the kill. The tension of the vocals is similar. Prepare for a bombing.

▶▶ Tracks: *Stinkfist; Eulogy; H; Useful idiot; Forty Six & 2; Message To Harry Manback; Hooker With A Penis; Intermission; Jimmy; Die Eier Von Satan; Pushit; Cesaro Summability; Aenima; (–) Ions; Third Eye.*

★ First released 1996
★ UK peak chart position: did not chart
★ USA peak chart position: 2
★ Previous Top 1000 position: 1998 (–): 1994 (–)

801 OCTOBER ↑
U2

On the cover the four members of the band look very ordinary. Bono, complete with a very 80s new romantic hairdo, looks like he's just seen a flying saucer. These youthful looks belie the maturity of the songs on this album and the progress made since the previous year's *Boy*. Edge's guitar is fluid and masterly, Bono's voice reaches new heights, and producer Steve Lillywhite has got into their music this time around. The album includes two spectacular future stage classics, 'Gloria' and 'Fire', but equally impressive are 'I Fall Down' and 'Stranger in A Strange Land'. A sonorous record that holds up well.

➤➤ Tracks: *Gloria; I Fall Down; I Threw A Brick Through A Window; Rejoice; Fire; Tomorrow; October; With A Shout; Stranger In A Strange Land; Scarlet; Is That All?*.

★ First released 1981
★ UK peak chart position: 11
★ USA peak chart position: 104
★ Previous Top 1000 position: 1998 (–): 1994 (–)

802 WHAT DOES ANYTHING MEAN? BASICALLY ↑
The Chameleons

The second and best album by this Manchester, England-based quartet improved upon the stylish pop of its predecessor. An edgy quality grips their melodies which are pieced together meticulously over layers of treated guitar work and atmospheric keyboards. Mark Burgess sings in a moody, resigned manner, but this does not undermine the emotive qualities he brings to the imaginative material. Cut from a cloth inspiring the Teardrop Explodes and the Psychedelic Furs, the Chameleons offer a resounding sound in which mystery pairs with tough beauty. Two extra tracks have been added to the CD.

➤➤ Tracks: *Silence, Sea and Sky; Perfume Garden; Intrigue In Tangiers; Return Of The Roughnecks; Singing Rule Britannia (While The Walls Close In); On The Beach; Looking Inwardly; One Flesh; Home Is Where The Heart Is; P.S. Goodbye; In Shreds; Nostalgia.*

★ First released 1985
★ UK peak chart position: 60
★ USA peak chart position: did not chart
★ Previous Top 1000 position: 1998 (-): 1994 (671)

803 BACKSTREET BOYS ↑
Backstreet Boys

Another manufactured boy band who may at some time in the future control their own destiny, but at the moment are scrapping for control of the transatlantic teenage pop market with 'N Sync (in the USA), and Boyzone and Westlife (in the UK). There is little to choose between any of these acts, such is the similarity in the way the songs are constructed and the vocal harmonies are layered. Yes, they can sing, the songs are all catchy, but how much more of this can we take before one of the boy bands wants to do something outrageous like, errr, rap or heavy metal. Fine rhymes with mine, and me rhymes with ecstasy. Now there's a thought.

➤➤ Tracks: *We've Got It Goin' On; Anywhere For You; Get Down (You're The One For Me); I'll Never Break Your Heart; Quit Playing Games (With My Heart); Boys Will Be Boys; Just To Be Close To You; I Wanna Be With You; Every Time I Close My Eyes; Darlin'; Let's Have A Party; Roll With It; Nobody But You.*

★ First released 1995
★ UK peak chart position: 12
★ USA peak chart position: 4
★ Previous Top 1000 position: 1998 (–): 1994 (–)

804 WAITING FOR COLUMBUS ↑
Little Feat

Getting straight to the point: this is one of the best live albums from one of the best bands in the history of popular music, ever. Little Feat's brand of funky southern rock 'n' roll had already delighted many over the course of six exceptional studio albums, but to experience them live was truly a joy to behold. In addition to the genius Lowell George they had a fantastic keyboard player (Bill Payne) and drummer (Richie Hayward), and their slippery way of playing around the off beat only added to their greatness. As you can see from the track listing all the classics are here, except, regretfully, the sublime 'Long Distance Love'.

➤➤ Tracks: *Join The Band; Fat Man In The Bathtub; All That You Dream; Oh Atlanta; Old Folks' Boogie; Time Loves A Hero; Day Or Night; Mercenary Territory; Spanish Moon; Dixie Chicken; Tripe Face Boogie; Rocket In My Pocket; Willin'; Sailin' Shoes; Feats Don't Fail me Now.*

★ First released 1978
★ UK peak chart position: 43
★ USA peak chart position: 18
★ Previous Top 1000 position: 1998 (-): 1994 (-)

805 POP ↑
U2

Bono and his chums made a conscious decision to stay 'with it' on *Pop*. In order to maintain their position as probably the most popular rock band of the past two decades they drew liberally from contemporary dance music sources. At the time, some critics and fans found the transformation hard to take. It's still the same band, just dressed up a bit with a vocoder, a drum machine and some new backing tracks. Four years on it sounds pretty good, and not too far removed from the Prodigy or the Chemical Brothers on their more rock-orientated numbers, although it is noticeable that the strongest track, 'Staring At The Sun', is the most traditional sounding. Improving with age.

➤ Tracks: *Discothèque; Do You Feel Loved; Mofo; If God Will Send His Angels; Staring At The Sun; Last Night On Earth; Gone; Miami; The Playboy Mansion; If You Wear That Velvet Dress; Please; Wake Up Dead Man.*

★ First released 1997
★ UK peak chart position: 1
★ USA peak chart position: 1
★ Previous Top 1000 position: 1998 (–): 1994 (–)

806 THREE DOLLAR BILL, Y'ALL$ ↑
Limp Bizkit

Although the Red Hot Chili Peppers may have defined metal/rap, it is Limp Bizkit who have taken over the mantle as leaders of the genre. It has to be said that this is pretty impressive stuff, although only a small percentage of listeners will find it their cup of Earl Grey. Outspoken frontman Fred Durst is a stunning stage performer, and part of their success on the college circuit has been the popularity of their incendiary live shows. Maybe it is irrelevant if the listener only understands a fraction of the garbled lyrics, the excitement generated is worth a container load of Leonard Cohen songbooks.

➤ Tracks: *Intro; Pollution; Counterfeit; Stuck; Nobody Loves Me; Sour; Stalemate; Clunk; Faith; Stink Finger; Indigo Flow; Leech; Everything.*

★ First released 1997
★ UK peak chart position: did not chart
★ USA peak chart position: 22
★ Previous Top 1000 position: 1998 (–): 1994 (–)

807 UNCLE MEAT ↑
Frank Zappa/The Mothers Of Invention

Over the two-record set, Frank Zappa manages to cover the entire spread of his interests. Masquerading as a movie in progress, it is a way of highlighting the struggle of trying to keep the band together against a pretty hostile, or worse, apathetic audience. The frustration of putting something out that is artistically brilliant has a particular significance, as music and film go hand in hand. The film dialogue is either hilarious or it will leave you cold. The former is the general consensus. Zappa was so far ahead that his earth life ended before we caught up with him. Weird but highly recommended.

➤ Tracks: *Uncle Meat; The Voice Of Cheese; Nine Types Of Industrial Pollution; Zolar Czakl; Dog Breath In The Year Of The Plague; The Legend Of The Golden Arches; Louie Louie; The Dog Breath Variations; Sleeping In A Jar; Our Bizarre Relationship; The Uncle Meat Variations; Electric Aunt Jemima; Prelude To King Kong; God Bless America; A Pound For A Brown On The Bus; Ian Underwood Whips It Out; Mr Green Genes; We Can Shoot You; If We'd All Been Living In California; The Air; Project X; Cruising For Burgers; Uncle Meat Film Excerpt Part 1; Tengo Na Minchia Tanta; Uncle Meat Film Excerpt Part 2; King Kong Itself; King Kong; 1-5.*

★ First released 1969
★ UK peak chart position: did not chart
★ USA peak chart position: 43
★ Previous Top 1000 position: 1998 (838): 1994 (–)

808 OXYGENE ↑
Jean-Michel Jarre

The 24 bit re-mastered CD announces that it contains 'new sleeve notes'. This must be an incentive to purchase the album because the music within contains nothing new under the sun. At the time this was pleasant background music and nothing more, and returning to the album twenty-five years later does little to alter this viewpoint. Choose your favourite track as you read the sleeve notes and wonder at the fact that 'Oxygene has sold 55 million copies worldwide and subsequent albums have seen Jarre not only broaden his horizons of electronic music, but attract many more fans to his vision bringing his total record sales to over 55 million.' Wow, that indicates that somebody must have bought his other albums.

➤ Tracks: *Oxygene (Part I); Oxygene (Part II); Oxygene (Part III); Oxygene (Part IV); Oxygene (Part V); Oxygene (Part VI).*

★ First released 1976
★ UK peak chart position: 2 ★ USA peak chart position: 78
★ Previous Top 1000 position: 1998 (–): 1994 (–)

809 PETER GABRIEL ↓
Peter Gabriel

The third of the former Genesis vocalist's self-titled releases, this is the album with Peter Gabriel's melting face on the cover. Any vestiges of Gabriel's prog-rock tendencies were completely banished on this strikingly modern album, which explored the psychotic extremes of the human mind in intense, character-based songs such as 'Intruder', 'I Don't Remember' and 'Family Snapshot'. Gabriel's use of computer-controlled synthesizer and electronic rhythm tracks marked an important break with chord-based rock music, aided by Steve Lillywhite's stark production. The album also yielded two of Gabriel's most endearingly popular songs, the sardonic 'Games Without Frontiers' and 'Biko', a moving eulogy to the murdered South African anti-apartheid leader Steve Biko, which paved the way for a glut of inferior rock anthems to political oppression.

▶ Tracks: *Intruder; No Self Control; Start; I Don't Remember; Family Snapshot; And Through The Wire; Games Without Frontiers; Not One Of Us; Lead A Normal Life; Biko.*

★ First Released 1980
★ UK peak chart position: 1 ★ USA peak chart position: 22
★ Previous Top 1000 position: 1998 (589): 1994 (–)

810 GHOST IN THE MACHINE ↑
The Police

After a brief shaky start the Police could suddenly do no wrong. They embraced the 80s and devoured it with their insatiable desire for success. On this transitional album they retained some of their patented white reggae sound, notably with the opener 'Spirits In The Material World'. This intense song is followed by the celebratory 'Every Little Thing She Does Is Magic' which in turn leads on to the politically-charged 'Invisible Sun' These were all massive hits, and the band can be forgiven for not being able to maintain the momentum over the remaining eight tracks. 'Omegaman' and 'Secret Journey' come pretty close.

▶ Tracks: *Spirits In The Material World; Every Little Thing She Does Is Magic; Invisible Sun; Hungry For You (j'aurais toujours faim de toi); Demolition Man; Too Much Information; Rehumanize Yourself; One World (Not Three); Omegaman; Secret Journey; Darkness.*

★ First released 1981
★ UK peak chart position: 1
★ USA peak chart position: 2
★ Previous Top 1000 position: 1998 (–): 1994 (–)

811 MOSELEY SHOALS ↓
Ocean Colour Scene

Riding on a crest of late 60s retro rock, Ocean Colour Scene have received a disproportionate dollop of criticism since their considerable success with this, their second album. Revealing influences ranging from 10cc and the Idle Race ('The Day We Caught The Train') to the Love Affair and Beatles ('The Circle'), the derivative nature of this record is nevertheless highly palatable. Even a Randy Newman soundalike rears up in 'Lining Your Pockets' and Eric Clapton's *Disraeli Gears* wah-wah guitar can also be found liberally sprinkled throughout ('The Riverboat Song', 'Policeman & Pirates'). A necessary album for anyone with a serious magpie complex.

▶ Tracks: *The Riverboat Song; The Day We Caught The Train; The Circle; Lining Your Pockets; Fleeting Mind; 40 Past Midnight; One For The Road; It's My Shadow; Policemen & Pirates; The Downstream; You've Got It Bad; Get Away.*

★ First released 1996
★ UK peak chart position: 1
★ USA peak chart position: did not chart
★ Previous Top 1000 position: 1998 (60): 1994 (–)

812 PARIS 1919 ↑
John Cale

Cale has coped well in the shadow of the far more famous Lou Reed, despite the fact that every interview he gives eventually gets round to asking about Reed or the Velvet Underground. Artistically Cale and Reed could not be more different, and though both are ambitious it is Cale's music that is the more bold and exploratory. This album is one of his most song-orientated and accessible, exploring fascinating lyrical concepts in tracks such as 'Child's Christmas In Wales', 'Andalucia', and 'Graham Greene'. In fact, every song draws the listener in to such an extent that for the first two or three listens you find yourself intrigued with the concept and forget that the music is quite wonderful.

▶ Tracks: *Child's Christmas In Wales; Hanky Panky Nohow; The Endless Plain Of Fortune; Andalucia; Macbeth; Paris 1919; Graham Greene; Half Past France; Antarctica Starts Here.*

★ First released 1973
★ UK peak chart position: did not chart
★ USA peak chart position: did not chart
★ Previous Top 1000 position: 1998 (–): 1994 (–)

813 BEFORE THESE CROWDED STREETS ↑ Dave Matthews Band

Recorded at a time when DMB was probably America's biggest band, they refused to rest on their laurels and produced some original and interesting music. 'Rapunzel' has some great pace changes and the Arabian sounding 'The Last Stop' puts you in a marketplace in Morocco. The unjustified criticism that the band is just too American is rebuffed by this album's veritable delicatessen of styles. The brilliant drummer Carter Beauford and the violinist Boyd Tinsley are particularly crucial to their cosmopolitan sound. Note for American fans: stick with it. Note for non-American fans: this band deserves your attention, starting with this album.

➠ Tracks: *Pantala Naga Pampa; Rapunzel; The Last Stop; Don't Drink The Water; Stay (Wasting Time); Halloween; The Stone; Crush; The Dreaming Tree; Pig; Spoon.*

★ First released 1998
★ UK peak chart position: did not chart
★ USA peak chart position: 1
★ Previous Top 1000 position: 1998 (–): 1994 (–)

814 I WANT TO SEE THE BRIGHT LIGHTS TONIGHT ↓
Richard and Linda Thompson

The debut album from Richard and Linda started a career that has placed Richard Thompson in the 'forever to be a huge cult figure' bracket. They did everything on this album, bar make the charts and sell records. Folk, rock, country and pop are brilliantly covered in a tasteful and controlled package that is a delight from beginning to end, with Linda singing beautifully. Concert favourites such as 'The Calvary Cross' and 'When I Get To The Border' are to be found here. It is not flippant to say that Richard Thompson is a world class songwriter and guitarist, albeit totally under-appreciated.

➠ Tracks: *When I Get To The Border; The Calvary Cross; Withered and Died; I Want To See The Bright Lights Tonight; Down Where The Drunkards Roll; We Sing Hallelujah; Has He Got A Friend For Me; The Little Beggar Girl; The End Of The Rainbow; The Great Valerio.*

★ First released 1974
★ UK peak chart position: did not chart
★ USA peak chart position: did not chart
★ Previous Top 1000 position: 1998 (150): 1994 (316)

815 FROM THE CHOIRGIRL HOTEL ↑ Tori Amos

The album sleeve contains a 'middle earth' map of Tori Amos' world. In pursuit of Rivendell but doomed to get stuck in the Misty Mountains, her career would probably stall if she ever sang of bliss and contentment. 'Jackie's Strength' is a wonderful song that compares her wedding day to Jackie Kennedy's, and throughout the album Amos is less abstract than she had been on her previous records. Recording with a full band for the first time, Amos fashioned her most adventurous and mature collection of songs to date. Indeed, the line 'I guess you go too far when pianos try to be guitars' from 'Northern Lad' can be read as a kiss off to her old piano balladeer image.

➠ Tracks: *Spark; Cruel; Black-Dove (January); Raspberry Swirl; Jackie's Strength; iieee; Liquid Diamonds; She's Your Cocaine; Northern Lad; Hotel; Playboy Mommy; Pandora's Aquarium.*

★ First released 1998
★ UK peak chart position: 6
★ USA peak chart position: 5
★ Previous Top 1000 position: 1998 (–): 1994 (–)

816 GET YER YA-YA'S OUT! ↑
The Rolling Stones

Subtitled The Rolling Stones In Concert, this is their second live album and the one on which then new guitarist Mick Taylor was able to show off quite magnificently. For a 1969 recording this is pretty good stuff. Everyone seems inspired by the new freedom that Taylor gave Keith Richards, the latter having carried Brian Jones for a year or two. The choice of blues material is particularly good and highpoints are 'Stray Cat Blues', 'Midnight Rambler', and Chuck Berry's frantic-paced 'Carol'. By the time they get to 'Street Fighting Man' the guitars are both turned up to eleven and, as Mick says, 'Charlie's good tonite innee'.

➠ Tracks: *Jumpin' Jack Flash; Carol; Stray Cat Blues; Love In Vain; Midnight Rambler; Sympathy For The Devil; Live With Me; Little Queenie; Honky Tonk Woman; Street Fighting Man.*

★ First released 1970
★ UK peak chart position: 1
★ USA peak chart position: 6
★ Previous Top 1000 position: 1998 (–): 1994 (–)

817 MORRISON HOTEL ↓
The Doors

Feted first as underground heroes, then reviled as teeny-bop stars, the Doors threw off such conundrums with this magnificent release. *Morrison Hotel* reaffirmed their blues roots, opening with the powerful 'Roadhouse Blues' before unfolding through a succession of songs showcasing all the group members' considerable strengths. Distinctively tight instrumental playing underscores memorable material, while Jim Morrison's authoritative vocal ranges from the demonstrative ('Maggie McGill') to the melancholic ('The Spy'). Despite contemporary problems, the Doors emerged with an album the equal of their first two stunning releases.

» Tracks: *Roadhouse Blues; Waiting For The Sun; You Make Me Real; Peace Frog; Blue Sunday; Ship Of Fools; Land Ho!; The Spy; Queen Of The Highway; Indian Summer; Maggie McGill.*

★ First released 1970
★ UK peak chart position: 12
★ USA peak chart position: 4
★ Previous Top 1000 position: 1998 (298): 1994 (123)

818 A BOY NAMED GOO ↑
Goo Goo Dolls

Any album that has six outstanding tracks is worth its weight in gold in the CD age. My CD has a self-made sticker that lists 3, 4, 6, 7, 9, 11 as the tracks to try before you buy. Each of these six songs is rich, guitar heavy and has one particularly uplifting moment. 'Naked' bursts into life after three seconds, 'Flat Top' has a glorious chorus, and 'Name' has a fabulous acoustic riff. Or get your head stuck into the Thin Lizzy riff that dominates 'Only One', or the wall of guitars on 'Ain't That Unusual' and 'Eyes Wide Open'. That's the six dealt with, and the rest are not too bad either.

» Tracks: *Long Way Down; Burnin' Up; Naked; Flat Top; Impersonality; Name; Only One; Somethin' Bad; Ain't That Unusual; So Long; Eyes Wide Open; Disconnected; Slave Girl.*

★ First released 1995
★ UK peak chart position: did not chart
★ USA peak chart position: 27
★ Previous Top 1000 position: 1998 (-): 1994 (-)

819 RIDE THE LIGHTNING ↑
Metallica

This is cultured thrash metal, if there can be such a thing. There is such a gap between Metallica and every other thrash protagonist. Even an outsider can appreciate that this may hurt the ears, but these boys certainly know their way around their instruments. At about 4 minutes into the title track, the band really let rip, and almost leave the drummer behind; it really is extraordinary. 'For Whom The Bell Tolls' is probably the stand out, made to sound grand and magnificent, it works, except for the lyrics that is. With instrumentation this good, the banality of the words can almost be forgiven.

» Tracks: *Fight Fire With Fire; Ride The Lightning; For Whom The Bell Tolls; Fade To Black; Trapped Under Ice; Escape; Creeping Death; The Call Of Ktulu.*

★ First released 1984
★ UK peak chart position: 87
★ USA peak chart position: 100
★ Previous Top 1000 position: 1998 (-): 1994 (-)

820 THE MODERN DANCE ↓
Pere Ubu

It is hard to believe that such noises could come from so deep in America's heartland, played by a group named after a character in a French absurdist play. The debut album by Pere Ubu, *The Modern Dance* is the realization of group leader David Thomas's (a.k.a. Crocus Behemoth) high-concept vision of a rock band whose sound was always just on the verge of falling apart. *Avant garde* and not terribly accessible, the album's noisy anarchy was a tonic for punks and intellectuals sick of the bloated, corporate sound that passed for commercial rock at the time. It became a major influence on the leading alternative bands of the following decade, including the Pixies and Hüsker Dü.

» Tracks: *Non-Alignment Pact; The Modern Dance; Laughing; Street Waves; Chinese Radiation; Life Stinks; Real World; Over My Head; Sentimental Journey; Humor Me.*

★ First released 1977
★ UK peak chart position: did not chart
★ USA peak chart position: did not chart
★ Previous Top 1000 position: 1998 (266): 1994 (-)

821 HIGH LAND, HARD RAIN ↑
Aztec Camera

For a short while the bands leader Roddy Frame was seen by many music journalists as the next great songwriting hope. This was a sparkling debut album that bucked the trend of the time by sounding acoustic and live, rather than the over crisp electronic productions. Frame could write great lyrics and managed to weave them naturally into the melody. 'Walk Out To Winter' has such a euphoric sequence of chords it's a wonder the classic gold stations have not placed it on the playlist, along with Alanis Morissette and the Bluebells. Frame has yet to equal this diamond, but the possibility should not be ruled out.

» Tracks: Oblivious; The Boy Wonders; Walk Out To Winter; The Bugle Sounds Again; We Could Send Letters; Pillar To Post; Release; Lost Outside The Tunnel; Back On Board; Down The Dip; Haywire; Orchid Girl; Queen's Tattoos.

★ First released 1983
★ UK peak chart position: 22
★ USA peak chart position: 129
★ Previous Top 1000 position: 1998 (–): 1994 (564)

822 HEAVY WEATHER ↓
Weather Report

Probably the best fusion album ever made, and the coming together of five precociously talented musicians. Joe Zawinul and Wayne Shorter assembled the unit with little knowledge that the complex music would become so accessible. Two compositions stand out; the graceful 'A Remark You Made', an evocative love song without words, and the hit single 'Birdland' (so successful it was even used by Akai for a major advertising campaign). On these two Zawinul compositions their genius bass player Jaco Pastorius gives a taste of what he was capable of. He bent the notes to make them talk, and that high octave bass solo on 'Birdland' is still a treasured moment.

» Tracks: Birdland; A Remark You Made; Teen Town; Harlequin; Rumba Mama; Palladium; The Juggler; Havona.

★ First released 1977
★ UK peak chart position: 43
★ USA peak chart position: 30
★ Previous Top 1000 position: 1998 (777): 1994 (–)

823 KORN ↑
Korn

If there is such a thing as a melodic hardcore band then Korn fit the description, and helps explain why they have such a broad following in their native US. This 1994 debut, released after the band had been touring non-stop for the best part of four years, is a ferocious slice of nu metal. Black Flag influences are to be expected but this debut was assured enough to prove instrumental in taking a specialist genre to the masses. Lead vocalist Jonathan Davis has the standard-issue gravel voice that is often complemented by the equally rough tonsils of Brian Welch. A lyric sheet would have helped, as 'Ball Tongue' sounds interesting.

» Tracks: Blind; Ball Tongue; Need To; Clown; Divine; Faget; Shoots and Ladders; Predictable; Fake; Lies; Helmet In The Bush; Daddy.

★ First released 1994
★ UK peak chart position: did not chart
★ USA peak chart position: 72
★ Previous Top 1000 position: 1998 (–): 1994 (–)

824 THIS IS HARDCORE ↑
Pulp

This was the third Pulp album to be released since their UK breakthrough in 1994. By this time the fickle masses had moved on to the latest smart young things, leaving the diehard Pulp fans to deal with a challenging collection of songs. The discordant and unsettling opening track 'The Fear' reminds the listener of latter day Cure epics. Jarvis Cocker reverts to his more familiar storytelling style on cuts such as 'Dishes' and the hit single 'Help The Aged'. Cocker is one of those songwriters who will often make the actual song secondary to his entertaining lyrics, so the fact that the rest of the band often gets the backing track spot on is a bonus.

» Tracks: The Fear; Dishes; Party Hard; Help The Aged; This Is Hardcore; TV Movie; A Little Soul; I'm A Man; Seductive Barry; Sylvia; Glory Days; The Day After The Revolution.

★ First released 1998
★ UK peak chart position: 1
★ USA peak chart position: did not chart
★ Previous Top 1000 position: 1998 (–): 1994 (–)

825 A LITTLE SOUTH OF SANITY ↑
Aerosmith

Even the most bigoted music fan should surely own up to liking Aerosmith and seeing them live confirms their status as one of the most exciting heavy rock acts of the last twenty years. In the late 90s (when this live album was recorded) Steven Tyler was still in excellent physical shape, prancing and dancing like a cat throughout an exhausting two hour show. This captures the atmosphere, replays all the favourite moments, and makes you realise that you should have been there. No live album can truly satisfy, but *A Little South Of Sanity* is a fine demonstration of how a bunch of formerly chemically charged dinosaurs are playing better than ever.

» Tracks: *Eat The Rich; Love In An Elevator; Falling In Love (Is Hard On The Knees); Same Old Song and Dance; Hole In My Soul; Monkey On My Back; Livin' On The Edge; Cryin'; Rag Doll; Angel; Janie's Got A Gun; Amazing; Back In The Saddle; Last Child; The Other Side; Walk On Down; Dream On; Crazy; Mama Kin; Walk This Way; Dude (Looks Like A Lady); What It Takes; Sweet Emotion.*

★ First released 1998
★ UK peak chart position: 36 ★ USA peak chart position: 12
★ Previous Top 1000 position: 1998 (–): 1994 (–)

826 SOLID AIR ↓
John Martyn

He began as a folksy minstrel but seemed drawn to experimental, freeform improvisation. *Solid Air* is where John Martyn's love affair with effects and echoplex became serious. The title track, dedicated to his close friend Nick Drake, became a eulogy, while the breezy 'Over The Hill' – one of the greatest songs written about a train journey – is a feathery delight. 'May You Never' and 'Don't Want To Know' continued the simple, stoned ballad approach, although it is his interpretation of Skip James's 'I'd Rather Be The Devil,' totally reshaped with hypnotic shifts, tidal echoes, and a slurred growl, which broods over the whole album. A record that remains Martyn's youthful zenith.

» Tracks: *Solid Air; Over The Hill; Don't Want To Know; I'd Rather Be The Devil; Go Down Easy; Dreams By The Sea; May You Never; The Man In The Station; Easy Blues.*

★ First released 1974
★ UK peak chart position: did not chart
★ USA peak chart position: did not chart
★ Previous Top 1000 position: 1998 (239): 1994 (125)

827 HELL FREEZES OVER ↑
The Eagles

It would be cruel to suggest that the Eagles got back together merely to make a huge mountain of dollars, especially as theirs was probably the most sought after reunion outside the Beatles. However, over six years later the promised new material has still not appeared. Apart from the ever-busy Don Henley the others have not, to my knowledge, broken into a sweat. The tour from which this live album was compiled was an artistic success and a nice little earner. Reprises of 'Desperado' and 'Wasted Time' are powerful rather than cloying and, out of the new songs, 'Learn To Be Still' hits the right spot.

» Tracks: *Get Over It; Love Will Keep Us Alive; The Girl From Yesterday; Learn To Be Still; Tequila Sunrise; Hotel California; Wasted Time; Pretty Maids All In A Row; I Can't Tell You Why; New York Minute; The Last Resort; Take It Easy; In The City; Life In The Fast Lane; Desperado.*

★ First released 1994
★ UK peak chart position: 28
★ USA peak chart position: 1
★ Previous Top 1000 position: 1998 (–): 1994 (–)

828 TIGERLILY ↓
Natalie Merchant

It is a pity that the record company felt the need to sticker the cover with 'former singer songwriter with 10,000 Maniacs'. Such is the fickle and forgetful pop public. The understated and underrated Merchant has a distinctive voice, and with concentration, this is a rewarding collection of songs that hark back to the Band's *Music From Big Pink* album. Not surprisingly, it was recorded down the road in Bearsville. Perhaps all back-catalogue 10,000 Maniacs albums should be stickered with 'featuring the highly original and talented Natalie Merchant, future solo singer and songwriter'. And maybe she does not want to sell as many records as Celine Dion.

» Tracks: *San Andreas Fault; Wonder; Beloved Wife; River; Carnival; I May Know The Word; The Letter; Cowboy Romance; Jealousy; Where I Go; Seven Years.*

★ First released 1995
★ UK peak chart position: 39
★ USA peak chart position: 13
★ Previous Top 1000 position: 1998 (653): 1994 (–)

829 MONK'S MUSIC ↑
Thelonious Monk

A surprisingly outstanding transfer to CD, considering how far Monk's piano seems to have been from the microphone compared to the high top end on both John Coltrane and Coleman Hawkins' tenors. Most of the time Monk seems content to sit back and bathe in the brilliance of his accompanying musicians. A glorious success all round, especially 'Ruby, My Dear' with its fabulous Hawkins solo, and 'Off Minor', on which all the players shine. Coltrane shines particularly well on the lengthy 'Epistrophy'. Little did Monk know at the time how important both himself and Coltrane were to become. The CD version has two alternate bonus tracks.

» Tracks: *Abide With Me; Well You Needn't; Ruby, My Dear; Off Minor (Take 5); Off Minor (Take 4); Epistrophy; Crepuscule With Nellie (Take 6); Crepuscule With Nellie (Takes 4 and 5).*

★ First released 1958
★ UK peak chart position: did not chart
★ USA peak chart position: did not chart
★ Previous Top 1000 position: 1998 (–): 1994 (–)

830 SKYLARKING ↑
XTC

All the usual words associated with XTC and Andy Partridge spring to mind here; painfully underrated, wacky genius, quirky, overlooked classic, national treasure, and so on depending on the quality of the thesaurus on your Macintosh. I have found myself constantly referring to Mr. Partridge in this way. The fact is, it is all absolutely true. *Skylarking* is a shimmering jewel, a shining diamond. 'Grass' is one of the band's greatest ever songs on a mature and funny album that deserved a better fate. The fact that there was no obvious hit singles didn't help, but their record label never understood that XTC didn't need chart success. After all, they are a national treasure.

» Tracks: *Summer's Cauldron; Grass; The Meeting Place; That's Really Super; Supergirl; Ballet For A Rainy Day; 1000 Umbrellas; Season Cycle; Earn Enough For Us; Big Day; Another Satellite; Mermaid Smiled; The Man Who Sailed Around His Soul; Dying; Sacrificial Bonfire.*

★ First released 1986
★ UK peak chart position: 90
★ USA peak chart position: 70
★ Previous Top 1000 position: 1998 (–): 1994 (–)

831 INTERNATIONAL VELVET ↑
Catatonia

Catatonia's big breakthrough came with this memorable and highly accessible album, backed by a concerted promotional push from their record company. Lead singer Cerys Matthews' photograph subsequently appeared everywhere in the press, but she retained her dignity by virtue of having a surprisingly wise head on young shoulders. Likeable hits such as 'Road Rage' and 'Mulder and Scully' are complemented by a clutch of catchy, upbeat songs. You would not argue with Matthews when she promises to 'put a horse in peoples beds' on 'I Am The Mob', and most listeners can only marvel at the source of her pride on the Welsh language title track.

» Tracks: *Mulder and Scully; Game On; I Am The Mob; Road Rage; Johnny Come Lately; Goldfish and Paracetamol; International Velvet; Why I Can't Stand One Night Stands; Part Of The Furniture; Don't Need The Sunshine; Strange Glue; My Selfish Gene.*

★ First released 1997
★ UK peak chart position: 1
★ USA peak chart position: did not chart
★ Previous Top 1000 position: 1998 (–): 1994 (–)

832 BOY ↑
U2

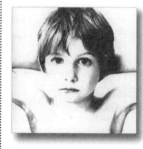

The small child staring out from the familiar cover must be in his late-20s by now. I wonder if he has followed U2's career since this inauspicious debut in 1980. Steve Lillywhite's polished production launched U2 on the route to world dominance, but in hindsight the band had yet to establish their own niche. Some early reviews compared them to late 60s progressive rock bands, a comparison which would be unthinkable nowadays. They could, and would do better, but on 'I Will Follow' and 'Into The Heart' U2 had already hiked themselves a few rungs up the ladder to the moon.

» Tracks: *I Will Follow; Twilight; An Cat Dubh; Into The Heart; Out Of Control; Stories For Boys; The Ocean; A Day Without Me; Another Time, Another Place; The Electric Co.; Shadows and Tall Trees.*

★ First released 1980
★ UK peak chart position: 52
★ USA peak chart position: 63
★ Previous Top 1000 position: 1998 (–): 1994 (–)

833 THE HEAD ON THE DOOR ↑
The Cure

With all the doom and despair that drips from Robert Smith's pen you would not naturally assume that here is a man who has been married to the same person for many years. Reading into lyrics usually tells the reader something about the composer, but Smith has managed to confuse us for two decades. When he sings 'yesterday I got so old, I felt like I could die', ('In Between Days') or 'I made myself so sick, I wish I'd stayed asleep today' ('Close To Me') you can be forgiven for thinking he is unhappy. All brilliant stuff, wrapped around the now familiar plinky-plonky, chiming guitar sound.

» Tracks: *Inbetween Days; Kyoto Song; The Blood; Six Different Ways; Push; The Baby Screams; Close To Me; A Night Like This; Screw; Sinking.*

★ First released 1985
★ UK peak chart position: 7
★ USA peak chart position: 59
★ Previous Top 1000 position: 1998 (–): 1994 (–)

834 WELCOME TO THE PLEASURE DOME ↑
Frankie Goes To Hollywood

Listening to 80s pop music in the new millennium does confirm that there was a special sound reserved only for that decade. Magnificent producer Trevor Horn probably has a lot to do with the way the synthetic drums blend with that 80s electric guitar ping on the 12th fret, when you lightly dampen your fingers over the strings. The lasting memory of the outrage that the Frankies' lyrics caused in a goody goody decade have helped these dynamic songs to stand the test of time. The title track, 'Relax' and 'The Power Of Love' are gigantic songs, and the cover versions of Bruce Springsteen's 'Born To Run', Edwin Starr's 'War' are equally inventive.

» Tracks: *The World Is My Oyster; Welcome To The Pleasure Dome; Relax; War; Two Tribes; Tag; Fury; Born To Run; San Jose; Wish The Lads Were Here; The Ballad Of 32; Krisco Kisses; Black Night White Light; The Only Star In Heaven; The Power Of Love; Bang.*

★ First released 1985
★ UK peak chart position: 1
★ USA peak chart position: 33
★ Previous Top 1000 position: 1998 (–): 1994 (–)

835 THE CAPTAIN AND ME ↓
The Doobie Brothers

Boasting three strong vocalists, two expert guitarists and a brace of rhythmic drummers, the Doobie Brothers burst to national prominence with a sound crossing AM pop-rock, soul-tinged R&B and strong musicianship. Traces of Moby Grape, whom the group adored, can be heard in their vibrant harmonies and flowing hooklines, but *The Captain and Me* showed an act of singular purpose. The effervescent urgency propelling 'Long Train Running' and 'China Grove' into the US singles charts is apparent on every selection, where melody combines with twin-lead arpeggios to create an undoubted excitement. The unified sound emerging from this cross-section imbues this album with its lasting strength.

» Tracks: *Natural Thing; Long Train Running; China Grove; Dark-eyed Cajun Woman; Clear As The Driven Snow; Without You; South City Midnight Lady; Evil Woman; Busted Down Around O'Connelly Corners; Ukiah; The Captain and Me.*

★ First released 1973
★ UK peak chart position: did not chart
★ USA peak chart position: 7
★ Previous Top 1000 position: 1998 (566): 1994 (434)

836 CAR WHEELS ON A GRAVEL ROAD ↑
Lucinda Williams

Probably the least prolific artist currently living, Williams has drip fed us five albums in twenty years. Her brand of country rock has never found favour with the masses, but this album certainly put her on the map with the critics. She has paid the bills by having her songs recorded by others, but this album has given her the opportunity to speak out, and the listener can relate her beautiful songs to her own situation. Those lucky enough to own this stellar album now realise that Williams is one of the finest songwriters of Americana to appear over the past two decades. She can sing as well.

» Tracks: *Right In Time; Car Wheels On A Gravel Road; 2 Kool 2 Be 4-Gotten; Drunken Angel; Concrete and Barbed Wire; Lake Charles; Can't Let Go; I Lost It; Metal Firecracker; Greenville; Still I Long For Your Kiss; Joy; Jackson.*

★ First released 1998
★ UK peak chart position: did not chart
★ USA peak chart position: 65
★ Previous Top 1000 position: 1998 (–): 1994 (–)

837 MUTATIONS ↑
Beck

This album was only meant to be a stopgap collection, not the official follow-up to the acclaimed *Odelay*. Beck originally planned to release *Mutations* on the small indie label Bong Load Records, but Geffen Records had other ideas and gave the album the big push. Some *Odelay* fans would have been disappointed by the laid back pace and stripped down production, but long-term acolytes were delighted by *Mutations'* lilting charm. At times the sound is not dissimilar to Eno's *Another Green World*, especially on 'Nobody's Fault But My Own'. In the same manner that Neil Young alternates between acoustic and rock albums, Beck proves equally adept at constructing multi-layered post-modern masterpieces or bashing out lo-fi winners such as this album.

➤ Tracks: *Cold Brains; Nobody's Fault But My Own; Lazy Flies; Canceled Check; We Live Again; Tropicalia; Dead Melodies; Bottle Of Blues; O Maria; Sing It Again; Static.*

★ First released 1998
★ UK peak chart position: 24
★ USA peak chart position: 13
★ Previous Top 1000 position: 1998 (–): 1994 (–)

838 PACIFIC OCEAN BLUE ↑
Dennis Wilson

The biggest threat to the Beach Boys crown was not the internal bickering and turmoil, but the fear that happy-go-lucky Dennis Wilson could really be the dark horse genius of the band. Indeed those lucky enough to own this album will already be aware of his talent. Dennis was brilliant, a crazy rogue who lived fast and died too young. From the luscious wall of vocals sound of the gospel influenced opening track 'River Song' to the last sad tinkle on the closing 'End Of The Show' this Wilson is in complete control. And just soak up the emotion as he sings 'it was you who said there won't be tomorrow' in 'Moonshine'. Easily on a par with *Pet Sounds*.

➤ Tracks: *River Song; What's Wrong; Moonshine; Friday Night; Dreamer; Thoughts Of You; Time; You and I; Pacific Ocean Blues; Farewell; Rainbows; End Of The Show.*

★ First released 1977
★ UK peak chart position: did not chart
★ USA peak chart position: 96
★ Previous Top 1000 position: 1998 (–): 1994 (–)

839 SEAL II ↑
Seal

Three albums in nine years is hardly prolific, especially coming from an artist who caused waves of excitement when his career was launched. This second album, produced by Trevor Horn, confirmed expectations of this great new voice whose effortless delivery combined the unusual combination of husky depth and tremendous power. Dreamy stuff on the surface, underpinnned by a funky underbelly, most of the tracks succeed well and some, notably 'Prayer For The Dying', 'Don't Cry' and 'Kiss From A Rose', are downright monumental. Seal is a major talent that we selfishly want to up his delivery rate.

➤ Tracks: *Bring It On; Prayer For The Dying; Dreaming In Metaphors; Don't Cry; Fast Changes; Kiss From A Rose; People Asking Why; Newborn Friend; If I Could; I'm Alive; Bring It On (Reprise).*

★ First released 1994
★ UK peak chart position: 1
★ USA peak chart position: 15
★ Previous Top 1000 position: 1998 (–): 1994 (–)

840 1999 ↑
Prince

The title track is rightly celebrated as one of Prince's finest moments, and one that had a healthy reprise in the run up to the hugely overrated millennium celebrations. After the title track comes the equally euphoric 'Little Red Corvette'. Although the remainder of the album fails to ignite the same sparks as these two opening tracks, Prince's talent is such that, as with the similarly chameleon-like David Bowie, the listener gratefully enjoys even the average tracks. In keeping with Bowie, Prince is also never afraid to try different things, even if he occasionally misses the mark. A Prince album which is highly rated by both fans and critics.

➤ Tracks: *1999; Little Red Corvette; Delirious; Let's Pretend We're Married; D.M.S.R.; Automatic; Something In The Water (Does Not Compute); Free; Lady Cab Driver; All The Critics Love U In New York; International Lover.*

★ First released 1982
★ UK peak chart position: 30
★ USA peak chart position: 9
★ Previous Top 1000 position: 1998 (–): 1994 (–)

841 USE YOUR ILLUSION I ↑
Guns N'Roses

The opening shot in Guns N'Roses two pronged assault on the transatlantic charts in 1991. Not since the days of the Beatles had one band dominated the album charts to such an extent, but in retrospect the success of the *Use Your Illusion* albums marked the beginning of the end for Guns N'Roses. In the ten years since, the band has disintegrated amid constant rumours of their final demise, leaving Axl Rose as the sole remaining original member. For many commentators, UK born guitarist Slash was the antidote to Axl's nasal whine. If at any time Rose's voice grated, and it certainly did on the cover of 'Live and Let Die', there was always the superb band behind him to appreciate.

» Tracks: *Right Next Door To Hell; Dust N' Bones; Live and Let Die; Don't Cry; Perfect Crime; You Ain't The First; Bad Obsession; Back Off Bitch; Double Talkin' Jive; November Rain; The Garden; Garden Of Eden; Don't Damn Me; Bad Apples; Dead Horse; Coma.*

★ First released 1991
★ UK peak chart position: 2
★ USA peak chart position: 2
★ Previous Top 1000 position: 1998 (–): 1994 (–)

842 THE SOUL CAGES ↑
Sting

The most powerful set of songs Mr. Sumner has so far recorded, The Soul Cages was released during a period of consolidation and reflection in his personal life after several years of non-stop touring and success. The album is really one long poem broken into sensible chapters, and writing about his parents and his working class upbringing made Sting seem a lot more real to many listeners. The sensitive arrangements subtly enhance the record and special mention must be given to the brilliant Branford Marsalis (saxophone), Kathryn Tickell (pipes) and Paola Paparelle (oboe). It is a pity, however, that a synclavier is used instead of real violins. A stunning record nonetheless.

» Tracks: *Island Of Souls; All This Time; Mad About You; Jeremiah Blues (Part 1); Why Should I Cry For You; Saint Agnes and The Burning Train; The Wild Wild Sea; The Soul Cages; When The Angels Fall.*

★ First released 1991
★ UK peak chart position: 1
★ USA peak chart position: 2
★ Previous Top 1000 position: 1998 (–): 1994 (–)

843 YES I AM ↑
Melissa Etheridge

Sharing the honours with *Never Enough* as the Melissa Etheridge album to own, *Yes I Am* continues in the up-tempo rock vein of the previous, Grammy-award winning album. Her voice is markedly rougher here. Presumably she had been gargling with gravel and sharp sand following the recording of *Never Enough*. Since the release of *Yes I Am* Etheridge has made no secret of her sexual leanings and so it is interesting, in hindsight, to take what seem like regular heterosexual rock lyrics and put them into a gay context. As she boldly states on 'Come To My Window', 'I don't care what they say, I don't care what they say, what do they know about this love anyway'. Right on sister.

» Tracks: *I'm The Only One; If I Wanted To; Come To My Window; Silent Legacy; I Will Never Be The Same; All American Girl; Yes I Am; Resist; Ruins; Talking To My Angel.*

★ First released 1993
★ UK peak chart position: did not chart
★ USA peak chart position: 15
★ Previous Top 1000 position: 1998 (–): 1994 (–)

844 DIRTY DANCING ↑
Soundtrack

Modern day film soundtracks often reek of the director's personal tastes from the rock 'n' roll era. The choice here is often inspired, and at the worst, interesting. The lead track is the Jennifer Warnes/Bill Medley monster '(I've Had) The Time Of My Life', but it is the older diamonds that really get the nostalgia juices flowing. Stand-outs include Bruce Channel's 'Hey Baby' (just listen to that harmonica intro from Delbert McClinton), and Brian Wilson's all time favourite recording, 'Be My Baby'. There is also 'She's Like The Wind', sung by the movie's star Patrick Swayze. Thank you Mr. Swayze, leave your name at the door.

» Tracks: *(I've Had) The Time Of My Life (Bill Medley and Jennifer Warnes); Be My Baby (The Ronettes); She's Like The Wind (Patrick Swayze); Hungry Eyes (Eric Carmen); Stay (Maurice Williams and The Zodiacs); Yes (Merry Clayton); You Don't Own Me (The Blow Monkeys); Hey Baby (Bruce Channel); Overload (Zappacosta); Love Is Strange (Mickey and Sylvia); Where Are You Tonight? (Tom Johnston); In The Still Of The Night (The Five Satins).*

★ First released 1987
★ UK peak chart position: 4
★ USA peak chart position: 1
★ Previous Top 1000 position: 1998 (–): 1994 (–)

845 IF YOU'RE FEELING SINISTER ↑ Belle and Sebastian

The importance of including a lyric sheet with a highly literate CD such as this one cannot be overstated. Our ears have gotten lazy over the years, and the joys of Belle and Sebastian really unfold with the whole story in front of your eyes. Musically this is simple, lightweight and pleasant stuff, with the band sounding like an incredibly happy and lively Nick Drake. The songs are wonderful, sometimes obscure, but never less than complete tales. If only everybody was old enough to understand the importance of the line (from the title track), 'when she got back, her spirituality was thrown into confusion, so she got a special deal on renting from the man at Rediffusion.'

➤➤ Tracks: *The Stars Of Track and Field; Seeing Other People; Me and The Major; Like Dylan In The Movies; The Fox In the Snow; Get Me Away From Here, I'm Dying; If You're Feeling Sinister; Mayfly; The Boy Done Wrong Again; Judy and The Dream Of Horses.*

★ First released 1996
★ UK peak chart position: did not chart
★ USA peak chart position: did not chart
★ Previous Top 1000 position: 1998 (–): 1994 (–)

846 TEMPLE OF LOW MEN ↑ Crowded House

The second album from New Zealand's most successful export after lamb. The Finn brothers had been around the music business for many years with Split Enz, and as a result this collection of songs dripped from Neil Finn's pen like water off a sheep's back. Few bands have enjoyed such an unprecedented level of affection throughout their career, yet Crowded House never became establishment fodder for journalistic snipers. Quality I guess is the key, with never a throwaway lyric or melody, and those reassuringly familiar harmonies. However, I'm sure you don't need to be told how good this album is.

➤➤ Tracks: *I Feel Possessed; Kill Eye; Into Temptation; Mansion In The Slums; When You Come; Never Be The Same; Love This Life; Sister Madly; In The Lowlands; Better Be Home Soon.*

★ First released 1988
★ UK peak chart position: did not chart
★ USA peak chart position: 40
★ Previous Top 1000 position: 1998 (–): 1994 (–)

847 COME ON COME ON ↑ Mary-Chapin Carpenter

By moving away from more traditionally based country folk into a harder edged country rock sound, Mary-Chapin Carpenter made the most commercial move of an already impressive career. The album is full of top-notch songs that stand up to repeated listening. 'The Hard Way' sets a standard that is maintained throughout, be it the sadly ironic tale of a dead marriage 'He Thinks He'll Keep Her' or the equally cheeky, yet demanding 'Passionate Kisses' (written by Lucinda Williams) where the singer claims 'shouldn't I have this, shouldn't I have all of this'. The title track is a tasteful and gentle end to an album that she may find hard to equal.

➤➤ Tracks: *The Hard Way; He Thinks He'll Keep Her; Rhythm Of The Blues; I feel Lucky; The Bug; Not Too Much To Ask; Passionate Kisses; Only A Dream; I Am A Town; Walking Through Fire; Take My Chances; Come On Come On.*

★ First released 1992
★ UK peak chart position: did not chart
★ USA peak chart position: 31
★ Previous Top 1000 position: 1998 (–): 1994 (879)

848 TERRAPIN STATION ↑ Grateful Dead

Some criticism was levelled at the Grateful Dead for allowing themselves to be produced by a real record producer, but revisiting this more than twenty years later it seems to hold up perfectly well. The strings accompanying the 'Terrapin' suite have become like old friends to familiar listeners. And frankly, new ones won't remember what the fuss was all about. Garcia's voice brings a tear to the eye and Robert Hunter's lyrics are as brilliantly obscure as ever. Strange but true – in 2000 Bob Weir's voice sounds absolutely fantastic on 'Estimated Prophet'. Was that down to inferior hi-fi systems in those days or maybe something else?

➤➤ Tracks: *Estimated Prophet; Dancin' In The Streets; Passenger; Samson & Delilah; Sunrise; Terrapin Station Part 1 – Lady With A Fan, Terrapin Station, Terrapin, Terrapin Transit, At A Siding, Terrapin Flyer, Refrain.*

★ First released 1977
★ UK peak chart position: 30
★ USA peak chart position: 28
★ Previous Top 1000 position: 1998 (–): 1994 (–)

849 THE MONKEES ↑
The Monkees

Created to perform roles in a television series, the Monkees were greeted with scepticism by certain sections of the rock fraternity. The quartet may not have played the instruments on their debut album, but this does not diminish the appeal of its content. Excellent songs by Tommy Boyce and Bobby Hart formed its core, while contributions by Carole King, David Gates and group member Mike Nesmith ensure that the quality remains consistently high. Mickey Dolenz possesses the ideal pop voice and the enthusiasm generated on each performance is completely captivating. The Monkees' grasp of teen angst and melodrama is sure and, now divorced from contemporary travails, this album stands as one of the era's most entertaining debuts.

➤ Tracks: *Theme From The Monkees; Saturday's Child; I Wanna Be Free; Tomorrow's Gonna Be Just Another Day; Papa Gene's Blues; Take A Giant Step; Last Train To Clarksville; This Just Doesn't Seem To Be My Day; Let's Dance On; I'll Be True To You; Sweet Young Thing; Gonna Buy Me A Dog.*

★ First released 1966
★ UK peak chart position: 1 ★ USA peak chart position: 1
★ Previous Top 1000 position: 1998 (933); 1994 (393)

850 BLOWS AGAINST THE EMPIRE ↓
Jefferson Starship

Before the Airplane metamorphosed into a Starship, there was a loose conglomeration assembled by science-fiction devotee Paul Kantner. This was a vehicle to release his great concept album. Friends such as David Crosby, Graham Nash and the Grateful Dead were roped in, and apart from one or two pompous lyrics ('Mau Mau (Amerikon)') the project was a success critically and commercially. Highlights, however, are the slower acoustic melodies that have great atmosphere, such as 'A Child Is Coming' and 'Have You Seen The Stars Tonite'. The idea was to hijack a starship, leave the Earth and live happily ever after. 'Yeah, wow, great man, but like, where do we get our drugs from?'

➤ Tracks: *Mau Mau (Amerikon); The Baby Tree; Let's Go Together; A Child Is Coming; Sunrise; Hijack; Home; Have You Seen The Stars Tonite; XM; Starship.*

★ First released 1970
★ UK peak chart position: did not chart
★ USA peak chart position: 20
★ Previous Top 1000 position: 1998 (811); 1994 (–)

851 IN IT FOR THE MONEY ↓
Supergrass

Eagerly awaited by both fans and critics, *In It For The Money* was an energetic and accomplished second album that inexplicably failed to make a long-term impact with the record-buying public. Like their debut, virtually every track was worthy of single release, and the singles themselves, notably the blistering punk of 'Richard III' and the classy brass arrangements of 'Going Out', were outstanding. Never afraid of slowing down the pace at the right moment, ballads such as 'It's Not Me' were as impressive as the rockers. Humorous and imaginative throughout, revealing a remarkable grasp of melody and knack for hooklines, Supergrass still promise much in the long haul of British pop music.

➤ Tracks: *In It For The Money; Richard III; Tonight; Late In The Day; G-Song; Sun Hits The Sky; Going Out; It's Not Me; Cheapskate; You Can See Me; Hollow Little Reign; Sometimes I Make You Sad.*

★ First released 1997
★ UK peak chart position: 1
★ USA peak chart position: did not chart
★ Previous Top 1000 position: 1998 (108); 1994 (–)

852 C'MON KIDS ↓
The Boo Radleys

A consistently imaginative album and one that reveals at least one clever hook or twist in every track. Returning to the spirit of *Giant Steps*, a screeching wall-of-guitar noise dominates the title track, which leads into increasingly strange subject matter ('Meltin's Worm') and fresh musical ideas throughout. The dub feel of 'Fortunate Son' recalls the mighty 'Lazarus', and the Simon and Garfunkel-style harmonies of 'New Brighton Promenade' emphasize the Boo Radleys' stunning ability to write crafted, melodic pop songs. Overall a highly uncommercial album, it nevertheless restored the band's reputation as inspired pop experimenters.

➤ Tracks: *C'mon Kids; Meltin's Worm; Melodies For The Deaf (Colours For The Blind); Get On The Bus; Everything Is Sorrow; Bullfrog Green; What's In The Box (See Whatcha Got); Four Saints; New Brighton Promenade; Fortunate Son; Shelter; Ride The Tiger; One Last Hurrah.*

★ First released 1996
★ UK peak chart position: 1
★ USA peak chart position: did not chart
★ Previous Top 1000 position: 1998 (695); 1994 (–)

853 TUSK ↑
Fleetwood Mac

Any album that had to follow Rumours was always going to be a problem. A double album on which Lindsay Buckingham tried to ease them in a different direction was greeted with howls. Christine McVie was otherwise occupied with her relationship with Dennis Wilson of the Beach Boys and Stevie Nicks was getting a bit reclusive. Buckingham took the helm and led them off into what is now seen as a great single album. Tracks such as 'What Makes You Think You're The One' can be forgotten. Surely the worst drum sound of any Mac recording. A good album for Mac completists or Buckingham devotees only.

» Tracks: *Over and Over; The Ledge; Think About Me; Save Me A Place; Sara; What Makes You Think You're The One; Storms; That's All For Everyone; Not That Funny; Sisters Of The Moon; Angel; That's Enough For Me; Brown Eyes; Never Make Me Cry; I Know I'm Not Wrong; Honey Hi; Beautiful Child; Walk A Thin Line; Tusk; Never Forget.*

★ First released 1979
★ UK peak chart position: 6
★ USA peak chart position: 4
★ Previous Top 1000 position: 1998 (–): 1994 (–)

854 ALL THINGS MUST PASS ↓
George Harrison

A preponderance of timeless Lennon/McCartney songs ensured that George Harrison's contribution to the Beatles' catalogue was held in check. This backlog ensured that his 'official' debut set was teeming with strong material. 'Isn't It A Pity' and 'My Sweet Lord' are among his finest songs, despite the charge of plagiarism directed at the latter. A suitably lush Phil Spector production cocooned Harrison's sometimes one-dimensional voice, creating a tapestry enhanced by contributions by Eric Clapton and the group that would later become Derek and The Dominoes. Three albums made up a set that showed Harrison's gifts to be mature and indicated that his talents had been too long obscured.

» Tracks: *I'd Have You Anytime; My Sweet Lord; Wah-wah; Isn't It A Pity; What Is Life; If Not For You; Behind That Locked Door; Let It Down; Run Of The Mill; Beware Of Darkness; Apple Scruffs; Ballad Of Sir Frankie Crisp (Let It Roll); Awaiting On You All; All Things Must Pass; I Dig Love; Art Of Dying; Isn't It A Pity; Hear Me Lord; Out Of The Blue; It's Johnny's Birthday; Plug Me In; I Remember Jeep; Thanks For The Pepperoni.*

★ First released 1970
★ UK peak chart position: 4   ★ USA peak chart position: 1
★ Previous Top 1000 position: 1998 (390): 1994 (211)

855 THE COLOUR AND THE SHAPE ↑
Foo Fighters

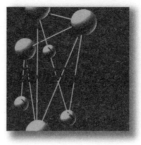

There were a few doubters who felt that, post-Nirvana, Dave Grohl's own musical ambitions would be short-lived. It was, they said, a bit like Noel Redding maintaining a hugely successful career post-Hendrix. Grohl has turned this theory on its head, with this sophomore album easily matching the success of the Foo Fighter's self-titled debut. 'Monkey Wrench' is instantly appealing and sets a pace for the rest of this fast and furious album to follow, and there are enough great hooks and crunching guitar chords here to satisfy former devotees (notably 'My Poor Brain' and 'My Hero'). Grohl's songwriting talent has grown in leaps and bounds, however, and Foo Fighters have now established themselves as a great band on their own terms.

» Tracks: *Doll; Monkey Wrench; Hey, Johnny Park!; My Poor Brain; Wind Up; Up In Arms; My Hero; See You; Enough Space; February Stars; Everlong; Walking After You; New Way Home.*

★ First released 1997
★ UK peak chart position: 3
★ USA peak chart position: 10
★ Previous Top 1000 position: 1998 (–): 1994 (–)

856 THE COLOUR OF MY LOVE ↑
Celine Dion

Some might say if you can't say something positive or constructive then don't say nuffink. I would like to align myself with the millions who love this artist, but my inability to do so is clearly a failing that I will never be able to correct. Celine Dion is very popular and her music makes a lot of people very happy. She does not write her own songs, has a powerful voice, and likes a big full production with lots of drama. On songs like 'Think Twice' she milks each note for all it's worth. And when I say milk, I mean milk.

» Tracks: *The Power Of Love; Misled; Think Twice; Only One Road; Everybody's Talkin' My Baby Down; Next Plane Out; Real Emotion; When I Fall In Love; Love Doesn't Ask Why; Refuse To Dance; I Remember L.A.; No Living Without Loving You; Lovin' Proof; The Colour Of My Love.*

★ First released 1993
★ UK peak chart position: 1
★ USA peak chart position: 4
★ Previous Top 1000 position: 1998 (–): 1994 (–)

857 KINGS OF THE WILD FRONTIER ↓ Adam and The Ants

Adam Ant succeeded in the pop charts as a result of style as much as music. He rode the crest of post-punk new wave, with his brand of pop leaning heavily on the drumming and chanting of African artists such as Burundi Black. 'Dog Eat Dog' and 'Antmusic' are two good examples of his sound. A track such as 'Feed Me To The Lions' attempts a more regular sound and, as such, falls short. The title track was the main hit, but spare a thought for 'The Magnificent Five', with its opening lyric: 'long ago in London town, a man called Ant sat deeply sighing'.

» Tracks: *Dog Eat Dog; Antmusic; Feed Me To The Lions; Los Rancheros; Ants Invasion; Killer In The Home; Kings Of The Wild Frontier; The Magnificent Five; Don't Be Square (Be There); Jolly Roger; Making History; The Human Beings.*

★ First released 1980
★ UK peak chart position: 1
★ USA peak chart position: 44
★ Previous Top 1000 position: 1998 (539): 1994 (–)

858 MUD SLIDE SLIM AND THE BLUE HORIZON ↑ James Taylor

The US bedsitter artist who defined a decade of singer-songwriters. Young James sang like an old James, and millions believed the sentiments of classics such as 'You've Got A Friend' and the title track. The short and sweet 'Soldiers' revisits the same place as 'Sweet Baby James' but at the time most listeners were too stoned to notice. The great love song on this one is 'You Can Close Your Eyes' still one of his most requested songs. The last 55 seconds of the album are wrapped up by the concise yet beautiful 'Isn't It Nice To Be Home Again'. Taylor's finger-picking on this album is exquisite.

» Tracks: *Love Has Brought Me Around; You've Got A Friend; Places In My Past; Riding On A Railroad; Soldiers; Mud Slide Slim; Hey Mister, That's Me Up On The Jukebox; You Can Close Your Eyes; Machine Gun Kelly; Long Ago and Far Away; Let Me Ride; Highway Song; Isn't It Nice To Be Home Again.*

★ First released 1971
★ UK peak chart position: 4
★ USA peak chart position: 2
★ Previous Top 1000 position: 1998 (–): 1994 (–)

859 SHEPHERD MOONS ↑ Enya

It is sometimes difficult to write objectively about music that is not quite in your own garden. Clearly it is a fault within me. After all Enya sells zillions of records. The underlying strength of this record resides in the pleasant, hymn-like chord changes. Musically it is hard to fault but, apart from the odd flourish such as the Phil Spector castanets on 'Book Of Days', dullness creeps in prior to nodding off. Her voice is quite beautiful. If you like Bach or the Mannheim Steamroller you will love this. If on the other hand you appreciate popular music ranging from Metallica to Frank Sinatra you will probably want to give this an extra wide berth.

» Tracks: *Shepherd Moon; Caribbean Blue; How Can I Keep From Singing?; Ebudæ; Angeles; No Holly For Miss Quinn; Book Of Days; Evacuee; Lothlorien; Marble Halls; After Ventus; Smaointe…*

★ First released 1991
★ UK peak chart position: 1
★ USA peak chart position: 17
★ Previous Top 1000 position: 1998 (–): 1994 (508)

860 THE REAL THING ↑ Faith No More

'From Out Of Nowhere', the excellent opening track on Faith No More's break-through third album, fools the listener into thinking this is a 70s rock band along the lines of Kiss, or even a heavier Todd Rundgren song. The second track 'Epic' reveals the band's true colours, retaining the duel guitars but introducing their familiar hard-edged neo rap/metal style. The commercial brightness of the album's sound fails to gloss over the lyrical darkness, which encompasses paedophilia on 'Edge Of The World' and the grim tale of 'Surprise! You're Dead!'. The most impressive thing about this album is how together the band sounds.

» Tracks: *From Out Of Nowhere; Epic; Falling To Pieces; Surprise! You're Dead!; Zombie Eaters; The Real Thing; Underwater Love; The Morning After; Woodpecker From Mars; War Pigs; Edge Of The World.*

★ First released 1989
★ UK peak chart position: 30
★ USA peak chart position: 11
★ Previous Top 1000 position: 1998 (–): 1994 (–)

861 BLACK WOMAN & CHILD ↑
Sizzla

Dancehall DJ Miguel Collins has taken on the mantle of Marcus Garvey, enjoying huge success in Jamaica as a modern day musical spokesperson for the repatriation of the 'suffering black masses' to Ethiopia. Presumably, this will have to find favour with those many Jamaicans who find the stunningly beautiful lush climate of their island quite agreeable, particularly in preference to a drought stricken hell. And where would you get a cold Red Stripe beer, or splash in the Dunn's River falls, or find the great record shops in downtown Kingston. Come off it Sizzla, let's just enjoy the great music, aye.

❱❱ Tracks: *Black Woman & Child; Hard Ground; More Guidance; Make It Secure; Oh What A Joy; Love Is Divine; One Away; Guide Over Us; Give Them The Ride; Babylon A Use Dem Brain; Princess Black; No Time To Gaze; Too Much To Bear; Mi Lord; Give Them The Ride (Remix).*

★ First released 1997
★ UK peak chart position: did not chart
★ USA peak chart position: did not chart
★ Previous Top 1000 position: 1998 (–): 1994 (–)

862 INVISIBLE TOUCH ↑
Genesis

Ooooh, those 80s electronic drums. Why were they allowed in? Perfect for digital recording but horrible on the ears. If you imagine a real fat acoustic drum kit this holds up as an excellent collection. Turn down the treble in your head and dream of beefy kettle drums and 'tiss tadah, tiss tadah' cymbals on 'Tonight Tonight Tonight'. Will the tinniness of Phil Collins's voice to go away, notably on 'Land Of Confusion' and the title track, and just pretend that is a valve amplifier driving Mike Rutherford's guitar. Only 'In Too Deep' lends itself to 80s technology, with every nasty digital blip sounding corny but acceptable.

❱❱ Tracks: *Invisible Touch; Tonight, Tonight, Tonight; Land Of Confusion; In Too Deep; Anything She Does; Domino (Part One – In The Glow Of The Night. Part Two – The Last Domino); Throwing It All Away; The Brazilian.*

★ First released 1986
★ UK peak chart position: 1
★ USA peak chart position: 3
★ Previous Top 1000 position: 1998 (–): 1994 (–)

863 THE SOFT PARADE ↑
The Doors

The continuing popularity of the Doors shows no signs of losing pace, and as such just about any official album will be applauded due to their short career. *The Soft Parade* is generally thought to be their weakest album, but presumably that still ranks it better than most of the thousands of albums released over the past 30 years or so. That said the album sometimes overuses the brass and strings to beef up the rather tinny sound. Stand-out tracks such as the hit single 'Touch Me' and the beautifully orchestrated 'Wishful Sinful' compensate for the over ambitious and lengthy title track.

❱❱ Tracks: *Tell All The People; Touch Me; Shaman's Blues; Do It; Easy Ride; Wild Child; Runnin' Blue; Wishful Sinful; The Soft Parade.*

★ First released 1969
★ UK peak chart position: did not chart
★ USA peak chart position: 6
★ Previous Top 1000 position: 1998 (–): 1994 (–)

864 MAYBE YOU'VE BEEN BRAINWASHED TOO ↑
New Radicals

One of the high points of the pop charts in 1998 was the success of the New Radicals single 'You Get What You Give'. This spectacular song, which espoused the old Indian wisdom 'the smile you give out returns to you', was a wonderful antidote to the 'me me me, why am I in so much pain' type lyric that is the staple of the alternative rock market. No sooner had the single and this excellent album dropped off the chart than songwriter/leader Gregg Alexander folded the band to retire to a career behind the scenes. Which would indicate that you get what you give, but you can't always get what you want, you just get what you need.

❱❱ Tracks: *Mother We Just Can't Get Enough; You Get What You Give; I Hope I Didn't Just Give Away The Ending; I Don't Wanna Die Anymore; Jehovah Made This Whole Joint For You; Someday We'll Know; Maybe You've Been Brainwashed Too; In Need Of A Miracle; Gotta Stay High; Technicolor Lover; Flowers; Crying Like A Church On Monday.*

★ First released 1998
★ UK peak chart position: 10
★ USA peak chart position: 41
★ Previous Top 1000 position: 1998 (–): 1994 (–)

865 LOOK SHARP! ↑
Joe Jackson

Joe Jackson was never really a punk, although he did adopt some of the genre's attitude and aggression. He failed as a punk because melody kept creeping into his songs, and his songs kept wandering way beyond four chords. This excellent album sounded angry in 1979 although it now sounds tame. Jackson's lyrics were often poignant, if not sometimes downright clever. To use the analogy that any other man that any other woman goes out with is a gorilla is a real man thing, and he is similarly scathing on tracks such as 'Happy Loving Couples' and the 'Sunday Papers'. Jackson is now a credible classical composer but he should never dismiss his punkish apprenticeship.

▶ Tracks: *One More Time; Sunday Papers; Is She Really Going Out With Him?; Happy Loving Couples; Throw It Away; Baby Stick Around; Look Sharp!; Fools In Love; (Do The) Instant Mash; Pretty Girls; Got The Time.*

★ First released 1979
★ UK peak chart position: 40
★ USA peak chart position: 20
★ Previous Top 1000 position: 1998 (–): 1994 (–)

866 A TRICK OF THE TAIL ↑
Genesis

Prior to the release of this ambitious project the post-Gabriel Genesis were still feeling their way. Phil Collins had an undeniably difficult task in stepping out from behind the drums and replacing the canonized angel. Fortunately for everybody it all turned out splendidly, and the likeable progsters delivered some of their finest epics of change and twiddle. 'Squonk' became a regular extended concert favourite and the title track is Genesis at their most delightful. Few would begrudge this track five stars. It's a great pity the lyrics cannot be clearly read on the CD. One point size type is not good. Fortunately 'Los Endos' is an instrumental.

▶ Tracks: *Dance On A Volcano; Entangled; Squonk; Mad Man Moon; Robbery, Assault & Battery; Ripples; A Trick Of The Tail; Los Endos.*

★ First released 1976
★ UK peak chart position: 3
★ USA peak chart position: 31
★ Previous Top 1000 position: 1998 (–): 1994 (–)

867 MR LUCKY ↑
John Lee Hooker

All Mr. Lucky needs to do is to continue to stay alive and he will be Mr. Immortal. He is the last of the giant old bluesmen and, with B.B. King and Muddy Waters, he surely represents the greatest. This album found him on a roll after the extraordinary success of *The Healer*. Although not quite as strong he was able to tap into a rich vein of material and call on dozens of famous artists and musicians. All of them would have queued up just to stand next to him in the studio, let alone play on the record. Hooker has incredible charisma, which this album amply demonstrates.

▶ Tracks: *I Want To Hug You; Mr. Lucky; Backstabbers; This Is Hip; I Cover The Waterfront; Highway 13; Stripped Me Naked; Susie; Crawlin' Kingsnake; Father Was A Jockey.*

★ First released 1991
★ UK peak chart position: 3
★ USA peak chart position: 101
★ Previous Top 1000 position: 1998 (–): 1994 (817)

868 THE ROYAL SCAM ↑
Steely Dan

How dare this lag behind other Steely Dan albums in the popular vote. It remains one of their best, although it is difficult to choose a favourite with such a rich back catalogue. A number of indispensable classics are present here, including the magnificent 'Haitian Divorce' which features a guitar solo so good you want to eat it. The title track and 'Kid Charlemagne' are other highlights, although every track has merit. Faultless apart from the lack of a lyric sheet on the CD, and the annoying debate as to which guitarist played on what. Choose between Walter Becker, Larry Carlton, Denny Dias, Elliott Randall or Dean Parks. And Jeff 'Skunk' Baxter has to be in there somewhere as well.

▶ Tracks: *Kid Charlemagne; The Caves Of Altamira; Don't Take Me Alive; Sign In Stranger; The Fez; Green Earrings; Haitian Divorce; Everything You Did; The Royal Scam.*

★ First released 1976
★ UK peak chart position: 11
★ USA peak chart position: 15
★ Previous Top 1000 position: 1998 (–): 1994 (–)

869 LIFE IS PEACHY ↑
Korn

One crucial thing had changed by the time Korn were ready to release this, their second album – they had become incredibly popular in American high schools. School authorities, in a typical knee jerk response, were objecting to the alleged 'bad influence' of the band's explicit lyrical content. In reality the band's lyrics were no better or worse than any other metal, hardcore or gangsta rap outfit. Certainly the band's appeal to US males in their early teens is quite extraordinary. This breakthrough album, which captures the band on the brink of becoming one of the most popular rock acts in the US, allows the listener to peek into the dark world of Korn without having to wear the T-shirt and baseball cap. Principals everywhere must have been shaking their heads in dismay.

❱❱ Tracks: Twist; Chi; Lost; Swallow; Porno Creep; Good God; Mr. Rogers; K@#%!; No Place To Hide; Wicked; A.D.I.D.A.S.; Lowrider; Ass Itch; Kill You.
★ First released 1996
★ UK peak chart position: 32 ★ USA peak chart position: 3
★ Previous Top 1000 position: 1998 (–): 1994 (–)

870 MUSIC FROM THE MOTION PICTURE PULP FICTION ↑
Soundtrack

Unlike most soundtrack albums of the 90s this juxtaposes music with snatches of dialogue from the movie. This clever ploy acts as a warm reminder to those who have seen the movie, and tempts others to go and see it for the first time. The use of the Dick Dale track 'Misirlou' was inspired and introduced a whole new generation to his slightly dodgy style of surf music. The use of well-worn classics is joyous rather than disappointing, although hearing Dusty Springfield and Al Green in this dark movie was a unique twist. This carefully and successfully chosen selection forms an integral part of the movie's appeal, and as a bonus the priceless 'Royale With Cheese' dialogue is also included.

❱❱ Tracks: 'Pumpkin and Honey Bunny'/Misirlou (Dick Dale and His Del-Tones); 'Royale With Cheese'; Jungle Boogie (Kool and The Gang); Let's Stay Together (Al Green); Bustin' Surfboards (Tornadoes); Lonesome Town (Ricky Nelson); Son Of A Preacher Man (Dusty Springfield); 'Zed's Dead, Baby'/Bullwinkle Part II (The Centurians); 'Jack Rabbit Slims Twist Contest'/You Never Can Tell (Chuck Berry); Girl, You'll Be A Woman Soon (Urge Overkill); If Love Is A Red Dress (Hang Me In Rags) (Maria McKee); 'Bring Out The Gimp'/Comanche (The Revels); Flowers On The Wall (The Statler Brothers); Personality Goes A Long Way; Surf Rider (The Lively Ones); 'Ezekiel 25:17'.
★ First released 1994 ★ UK peak chart position: 5
★ USA peak chart position: 21
★ Previous Top 1000 position: 1998 (–): 1994 (–)

871 PILGRIM ↑
Eric Clapton

This recent album features some of the most important lyrical statements made by Clapton in his lengthy career. Having shaken off his past excesses he felt free to talk honestly about his life, previously a subject that was a closed door. Clapton's vocals are also more soulful, and the overall groove is relaxed. The opening track 'My Father's Eyes' is about his own absent father, while 'Circus' alludes to his late son. The tour de force, 'You Were There', is not about Patti Boyd but his former manager Roger Forrester, a man who also helped him through his dark days 'of wine and madness'. A much deeper and better album than many of you noticed.

❱❱ Tracks: My Father's Eyes; River Of Tears; Pilgrim; Broken Hearted; One Chance; Circus; Going Down Slow; Fall Like Rain; Born In Time; Sick and Tired; Needs His Woman; She's Gone; You Were There; Inside Of Me.

★ First released 1998
★ UK peak chart position: 6
★ USA peak chart position: 4
★ Previous Top 1000 position: 1998 (–): 1994 (–)

872 IT'S MY LIFE ↓
Talk Talk

As an early 80s band, Talk Talk spent some time trying to disassociate themselves from their New Romantic contemporaries. Vocalist Mark Hollis had a problem in as much that his voice shares a pristine, pitch-perfect singing style with Tony Hadley (Spandau Ballet) and Martin Fry (ABC). Still, Hollis' distinctive voice made some good pop songs sound great. The title track, for example, has every synth gimmick under the sun but cannot fail in its infectious spirit. Some trusty old-timers are added to the proceedings; jazz trumpeter Henry Lowther wails beautifully and guitarist Robbie McIntosh (Average White Band) excels. Splendid, unchallenging stuff.

❱❱ Tracks: Dum Dum Girl; Such A Shame; Renée; It's My Life; Tomorrow Started; The Last Time; Call In The Night Boy; Does Caroline Know?; It's You.

★ First released 1984
★ UK peak chart position: 35
★ USA peak chart position: 42
★ Previous Top 1000 position: 1998 (822): 1994 (–)

873 ELECTRIC WARRIOR ↓
T. Rex

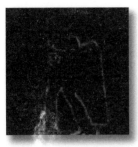

Marc Bolan emerged from the petals of Britain's underground scene to become one of the 70s' bona fide rock stars. *Electric Warrior* followed the pattern of his group's highly successful singles in that every track boasted nagging hooklines and incessant charm. Bolan understood pop history and his work drew on the immediacy of classic rock 'n' roll and the charm of its icons. He infused his music with an ebullient energy impossible to ignore, while offering a mythology to enhance its appeal. The antithesis of contemporaneous progressive rock, *Electric Warrior* was fresh and uncluttered, and therein lies its continued attraction.

» Tracks: *Mambo Sun; Cosmic Dancer; Jeepster; Monolith; Lean Woman Blues; Get It On; Planet Queen; Girl; The Motivator; Life's A Gas; Rip Off.*

★ First released 1971
★ UK peak chart position: 1
★ USA peak chart position: 32
★ Previous Top 1000 position: 1998 (303): 1994 (69)

874 DRY ↓
PJ Harvey

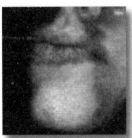

This West Country chanteuse with a credible line in extolling the virtues of sex, came with a wealth of emotional baggage that she was more than willing to share. Her public persona was a mix of nudity wrapped in clingfilm, or draped with a feather boa and arch, accentuated sunglasses, while her songs bristled with fragility and pain and a surly inner strength. Now more widely acknowledged for her excellent *Rid Of Me* and *To Bring You My Love, Dry* was the bedrock on which she built her tower of emotions. The gritty 'Victory', the surprisingly light 'Water', the evocative 'Happy and Bleeding' – all made for a crushing masterpiece.

» Tracks: *Oh My Lover; O Stella; Dress; Victory; Happy and Bleeding; Sheela-Na-Gig; Hair; Joe; Plants and Rags; Fountain; Water.*

★ First released 1992
★ UK peak chart position: 11
★ USA peak chart position: did not chart
★ Previous Top 1000 position: 1998 (386): 1994 (532)

875 LISTEN WITHOUT PREJUDICE, VOL. 1 ↑
George Michael

Probably the best career move that George Michael made was to get caught with his trousers down. His make or break honesty in dealing with the situation has worked well, and many people have subsequently listened to his music without prejudice. This album, recorded way back at the end of the 80s, stands up well to the test of time. The slower tracks are particularly suited to his voice, especially 'Praying For Time', an exceptional version of Stevie Wonder's 'They Won't Go When I Go', and 'Cowboys and Angels' – the latter, a gamble that paid off. Michael has a sensational voice but he should skip the chat show appearances and concentrate on his music. Keep the profundity for the songs.

» Tracks: *Praying For Time; Freedom '90; They Won't Go When I Go; Something To Save; Cowboys and Angels; Waiting For That Day/You Can't Always Get What You Want; Mothers Pride; Heal The Pain; Soul Free; Waiting (Reprise).*

★ First released 1990
★ UK peak chart position: 1
★ USA peak chart position: 2
★ Previous Top 1000 position: 1998 (–): 1994 (–)

876 TREASURE ↑
Cocteau Twins

Although not as lush as *Heaven Or Las Vegas*, *Treasure* remains the other essential Cocteau Twins album to acquire. Elizabeth Fraser's astonishing voice alternates between angelic thoughts and deep despair as she swoops above and below Robin Guthrie's beautifully flanged guitar. 'Persephone' is a breathtaking piece that needs to be played loud to appreciate its chiming power. I doubt if more than a dozen fans could reel off any of Fraser's lyrics, which for the most part are indecipherable and irrelevant to the surreal wash of sound. Astral and cosmic are the words that spring to mind as your ears are given an aural treat.

» Tracks: *Ivo; Lorelei; Beatrix; Persephone; Pandora; Amelia; Aloysius; Cicely; Ottereley; Donimo.*

★ First released 1984
★ UK peak chart position: 29
★ USA peak chart position: did not chart
★ Previous Top 1000 position: 1998 (–): 1994 (–)

877 THE LION AND THE COBRA
↑ Sinéad O'Connor

Sadly it appears that Sinéad O'Connor's star has waned as more and more her exploits outside the music business attract more media attention than her recording career. Certainly her outspokenness has alienated her from many early fans who latched on to this fine debut album. A well-produced record with lyrical depth was as rare as a square CD at the end of the 80s, and O'Connor was deservedly praised for an original collection of songs that combined Kate Bush's quirkiness with late 70s angst. The wailing 'Jerusalem' and the passionate 'Troy' are particular highlights. If the latter had left out the plonky Genesis banjo guitar tone it would have been even better.

❱❱ Tracks: *Jackie; Mandinka; Jerusalem; Just Like U Said It Would B; Never Get Old; Troy; I Want Your (Hands On Me); Drink Before The War; Just Call Me Joe.*

★ First released 1987
★ UK peak chart position: 27
★ USA peak chart position: 36
★ Previous Top 1000 position: 1998 (–): 1994 (–)

878 IT'S GREAT WHEN YOU'RE STRAIGHT, YEAH! ↓ Black Grape

Few could have been expecting great things from ex-Happy Mondays singer Shaun Ryder, last seen drug-addled and artistically barren when that group fizzled out unceremoniously. However, his return was glorious – harnessing the remixing talents of Danny Saber and the croaky rapping of Kermit, *It's Great ...* offered an instant high for party people. Ryder's slurred rantings and nonsense lyrics seemed more at home than ever: 'A Big Day In The North' most clearly recalled the Happy Mondays sound, but the mighty 'Reverend Black Grape', 'Kelly's Heroes' and the irresistible invitation to 'Shake Your Money' defined the in-yer-face Black Grape sound.

❱❱ Tracks: *Reverend Black Grape; In The Name Of The Father; Tramazi Parti; Kelly's Heroes; Yeah Yeah Brother; A Big Day In The North; Shake Well Before Opening; Submarine; Shake Your Money; Little Bob.*

★ First released 1995
★ UK peak position: 1
★ USA peak position: did not chart
★ Previous Top 1000 position: 1998 (127): 1994 (–)

879 K ↓
Kula Shaker

Crispin Mills' mother (actress Hayley) must have fed her baby son a balanced diet of Jimi Hendrix, Beatles and late 60s rock. All these styles are beautifully honed on this stunning debut album. Creamy guitars, crybaby wah-wahs, and chiming sitars are all-pervading. Even the record-cover collage of famous 'K's (Ken Dodd and Lord Kitchener among them) reflects the band's mish-mash of influences. The mystical Eastern themes of 'Govinda' and 'Tattva' sit alongside unapologetically retro rockers such as 'Grateful When You're Dead/Jerry Was There' and 'Hey Dude', merely serving to reinforce the atmosphere: you can almost picture the cheesecloth and smell the patchouli from here.

❱❱. Tracks: *Hey Dude; Knight On The Town; Temple Of Everlasting Light; Govinda; Smart Dogs; Magic Theatre; Into The Deep; Sleeping Jiva; Tattva; Grateful When You're Dead/Jerry Was There; 303; Start All Over; Hollow Man.*

★ First released 1996
★ UK peak chart position: 1
★ USA peak chart position: did not chart
★ Previous Top 1000 position: 1998 (55): 1994 (–)

880 CLOSING TIME ↑
Tom Waits

It's hard to imagine that Tom Waits could ever sound young, but hearing this album's opening track 'Ol' 55' again there is definitely a youthful timbre in his voice. 'Ol' 55' was popularised by the Eagles and helped give Waits reputation, a much needed shot in the arm. Producer Jerry Yester handled this idiosyncratic artist well and this is an important addition for those looking to build a Tom Waits library. These are simple melodic songs that eschew the rich drama of his later recordings. 'I Hope That I Don't Fall In Love With You' is a fine example of him pretending to be James Taylor when all along he really wanted to be Howlin' Wolf. Character building stuff.

❱❱ Tracks: *Ol' 55; I Hope That I Don't Fall In Love With You; Virginia Avenue; Old Shoes (& Picture Postcards); Midnight Lullaby; Martha; Rosie; Lonely; Ice Cream Man; Little Trip To Heaven (On The Wings Of Your Love); Grapefruit Moon; Closing Time.*

★ First released 1973
★ UK peak chart position: did not chart
★ USA peak chart position: did not chart
★ Previous Top 1000 position: 1998 (–): 1994 (–)

881 EUROPE '72 ↑
Grateful Dead

A 3-RECORD SET ON 2 SPECIALLY-PRICED COMPACT DISCS

Europe '72

They came, they played, they indulged, they conquered. A massive entourage of hipness invaded and made swinging Carnaby Street look as dull as Savile Row. European Deadheads will always envy America for having the band on their doorstep, as regular as *Coronation Street*. Fortunately this is an admirable reminder of how good they were at one of their many peaks. So much material now exists via the *Dick's Picks* series that choosing stand-outs has become almost academic, but 'Truckin' is particularly sprightly, and Weir sings 'Sugar Magnolia' like he really means it. There have been many better Grateful Dead live albums but this one means the most to Europeans.

» Tracks: *Cumberland Blues; He's Gone; One More Saturday Night; Jack Straw; You Win Again; China Cat Sunflower; I Know You Rider; Brown-Eyed Woman; Hurts Me Too; Ramble On Rose; Sugar Magnolia; Mr. Charlie; Tennessee Jed; Truckin'; Epilogue; Prelude; (Walk Me Out In The) Morning Dew.*

★ First released 1972
★ UK peak chart position: did not chart
★ USA peak chart position: 24
★ Previous Top 1000 position: 1998 (–): 1994 (–)

882 NEW GOLD DREAM (81, 82, 83, 84) ↓ Simple Minds

Simple Minds began their career indebted to Roxy Music, David Bowie and Magazine, but over successive releases emerged as a distinctive act. On *New Gold Dream* the group's ambitions came to full fruition, the awkward dissonance of early recordings replaced by a warm, textured sound. The content ranged from brash stadium rock to melodic ballad, but a singleness of purpose ensured such contrasts enhanced the set's overall cohesion. The quintet had never sounded so confident or assured and the resultant lush textures launched them into the international arena, fulfilling their undoubted promise. On 'Promised You A Miracle' did Kerr really sing 'guinea pigs are guinea pigs'?

» Tracks: *Someone Somewhere (In Summertime); Colours Fly and Catherine Wheel; Promised You A Miracle; Big Sleep; Somebody Up There Likes You; New Gold Dream; Glittering Prize; Hunter and The Hunted; King Is White and In The Crowd.*

★ First released 1982
★ UK peak chart position: 3
★ USA peak chart position: 69
★ Previous Top 1000 position: 1998 (292): 1994 (155)

883 SUPPOSED FORMER INFATUATION JUNKIE ↑
Alanis Morissette

If it ain't broke it ain't worth fixing, or something like that. The trouble is, there is only one way to skin a rabbit, or something like that. Of course, their was massive pressure on to follow up the phenomenon that was *Jagged Little Pill*, and of course this fell way short of the mark. Morissette clearly has tons of lyrics to pour out, and good lyrics at that, but her vocal intonation becomes repetitive and boring after a while as she rolls each word into the next. And surely standing on the pavement Botticelli style, with no clothes on will give her a nasty chill.

» Tracks: *Front Row; Baba; Thank U; Are You Still Mad; Sympathetic Character; That I Would Be Good; The Couch; Can't Not; UR; I Was Hoping; One; Would Not Come; Unsent; So Pure; Joining You; Heart Of The House; Your Congratulations.*

★ First released 1998
★ UK peak chart position: 3
★ USA peak chart position: 1
★ Previous Top 1000 position: 1998 (–): 1994 (–)

884 ENGLISH SETTLEMENT ↑
XTC

The wonderful and criminally underrated XTC almost made the very big time after this ambitious double album received across the board positive reviews and scaled the charts. Everything in XTC's garden seemed fine, and Andy Partridge was even seen strumming his Martin guitar on *Top Of The Pops* singing 'Senses Working Overtime'. That was until Partridge fell ill and decided to retreat to his attic room in Swindon. Surrounded by his lead soldiers he announced that XTC would never perform live again. In hindsight, this was the best thing that could have happened because it allowed the eccentric Partridge to devote his time to making more wonderful records like this one.

» Tracks: *Runaways; Ball and Chain; Senses Working Overtime; Jason and The Argonauts; No Thugs In Our House; Yacht Dance; All Of A Sudden (It's Too Late); Melt The Guns; Leisure; It's Nearly Africa; Knuckle Down; Fly On The Wall; Down In The Cockpit; English Roundabout; Snowman.*

★ First released 1982
★ UK peak chart position: 5
★ USA peak chart position: 48
★ Previous Top 1000 position: 1998 (–): 1994 (–)

885 BODY AND SOUL ↑
Joe Jackson

Oh dear! How dare he mimic a Reid Miles designed Blue Note cover (*Sonny Rollins Vol. 2*), even down to the typography (take a look at no. 564). Believe it or not some critics were more concerned with that, than the music. Jackson boldly moved forward into scoring pieces of instrumental music, a continued development from the previous *Night and Day*. Although not as commercially successful *Body and Soul* reeked of class and move punkish Joe into higher ground towards his now realised goal as a pure composer. One last look over his shoulder towards the pop charts was with the excellent 'Be My Number Two'. A nice way to move on.

» Tracks: *The Verdict; Cha Cha Loco; Not Here, Not Now; You Can't Get What You Want (Till You Know What You Want); Go For It; Loisaida; Happy Ending; Be My Number Two; Heart Of Ice.*

★ First released 1984
★ UK peak chart position: 14
★ USA peak chart position: 20
★ Previous Top 1000 position: 1998 (–): 1994 (–)

886 OMMADAWN ↓
Mike Oldfield

Ommadawn represents a creative peak for Mike Oldfield that is often overshadowed by the huge commercial success of his debut *Tubular Bells*. Oldfield employed the same format he had used on his previous two albums, with both sides of the record comprising a lengthy instrumental collage. This time he drew on a greater range of musical styles, using recurring motifs that had recognizable African, Eastern European and Irish sources (Paddy Moloney of The Chieftains being responsible for the latter). The recording was also notable for the way Oldfield collaborated with the other musicians, drawing attention away from his image as the self-styled studio recluse.

» Tracks: *Ommadawn Part 1; Ommadawn Part 2.*

★ First released 1975
★ UK peak chart position: 4
★ USA peak chart position: 146
★ Previous Top 1000 position: 1998 (403): 1994 (–)

887 READING, WRITING AND ARITHMETIC ↑
The Sundays

The pop market was deprived of this charming record for over three years, during which time the Sundays became the yesterdays in the short memories of the record buying public. Parlophone Records reissued this debut album in 1996, and although sales were still minimal the album stands up as a minor gem. 'Can't Be Sure' was the surprise hit single, but other tracks now have greater impact, notably the gorgeous 'Here's Where The Story Ends' (a recent dance hit for Tin Tin Out). Harriet Wheeler has a sweet voice with just enough steel to make it palatable, which laid over the top of David Gavurin's imaginative guitar work makes for an agreeable 38 minutes of indie pop.

» Tracks: *Skin & Bones; Here's Where The Story Ends; Can't Be Sure; I Won; Hideous Towns; You're Not The Only One I Know; A Certain Someone; I Kicked A Boy; My Finest Hour; Joy.*

★ First released 1990
★ UK peak chart position: 4
★ USA peak chart position: 39
★ Previous Top 1000 position: 1998 (–): 1994 (–)

888 TONIGHT'S THE NIGHT ↓
Neil Young

For many years this was the critics' favourite. The cognoscenti loved its rawness and the depression the album both portrayed and induced. The title track chronicles roadie Bruce Berry and Crazy Horse member Danny Whitten's deaths. Other songs address the fact that Young was not a happy bunny at this time in his life. The sloppy piano and most guitar parts are played by Nils Lofgren. The bar-room atmosphere has been repeated on many Neil Young albums over the years, but never as home-grown as this. Of all the excellent records Young has made, this is definitely not the one for sunny Sunday mornings.

» Tracks: *Tonight's The Night; Speakin' Out; World On A String; Borrowed Tune; Come On Baby Let's Go Downtown; Mellow My Mind; Roll Another Number (For The Road); Albuquerque; New Mama; Lookout Joe; Tired Eyes; Tonight's The Night Part II.*

★ First released 1975
★ UK peak chart position: 48
★ USA peak chart position: 25
★ Previous Top 1000 position: 1998 (199): 1994 (–)

889 TELLIN' STORIES ↓
The Charlatans

One UK indie band to have well and truly lasted the course, the Charlatans are now seen as old lags of a new scene. With this, their most successful album to date, they lifted themselves from a pit of despair after the tragic death of keyboard player Rob Collins. Tragic and ironic because Collins gave their sound an original edge with his full-sounding Hammond organ. His replacement to complete the recording of this album was Martin Duffy from Primal Scream. Excellent songs such as 'North Country Boy' and 'How High' are minor classics and the final instrumental doodle, 'Rob's Theme', is a fitting tribute to Collins.

» Tracks: *With No Shoes; North Country Boy; Tellin' Stories; One To Another; You're A Big Girl Now; How Can You Leave Us; Area 51; How High; Only Teethin'; Get On It; Rob's Theme.*

★ First released 1997
★ UK peak chart position: 1
★ USA peak chart position: did not chart
★ Previous Top 1000 position: 1998 (180): 1994 (–)

890 LET IT BE ↓
The Beatles

On the back of the sleeve is the ironic note: 'This is a new phase Beatles album'. The new phase being, here are four maturing men growing apart and desperately needing a break from each other. The accompanying film is too painful to watch, as tempers fray and tension is in the air. In addition to the title track, only 'Get Back' and maybe 'Long and Winding Road' rate as great Beatles songs. The others are all brief entertainments and scraps of tunes. Lennon and Harrison had already moved on in their heads and McCartney was left to paste it together. The overwhelming feeling of this album is one of incredible sadness.

» Tracks: *Two Of Us; Dig A Pony; Across The Universe; I Me Mine; Dig It; Let It Be; Maggie Mae; I've Got A Feeling; One After 909; The Long and Winding Road; For You Blue; Get Back.*

★ First released 1970
★ UK peak chart position: 1
★ USA peak chart position: 1
★ Previous Top 1000 position: 1998 (561): 1994 (–)

891 LUST FOR LIFE ↓
Iggy Pop

Iggy Pop and David Bowie at the height of their respective powers presented a formidable artistic engine, and *Lust For Life* saw them working up a full head of steam. Two songs will need little introduction – 'Lust For Life' and 'The Passenger' are as intrinsic to the tapestry of 70s rock music as sundry Beatles efforts were to the previous decade (their influence on 90s film soundtracks is a testament to their durability). Those monolithic jukebox favourites aside, listeners may also find space in their hearts for the swaggering 'Neighbourhood Threat' (shades of the Stooges, without the musical clatter) and the disquieting 'Turn Blue', written from the viewpoint of an overdosing junkie.

» Tracks: *Lust For Life; Sixteen; Some Weird Sun; The Passenger; Tonight; Success; Turn Blue; Neighbourhood Threat; Fall In Love With Me.*

★ First released 1977
★ UK peak chart position: 28
★ USA peak chart position: 120
★ Previous Top 1000 position: 1998 (219): 1994 (–)

892 SAVAGE GARDEN ↑
Savage Garden

Another of those albums you hate to like, chock full of well-recorded, hummable, and undeniably catchy songs. Poor Savage Garden has done little to warrant the torrent of hostility reserved for them in the music press. To put elitism in its place, this sparkling album contains a lot of easy on the ear tunes that fall somewhere between 70s AOR and 80s mainstream pop. Darren Hayes and Daniel Jones must have been doing something right, however, translating chart-topping records in their native Australia into lucrative success on the transatlantic market. Highly pleasant songs such as 'Truly Madly Deeply' and 'To The Moon and Back' are fine examples of lightweight pop at its best.

» Tracks: *To The Moon and Back; I Want You; Truly Madly Deeply; Tears Of Pearls; Universe; Carry On Dancing; Violet; Break Me Shake Me; A Thousand Words; Promises; Santa Monica.*

★ First released 1997
★ UK peak chart position: 2
★ USA peak chart position: 3
★ Previous Top 1000 position: 1998 (–): 1994 (–)

893 NEW YORK DOLLS ↓
New York Dolls

It's hard in retrospect, with all water that's passed under the bridge in the genre of alternative rock, to articulate the impact this incendiary debut had on its release. The Stooges apart (and they were a different kettle of garage band entirely, in content as much as style), there simply hadn't ever been anything quite as confrontational, cocky and in-your-face as the New York Dolls. From the classic Thunders/Johansen opener 'Personality Crisis' onwards, the Dolls revealed themselves as the new rock outsiders. The album's pungent undertones of low-life street hassle and edgy drug deals and sharply observed narcissism set them apart. And every subsequent punk rock icon, from Joey Ramone to Johnny Rotten, took note.

» Tracks: *Personality Crisis; Looking For A Kiss; Vietnamese Baby; Lonely Planet Boy; Frankenstein (Orig); Trash; Bad Girl; Subway Train; Pills; Private World; Jet Boy.*

★ First released 1973
★ UK peak chart position: did not chart
★ USA peak chart position: 116
★ Previous Top 1000 position: 1998 (220): 1994 (–)

894 COME CLEAN ↑
Curve

Curve have been a familiar name on the UK indie scene for nearly a decade (including a three years hiatus), having watched dozens of upstarts and pretenders come and go but always remaining on the periphery of success. *Come Clean* is excellent, uncompromising electronic rock music that may not be as catchy as Garbage, whose sound they share, but is of equal quality. The album's biting production allows the rich waves of guitar sound to spit out of the speakers. The excellent opening track 'Chinese Burn', which surprisingly failed to hit the charts, is followed by two further stand-outs, 'Coming Up Roses' and 'Something Familiar'. This album is highly recommended for those of you who may have missed it.

» Tracks: *Chinese Burn; Coming Up Roses; Something Familiar; Dog Bone; Alligators Getting Up; Dirty High; Killer Baby; Sweetback; Forgotten Sanity; Cotton Candy; Beyond Reach; Come Clean; Recovery.*

★ First released 1998
★ UK peak chart position: did not chart
★ USA peak chart position: did not chart
★ Previous Top 1000 position: 1998 (–): 1994 (–)

895 FLOOD ↓
They Might Be Giants

It is fair to say that listening to this, their second album, in one hit is a little hard on the ear. Individually, the pathos and humour these chaps manage to put into every song is admirable – very much like a 90s version of Tom Lehrer, but without the satire. The jokes are ironic rather than obvious. Their success is, of course, due to the songs' accessibility, the most commercial being the wonderful 'Birdhouse In Your Soul', a deserved hit single. The story of a back-stabbing office ogre is chronicled in the shape of 'Someone Keeps Moving My Chair'. Some tracks are clearly private jokes and pass by the listener, although self-interpretation can come into play.

» Tracks: *Theme From Flood; Birdhouse In Your Soul; Lucky Ball & Chain; Istanbul (Not Constantinople); Dead; Your Racist Friend; Particle Man; Twisting; We Want A Rock; Someone Keeps Moving My Chair; Hearing Aid; Minimum Wage; Letterbox; Whistling In The Dark; Hot Cha; Women & Men; Sapphire Bullets Of Pure Love; They Might Be Giants; Road Movie To Berlin.*

★ First released 1990
★ UK peak chart position: 14
★ USA peak chart position: 75
★ Previous Top 1000 position: 1998 (691): 1994 (–)

896 STUNT ↑
Barenaked Ladies

After six years spent destined to be another Canadian band who failed to sell records outside the land of check shirts, this album suddenly took off and broke the band on the international market. At times there are too many words to take in, especially on the chart-topping hit 'One Week'. Thankfully lyrics are supplied, which help to confirm what a funny, clever and entertaining bunch of chaps the Barenaked Ladies are. 'Alcohol' is a particularly enlightening observation, and 'It's All Been Done' and 'Told You So' unearth a cruel streak, but the overall mood of the album is so positive the listener can't help feel anything other than good.

» Tracks: *One Week; It's All Been Done; Light Up My Room; I'll Be That Girl; Leave; Alcohol; Call and Answer; In The Car; Never Is Enough; Who Needs Sleep?; Told You So; Some Fantastic; When You Dream.*

★ First released 1998
★ UK peak chart position: 20
★ USA peak chart position: 3
★ Previous Top 1000 position: 1998 (–): 1994 (–)

897 SHE'S SO UNUSUAL ↓
Cyndi Lauper

Once the orange-haired Cyndi Lauper dropped the contrived, dumb, cutesy, lispy broad persona, she was seen as a credible artist, and has subsequently become highly respected as a terrific songwriter. On this, her pen was sharpened with the magnificent song of unconditional love, 'Time After Time', a track that has since been recorded by several others, including beautiful cover versions by Miles Davis and the jazz husband-and-wife duo, Tuck and Patti. Less sophisticated, but of equal fun, is 'She Bop', and then there are well-chosen cover versions such as Jules Shear's 'All Through The Night' and Prince's 'When You Were Mine'.

▶ Tracks: *Money Changes Everything; Girls Just Want To Have Fun; When You Were Mine; Time After Time; She Bop; All Through The Night; Witness; I'll Kiss You; He's So Unusual; Yeah Yeah.*

★ First released 1983
★ UK peak chart position: 16
★ USA peak chart position: 4
★ Previous Top 1000 position: 1998 (637): 1994 (–)

898 ELEPHANT MOUNTAIN ↓
The Youngbloods

This was the closest that the Youngbloods came to making a fully realized album. It remains their finest work, even though fans and critics felt, and still feel, that they were capable of something much better. The disposable snippets and vignettes help to fill up an album of a 'few great songs'. 'Darkness Darkness' is one of the great ones, with a guitar break that seems to go above the last fret on the neck. 'Quicksand', 'Ride the Wind' and 'Beautiful' are further examples of clever but unpretentious pop masquerading as rock. Jesse Colin Young was a fine songwriter and the undisputed brains behind Bauer and Banana.

▶ Tracks: *Darkness Darkness; Smug; On Sir Francis Drake; Sunlight; Double Sunlight; Beautiful; Turn It Over; Rain Song; Trillium; Quicksand; Black Mountain Breakdown; Sham; Ride The Wind.*

★ First released 1969
★ UK peak chart position: did not chart
★ USA peak chart position: 118
★ Previous Top 1000 position: 1998 (737): 1994 (–)

899 CHEAP THRILLS ↓
Big Brother and The Holding Company

This ramshackle, sparkling and ear-shattering album from the band 'featuring' lead vocalist Janis Joplin came out of the San Francisco rock scene in 1968. The full-blown vocals from Joplin sparred with the loose electric guitar of Sam Andrew and the finger-picking style of James Gurley, and kept them apart from other bands in the area who courted folk and psychedelia. Both 'Piece Of My Heart' and 'Ball and Chain' are classics of their time and place and although the recording is flawed the atmosphere Joplin creates is riveting and has never been bettered by any of the Janisalike rock chicks of the past three decades.

▶ Tracks: *Combination Of The Two; I Need A Man To Love; Summertime; Piece Of My Heart; Turtle Blues; Oh Sweet Mary; Ball and Chain.*

★ First released 1968
★ UK peak chart position: did not chart
★ USA peak chart position: 1
★ Previous Top 1000 position: 1998 (830): 1994 (355)

900 461 OCEAN BOULEVARD ↓
Eric Clapton

It is really only 'Give Me Strength' that provides a hint of the emergence from anguish and peril represented by *461 Ocean Boulevard*. Eric Clapton had descended into the depths of a serious heroin habit, invisible to the world for two years until Pete Townshend organized his comeback concert at the Rainbow. *461* followed, and showcases a relaxed Clapton, drawing as much on his songwriting ability and gentle vocal style as on his legendary guitar skills. Bob Marley's 'I Shot The Sheriff' was a worldwide hit, and 'Let It Grow' and 'Get Ready' (written with Yvonne Elliman) are still regular concert favourites. This was Clapton's new dawn.

▶ Tracks: *Get Ready; Give Me Strength; I Can't Hold Out Much Longer; I Shot The Sheriff; Let It Grow; Mainline Florida; Motherless Children; Please Be With Me; Steady Rollin' Man; Willie and The Hand Jive.*

★ First released 1974
★ UK peak chart position: 3
★ USA peak chart position: 1
★ Previous Top 1000 position: 1998 (490): 1994 (265)

901 MELISSA ETHERIDGE ↑
Melissa Etheridge

This artist does have a considerable following in the USA and the support for this, her debut album, is exclusively from that country. This type of late 80s guitar rock now seems stultifyingly ordinary. 'Similar Features' is a dull start to the album, and the following 'Chrome Plated Heart' is only saved by Etheridge's great vocals and spunky acoustic guitar. The album picks up towards the end with the charming hit single, 'Bring Me Some Water'. It is not that this is a bad record, but there is something that makes the listener want to move on to something better and more original. This attempts to be a great album, but sadly misses the mark.

❯❯ Tracks: Similar Features; Chrome Plated Heart; Like The Way I Do; Precious Pain; Don't You Need; The Late September Dogs; Occasionally; Watching You; Bring Me Some Water; I Want You.

★ First released 1988
★ UK peak chart position: did not chart
★ USA peak chart position: 22
★ Previous Top 1000 position: 1998 (–): 1994 (–)

902 GOOD OLD BOYS ↓
Randy Newman

Randy Newman's first concept album tackled a prickly subject, the culture of the American south. The opening 'Rednecks' may have gained Newman notoriety, but on tracks such as 'Marie', 'Louisiana 1927' and 'A Wedding In Cherokee Country', the tender heart beneath his withering irony was exposed. The album documents a complex mix of revulsion and empathy that touch on Newman's own New Orleans upbringing and his Jewishness. It was an unexpected irony, however, that the arch-satirist reached his songwriting peak on an album featuring the pick of America's session players and a glossy west coast production.

❯❯ Tracks: Rednecks; Birmingham; Marie; Mr. President (Have Pity On The Working Man); Guilty; Louisiana 1927; Every Man A King; Kingfish; Naked Man; A Wedding In Cherokee County; Back On My Feet Again; Rollin'.

★ First released 1974
★ UK peak chart position: did not chart
★ USA peak chart position: 36
★ Previous Top 1000 position: 1998 (387): 1994 (–)

903 GENTLEMEN ↑
The Afghan Whigs

The threatening opening created by the electric strum on 'If I Were Going' immediately enthralls the listener, and by the time Greg Dulli announces 'your attention please' on the following 'Gentleman' the listener is hooked. On 'Debonair', he commands 'hear me now and don't forget', and we do and we don't. The Afghan Whigs' lead singer has a dangerously raw edge that demands the listener's attention. None of his band's experimental edge and indie originality was lost on this, their major label debut, which allowed Dulli's disarming little sermons to reach a wider audience. Seven years on and this still sounds as if it was recorded only a few months ago.

❯❯ Tracks: If I Were Going; Gentlemen; Be Sweet; Debonair; When We Two Parted; Fountain and Fairfax; What Jail Is Like; My Curse; Now You Know; I Keep Coming Back; Brother Woodrow/Closing Prayer.

★ First released 1993
★ UK peak chart position: 58
★ USA peak chart position: did not chart
★ Previous Top 1000 position: 1998 (–): 1994 (–)

904 ...NOTHING LIKE THE SUN...
↑ Sting

Another masterful collection from undeniably one of the most consistent songwriters of the past quarter of a century. To think that the former spiky-headed punk is now part of the establishment alongside the likes of Elton John and Phil Collins. This may rankle some, but Sting always wanted the fame. 'Be Still My Beating Heart', 'Englishman In New York' and the stunning 'They Dance Alone' are three classics, but it is the cover version of 'Little Wing', written by Jimi Hendrix and orchestrated by the brilliant Gil Evans, which raises the emotions. Shed a tear for these two heroes who are no longer with us.

❯❯ Tracks: The Lazarus Heart; Be Still My Beating Heart; Englishman In New York; History Will Teach Us Nothing; They Dance Alone (Gueca Solo); Fragile; We'll Be Together; Straight To My Heart; Rock Steady; Sister Moon; Little Wing; The Secret Marriage.

★ First released 1987
★ UK peak chart position: 1
★ USA peak chart position: 9
★ Previous Top 1000 position: 1998 (–): 1994 (–)

905 LOW-LIFE ↓
New Order

New Order evolved from the rump of Joy Division following the death of vocalist Ian Curtis. The course they followed contrasted with that of their former incarnation, exploring a heady mix of techno-styled dance tracks and melodic soundscapes. *Low-Life* captured the quartet in eclectic mood, taking an electronic muse through diffuse material. It boasts two of New Order's finest ever songs, the ballad-styled 'Love Vigilantes' and the lush 'The Perfect Kiss', while elsewhere the quartet explore different facets of their sound without losing cohesion. This acclaimed release finally confirmed New Order as an act in its own right.

➤ Tracks: *Love Vigilantes; The Perfect Kiss; This Time Of Night; Sunrise; Elegia; Sooner Than You Think; Sub-Culture; Face Up.*

★ First released 1985
★ UK peak chart position: 7
★ USA peak chart position: 94
★ Previous Top 1000 position: 1998 (405): 1994 (446)

906 ORANGES & LEMONS ↓
XTC

Using a 60s Milton Glaser-type cover illustration, this purported to be a retro album. In reality it was another extremely fine XTC album, their ninth in a series of classy, offbeat pop exercises from the musically fertile brain of Andy Partridge, who hated touring and loved to stay at home as a reclusive pop star. This is probably their best album and features Partridge's most complete and satisfying songs. 'The Loving' and 'The Mayor Of Simpleton' are both excellent compositions, but they pale against the exceptional 'Chalkhills and Children'. On this, Partridge celebrates that his home (the nearby chalkhills) and children keep him sane and well-grounded against the possible excesses to which he would succumb as a touring popster.

➤ Tracks: *Garden Of Earthly Delights; The Mayor Of Simpleton; King For A Day; Here Comes President Kill Again; The Loving; Poor Skeleton Steps Out; One Of The Millions; Scarecrow People; Merely A Man; Cynical Days; Across This Antheap; Hold Me My Daddy; Pink Thing; Miniature Sun; Chalkhills and Children.*

★ First released 1989
★ UK peak chart position: 28
★ USA peak chart position: 44
★ Previous Top 1000 position: 1998 (430): 1994 (–)

907 RELOAD ↑
Metallica

Recorded at the same sessions as the previous year's *Load*, Metallica paid their debts to their loyal fans who had to wait over five years for *Load*. This is more immaculate metal from the undisputed leaders of the genre, not just the left overs ready for the dustbin. So good, it is now used by many hi-fi shops to show off their gear, *Reload* is one of the albums to play a visiting Martian to explain this phenomenon called heavy metal. As daft as it is, the genre refuses to go away. Even Marianne Faithfull appears on this album. Did Led Zeppelin sound this good and this fresh at this stage in their career?

➤ Tracks: *Fuel; The Memory Remains; Devil's Dance; The Unforgiven II; Better Than You; Slither; Carpe Diem Baby; Bad Seed; Where The Wild Things Are; Prince Charming; Low Man's Lyric; Attitude; Fixxxer.*

★ First released 1997
★ UK peak chart position: 4
★ USA peak chart position: 1
★ Previous Top 1000 position: 1998 (–): 1994 (–)

908 THE LAMB LIES DOWN ON BROADWAY ↑
Genesis

According to the fans, this was Peter Gabriel's finest moment with Genesis according to the fans. It must have been a shock when he announced his departure a few months after this album was released, especially in view of the fact that these songs formed the bulk of their stage show at the time. Much criticism has been aimed at Genesis and their progressive rock counterparts, but apart from being too long, this is a fine piece of music. The problem is, trying to get your head around the story that accompanies the set. My suggestion is to bin the story and simply concentrate on the music and lyrics. That way you might end up liking the music a lot and understand what some of the lyrics are about.

➤ Tracks: *The Lamb Lies Down On Broadway; Fly On A Windshield; Broadway Melody Of 1974; Cuckoo Cocoon; In The Cage; The Grand Parade Of Lifeless Packaging; Back In N.Y.C.; Hairless Heart; Counting Out Time; Carpet Crawlers; The Chamber Of 32 Doors; Lilywhite Lilith; The Waiting Room; Anyway; Here Comes The Supernatural Anaesthetist; The Lamia; Silent Sorrow In Empty Boats; The Colony Of Slippermen; Ravine; The Light Dies Down On Broadway; Riding The Scree; In The Rapids; It.*

★ First released 1974
★ UK peak chart position: 10 ★ USA peak chart position: 41
★ Previous Top 1000 position: 1998 (–): 1994 (–)

909 RAM ↓
Paul and Linda McCartney

On *Ram* Paul McCartney moved further away from the studio polish of the Beatles' swan-song, *Abbey Road*, with a wonderfully unforced and ramshackle collection of songs. On 'Smile Away' and 'Monkberry Moon Delight', he proved that he could still play the unrepentant rocker, while 'Uncle Albert/Admiral Halsey' was an utterly charming slice of McCartney whimsy that managed to avoid the tweeness that was sometimes his bugbear. The closing track, 'The Back Seat Of My Car', contained more hooks than are usually found on the average album, proving that even at his most spontaneous McCartney was still melodic to the core.

» Tracks: *Too Many People; 3 Legs; Ram On; Dear Boy; Uncle Albert/Admiral Halsey; Smile Away; Heart Of The Country; Monkberry Moon Delight; Eat At Home; Long Haired Lady; Ram On; The Back Seat Of My Car.*

★ First released 1971
★ UK peak chart position: 1
★ USA peak chart position: 2
★ Previous Top 1000 position: 1998 (654): 1994 (–)

910 UNDERTOW ↑
Tool

If you can skip the disturbing sleeve images of the large lady and the fat pig on a sacrificial bed of forks and just concentrate on the music then this album is an unqualified success. One of the leading new heavy metal acts to emerge during the 90s, Tool proudly wear their Metallica, Rollins Band, and Soundgarden influences on their sleeves. Vocalist Maynard James Keenan wrestles with his own inner demons, and it is a pity some of the pointless images on the CD sleeve were not replaced by the lyrics so we can all share his troubles. Henry Rollins joins in on 'Bottom', while the band's underrated sense of humour is evident in the credits for Keenan (mastresticator), Adam Jones (bastardometer), Danny Carey (membranophones) and Paul D'Amour (bottom feeder).

» Tracks: *Intolerance; Prison Sex; Sober; Bottom; Crawl Away; Swamp Song; Undertow; 4º; Flood; Disgustipated.*

★ First released 1993
★ UK peak chart position: did not chart
★ USA peak chart position: 50
★ Previous Top 1000 position: 1998 (–): 1994 (–)

911 LOVE ↑
The Cult

Never quite goths, never quite new romantics, never quite metal, never quite U2. What ever they never quite were, the Cult commanded a sizeable following during their 80s heyday. Ian Astbury was the distinctive lead singer who flaunted himself with style. Two hits were culled from this, 'She Sells Sanctuary' and the fiery 'Rain'. Both were distinctive at the time, but unfortunately now the bell-chime guitar, overdosing on wah wah and flanger, sounds as palatable as Gary Burton's vibraphone. This remains the Cult's most commercial album, and for those who relished guitar bands in a decade barren of them, this is perfect nostalgia.

» Tracks: *Nirvana; Big Neon Glitter; Love; Brother Wolf Sister Moon; Rain; The Phoenix; Hollow Man; Revolution; She Sells Sanctuary; Black Angel.*

★ First released 1985
★ UK peak chart position: 4
★ USA peak chart position: 87
★ Previous Top 1000 position: 1998 (–): 1994 (–)

912 COOKIN' ↓
Miles Davis

One of a series of important albums recorded for Prestige Records during the 50s that also included the excellent *Workin'* and *Steamin'*. Miles Davis's dream quintet also included John Coltrane and Red Garland (piano), Paul Chambers (bass) and the breathing brushwork of Philly Joe Jones. Of the dozens of line-ups over many years, this unit is still spoken of with sparkling eyes by those who saw them play during their two years together. One of his best recordings of 'My Funny Valentine' is on this disc, as well as a definitive 'Blues By Five'. The title was Davis's: 'after all, that's what we did, came in and cooked'.

» Tracks: *My Funny Valentine; Blues By Five; Airegin; Tune Up.*

★ First released 1957
★ UK peak chart position: did not chart
★ USA peak chart position: did not chart
★ Previous Top 1000 position: 1998 (814): 1994 (–)

913 NO WAY OUT ↑
Puff Daddy and The Family

The intro features helicopters and police sirens and Puff Daddy in heaven, looking down and asking for forgiveness. This threatening opening sets the mood for the whole album leaving the listener in no doubt that Puff is a serious rapper. The family that plays together includes Faith Evans, the late Notorious B.I.G. And Ginuwine. There is some exceptional choice of sampling, the pinnacle being the use of Lisa Stansfield's 'All Around The World' and David Bowie's 'Let's Dance'. Elsewhere the invisible presence of Stevie Wonder is consistently felt and the Police are sampled on the tribute to B.I.G., 'I'll Be Missing You'. A wondrous CD.

» Tracks: *No Way Out (Intro); Victory; Been Around The World; What You Gonna Do?; Don't Stop What You're Doing; If I Should Die Tonight (Interlude); Do You Know?; Young G's; I Love You Baby; It's All About The Benjamins (Remix); Pain; Is This The End?; I Got The Power; Friend; Señorita; I'll Be Missing You; Can't Nobody Hold Me Down.*

★ First released 1997
★ UK peak chart position: 8
★ USA peak chart position: 1
★ Previous Top 1000 position: 1998 (–): 1994 (–)

914 FROM THE CRADLE ↑
Eric Clapton

The most up front blues album that Clapton has recorded since his brief days as a Bluesbreaker. Clearly he is at his loosest and probably happiest singing the blues. You can feel his joy in the sadness of 'How Long Blues' and sense how comfortable he is performing Willie Dixon's 'Hoochie Coochie Man'. 'Motherless Child' however is plodding and dull and the weakest track, but things perk up with the following 'It Hurts Me Too', complete with the routine Elmore James slide solo. Carping aside, Clapton has mastered acoustic blues and electric blues, and plays both with equal passion on this excellent recording.

» Tracks: *Blues Before Sunrise; Third Degree; Reconsider Baby; Hoochie Coochie Man; Five Long Years; I'm Tore Down; How Long Blues; Goin' Away Baby; Blues Leave Me Alone; Sinner's Prayer; Motherless Child; It Hurts Me Too; Someday After A While; Standin' Round Crying; Driftin'; Groaning The Blues.*

★ First released 1994
★ UK peak chart position: 1
★ USA peak chart position: 1
★ Previous Top 1000 position: 1998 (–): 1994 (–)

915 5150 ↑
Van Halen

It's only when having to really concentrate for review purposes that the critic is able to pick up on the hidden strengths of artists he/she may have never really listened to properly. Van Halen fit this mould, specifically regarding the technique and sound of guitarist Edward Van Halen. At times he is so good it is ridiculous. This was the first album with new vocalist Sammy Hagar, who stepped in after David Lee Roth foolishly jumped ship. Hagar proved to be an ideal replacement and the band celebrated with their first chart-topping album and a huge hit single with the positively uplifting 'Why Can't This Be Love'. This album barely pauses for breath and remains one of their best efforts to date.

» Tracks: *Good Enough; Why Can't This Be Love; Get Up; Dreams; Summer Nights; Best Of Both Worlds; Love Walks In; '5150'; Inside.*

★ First released 1986
★ UK peak chart position: 16
★ USA peak chart position: 1
★ Previous Top 1000 position: 1998 (–): 1994 (–)

916 DIZZY HEIGHTS ↓
Lightning Seeds

This album is one of those pop records that has something memorable in every track. Ian Broudie has the combined talent of pop eccentrics such as Andy Partridge (XTC) and Paddy McAloon (Prefab Sprout). However, the feeling is that the last two write great songs for themselves, whereas Broudie writes for a pop audience, with elements of the Beach Boys, Beatles and late 60s summer fun songs mastered by writers like John Carter. It would be the ultimate treat to be able to read the lyrics supplied, but the typographic designer decided to make this just impossible. Fortunately, while we curse the CD sleeve, we still have our ears.

» Tracks: *Imaginary Friends; You Bet Your Life; Waiting For Today To Happen; What If; Sugar Coated Iceberg; Touch and Go; Like You Do; Wishaway; Fingers and Thumbs; You Showed Me; Ready Or Not; Fish On The Line.*

★ First released 1996
★ UK peak chart position: 11
★ USA peak chart position: did not chart
★ Previous Top 1000 position: 1998 (534): 1994 (–)

917 MARC COHN ↑
Marc Cohn

Yes, this is the one with 'Walking In Memphis' on it. It may come as a surprise but the other songs are good as well. Cohn is blessed with a smooth husky voice, sort of like Joe Cocker after swallowing a tub of butter, and he uses it to great effect on this, his debut album. 'Silver Thunderbird' is yet another car song, but Cohn manages to differentiate his lyrics from the car showroom manager Springsteen, although there is a similarity in the style of storytelling. Cohn sits firmly in the 'profound' songwriter camp, alongside the likes of Billy Joel. 'True Companion' is the other real gem on the album.

➤➤ Tracks: *Walking In Memphis; Ghost Train; Silver Thunderbird; Dig Down Deep; Walk On Water; Miles Away; Saving The Best For Last; Strangers In A Car; 29 Ways; Perfect Love; True Companion.*

★ First released 1991
★ UK peak chart position: 27
★ USA peak chart position: 38
★ Previous Top 1000 position: 1998 (–): 1994 (–)

918 LIVE RUST ↑
Neil Young and Crazy Horse

This was recorded at a time when Young's star was once again in the ascendant. He combined songs from *Rust Never Sleeps* with some carefully chosen old material. The acoustic 'Sugar Mountain' and 'I Am A Child' clearly delight the enthusiastic audience who fondly remember Buffalo Springfield, but it is when he plugs in his black Gibson you sense he really begins to buzz. No wonder he goes back to Crazy Horse time and time again, no one else (not even Stephen Stills) can fire him up so well. 'When You Dance I Can Really Love' opens the electric side and from then on his course is set. Dirty, grungy, exciting music that is almost perfect.

➤➤ Tracks: *Sugar Mountain; I Am A Child; Comes A Time; After The Gold Rush; My My, Hey Hey (Out Of The Blue); When You Dance I Can Really Love; The Loner; The Needle and The Damage Done; Lota Love; Sedan Delivery; Powderfinger; Cortez The Killer; Cinnamon Girl; Like A Hurricane; Hey Hey, My My (Into The Black; Tonight's The Night.*

★ First released 1979
★ UK peak chart position: 55
★ USA peak chart position: 15
★ Previous Top 1000 position: 1998 (–): 1994 (–)

919 LAID ↑
James

This is James's most original album by a mile, and one that bears the influence of the remarkable producer Brian Eno, a man who indelibly shapes every project he works on. Tim Booth's voice is given space to work in, and not buried in sound as it has been on more recent albums. Likewise, each instrument is recorded with respect and clarity. On the beautiful opening track 'Out To Get You', Booth's rich voice is complemented by some exquisite slide guitar. The following 'Sometimes (Lester Piggott)' features a ringing single chord motif which never grates. This is a fabulous record that deserves a quiet half-hour to let its beauty wash over you.

➤➤ Tracks: *Out To Get You; Sometimes (Lester Piggott); Dream Thrum; One Of The Three; Say Something; Five-O; P.S.; Everybody Knows; Knuckle Too Far; Low Low Low; Laid; Lullaby; Skindiving.*

★ First released 1993
★ UK peak chart position: 3
★ USA peak chart position: 72
★ Previous Top 1000 position: 1998 (–): 1994 (–)

920 THE SECOND COMING ↓
Stone Roses

Five fruitless years after the most acclaimed and influential album of the 80s, the Stone Roses returned, having swapped Byrdsian guitar pop for swaggering Jimmy Page riffs. Predictably, the critics disapproved. Labelled overblown and self-indulgent, *The Second Coming* was woefully undervalued. Since its release, however, appreciation for this remarkable record has increased enormously: the sheer scope of 'Breaking Into Heaven' astonishes; the self-mocking 'Driving South', the sparkling 'Ten Storey Love Song', the frenzied 'Begging You' and the glorious 'Love Spreads' alone distinguish this album as a worthy successor. As the last, mighty gasp from a great band, all too aware of their own importance and on the verge of spectacular implosion, it stands as a fitting and poignant epitaph.

➤➤ Tracks: *Breaking Into Heaven; Driving South; Ten Storey Love Song; Daybreak; Your Star Will Shine; Straight To The Man; Begging You; Tightrope; Good Times; Tears; How Do You Sleep; Love Spreads.*

★ First released 1994
★ UK peak position: 4
★ USA peak position: 47
★ Previous Top 1000 position: 1998 (137): 1994 (–)

921 TECHNIQUE ↑
New Order

The acceptable face of rock's flirtation with the Balearic craze of the late 80s. New Order rarely put a foot wrong throughout the 80s following their birth from the ashes of Joy Division, and was one of the most influential rock-based bands of the decade. This was their fifth album, and although they did not deviate too far from the bass heavy sound of old it was also the band's most dance-orientated outing. This could be explained by the fact that *Technique* was partly recorded in the new Mecca for dance music, Ibiza, at the height of acid house. It is impossible to cite any particular track, as this underrated album is an unmitigated joy from start to finish.

▶ Tracks: *Fine Time; All The Way; Love Less; Round & Round; Guilty Partner; Run; Mr. Disco; Vanishing Point; Dream Attack.*

★ First released 1989
★ UK peak chart position: 1
★ USA peak chart position: 32
★ Previous Top 1000 position: 1998 (–): 1994 (–)

922 SELECTED AMBIENT WORKS 1985-1992 ↓ Aphex Twin

Very occasionally in music, something will come at you from so far out on the left field, that not only do you not note its immediate import, you scarcely recognize it as music at all. This is the record that cemented the media's fascination with Richard James, a Cornwall bedroom DJ. *Selected Ambient Works* is not an entirely representative recording, as these are essentially mood pieces, unlike the more instantaneous, dancefloor-targeted material that originally brought him to the nation's attention. Nevertheless if you are prepared to make the journey, and can see past the album's intimidating length and its lack of linear framework, there are some exquisite moments – ranging in texture from melodic delirium to sweeping melancholy.

▶ Tracks: *Xtal; Tha; Pulsewidth; Ageispolis; Green CALX; Heliospan; We Are The Music Makers; Schotkey; Ptolemy; Hedphelym; Delphium; Actium; I.*

★ First released 1994
★ UK peak chart position: did not chart
★ USA peak chart position: did not chart
★ Previous Top 1000 position: 1998 (575): 1994 (–)

923 SONGS FROM THE BIG CHAIR ↑ Tears For Fears

Go on, admit it, Tears For Fears had completely slipped out of your memory bank. Their albums are the ones in that pile of 80s stuff which never get played, and radio stations rarely program anything other than the worldwide hits 'Everybody Wants To Rule the World' and 'Shout'. Curt Smith left for a solo career and was never heard of again, while Roland Orzabal struggled to retain credibility in the 90s. So here is an opportunity to reclaim Tears For Fears and put this album up there with 80s classics such as *The Lexicon Of Love* and *Rio*. Strip away those horrible synthetic drums and bell-ringer guitars that were so much a part of the decade and you are left with a sterling bunch of songs. Splendid.

▶ Tracks: *Shout; The Working Hour; Everybody Wants To Rule The World; Mothers Talk; I Believe; Broken; Head Over Heels/Broken; Listen.*

★ First released 1985
★ UK peak chart position: 2
★ USA peak chart position: 1
★ Previous Top 1000 position: 1998 (–): 1994 (–)

924 JANET JACKSON'S RHYTHM NATION 1814 ↓
Janet Jackson

Little did you know that the American national anthem, 'God Bless America', was written in 1814. Janet Jackson did, and she sets out in 'Rhythm Nation' to dish out a bit of 'let's all work together for a better world and improve our way of life' type thing. This vein continues for a number of tracks, and admirable though it is, she sounds so much more convincing singing a good old-fashioned love song. The Jacksons were meant to dance, not to sermonize. That said, 'Miss You Much', 'Lonely' and 'Come Back To Me' are fabulous. Slick, sweet soul sung and played perfectly.

▶ Tracks: *Interlude: Pledge; Rhythm Nation; Interlude: TV; State Of The World; Interlude: Race; The Knowledge; Interlude: Let's Dance; Miss You Much; Interlude: Come Back; Love Will Never Do (Without You); Livin' In A World (They Didn't Make); Alright; Interlude: Hey Baby; Escapade; Interlude: No Acid; Black Cat; Lonely; Come Back To Me; Someday Is Tonight; Interlude: Livin' In Complete Darkness.*

★ First released 1989
★ UK peak chart position: 4
★ USA peak chart position: 1
★ Previous Top 1000 position: 1998 (904): 1994 (–)

925 THIS FIRE ↑
Paula Cole

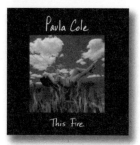

Nestling somewhere between Sarah McLachlan and Tori Amos, Cole has enjoyed several hit singles but fortunately avoided the mass sales that have put damaging pressure on several of her contemporaries. This is deep and powerful pop music, with the opening track 'Tiger' featuring Cole stretching her tonsils to breaking point. 'Where Have All The Cowboys Gone?' is a wonderful tongue in cheek plea for good old-fashioned romance, while 'Carmen' is a fragile song reminiscent of early Cowboy Junkies. The disturbing pauses on 'Hush, Hush, Hush' add to its spacey sadness, with Peter Gabriel's backing vocals recalling his duet with Kate Bush on 'Don't Give Up'.

» Tracks: *Tiger; Where Have All The Cowboys Gone?; Throwing Stones; Carmen; Mississippi; Nietzsche's Eyes; Road To Dead; Me; Feelin' Love; Hush, Hush, Hush; I Don't Want To Wait.*

★ First released 1996
★ UK peak chart position: 60
★ USA peak chart position: 33
★ Previous Top 1000 position: 1998 (–): 1994 (–)

926 JAZZ SAMBA ↑
Stan Getz

The album that launched Antonio Carlos Jobim's now classic 'Desafinado', *Jazz Samba* was released in 1962, in the early days of America's bossa nova craze and before the music lost its charm to cliché. Joined by fellow Latin jazz pioneer Charlie Byrd on classical guitar, and a discreet bass and drums team, tenor saxophonist Getz makes light and elegant music out of a collection of catchy bossas and sambas. His virtuosity, bluesy drive and smooth, soft tone make the music cook like bossa jazz rarely has since. There are still enough surprises to make this record more than just a period piece, and it stands as a fine example of Stan Getz's lyrical genius.

» Tracks: *Desafinado; Samba Dees Days; O Pato; Samba Triste; Samba De Uma Nota So; E Luxo So; Baia.*

★ First released 1962
★ UK peak chart position: 15
★ USA peak chart position: 1
★ Previous Top 1000 position: 1998 (963): 1994 (594)

927 STAND ↓
Sly and The Family Stone

Sly Stone was too busy having a good time and living life to the excess to begin to realize how influential his brand of funky soul would become. Early signs of rap also surfaced on this album. Confident, hard rocking and marvellously arrogant, the band were outrageous and exciting; even five minutes of a cappella handclapping was riveting. Two classics appear on this – 'I Want To Take You Higher' and 'Everyday People' – but the whole album is a necessary purchase for students of goodtime soul, dance, rap and funk. This family is the acknowledged leader.

» Tracks: *Stand!; Don't Call Me Nigger, Whitey; I Want To Take You Higher; Somebody's Watching You; Sing A Simple Song; Everyday People; Sex Machine; You Can Make It If You Try.*

★ First released 1969
★ UK peak chart position: did not chart
★ USA peak chart position: 13
★ Previous Top 1000 position: 1998 (155): 1994 (59)

928 EVIL EMPIRE ↑
Rage Against The Machine

Radical politics is Rage Against The Machine's cause, and they expound it with ferocious determination. A selected bibliography is photographed in the CD sleeve, indicating that this is one band who does its research before opening their mouths. The mix of hip-hop and metal perfectly complements the lyrics, which are not without their own sly humour either; 'I wanna be Jackie Onassis, I wanna wear a pair of dark sunglasses' ('Tire Me'). 'Down Rodeo' ('one God, one market, one truth, one consumer') is one of the album's most thought provoking and blisteringly accurate tracks. Rage Against The Machine are refreshingly sincere prophets in a ruthless music business.

» Tracks: *People Of The Sun; Bulls On Parade; Vietnow; Revolver; Snakecharmer; Tire Me; Down Rodeo; Without A Face; Wind Below; Roll Right; Year Of Tha Boomerang.*

★ First released 1996
★ UK peak chart position: 4
★ USA peak chart position: 1
★ Previous Top 1000 position: 1998 (–): 1994 (–)

929 40oz. TO FREEDOM ↑
Sublime

Just prior to the release of their breakthrough third album Sublime were rocked by the death, at the age of 28 from an overdose, of their troubled leader Brad Nowell. For six years they had built a solid live following for their exhilarating fusion of rock, ska and hip-hop. Their debut *40oz. To Freedom* was re-promoted following the events of 1996. It is a highly recommended album which is destined to languish in the collections of only a few. Alongside the excellent originals have great quality and the three non-originals include a ska version of the Grateful Dead's 'Scarlet Begonias'. Investigate before it is deleted.

» Tracks: *Waiting For My Ruca; 40oz. To Freedom; Smoke Two Joints; We're Gonna Die For Our Arrogance; Don't Push; 5446 That's My Number/Ball and Chain; Badfish; Let's Go Get Stoned; New Thrash; Scarlet Begonias; Live At E's; D.J.s; Chica Me Tipo; Right Back; What Happened; New Song; Ebin; Date Rape; Hope; KRS-One.*

★ First released 1992
★ UK peak chart position: did not chart
★ USA peak chart position: did not chart
★ Previous Top 1000 position: 1998 (–): 1994 (–)

930 COMPUTER WORLD ↓
Kraftwerk

Although it coincided with their period of greatest commercial success and popularity, *Computer World* also marked the beginning of Kraftwerk's decline as a pioneering force in electronic music. Tracks such as 'Pocket Calculator' and 'It's More Fun To Compute' indicated that the seemingly endless musical inventiveness of Ralf Hütter and Florian Scheider was drying up, although the hypnotic beats of 'Numbers' put the group on the dancefloors courtesy of Afrika Bambaataa's sampling on his 'Planet Rock' the following year. Easily their most accessible collection, *Computer World* marked a slightly disappointing end to Kraftwerk's run of brilliant albums.

» Tracks: *Computer World; Pocket Calculator; Numbers; Computer World 2; Computer Love; Homecomputer; It's More Fun To Compute.*

★ First Released 1981
★ UK peak chart position: 15
★ USA peak chart position: 72
★ Previous Top 1000 position: 1998 (174): 1994 (–)

931 HEARTS AND BONES ↑
Paul Simon

The CD sleeve is at pains to point out that this is Paul Simon's second album of new material on the Warner Brothers label, just in case people were seeing him as an oldies act who occasionally teamed up with the thin blonde one. In fact this should be seen as one of his finest works. It contains some evocative and beautiful songs combining Simon's precious, vulnerable vocals with incisive lyrics. 'Allergies' and the title track stamp their authority over the record, although it is 'The Late Great Johnny Ace' and 'Rene and Magritte With Their Dog After The War' that brings out a nostalgic tear and sways the listener to investigate classic 50s doo wop.

» Tracks: *Allergies; Hearts and Bones; When Numbers Get Serious; Think Too Much (b); Song About The Moon; Think Too Much (a); Train In The Distance; Rene and Georgette Magritte With Their Dog After The War; Cars Are Cars; The Late Great Johnny Ace.*

★ First released 1983
★ UK peak chart position: 34
★ USA peak chart position: 35
★ Previous Top 1000 position: 1998 (–): 1994 (–)

932 PRESENCE ↑
Led Zeppelin

At this stage in their remarkable career Led Zeppelin could have recorded anything they wanted and it would still have gone straight to number one. Nearly a quarter of a century later *Presence* is regarded as an OK album which by today's standards would probably have scraped into the Top 50 on both sides of the Atlantic. Nothing really grabs you, and both 'For Your Life' and 'Royal Orleans' have irritating stop/start structures. Page and Plant are not on top form here, although Bonham and Jones are as reliable as ever. The presence of a fantastic singer and guitar hero in the same band counts for nothing if they don't have some good songs to play.

» Tracks: *Achilles Last Stand; For Your Life; Royal Orleans; Nobody's Fault But Mine; Candy Store Rock; Hots On For Nowhere; Tea For One.*

★ First released 1976
★ UK peak chart position: 1
★ USA peak chart position: 1
★ Previous Top 1000 position: 1998 (–): 1994 (–)

933 WITHOUT YOU I'M NOTHING ↑
Placebo

This is a vast improvement over Placebo's good but derivative debut. This time around lead singer Brian Molko's image is pushed into the background, which is welcome as he was in danger of becoming more famous for his androgynous looks than his lyrics. This is a confessional, come down album, with producer Steve Osborne deserving particular praise for the songs' added depth. New drummer Steve Hewitt also adds a lot to the band's sound providing a steady backbeat for Molko's buzzing glam rock guitar chords. 'Pure Morning', 'You Don't Care About Us' and 'Allergic (To Thoughts Of Mother Earth)' are absolute corkers, although the latter threatens for Lou Reed to walk through the door any moment.

» Tracks: Pure Morning; Brick Shithouse; You Don't Care About Us; Ask For Answers; Without You I'm Nothing; Allergic (To Thoughts Of Mother Earth); The Crawl; Every You Every Me; My Sweet Prince; Summer's Gone; Scared Of Girls; Burger Queen.

★ First released 1998 ★ UK peak chart position: 7
★ USA peak chart position: did not chart
★ Previous Top 1000 position: 1998 (–): 1994 (–)

934 TURN! TURN! TURN! ↓
The Byrds

Uncomfortably hot on the heels of their debut album, this record had no right to be so good. Once again Gene Clark had enough great songs to complement the Bob Dylan and traditional material, especially 'Set You Free This Time' and 'The World Turns All Around Her'. Their cover of the title track is untouchable in terms of sound and emotion and just behind is the gorgeous 'Lay Down Your Weary Tune'. The excellent reissue contains among others the David Crosby instrumental 'Stranger In A Strange Land'. Commercially, they had already peaked, but creatively they were just getting started. As good as this is, the best was still to come.

» Tracks: Turn! Turn! Turn!; It Won't Be Wrong; Set You Free This Time; Lay Down Your Weary Tune; He Was A Friend Of Mine; The World Turns All Around Her; Satisfied Mind; If You're Gone; The Times They Are A-Changin'; Wait and See; Oh! Susannah; The Day Walk (Never Before); She Don't Care About Time; The Times They Are A Changin'; It's All Over Now, Baby Blue; She Don't Care About Time; The World Turns All Around Her; Stranger In A Strange Land.

★ First released 1965
★ UK peak chart position: 11 ★ USA peak chart position: 17
★ Previous Top 1000 position: 1998 (209): 1994 (–)

935 A WIZARD/A TRUE STAR ↓
Todd Rundgren

Even among Todd Rundgren fans this album is likely to evoke a mixed response. Whether it is listened to as the recording peak of a maverick genius or a failed attempt to reproduce an acid trip on vinyl, A Wizard/A True Star is never less than interesting. The 22 tracks career wildly between the sublime ('International Feel', 'Zen Archer' and 'Sometimes I Don't Know What To Feel') and the ridiculous ('Rock and Roll Pussy', 'Dogfight Giggle', 'Just Another Onionhead'), via the inspired white soulboy medley on side two. In retrospect, A Wizard/A True Star should be honoured as an album where one of pop's godlike genii revealed his human frailties.

» Tracks: International Feel; Never Never Land; Tic Tic Tic It Wears Off; You Need Your Head; Rock and Roll Pussy; Dogfight Giggle; You Don't Have To Camp Around; Flamingo; Zen Archer; Just Another Onionhead/Da Da Dali; When The Shit Hits The Fan/Sunset Blvd; Le Feel Internacionale; Sometimes I Don't Know What To Feel; Does Anybody Love You?; Medley: I'm So Proud/Ooh Baby Baby/La La Means I Love You/Cool Jerk; Hungry For Love; I Don't Want To Tie You Down; Is It My Name; Just One Victory.

★ First released 1973 ★ UK peak chart position: did not chart
★ USA peak chart position: 86
★ Previous Top 1000 position: 1998 (235): 1994 (–)

936 EXODUS ↓
Bob Marley

Bob Marley's consistent (certainly by reggae standards) album career has proffered many great songbooks, of which Exodus is just one good example. The singles 'One Love' and 'Jamming' will be familiar to anyone with even a passing acquaintance with Jamaican music, but just as vital are the touchingly vulnerable love song 'Waiting In Vain', the magnificent title track, and the splendid 'Guiltiness'. This was the first album to feature Junior Marvin on guitar, while the expressive use of horns adds new texture to the established quality of the Wailers' familiar steady backing. Like most of Marley's work, this is vital for any comprehensive collection.

» Tracks: Natural Mystic; So Much Things To Say; Guiltiness; The Heathen; Exodus; Jamming; Waiting In Vain; Turn Your Lights Down Low; Three Little Birds; One Love – People Get Ready.

★ First released 1977
★ UK peak chart position: 8
★ USA peak chart position: 20
★ Previous Top 1000 position: 1998 (391): 1994 (602)

937 FANMAIL ↑
TLC

What a brilliant sales idea. The trio announces on the opening title track that they have dedicated the album cover to anybody who has ever sent them fan mail. That way, even if you had gone off Left Eye, Chilli and T-Boz the purchase of the album is a must so you can see your name in print. An even nicer gesture would have been for the record company to give every named person a copy of the record. *Fanmail* came close to matching the runaway commercial success of *CrazySexyCool*, although from a musical point of view the space age burps and squeals fail to improve on the sweet, soulful charm of the former album.

)) Tracks: *Fanmail; The Vic-E Interpretation – Interlude; Silly Ho; Whispering Playa – Interlude; No Scrubs; I'm Good At Being Bad; If They Knew; I Miss You So Much; Unpretty; My Life; Shout; Come On Down; Dear Lie; Communicate – Interlude; Lovesick; Automatic; Don't Pull Out On Me Yet.*

★ First released 1999
★ UK peak chart position: 7
★ USA peak chart position: 1
★ Previous Top 1000 position: 1998 (–): 1994 (–)

938 MARCUS GARVEY ↓
Burning Spear

One of the most distinctive and original talents in the history of reggae, Burning Spear – né Winston Rodney – was launched internationally with this striking album. His deep, preaching vocal is immediately arresting, a characteristic enhanced by a dense and brooding accompaniment. Taking cues from Rastafarian chants, Spear subtly builds an intensity, locking each track into a seamless whole. His knowledge of black history brings a chilling realism to the album's lyrics, resulting in what is incontestably a milestone in the development of reggae. Listening to it is an education itself. The CD reissue has the bonus of the dub version *Garvey's Ghost*.

)) Tracks: *Marcus Garvey; Slavery Days; Invasion; Live Good; Give Me; Old Marcus Garvey; Tradition; Jordan River; Red, Gold and Green; Resting Place.*

★ First released 1975
★ UK peak chart position: did not chart
★ USA peak chart position: did not chart
★ Previous Top 1000 position: 1998 (419): 1994 (204)

939 MERMAID AVENUE ↑
Billy Bragg and Wilco

This album proves that there are still unmined treasures to be found in the music world. Hundreds of lyrics to unrecorded songs by the pioneering songwriter Woody Guthrie were lovingly sifted through and studied by his daughter Nora, Billy Bragg, and Wilco. The result not only enhances the reputation of the artists involved, but also ensures that a younger generation will be exposed to Guthrie's magnificent prose. 'Way Over Yonder In The Minor Key' is a prime example, with a Guthrie lyric from 1946 perfectly complemented by Bragg's new music and an overwhelmingly emotional performance by all concerned. He is to be congratulated for never letting his ego get in the way during the recording of this outstanding project.

)) Tracks: *Walt Whitman's Niece; California Stars; Way Over Yonder In The Minor Key; Birds and Ships; Hoodoo Voodoo; She Came Along To Me; At My Window Sad and Lonely; Ingrid Bergman; Christ For President; I Guess I Planted; One By One; Eisler On The Go; Hesitating Beauty; Another Man's Done Gone; The Unwelcome Guest.*

★ First released 1998
★ UK peak chart position: 34 ★ USA peak chart position: 90
★ Previous Top 1000 position: 1998 (–): 1994 (–)

940 MINGUS AT ANTIBES ↑
Charles Mingus

Time and time again the wonders of the CD hit home. Remember what a drag it was to have to deal with this double vinyl album. Six tracks spread over four sides meant the listener was up and down on the beanbag like the stock market. Now on one wondrous disc, this is seventy-one minutes of Mingus in his prime, playing and coaxing his musicians on like a demon. Eric Dolphy (saxophone/clarinet) and Dannie Richmond (drums) are particularly outstanding, although to not credit Booker Ervin (saxophone) and Ted Curson (piano) would be unfair. This album remains one of the best live jazz recordings ever released because its sounds alive and in the open air.

)) Tracks: *Wednesday Night Prayer Meeting; Prayer For Passive Resistance; What Love?; I'll Remember April; Folk Forms I; Better Git Hit In Your Soul.*

★ First released 1960
★ UK peak chart position: did not chart
★ USA peak chart position: did not chart
★ Previous Top 1000 position: 1998 (–): 1994 (–)

941 DAYS OF FUTURE PASSED ↓
Moody Blues

From British R&B combo to classical pop with no transitional album in between, all the Moody Blues lost was lead singer Denny Laine while they gained John Lodge and Justin Hayward. This was an ambitious record from a group who had stopped having hits in the UK, and their record company Decca/Deram should be applauded in allowing them down this untried road. This is the album that features Justin Hayward's epic song 'Nights In White Satin', together with some other fine, melancholic pop songs. What makes the album work is not the band, but the sensitive and rich orchestration throughout from the London Festival Orchestra and, in particular, the great contribution from conductor Peter Knight.

» Tracks: *The Day Begins; Dawn, i Dawn Is A Feeling; The Morning, i Another Morning; Lunch Break, i Peak Hour; The Afternoon, i Forever Afternoon, ii Time To Get Away; Evening, i The Sun Set, ii Twilight Time; The Night, i Nights In White Satin.*

★ First released 1967
★ UK peak chart position: 27
★ USA peak chart position: 3
★ Previous Top 1000 position: 1998 (571): 1994 (–)

942 CHICAGO TRANSIT AUTHORITY ↓ Chicago

This debut has surprisingly endured, whereas all their following 18,000 albums with the same title (other than a number change) have little or no credibility in the public's memory. This album can be interchanged with the second and third Blood Sweat and Tears albums; all represent the very best of late 60s American jazz/rock. The band changed their name soon afterwards as they ploughed a successful path into smooth AOR. Lengthy tracks such as 'South California Purples' and their excellent cover version of Spencer Davis Group's 'I'm A Man' prove beyond doubt that these chaps can really play. Maybe they were smarter than most in seeing the limitations of jazz/rock and moving on to play Russian roulette.

» Tracks: *Introduction; Does Anybody Really Know What Time It Is?; Beginnings; Questions 67 & 68; Listen; Poem 58; Free Form Guitar; South California Purples; I'm A Man; Prologue, August 29, 1968; Someday August 29 1968; Liberation.*

★ First released 1969
★ UK peak chart position: 9
★ USA peak chart position: 17
★ Previous Top 1000 position: 1998 (699): 1994 (–)

943 SHOOTING AT THE MOON ↑
Kevin Ayers

Idiosyncratic and slightly bonkers, Kevin Ayers' increasingly infrequent contributions to popular music is a source of much dismay to his loyal following. This former Soft Machine member's promising solo career arguably reached a peak on this, his second album, on which he is supported by such excellent musicians as a pre-*Tubular Bells* Mike Oldfield, Lol Coxhill, and the hugely talented arranger David Bedford. Although feted by progressive rock followers Ayers always had a great pop sensibility, and every track here has at least one gorgeously melodic moment. If by any chance there is a hole in your CD wants list I recommend you fill it with this unforgettable little pearl.

» Tracks: *May I; Rheinhardt and Geraldine; Colores Para Dolores; Lunatic Lament; Pisser Dans Un Violon; The Oyster and The Flying Fish; Underwater; Clarence In Wonderland; Red Green and You Blue; Shooting At The Moon.*

★ First released 1970
★ UK peak chart position: did not chart
★ USA peak chart position: did not chart
★ Previous Top 1000 position: 1998 (–): 1994 (–)

944 TUPELO HONEY ↑
Van Morrison

After the disappointment of *Van Morrison, His Band and The Street Choir*, the man sought refuge in the redwoods near his home in Marin County. Recently married to Janet Planet, this album is a celebration of Morrison's happiness at that point in his life. Over the years *Tupelo Honey*'s initial impression of dullness has subsided into warm affection. Certainly there is a ton of joy in '(Straight To Your Heart) Like A Cannonball', 'You're My Woman' and 'Moonshine Whiskey'. The magnificent title track is the stand-out, and is probably his most open love song. Note: there is not one mention of 'gardens wet with rain' throughout this record.

» Tracks: *Wild Night; (Straight To Your Heart) Like A Cannonball; Old Old Woodstock; Starting A New Life; You're My Woman; Tupelo Honey; I Wanna Roo You (Scottish Derivative); When That Evening Sun Goes Down; Moonshine Whiskey.*

★ First released 1971
★ UK peak chart position: did not chart
★ USA peak chart position: 27
★ Previous Top 1000 position: 1998 (–): 1994 (–)

945 DESERTER'S SONGS ↑
Mercury Rev

A dark horse of a record that ended up as album of the year on the lists of many music journalists. Jonathan Donahue's delicate vocals lend a deceptively winsome air to his tales of love and despair. Not everything works as intended, and 'Endlessly' struggles to stay on the right side of fey. The successes are magnificent, however, and bring comfort to longstanding music lovers who still crave the warmth of a good old-fashioned melodic song. 'Opus 40' has the right ingredients, and 'Holes' has them all and more. *Deserter's Songs* is an accessible, varied collection which kicks the current wave of negativity favoured by alternative rock outfits in the crotch.

» Tracks: *Holes; Tonite It Shows; Endlessly; I Collect Coins; Opus 40; Hudson Line; The Happy End (The Drunk Room); Goddess On A Hiway; The Funny Bird; Pick Up If You're There; Delta Sun Bottleneck Stomp.*

★ First released 1998
★ UK peak chart position: 27
★ USA peak chart position: did not chart
★ Previous Top 1000 position: 1998 (–): 1994 (–)

946 SUNDAY AT THE VILLAGE VANGUARD ↑ Bill Evans

If you were only allowed two Bill Evans albums in your collection few would disagree that this (also known as *Live At The Village Vanguard*) and its sister album *Waltz For Debby* are the pair to own. Recorded with such perfect spontaneity it is hard to believe that there is a lucky audience experiencing this in a club of shoebox proportions. This features the best ever Evans trio, with two other outstanding jazz masters, drummer Paul Motian and the late Scott LaFaro. The latter is surely the greatest bass player of that era, and one who influenced dozens of lesser players. The CD has four bonus alternate takes. Every track is pure perfection.

» Tracks: *Gloria's Step (Take 2); Gloria's Step (Take 3); My Man's Gone Now; Solar; Alice In Wonderland (Take 2); Alice In Wonderland (Take 1); All Of You (Take 2); All Of You (Take 3); Jade Visions (Take 2); Jade Visions (Take 1).*

★ First released 1961
★ UK peak chart position: did not chart
★ USA peak chart position: did not chart
★ Previous Top 1000 position: 1998 (–): 1994 (–)

947 SLOWHAND ↑
Eric Clapton

The opening track 'Cocaine' is not, as many of us innocent children would have thought, about visiting the dentist, but JJ Cale's song refuses to be sinister. Clapton had already gone way past cocaine by the time this Glyn Johns-produced LP was recorded, at the time the best thing he had put out since *461 Ocean Boulevard*. Even though he had swapped the heroin for booze it was a remarkably together recording, and Johns must take credit for cajoling Clapton into working so hard. In addition to the twee hit singles 'Wonderful Tonight' and 'Lay Down Sally' the album includes the feisty 'The Core', featuring the vocals of Marcy Levy.

» Tracks: *Cocaine; Wonderful Tonight; Lay Down Sally; Next Time You See Her; We're All The Way; The Core; May You Never; Mean Old Frisco; Peaches and Diesel.*

★ First released 1977
★ UK peak chart position: 23
★ USA peak chart position: 2
★ Previous Top 1000 position: 1998 (–): 1994 (–)

948 ONE WORLD ↑
John Martyn

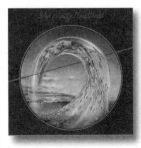

Black and white, dark and light, good or bad, but never indifferent, just like John Martyn's temperament. From tales of drugs and deals in 'Big Muff' and 'Dealer', to blissful love in the gorgeous slurred 'Certain Surprise', and arguably his ultimate song of unconditional love, 'Couldn't Love You More'. The thought-provoking title track has Martyn delivering the uncompromising lines 'some of us live like Princes and some of us live like Queens, most of us live just like me and don't know what it means'. Martyn is one of Britain's most vital singer songwriter's and this is one of the most durable albums in an incredible catalogue.

» Tracks: *Dealer; One World; Smiling Stranger; Big Muff; Couldn't Love You More; Certain Surprise; Dancing; Small Hours.*

★ First released 1977
★ UK peak chart position: 54
★ USA peak chart position: did not chart
★ Previous Top 1000 position: 1998 (–): 1994 (–)

949 WELD ↓
Neil Young and Crazy Horse

Neil Young hit yet another peak in the 90s and this blisteringly distorted album was probably the best, following on from the standards set by *Freedom*. He out-grunges everybody with Crazy Horse, the best support band in the world (ask Ian McNabb). 'Cortez The Killer' from *Zuma* is given new life, as is his gentle rocker 'Cinnamon Girl' from 1968. The excitement level of the double set is extraordinary as the gut-wrenching volume of playing fails to irritate – it only ignites the soul for more. The low point is the overlong and ponderous 'Farmer John', which should be left with the Searchers.

》 Tracks: *Hey Hey, My My (Into The Black); Crime In The City; Blowin' In The Wind; Welfare Mothers; Love To Burn; Cinnamon Girl; Mansion On The Hill; F*!#In' Up; Cortez The Killer; Powderfinger; Love and Only Love; Rockin' In The Free World; Like A Hurricane; Farmer John; Tonight's The Night; Roll Another Number.*

★ First released 1991
★ UK peak chart position: 20
★ USA peak chart position: 154
★ Previous Top 1000 position: 1998 (547): 1994 (574)

950 WHITECHOCOLATESPACEEGG
↑ Liz Phair

Liz Phair's acclaimed debut *Exile In Guyville* helped inspire a new generation of articulate female singer-songwriters. Phair is blessed with the same songwriting talents as Aimee Mann, and like her, deserves as much attention as Alanis Morissette and Sheryl Crow. There is a ton of feisty home truths in her lyrics, and although she has tempered her tone of late, male listeners should pay particular attention. Make a mental note of cryptic humour of 'Polyester Bride' and dream on about becoming 'Johnny Feelgood'. A rich, creamy and delicious album that, no doubt, is very similar to a whitechocolatespaceegg.

》 Tracks: *White Chocolate Space Egg; Big Tall Man; Perfect World; Johnny Feelgood; Polyester Bride; Love Is Nothing; Baby Got Going; Uncle Alvarez; Only Son; Go On Ahead; Headache; Ride; What Makes You Happy; Fantasize; Shitloads Of Money; Girls' Room.*

★ First released 1998
★ UK peak chart position: did not chart
★ USA peak chart position: 35
★ Previous Top 1000 position: 1998 (–): 1994 (–)

951 BACK TO BACK ↑
Duke Ellington and Johnny Hodges

A welcome reissue, with a quite magnificent 20 bit digital transfer that highlights the quality of the original recording. Hodges' alto saxophone threatens to burst through the right speaker cloth on 'Wabash Blues', until you are distracted by Harry Edison's trumpet coming out of the left one. The seven blues on this album make for sumptuous listening, although personal highlights are the aforementioned 'Wabash Blues', the moody 'Weary Blues', and the lilting 'Royal Garden Blues'. 'The St. Louis Blues' and 'Basin Street Blues' have been heard a million times before and deserve a rest in favour of these lesser known gems. An immaculate album, much better appreciated on CD forty years later.

》 Tracks: *Wabash Blues; Basin Street Blues; Beale Street Blues; Weary Blues; The St. Louis Blues; Loveless Love; Royal Garden Blues.*

★ First released 1959
★ UK peak chart position: did not chart
★ USA peak chart position: did not chart
★ Previous Top 1000 position: 1998 (–): 1994 (–)

952 THIRD EYE BLIND ↑
Third Eye Blind

Straightforward contemporary US rock, with enough melodic choruses and chiming guitars to retain that all important pop sensibility. San Francisco's Third Eye Blind enjoyed instant success with this debut album, boosted by the excellent chart performance of the college rock favourite, 'Semi-Charmed Life'. Great harmonies and a nod backwards to Mick Ronson's *Ziggy Stardust* chords, with wah wah pedals ringing out loud during the short and snappy guitar breaks. Stephan Jenkins, the main lyricist and singer, has the perfect voice with which to vent his tales of romantic woe. 'Losing A Whole Year' for example; bitter, who me? He will get over his loss eventually, although such is the strength of the songs on this album that the selfish listener hopes it will happen again and again.

》 Tracks: *Losing A Whole Year; Narcolepsy; Semi-Charmed Life; Jumper; Graduate; How's It Going To Be; Thanks A Lot; Burning Man; Good For You; London; I Want You; The Background; Motorcycle Drive By; God Of Wine.*

★ First released 1997
★ UK peak chart position: did not chart
★ USA peak chart position: 25
★ Previous Top 1000 position: 1998 (–): 1994 (–)

953 MILES DAVIS AT CARNEGIE HALL ↑ Miles Davis

The familiar introduction of 'So What' opens this concert, suddenly interrupted by a distorted shriek of top end trumpet warning the microphones that 'we can't cope with the recording dynamics'. After that blip, the VU meters were obviously turned down and the recording for most part is exceptional. The CD transfer, now on two full discs, is second only to having been at the concert. His quintet on this occasion was Hank Mobley (tenor), Paul Chambers (bass), Jimmy Cobb (drums) and a particularly lively Wynton Kelly (piano). Life is made complete by Gil Evans and his 21 piece orchestra. Mmmmm, now that's nice.

➤➤ Tracks: So What; Spring Is Here; Teo; Walkin'; The Meaning Of The Blues/Lament; New Rhumba; Someday My Prince Will Come; Oleo; No Blues; I Thought About You; En Aranjuez Con Tu Amor.

★ First released 1962
★ UK peak chart position: did not chart
★ USA peak chart position: 59
★ Previous Top 1000 position: 1998 (–): 1994 (–)

954 HAPPY SAD ↑ Tim Buckley

The critical success of Buckley's late son Jeff has reactivated interest in his estranged father's catalogue, which had never been viewed as anything more than a cult oddity. Two previous albums established Tim Buckley as an imaginative folk-singer. On this release he extended his musical range by incorporating jazz structures into his songs. Formal meter was broken down to allow the artist's voice fuller expression, a freedom he embraced with relish. Vibes and conga drums provide a rhythmic pulse on material ranging from intense reflection to scat-singing association, the latter encapsulated on the extended tour de force, 'Gypsy Woman'. The contrast between its stridency and the beautiful melancholia of the remaining selections is the album's abiding strength.

➤➤ Tracks: Strange Feelin'; Buzzin' Fly; Love From Room 109 At The Islander (On Pacific Coast Highway); Dream Letter; Gypsy Woman; Sing A Song For You.

★ First released 1968
★ UK peak chart position: did not chart
★ USA peak chart position: 81
★ Previous Top 1000 position: 1998 (–): 1994 (897)

955 SONGS FOR A TAILOR ↑ Jack Bruce

Bruce released this fine solo debut shortly after the demise of Cream, the power trio in which he helped define rock bass and became a much-emulated role model. Bruce sounds happy and free on Songs For A Tailor, utilising great brass players such as Dick Heckstall-Smith and calling upon Pete Brown for some of his lyrical poems. This album includes three truly great songs. 'Weird Of Hermiston', the snappy 'Never Tell Your Mother She's Out Of Tune' (written about Chris Spedding's mum), and the magnificent opus 'Theme For An Imaginary Western', an emotional eulogy about life on a motorway, in a van, in a band, in the 60s.

➤➤ Tracks: Never Tell Your Mother She's Out Of Tune; Theme For An Imaginary Western; Tickets To Water Falls; Weird Of Hermiston; Rope Ladder To The Moon; The Ministry Of Bag; He The Richmond; Boston Ball Game, 1967; To Isengard; The Clearout.

★ First released 1969
★ UK peak chart position: 6
★ USA peak chart position: 55
★ Previous Top 1000 position: 1998 (–): 1994 (–)

956 ME AGAINST THE WORLD ↑ 2Pac

2Pac holds the record for being the only person to debut at number one in the US album chart while serving a prison sentence for an alleged sexual assault. He continued to write and sing about his innocence until he was fatally gunned down in September 1996. His legacy is immense, and whatever the rights and wrongs of his involvement in the east coast/west coast gangsta rap feud he remains a gigantic figure as a master of hip-hop and poet for black equality. Nobody should fail to be affected by the sentiments of tracks such as 'Me Against The World', 'So Many Tears', or the spookily prophetic 'Death Around The Corner'.

➤➤ Tracks: Intro; If I Die 2 Nite; Me Against The World; So Many Tears; Temptations; Young Niggaz; Heavy In The Game; Lord Knows; Dear Mama; It Ain't Easy; Can U Get Away; Old School; F*** The World; Death Around The Corner; Outlaw.

★ First released 1995
★ UK peak chart position: did not chart
★ USA peak chart position: 1
★ Previous Top 1000 position: 1998 (–): 1994 (–)

957 SOUL'S CORE ↑
Shawn Mullins

How the CD cover belies what is within. A puppy face trying to grow a beard gazes out. Inside is an incredible collection of mature electric folk songs, sung with the raspy voice of a man three times his age. Pitching somewhere between Robbie Robertson's growl and Tom Petty's high register, Mullins matches both of them with precocious ease. His grasp of Americana is both entertaining and intriguing, the latter because it is a baby boomer's view of the American Dream. This recording can sit proudly alongside those Band and Little Feat albums on the shelf. And to think that these young whippersnappers now read Richard Brautigan books as well!

>> Tracks: *Anchored In You; Lullaby; The Gulf Of Mexico; September In Seattle; Twin Rocks, Oregon; And On A Rainy Night; Tannin Bed Song; Soul Child; Ballad Of Billy Jo McKay; Patrick's Song; Sunday Mornin' Comin' Down; You Mean Everything To Me; Shimmer.*

★ First released 1998
★ UK peak chart position: 60
★ USA peak chart position: 54
★ Previous Top 1000 position: 1998 (–): 1994 (–)

958 SMALL CHANGE ↑
Tom Waits

Tom Waits is another one of those national treasure types with a totally unique style. That voice is for real, although thousands of cigarettes and whiskey may have helped on the way. *Small Change* is yet another masterpiece from the man, and despite being his most commercially successful album for a long time the derisory chart position is still an insult. The album is worth the price of admission alone for the beautiful 'Tom Traubert's Blues' ('Waltzing Matilda' to you) and the title track. The latter is so smoky it makes you wish that in an earlier life Waits could have made wonderful music with John Coltrane or Ben Webster.

>> Tracks: *Tom Traubert's Blues (Four Sheets To The Wind In Copenhagen); Step Right Up; Jitterbug Boy; I Wish I Was In New Orleans (In The Ninth Ward); The Piano Has Been Drinking (Not Me); Invitation To The Blues; Pasties and A G-String (At The Two O'Clock Club); Bad Liver and A Broken Heart (In Lowell); The One That Got Away; Small Change (Got Rained On With His Own .38); I Can't Wait To Get Off Work (And See My Baby On Montgomery Avenue).*

★ First released 1976 ★ UK peak chart position: did not chart
★ USA peak chart position: 89
★ Previous Top 1000 position: 1998 (–): 1994 (–)

959 MOANIN' ↑
Art Blakey and The Jazz Messengers

Blakey attracted great musicians like a rat up a drainpipe. On this he had the good fortune to have his pianist Bobby Timmons contribute a song, 'Moanin'', which has gone on to become a jazz classic and been played and sung by hundreds of artists. The author's lightness of touch and understated tone on this particular recording is pure joy. Lee Morgan also shines throughout, his crisp trumpet playing slicing through the even sound. The only weak moment comes from Blakey himself on Benny Golson's 'The Drum Thunder (Miniature) Suite', adding little to a woefully dull piece which makes Sandy Nelson look good. The CD bonus track, the alternate take of 'Moanin', more than makes up for it.

>> Tracks: *Moanin'; Moanin' (Alternate Take); Are You Real; Along Came Betty; The Drum Thunder Suite; Blues March; Come Rain Or Come Shine.*

★ First released 1958
★ UK peak chart position: did not chart
★ USA peak chart position: did not chart
★ Previous Top 1000 position: 1998 (–): 1994 (–)

960 TRAILER PARK ↑
Beth Orton

When the beautifully sparse *Trailer Park* was released no record company hype was needed to gain the public's attention. After only a few seconds of the opening track the listener was already entranced by this fresh, original talent. The album was scheduled to be called *Winnebago* but for some stupid reason the camper van manufacturers objected. *Trailer Park* was quickly established as one of the cult highlights of 1996 and Orton became a reluctant star. Her voice is highly original, waif-like but with enough edge to cut through the sensitive instrumental arrangements. On other tracks she accompanies herself on guitar, but never lapses into folk cliché.

>> Tracks: *She Cries Your Name; Tangent; Don't Need A Reason; Live As You Dream; Sugar Boy; Touch Me With Your Love; Whenever; How Far; Someone's Daughter; I Wish I Never Saw The Sunshine; Galaxy Of Emptiness.*

★ First released 1996
★ UK peak chart position: 68
★ USA peak chart position: did not chart
★ Previous Top 1000 position: 1998 (–): 1994 (–)

961 WHATEVER ↓
Aimee Mann

Perhaps the end of her relationship with Jules Shear gave Aimee Mann a real kick to her songs – certainly the energy and the powerful lyrics succeed where her former band, 'Til Tuesday, failed. This album won over many critics in 1993, both old and young – mainly those of us who love anything that sounds like the Byrds and others who see indie guitar pop as an extension of punk. Whatever, the album is a corker and tracks such as 'I Should've Known', 'Fifty Years After The Fair' and 'Stupid Thing' are enduring classics. P.S. Roger McGuinn guests on guitar as well. It's a pity she has faded after the early promise of this LP.

❱❱ Tracks: *I Should've Known; Fifty Years After The Fair; 4th Of July; Could've Been Anyone; Put Me On Top; Stupid Thing; Say Anything; Jacob Marley's Chain; Mr Harris; I Could Hurt You Now; I Know There's A Word; I've Had It; Way Back When.*

★ First released 1993
★ UK peak chart position: 39
★ USA peak chart position: did not chart
★ Previous Top 1000 position: 1998 (264): 1994 (380)

962 THE DANCE ↑
Fleetwood Mac

Mick Fleetwood must have breathed a huge sigh of relief when this line-up buried the hatchet soon after the dreadful Dave Mason/Bekka Bramlett release *Time*. Predictably it is Lindsey Buckingham who steals the show with his strangely refreshing performances of mostly old hits. His acoustic guitar on 'Big Love' is formidable. Stevie Nicks' vocals have not weathered particularly well, and she finds her lower register running out of puff. Although many of these tracks have been heard time and time again, the slightly updated arrangements still warm the heart. Of the new songs 'Bleed To Love Her' is the strongest, and of the old songs 'Go Your Own Way', featuring Buckingham's low-mixed guitar solo, is an absolute blinder.

❱❱ Tracks: *The Chain; Dreams; Everywhere; Rhiannon; I'm So Afraid; Temporary One; Bleed To Love Her; Big Love; Landslide; Say You Love Me; My Little Demon; Silver Springs; You Make Loving Fun; Sweet Girl; Go Your Own Way; Tusk; Don't Stop.*

★ First released 1997
★ UK peak chart position: 15
★ USA peak chart position: 1
★ Previous Top 1000 position: 1998 (–): 1994 (–)

963 DID I SHAVE MY LEGS FOR THIS? ↑
Deana Carter

Deana Carter, who looks like a California babe but sounds like a cross between Dolly Parton and Reba McEntire, had one of the smash country hits of 1996 with this album. She made her mark on the notorially territorial country music fraternity with a mixture of excellent originals and material by some of the best new country writers, including Matraca Berg and Kim Carnes. The title track is a witty and clever tale that indicates that the days of the subservient, gingham-clad mid-western wife are long gone. Carter may be a little more country than Shania Twain or Faith Hill, but your attention is still highly advised.

❱❱ Tracks: *I've Loved Enough To Know; We Danced Anyway; Count Me In; If This Is Love; Love Ain't Worth Making; Before We Ever Heard Goodbye; How Do I Get There; Strawberry Wine; That's How You Know It's Love; Did I Shave My Legs For This?; To The Other Side.*

★ First released 1996
★ UK peak chart position: did not chart
★ USA peak chart position: 10
★ Previous Top 1000 position: 1998 (–): 1994 (–)

964 BRILLIANT CORNERS ↑
Thelonious Monk

Another classic Riverside album remastered on CD. This December 1956 recording features Monk once again democratically sharing his solos with musicians including Sonny Rollins (tenor), Max Roach (drums), Oscar Pettiford (bass) and Ernie Henry (alto). For Monk fans this came as quite a surprise as the eccentric solos are replaced by an almost traditional sounding Monk, and even in a jazz framework the mad pianist is tamed. Having to discipline himself occasionally was no bad thing, however, and this album is an artistic success. The foxy 'Bemsha Swing' and the lengthy 'Ba-Lue Bolivar Ba-Lues-Are' win by a piano key.

❱❱ Tracks: *Brilliant Corners; Ba-Lue Bolivar Ba-Lues-Are; Pannonica; I Surrender, Dear; Bemsha Swing.*

★ First released 1957
★ UK peak chart position: did not chart
★ USA peak chart position: did not chart
★ Previous Top 1000 position: 1998 (–): 1994 (–)

965 SPEAKING IN TONGUES ↑
Talking Heads

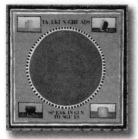

Talking Heads' return to the studio after a three year gap came at a time when they were being challenged by a clutch of new and exciting young things who were suddenly making them sound old. For years they had been routinely cited as America's most interesting and influential band, but now they were having to work hard to justify the accolades. This album received mixed reviews when it was first released, but time has now accepted it into the fold. The two strongest tracks, 'Burning Down The House' and 'This Must Be The Place (Naïve Melody)', act like a sandwich holding together some indifferent filling. The latter hits an attractive groove, although the guitars constantly threaten to break away into a Bhundu Boys track.

» Tracks: *Burning Down The House; Making Flippy Floppy; Girlfriend Is Better; Slippery People; I Get Wild/Wild Gravity; Swamp; Moon Rocks; Pull Up The Roots; This Must Be The Place (Naïve Melody).*

★ First released 1983
★ UK peak chart position: 21
★ USA peak chart position: 15
★ Previous Top 1000 position: 1998 (–): 1994 (–)

966 SONGS FROM NORTHERN BRITAIN ↑ Teenage Fanclub

When oh when will the rest of the world wake up to the fantastic Fannies. Admittedly, the Big Star and Byrds influences are rather obvious at times, but these derivatives aside, Teenage Fanclub are a good thing to have around. This was their final album for Creation Records (although they did not know it at the time) and contains 12 tracks of pure melodic joy, including such corkers as 'Start Again' and 'I Don't Want Control Of You'. It sold as moderately as all their others, however. Maybe they should have a preservation order slapped on them, like the ones bestowed on XTC and the Kinks.

» Tracks: *Start Again; Ain't That Enough; Can't Feel My Soul; I Don't Want Control Of You; Planets; It's A Bad World; Take The Long Way Round; Winter; I Don't Care; Mount Everest; Your Love Is The Place Where I Come From; Speed Of Light.*

★ First released 1997
★ UK peak chart position: 3
★ USA peak chart position: did not chart
★ Previous Top 1000 position: 1998 (–): 1994 (–)

967 CRIME OF THE CENTURY ↓
Supertramp

The punishment befits the crime, and a quarter of a century later, Supertramp have been forgiven by critics. Quite why they induced such negative press seems unjustified, as 'Bloody Well Right' and 'Dreamer' sound as fresh as ever. The electric piano cuts through the speakers like a knife through butter, the treble at times hurting the ear like a heavy rock guitar solo. Both Roger Hodgson's and Richard Davies' voices sound rich and confident, although both are quite different. Maybe the pace slackens with the slightly indulgent 'If Everyone Was Listening' and the title track, but there are enough musical highlights to recommend this for any would-be 90s progster's wants list.

» Tracks: *School; Bloody Well Right; Hide In Your Shell; Asylum; Dreamer; Rudy; If Everyone Was Listening; Crime Of The Century.*

★ First released 1974
★ UK peak chart position: 4
★ USA peak chart position: 38
★ Previous Top 1000 position: 1998 (689): 1994 (–)

968 HARD PROMISES ↑
Tom Petty

Tom Petty gives the impression of being able to bash out an album's worth of songs while still keeping one eye on the television screen During the period between 1978 and 1982 there was little to choose between several excellent albums. All adhered to the same patented formula, albeit one borrowed and honed from Roger McGuinn. This is as straightforward as rock can ever get, with just enough subtle chord changes and twists to keep it interesting. The best moment is 'The Waiting', a positive love song sung with rock 'n' roll abandon; 'I'll be your bleedin' heart, I'll be your cryin' fool'.

» Tracks: *The Waiting; A Woman In Love (It's Not Me); Nightwatchman; Something Big; Kings Road; Letting You Go; A Thing About You; Insider; The Criminal Kind; You Can Still Change Your Mind.*

★ First released 1981
★ UK peak chart position: 32
★ USA peak chart position: 5
★ Previous Top 1000 position: 1998 (–): 1994 (–)

969 PRIVATE DANCER ↓
Tina Turner

Enlisting the help of notable producers such as Joe Sample, Martyn Ware and Rupert Hine, Tina Turner out-performed even the original artists as she strutted her way into rock music, having been on the periphery for years with her screaming R&B and her ex-husband's strong influence. Al Green's 'Let's Stay Together' is made her own and even without the thin-sounding organ on the Ann Peebles original, her interpretation of 'I Can't Stand The Rain' is wholly acceptable. Mark Knopfler's standing benefited from having written the title track, and if that isn't enough, there is also 'What's Love Got To Do With It'.

⟩⟩ Tracks: I Might Have Been Queen; What's Love Got To Do With It; Show Some Respect; I Can't Stand The Rain; Private Dancer; Let's Stay Together; Better Be Good To Me; Steel Claw; Help; 1984.

★ First released 1984
★ UK peak chart position: 2
★ USA peak chart position: 3
★ Previous Top 1000 position: 1998 (242): 1994 (25)

970 DIZZY UP THE GIRL ↑
Goo Goo Dolls

Surprisingly more successful than the band's previous album A Boy Named Goo, the single 'Iris' suddenly took off after it was featured in the Nicolas Cage movie City Of Angels and the album followed suit. It went on to sell 3 million copies in the USA in a very short time. Goo Goo Dolls are a straight ahead US rock group who avoid falling into punk or alternative rock categories, but with enough metal in their guitars to appeal to both markets. 'Slide' is the album's star. A memorable song that bursts into life after a catchy intro with a descending guitar doodle.

⟩⟩ Tracks: Dizzy; Slide; Broadway; January Friend; Black Balloon; Bullet proof; Amigone; All Eyes on Me; Full Forever; Acoustic No.3; Iris; Extra Pale; Hate This Place.

★ First released 1998
★ UK peak chart position: 47
★ USA peak chart position: 15
★ Previous Top 1000 position: 1998 (–): 1994 (–)

971 SOLITUDE STANDING ↑
Suzanne Vega

Suzanne Vega followed in the footsteps of Carly Simon and Joni Mitchell and predated the rise of feisty female singer-songwriters such as Alanis Morissette in the 90s. She came along on her own in the mid 80s when intelligent female singers were largely ignored. Her debut album and this 1987 follow-up are essential. She writes sensitively and sings like a dream. 'Luka' may sound like a perky pop song but it uncovers a dark story of child abuse. Similarly, the title track alludes to the comfort of loneliness, deep, dark and beautiful and giving hope through despair. It was a great pity that she was unable to maintain the creative peak she reached on this recording.

⟩⟩ Tracks: Tom's Diner; Luka; Ironbound/Fancy Poultry; In The Eye; Night Vision; Solitude Standing; Calypso; Language; Gypsy; Wooden Horse; Tom's Diner (Reprise).

★ First released 1987
★ UK peak chart position: 2
★ USA peak chart position: 11
★ Previous Top 1000 position: 1998 (–): 1994 (–)

972 ENDLESS SUMMER ↓
The Beach Boys

Just as everybody had written off the Beach Boys as passé, we were reminded of the colossal contribution that Brian Wilson had made to popular music with this inspired compilation. New Beach Boys albums were selling badly at the time of this release, and then somebody had the idea of packaging this superb collection of surf and car songs that reeked of sand, sea, sun and innocence. There is something special about 'catching a wave', even though most followers have never been near a surfboard in their lives, let alone a clean beach.

⟩⟩ Tracks: Surfin' Safari; Surfer Girl; Catch A Wave; Warmth Of The Sun; Surfin' USA; Be True To Your School; Little Deuce Coup; In My Room; Shut Down; Fun Fun Fun; I Get Around; Girls On The Beach; Wendy; Let Him Run Wild; Don't Worry Baby; California Girls; Girl Don't Tell Me; Help Me Rhonda; You're So Good To Me; All Summer Long; Good Vibrations.

★ First released 1974
★ UK peak chart position: did not chart
★ USA peak chart position: 1
★ Previous Top 1000 position: 1998 (531): 1994 (542)

973 THE WONDERFUL AND FRIGHTENING WORLD OF ↓
The Fall

The eighth Fall album consolidated the abrasive sextet's relationship with producer John Leckie, who helped expand their musical palate without sacrificing individuality. The presence of guitarist Laura Elise, better known as Brix Smith, expanded the unit's tonal capabilities, but they remained firmly a vehicle in which singer Mark E. Smith vented his spleen. His vitriolic lyrics were as uncompromising as ever, even if now-accustomed dissonance is occasionally paired with neo-psychedelic nuances. *The Frightening World* captures the Fall as they expanded their frame of reference, and in the process, gained recognition for their highly original music.

▶ Tracks: *Lay Of The Land; 2 x 4; Copped It; Elves; Oh! Brother; Draygo's Guilt; God-box; Clear Off; C.R.E.E.P.; Pat-Trip Dispenser; Slang King; Bug Day; Stephen Song; Craigness; Disney's Dream Debased; No Bulbs.*

★ First released 1984
★ UK peak chart position: 62
★ USA peak chart position: did not chart
★ Previous Top 1000 position: 1998 (836): 1994 (397)

974 VIOLENT FEMMES ↓
Violent Femmes

A band with a surfeit of natural charm, the Violent Femmes can also boast of a prodigious back-catalogue of easily accessible, effortlessly original songs. This is the best place to start. Their ramshackle Milwaukee hillbilly punk is complemented by Gordon Gano's geek with attitude lyrics, by turns hilarious and tragic, often within a few lines. Sample the emotional simplicity of 'Kiss Off' or 'Please Do Not Go'. Unlike many of their contemporaries, you feel nobody else on the planet could have written or performed something like 'Gone Daddy Gone', which single-handedly redefines the essential elements of a great pop song (imagine Brian Wilson writing his surf instrumentals on a xylophone).

▶ Tracks: *Blister In The Sun; Kiss Off; Please Do Not Go; Add It Up; Confessions; Prove My Love; Promise; To The Kill; Gone Daddy Gone; Good Feeling.*

★ First released 1991
★ UK peak chart position: did not chart
★ USA peak chart position: 171
★ Previous Top 1000 position: 1998 (734): 1994 (–)

975 IF I SHOULD FALL FROM GRACE WITH GOD ↑ The Pogues

The cover depicts eight young men unspoiled by the ravages of time. The perkiest and youngest looking is Shane MacGowan, who since the picture was taken has nearly succeeded in wearing out his lungs and liver. For all this, the unbridled joy that the Pogues unleashed on the public was as fresh as a pint of freshly pumped Murphys. They perfectly captured the bawdy Irish spirit while embracing sounds from the Middle East and Spain. A beautiful, ramshackle record that manages to clean up its act when Kirsty MacColl joins the party on Christmas eve for 'Fairytale Of New York'.

▶ Tracks: *If I Should Fall From Grace With God; Turkish Song Of The Damned; Bottle Of Smoke; Fairytale Of New York; Metropolis; Thousands Are Sailing; Fiesta; Medley; Streets Of Sorrow/Birmingham Six; Lullaby Of London; Sit Down By The Fire; The Broad Majestic Shannon; Worms.*

★ First released 1988
★ UK peak chart position: 3
★ USA peak chart position: 88
★ Previous Top 1000 position: 1998 (–): 1994 (–)

976 THE ORIGINAL SOUNDTRACK
↑ 10cc

Stamped indelibly as 70s music, 10cc have slid from grace much the way that ELO did. No one can deny it is clever stuff, but sometimes too many changes within a single track can be irritating. 10cc were masters of the effortless segue, but occasionally it would be nice to have just one long lovely bit. This theory is perfectly typified by the opening track 'Une Nuit A Paris (Part 1)'; too damn clever by half. Even the poppy 'Life Is A Minestrone' has more changes than the weather. It does however contain 'I'm Not In Love', the ONLY best slow dance song to end a party with in the 70s.

▶ Tracks: *Une Nuit A Paris (Part 1); The Same Night In Paris (Part 2); Later The Same Night In Paris (Part 3); I'm Not In Love; Blackmail; The Second Sitting For The Last Supper; Brand New Day; Flying Junk; Life Is A Minestrone; The Film Of My Love.*

★ First released 1975
★ UK peak chart position: 4
★ USA peak chart position: 15
★ Previous Top 1000 position: 1998 (–): 1994 (–)

977 NO GURU, NO METHOD, NO TEACHER ↑ Van Morrison

Although he had barely put a foot wrong in the 80s, other than a poor live set recorded in Belfast, this is the album that tweaked the critics' hearts. Morrison acknowledged his past with the punningly titled 'Here Comes The Knight' and sniped at his plagiarists on 'A Town Called Paradise'. 'In The Garden' reprises themes first aired on *Astral Weeks* (imagine the line 'gardens wet with rain' on a repeat royalty). 'Tir Na Nog' is shamelessly nostalgic and more revealing and less oblique than much of his material prior to this rebirth. If only casual listeners realised that, alongside this excellent album, there are at least six or seven other worthy Morrison albums besides *Astral Weeks*.

» Tracks: *Got To Go Back; Oh The Warm Feeling; Foreign Window; A Town Called Paradise; In The Garden; Tir Na Nog; Here Comes The Knight; Thanks For The Information; One Irish Rover; Ivory Tower.*

★ First released 1986
★ UK peak chart position: 27
★ USA peak chart position: 70
★ Previous Top 1000 position: 1998 (–): 1994 (–)

978 THERE'S A RIOT GOIN' ON ↓ Sly and The Family Stone

During the late 60s Sly and The Family Stone changed the nature of soul music by infusing it with elements of psychedelic pop. Their exciting, effervescent singles included 'Dance To The Music', 'Stand' and 'I Want To Take You Higher', but with the release of this album, group leader Sly Stone exorcised personal and cultural psychoses. Its brooding funk was distilled through a deep, somnambulist sound in which even the lightest of songs, 'Runnin' Away' or 'Family Affair', were tinged with discomfort. The set culminates with bitter, twisted rhythms, disembodied vocals and a ravaged intensity quite unlike anything previously heard in soul music.

» Tracks: *Luv 'N' Haight; Just Like A Baby; The Poet; Family Affair; Africa Talks To You 'The Asphalt Jungle'; Brave and Strong; (You Caught Me) Smilin'; Time; Spaced Cowboy; Runnin' Away; Thank You For Talking To Me Africa.*

★ First released 1971
★ UK peak chart position: 31
★ USA peak chart position: 1
★ Previous Top 1000 position: 1998 (216): 1994 (277)

979 FOLLOW THE LEADER ↓ Eric B & Rakim

A New York team who met in 1985 and have gone on to become an important duo in Rap's short history. Their debut album, *Paid In Full*, caused great legal waves via its explicit use of samples (Eric B is often credited with putting the funk back into rap music via his James Brown signatures). Rakim was responsible for introducing a more relaxed, intuitive delivery which was a distinct advance on the thumping bravado of Run DMC and LL Cool J, and is best sampled on this influential and instructive album. The title track, 'Lyrics Of Fury' and 'Microphone Fiend' provided the fullest possible evidence of the duo's skill.

» Tracks: *Follow The Leader; Microphone Fiend; Lyrics Of Fury; Eric B Never Scared; Just A Beat; Put Your Hands Together; To The Listeners; No Competition; The R; Musical Massacre; Beats For The Listeners.*

★ First released 1988
★ UK peak chart position: did not chart
★ USA peak chart position: 22
★ Previous Top 1000 position: 1998 (482): 1994 (952)

980 LIVE THROUGH THIS ↓ Hole

With the world and its dog besotted with the latest hybrid of punk rock (grunge) and its finest exponents (Nirvana), *Live Through This* almost slipped through the net. With Kurt Cobain dead a week before its release, journalists were more interested in his widow's reactions than her music. Little wonder – it was hard to overlook lyrics such as 'With a bullet, number one/Kill the family, save the son' ('Jennifer's Boy'). Courtney Love had just released the best album of her career. *Live Through This* saw her songwriting develop accessibility and personality. Most songs provided a happy halfway house between brash pop and blazing guitar workouts. There are some truly startling lyrical images that make *Live Through This* a thrilling experience.

» Tracks: *Violet; Miss World; Plump; Asking For It; Jennifer's Body; Doll Parts; Credit In The Straight World; Softer, Softest; She Walks On Me; I Think That I Would Die; Gutless; Rock Star.*

★ First released 1994
★ UK peak chart position: 13
★ USA peak chart position: 52
★ Previous Top 1000 position: 1998 (468): 1994 (–)

981 SURRENDER ↑
The Chemical Brothers

Dance music definitely, but of such broad crossover appeal that even people who don't like dance will warm to this album. Tom Rowlands and Edward Simons are unlikely stars, but their recorded output represents the pinnacle of the 'big beat' style of dance music. They are constantly sought after by others to add their quality stamp to their projects, and several of those artists repay the favour on *Surrender*. Guest vocals come courtesy of the lead vocalists of New Order, Primal Scream and Mazzy Star, but it is the Brothers who are in absolute control. One of 1999's highlights, in any genre.

» Tracks: *Music: Response; Under The Influence; Out Of Control; Orange Wedge; Let Forever Be; The Sunshine Underground; Asleep From Day; Got Glint?; Hey Boy Hey Girl; Surrender; Dream On.*

★ First released 1999
★ UK peak chart position: 1
★ USA peak chart position: 32
★ Previous Top 1000 position: 1998 (–): 1994 (–)

982 CENTRAL RESERVATION ↑
Beth Orton

The third album in what promises to be a career worth following. Orton has captivated many listeners with her unaffected personality and her needle sharp observations. This is a fuller sounding recording than her excellent *Trailer Park*. Both were nominated for several awards, with Orton winning a BRIT in March 2000 despite facing fierce competition from some formidable chart divas. Tim Buckley and Tim Hardin spring to mind when listening to the evocative and beautifully arranged 'Sweetest Decline'. From acoustic folk ballads to trip-hop, her captivating voice, creamy with a slightly rough edge, is the one defining link. Her lyrics should also be given the close attention they merit.

» Tracks: *Stolen Car; Sweetest Decline; Couldn't Cause Me Harm; So Much More; Pass In Time; Central Reservation (Original Version); Stars All Seem To Weep; Love Like Laughter; Blood Red River; Devil Song; Feel To Believe; Central Reservation (The Then Again Version).*

★ First released 1999
★ UK peak chart position: 17
★ USA peak chart position: 110
★ Previous Top 1000 position: 1998 (–): 1994 (–)

983 CORE ↑
Stone Temple Pilots

It is bizarre to think that after just two listens to the opening track 'Dead & Bloated', days later you could find yourself in any situation singing 'I am smelling like the rose that somebody gave me on my birthday deathbed'. Not quite Gershwin-style sentiment, but haunting nonetheless. The Stone Temple Pilots are irritatingly good, reeling off memorable choruses that the listener cannot resist even on crudely ironic fare such as 'Sex Type Thing'. Although this album was criticised at the time for sounding too similar to Pearl Jam and Nirvana, the massive guitar chords, drums played with lead weights and Scott Weiland's deep expressive voice in hindsight capture grunge at its best.

» Tracks: *Dead & Bloated; Sex Type Thing; Wicked Garden; No Memory; Sin; Naked Sunday; Creep; Piece Of Pie; Plush; Wet My Bed; Crackerman; Where The River Goes.*

★ First released 1992
★ UK peak chart position: 27
★ USA peak chart position: 3
★ Previous Top 1000 position: 1998 (–): 1994 (–)

984 PAUL SIMON ↑
Paul Simon

This was very much a 'test the breeze' album for Paul Simon following his parting with Art Garfunkel. Having to follow *Bridge Over Troubled Water* must have been intimidating, and even though this sold one tenth as many copies the quality is the same. Simon has always had a knack for writing catchy pop, exemplified here by 'Mother and Child Reunion' and 'Me and Julio Down By The Schoolyard'. Pleasant though these two songs are they cannot hold a candle to the outstanding 'Run That Body Down' and the delicate 'Everything Put Together Falls Apart', two examples of the type of sweet confessional that Simon is a master of.

» Tracks: *Mother and Child Reunion; Duncan; Everything Put Together Falls Apart; Run That Body Down; Armistice Day; Me and Julio Down By The School Yard; Peace Like A River; Papa Hobo; Hobo's Blues; Paranoia Blues; Congratulations.*

★ First released 1972
★ UK peak chart position: 1
★ USA peak chart position: 4
★ Previous Top 1000 position: 1998 (–): 1994 (–)

985 OKLAHOMA! ↓
Various

Twelve years after it opened on Broadway, Richard Rodgers and Oscar Hammerstein II's first musical burst onto the screen in the Todd-AO widescreen process, with a fine cast that included Gordon MacRae, Shirley Jones, Charlotte Greenwood, Rod Steiger, Gloria Grahame, Gene Nelson and James Whitmore. All the marvellous songs heard in the stage production are here, with the highlights being 'Oh, What A Beautiful Mornin'', 'The Surrey With The Fringe On Top', 'People Will Say We're In Love', and the rousing title number. A spell of over four years in the US charts (four weeks at number 1) says it all.

» Tracks: *Oklahoma Overture; Oh, What A Beautiful Morning; Surrey With The Fringe On Top; Kansas City; I Can't Say No; Many A New Day; People Will Say We're In Love; Poor Jud Is Dead; Out Of My Dreams; Farmer and The Cowman; All Or Nothin'; Oklahoma.*

★ First released 1955
★ UK peak chart position: 4
★ USA peak chart position: 1
★ Previous Top 1000 position: 1998 (380): 1994 (81)

986 SUPERFLY ↓
Curtis Mayfield

As leader of the Impressions, Curtis Mayfield brought a lyricism to soul music. As a solo artist he chronicled society's travails and street culture, which in turn inspired *Superfly*, the soundtrack to one of the era's most popular 'blaxploitation' movies. Mayfield's gift for combining light melody with simple, but chilling, wordplay ensured that the album stood up on its own terms without visual images, and its lynchpin selection, 'Freddie's Dead', was a million-selling single in its own right. Sympathetic but not sentimental, *Superfly* set new standards for soul music.

» Tracks: *Little Child Runnin' Wild; Pusherman; Freddie's Dead; Junkie Chase; Give Me Your Love; Eddie You Should Know Better; No Thing On Me; Think; Superfly.*

★ First released 1972
★ UK peak chart position: 26
★ USA peak chart position: 1
★ Previous Top 1000 position: 1998 (359): 1994 (596)

987 THIS IS MY TRUTH TELL ME YOURS ↑
Manic Street Preachers

The Manic Street Preachers still couldn't get arrested in the biggest market in the world, the USA. Elsewhere they are huge, and in the UK they are probably more popular than U2. Wales has taken over from Ireland as the prime location for adventurous indie rock bands, although it is by refining their brand of angry pop, left wing politics and power to the people lyrics that the Manics have become so successful. It is not surprising that rich, melody-laden epics such as 'The Everlasting' and 'You Stole The Sun From My Heart' have captured the hearts of so many. Now back to America; why can't they get a foot in the door? Any suggestions?

» Tracks: *The Everlasting; If You Tolerate This Your Children Will Be Next; You Stole The Sun From My Heart; Ready For Drowning; Tsunami; My Little Empire; I'm Not Working; You're Tender and You're Tired; Born A Girl; Be Natural; Black Dog On My Shoulder; Nobody Loved You; S.Y.M.M..*

★ First released 1998
★ UK peak chart position: 1
★ USA peak chart position: did not chart
★ Previous Top 1000 position: 1998 (–): 1994 (–)

988 FLAMING PIE ↑
Paul McCartney

Who would have expected Macca after many years of indifferent to poor albums to come back with such a storming record. Hear the rejuvenated McCartney duelling with Steve Miller on the excellent rocker 'Used To Be Bad' and sense his own satisfaction at writing such new gems as 'Young Boy' and 'The Song We Were Singing'. This is all the more remarkable because during the making of this album he knew that Linda's cancer was terminal. And therefore the saddest and most important song is 'Somedays', complete with a weepy string octet. Now that's a song from a chap who *really* loved his wife.

» Tracks: *The Song We Were Singing; The World Tonight; If You Wanna; Somedays; Young Boy; Calico Skies; Flaming Pie; Heaven On A Sunday; Used To Be Bad; Souvenir; Little Willow; Really Love You; Beautiful Night; Great Day.*

★ First released 1997
★ UK peak chart position: 2
★ USA peak chart position: 2
★ Previous Top 1000 position: 1998 (–): 1994 (–)

989 LIVE 1966: THE ROYAL ALBERT HALL CONCERT ↑
Bob Dylan

Bootlegged for years, this brilliantly ramshackle album is a vital document in the history of popular music. Even Dylan doubters should not fail to see the greatness in being able to move between folk and rock with equal passion. The folkies in Manchester's Free Trade Hall moaned and walked out, the fans, open-mouthed, stayed, and have done so for more than 30 years. As a stoned Dylan says at the intro to 'I Don't Believe You (She Acts Like We Never Have Met)'; 'this is called I don't believe you, it used to be like that, and now it goes like this'. In one sentence he dealt a devastating blow for musical change; listen to the nervous titters after the delivery. A monumental record.

❱❱ Tracks: *She Belongs To Me; Fourth Time Around; Visions of Johanna; It's All Over Now, Baby Blue; Desolation Row; Just Like A Woman; Mr. Tambourine Man; Tell Me Momma; I Don't Believe You (She Acts Like We Never Have Met); Baby, Let Me Follow You Down; Just Like Tom Thumb's Blues; Leopard-Skin Pill-Box Hat; One Too Many Mornings; Ballad Of A Thin Man; Like Rolling Stone.*

★ First released 1998
★ UK peak chart position: 19
★ USA peak chart position: 31
★ Previous Top 1000 position: 1998 (–): 1994 (–)

990 ATOM HEART MOTHER ↑
Pink Floyd

When this album was first previewed live some music critics thought that by experimenting with orchestrated art-rock Pink Floyd had strayed too far from the wacky psyched-out Syd Barrett days. As a result this album became more famous for the picture of the cow on the cover. Everybody knew about it, it was in every vinyl collection, but few dared listen. Now of course it marks an important developmental stage in the back catalogue of one of the most successful bands of all time. The only real problem is that you have to wait 10 minutes and 48 seconds before you hear a bloody guitar!

❱❱ Tracks: *Atom Heart Mother; If; Summer '68; Fat Old Sun; Alan's Psychedelic Breakfast.*

★ First released 1970
★ UK peak chart position: 1
★ USA peak chart position: 55
★ Previous Top 1000 position: 1998 (–): 1994 (–)

991 SPEAK & SPELL ↑
Depeche Mode

I suppose if this book has to feature electronic music from the early 80s then Depeche Mode are the most acceptable representatives of what is a much-maligned genre. Nearly twenty years on it is hard to appreciate that the simple electronic sounds coming out of Basildon, Essex helped influence the textured dance music of the late 90s. *Speak & Spell* (the CD reissue with five bonus tracks is listed here) is a difficult album to listen to today, coming across as charming, quaint and lacking in guts. These days Depeche Mode is a fully-fledged stadium rock act, with the onstage reel to reel a distant memory from the early 80s.

❱❱ Tracks: *New Life; I Sometimes Wish I Was Dead; Puppets; Boys Say Go!; Nodisco; What's Your Name?; Photographic; Tora! Tora! Tora!; Big Muff; Any Second Now (Voices); Just Can't Get Enough; Dreaming Of Me; Ice Machine; Shout; Any Second Now; Just Can't Get Enough (Schizo).*

★ First released 1981
★ UK peak chart position: 10
★ USA peak chart position: 192
★ Previous Top 1000 position: 1998 (–): 1994 (–)

992 3+3 ↓
The Isley Brothers

The day Ernie Isley picked up his electric guitar with a fuzzbox connected was the day the Isleys' fortunes changed for the better. The slick, besuited Tamla/Motown soul was replaced by funkier stuff with some truly spectacular guitar solos. 'That Lady' is present here in its full-length glory, as is the lengthy workout on 'Summer Breeze'. Ernie became a guitar hero with those two tracks and spawned a host of second-rate imitators. Other highlights are 'The Highways Of My Life' and James Taylor's 'Don't Let Me Be Lonely Tonight'. The version of the Doobie Brothers' 'Listen To The Music' can be dispensed with. Almost a rock album, but not quite.

❱❱ Tracks: *That Lady; Don't Let Me Be Lonely Tonight; If You Were There; You Walk Your Way; Listen To The Music; What It Comes Down To; Sunshine (Go Away Today); Summer Breeze; The Highways Of My Life.*

★ First released 1973
★ UK peak chart position: did not chart
★ USA peak chart position: 8
★ Previous Top 1000 position: 1998 (385): 1994 (718)

993 THE GOOD WILL OUT ↑
Embrace

For some reason the vast amount of coverage Embrace receive in the music press has brought out an unhealthy amount of professional snipers. This debut album, eagerly awaited following an acclaimed series of singles and EPs, had to be good to live up to the hype. In the end, *The Good Will Out* was a notable debut but was certainly not the expected *Sgt. Pepper's Lonely Hearts Club Band*. The critical griping centred on Danny McNamara's vocals which are a shade off sharp throughout. On songs such as 'All You Good Good People', where McNamara's vocal is buried in the mix, this is not a problem. Where he is vulnerable to attack is on the more restrained 'My Weakness Is None Of Your Business' and 'Come Back To What You Know'.

» Tracks: *Intro; All You Good Good People; My Weakness Is None Of Your Business; Come Back To What You Know; One Big Family; Higher Sights; Retread; I Want The World; You've Got To Say Yes; Fireworks; The Last Gas; That's All Changed Forever; Now You're Nobody; The Good Will Out.*

★ First released 1998
★ UK peak chart position: 1
★ USA peak chart position: did not chart
★ Previous Top 1000 position: 1998 (–): 1994 (–)

994 SOMEDAY MY PRINCE WILL COME ↓ Miles Davis

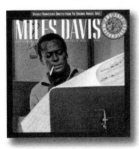

Quintessential Miles Davis, laid-back, confident and spacious, together with, for many, his best musical unit of John Coltrane, Wynton Kelly, Paul Chambers and Philly Joe Jones, further augmented by Hank Mobley (tenor) and Jimmy Cobb. Although Coltrane was only guesting, his strong spirit is felt and his vignettes are faultless. The title track builds beautifully until a wonderful drone-like, booming bass line closes it. The other stand-out tracks are 'Pfrancing', with some glorious light fingers from Kelly and on 'Teo' the groove is very much in the *Kind Of Blue* mould. This is an exceptional Miles Davis album that often gets overlooked.

» Tracks: *Someday My Prince Will Come; Old Folks; Pfrancing; Drad-Dog; Teo; I Thought About You.*

★ First released 1961
★ UK peak chart position: did not chart
★ USA peak chart position: did not chart
★ Previous Top 1000 position: 1998 (966): 1994 (505)

995 DIAMOND DOGS ↑
David Bowie

'This ain't rock 'n' roll, this is genocide' shouts the thin white duke, even though he clearly loved the madness of it all. Since the creation of Ziggy Stardust Bowie had remained on a non-stop trip that was still in full flight as this album was being recorded. Glam rock's credibility was only kept alive by the extravagance and quality of songs such as 'Sweet Thing', Diamond Dogs' and the unforgettable 'Rebel Rebel'. 'Your face is a mess, you've torn your dress' he sang, riding a creative wave that nearly killed him. We were the fortunate beneficiaries, viewing riff-laden pop at its best through the safety of our Celestion speakers.

» Tracks: *Future Legend; Diamond Dogs; Sweet Thing; Candidate; Sweet Thing (Reprise); Rebel Rebel; Rock 'N' Roll With Me; We Are The Dead; 1984; Big Brother; Chant Of The Ever Circling Skeletal Family.*

★ First released 1974
★ UK peak chart position: 1
★ USA peak chart position: 5
★ Previous Top 1000 position: 1998 (–): 1994 (–)

996 FREEDOM ↓
Neil Young

During the 80s Neil Young managed to change his ways and confuse his audience. The last major album before this was the R&B-influenced *This Note's For You* – and just when everyone least expected it, he made a dynamite 'regular' Neil Young album. *Freedom* was the beginning of a run of acclaimed albums that now put Young up on a pedestal with Bob Dylan and Van Morrison as one of the all-time great singing troubadours. The difference, however, is that Young still rocks, and he likes his guitar to sound loud and dirty. *Freedom* was a restatement of his immense varied talent, but with enough new chunky chord structures to make his familiar patterns sound exciting and different.

» Tracks: *Rockin' In The Free World; Crime In The City (Sixty To Zero Part 1); Don't Cry; Hangin' On A Limb; Eldorado; The Ways Of Love; Someday; On Broadway; Wrecking Ball; No More; Too Far Gone; Rockin' In The Free World.*

★ First released 1989
★ UK peak chart position: 17
★ USA peak chart position: 35
★ Previous Top 1000 position: 1998 (409): 1994 (–)

997 NO SECRETS ↑
Carly Simon

Before she married James Taylor and they became the most photographed couple in rock there was a time when Carly Simon could sit down quietly and write songs. Some of her all-time greats are on this album including the alleged musical biography of Warren Beatty, 'You're So Vain'. True or false, the mud has stuck to poor Warren for many years. Equally impressive is the track 'We Have No Secrets' which deals with the problems past relationships cause in a current affair. The poignant line after the innocent 'we have no secrets' is the killer; 'sometimes I wish that I never knew some of the secrets of yours'.

▶ Tracks: *The Right Thing To Do; The Carter Family; You're So Vain; His Friends Are More Than Fond Of Robin; We Have No Secrets; Embrace Me, You Child; Waited So Long; It Was So Easy; Night Owl; When You Close Your Eyes.*

★ First released 1972
★ UK peak chart position: 3
★ USA peak chart position: 1
★ Previous Top 1000 position: 1998 (–): 1994 (–)

998 STILL WARM ↑
John Scofield

John Scofield has really come of age since this album was released, winning awards and nominations galore, and in doing so has become one of the world's leading jazz guitarists. His popularity increased with this record as his funk and rock influences shone through. 'Techno' is the type of music we might have imagined Jimi Hendrix playing, had he lived. The title track is both romantic and highly erotic, the rhythm is almost Latin and the song builds continuously as the musical scale ascends, yet the listener is completely fooled because the climax is only one octave. This is a fantastic and funky jazz record which purists will hate.

▶ Tracks: *Techno; Still Warm; High and Mighty; Protocol; Rule Of Thumb; Picks and Pans; Gil B 643.*

★ First released 1987
★ UK peak chart position: did not chart
★ USA peak chart position: did not chart
★ Previous Top 1000 position: 1998 (–): 1994 (802)

999 THE TRINITY SESSION ↑
Cowboy Junkies

The ghostly quality of this record is probably due to the fact that it was recorded in a church, and not the layers of echo and reverb. Considering the shoestring budget it was recorded on this is a remarkable session. The sloppy do be do be do be do be do style that permeates most of their material is more compelling than annoying here. After two or three tracks the listener is won over by the band's lethargic swagger. The stand-out track is 'Blue Moon Revisited (Song For Elvis)', more Kentucky than Richard Rogers' Broadway. A special mention also for their spooky interpretation of the Velvet Underground's 'Sweet Jane'.

▶ Tracks: *Mining For Gold; Misguided Angel; Blue Moon Revisited (Song For Elvis); I Don't Get It; I'm So Lonesome I Could Cry; To Love Is To Bury; 200 More Miles; Dreaming My Dreams With You; Working On A Building; Sweet Jane; Postcard Blues; Walking After Midnight.*

★ First released 1988
★ UK peak chart position: did not chart
★ USA peak chart position: 26
★ Previous Top 1000 position: 1998 (–): 1994 (–)

1000 TODD ↑
Todd Rundgren

The excellent reissue program recently under-taken by Essential Records has allowed critics to reappraise this talented artist's 70s oeuvre. As a cult favourite Rundgren has few peers, but do his albums really stand up twenty years on? Some do and some don't, with *Todd* just about slipping into the former category. Despite some questionable electronic filler, enough of Rundgren's trademark melodic genius shine through to make this an essential purchase. And so much of his work has influenced others, with 'An Elpee's Worth Of Toons' surely giving the Barenaked Ladies their start in life. This retiring genius now has his impressive back catalogue in print, so don't pass it by.

▶ Tracks: *How About A Little Fanfare?; I Think You Know; The Spark Of Life; An Elpee's Worth Of Toons; A Dream Goes On Forever; Lord Chancellor's Nightmare Song; Drunken Blue Rooster; The Last Ride; Everybody's Going To Heaven/King Kong Reggae; No.1 Lowest Common Denominator; Useless Begging; Sidewalk Cafe; Izzat Love?; Heavy Metal Kids; In and Out The Chakras We Go (Formerly: Shaft Goes To Outer Space); Don't You Ever Learn?; Sons Of 1984.*

★ First released 1974
★ UK peak chart position: did not chart
★ USA peak chart position: 54
★ Previous Top 1000 position: 1998 (–): 1994 (–)

An All-Time Top 100 Singles

The most opinionated list in the book. I will not even begin to defend the absence of Chuck Berry, Abba, Queen, the Smiths, Frank Sinatra, and so on. This is the choice of the author, as of today. The fact is that 'Mr Tambourine Man' still does make me shiver, and a new song, like the New Radicals one, has a similar effect. Time will tell of course. Tomorrow, at least half the list could be replaced.

The criteria was that they had to have been officially issued as a single in the UK. Only one choice per artist (except the Beatles, Bob Dylan and the Byrds, because it's my list and I'm in charge).

This is a taster for the forthcoming *All-Time Top 1000 Singles*, which is being prepared as I write. Trust me with this list, it would make a spiffing 5-CD set for the longest of car journeys. Oh, and before you skin spotters contact me, the list is made up of 26 black and 74 white, 0 blue.

The UK/USA mix is 51 USA and 47 UK (2 Jamaica).

The decades represented are; 3 from the 50s, 56 from the 60s, 10 from the 70s, 11 from the 80s, and 20 from the 90s. And yes, naturally, there are more 60s hits than anything else. It could not have happened to a better decade. Letters of disagreement to the usual address please.

1 The Byrds – Mr Tambourine Man (1965)
Still a rush to flatten the hairs on the forearm every time it is played on the radio. McGuinn's 12-string opener has to be the definitive. Four of the five original Byrds sound like sweet little angels on the vocals.
● *Best line:* 'Take me for a trip upon your magic swirling ship'.

2 Spencer Davis Group – Gimme Some Loving (1966)
Don't get fooled by the horrible version played on radio all over the world. That is the re-recording with unnecessary girly chorus, extra clunky percussion and pointless piano. You only need Hammond and bass, just like this original.
● *Best line:* 'Well my head's exploding and a-floating to sound, too much is happening cos you're around'.

3 Bob Dylan – Like A Rolling Stone (1965)
Another showcase for the Hammond organ, this time played by Al Kooper. His frills add to Dylan's first masterpiece of the modern rock era. Truth, pathos, irony and life, dusted off in a few minutes.
● *Best line:* 'Ah you never turned around to see the frowns on the jugglers and the clowns, when they all did tricks for you'.

4 Scarlet Party – 101 Dam-Nations (1982)
It reached 44 in the UK chart. One of the greatest power pop singles, it should have been an anthemic monster number one. It sounds like the Beatles, it was on their label. Any chance of Parlophone reissuing this on CD please?
● *Best line:* 'One hundred and one damnations, marching off to find a war'.

5 Booker T and The MGs – Green Onions (1962)
Although the Hammond organ once again features prominently, the real clincher is the fruity sound it makes in combination with Steve Cropper's Telecaster guitar. An incredible, unrepeatable piece of music, copied by millions but never remotely challenged.

6 The Kingsmen – Louie Louie (1963)
It doesn't matter what they are singing about. Richard Berry may have taken the lyrics to the grave with him, but he left us with this magnificent opus of sound. To think the Beach Boys did it as well. Take another listen to the drummer, he comes in at least half an hour late.
● *Decipherable line:* 'OK, let's give it to em right now'.

7 The Beatles – A Hard Day's Night (1964)
Jannng goes the opening chord as the moptops effortlessly launch into this perfectly constructed song. And Lennon really sounds sincere when he sings 'you know I work all day, to get you money, to buy you things'.
● *Best line:* 'I should be sleeping like a log'.

8 The Kinks – Waterloo Sunset (1967)
Was it Terry Stamp meeting Julie Christie on Hungerford railway bridge or not? Either way, millions of other couples have experienced the same sunset. Ray Davies' most evocative song, beautifully opened by Pete Quaife's rumbling bass.
● *Best line:* 'Chilly chilly is evening time, Waterloo sunset's fine'.

9 Big Youth – Concrete Jungle (1973)
Never has reggae bass sounded so deep and fluffy. Like a punch in the stomach with a candy floss. DJ Youth has an equally impressive voice. 'Screaming Target' is the b-side. Amazingly good.
● *Best line:* 'If you want to go to Zion, then you've got to be an irie ites lion'.

10 The Beatles – Strawberry Fields Forever (1967)
Nothing original in picking this, other than it really is a piece of music that was forty years ahead of its time, but that's 'nothing to get hung about'. In seven years time we will have caught up with it. Sweet little 'Penny Lane' on the other side.
● *Best line:* 'No one, I think, is in my tree'.

11 James Brown – **Papa's Got A Brand New Bag** (1965)

Split into parts one and two. Unfortunately the Dansette could not turn it over, and manually it was a pain. Apart from Brown's incredible delivery the brass section's 'duddle dada' is priceless.
● *Best line:* 'He's doin' the joik, he's doin' the fly, don't play and cheat cos you know he ain't shy'.

12 The Byrds – **Eight Miles High** (1966)

The first song that ever threatened to wobble the speakers off the shelf. Hillman's opening bass is extraordinary because you can hear it rattle the drummer's cymbals, but if you think that is good wait till McGuinn's solo comes along. Space Rock never bettered.
● *Best line:* 'Rain grey town, known for it's sound, in places small faces unbound'.

13 Buffalo Springfield – **For What It's Worth** (1967)

If only Stills would revert to this version at live gigs instead of the 'woah yeah, what's that sound' funky groove. This after all is a beautiful, gentle and sensitive song. It deserves to be treated as it was intended.
● *Best line:* 'Paranoia strikes deep, into your mind it will creep'.

14 Jimi Hendrix – **The Wind Cries Mary** (1967)

Only Hendrix could have sung, 'the traffic lights turn blue' and made the listener believe it possible. The guitar solo ending, mixed with Redding's three bass notes (glung glung, glung), is breathtaking.
● *Best line:* 'A broom is drearily sweeping up the pieces of yesterday's life'.

15 Sugar Pie DeSanto – **Soulful Dress** (1964)

Released in the UK thanks to Dusty Springfield's crusading. Sugar Pie sounds like she really knows how to enjoy her Saturday night, and still remain in charge of the proceedings. Raw 60s R&B at its best.
● *Best line:* 'Don't you girls go a getting jealous if I round up all of your fellas'.

16 Lovin' Spoonful – **You Didn't Have To Be So Nice** (1965)

The unforgettable guitar sound on this, after the deliberately sloppy drum opening, is the descending 'gling gling gling'. The great John Sebastian showering us with his romantic happiness.
● *Best line:* 'Today said the time was right for me to follow you'.

17 Dusty Springfield – **Some Of Your Loving** (1965)

A gorgeous paused piano and slushy strings opens strongly with Dusty sounding like she's singing in another room. One of many beautiful Goffin and King songs she made her own.
● *Best line:* 'Now I'm not a jealous child, my demands are mild, just give me some of your loving'.

18 Blur – **She's So High** (1990)

The first single from the pride of Colchester. When Damon finally sings after the gloriously long Beatlesque intro you can believe that he wants to 'crawl over her'. A much overlooked single in their catalogue.
● *Best line*, not surprisingly: 'She's so high, I want to crawl over her'.

19 Strawberry Alarm Clock – **Incense and Peppermints** (1967)

The first *Austin Powers* movie gave this a much deserved showcase. The Mamas and The Papas' style harmony intro, beautiful cheesy organ, handclaps and bells made this, with 'Paper Sun' the most evocative pop song of 1967.
● *Best line:* 'Who cares what games we chose, little to win, but nothing to lose'.

20 Etta James – **At Last/I Just Want To Make Love To You** (1961)

There is not enough space to get to the incredible b-side, but the original hit featured both. Her soulful version of this ancient classic by Harry Warren is the best. The swirly strings are wonderful, and she sounds convinced she really has found her man.
● *Best line:* 'I found a thrill to rest my chin to, a thrill that I have never known'.

21 The Beach Boys – **Good Vibrations** (1966)

Try as you might, there is no denying that this familiar chestnut still sounds ridiculously good and unbelievably fresh. So many different bits to choose from in Brian Wilson's greatest achievement.
● *Best line:* 'I don't know what where but she sends me there'.

22 Bruce Channel – **Hey! Baby** (1962)

This slice of pop R&B has been cited as having the greatest harmonica intro ever, but spare a thought for Bruce, he sang the song like an angel. As good as 'the' Delbert McClinton solo is, Channel's voice is as frail as a lost sheep yet as rich as a farmer.
● *Best line:* 'Come on baby give me a whirl, I wanna know if you'll be my girl'.

23 Muddy Waters – **Mannish Boy** (1955)

Often confused with Bo Diddley's 'I'm A Man' because of the similar riff; dada da dah. This is the real dog's undercarriage. A piece of blues that has influenced thousands and been ingloriously ripped off by millions.
● *Best line:* 'I'm a rolling stone, I'm a mayn, I'm a hoochie coochie mayn'.

24 Cream – **Badge** (1969)

Glung glung glung orommpumpumpumpummp. That's the intro in my head. It has to be one of the best openers of all time, and combined with a classic Clapton vocal the lyrical nonsense almost slips by. Almost.

● *Best line:* 'And you'd better pick yourself up off the ground, before they bring the curtain down'.

25 Tommy Tucker – **Hi-Heel Sneakers** (1964)

Featuring a delicate guitar intro that almost gets lost and which radio presenters hate because it's so quiet and leaves a painful few seconds before the incredible vocal finally arrives. And there really were wighats and high heeled sneakers, apparently.

● *Best line:* 'Gonna wear some boxing gloves, in case some fool might wanna fight'.

26 Bob Dylan – **Positively Fourth Street** (1965)

The second great Al Kooper organ trill, and another gigantic anthem that made listening to pirate radio in 1965 so rewarding. Dylan and the Byrds dominated from spring to autumn, and at the time who cared what they were singing about?

● *Best line:* 'When you know as well as me, you'd rather see me paralysed'.

27 Aretha Franklin – **Baby I Love You** (1967)

Quite apart from Aretha's foxiest vocal, the support from the musicians is incredible. The way Steve Cropper chops his guitar throughout adds great sexuality to the song.

● *Best line:* 'I love ya, I love ya, I love ya, I love ya, baby I love you'.

28 The Hollies – **I Can't Let Go** (1966)

Another amazing intro, this time it is the treble-laden bass guitar. Chungchunchungchunchungchun, 'woh I try . . .' Allan Clarke's best vocal, and little Graham Nash hits the highest note ever known on the 'weeeeeeeeeeees'.

● *Best line:* 'But the thought of you gone makes me want to hold on'.

29 The Who – **I Can See For Miles** (1967)

And another killer 5 seconds. This time John Entwhistle turns up the bass for one extended note, prior to Daltrey letting rip on what many think is his finest vocal. Moon's drums are also amazing.

● *Best line:* 'Well here's a poke at you, you're gonna choke on it too'.

30 Elvis Costello – **Pills and Soap** (1983)

Any anger and frustration felt against the prevailing government led by Margaret Thatcher was none better spat out than by Elvis. His subtle denunciation is untouchable.

● *Best line:* 'There are ashtrays of emotion for the fag ends of the aristocracy'.

31 The Pretty Things – **Come See Me** (1966)

Without labouring the point, this is the greatest bass intro of any song, ever. So loud and distorted it delivers a boxing glove through the speaker cloth. This had to be a mistake, as the levels are suddenly turned down for Phil May's voice to cut through.

● *Best line:* 'If you need a hug babe, come see me babe'.

32 The Sex Pistols – **Pretty Vacant** (1977)

There were any number to choose from, but the clash and clamour of this particular little gem is the best starter for the punk single to end all punk singles. To think there were those who said they couldn't play.

● *Best line,* of course: 'We're so pretty, oh so pretty, we're vaaaycunt'.

33 Bruce Springsteen – **Born To Run** (1975)

As the upstroke of his Telecaster meets Phil Spector, this is likely to remain Springsteen's anthem. Although not a song that would slip on the turntable through choice, when it comes out of the radio nobody can fail to be moved.

● *Best line:* 'Just wrap your legs round these velvet rims, and strap your hands cross my engines'.

34 Nirvana – **Smells Like Teen Spirit** (1991)

Once familiar with this incredible song it remains a joy for the listener to still anticipate the change when it kicks in after the first verse. Very few heavy rock songs sound so inspired and exciting after repeated play. This has it all and melody.

● *Best line:* 'Life is stupid and contagious, here we are now, entertain us'.

35 The O'Jays – **Backstabbers** (1972)

If the soul of the 60s belonged to Detroit, the 70s belonged to Philadelphia, and notably the superlative Gamble and Huff arrangements. Swirling violins, a hint of guitar and a timeless vocal sound that matched the Four Tops.

● *Best line:* 'What can I do to get on the right track, I wish they'd take some of these knives outta my back'.

36 Duane Eddy – **Because They're Young** (1960)

This magnificent instrumental from the movie of the same name was adopted in 1965 by dear ol' Johnnie Walker, the finest of all the pirate radio DJs. Its familiarity masks the beauty of the song, as Duane hardly gets a look in for a quick twang from behind the lush orchestration.

37 Fleetwood Mac – **Need Your Love So Bad** (1968)

Never had Peter Green played so sparsely, and yet he managed to eke an ocean of sound and emotion from so few notes. On top of that his vocal delivery is at his pleading best, and then producer Mike Vernon added some gorgeous strings.

● *Best line:* 'Or write it on a piece of paper baby, so it can be read to me'.

38 The Temptations – **Ain't Too Proud To Beg** (1966)

Recorded at the height of Motown, it is almost impossible to select just one song or even one performer. The richest vein of music, ever. Writers Whitfield and Holland were dashing off songs with embarrassing ease.

● *Best line:* 'If I have to beg, plead for your sympathy, I don't mind, cos you mean that much to me'.

39 Everly Brothers – **Cathy's Clown** (1960)

The opening thunderous drum roll of this opus was this writer's first true love. The moment that something (in this case a song, not a woman) often moved him to tears. The euphoric happiness the song delivers completely masks the sad lyrics.

● *Best line:* 'Doncha think it's kinda sad, that you're treating me so bad, or don't you even care'.

40 John Lee Hooker – **Dimples** (1964)

The greatest living bluesman (I refuse to accept he can ever pop his clogs) gave the Animals a run for their money in 1964. Their blues was one thing, but when Hooker opened his mouth it was something else – something dirtier and deeper.

● *Best line:* 'You got dimples in yo jaw, you're my babe, I got my eyes on you'.

41 Marvin Gaye – **Let's Get It On** (1973)

Gaye's voice duels with the understated wah-wah guitar from the opening note. Nobody has ever quite put sexual frustration on record quite like this man. This and 'Sexual Healing' are two perfect examples.

● *Best line* begins with: 'There's nothing wrong with me'.

42 Them – **Baby Please Don't Go** (1965)

One of the most familiar openings of all time gave us a shot of something that we now know as Van Morrison. As distinctive as his voice is on this, spare a minute for those fine lads who followed him across the Irish Sea. The musical texture they create is equal to Van's superb delivery.

● *Best line:* 'Fourbeadoll, fourbeadoll, fourbeadoll gecha way down here, anmakyawolkalong, baby please don't go'.

43 Fatboy Slim – **The Rockafeller Skank** (1998)

One of only a handful of 'irritating' songs that refuse to irritate. Any time, any place, this great piece of mood changing nonsense will do the trick. To think that the elongated 'doinnng' bit near the end used to be done by flicking your wooden school rule on the desk.

● *Best line*, of course: 'Check it out now, the funk soul brother'.

44 Robert Wyatt – **Shipbuilding** (1983)

Elvis Costello wrote it to express his anger over the pointless stupidity of the Falklands war. Nobody however, could ever have sung it like Wyatt. Delicate and pleading, he almost hides his cynicism but nails political dogma in the most subtle way.

● *Best line:* 'With all the will in the world, diving for dear life, when we could be diving for pearls'.

45 Love – **Alone Again Or** (1967)

Surely the most surprising record never to top the charts. Everyone has heard the song, but for many, Love remain a four letter word of endearment. Just for the record they also did '7 & 7 Is' and the theme tune to Cliff Michelmore's travel programme on the BBC.

● *Best line:* 'You know that I could be in love with almost everyone'.

46 Brenda Holloway – **Every Little Bit Hurts** (1964)

Once upon a time, in the first part of the 60s, white boys and girls introduced black music to the UK for the first time. Dusty Springfield and Steve Winwood were two leading pioneers. The Spencer Davis Group single led you to the original. You never need go any further.

● *Best line:* 'Every night I cry, every night I sigh, every night I wonder why you treat me so'.

47 Oasis – **Wonderwall** (1995)

Whatever happens to the troubled Gallagher boys in the future, they have left a mark with some truly exceptional singles. Lennonesque they might be, but this is a magnificent semi-acoustic number. And the original 'Wonderwall' was George Harrison's actually.

● *Best line:* 'Backbeat the word is on the street that the fire in your heart is out'.

48 Brenda Lee – **Sweet Nuthin's** (1959)

Recent success as a mature country singer clouds the glorious past of this tiny rock 'n' roller with a concrete mixer voice. 'My baby whispers in my ear', innocent Brenda sings. 'Uhhhaaahaaahaaaahh', go the knowing female backing singers.

● *Best line:* 'Mama turned on the front porch light, said "come in daughter that's enough for tonight"'.

49 The Commodores – **Nightshift** (1985)

A song that creeps in to your psyche unnoticed. Unlike their nauseating 'Three Times A Lady', this evocative piece, notably the 12-inch extended version, is a perfect example of how 60s soul had developed by the 80s. And still Marvin and Jackie were along for the ride.

● *Best line:* 'Marvin sang of the joy of pain, he opened up our minds and I still can hear him say'.

50 The Four Seasons – **Walk Like A Man** (1963)

So loud and full of pomp, this remains a classic of 60s over-production. The high notes meet the low notes in a crescendo of lavish sound. Even the marching band drum

roll can be forgiven.
● *Best line:* 'Oh how you try, to put me down to sy-yize, telling dirty lie-yize to mah friends'.

51 Del Shannon – **Hats Off To Larry** (1961)
Poor old Del, always sang about losing his girl, breaking up and being cheated on. This is better than 'Runaway' because the trademark falsetto is just a tad more convincing. Anyway, any woman who runs off with a Larry couldn't have been much in the first place.
● *Best line:* 'It may sound cruel, but you laughed at me, when you said we were through'.

52 Otis Redding – **My Girl** (1965)
Possessive it might be, but this is still the classic example of a love song full of pride. Grittier than the Smokey Robinson original as if Otis has just swallowed a spoonful of sharp sand. Much better sung by fathers to small daughters than boy to girl.
● *Best line:* 'I got sunshine on a cloudy day'.

53 The Rolling Stones – **I Wanna Be Your Man** (1963)
Although there are dozens of classic Stones singles to adorn any collection, this little Lennon/McCartney gem reveals inner treasure. The most fluid Brian Jones slide guitar is hidden in the background, and the most incredible Wyman bass chunking along throughout in the foreground.
● *Best line*, the repeated chorus: 'Wanna be your man'.

54 Al Green – **Let's Stay Together** (1972)
Another soul singer who sounds like he has a toffee stuck in his throat. On this the good Reverend has a whole jar of them. It is however one of the best songs about unconditional love and is sung with quivering sincerity.
● *Best line:* 'Whether times are good or bad, happy or sad'.

55 The Four Tops – **Reach Out I'll Be There** (1966)
After the memorable intro there is another g-spot moment when the trombones really greet the voices at about 1 minute 4 seconds in. One of the most uplifting two minutes in the history of the world.
● *Best line:* 'I can tell the way you hang your head, you were in lurve, now you're afraid'.

56 Joy Division – **Love Will Tear Us Apart** (1980)
This song of inevitable doom is underpinned by a powerful unrelenting drum smack throughout, and Peter Hook's driving bass line, mixed with a thin organ, adds to the atmosphere. Ian Curtis' almost deadpan delivery underlines his belief in the sentiments of the lyric.
● *Best line:* 'You cry out in your sleep, all my failings are exposed'.

57 Tom Waits – **In The Neighbourhood** (1986)
The most ramshackle and sloppy single in this list. This is one of the few singles that is enhanced by a video. Normally I detest having to prop up a song with a video, but this one's sepia filmed, scruffy carnival procession, led by Tom, is overpowering.
● *Best line:* 'And the kids can't get ice cream cos the market burned down'.

58 Madness – **Our House** (1982)
Another hit that is improved by the accompanying video. Madness reached pop maturity with this entertaining and intelligent tale of ordinary lives, matched by the faultless arrangement.
● *Best line:* 'Our mum she's so houseproud, nothing ever slows her down and a mess is not allowed'.

59 Animals – **House Of The Rising Sun** (1964)
Imagine a song 4 mins 32 secs in length about a brothel. How could it ever be played on the radio, they said. The first ever single to break the barrier is still the favoured choice (along with Stairway To Heaven) as the aspiring guitarist's first song to learn.
● *Best line:* 'My mother was a tailor, sold my new blue jeans, my father was a gambler, down in New Orleans'.

60 Plastic Penny – **Everything I Am** (1967)
Another lost jewel, in the wacky and yet cruel pop world of here today and forgotten tomorrow. More famous now for its Page One label, this is a tremendous burst of intelligent, quality pop. I almost forgot to mention the pizzicato plucked piano opening.
● *Best line:* 'Got my feet on the ground, you found some good in me'.

61 The Police – **Every Breath You Take** (1983)
Few would not argue that this is Sting's masterpiece. A song that is as indelible as the power the subject has over his victim and a convincing tale of believable obsession.
● *Best line:* 'Every move you make, every vow you break, every smile you fake, every claim you stake, I'll be watching you'.

62 Barry White – **Just The Way You Are** (1978)
The perfect match. Unfashionable disco dude Barry White takes corny, sentimental Billy Joel song and turns it into a fantastic slab of acceptable slush. The voice was made for this song. The song was made for this voice.
● *Best line:* 'All of the bad times, all of the good times'.

63 The Swinging Blue Jeans – **You're No Good** (1964)
This beat combo peaked with their incredibly mature cover version of Clint Ballard's song, first recorded by Betty Everett.

Their gutsy version has great vocal presence. A song that deserved to be a number one.
- *Best line:* 'I've learned my lesson, it left a scar, and now I see how you really are'.

64 Georgie Fame – **Because I Love You** (1967)
At the time it seemed that Georgie was singing flat at the end of every line. Having learned a bit since then, it is appreciated that he was rounding off those blue notes like a jazz singer. Fame has been cruelly underrated, and this single has been completely overlooked.
- *Best line:* 'Cos darlin' you got me on a string, I'll give up everything'.

65 Summercamp – **Drawer** (1997)
Little known alternative rockers. Summercamp came to our ears thanks to the likes of vital radio stations such as XFM. A snare drum smack announces a highly commercial opus that somehow slipped the net.
- *Best line:* 'You don't care who lies to you, you've finally found something to do'.

66 Johnny Kidd – **Shakin' All Over** (1960)
The twangy guitar intro and solo, allegedly by the legendary Mick Green, has been attempted by a cast of thousands. Even Pete Townshend couldn't quite get it right. Kidd's strident vocal shines on this, the best of British rock 'n' roll, before the Beatles.
- *Best line:* 'Quivers down the backbone' to 'tremors in the thigh bone'.

67 New Radicals – **You Get What You Give** (1998)
An emphatic positive in the midst of a sea of negativity. A song that gave great hope at the dusk of the 90s. The singer sounds convinced and sincere, and the band genuinely sound happy to be alive. Ten minutes after it dropped off the charts they broke up.
- *Best line:* 'You've got the music in you, don't let go, you've got the music in you, one dance left'.

68 Lorraine Ellison – **Stay With Me Baby** (1966)
The absolute definitive version of this belter, and there have been quite a few fine attempts from Terry Reid to Ruby Turner. None come near the passion of Ellison. Clearly she was really living the song.
- *Best line:* 'No no, I can't believe, you're leaving me'.

69 Howlin' Wolf – **Smokestack Lightnin'** (1964)
Recently popularized by exposure on an advertisement. This great bluesman gave us Captain Beefheart and Tom Waits, without even knowing it. And if you analyse the title, what a great combination of word and concept.
- *Best line:* 'Why doncha hear me crying, woooohooo woooohooo'.

70 The Shadows – **Theme For Young Lovers** (1964)
Out of the dozens of instrumental hits by Britain's answer to the Ventures, none have the watery eye potential more than this Bruce Welch stunner. 'Apache' and 'FBI' were for blokes with sideburns, but this evocative arrangement appealed to the girls (and the girly blokes).

71 Aimee Mann – **I Should've Known** (1993)
With this song Mann reached out to spurned females and connected. At the same time she let us know that she ain't quite the fool. The pace and snappy lead guitar break should be a warning, not to mess with her. Infidels beware.
- *Best line:* 'I should've known, you'd betray me but without the kiss'.

72 The Supremes – **Nathan Jones** (1971)
Out of their many huge hits, this late in the day single is a minor classic. The heavily phased background was a pathetic attempt to align the Supremes with the underground scene. As great as the song was, nobody but nobody could picture them smoking reefers.
- *Best line:* 'Winter's past, spring and fall, you never wrote me, you never called'.

73 The Raspberries – **Overnight Sensation (Hit Record)** (1974)
Before the painful 'All By Myself', there was Eric Carmen's pop band. And what a storming bunch of songs they put out in a short time. This was their 'epic', with lots of changes, lifts and drops. A perfect summer record.
- *Best line:* 'And I wanna hear the record, wanna hear it on the radio'.

74 Jimmy Jones – **Good Timin'** (1960)
Following 'Handy Man' with another gigantic hit boded well for the future, it seemed. Little was ever heard from him again. The Hank Ballard song is sublime, the lyrics are, frankly, quite bonkers.
- *Most ridiculous approximate line:* 'Big toe lying by the stump post him, instead of the other way round'!

75 Robbie Williams – **She's The One** (1999)
Thank goodness Robbie rescued this Karl Wallinger song from World Party's excellent *Egyptology* album, and saved it from possible extinction. A perfect example of the art of building a beautiful song around an uncannily simple riff, and even simpler lyric.
- *Best line:* 'When you get to where you wanna go, and you know the things you wanna know.'

76 Adam Faith – **Poor Me** (1960)
Sung with a slight speech impediment and a limited vocal range, Faith's voice was the perfect foil to John Barry's magnificent plinky plonky strings. One of the shortest ever singles, it clocks in at a delightful 1 min 45 secs.

● *Best line:* 'Sorrow's leaping around my head, it's been heard and it's been said'.

77 The Zombies – **Time Of The Season** (1968)

Boom boom boom, aah, boom boom boom, aah. Bless his heart, Colin Blunstone attempts sex on record. Carping aside, this is the peak of Rod Argent and Chris White's songwriting partnership. A much deserved hit in the USA, a total flop in the UK.

● *Best line:* 'What's your name, who's your daddy, is he rich like me'.

78 Julian Lennon – **Day After Day** (1998)

Nobody was prepared to give Julian the time of day when this snuck out. A great pity because his songwriting skills had never been sharper or more mature. His debt to his father is complimentary rather than competitive. Sometimes there ain't no justice.

● *Best line:* 'Darlin' you know the winds of peace are blowing'.

79 Little Richard – **Tutti Frutti** (1957)

Is it 'awopbopaloobop awopbamboom', or not? The most famous line in all of rock 'n' roll is easier to sing than to write down. Little Richard was outrageous to look at and equally shocking to the ear. The perfect weapon and one of many essential singles from the true queen of rock.

● *Best line:* The often misspelt chorus.

80 Ian McNabb – **You Must Be Prepared To Dream** (1994)

Imagine a scouser mixed together with Crazy Horse. This is what you get from an unlikely combination. McNabb really revels in the moment, and you can sense the joy in having borrowed Neil's boys for half an hour.

● *Best line:* 'You're looking at the higher ground, you're swimming in a sea of sound, you're a chosen soul, you've got a vision'.

81 Michael Jackson – **Stranger In Moscow** (1995)

Arranged and performed to the perfectionist standards of a Stevie Wonder. Having to fight against a tide of bad publicity and mockery Jackson demonstrated that the knack of writing a really classy song had not left him. Swathed in emotion.

● *Best line:* 'How does it feel when you're alone and cold inside'.

82 Mojos – **Everything's Alright** (1964)

They came and went, leaving behind one of the best band names ever used. Little Stu James (now a Virginal music editor Stuart Slater) belted out this beat era one-off, with youthful ease. One of the few beat group songs to actually exhaust the listener.

● *Best line:* 'Oh little baby, you know I feel so good, oh little baby, I never knew I could'.

83 Teenage Fanclub – **I Don't Want Control Of You** (1997)

The fabulous Fannies get right to the heart with this mid-paced corker. Loads of chung chung chung happy chords, an inspired key change half way through, and some of the finest sentiments ever expressed.

● *Best line:* 'Don't want this love to stay the same, grow with every year'.

84 Elvis Presley – **A Mess Of Blues** (1960)

This was the last of the real Elvis. Featuring full production and the brilliant Jordanaires, this was released just before he got into the opera singing phase, which was a precursor to the appalling material that followed him around like a bad smell. It sounds like his last real sneer.

● *Best line:* 'I ain't slept a wink since Sunday, I can't eat a thing all day'.

85 XTC – **The Ballad Of Peter Pumpkinhead** (1992)

Ours it not to wonder what goes on in the head of Andy Partridge. Where it comes from nobody knows, but he can conjure up wondrous characters like Peter Pumpkinhead, who all seem believable.

● *Best line:* 'Peter merely said, any kind of love is alright'.

86 Moody Blues – **Go Now** (1964)

For about ten minutes the original Moody Blues (with Denny Laine) looked a threat to the Beatles. On *Ready Steady Go* they played like demons. Sad to say, the Bessie Banks original never had this amount of power or emotion. The piano solo still sounds good.

● *Best line:* 'Cos darlin' darlin', can't you see I want you to stay'.

87 Stereolab – **Wow and Flutter** (1994)

I have not one clue as to what she is singing about, other than 'it's not eternal', but the combination of Laetitia Sadier's Françoise Hardy-style vocal and the corny organ sound is enough to sway me over. Unbeatable in the car:

● *Best line:* 'ajestimersuizjerajunper' or something.

88 Ian Dury – **Very Personal** (1984)

Hard to believe, but this little corker failed to trouble the charts. Dury reaches low bass notes normally heard only at the bottom of a deep well. Listen out for the subtle echo on 'personal', to make the word seem very 'pers-nnal'.

● *Best line:* 'You can say I like it here, wiv my mouth right in your earole'.

89 The Dandy Warhols – **Not If You Were The Last Junkie On Earth** (1998)

With an intro that threatens to turn into ELO's and 'Don't

Bring Me Down', the band fortunately manage to change gear and start singing. Amazing how familiar and often used chord patterns can still stir the soul. Just enough tinny organ to add to the sparkling 60s retro sound.

● *Best line:* 'Heroin is so passé'.

90 The Smithereens – Behind The Wall Of Sleep (1986)

They never get cited as being an influence on anybody, but America's the Smithereens trotted out a few magnificent chunks of gutsy power pop, such as this unheralded classic.

● *Best line:* 'Well she held the bass guitar and she was playing in a band, and she stood just like Bill Wyman, now I am her biggest fan'.

91 Sting – If I Ever Lose My Faith In You (1993)

He has a knack of attempting to sound profound and then hitting the button and being very profound. This love song to his wife is one of many Sting confessions. Don't ignore the inspiring, driving bass line which fights against the beat.

● *Best line:* 'You will say I lost my belief in our politicians, they all seem like game show hosts to me'.

92 Kula Shaker – Hey Dude (1996)

Very uncool to like this. The late Kula Shaker are currently going through the 'wiped off the face of the earth phase' in people's memories. To refresh, they brought back the rock spirit of 1968. Derivative maybe, but blinking good.

● *Best line:* 'Smell the rose, the sweet sweet rose, catch the sun and find where it grows'.

93 The Stone Roses – I Wanna Be Adored (1989)

A big, fat, impressive, chiming intro that can't fail in alerting the listener to an unforgettable piece of music. Ian Brown was succinctly putting in song what is, after all, a basic human requirement of us all. Unflinchingly honest.

● *Best line:* The repeated title line.

94 Traffic – Paper Sun (1967)

Oh, to have been a fly on the wall down at that cottage in Aston Tirrold when they got this one together. Probably the most hippie-inspired song ever. Phased sitars and joss sticks mix with bongos and beads.

● *Best line:* 'But if you look around and see a shadow on the run, don't be too upset it's just a paper sun'.

95 Desmond Dekker and The Aces – 007 (Shanty Town) (1967)

This profound tale of shooting and looting rude boys from Jamaica. is much more significant than just a catchy melody and danceable beat. Get your ear in and concentrate on the lyrics, it is well worth it.

● *Best line:* 'I'm a rude boy gonna bum (burn) up the town'.

96 Jethro Tull – Living In The Past (1969)

An early hit just after they stopped playing the blues, and before they became an albums band. Anderson's vocals have never sounded so clear and relaxed, aided by the beautiful mix of flute and bass. And another very fine into.

● *Best line:* 'Now there's revolution but they don't know what they're fighting'.

97 Lindisfarne – Lady Eleanor (1972)

So what if it is a bit soppy, the fact is that Alan Hull wrote it for his wife and he stayed madly in love with her until his heart gave out in 1995. Furthermore he continued to perform the song with enthusiasm and passion. A good tune is a good tune.

● *Best line:* 'Belly dancing beauty with a power drilling saw'.

98 Joan Osborne – One Of Us (1996)

I take great pride in being the first person to play this maverick hit on UK radio. Osborne and her gritty band sound like a female Neil Young and Crazy Horse. The guitar solo is rudely cut on the single however.

● *Best line:* 'Just a stranger on the bus, trying to find his way home'.

99 Jellyfish – Baby's Coming Back (1991)

Two fantastic albums, a clutch of memorable singles and that's yer lot. Implosion, musical differences, the usual stuff. Jellyfish were one of the cleverest and happiest pop bands of the 90s.

● *Best line:* 'But that couldn't shoot away the bullseye that you made on my heart'.

100 Lightning Seeds – The Life Of Riley (1992)

Similarly uplifting were the excellent songs of Ian Brodie and the Lightning Seeds. There were a good half a dozen to choose from but this has the edge for its euphoric bounce and great main chorus.

● *Best line:* 'In this world we've got to find the time, for the life of Riley'.

And finally: 'American Pie' by Don McLean, 'Young At Heart' by the Bluebells, and the diabolical 'In The Year 2525' by Zager and Evans are the three singles that should be burnt in bulk. I don't just mean burn, I mean disappear for ever. How is it that pop music can cause such a wide range of emotion. Whenever I hear them on the radio they make me swear and shout. Why is it I hate them with such a vengeance?

★ LET ME KNOW BY EMAIL THE PARTICULAR TRACK THAT RAISES YOUR HACKLES AND ACTUALLY MAKES YOU ANGRY. YOU CAN REACH ME AT: colin@muze.co.uk

ALL TIME TOP 5 ALBUMS
BY 100 KEY ARTISTS

The recommendations for 100 key artists are purely subjective. We think we have approached it responsibly, and have selected the best five albums by these artists in our opinion. This may not coincide with the votes and the final listing. As for the choice of the 100 key artists, they were selected by the author. My choice is justified by the fact that you really need five good albums under your belt to qualify. Recent history shows that most artists run out of steam, or, in the case of a band, have broken up. We have deliberately not included compilations. Complaints, to the Assistant Editor Nic Oliver, at the usual address please.

AEROSMITH
Toys In The Attic
Pump
Get A Grip
Permanent Vacation
Nine Lives

AC/DC
Back In Black
Highway To Hell
Let There Be Rock
Ballbreaker
For Those About To Rock (We
    Salute You)

THE BAND
The Band
Music From Big Pink
Stage Fright
Rock Of Ages
Northern Lights-Southern Cross

BASIE, COUNT
Atomic Mr Basie
April In Paris
The Original American Decca
    Recordings
On My Way and Shouting Again
At Newport

THE BEACH BOYS
Sunflower
Pet Sounds
Surfs Up
Smiley Smile
Holland

THE BEASTIE BOYS
Paul's Boutique
Hello Nasty
III Communication
Check Your Head
Licensed To III

BEATLES
Revolver
Sgt. Peppers Lonely Hearts Club
    Band
The Beatles (White Album)
Abbey Road
Rubber Soul

BLUR
Parklife
13
Blur
Leisure
The Great Escape

BOB JOVI
Crossroad
Keep The Faith
Slippery When Wet
New Jersey
These Days

BOWIE, DAVID
The Rise and Fall Of Ziggy
    Stardust
Hunky Dory
Low
Heroes
Aladdin Sane

BRAGG, BILLY
Talking With The Taxman About
    Poetry
Don't Try This At Home
William Bloke
Mermaid Avenue
Brewing Up With Billy Bragg

BROOKS, GARTH
No Fences
In Pieces
Garth Brooks
Ropin' The Wind
The Chase

BROWN, JAMES
Live At The Apollo Vol. 1
Pure Dynamite! Live At The Royal
Live At The Garden
I Got You (I Feel Good)
Papa's Got A Brand New Bag

BROWNE, JACKSON
Late For The Sky
For Everyman
I'm Alive
The Pretender
Jackson Browne aka Saturate
    Before Using

BUCKLEY, TIM
Starsailor
Goodbye & Hello
Dream Letter (Live In London,
    1968)
Happy Sad
Blue Afternoon

BUSH, KATE
Hounds Of Love
The Dreaming
The Kick Inside
The Sensual World
Never For Ever

THE BYRDS
The Notorious Byrd Brothers
Younger Than Yesterday
Mr Tambourine Man
Turn! Turn! Turn!
Fifth Dimension

CAN
Future Days
Ege Bamyasi
Soon Over Babaluma
Tago Mago
Monster Movie

CAPTAIN BEEFHEART
Trout Mask Replica
Clear Spot
Safe As Milk
Strictly Personal
Lick My Decals Off Baby

CASH, JOHNNY
Johnny Cash At Folsom Prison
Johnny Cash At San Quentin
Orange Blossom Special
Ride This Train
American Recordings

CHARLES, RAY
Genius + Soul = Jazz
The Genius Of Ray Charles
Ray Charles In Person
Modern Sounds In Country and
    Western
Ingredients In A Recipe For Soul

CLAPTON, ERIC
461 Ocean Boulevard
MTV Unplugged
From The Cradle
Pilgrim
Slowhand

COLTRANE, JOHN
A Love Supreme
Blue Train
Giant Steps
My Favorite Things
Coltrane Jazz

COSTELLO, ELVIS
Imperial Bedroom
This Year's Model
My Aim Is True
Get Happy!!
King Of America

CSN FAMILY
Crosby, Stills and Nash – Crosby,
    Stills and Nash
Stephen Stills 1 – Stephen Stills
Deja Vu – Crosby, Stills, Nash and Young
If I Could Only Remember My
    Name – David Crosby
Wind On The Water – David
    Crosby and Graham Nash

THE CURE
Pornography
Kiss Me, Kiss Me, Kiss Me
Disintegration
Wish
Bloodflowers

DAVIS, MILES
Kind Of Blue
In A Silent Way
Birth Of The Cool
Sketches Of Spain
Bitches Brew

THE DOORS
The Doors
L.A. Woman
Morrison Hotel
Strange Days
Waiting For The Sun

DYLAN, BOB
Blonde On Blonde
Blood On The Tracks
Highway 61 Revisited
Bringing It All Back Home
Time Out Of Mind

ELLINGTON, DUKE
The Blanton-Webster Years
Money Jungle
Ellington Indigos
Ellington At Newport '56
Newport '58

FAIRPORT CONVENTION
Liege and Lief
What We Did On Our Holidays
Unhalfbricking
Full House
Jewel In The Crown

THE FALL
This Nation's Saving Grace
Shift Work
Dragnet
The Wonderful and Frightening
    World Of
Hex Induction Hour

FITZGERALD, ELLA
Ella Fitzgerald Sings The Cole
    Porter Songbook
Ella Fitzgerald Sings The George
    and Ira Gershwin Songbook
Ella and Louis
Ella Fitzgerald Sings The Rodgers
    and Hart Songbook
Like Someone In Love

FLEETWOOD MAC
Rumours
Peter Green's Fleetwood Mac
Tango In The Night
Fleetwood Mac
Then Play On

FRANKLIN, ARETHA
Aretha: Lady Soul
I Never Loved A Man The Way I
    Love You
Aretha Now
Soul '69
Amazing Grace

GAYE, MARVIN
What's Going On
Let's Get It On
I Want You
Trouble Man
Here My Dear

THE GRATEFUL DEAD
American Beauty
Workingman's Dead
Anthem Of The Sun
Live Dead
From The Mars Hotel

HARRIS, EMMYLOU
Wrecking Ball
Pieces Of The Sky
Luxury Liner
Roses In The Snow
Quarter Moon In A Ten Cent Town

HENDRIX, JIMI
Electric Ladyland
Are You Experienced
Axis: Bold As Love

Band Of Gypsies
Live At Monterey

HOOKER, JOHN LEE
The Healer
Real Folk Blues
Mr Lucky
Don't Look Back
That's My Story

IRON MAIDEN
The Number Of The Beast
Piece Of Mind
Seventh Son Of A Seventh Son
Iron Maiden
No Prayer For The Dying

JACKSON, MICHAEL
Thriller
Bad
Off The Wall
HIStory Past, Present & Future,
    Book 1
Dangerous

JARRETT, KEITH
The Köln Concert
Facing You
Belonging
Standards Volume 1
Solo Concerts: Bremen and Lausanne

THE JEFFERSON AIRPLANE
Surrealistic Pillow
After Bathing At Baxter's
Volunteers
Crown Of Creation
Bless Its Pointed Little Head

JETHRO TULL
Stand Up
This Was
Songs From The Wood
Thick As A Brick
Aqualung

JOHN, ELTON
Tumbleweed Connection
Elton John
Goodbye Yellow Brick Road
Don't Shoot Me I'm Only The Piano
    Player
Captain Fantastic and The Brown
    Dirt Cowboy

KING, B.B.
Live At The Regal
Deuces Wild
Live At San Quentin
There's Always One More Time
Lucille

THE KINKS
The Kinks Are The Village Green
    Preservation Society

Face To Face
Something Else
Misfits
To The Bone

KISS
Dressed To Kill
Destroyer
Alive
Kiss
Love Gun

LED ZEPPELIN
Led Zeppelin IV
Physical Graffiti
Led Zeppelin II
Led Zeppelin
Houses Of The Holy

LITTLE FEAT
Feats Don't Fail Me Now
The Last Record Album
Sailin' Shoes
Dixie Chicken
Waiting For Columbus

MARLEY, BOB
Kaya
Catch A Fire
Natty Dread
Live
Burnin'

MADONNA
Like A Prayer
Like A Virgin
Ray Of Light
Madonna
Bedtime Stories

MARTYN, JOHN
Solid Air
Grace and Danger
One World
Well Kept Secret
Glorious Fool

MAYALL, JOHN
Bluesbreakers with Eric Clapton
A Hard Road
Bare Wires
Turning Point
Wake Up Call

METALLICA
Metallica
Master Of Puppets
Kill 'Em All
Load
... And Justice For All

METHENY, PAT
Travels
Offramp
American Garage

As Falls Wichita, So Fall Wichita Falls
Letter From Home

MILLER, STEVE, BAND
Sailor
Brave New World
Number 5
Children Of The Future
Fly Like An Eagle

MINGUS, CHARLES
The Black Saint and The Sinner Lady
Mingus, Mingus, Mingus, Mingus, Mingus
Mingus Ah Um
Oh Yeah!
Mingus At Antibes

MITCHELL, JONI
Blue
Hejira
Court and Spark
The Hissing Of Summer Lawns
Ladies Of The Canyon

MONK, THELONIOUS
Genius Of Modern Music Volumes 1 & 2
Mysterioso
Thelonious Alone In San Francisco
Pure Monk
Monk's Music

MORRISON, VAN
Astral Weeks
Moondance
It's Too Late To Stop Now
Saint Dominic's Preview
No Guru, No Method, No Teacher

MULLIGAN, GERRY
Gerry Mulligan Meets Ben Webster
Jeru
What Is There To Say?
Two Of A Kind
Mulligan Plays Mulligan

NEWMAN, RANDY
Good Old Boys
Lonely At The Top
12 Songs
Little Criminals
Randy Newman

PEARL JAM
Vitalogy
No Code
Ten
Vs
Yeild

PETTY, TOM
Damn The Torpedoes

Full Moon Fever
Into The Great Wide Open
Southern Accents
Wildflowers

PINK FLOYD
Dark Side Of The Moon
Wish You Were Here
The Wall
The Piper At The Gates Of Dawn
Meddle

PRESLEY, ELVIS
Sun Collection
Elvis Presley
King Creole
Loving You
Elvis

PRINCE
Sign O' The Times
Purple Rain
Parade
Dirty Mind
1999

PUBLIC ENEMY
It Takes A Nation Of Millions To Hold Us Back
Fear Of A Black Planet
Apocalypse '91 The Enemy Strikes Back
Yo! Bum Rush The Show
There's A Poison Going On

QUEEN
A Night At The Opera
Sheer Heart Attack
A Kind Of Magic
A Day At The Races
Queen 2

R.E.M.
Automatic For The People
Out Of Time
New Adventures In Hi-Fi
Green
Murmur

REDDING, OTIS
Otis Blue
Complete & Unbelievable ... The Dictionary Of Soul
The Dock Of The Bay
The Soul Album
The Great Otis Redding Sings Soul Ballads

REED, LOU
Transformer
New York
Berlin
Rock N Roll Animal
Sally Can't Dance

THE ROLLING STONES
Exile On Main Street
Let It Bleed
Beggars Banquet
Sticky Fingers
Aftermath

ROXY MUSIC
For Your Pleasure
Avalon
Roxy Music
Stranded
Country Life

RUNDGREN, TODD
Something/Anything
A Wizard, A True Star
The Ballad Of Todd Rundgren
The Hermit Of Mink Hollow
Todd

SANTANA
Abraxas
Santana
Caravanserai
Santana III
Supernatural

SIMON, PAUL
There Goes Rhymin' Simon
Hearts and Bone
Still Crazy After All These Years
Graceland
Paul Simon

SINATRA, FRANK
Songs For Swingin' Lovers!
In The Wee Small Hours
Frank Sinatra Sings For Only The
    Lonely
Swing Easy!
A Swingin' Affair!

THE SMITHS
The Queen Is Dead
The Smiths
Hatful Of Hollow
Meat Is Murder
Strangeways, Here We Come

SPIRIT
The Twelve Dreams Of Dr
    Sardonicus
Future Games
The Family That Plays Together
Spirit
Spirit Of '76

SPRINGFIELD, DUSTY
Dusty In Memphis
Everything's Coming Up Dusty
A Brand New Me
Where Am I Going?
Dusty Definitely

SPRINGSTEEN, BRUCE
Born To Run
Tunnel Of Love
Darkness At The Edge Of Town
Born In The USA
The River

SQUEEZE
East Side Story
Argybargy
Cosi Fan Tutti Frutti
Ridiculous
Cool For Cats

STEELY DAN
Countdown To Ecstasy
Can't Buy A Thrill
Pretzel Logic
Aja
Gaucho

STEWART, ROD
Every Picture Tells A Story
An Old Raincoat Will Never Let
    You Down
Gasoline Alley
Never A Dull Moment
Unplugged and Seated

THE STRANGLERS
Rattus Norvegicus
No More Heroes
The Raven
La Folie
Black and White

TALKING HEADS
Remain In Light
Fear Of Music
Talking Heads '77
Stop Making Sense
More Songs About Buildings and
    Food

TAYLOR, JAMES
Sweet Baby James
Mud Slide Slim
J.T.
That's Why I'm Here
One Man Dog

THE TEMPTATIONS
Cloud Nine
Wish It Would Rain
Temptin' Temptations
Gettin' Ready
With A Lot O' Soul

THOMPSON, RICHARD
I Want To See The Bright Lights
    Tonight (with Linda)
Shoot Out The Lights (with Linda)
Pour Down Like Silver (with Linda)
Hand Of Kindness
Hokey and Pokey (with Linda)

TRAFFIC
The Low Spark Of High Heeled
    Boys
Traffic
John Barleycorn Must Die
Dear Mr Fantasy
When The Eagle Flies

U2
The Joshua Tree
The Unforgettable Fire
Achtung Baby
Zooropa
War

WAITS, TOM
Rain Dogs
Swordfishtrombones
Blue Valentine
Small Change
Bone Machine

THE WHO
Live At Leeds
Who's Next
Quadrophenia
Tommy
Sings My Generation

WONDER, STEVIE
Songs In The Key Of Life
Innervisions
Talking Book
Fulfillingness' First Finale
Music Of My Mind

XTC
Oranges & Lemons
Nonsuch
Skylarking
English Settlement
Apple Venus Vol 1

YOUNG, NEIL
After The Goldrush
On The Beach
Everybody Knows This Is Nowhere
Rust Never Sleeps
Freedom

ZAPPA, FRANK
Hot Rats
We're Only In It For The Money
Freak Out
Joe's Garage
Apostrophe (')

Top 1000 Check List

1 **Revolver** – The Beatles
2 **The Bends** – Radiohead
3 **Sgt. Pepper's Lonely Hearts Club Band** – The Beatles
4 **OK Computer** – Radiohead
5 **The White Album** – The Beatles
6 **Automatic For The People** – R.E.M.
7 **Blood On The Tracks** – Bob Dylan
8 **Abbey Road** – The Beatles
9 **Dark Side Of The Moon** – Pink Floyd
10 **The Queen Is Dead** – The Smiths
11 **The Stone Roses** – The Stone Roses
12 **Forever Changes** – Love
13 **The Velvet Underground & Nico** – The Velvet Underground
14 **Kind Of Blue** – Miles Davis
15 **The Unforgettable Fire** – U2
16 **Astral Weeks** – Van Morrison
17 **Nevermind** – Nirvana
18 **Pet Sounds** – The Beach Boys
19 **Sign 'O' The Times** – Prince
20 **Born To Run** – Bruce Springsteen
21 **(What's The Story) Morning Glory?** – Oasis
22 **A Hard Day's Night** – The Beatles
23 **Hunky Dory** – David Bowie
24 **Blue** – Joni Mitchell
25 **The Joshua Tree** – U2
26 **Highway 61 Revisited** – Bob Dylan
27 **The Rise and Fall Of Ziggy Stardust and The Spiders From Mars** – David Bowie
28 **Blue Lines** – Massive Attack
29 **Never Mind The Bollocks Here's The Sex Pistols** – The Sex Pistols
30 **The Wall** – Pink Floyd
31 **Rumours** – Fleetwood Mac
32 **Electric Ladyland** – Jimi Hendrix
33 **Blonde On Blonde** – Bob Dylan
34 **Rubber Soul** – The Beatles
35 **Exile On Main Street** – The Rolling Stones
36 **Achtung Baby** – U2
37 **London Calling** – The Clash
38 **Wish You Were Here** – Pink Floyd
39 **What's Going On** – Marvin Gaye
40 **Let It Bleed** – The Rolling Stones
41 **Dummy** – Portishead
42 **Led Zeppelin IV** – Led Zeppelin
43 **Graceland** – Paul Simon
44 **Definitely Maybe** – Oasis
45 **The Band** – The Band
46 **The Doors** – The Doors
47 **Low** – David Bowie
48 **Who's Next** – The Who
49 **Out Of Time** – R.E.M.
50 **Trout Mask Replica** – Captain Beefheart and The Magic Band
51 **Jagged Little Pill** – Alanis Morissette
52 **Tommy** – The Who
53 **Marquee Moon** – Television
54 **Odelay** – Beck
55 **Five Leaves Left** – Nick Drake
56 **The Smiths** – The Smiths
57 **Parallel Lines** – Blondie
58 **Transformer** – Lou Reed
59 **Leftism** – Leftfield

60 **Legend** – Bob Marley and The Wailers
61 **Led Zeppelin** Led Zeppelin
62 **After The Goldrush** – Neil Young
63 **Are You Experienced** – Jimi Hendrix
64 **Thriller** – Michael Jackson
65 **Loveless** – My Bloody Valentine
66 **Bridge Over Troubled Water** – Simon and Garfunkel
67 **Hotel California** – The Eagles
68 **Moon Safari** – Air
69 **Performance and Cocktails** The Stereophonics
70 **Ten** – Pearl Jam
71 **Saint Dominic's Preview** – Van Morrison
72 **Purple Rain** – Prince
73 **Little Earthquakes** – Tori Amos
74 **Tapestry** – Carole King
75 **The Man Who** – Travis
76 **Mellon Collie and The Infinite Sadness** – The Smashing Pumpkins
77 **Debut** – Björk
78 **Talk On Corners** – The Corrs
79 **Moondance** – Van Morrison
80 **Woodface** – Crowded House
81 **Led Zeppelin II** – Led Zeppelin
82 **So** – Peter Gabriel
83 **Crosby, Stills and Nash** – Crosby, Stills and Nash
84 **Sticky Fingers** – The Rolling Stones
85 **A Love Supreme** – John Coltrane
86 **Goodbye Yellow Brick Road** – Elton John
87 **Hounds Of Love** – Kate Bush
88 **Metallica** – Metallica
89 **Songs In The Key Of Life** – Stevie Wonder
90 **Otis Blue** – Otis Redding
91 **Synchronicity** – The Police
92 **It Takes A Nation Of Millions To Hold Us Back** – Public Enemy
93 **Harvest** – Neil Young
94 **Disintegration** – The Cure
95 **Parklife** – Blur
96 **A Night At The Opera** – Queen
97 **Licensed To III** – The Beastie Boys
98 **Moby Grape** – Moby Grape
99 **Grace** – Jeff Buckley
100 **Songs For Swingin' Lovers!** – Frank Sinatra
101 **Paul's Boutique** – The Beastie Boys
102 **Tubular Bells** – Mike Oldfield
103 **American Beauty** – The Grateful Dead
104 **Van Halen** – Van Halen
105 **Master Of Puppets** – Metallica
106 **Déjà Vu** – Crosby, Stills, Nash and Young
107 **Back In Black** – AC/DC
108 **Hysteria** – Def Leppard
109 **Siamese Dream** – The Smashing Pumpkins
110 **August and Everything After** – Counting Crows
111 **Physical Graffiti** – Led Zeppelin
112 **Garbage** – Garbage
113 **Don't Shoot Me I'm Only The Piano Player** – Elton John

114 **Doolittle** – The Pixies
115 **Gold: Greatest Hits** – Abba
116 **Court and Spark** – Joni Mitchell
117 **Houses Of The Holy** – Led Zeppelin
118 **Aja** – Steely Dan
119 **Help!** – The Beatles
120 **Like A Prayer** – Madonna
121 **Bat Out Of Hell** – Meat Loaf
122 **War** – U2
123 **Hot Rats** – Frank Zappa
124 **Everybody Knows This Is Nowhere** – Neil Young
125 **Frank Sinatra Sings For Only The Lonely** – Frank Sinatra
126 **Clear Spot** – Captain Beefheart and The Magic Band
127 **The Freewheelin' Bob Dylan** – Bob Dylan
128 **Imagine** – John Lennon
129 **Stephen Stills** – Stephen Stills
130 **Close To The Edge** – Yes
131 **Pink Moon** – Nick Drake
132 **Fun House** – The Stooges
133 **Another Side Of Bob Dylan** – Bob Dylan
134 **Meat Is Murder** – The Smiths
135 **Screamadelica** – Primal Scream
136 **The Chronic** – Dr. Dre
137 **Appetite For Destruction** – Guns N'Roses
138 **3 Feet High and Rising** – De La Soul
139 **Green** – R.E.M.
140 **Slanted and Enchanted** – Pavement
141 **The Kinks Are The Village Green Preservation Society** – The Kinks
142 **Blood Sugar Sex Magik** – The Red Hot Chili Peppers
143 **Innervisions** – Stevie Wonder
144 **Rum, Sodomy & The Lash** – The Pogues
145 **Enter The Wu-Tang (36 Chambers)** – Wu-Tang Clan
146 **Aladdin Sane** – David Bowie
147 **Axis: Bold As Love** – Jimi Hendrix
148 **For The Roses** – Joni Mitchell
149 **Songs Of Leonard Cohen** – Leonard Cohen
150 **Older** – George Michael
151 **Parade** Prince
152 **This Year's Model** Elvis Costello
153 **In A Silent Way** Miles Davis
154 **Quadrophenia** The Who
155 **Sketches Of Spain** Miles Davis
156 **If Only I Could Remember My Name** – David Crosby
157 **1962-1966 (Red Album)** The Beatles
158 **The Notorious Byrd Brothers** – The Byrds
159 **The Lexicon Of Love** – ABC
160 **Born In The USA** – Bruce Springsteen
161 **Fresh Fruit For Rotting Vegetables** – The Dead Kennedys
162 **Lifes Rich Pageant** – R.E.M.
163 **The Piper At The Gates Of Dawn** – Pink Floyd
164 **Americana** – The Offspring
165 **Buffalo Springfield Again** – Buffalo Springfield
166 **Machine Head** – Deep Purple

338 **Bookends** – Simon and Garfunkel
339 **Blue Train** – John Coltrane
340 **Erotica** – Madonna
341 **Faith** – George Michael
342 **Tea For The Tillerman** – Cat Stevens
343 **We're Only In It For The Money** – Frank Zappa
344 **Life After Death** – The Notorious B.I.G.
345 **Hats** – Blue Nile
346 **Out Of The Blue** – Electric Light Orchestra
347 **Slippery When Wet** – Bon Jovi
348 **Paranoid** – Black Sabbath
349 **Birth Of The Cool** – Miles Davis
350 **Music For The Masses** – Depeche Mode
351 **The Number Of The Beast** – Iron Maiden
352 **I Never Loved A Man The Way I Love You** – Aretha Franklin
353 **Sailor** – The Steve Miller Band
354 **Come On Over** – Shania Twain
355 **Eliminator** – ZZ Top
356 **Live At Leeds** – The Who
357 **The Köln Concert** – Keith Jarrett
358 **The Wild, The Innocent & The E Street Shuffle** – Bruce Springsteen
359 **In The Wee Small Hours** – Frank Sinatra
360 **Genius + Soul = Jazz** – Ray Charles
361 **Led Zeppelin III** – Led Zeppelin
362 **The Fillmore Concerts/Live At Fillmore East** – The Allman Brothers Band
363 **Generation Terrorists** – The Manic Street Preachers
364 **Let's Get It On** – Marvin Gaye
365 **The Dreaming** – Kate Bush
366 **Boys For Pele** – Tori Amos
367 **Savage** – The Eurythmics
368 **Swing Easy!** – Frank Sinatra
369 **John Barleycorn Must Die** – Traffic
370 **The Dream Of The Blue Turtles** – Sting
371 **Workingman's Dead** – The Grateful Dead
372 **Bring It On** – Gomez
373 **Elton John** – Elton John
374 **Swordfishtrombones** – Tom Waits
375 **Outlandos D'Amour** – The Police
376 **Anthem Of The Sun** – The Grateful Dead
377 **Here Come The Warm Jets** – Brian Eno
378 **The Times They Are A-Changin'** – Bob Dylan
379 **On How Life Is** – Macy Gray
380 **Sweet Dreams** – The Eurythmics
381 **Psychocandy** – Jesus and Mary Chain
382 **Rock 'N' Roll Animal** – Lou Reed
383 **Burnin'** – The Wailers
384 **The Cars** – The Cars
385 **Seal** – Seal
386 **Bandwagonesque** – Teenage Fanclub
387 **Aftermath** – The Rolling Stones
388 **1984** – Van Halen
389 **Once Upon A Time** – Simple Minds
390 **The Genius Of Ray Charles** – Ray Charles
391 **Bluesbreakers With Eric Clapton** – John Mayall
392 **My Favorite Things** – John Coltrane
393 **Tumbleweed Connection** – Elton John
394 **Stop Making Sense** – Talking Heads
395 **Wrecking Ball** – Emmylou Harris
396 **Talking Heads '77** – Talking Heads
397 **Doggystyle** – Snoop Doggy Dogg
398 **Reggatta De Blanc** – The Police
399 **Miles Smiles** – Miles Davis
400 **Fly Like An Eagle** – The Steve Miller Band
401 **Foo Fighters** – Foo Fighters
402 **The Buddy Holly Story** – Buddy Holly
403 **Pretenders II** – The Pretenders
404 **Genius Of Modern Music Vols 1 & 2** – Thelonious Monk
405 **Saxophone Colossus** – Sonny Rollins
406 **The Hangman's Beautiful Daughter** – Incredible String Band
407 **A Walk Across The Rooftops** – Blue Nile
408 **My Own Prison** – Creed
409 **... and Justice For All** – Metallica
410 **Zuma** – Neil Young
411 **The Atomic Mr. Basie** – Count Basie
412 **Copperhead Road** – Steve Earle
413 **Fulfillingness' First Finale** – Stevie Wonder
414 **The Low End Theory** – A Tribe Called Quest
415 **Smiley Smile** – The Beach Boys
416 **Vs.** – Pearl Jam
417 **The Complete Savoy Sessions** – Charlie Parker
418 **The Rolling Stones** – The Rolling Stones
419 **Spirit Of Eden** – Talk Talk
420 **Kick** – INXS
421 **There Goes Rhymin' Simon** – Paul Simon
422 **Shoot Out The Lights** – Richard & Linda Thompson
423 **I Want You** – Marvin Gaye
424 **The Healer** – John Lee Hooker
425 **Nebraska** – Bruce Springsteen
426 **The Black Saint and The Sinner Lady** – Charles Mingus
427 **No More Heroes** – The Stranglers
428 **Saucerful Of Secrets** – Pink Floyd
429 **Bossanova** – The Pixies
430 **Tim Hardin II** – Tim Hardin
431 **Veedon Fleece** – Van Morrison
432 **Risqué** – Chic
433 **Be Yourself Tonight** – The Eurythmics
434 **Maiden Voyage** – Herbie Hancock
435 **Peter Green's Fleetwood Mac** – Fleetwood Mac
436 **Tragic Kingdom** – No Doubt
437 **Blind Faith** – Blind Faith
438 **Oh Mercy** – Bob Dylan
439 **Buena Vista Social Club** – Ry Cooder & Various
440 **Revenge** – The Eurythmics
441 **This Nation's Saving Grace** – The Fall
442 **Dressed To Kill** – Kiss
443 **For Everyman** – Jackson Browne
444 **The Downward Spiral** – Nine Inch Nails
445 **Club Classics Vol. 1** – Soul II Soul
446 **Fear Of Music** – Talking Heads
447 **Rastaman Vibration** – Bob Marley and The Wailers
448 **Gerry Mulligan Meets Ben Webster** – Gerry Mulligan & Ben Webster
449 **Sunflower** – The Beach Boys
450 **Paid In Full** – Eric B & Rakim
451 **Genius Hits The Road** – Ray Charles
452 **Music From Big Pink** – The Band
453 **The Patsy Cline Showcase** – Patsy Cline
454 **The Man and His Music** – Sam Cooke
455 **Arc Of A Diver** – Steve Winwood
456 **I'm Alive** – Jackson Browne
457 **These Days** – Bon Jovi
458 **Up** – R.E.M.
459 **Be Here Now** – Oasis
460 **At Newport** – Duke Ellington
461 **Sinatra At The Sands** – Frank Sinatra
462 **The Kick Inside** – Kate Bush
463 **Trouble Man** – Marvin Gaye
464 **Yield** – Pearl Jam
465 **Waltz For Debby** – Bill Evans
466 **Big Willie Style** – Will Smith
467 **African Herbsman** – Bob Marley and The Wailers
468 **Little Criminals** – Randy Newman
469 **Sailin' Shoes** – Little Feat
470 **My Funny Valentine** – Miles Davis
471 **Sixteen Stone** – Bush
472 **Oliver!** – Various
473 **The George and Ira Gershwin Songbook** – Ella Fitzgerald
474 **Goodbye Jumbo** – World Party
475 **Blood & Chocolate** – Elvis Costello
476 **Lonely At The Top** – Randy Newman
477 **Milestones** – Miles Davis
478 **Midnight Love** – Marvin Gaye
479 **Nuggets: Original Artyfacts From The First Psychedelic Era 1965-1968** – Various
480 **Body and Soul** – Coleman Hawkins
481 **Young Americans** – David Bowie
482 **Permanent Vacation** – Aerosmith
483 **The Fabulous Little Richard** – Little Richard
484 **Country Life** – Roxy Music
485 **Heaven Up Here** – Echo and The Bunnymen
486 **Kick Out The Jams** – MC5
487 **Avalon Sunset** – Van Morrison
488 **Complete & Unbelievable: The Otis Redding Dictionary Of Soul** – Otis Redding
489 **Keep The Faith** – Bon Jovi
490 **Ella Fitzgerald Sings The Cole Porter Songbook** – Ella Fitzgerald
491 **Mingus, Mingus, Mingus, Mingus, Mingus** – Charles Mingus
492 **Sheer Heart Attack** – Queen
493 **Spice** – The Spice Girls
494 **Waiting For The Sun** – Doors
495 **I'm Your Man** – Leonard Cohen
496 **Kaya** – Bob Marley and The

Wailers
497 **Night and Day** – Joe Jackson
498 **Here, My Dear** – Marvin Gaye
499 **Workers Playtime** – Billy Bragg
500 **Songs Of Love and Hate** –
Leonard Cohen
501 **Tres Hombres** – ZZ Top
502 **In Search Of The Lost Chord**
– The Moody Blues
503 **Eden** – Everything But The Girl
504 **Gaucho** – Steely Dan
505 **Last Time Around** – Buffalo
Springfield
506 **Hypocrisy Is The Greatest
Luxury** – The Disposable
Heroes Of Hiphoprisy
507 **Starsailor** – Tim Buckley
508 **New Boots and Panties!!** –
Ian Dury and The Blockheads
509 **The Pretender** – Jackson Browne
510 **Oar** – Alexander 'Skip' Spence
511 **Can't Slow Down** – Lionel Richie
512 **The Sky Is Crying** – Stevie Ray
Vaughan
513 **Stand Up** – Jethro Tull
514 **What's The 411?** – Mary J.
Blige
515 **Band On The Run** – Wings
516 **Goodbye and Hello** – Tim Buckley
517 **Mr. Fantasy** – Traffic
518 **Bedtime Stories** – Madonna
519 **The "Chirping" Crickets** – The
Crickets
520 **Songs From The Wood** – Jethro
Tull
521 **In The Dark** – The Grateful Dead
522 **Reggae Greats** – Toots and
The Maytals
523 **The Singles 1969-1973** –
The Carpenters
524 **The River** – Bruce Springsteen
525 **Here's Little Richard** – Little
Richard
526 **Round About Midnight** – Miles
Davis
527 **Lady In Autumn** – Billie Holiday
528 **One Of These Nights** – The
Eagles
529 **Band Of Gypsies** – Jimi Hendrix
530 **One Step Beyond** – Madness
531 **Money Jungle** – Duke Ellington
532 **Janet** – Janet Jackson
533 **Burn** – Deep Purple
534 **Full Moon Fever** – Tom Petty
535 **Pink Flag** – Wire
536 **Black and Blue** – The Rolling
Stones
537 **Damn The Torpedoes** – Tom
Petty and The Heartbreakers
538 **Rocks** – Aerosmith
539 **Teaser and The Firecat** – Cat
Stevens
540 **King Of America** – Elvis Costello
541 **Darkness At The Edge Of
Town** – Bruce Springsteen
542 **Baduizm** – Erykah Badu
543 **Collective Soul** – Collective Soul
544 **Unleashed In The East** – Judas
Priest
545 **Nice 'n' Easy** – Frank Sinatra
546 **Republic** – New Order
547 **Stranded** – Roxy Music
548 **Ellington Indigos** – Duke
Ellington
549 **Kate & Anna McGarrigle** –
Kate and Anna McGarrigle
550 **Modern Sounds In Country
and Western Music** – Ray
Charles
551 **Wild Wood** – Paul Weller

552 **Damned Damned Damned** –
The Damned
553 **Happy Trails** – Quicksilver
Messenger Service
554 **Face To Face** – The Kinks
555 **The Last Record Album** – Little
Feat
556 **From The Mars Hotel** – The
Grateful Dead
557 **Bellybutton** – Jellyfish
558 **Aretha Now** – Aretha Franklin
559 **My Fair Lady** – Original
Broadway Cast
560 **Organ Grinder Swing** – Jimmy
Smith
561 **Pieces Of The Sky** – Emmylou
Harris
562 **Hello, I Must Be Going!** – Phil
Collins
563 **Dixie Chicken** – Little Feat
564 **Sonny Rollins Vol. 2** – Sonny
Rollins
565 **Shift Work** – The Fall
566 **Bare Wires** – John Mayall
567 **Van Halen II** – Van Halen
568 **Steel Wheels** – The Rolling
Stones
569 **The Soul Album** – Otis Redding
570 **Travels** – Pat Metheny
571 **Vivid** – Living Colour
572 **Our Man In Paris** – Dexter
Gordon
573 **Hot Buttered Soul** – Isaac Hayes
574 **This Was** – Jethro Tull
575 **The Family That Plays
Together** – Spirit
576 **Kill 'Em All** – Metallica
577 **Together Alone** – Crowded
House
578 **No Need To Argue** – The
Cranberries
579 **Nashville Skyline** – Bob Dylan
580 **Operation Radication** –
Yellowman
581 **Your Arsenal** – Morrissey
582 **Sail Away** – Randy Newman
583 **E.1999 Eternal** – Bone Thugs-
N-Harmony
584 **The Sidewinder** – Lee Morgan
585 **I Do Not Want What I Haven't
Got** – Sinéad O'Connor
586 **Live At The Regal** – B.B. King
587 **The Song Remains The Same**
– Led Zeppelin
588 **Big Ones** – Aerosmith
589 **Stanley Road** – Paul Weller
590 **Between The Lines** – Janis Ian
591 **Crown Of Creation** – Jefferson
Airplane
592 **Bone Machine** – Tom Waits
593 **X** – INXS
594 **Late For The Sky** – Jackson
Browne
595 **After Bathing At Baxters** –
Jefferson Airplane
596 **One Size Fits All** – Frank Zappa
597 **Word Gets Around** – The
Stereophonics
598 **Dreadlocks Dread** – Big Youth
599 **Making Movies** – Dire Straits
600 **Substance** – New Order
601 **Strangeways, Here We Come**
– Smiths
602 **For Those About To Rock We
Salute You** – AC/DC
603 **For Your Pleasure** – Roxy Music
604 **Hokey Pokey** – Richard & Linda
Thompson
605 **Apostrophe (')** – Frank Zappa
606 **Music In A Doll's House** –

Family
607 **Volunteers** – Jefferson Airplane
608 **Song For My Father** – Horace
Silver Quintet
609 **Caravanserai** – Santana
610 **Nine Lives** – Aerosmith
611 **Cracked Rear View** – Hootie
and The Blowfish
612 **Stutter** – James
613 **The Scream** – Siouxsie and
The Banshees
614 **East Side Story** – Squeeze
615 **Nick Of Time** – Bonnie Raitt
616 **Come Fly With Me** – Frank
Sinatra
617 **Fear Of A Black Planet** –
Public Enemy
618 **Being There** – Wilco
619 **Elvis Presley** – Elvis Presley
620 **The Gilded Palace Of Sin** –
Flying Burrito Brothers
621 **52nd Street** – Billy Joel
622 **Please Please Me** – The Beatles
623 **Document** – R.E.M.
624 **Grand Prix** – Teenage Fanclub
625 **The Low Spark Of High
Heeled Boys** – Traffic
626 **Dread Inna Babylon** – U-Roy
627 **Pills 'N' Thrills and Bellyaches**
– Happy Mondays
628 **Permanent Waves** – Rush
629 **King Of The Delta Blues
Singers** – Robert Johnson
630 **His Band and The Street
Choir** – Van Morrison
631 **Desperado** – The Eagles
632 **Pearl** – Janis Joplin
633 **The Cross Of Changes** – Enigma
634 **Secrets** – Toni Braxton
635 **Purple** – Stone Temple Pilots
636 **Ella and Louis** – Ella Fitzgerald
and Louis Armstrong
637 **Odessey & Oracle** – The Zombies
638 **A Hard Road** – John Mayall
639 **With A Little Help From My
Friends** – Joe Cocker
640 **Dare** – The Human League
641 **Equal Rights** – Peter Tosh
642 **Ella Fitzgerald Sings The
Rodgers and Hart Songbook**
– Ella Fitzgerald
643 **The Great Otis Redding Sings
Soul Ballads** – Otis Redding
644 **In My Tribe** – 10,000 Maniacs
645 **Music Of My Mind** – Stevie
Wonder
646 **Wish** – The Cure
647 **Smash** – The Offspring
648 **Holland** – The Beach Boys
649 **Bert Jansch** – Bert Jansch
650 **The Slim Shady LP** – Eminem
651 **Greetings From Asbury Park
N.J.** – Bruce Springsteen
652 **Time Out Of Mind** – Bob Dylan
653 **The La's** – The La's
654 **If You're Feeling Sinister** –
Belle and Sebastian
655 **One For All** – Brand Nubian
656 **New Jersey** – Bon Jovi
657 **Phaedra** – Tangerine Dream
658 **Spirit** – Spirit
659 **I Still Believe In You** – Vince Gill
660 **Blood, Sweat & Tears** –
Blood, Sweat and Tears
661 **Strictly Personal** – Captain
Beefheart and The Magic Band
662 **Friends** – The Beach Boys
663 **The Complete Live At The
Plugged Nickel 1965** – Miles
Davis

664 **Love Chronicles** – Al Stewart
665 **Rumor and Sigh** – Richard Thompson
666 **Beautiful Freak** – The Eels
667 **Tell Mama** – Etta James
668 **On The Threshold Of A Dream** – The Moody Blues
669 **Offramp** – Pat Metheny
670 **The Southern Harmony and Musical Companion** – The Black Crowes
671 **I've Been Expecting You** – Robbie Williams
672 **Another Green World** – Brian Eno
673 **Jailbreak** – Thin Lizzy
674 **Aoxomoxoa** – The Grateful Dead
675 **154** – Wire
676 **Brave New World** – The Steve Miller Band
677 **Johnny Cash At Folsom Prison** – Johnny Cash
678 **The Eagles** – The Eagles
679 **Got My Mojo Workin'** – Jimmy Smith
680 **Eat A Peach** – The Allman Brothers Band
681 **Duke** – Genesis
682 **Eve6** – Eve6
683 **The Miseducation Of Lauryn Hill** – Lauryn Hill
684 **Bless The Weather** – John Martyn
685 **The Grand Illusion** – Styx
686 **In Rock** – Deep Purple
687 **Impressions** – John Coltrane
688 **Unhalfbricking** – Fairport Convention
689 **Forrest Gump** – Original Soundtrack
690 **More Songs About Buildings and Food** – Talking Heads
691 **12 Songs** – Randy Newman
692 **Euphoria** – Def Leppard
693 **It's Too Late To Stop Now** – Van Morrison
694 **Joan Armatrading** – Joan Armatrading
695 **Coming Up** – Suede
696 **Aqualung** – Jethro Tull
697 **Daydream Nation** – Sonic Youth
698 **Space Oddity** – David Bowie
699 **Copper Blue** – Sugar
700 **Damn Right, I've Got The Blues** – Buddy Guy
701 **Nimrod** – Green Day
702 **Dire Straits** – Dire Straits
703 **The Madcap Laughs** – Syd Barrett
704 **Stage Fright** – The Band
705 **Under The Pink** – Tori Amos
706 **Our Favourite Shop** – The Style Council
707 **Diamond Life** – Sade
708 **Trust** – Elvis Costello
709 **Wide Open Spaces** – Dixie Chicks
710 **Talking With The Taxman About Poetry** – Billy Bragg
711 **Tim Hardin I** – Tim Hardin
712 **The Woman In Me** – Shania Twain
713 **The Cat** – Jimmy Smith
714 **Joe's Garage** – Frank Zappa
715 **Soft Machine Volume Two** – Soft Machine
716 **Randy Newman** – Randy Newman
717 **Vitalogy** – Pearl Jam
718 **Feats Don't Fail Me Now** – Little Feat
719 **The Division Bell** – Pink Floyd
720 **Sparkle and Fade** – Everclear
721 **Mezzanine** – Massive Attack
722 **Pretenders** – The Pretenders
723 **Adore** – The Smashing Pumpkins
724 **Antichrist Superstar** – Marilyn Manson
725 **The Great Escape** – Blur
726 **Crazy Sexy Cool** – TLC
727 **Celebrity Skin** – Hole
728 **Hergest Ridge** – Mike Oldfield
729 **Follow The Leader** – Korn
730 **Whatever and Ever Amen** – Ben Folds Five
731 **Ladies Of The Canyon** – Joni Mitchell
732 **Hello Nasty** – The Beastie Boys
733 **Third/Sister Lovers** – Big Star
734 **The Score** – Fugees
735 **Manassas** – Stephen Stills
736 **Ready To Die** – The Notorious B.I.G.
737 **Vulgar Display Of Power** – Pantera
738 **2112** – Rush
739 **No Fences** – Garth Brooks
740 **Whitney Houston** – Whitney Houston
741 **Cross Road** – Bon Jovi
742 **Love Is The Thing** – Nat 'King' Cole
743 **Spirit** – Jewel
744 **Pump** – Aerosmith
745 **Destroyer** – Kiss
746 **The B-52's** – The B-52's
747 **Solo Monk** – Thelonious Monk
748 **Burgers** – Hot Tuna
749 **A Day At The Races** – Queen
750 **III Communication** – The Beastie Boys
751 **Promenade** – The Divine Comedy
752 **Mellow Gold** – Beck
753 **No Code** – Pearl Jam
754 **Backstabbers** – The O'Jays
755 **Harvest Moon** – Neil Young
756 **Dream Letter (Live In London 1968)** – Tim Buckley
757 **Wheels Of Fire** – Cream
758 **Ropin' The Wind** – Garth Brooks
759 **Tattoo You** – The Rolling Stones
760 **Scott 4** – Scott Walker
761 **Desire** – Bob Dylan
762 **Heavy Soul** – Paul Weller
763 **Load** – Metallica
764 **Giant Steps** – John Coltrane
765 **Rid Of Me** – PJ Harvey
766 **Rattus Norvegicus** – The Stranglers
767 **Daydream** – Lovin' Spoonful
768 **Actually** – The Pet Shop Boys
769 **Everywhere** – Tim McGraw
770 **Still Crazy After All These Years** – Paul Simon
771 **To Bring You My Love** – PJ Harvey
772 **Eponymous** – R.E.M.
773 **13** – Blur
774 **You've Come A Long Way, Baby** – Fatboy Slim
775 **Boys Don't Cry** – The Cure
776 **Hejira** – Joni Mitchell
777 **Bleach** – Nirvana
778 **... Baby, One More Time** – Britney Spears
779 **Let's Stay Together** – Al Green
780 **Crash** – The Dave Matthews Band
781 **Songs Of Faith and Devotion Live** – Depeche Mode
782 **Play** – Moby
783 **In-A-Gadda-Da-Vida** – Iron Butterfly
784 **Surfacing** – Sarah McLachlan
785 **Porgy and Bess** – Miles Davis
786 **Monster** – R.E.M.
787 **Don't Look Back** – Boston
788 **Unplugged** – Eric Clapton
789 **A Momentary Lapse Of Reason** – Pink Floyd
790 **The Globe Sessions** – Sheryl Crow
791 **The Dock Of The Bay** – Otis Redding
792 **Under The Table and Dreaming** – The Dave Matthews Band
793 **Ben Folds Five** – Ben Folds Five
794 **Full Moon, Dirty Hearts** – INXS
795 **Piano Man** – Billy Joel
796 **So Much For The Afterglow** – Everclear
797 **Something/Anything** – Todd Rundgren
798 **Suzanne Vega** – Suzanne Vega
799 **Reckless** – Bryan Adams
800 **Aenima** – Tool
801 **October** – U2
802 **What Does Anything Mean? Basically** – The Chameleons
803 **Backstreet Boys** – The Backstreet Boys
804 **Waiting For Columbus** – Little Feat
805 **Pop** – U2
806 **Three Dollar Bill, Y'all$** – Limp Bizkit
807 **Uncle Meat** – Frank Zappa
808 **Oxygene** – Jean-Michel Jarre
809 **Peter Gabriel 3** – Peter Gabriel
810 **Ghost In The Machine** – The Police
811 **Moseley Shoals** – Ocean Colour Scene
812 **Paris 1919** – John Cale
813 **Before These Crowded Streets** – The Dave Matthews Band
814 **I Want To See The Bright Lights Tonight** – Richard & Linda Thompson
815 **From The Choirgirl Hotel** – Tori Amos
816 **Get Yer Ya-Ya's Out!** – The Rolling Stones
817 **Morrison Hotel** – The Doors
818 **A Boy Named Goo** – Goo Goo Dolls
819 **Ride The Lightning** – Metallica
820 **The Modern Dance** – Pere Ubu
821 **High Land, Hard Rain** – Aztec Camera
822 **Heavy Weather** – Weather Report
823 **Korn** – Korn
824 **This Is Hardcore** – Pulp
825 **A Little South Of Sanity** – Aerosmith
826 **Solid Air** – John Martyn
827 **Hell Freezes Over** – The Eagles
828 **Tigelily** – Natalie Merchant
829 **Monk's Music** – Thelonious Monk
830 **Skylarking** – XTC
831 **International Velvet** – Catatonia
832 **Boy** – U2
833 **The Head On The Door** – The Cure
834 **Welcome To The Pleasure Dome** – Frankie Goes To Hollywood
835 **The Captain and Me** – The

Doobie Brothers
836 **Car Wheels On A Gravel Road** – Lucinda Williams
837 **Mutations** – Beck
838 **Pacific Ocean Blue** – Dennis Wilson
839 **Seal (2nd Album)** – Seal
840 **1999** – Prince
841 **Use Your Illusion I** – Guns N'Roses
842 **The Soul Cages** – Sting
843 **Yes I Am** – Melissa Etheridge
844 **Dirty Dancing** – Original Soundtrack
845 **The Boy With The Arab Strap** – Belle and Sebastian
846 **Temple Of Low Men** – Crowded House
847 **Come On Come On** – Mary-Chapin Carpenter
848 **Terrapin Station** – The Grateful Dead
849 **The Monkees** – The Monkees
850 **Blows Against The Empire** – Jefferson Starship
851 **In It For The Money** – Supergrass
852 **C'Mon Kids** – The Boo Radleys
853 **Tusk** – Fleetwood Mac
854 **All Things Must Pass** – George Harrison
855 **The Colour & The Shape** – Foo Fighters
856 **The Colour Of My Love** – Celine Dion
857 **Kings Of The Wild Frontier** – Adam and The Ants
858 **Mud Slide Slim and The Blue Horizon** – James Taylor
859 **Shepherd Moons** – Enya
860 **The Real Thing** – Faith No More
861 **Black Woman & Child** – Sizzla
862 **Invisible Touch** – Genesis
863 **Soft Parade** – The Doors
864 **Maybe You've Been Brainwashed Too** – The New Radicals
865 **Look Sharp!** – Joe Jackson
866 **Trick Of The Tail** – Genesis
867 **Mr Lucky** – John Lee Hooker
868 **The Royal Scam** – Steely Dan
869 **Life Is Peachy** – Korn
870 **Pulp Fiction** – Original Soundtrack
871 **Pilgrim** – Tim Buckley
872 **It's My Life** – Talk Talk
873 **Electric Warrior** – T. Rex
874 **Dry** – PJ Harvey
875 **Listen Without Prejudice, Vol.1** George Michael
876 **Treasure** – The Cocteau Twins
877 **The Lion and The Cobra** – Sinéad O'Connor
878 **It's Great When You're Straight, Yeah!** – Black Grape
879 **K** – Kula Shaker
880 **Closing Time** – Tom Waits
881 **Europe '72** – The Grateful Dead
882 **New Gold Dream (81,82, 83, 84)** – Simple Minds
883 **Supposed Former Infatuation Junkie** – Alanis Morissette
884 **English Settlement** – XTC
885 **Body and Soul** – Joe Jackson
886 **Ommadawn** – Mike Oldfield
887 **Reading, Writing and Arithmatic** – The Sundays
888 **Tonight's The Night** – Neil Young
889 **Tellin' Stories** – The Charlatans
890 **Let It Be** – The Beatles

891 **Lust For Life** – Iggy Pop
892 **Savage Garden** – Savage Garden
893 **The New York Dolls** – The New York Dolls
894 **Come Clean** – Curve
895 **Flood** – They Might Be Giants
896 **Stunt** – The Barenaked Ladies
897 **She's So Unusual** – Cyndi Lauper
898 **Elephant Mountain** – The Youngbloods
899 **Cheap Thrills** – Big Brother and The Holding Company
900 **461 Ocean Boulevard** – Eric Clapton
901 **Melissa Etheridge** – Melissa Etheridge
902 **Good Old Boys** – Randy Newman
903 **Gentlemen** – The Afghan Whigs
904 **... Nothing Like The Sun ...** – Sting
905 **Low-Life** – New Order
906 **Oranges & Lemons** – XTC
907 **ReLoad** – Metallica
908 **The Lamb Lies Down On Broadway** – Genesis
909 **Ram** – Paul & Linda McCartney
910 **Undertow** – Tool
911 **Love** – The Cult
912 **Cookin'** – Miles Davis
913 **No Way Out** – Puff Daddy & The Family
914 **From The Cradle** – Eric Clapton
915 **5150** – Van Halen
916 **Dizzy Heights** – The Lightning Seeds
917 **Marc Cohn** – Marc Cohn
918 **Live Rust** – Neil Young
919 **Laid** – James
920 **The Second Coming** – The Stone Roses
921 **Technique** – New Order
922 **Selected Ambient Works: 1985-1992** – Aphex Twin
923 **Songs From The Big Chair** – Tears For Fears
924 **Janet Jackson's Rhythm Nation 1814** – Janet Jackson
925 **This Fire** – Paula Cole
926 **Jazz Samba** – Stan Getz
927 **Stand!** – Sly and The Family Stone
928 **Evil Empire** – Rage Against The Machine
929 **40oz. To Freedom** – Sublime
930 **Computer World** – Kraftwerk
931 **Hearts and Bones** – Paul Simon
932 **Presence** – Led Zeppelin
933 **Without You I'm Nothing** – Placebo
934 **Turn! Turn! Turn!** – The Byrds
935 **A Wizard, A True Star** – Todd Rundgren
936 **Exodus** – Bob Marley and The Wailers
937 **Fanmail** – TLC
938 **Marcus Garvey** – Burning Spear
939 **Mermaid Avenue** – Billy Bragg & Wilco
940 **Mingus At Antibes** – Charles Mingus
941 **Days Of Future Passed** – The Moody Blues
942 **Chicago Transit Authority** – The Chicago Transit Authority
943 **Shooting At The Moon** – Kevin Ayers
944 **Tupelo Honey** – Van Morrison
945 **Deserter's Songs** – Mercury Rev

946 **Sunday At The Village Vanguard** – Bill Evans
947 **Slowhand** – Eric Clapton
948 **One World** – John Martyn
949 **Weld** – Neil Young
950 **Whitechocolatespaceegg** – Liz Phair
951 **Back To Back** – Duke Ellington
952 **Third Eye Blind** – Third Eye Blind
953 **Miles Davis At Carnegie Hall** – Miles Davis
954 **Happy Sad** – Tim Buckley
955 **Songs For A Tailor** – Jack Bruce
956 **Me Against The World** – 2Pac
957 **Soul's Core** – Shawn Mullins
958 **Small Change** – Tom Waits
959 **Moanin'** – Art Blakey
960 **Trailer Park** – Beth Orton
961 **Whatever** – Aimee Mann
962 **The Dance** – Fleetwood Mac
963 **Did I Shave My Legs For This?** – Deana Carter
964 **Brilliant Corners** – Thelonious Monk
965 **Speaking In Tongues** – Talking Heads
966 **Songs From Northern Britain** – Teenage Fanclub
967 **Crime Of The Century** – Supertramp
968 **Hard Promises** – Tom Petty and The Heartbreakers
969 **Private Dancer** – Tina Turner
970 **Dizzy Up The Girl** – Goo Goo Dolls
971 **Solitude Standing** – Suzanne Vega
972 **Endless Summer** – The Beach Boys
973 **The Wonderful and Frightening World Of** – The Fall
974 **Violent Femmes** – Violent Femmes
975 **If I Should Fall From Grace With God** – The Pogues
976 **Original Soundtrack** – 10cc
977 **No Guru, No Method, No Teacher** – Van Morrison
978 **There's A Riot Goin' On** – Sly and The Family Stone
979 **Follow The Leader** – Eric B & Rakim
980 **Live Through This** – Hole
981 **Surrender** – The Chemical Brothers
982 **Central Reservation** – Beth Orton
983 **Core** – Stone Temple Pilots
984 **Paul Simon** – Paul Simon
985 **Oklahoma!** – Various
986 **Superfly** – Curtis Mayfield
987 **This Is My Truth Tell Me Yours** – The Manic Street Preachers
988 **Flaming Pie** – Paul McCartney
989 **Live 1966: The Royal Albert Hall Concert** – Bob Dylan
990 **Atom Heart Mother** – Pink Floyd
991 **Speak & Spell** – Depeche Mode
992 **3+3** – The Isley Brothers
993 **The Good Will Out** – Embrace
994 **Someday My Prince Will Come** – Miles Davis
995 **Diamond Dogs** – David Bowie
996 **Freedom** – Neil Young
997 **No Secrets** – Carly Simon
998 **Still Warm** – John Scofield
999 **The Trinity Session** – Cowboy Junkies
1000 **Todd** – Todd Rundgren

Index

This is an index of artists appearing in the main section of ALL TIME TOP 1000 ALBUMS. The number refers to the position of the album and not the page number.